Complete Encyclopedia *of the*

Freshwater Aquarium

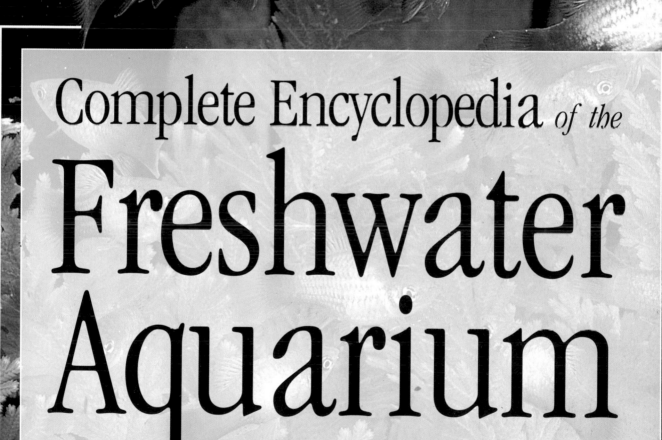

Complete Encyclopedia *of the*

Freshwater
Aquarium

John Dawes

INTERPET PUBLISHING

Conceived and produced
by Andromeda Oxford Limited
11–13 The Vineyard, Abingdon
Oxon OX14 3PX
www.andromeda.co.uk

Published by Interpet Publishing,
Vincent Lane, Dorking,
Surrey RH4 3YX
United Kingdom

ISBN 1-84286-041-0

PROJECT DIRECTOR Graham Bateman
MANAGING EDITOR Shaun Barrington
EDITING AND DESIGN D & N Publishing,
Marlborough, Wiltshire
EDITORIAL ASSISTANT Marian Dreier
INDEX Janet Dudley
PICTURE MANAGER Claire Turner
PRODUCTION Clive Sparling

Printed in Poland

DEDICATION

To Vivian.

CONTENTS

P. 1 CLOCKWISE FROM TOP LEFT: *BRILLIANT RUMMY-NOSED TETRA* (HEMIGRAMMUS BLEHERI); *RUBY BARB* (BARBUS NIGROFASCIATUS); *FLORIDA FLAGFISH* (JORDANELLA FLORI-DAE); *REDFIN OTOCINCLUS* (PAROTOCINCLUS MACULICAUDA); *ARCHER FISH* (TOXOTES JACULATRIX); *INDIAN GLASSFISH* (PARAMBASSIS RANGA). PP.2–3: *SOUTHERN PLATY* (XIPHOPHORUS MACULATUS VAR.). THIS PAGE, TOP TO BOTTOM: *BURNISHED GOLD SUNSET PLATY* (XIPHOPHORUS MACULATUS VAR.); *BIG-FINNED BRISTLENOSE* (ANCISTRUS DOLICHOPTERUS); *CATEMACO LIVEBEARER* (XIPHOPHORUS MILLERI).

PICTURE CREDITS AND ACKNOWLEDGMENTS

The Author and Publishers would like to thank in particular Frank Schäfer of the Aqualog Archive for his tireless cooperation—and knowledge—in finding illustrations; and also the incomparable aquarium fish photographer Max Gibbs.

Andromeda Oxford Limited 34tcl, 34tcr, 34tr, 34cl, 34cr, 46, 52, 53; Phil Jane/Andromeda Oxford Limited 257b; Aqualog Archive 1bcl, 86, 87, 88r, 89, 91b, 92c, 92b, 93, 96b, 130b, 131b, 132, 134c, 136–138, 139t, 140, 141, 142c, 144l, 145b, 146b, 147, 148b, 190–196, 197b, 199c, 200–205, 207, 209tr, 209c, 209b, 210, 211c, 212t, 213b, 214–218, 219b, 220–227, 228b, 229t, 230t, 231t, 268, 277t, 278t, 280b x3, 286–289, 290t, 291–297; Aquarian Fish Foods 20; Staffan Widstrand/BBC Natural History Unit 17; Dennis Barrett 5b, 6, 59; Dieter Bork 7b, 268b, 269; Jane Burton/Bruce Coleman Collection 12; Andrew Davies/Bruce Coleman Collection 19; D.J. Lambert 283; Max Gibbs/Photomax 1tl, 1cr, 1b, 1bcl, 1tcl, 2–3, 5t, 5c, 7t, 10–11, 13–16, 21, 23–31, 34tl, 37–39, 41–45, 48, 50, 51, 54, 56–58, 61–85, 88l, 90, 91t, 92t, 94, 95, 96t, 97–129, 130t, 131t, 133, 134b, 135, 139b, 142b, 143, 144r, 145t, 146c, 148t, 149–177, 178t, 179–189, 197t, 198, 199t, 206, 208, 209tl, 211b, 212b, 213t, 219t, 228, 229b, 230b, 231b, 232–256, 257t, 258–267, 270–276, 277c, 278b, 279, 280t, 281, 282, 285, 290c; M. Sandford 35, 55; W. Tomey 1tr, 9, 18, 22, 40, 49, 178b.

THIS PAGE: (TOP LEFT) *CELEBES HALFBEAK (NOMORHAMPHUS LIEMI)*; (TOP RIGHT) *SPOTTED GOODEID (CHAPALICHTHYS ENCAUSTUS)*; (ABOVE) *PIKE TOP LIVEBEARER (BELONESOX BELIZANUS)*. OPPOSITE PAGE: (TOP) *PEPPERED CORYDORAS (CORYDORAS PALEATUS)*; (BOTTOM) *BAR-TAILED RIVULUS (RIVULUS MAGDALENAE)*.

INTRODUCTION

Little could I have guessed when I took up aquarium keeping about 50 years ago, that I was choosing one of the most absorbing, interesting and colorful hobbies in the world. Equally, there was no way I could have known then that those initial, exciting, error-riddled steps would lead to a lifelong involvement that has taken me almost round the world.

Seeing Cardinal Tetras (*Paracheirodon axelrodi*) for the first time in a flooded Rio Negro forest; netting Mosquito Fish (*Gambusia holbrooki*) in swamps in Florida; collecting Ornate Paradise Fish (*Malpulutta kretseri*) for a captive breeding project in the jungles of Sri Lanka; observing Threadjaw Halfbeaks (*Hemirhamphodon pogonognathus*) in a tiny stream in Malaysia—these, along with so many other experiences, have contributed to a fascination that continues to deepen with every passing day, fueling my enthusiasm to continue to search for knowledge about fish and aquatic plants. The more I have traveled, and the more people I have had the privilege of meeting, exchanging experiences with and learning from, the more I've come to appreciate that we all share the same "affliction"—we are all crazy about fish!

My teachers have been many. Sará—an Amazonian caboclo—taught me how to "call" cardinals out of hiding; Dharmadasa taught me, likewise, how to call *Rasbora vaterifloris* in Sri Lanka; Yong taught me how to spot Snakehead fry among water plants in Malaysia; Marco showed me just how tough some species of molly, such as *Poccilia vivipara*, can be (they thrive in the often-polluted waters of Lago Rodrigo de Freitas in Rio de Janeiro). Countless other unselfish people—including many hundreds of fellow aquarists—have generously given me their time and shared their hard-earned knowledge with me over the years. So while the pages that follow may have come from my pen, the information they contain bears witness to innumerable invaluable contributions made by many. To each and every one of them, I extend my respectful and most sincere thanks.

What I have attempted to do is present an overall picture of the modern hobby, outlining some of the latest thinking in aquarium management techniques and philosophies, and presenting an extensive selection of fish and plants. I also hope to have highlighted the tremendous responsibility that all of us who keep fish need to shoulder.

The fish section—the largest in the book—is arranged in families. There are some families, though, that are represented in the hobby by only one or a few species, and these have been grouped together in the final section. Owing to the large number of species featured, allied to space and other limitations, it has not been possible to illustrate every single fish. Readers are therefore encouraged to consult the specialist literature cited in the Bibliography for further illustrations.

Within the families, species are listed in alphabetical order of scientific name. The common name for the species is given on the first line. Common names vary from country to country—or even within a single country—and, in some cases, one common name may be applied to more than one species, something that does not, or should not, apply to the scientific equivalents. Therefore, *Dianema longibarbis* precedes *D. urostriata* in this book, even though this means that their respective common names, Porthole Catfish and Flag-Tailed Catfish, do not appear in alphabetical order.

Although, at any one time, there is (or should be) only one valid scientific name for each species, complications can, and do, occur. For instance, opinions may differ between scientists, with some claiming that two or more species are sufficiently similar to each other to warrant their inclusion within a single species. Alternatively, a variable species may be deemed by some to consist of not just one but several very closely related species. Further, one authority may deem an individual species to belong to a particular genus while others disagree and assign it to another. Genera may be considered members of different families or subfamilies, and so on.

Intimately associated with taxonomy (the science of classifying living organisms into hierarchical groups, i.e. subspecies, species, genera, subfamilies, families, and so on), is the science of systematics, which attempts to classify organisms according to their "natural" relationships by taking into consideration matters relating to their evolutionary biology. The end result is that, while universal agreement may exist regarding the identity and therefore, the name, of numerous species, there are also areas of disagreement and debate. Even when, or if, a consensus is reached, it may take some time (years) before the latest, agreed, valid name becomes accepted. Consequently, a particular species may be listed under one scientific name by some authors and under a different one by others.

A good example of this complex and "fluid" situation exists with the beautiful and highly variable African Rift Lake cichlid commonly known as the Zebra Cichlid. Traditionally this species is listed as *Pseudotropheus zebra*. In 1997, it was renamed *Metriaclima zebra*, but this move has yet to receive universal acceptance. To complicate matters further, some authors regard this species as *Maylandia zebra*.

Where such situations exist, I have highlighted some of the issues concerned and have listed such species according to how convincing, or otherwise, the arguments for and against appear to be, or how widely accepted, or otherwise, the various names have become. As a result, some species in this book, such as the Dwarf Rasbora (*Boraras maculata*) are listed differently than they are in some other literature. In the case of the Harlequin, which is still regarded as *Rasbora heteromorpha* by many authors, the new name, *Trigonostigma heteromorpha*, erected in 1999, is also listed and acknowledged because, in the foreseeable future, the new name is likely to replace the old one.

The above examples help to illustrate that, far from being a static science, fish classification is dynamic and "changing." To some, i.e. those who like their science presented in neat little packages, this situation causes problems. To many others (and I include myself in this group), problems are challenges in disguise. To us, the dynanism, subjectiveness, openness and everevolving nature of the subject is one of its major attractions.

Fish classification, aquarium science, and every single aspect of our hobby and the industries that service it, will continue to evolve apace, and we need to grow and adapt accordingly. New areas of debate and controversy will continue to challenge us, and all need to be faced openly and honestly. Two issues that have been "bubbling" for some time, and that have been gradually gaining momentum to the point that they are making headlines worldwide, are biopiracy and genetically modified fish. Both are of obvious and direct relevance to the hobby, as well as to the ornamental aquatic industry, and both will, undoubtedly, play significant roles in years to come. They are an integral part of aquatics in the new millennium—a millennium that will see us attain new levels of success in areas of activity that we don't even know exist yet. The ride will be exciting, though not always easy. Welcome aboard!

John Dawes
Sabinillas, Spain

THE RED PARROT, A RECENT ADDITION TO THE HUGE RANGE OF FISH THAT ARE TODAY KEPT IN AQUARIA.

NATURAL HISTORY OF FISH

F ish are fascinating creatures, but what is a fish? It is actually difficult to define the term "fish" concisely and unambiguously. The pages that follow therefore begin with a discussion of this important topic. They then detail the various characteristics of fish. Some of the most important habitats from which aquarium fish originate are also described. This is important because a better understanding of the conditions that fish encounter in the wild can help us to cater to their needs in aquaria.

Also of great relevance to aquarists is the status of fish species in the wild. Some are extinct in nature, but exist in captivity; others are close to extinction, while many are threatened. Efforts to save many such species are, however, under way, both at national and international levels, and some of these measures are described. Finally, the commercial aspects of ornamental fish breeding are examined.

WHAT IS A FISH?

There are well over 24,000 species of fish known to science, a number that appears to be increasing as quickly today as it did during the early period of plant and animal classification. However, although research may be more meticulous now, and communications are certainly more efficient—minimizing the risks of double, or even multiple, naming—there are still instances of the same fish (or other organism) being described and assigned different names by different scientists.

With so many thousands of species in existence, from whale sharks to minnows, we should all know what a fish actually is. We do not. It would be fair to say that there is no categorical definition of the term "fish." While we can all identify, say, any variety of goldfish as a fish, when it comes down to listing all the characteristics that would identify any fish as a fish, we immediately run into difficulties. It is, for example, quite ridiculous to say that an animal is a fish if it lives in water. Dolphins, whales, leeches, lobsters, sea cucumbers, sponges and numerous other aquatic organisms do likewise. Fish have scales on their bodies, but so do reptiles (crocodiles, turtles, lizards and the like). Conversely, not all animals that we definitely regard as fish have scales: catfish belonging to the family Pimelodidae are, in fact, quite naked, and there are numerous other examples of scaleless fish. Matters do not improve much when another fish characteristic—gills—is considered. Newt larvae and salamander tadpoles, including the incredible neotenous axolotl, all possess gills, yet they are amphibians—definitely not fish.

Combining fish characteristics, such as an aquatic lifestyle, and the possession of gills and fins might, at first sight, bring a definition a little closer, but not when you consider that other animals such as cuttlefishes (*Sepia, Sepiola* etc.) and squids exhibit the same characteristics. One important difference (there are others) is that in cuttlefishes and squids, which are both mollusks, the internal organs are found inside a mantle cavity. Fish do not possess a mantle cavity. Fish have an internal skeleton, but, then again, so do cuttlefishes and squids (the cuttlebone and pen, respectively), starfishes, and their close relatives the urchins (their skeleton consists of calcareous plates overlaid with thin surface tissue). What cuttlefishes and urchins do not possess is a cranium (braincase or skull). However, not even this apparently unassailable criterion is

sufficient to distinguish fish from other marine organisms. If it did then lampreys and the other "jawless fishes," the hagfishes, would also be "true" fish, but they are not. They do have a skull of sorts, even though it is largely a covered cartilage "trough" (particularly in hagfishes), but they also have many other "nonfish" characteristics, such as the absence of a backbone, two (instead of three) semicircular canals in the ear, and gills that are arranged almost back to front when compared with "normal" fish (in jawless fishes they are directed internally). In addition, jawless fishes (Agnatha), unsurprisingly, do not possess jaws. Therefore, even combining characteristics, the term "fish" is still impossible to define concisely and unambiguously.

Keith Banister, in *The Encyclopaedia of Underwater Life* (*see* Bibliography) puts the matter succinctly. Referring to the four groups of "fishes" that exist today, namely the lampreys, hagfishes, cartilaginous fishes, and bony fishes, he says that classifying all these under the common heading of fish is like "lumping all flying vertebrates, i.e., bats, birds and even the flying lizard, under the heading 'birds' just because they all fly."

If we consider the relationship between say, a lamprey and a guppy, we come to the conclusion that

THE POSSESSION OF GILLS DOES NOT DEFINE AN ANIMAL AS A FISH. THE AXOLOTL, A SALAMANDER, KEEPS GILLS THROUGHOUT ITS LIFE, WHICH IS UNUSUAL FOR AN AMPHIBIAN.

they are as different from each other as a bat from a chicken. It must be inappropriate to refer to them both as fish. Quoting Banister again, "'Fish' is simply a shorthand notation for an aquatic vertebrate that is not a mammal, a turtle, or anything else."

In practice, when we use the word "fish," we refer to those species of aquatic vertebrates identified as fish by Banister, some of which are eaten, some of which are maintained in aquaria and ponds. (Despite the fact that lampreys are eaten in some parts of the world, they are not included.) Common usage of the term "fish" is restricted to members of two large groups:

1. Cartilaginous fishes (Class Chondrichthyes)
   Sharks, rays and chimaeras (approximately 700 species).
2. Bony fishes (Class Osteichthyes)
   A large class of species from guppies to seahorses (over 23,000 species).

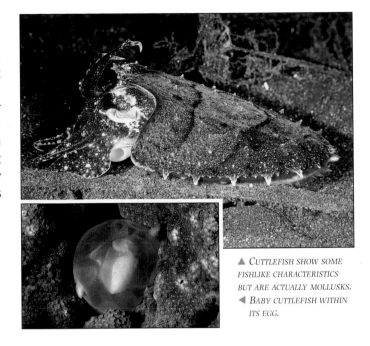

▲ CUTTLEFISH SHOW SOME FISHLIKE CHARACTERISTICS BUT ARE ACTUALLY MOLLUSKS.
◄ BABY CUTTLEFISH WITHIN ITS EGG.

Of these two categories, the one that is encountered almost (but not quite) exclusively in aquaria and in ponds, is the Class Osteichthyes, or bony fishes. It is possible, with difficulty and numerous exceptions and qualifications, to list the characteristics that, in combination, allow us to recognize a bony fish as such. Bony fish:

- Possess a braincase and limb (fin) skeleton consisting, at least in part, of bone
- Possess fins, usually with spines and/or rays
- Breathe through outwardly directed gills covered by an operculum (gill cover) that, externally, appears as a slitlike aperture
- Have bodies totally or partially covered in scales (with some important exceptions)
- Possess an air/gas/swimbladder used in buoyancy control (with a few exceptions)
- Possess a sensory mechanism called the lateral line system, which runs in a head–tail direction
- Are poikilothermic (cold-blooded): their body temperature is determined by that of the environment. (Again, there are some significant exceptions, such as tuna, which are capable of raising their body temperature above that of the surrounding water.)

THE SKULL

The skull or cranium of bony fishes is made up of two main parts: the neurocranium and the branchiocranium.

The neurocranium consists of the part of the skull that encloses the brain itself, plus the associated bones that make up the top half of the skull and extend forward to the "internal" upper tip of the snout (ending with the ethmoid and vomer bones). The neurocranium is subdivided into two further parts: the chondrocranium, which is the original cartilaginous braincase that ossifies (changes into bone) during development, and the dermatocranium, which consists of components that are ossified from the outset.

The branchiocranium consists of five separate composite components, referred to as arches, which include the maxillae (jaws) and the operculi (gill covers). One of the bones of the upper jaw, the premaxilla, covers the ethmoid and vomer bones mentioned above, which are thus not visible externally—hence the reference to their constituting the "internal" upper tip of the snout.

THE SKELETON

The limb part of the skeleton consists of a pelvic (hip) and pectoral (chest) girdle, and associated bones that support the pelvic or ventral fins and the pectoral fins. However, since fish also have other appendages—such as anal (belly), caudal (tail), and dorsal (back) fins, plus, in some types, adipose (second dorsal) fins—they also possess additional supporting bones.

Running the length of the body, from the back of the skull to the caudal fin, lies the backbone or vertebral column. In the posterior half of the body, the individual

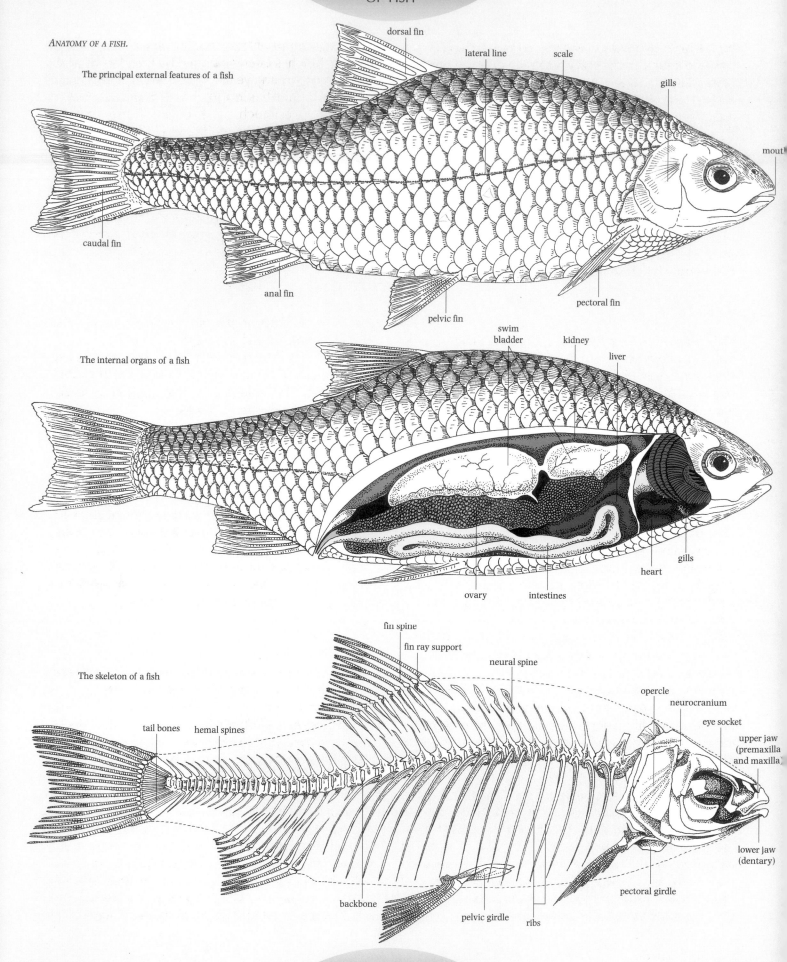

ANATOMY OF A FISH.

The principal external features of a fish

dorsal fin

lateral line

scale

gills

mout[h]

caudal fin

anal fin

pelvic fin

pectoral fin

The internal organs of a fish

swim bladder

kidney

liver

ovary

intestines

heart

gills

The skeleton of a fish

fin spine

fin ray support

neural spine

opercle

neurocranium

eye socket

upper jaw (premaxilla and maxilla)

tail bones

hemal spines

lower jaw (dentary)

backbone

pelvic girdle

ribs

pectoral girdle

bones have two vertical spines, an upwardly directed one (the neural spine) and a ventrally directed one (the hemal spine). Further forward, in the region that lies above the abdominal cavity, the hemal spines are much reduced or absent, leaving space for the internal organs as well as acting as basal supports for the ribs.

The tail of a fish is a highly complicated and beautifully put together structure referred to as the caudal complex. The base itself consists of modified neural and hemal spines, the most modified of which are referred to as hypurals; these act as supports for the fin rays. Fish tails are superb examples of biological engineering. Their exceptional qualities can be fully appreciated only by close microscopic examination.

THE FINS

Fish usually possess two sets of paired fins (the pectorals and the pelvics), and two single ones (though they may be divided into finlets), the so-called median fins consisting of the dorsal and the anal, plus the single caudal complex. In addition, some fish—for example, characins such as piranhas and tetras—possess a "second" dorsal fin. This is called the adipose fin, and it can be a small, singular structure (as in characins) or a more elaborate one (as in some catfishes). Either way, the term "adipose fin" is misleading, since adipose suggests that these fins—the function of which is not clearly understood—are fat stores or fatty in composition, which, generally speaking, they are not. Some authorities regard the dorsal as two separate fins: an anterior one (the first dorsal, made up of one or more rigid, unbranched spines) and a posterior one (the second dorsal, made up largely or exclusively of soft, usually branched, rays, sometimes preceded by a spine-like structure composed of a bundle of fused rays).

While adhering to this basic format—which also includes an assortment of unbranched spines and branched soft rays—fins have undergone major modifications during the course of evolution. In some cases, these modifications have been so extreme that the resulting structures are difficult to recognize as fins at all. The pelvics of gouramis belonging to the genera *Trichogaster* and *Colisa* for example have evolved into long, hairlike feelers that are virtually useless for locomotion or balance. In other fish, such as the seahorses with their upright posture, some fins have actually disappeared altogether and the locomotory functions of the caudal fin have been assumed by the dorsal. In livebearers, the anal fin of males has been modified, through natural selection, into an intromittent sexual organ.

The possibility of transforming fins through selective breeding has been exploited by breeders of ornamental fish for many years (a few centuries in the case of goldfish), and has resulted in a plethora of commercial varieties much sought after within the hobby. The most frequently encountered variations occur in the most popular species such as guppies, swordtails, platies, angels, Siamese fighters and goldfish. In most cases, the modifications consist of enlarged fins, while in others, such as Ranchu and Lionhead (varieties of goldfish), these modifications include the total elimination of the dorsal fin and the doubling of both the anal and caudal fins.

THE SCALES

Scales can be categorized into four basic types: placoid, cosmoid, ganoid, and cycloid.

Placoid scales are usually found in sharks, rays and their relatives. The term "dermal denticles" often (but inadequately, in biological terms) applied to sharks refers to modified placoid scales.

Cosmoid scales are frequently encountered in fossil fishes. Modern-day lungfishes have scales that have evolved from the basic cosmoid design.

Ganoid scales are found in some of the more "primitive" aquarium fishes, such as gars, bowfins and birchirs. This type of scale is generally rhomboid-shaped with an articulated joint between each scale.

Cycloid—also known as ctenoid—scales are possessed by the vast majority of bony fishes. They overlap each other, rather like roof tiles. Also typical of these scales is a spinous posterior margin.

THE GILLS

Gills are remarkable structures that act as super-efficient gas exchangers. They are constructed of finely divided, thin, platelike structures or lamellae (filaments), with each of these being further divided into even finer lamellae. The lamellae are served by a rich blood supply. Oxygen from the water diffuses across the gill membrane into the bloodstream, whence it is taken to the heart and then around the fish's body. As it circulates, it supplies tissues with oxygen and picks up waste carbon dioxide. As the carbon dioxide-rich, deoxygenated blood is returned to the gill lamellae, the toxic carbon dioxide diffuses out and new oxygen diffuses in.

This mechanism works perfectly for most species. However, not all fish live in oxygen-rich waters. Some, including the well-known gouramis and fighters as well as many catfish, inhabit waters that are either permanently or seasonally deficient in oxygen. Were such species to rely exclusively on their gills for their oxygen supply, they would, quite simply, asphyxiate. Through time, these species have evolved a variety of mechanisms that assure them of an adequate oxygen supply and an efficient carbon dioxide elimination mechanism. In catfish, for example, part of the gut can be used for this purpose, while in gouramis and other anabantoids, some of the gills have actually been reduced and the resulting space in the gill chamber has become occupied by the labyrinth, a convoluted, blood-rich organ that allows these fish to inhale oxygen direct from the air and expel carbon dioxide in the form of a bubble.

In addition to "breathing," gills also perform another vitally important function. They are one of the two main organs (the other one being the kidneys) via which ammonia, a highly toxic metabolic waste product generated by fish, is expelled from the body.

THE LATERAL LINE OF THE COMMON GOLDFISH (CARRASIUS AURATUS VAR.) CAN BE SEEN RUNNING THE LENGTH OF ITS BODY.

THE SWIMBLADDER

The swimbladder is the main buoyancy mechanism used by bony fishes, although the actual composition of the body tissues may also play a part in maintaining buoyancy. In many books, the swimbladder is referred to as the air bladder. Strictly speaking, though, both terms are inaccurate, for the bladder is not used for swimming and, though it contains the three main atmospheric gases, i.e., oxygen, carbon dioxide and nitrogen, their relative percentages are different to those found in air. A more appropriate term would therefore be "gas bladder."

The gas bladder enables a fish to control its buoyancy by adjusting the amount of gas it contains. This movement of gas enables a fish to acquire neutral buoyancy—

it neither sinks nor floats—which is the least energy-costly state for any animal that lives in water.

However, for benthic (bottom-dwelling) species, the presence of gas in the bladder would present them with a metabolic disadvantage in that they would need to expend large amounts of energy just to remain on the bottom. Not surprisingly therefore, such species have either a reduced gas bladder or no bladder at all.

Besides using it as a buoyancy mechanism, certain fish can use the gas bladder either to produce sound, or as an organ to receive ("hear") sound.

THE LATERAL LINE SYSTEM

The lateral line system is a sensory apparatus that reacts to wave vibrations in the water. This helps a fish detect potential prey, predators, or any submerged objects. It is made up of two main components: the cephalic lateral line canals, located in the head, and the lateral line, which runs longitudinally along the body.

Of the two, the lateral line is more easily visible to the naked eye as a row of dots. These may extend the whole length of the body, either in a single, usually gently undulating or curved line, as an anterior (shorter and higher) section separated by several lines of scales from a posterior portion, or as a single line that may extend only partially down the body. Each "dot" is, in fact, a pore (a neuromast) containing a number of sensory hair cells, supporting cells, and nerve endings. It is these that are stimulated by vibrations, enabling a fish to be aware of changes in its environment.

TEMPERATURE CONTROL

Fish are usually referred to as poikilothermic or "cold-blooded." More accurately, they are "ectothermic." The term cold-blooded suggests that the temperature of a fish's blood is consistently cold, irrespective of external conditions, just as endothermic animals—humans, other mammals and birds—have "warm blood" irrespective of the ambient temperature. In reality, it means that the temperature of a fish's blood fluctuates to match that of its environment, so, in coldwater conditions, a fish's blood temperature is low; in tropical, warm-water environments, the blood temperature is warm.

While the vast majority of fish are ectotherms, a few—most notably, tuna and their closest relatives—are endotherms, conserving internal body heat generated by their constantly active swimming muscles.

Natural Habitats

River rushing through tropical rainforest in Mazaruni, Guyana.

Fish occupy habitats as diverse as the so-called Arctic "wastes," tiny mudpools no bigger than an elephant's footprint, the coldest, darkest recesses of the midocean abysses, and the illuminated, warm, crystal-clear shallows of coral reefs.

A little over 70 percent of the planet's surface is covered by seas and oceans. Add to this the areas taken up by landmasses, and what is left—the freshwater areas—appears meager, especially given that four fifths of the world's freshwater is tied up in glaciers, polar ice sheets and ground water. However, the tiny fraction that remains still includes the vast expanses of the Amazon basin, the inland "seas" such as the African Rift Lakes and the Great Lakes, plus all the other countless rivers, lakes, streams, rivulets and ditches that help to make up an environment of untold richness and potential. Of the available freshwater— about 30,000 cubic miles (125,000 cubic km)—four

fifths is contained in some 40 lakes. The remaining one fifth is accounted for by all the other bodies of freshwater, including mighty rivers such as the Amazon, Yangtze and Mississippi.

The Amazon and Its Tributaries

One fifth may not sound like much, but it is estimated that the Amazon is fed by no fewer than 1,100 tributaries, together disgorging enough water into the Atlantic Ocean for it to be detectable some 100 miles (160km) from land. It takes a largish European river such as the Thames a whole year to match the volume of water that flows out of the Amazon in a single day. While the main Amazon river system is an awe-inspiring 4,000 miles (6,400km) or so long, even this pales into insignificance when compared with the approximate 50,000 miles (80,500km) of navigable waters spread out over the basin itself. If this isn't enough to convey the scale of this giant river, consider that the island of Marajó, which nestles between the banks of the Amazon's gaping mouth, is approximately the same size as Switzerland.

A closer look at the nature of Amazonian water itself reveals that the one thing it lacks is uniformity. It could be said that there are as many Amazons as there are tributaries. Nowhere is this more vividly illustrated than around the city of Manáus, in Brazil. Here, the two mighty tributaries of the Amazon proper—the Rio Negro and the Solimões—converge. The dark-stained, but clear, sediment-free, black waters of the Rio Negro meet the sediment-laden, milky-tea-col-

LAKE TANGANYIKA IN EAST AFRICA IS HOME TO MANY ENDEMIC CICHLIDS.

ored waters of the Solimões in a dramatic confluence known as the "Encontro das Aguas," or "Meeting of the Waters." Such is the awesome power of these two tributaries, that their distinct waters flow side by side for some 50 miles (80km) downriver, only gradually mixing until they form the uniformly brown waters of the lower Amazon.

The main channels of the Amazonian tributaries yield remarkably few aquarium fishes. The waters here are too open and fast-flowing for most of the small species adored by aquarists worldwide. Yet move away from these major arteries, and a spellbinding world unfolds. This is the world of creeks (agarapé), flooded

blackwater forests (igapó), and the floodplain lakes of the turbid tributaries (várzea). Differing in depth and expanse—and even in degree of permanence—the waters of these habitats show a range of properties from clear, almost uncolored, waters, through yellow-stained waters, to the true blackwaters for which the Rio Negro is famous, and the turbid, silty waters bordering the Solimões. The chemical composition also varies, not just from place to place, but from season to season.

Not surprisingly, such a diverse assortment of habitats supports an unknown, and perhaps unknowable, complement of species, each subtly tuned and in harmony with its environment. It is quite impossible to give an accurate figure for the number of fish species that the Amazon holds. New species are constantly being discovered, numerous others remain to be discovered, and there are some that may never be discovered—such is the immensity of the basin and the inaccessibility of some of its remotest backwaters. A rough estimate would place the number of fish species distributed throughout the Amazon at somewhere around 3,000.

THE AFRICAN RIFT LAKES

In sharp contrast to the soft, acid waters of the Amazon, those of the African Rift Lakes are hard and alkaline. Just as Amazonian tributaries are very different from each other, so are the African Rift Lakes. However, the range of species they contain, while being much wider than indicated in popular aquarium literature, is restricted when compared with that of the Amazon basin. Within the aquarium hobby, the African Rift Lakes are famous for their cichlids, most notably the mouthbrooding species, which include the rockdwellers or mbuna.

Of the three lakes making up the African Rift Lakes, Lake Tanganyika is, at 4,800 feet (1,470m), by far the deepest, followed by Lake Malawi at 2,300 feet (700m) and, finally, Lake Victoria at no more than 145 feet (45m). (Lake Tanganyika is in fact the second deepest lake in the world, the deepest being the Siberian Lake Baikal at 5,315 feet/1,620m.) Other statistics are equally impressive. Lake Tanganyika, for example, is about 420 miles (675km) long and around 85 miles (140km) wide, while Lake Malawi is around 360 miles (580km) long and 50 miles (80km) wide, and Lake Victoria is approximately 200 miles (320km) long and only slightly less (about 185 miles/300km) wide. In terms of surface area; Lake Victoria is the largest at around 26,540 sq. miles (68,800 sq. km)—making it the third largest in the world, behind the Caspian Sea and Lake Superior—followed by Lake Tanganyika at around 13,120 sq. miles (34,000 sq. km) and Lake Malawi at 11,570 sq. miles (30,000 sq. km). In practice, though not necessarily by strict definition, the African Rift Lakes can be considered inland seas.

Alkalinity—a feature all three lakes share—varies from lake to lake and between areas within each lake: approximate pH value 7.8–8.5 in Lake Malawi, pH 8.0–9.5 in Lake Tanganyika, and pH 7.1–9.0 in Lake Victoria. A further common characteristic is that the cichlid species of all three lakes are largely endemic, being found in these lakes and nowhere else. Each lake in turn has its own array of endemic cichlids. The world-famous *Pseudotropheus*, *Aulonocara* and *Melanochromis* species for example are endemic to Lake Malawi; the equally celebrated *Lamprologus*, *Neolamprologus* and *Julidochromis* species are restricted to Lake Tanganyika; and the very distinct *Haplochromis* species occur only in Lake Victoria.

OTHER HABITATS

While the Amazon and the African Rift Lakes may be the two best-known regions, there are others that aquarists should know about. Mexico, for example, is particularly rich in livebearing species, with the fascinating goodeids (family Goodeidae)—sometimes referred to as Mexican Livebearers—endemic to the country. Tropical far-eastern stillwater regions are particularly rich in labyrinth species, including all the *Trichogaster* gouramis and the numerous species of "fighters" (genus *Betta*), while Papua New Guinea, Irian Jaya, neighboring countries, and Australia, are home to the impressive rainbowfishes.

The Indian subcontinent is a relative newcomer in supplying fish for the international aquarium hobby (although it is the home of many barbs and the *Colisa* gouramis). However, its vastness encompasses a wide diversity of aquatic habitats, from torrential mountain streams to still, weed-choked waters. Not surprisingly, the range of species found in its waters is extremely varied. The habitats found in mainland China are equally varied, encompassing (as in India) everything from mountain streams to still, heavily vegetated waters, with the added variable of a larger temperature range: from cold, oxygen-rich waters at one end of the spectrum, to permanently warm waters at the other. As a result, China has a vast range of fish species, some of which began to reach the hobby market during the early 1990s. Similar in terms of habitat diversity (though not in temperature or size) is Sri Lanka, whose tropical waters are home to numerous magnificent species of barb, such as the Ruby Barb (*Barbus nigrofasciatus*) and the Cherry Barb (*B. titteya*), along with some fascinating anabantoids such as the Combtail (*Belontia signata*) and *Malpulutta kretseri*.

In the United States, most of the aquarium fish natural habitats—while varying in water composition, levels of oxygenation and intensity of flow—are temperate, rather than tropical, with some subtropical areas in the extreme south, where species such as the Everglades Pygmy Sunfish (*Elassoma evergladei*) originate.

Although they may differ significantly in temperature, softness/hardness, acidity/alkalinity, level of oxygenation and a host of other parameters, the habitats mentioned so far are all strictly freshwater. So-called "freshwater" aquarium fish are, however, also found in waters whose salt content (mainly sodium chloride) varies from mere traces to almost fully marine levels. Such waters are found in estuaries and mangrove swamps and are referred to as "brackish." Perhaps the best-known freshwater aquarium species originating from such waters are the scats (*Scatophagus*), monos (*Monodactylus*), glassfish (*Parambassis* or *Chanda*) and archerfish (*Toxotes*), but there are others, many of which are featured in the Aquarium Fish section (pp.82–297).

Aquarium fish come from many (and diverse) corners of the globe, not all of which I have referred to. The result is that aquarists have an almost inexhaustible range of species from which they can stock their aquaria.

MANGROVES PROVIDE THE COASTLINE WITH VITAL NATURAL PROTECTION AGAINST HURRICANES, AS WELL AS OFFERING SUITABLE HABITATS FOR MANY SPECIES OF FISH.

FISH CONSERVATION

Fish conservation involves conserving habitats as diverse as coral reefs and rainforests. Without the survival of these habitats, species conservation can only, at best, achieve modest success. Sometimes species-centered conservation programs—in which species are conserved in aquaria rather than the wild—are the only option available. Where this is the case, as with the Gold Sawfin Goodeid (*Skiffia francesae*) from Mexico, such programs can make the difference between survival, albeit in captivity, and extinction.

INTERNATIONAL MEASURES

The International Union for the Conservation of Nature and Natural Resources (IUCN) publishes and updates the "Red List," which categorizes species according to the levels of threat that they are actually (or believed to be) under in the wild. The current Red List classifies animals and plants in the following categories: Extinct, Extinct in the Wild, Critically Endangered, Endangered, Vulnerable, Lower Risk (subdivided into Conservation Dependent, Near Threatened, and Least Concern), Data Deficient and Not Evaluated.

According to this list, there are just over 80 species of bony fishes that are either Extinct or Extinct in the Wild and just over 700 considered to fall within one or other of the higher categories of threat, i.e. Critically Endangered, Endangered and Vulnerable. Within the Lower Risk and Data Deficient categories, there are nearly 350 further species.

THE GOLD SAWFIN GOODEID (SKIFFIA FRANCESAE) BECAME EXTINCT IN THE WILD ONLY A DECADE AFTER ITS DISCOVERY IN 1978. IT CONTINUES TO SURVIVE IN CAPTIVITY, HOWEVER.

At the time of writing, the revised fish list details had not yet been determined. However, it is known from previous lists that several barbs (family Cyprinidae), livebearers (families Poeciliidae and Goodeidae), bony tongues (family Osteoglossidae), and lungfishes (family Ceratodontidae) are among freshwater species generally regarded as "aquarium" fish that are, and will be, officially classified under one or other of the IUCN Red List categories. These, however, represent only a small number of the grand total, which also includes marine species.

The IUCN Red List is compiled exclusively on scientific criteria and for scientific purposes. The Convention on International Trade in Endangered Species of Wild Fauna and Flora (CITES), on the other hand, is concerned with trade in threatened species. CITES compiles three Appendixes that list known (or perceived) levels of threat to wild populations as a result of trade. Species listed in Appendix I "are endangered … and commercial import, export and sale is normally prohibited." Some flexibility exists over prohibition in that specimens may be legally traded if they have been bred in captivity and are able to fulfil certain CITES criteria. There are currently only eight fish species listed in Appendix I. These are the famous Coelacanth (*Latimeria chalumnae*), the Dragon Fish (*Scleropages formosus*), two sturgeons, a cyprinid, a schilbeid catfish, a catostomid (sucker) and a scianid (croaker or drum).

The species included in Appendix II "are vulnerable but … may be traded commercially provided that import or export permits have been obtained." The controls imposed by Appendix II listing are designed to protect wild populations of the listed species so that they don't slip into the endangered (Appendix I) category. Currently, only five fish species are listed in Appendix II: the Australian Lungfish (*Neoceratodus forsteri*), the Atlantic Sturgeon (*Acipenser oxyrhynchus*), the Paddlefish (*Polyodon spathulae*), the Arapaima or Pirarucu (*Arapaima gigas*) and the African Blind Barb (*Caecobarbus geertsi*).

Appendix III lists species that are not deemed to be under major threat. Trade in Appendix III species is controlled on a domestic, rather than an international, basis. Nevertheless, countries can call upon collaboration from other countries should they feel that trade needs to be internationally controlled.

The CITES Appendixes are continuously evolving and should not be considered as permanent diktats. Species are proposed for inclusion, deletion or transfer according to the changing status of wild populations. The species referred to above are therefore those that were included at the time of writing. Major changes are not expected overnight, but some will occur over time.

Conservation efforts extend well beyond the IUCN and CITES lists. Even in cases where CITES permits the legal export of listed species, as occurs with a number of farms that breed the Dragon Fish, importing countries may impose their own controls if they feel that imports could endanger the status of their native fish populations. History has shown such measures to be occasionally essential and often desirable. For example, the widespread and unrestricted introduction of species such as the Mosquito Fish (*Gambusia holbrooki*) as a biological means of malaria control in the first half of the twentieth century not only failed to eradicate the disease but also drove some native species to the verge of extinction. Similarly, the introduction of the Nile Perch (*Lates niloticus*) into Lake Victoria has wreaked untold damage among the endemic haplochromine cichlid populations.

THE EMERALD-BACKED CICHLID (ABOVE) OF LAKE VICTORIA IS THREATENED IN THE WILD BY THE INTRODUCTION OF THE NILE PERCH (BELOW).

CAPTIVE BREEDING

While some countries impose bans on the collection and export of threatened species for aquaria, others adopt a different approach. Sri Lanka, for example, is very rich in both freshwater and marine fish species, many of the former being endemic to the island. Among the best known of these are several barbs, most notably the Ruby Barb (*Barbus nigrofasciatus*), the Cherry Barb (*B. titteya*), Cuming's Barb (*B. cumingi*) and (more obscure) the Bandula Barb (*B. bandula*). In the past (and despite the availability of commercially bred varieties of the first three species in other countries) demand for wild-caught Sri Lankan specimens, rather than commercial varieties with more intense coloration or longer fins, remained at a high level. This, allied to habitat destruction and pollution, raised concern within Sri Lanka for the longterm survival of these and other species in sufficient quantities for sustainable harvesting.

As a result, in the mid-1990s, captive breeding programs were set up by a number of exporters under the aegis of the Sri Lankan authorities. They were permitted to collect sufficient specimens of the first three species of barb to set up broodstock populations. Over a number of years, the exporters bred these species on their farms—monitored by a government agency—

until stocks were deemed to be sufficiently high to resume their exportation under a quota system. The Bandula Barb was apparently "rescued" from its only known, and very restricted, locality which appeared to be under environmental threat. Some of the collected specimens were placed in the hands of an experienced breeder/exporter who, over a period of time, was able to produce several thousand specimens. The species was saved from extinction, but, owing to the precarious state of its natural habitat, controlled reintroduction to the wild has only recently been possible.

In the case of another endangered Sri Lankan species, the beautiful anabantoid *Malpulutta kretseri* (Labyrinth Fish), it was the exporters themselves who proposed that no specimens be exported until a sufficient level of captive-bred stock had been achieved. This being a relatively slow-breeding species, the program was expected to take several years, so it may well be that the first exports of captive-bred *Malpulutta* will become available some time during the first decade of the new millennium.

In another fish-producing country, Singapore, as well as in other parts of the Far East, the legendary Dragon Fish (*Scleropages formosus*) is held in high esteem, since owning one is believed to bring the owner health and wealth. It is also a species that has long been listed under CITES Appendix I as endangered (although there does not appear to be conclusive proof that this is the case). As mentioned earlier, Appendix I species may be traded, but only if certain strict criteria are met, one of these being proof that the specimens in question have been bred in captivity for at least two generations. In order to document proof, the government of Singapore, through its then Primary Production Department (PPD)—now the Agri-food and Veterinary Authority (AVA)—set up a collaborative captive breeding project with a local breeder/exporter, which, over a number of years, resulted in the certified data required by CITES for legal exports of the species to recommence. As a result, legally certified captive-bred Singaporean Dragon Fish first became available for export on December 4, 1994. The first batch consisted of 300 Red Dragons, which were exported to Japan. Since then, many thousands have been exported worldwide. Each specimen is implanted with a uniquely coded microchip and is sold with a government-issued Certificate of Identity. This certificate carries the same 30-digit code that can be read by a scanner, authenticating the identity of the fish and its official source (*see* Bibliography). Since then, other farms in Singapore and elsewhere have applied for, and been granted, CITES approval for exports of this species.

A CAPTIVE-BRED DRAGON FISH (SCLEROPAGES FORMOSUS): AN ENDANGERED SPECIES CITED UNDER APPENDIX I OF CITES.

HOBBYIST PARTICIPATION

Captive breeding programs will, no doubt, continue to play a large part in the conservation of endangered species the world over. Aquarists have contributed, and continue to contribute, to these projects in several very important ways. For example, in the case of *Skiffia francesae*, it was (and is) the dedicated efforts of aquarists belonging to specialist livebearer societies in the U.S. and Europe that have ensured the continued survival of the species; repeated attempts at rediscovering this fish in the wild having failed.

In the case of *Malpulutta kretseri*, aquarists belonging to the Anabantoid Association of Great Britain played a very important role by providing the Sri Lankan exporter involved in the government-approved program with details of the maintenance and breeding techniques that they had successfully employed in their own aquaria.

Groups of aquarists that specialize in the breeding of threatened species exist in virtually all the leading fishkeeping countries. They form part of both national and international networks, sometimes working exclusively with other aquarists, sometimes in collaboration with scientific institutions, public aquaria and other official bodies. Without a doubt, today's aquarists have a very important part to play in fish conservation.

INDUSTRY PARTICIPATION

The modern-day ornamental aquatic industry also plays its part in fish, as well as habitat, conservation. As conservationists began embracing the concept of sustainable use of natural resources as vital to the conservation of species and their habitats, so did the ornamental aquatic industry, particularly from the mid-1990s. Today, the industry is actively involved in conservation and sustainable use projects as diverse as the successful Ocean Voice International and International Marinelife Alliance net-training programs in the Philippines (designed to replace cyanide collecting with net collecting), and the development of sustainable fisheries strategies in the Amazon. The closeness of the collaboration between the industry and Bio-Amazonia Conservation International is such that the conservation organization now uses the slogan: "Buy an ornamental fish; help save the rainforest."

In 1999 the Amazonian fish exporters set up a scheme under which each box of ornamental fish leaving Manáus was to carry a conservation "levy" or fee—half of which was to be paid by the exporters and half by the importers. This levy was designed to raise many thousands of U.S. dollars every year, all of which were to be invested in research on Amazonian fish species and their sustainable harvesting, as well as analysis of their fundamental importance to the economies of the human riverine communities.

COMMERCIAL BREEDING OF AQUARIUM FISH

Over 90 percent of all freshwater aquarium and pond fish are bred in captivity. The figure for marines is the reverse, with considerably less than 10 percent (probably around 5 percent) being commercially bred for the hobby. At first sight, the relatively low percentage of captive-bred marines might appear worrying, but the marine hobby is only approximately one tenth the size of the freshwater one. It is estimated that world demand for marine aquarium fish species amounts to something like 70–100 tonnes per year. The food fish industry accounts for around 100 million tonnes annually. Even the bycatch—the "waste" fish that are thrown overboard by trawlers—accounts for some 17 million tonnes every year.

Wild-caught fish for the marine aquarium hobby are collected from reefs spread out over an area of some 150,000 sq. miles (400,000 sq.km), thus avoiding to a large extent excessive pressure on individual reefs. Many programs are also now in place—and more are being developed—either to ensure that reefs do not suffer overexploitation, or to reverse the effects of past overexploitation.

Some of the programs include fish captive breeding or invertebrate culture projects *in situ*, and these, allied to *ex situ* programs as well as improved knowledge and husbandry techniques, are resulting in successes with species that had hitherto been considered impossible or

PART OF THE OUTDOOR HOLDING AREA IN A SINGAPOREAN FISH FARM.

very difficult to breed in captivity, such as marine angelfishes (Pomacanthidae). These successes are certain to continue and will gradually raise the percentage of commercially captive-bred marine species well above the current, modest level.

On the freshwater side, while the vast majority of so-called coldwater species and varieties available to aquarists and pondkeepers are bred commercially, a small number are still collected from the wild. In the main these consist of a restricted selection of Asiatic temperate species that have become available in recent years and for which demand is likely to remain low at least for the foreseeable future.

Most tropical freshwater species and varieties are bred in captivity for the hobby. However, the majority of the 10 percent or so of all freshwater species that are wild-collected are tropical in origin; coldwater species probably account for only about 1–2 percent. In some cases, it is perfectly feasible to breed these wild-caught species in captivity, and in quite large numbers. However, costs and consequently sale prices can be high when compared with those of wild-caught specimens. Certain species are therefore still usually wild-caught. The Sucking Loach or Chinese Algae Eater (*Gyrinocheilus aymonieri*) is one such species. It occurs in great abundance in its native waters in Thailand (not China as the species name implies) and is therefore widely available at reasonable prices. While it can be bred in captivity, only the golden and mottled varieties are captive-bred on a commercial basis; wild-type, i.e. "wild-colored," specimens are still collected from Thai hillstreams. Similarly, the abundance of the strikingly colored Clown Loach (*Botia macracantha*) from Indonesia makes captive breeding pointless. Shortly after the spawning season, gigantic shoals of juveniles occur downstream from the spawning grounds, and it is from these that the existing world demand for the species can be met without, apparently, affecting total populations.

The Cardinal Tetra (*Paracheirodon axelrodi*) is another popular aquarium species that occurs in vast numbers, this time in the Rio Negro basin in Brazil. During the middle to late 1990s, severe droughts were caused by the Pacific climatic phenomenon known as El Niño, and Cardinals became unavailable although they were not wiped out. As their native waters receded, the fish

retreated into areas that were difficult to get to or too far from the fishermen's bases to make the harvesting exercise economically viable. As numbers of wild-caught Cardinals gradually dried up, captive-bred stocks—primarily from the Czech Republic—took over. They were more expensive, but at least they were obtainable. Eventually, as the El Niño effects gradually disappeared and normal conditions returned in the Rio Negro, wild-caught Cardinals once more became the main source of supply.

As can be seen, when it comes to deciding whether or not to breed a particular species in captivity, it is not just the ease of breeding that needs to be taken into consideration. Economics and relative abundance in the wild are also important factors, alongside fecundity, speed of maturation and size. As a result, while highly prolific and abundant species like the three cited above are largely collected from the wild, other, less productive and sometimes more expensive, species are mainly bred in captivity. Captive breeding is also favored if the species in question shows inherent variability, as happens with the Angelfish (*Pterophyllum scalare*) and Discus (*Symphysodon discus* and *S. aequifasciatus*). All three, including the three main nominal subspecies of *S. aequifasciatus*, are still collected from the wild, but this accounts for only a small percentage of the total numbers available to hobbyists, the vast majority now being produced commercially by breeders in a number of countries, including Germany, the United States, Singapore, Thailand, Taiwan and Malaysia.

Where the wild-type of a species has been completely replaced by cultivated varieties—as has happened with many of the most popular aquarium fishes such as guppies, swordtails, platies, mollies, Siamese fighters, goldfish and numerous others—world demand for these fancy varieties is of course met exclusively by captive-bred stocks.

BREEDING ESTABLISHMENTS

Breeding aquarium and pond fish to meet aquarists' ever-growing demands is big business these days. Commercial ornamental fish breeding farms are now found in numerous temperate and tropical regions. In Japan, for example, Koi farms exist in many areas of the country, particularly Niigata, where the very best pedigree specimens are bred to be distributed the world over. This can be such a specialist activity that some families or breeding enterprises dedicate all their energies and expertise to the production of a single bloodline or variety such as, say, the Kohaku (a red and white variety of Koi). In China, some communities are equally dedicated to the production of a single variety of goldfish—the Oranda, for example.

Apart from these, there are less specific specialist breeders, concentrating on, say, a range of varieties of goldfish, or guppy, or Koi, or barbs. Even more wide-ranging are those breeders that specialize in, for instance, livebearers, or the "bread-and-butter" species and varieties, i.e. the most popular types.

The size of breeding establishment also varies widely. In the Czech Republic, for example, large numbers of tropical fish are bred in modestly sized premises, sometimes consisting of a single, medium-sized room. Such facilities dictate that careful thought be given to the types of fish chosen. These need to be either small—guppies, tetras, etc.—or types that can generate a reasonable return, such as discus or dwarf cichlids. Owing to the compact size of most of these breeding units, which can also be quite expensive to run, large or medium-sized inexpensive species are usually left for other, larger, breeding establishments to handle. This is where the major producers—Singapore, Malaysia, the United States, Sri Lanka and Israel—really excel, although they also breed small and high-revenue-generating species and varieties.

The largest share of the international demand for aquarium fish (around 30 percent) is met by Singapore, which is sometimes referred to as the "ornamental fish capital of the world." Other

THE TIGER BARB (BARBUS TETRAZONA)—SEE DESCRIPTION P.169—HAS BEEN BRED IN VAST NUMBERS BY AQUARISTS AND COMMERCIAL BREEDERS SINCE THE 1930s.

countries, such as Malaysia, also hold a large share of the market. Some of the apparently Singapore-bred fish that we keep in our tanks have, in fact, been bred in Singaporean-owned facilities in Malaysia.

Such is the global demand for freshwater ornamentals that some of the farms dedicated to captive breeding are huge. In Florida, some of the largest producers own not just a main farm, but "satellite" farms as well. Young fish, bred at the main farm, are regularly flown to these satellites for growing on and then reflown back to base once they attain sale size. Despite the vast numbers and varieties of fish bred and reared in this way, most Florida-produced tropicals are destined for the home (U.S.) market.

A number of countries employ a version of the satellite scheme operated by some Florida breeders. Whereas in Florida both the main farm and the satellites are owned by the same breeding establishment, in some countries the main breeder supplies juvenile fish to one or more independently owned satellite farms. They are contracted to grow the fish on to marketable size for the main breeder, who then buys back the fish prior to export. In this way, breeders that may have restricted facilities for rearing fish, but may be very good at breeding them, can greatly increase their production.

Another commercial breeding system is the community-based farm, as in some *kibbutzim* in Israel. A number of breeders contribute to a centralized breeding/exporting cooperative. Again, as with the satellite systems, this arrangement results in large numbers of fish being bred under controlled conditions, with each type being cultured by specialists.

A TYPICAL CAPTIVE-BRED SPECIES, THE BLUE VARIEGATED DELTA GUPPY (POECILIA RETICULATA).

FISH CARE IN THE AQUARIUM

Looking after fish is not just a question of setting up an aquarium and making sure that its inhabitants receive enough food. Such a simplistic approach will lead, sooner or later, to disaster. Success depends on numerous factors, many of them associated with the water itself, but there are many parameters that need to be considered to establish and maintain appropriate water conditions.

Even when water conditions are good, other factors will have a direct bearing on success or failure. For example, combining incompatible fish in a "community" aquarium must be avoided at all costs. All relevant factors, along with the main types of aquaria and how to set them up, are given individual attention in the following sections.

With due attention paid to the above, breeding will almost inevitably follow. Hence, a section that reviews the main reproductive strategies of aquarium fish is included.

AQUARIUM SETUP AND MAINTENANCE

Today's freshwater aquarist has several thousand species and varieties to choose from. With such a diversity of shape, size, requirement and habit, it follows that there is no single, infallible aquarium setup that can cater for all aquarium fish. However, many species have broadly similar requirements and can be grouped together from the maintenance, if not always from the breeding, point of view.

This chapter deals with the main groupings and how to set up aquaria suited to each. For special requirements, refer to the individual entries in the Aquarium Fish section.

COLDWATER OR TROPICAL?

It is important to attempt to distinguish between coldwater fish on the one hand, and tropical fish on the other. The dividing line between one and the other is nowhere near as precise as the terms imply.

What, for example, constitutes cold water? There is no debate if the temperature is at one or other end of the scale: 50°F (10°C) is undoubtedly coldwater, just as 86°F (30°C) must be tropical. However, at what point does a coldwater environment cease to be so and become tropical in nature? Turning to the fish themselves, species and varieties such as koi and goldfish are universally referred to as coldwater fish: true enough of specimens kept in, say, northern Europe, but what of those kept in Singapore, or Fiji, or Hawaii, where the ambient temperature is firmly within the tropical part of the spectrum?

The survival of the traditional application of both terms to aquaria has to do with the origins of aquarium keeping as a leisure activity. For a long time the hobby was far more popular in western temperate regions than in the tropics. As a result, many of the terms that we use were coined from the temperate perspective. If a fish could be kept in an unheated aquarium in a temperate country, it could justifiably be regarded as "coldwater." Any species requiring additional heat would be regarded as "tropical."

As the hobby expanded, and imports of goldfish and koi from the temperate regions of China and from Japan became progressively more popular, the term coldwater could still be regarded as appropriate. Then, as large-scale breeding and export of these fish spread to the tropics, the coldwater label was retained, so that today goldfish and Koi bred in tropical countries are still referred to as coldwater fish.

In summary, the term "coldwater" is applied to those fish that may be kept in unheated aquaria in temperate zones. Those that require supplementary heat in these regions, either for routine maintenance or for breeding, are referred to as "tropical." Therefore, even in tropical countries, a goldfish is still regarded as a coldwater fish because it would require no heat if it were being kept in a temperate country. Similarly, angels are still universally regarded as tropical because they can only be kept in heated aquaria. Most of the time, this interpretation works perfectly well, but there are numerous exceptions, fish that are perfectly capable of surviving in unheated aquaria in many temperate zones but are traditionally regarded as tropical. The Paradise Fish (*Macropodus opercularis*), the Medaka (*Oryzias latipes*), the Mosquito Fish (*Gambusia affinis* and *G. holbrooki*) and the White Cloud Mountain Minnow (*Tanichthys albonubes*) are just a few of the many examples of fish that originate either in temperate zones with a relatively mild winter climate, or in the so-called subtropical regions.

COMMUNITY AND SPECIES AQUARIA

The term "community aquarium" is used for any setup that includes a range of species and/or varieties of fish and/or invertebrates that can live in harmony with each other. In its broadest sense, it can be applied to any type of community-containing aquarium, whether this is a coldwater one consisting of goldfish, Koi, shiners,

ALBINO PARADISE FISH (MACROPODUS OPERCULARIS VAR.)

minnows and the like, a tropical one consisting of guppies, Corydoras catfish, neons or cardinals, hatchetfish, and other peaceful species, or an equivalent marine system. Taking the definition a little further, it can also be applied to, say, an African Rift Lake cichlid community, an Amazonian species community, a brackish-water selection of compatible species, a reef fish community, a mixed collection of compatible marine fish and invertebrates, and so on.

To the hobbyist, the term "community aquarium" most usually denotes a setup containing a selection of compatible, modestly sized, hardy, freshwater tropical species. This is the type of aquarium that the majority of aquarists install when they first enter the hobby; it is also, globally, the most popular system, even among the more experienced hobbyists.

In contrast, a "species" aquarium is one set up, strictly speaking, to house specimens of a single species. In the case of species that have been developed into cultivated varieties, such as mollies or guppies, the tank often contains representatives of a number of varieties. However, if an attempt is being made to breed a specific species or variety then only representatives of the selected type are included. If, further, the type of fish being bred is a poeciliid livebearer, the selection of suitable female specimens is made very early on, that is, before they have been mated. The reason is that poeciliid livebearer females can store sperm and use these to fertilize a sequence of egg batches (as many as ten or more). Therefore, if mated by a male of the "wrong" type, an inseminated poeciliid female is virtually useless for line-breeding purposes. (This does not apply to all types of livebearer. Goodeids, for example, do not store sperm; and for egglayers of course, each spawning is a completely "new" and separate event.)

Sometimes, species tanks can look a little empty, especially if the fish in question is a surface or bottom dweller. Such aquaria are therefore often stocked with a second species, compatible in terms of behavior, but not breeding characteristics, which will occupy the "empty" level. Corydoras catfish, for example, are excellent "companion" choices for a wide range of other species.

BASIC AQUARIUM NEEDS

Every aquarium, irrespective of type or size, needs to provide a minimum number of essentials if fish and plants are going to thrive in it. The water needs to be of good quality and of the appropriate composition, the temperature must match the needs of the fish and plants, there must be sufficient oxygen for the aquarium inhabitants, and—where plants are being cultivated—the light must be of the right type, intensity and duration. Aquaria must also provide adequate shelter, especially for retiring species.

Water is, of course, at the very heart of aquarium keeping. In some ways aquarists are "water keepers" rather than fish keepers. New aquarists are sometimes surprised by this, seeing themselves in the first instance as fish guardians and doctors, but even a moment's consideration will indicate that looking after the fish is quite impossible without looking after the water. The water's importance is illustrated by an old—and perfectly valid—saying in the hobby: "Look after the water, and the water will look after your fish."

"Water keeping" involves the setting up and management of equipment designed to help us control the enclosed environment within our aquaria. The key pieces of essential equipment available for this purpose are filters, aerators, heaters, thermostats, and lighting systems.

Filters and Filtration

In the confined space of an aquarium, fish cannot swim away to a better, cleaner location—as they can in the wild—if water conditions deteriorate. Unless some way of treating their waste products is found, they will end up swimming in their own excreta (both liquid and solid). This is not only unpleasant; the highly toxic nature of some of the waste can actually kill the fish. In particular, fish and other aquatic creatures generate ammonia as one of their primary excretory products. Unfortunately, ammonia is highly toxic (although more so in hard, alkaline water than in soft, acid conditions). In fact, a concentration as low as 0.025 milligrams per liter (parts per million) can prove toxic to delicate fish, while a concentration of 0.2–0.5mg/l (parts per million) can kill many species in a relatively short time. Certain bacteria are capable of converting ammonia into nitrites, which, while being less toxic, can still cause problems at 0.1mg/l (parts per million). Other bacteria are able to oxidize nitrites into nitrates, which need to rise to around 50mg/l (parts per million) before they begin to become a serious threat to delicate species.

There is currently a degree of uncertainty concerning the actual identity of the bacteria responsible for this detoxification of wastes. Traditionally, bacteria belonging to the genus *Nitrosomas* have been regarded as the prime ammonia-to-nitrites converters, with *Nitrobacter* bacteria continuing the process from nitrites to nitrates. In the latter half of the 1990s, though, research results obtained in the United States threw this longheld belief into doubt, and while the matter has not yet been cleared up there is a distinct possibility that neither of these genera play key roles in the ammonia-nitrite-nitrate oxidation process.

Whatever the eventual answer turns out to be, there is no denying that there are some microorganisms universally present in aquarium water that are capable of detoxifying soluble fish wastes. The processes involved are aerobic and therefore require oxygen. The end products of the oxidation of ammonia are nitrates that, while being relatively nontoxic, can eventually become so if their concentration is allowed to rise indefinitely. Fortunately, there are also waterborne microorganisms that, through a series of biochemical reactions, have the effect of converting nitrates back into nitrogen which then diffuses back into the atmosphere. These processes—unlike the ones that convert ammonia to nitrites and nitrates—are anaerobic, and can therefore occur in the absence of oxygen.

Armed with this knowledge, aquarium equipment manufacturers have developed a wide range of filters that allow us to control waste treatment in our aquaria using similar principles to those employed in sewage treatment plants. Some filters are placed under the aquarium gravel, using the grains not just as mechanical sediment traps, but also as surfaces on which detoxifying bacteria and other micro-organisms can become established. Other filters use canisters, located either inside or outside the aquarium, to perform similar functions. In addition, many of these filters provide a third facility: highly porous media such as activated carbon or zeolite (clay-based granules) can adsorb (not absorb) certain chemicals, including ammonia, directly from the water.

Such media are said to perform "chemical filtration." Physical removal of solid wastes is termed "mechanical filtration," and bacteria-mediated detoxification is referred to as "biological filtration." Strictly speaking, only physical entrapment qualifies as filtration; the two other processes are more accurately categorized as purification or detoxification.

From the late 1980s onward, filter technology advanced enormously, as a result of which home aquaria can now be fitted not just with the long-established types of filter, such as undergravel, box or canister systems, but also with trickle, or wet/dry filters (both internal and external), high-speed sand filters, or even a system increasingly employed in commercial establishments (after a period of popularity with marine hobbyists)—fluidized bed filters. (Ultraviolet sterilizers, which are sometimes referred to as "filters," are not filters and will be discussed in the Health section, *see* p.62.)

Filter media, too, have undergone constant development and refinement to the extent that some of today's

MECHANICAL FILTRATION · CHEMICAL FILTRATION · BIOLOGICAL FILTRATION

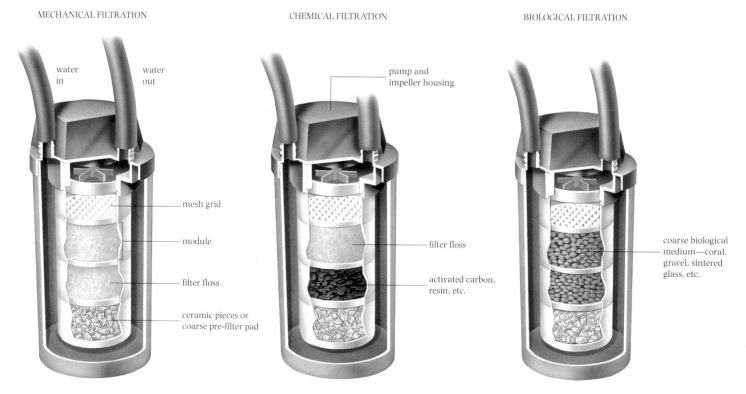

THE THREE MAIN WAYS TO UTILIZE A CANISTER FILTER. THESE MODELS USE INTERNAL CLIP-TOGETHER MODULES, EACH HOLDING A DIFFERENT MEDIUM.

spray bar

filter wool or sand

filtered water returns
to main aquarium

plastic trays with
drainage holes

*A KILLIFISH AQUARIUM INCORPORATING A FOAM SPONGE FILTER AND A COMBINED
HEATER/THERMOSTAT UNIT.*

▲ *A BASIC TRICKLER FILTER SYSTEM. UNITS SUCH AS THESE
ARE SITED ABOVE THE MAIN TANK. THEY ARE SUPPLIED BY
WATER PUMPED THROUGH A SPRAY BAR FROM A POWER
FILTER. TRICKLE FILTERS HELP OXYGENATE THE WATER
FLOWING THROUGH THEM AND SO INCREASE BACTERIAL
ACTIVITY.*

▶ *A GRAVITY-FED RAPID SAND FILTER. THIS UNIT COMPRISES
A SERIES OF COMPARTMENTS CONTAINING TRAYS, THROUGH
WHICH THE TANK WATER IS PASSED. THE FILTER MEDIA
INCLUDE COARSE, MEDIUM AND FINE FILTER SANDS.*

▼ *SMALL SINGLE-TRAY TRICKLE FILTERS SITED ABOVE THE
TANK CAN BE USED EFFECTIVELY ON BREEDING AND REARING
TANKS, OR WHERE IT IS IMPRACTICAL TO FIT A LARGE
MULTI-TRAY UNIT.*

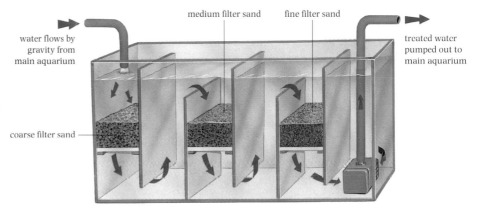

water flows by
gravity from
main aquarium

medium filter sand

fine filter sand

treated water
pumped out to
main aquarium

coarse filter sand

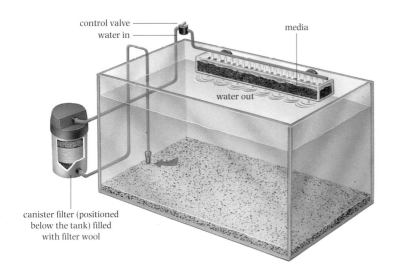

control valve

water in

media

water out

canister filter (positioned
below the tank) filled
with filter wool

super porous types can perform both nitrification (ammonia–nitrites–nitrates conversion) and denitrification (nitrates–nitrogen conversion) simultaneously. The old stalwart, filter floss or wool, is still around and still doing a great job as a mechanical medium. In between this and the latest "double-action" media, there is now a vast array of types and prices to choose from.

If a filter is well-matched with the job it needs to do, it will perform efficiently. However, push any system beyond its limits (commonly by overstocking or overfeeding), and not even the most efficient, sophisticated and expensive units will be able to cope. It is therefore vitally important to choose sensibly, seeking advice not just from manufacturers' literature but from experienced aquarists and professionals: speak to your dealer and explain your existing or proposed setup.

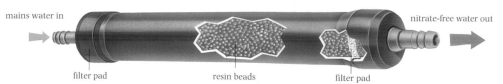

mains water in

filter pad   resin beads   filter pad

nitrate-free water out

NITRATE FILTER. WHILE NITRATE IS NOWHERE NEAR AS TOXIC AS AMMONIA OR NITRITE, IT CAN STILL WEAKEN FISH AND LEAVE THEM VULNERABLE TO DISEASE. A RECHARGEABLE RESIN FILTER LIKE THIS ELIMINATES WHAT CAN BE UNDULY HIGH NITRATE LEVELS IN MAINS WATER IN SOME AREAS; AND ANY BUILDUP AS PART OF THE BIOLOGICAL FILTRATION CYCLE.

The accompanying diagrams will help you familiarize yourself with some of the most commonly encountered filtration systems. Although individual brands differ in details, the basic principles do not change. When choosing any system, it is advisable to opt for one that not only performs the mechanical/chemical/biological functions required (including, if at all possible, denitrification), but one that has capacity spare to cope with emergencies or increases in stocking levels.

Aeration

Aquarium aerators do not just supply oxygen to the water. They also eliminate toxic gases, such as carbon dioxide, into the air. It is not the actual bubbles of air produced by an aerating device that are the primary source of dissolved oxygen. Indeed, very little, if any, oxygen can dissolve out of a bubble in the few seconds that it takes to travel to the surface of the water. The finer the bubbles produced from an aerating unit, either via a diffuser or air stone or via a venturi built into a filter powerhead, the greater the likelihood of oxygen dissolving from these bubbles into the water. However, even in these cases, the primary role of the airstream is to cause disturbance of the water surface, thus facilitating the absorption of oxygen from the air above the aquarium into the water, and the diffusion of toxic gases (predominantly carbon dioxide) from the aquarium into the air.

An effective interchange between air and water also helps to oxidize some potentially harmful chemicals and render them safe. This is one of the reasons that stale or foul-smelling water (which has no place in an aquarium, of course!) will quickly improve under vigorous aeration. Another valuable function of aeration is that, by circulating water, it prevents "hotspots" and "coldspots," distributing the warm water generated by the heating unit evenly throughout the aquarium. This distribution is important, even in unheated aquaria: layering (stratification) of warm water above cooler water can occur in the absence of adequate circulation.

Since aeration depends to a large extent on the creation of water-surface turbulence, the mechanism by which this is achieved can vary. Air bubbles from an aerator or venturi can be replaced by some other form of "turbulence-generator," such as fine streams of water from a spraybar attached to the outflow of a power filter. Most modern-day power filters now come with detachable spraybars, thus offering the user maximum flexibility.

In the earlier days of aquarium keeping, undergravel filters were exclusively operated by introducing the air line from an aerator (with or without an attached air stone) down the filter uplift tube. Today, while this practice is still widespread, a powerhead is often fitted in the top (open) end of the filter uplift tube. The principle remains the same. A stream of air bubbles (in the case of an air-driven system) or water (in the case of a powerhead-driven one) rises within the uplift tube, and, in so doing, creates a negative pressure under the filter plate. Waste-laden water is drawn in from above the gravel, under the filter plate, whence it is eventually pulled up the filter tube and back into the aquarium.

Where powerheads are used instead of an air-operated system, it is possible to reverse the flow of water, down the uplift tube, into the space under the filter plate and upward through the gravel. One of the advantages claimed for this method (known as reverse

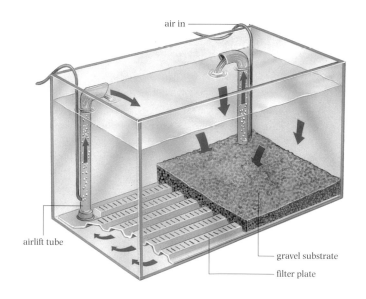

air in

airlift tube

gravel substrate

filter plate

A TANK FITTED WITH A CONVENTIONAL-FLOW UNDERGRAVEL FILTER. IN THIS SYSTEM, WATER IS DRAWN DOWN THROUGH THE FILTER BED (SUBSTRATE) AND RETURNED VIA THE AIRLIFT TUBE TO THE TOP OF THE AQUARIUM.

flow) is that solid matter is taken directly from the aquarium to the underplate space, thus reducing the degree of clogging of the gravel that inevitably occurs in normal flow filtration.

Aeration of aquaria can also be achieved, or enhanced, during the hours of daylight or under artificial illumination, with aquatic plants. In the presence of light, green plants perform a series of biochemical reactions collectively referred to as photosynthesis, one by-product of which is oxygen. This process (which is dealt with more fully in Aquarium Plants section), ceases at night. As a result, the oxygen level of a planted aquarium (even one that is not artificially aerated) will rise during the morning, reaching a peak in the early afternoon, and then gradually decrease during the hours of darkness, with the lowest concentration occurring during early morning. The actual quantities of oxygen dissolved in aquarium water depends on three main factors: the efficiency of the aerator, the surface area of the aquarium, and the temperature. A word of caution: some timid or retiring fish species do not welcome a turbulent environment, so this must be taken into account when planning the aeration system.

The cooler the water, the higher the level of oxygen that can be absorbed. The presence of pollutants and other compounds will also have an effect. In nature, many waters contain much less dissolved oxygen than the maximum (saturation) level possible, often as low as 2–5mg/l (parts per million)—a level that is too low for aquaria.

In aquaria, we should aim for levels close to saturation. We should also aim at keeping the dissolved-oxygen content as constant as possible. Both these criteria can be achieved with ease by employing an efficient aerating system, maintaining reasonable stocking levels, and following an adequate aquarium maintenance program. The table below gives approximate oxygen saturation levels for freshwater aquaria.

TEMPERATURE (°F/°C)	OXYGEN SATURATION LEVEL (mg/l—PARTS PER MILLION)
41/5	13.0–14.8
50/10	10.0–13.0
59/15	9.5–10.0
68/20	8.8–9.4
77/25	8.0–8.5
86/30	7.4–7.8

Although the highest levels of dissolved oxygen occur at the lowest temperatures, these are encountered only in home aquaria kept during winter in unheated rooms. Few aquaria experience such conditions. At the other end of the scale, aquaria designed for warmth-loving species such as *Discus* or mollies, are under threat of low oxygen saturation. Care with stocking such systems is therefore essential.

Temperature Control

Coldwater aquaria, as discussed earlier, do not require additional heat at any stage. Indeed, in warmer regions, particularly during the hottest periods of the year, they may even benefit from being kept cooler than the ambient temperature. In such cases, the use of an aquarium chilling unit may be found helpful, though not essential. There are some models available in a number of countries and professional advice from a specialist dealer should be sought before buying. Alternatively, switching the aquarium lights off during the hottest period of each day, ensuring that no direct sun hits the aquarium, vigorous aeration, and (even) floating a plastic bag with several ice cubes in it, may prove sufficient to lower the temperature by a few (and only a few) degrees.

In most homes, aquaria are kept in rooms that are either heated in winter—in those countries where this is necessary—or cooled by fans or air conditioners. Either way, the temperature of a coldwater aquarium will generally fall within acceptable limits without the need for additional heating or cooling. However, in the case of tropical setups, ambient (room) temperature is often several degrees below the optimum for fish, particularly in temperate zones (but the difference is rarely more than 15°F/8°C).

There are several ways in which an aquarium may be heated, and these methods may be direct or indirect. Space heating, where the room, rather than the aquarium, is heated to the required temperature, is an indirect method employed primarily by specialist hobbyists that have one or more rooms set aside exclusively for aquaria. Even in these cases, though, there is usually a backup direct system consisting of individual heater/thermostat units in each aquarium.

Submersible heater/thermostats—often referred to as heater/stats—are the most frequently used method of aquarium temperature control. So popular are they that there are units to match any size of aquarium, differing in heat output, sophistication, and price. They do not, however, differ in their essential function of heating the water up to a particular temperature and then switching off until the temperature drops once more to the level at which the unit has been set to reactivate.

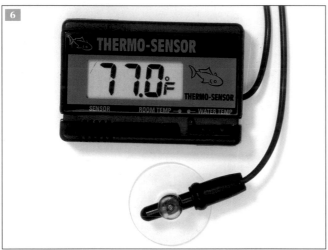

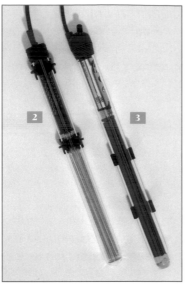

1. *ALCOHOL-FILLED THERMOMETER, WITH A GREEN "SAFETY ZONE" AND DUAL SCALE;* 2. & 3. *HEATERS WITH BUILT-IN THERMOSTATS;* 4. *HEATER ONLY, TO BE USED WITH* 5., *A TEMPERATURE CONTROLLER AND SENSOR PROBE;* 6. *LIQUID CRYSTAL DISPLAY (LCD) UNIT, ACCURATE AND EASY TO READ;* 7. *STANDARD ALCOHOL THERMOMETER;* 8. *COMBINED HYDROMETER/THERMOMETER;* 9. *STICK-ON LCD STRIP FOR BROAD-BASED READINGS.*

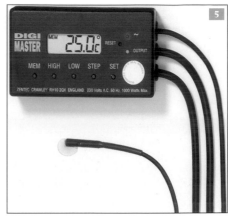

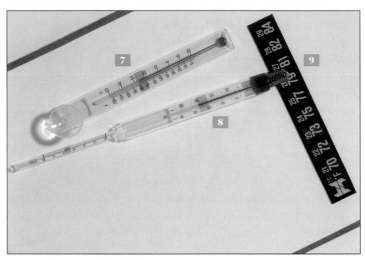

Other forms of heating include low-voltage undergravel cables and infilter heating units. Undergravel cables are very efficient and have the added advantage that they are never so hot that they can damage plant roots or gravel micro-organisms. Infilter heating units have the advantage that the heat source is removed from the aquarium and located inside a power filter instead, where it warms the water as it passes through the filter chamber. Another method, often employed in multichamber undertank filtration systems, uses this same principle: the heating unit is located in one of the filter compartments and is, thus, warmed within the filter, rather than within the aquarium.

Whichever method is employed (the choice depends on personal preference, budget and circumstances), one thing that needs to be determined is just how powerful a heating unit is required. Traditionally, the rule has been to allow about 4 watts per gal (4.5 watts per Imp. gal/1 watt per liter) of water. However, modern thinking has moved away toward lower figures, where (depending on the amount of heat estimated to be generated from aquarium lighting, etc.), we now recommend a maximum of just over 2 watts per gal (2 watts per Imp. gal/0.5 watts per liter)—or just under—but, preferably, around a little less than 1 watt per gal (around I watt per Imp. gal/0.2 watts per liter), depending on size of aquarium, ambient temperature, number and intensity of lights, and so on.

Using these figures, we can estimate the total approximate power (in watts) of the heating required for aquaria of different sizes kept in rooms whose temperatures differ from that of the aquarium water itself. The accompanying table shows some approximate figures for a range of aquarium capacities. (Note, though, that the figures are approximate and that the thermostatic unit of the heater will require adjustment to suit individual circumstances. The wattage/liter required increases relative to the temperature difference, as you would

TOTAL WATTAGE REQUIRED

AQUARIUM CAPACITY IN LITERS (APPROX. GAL/IMP GAL)	DIFFERENCE BETWEEN REQUIRED WATER AND ROOM TEMPERATURES IN °C				
	2	4	6	8	10
45 (12/10)	9W	19	29	39	48
60 (16/13)	11	23	34	45	57
80 (21/18)	14	27	41	55	69
100 (26/22)	16	32	48	64	80
150 (40/33)	21	42	56	76	95
200 (53/44)	25	51	76	101	127
250 (66/55)	29	57	86	114	143
300 (79/66)	33	66	99	133	166

expect. It also decreases as the tank capacity increases because larger volumes of water retain heat more effectively than smaller ones and, thus, require less input to maintain a constant temperature once the required level has been reached.

Comparing the figures in the capacity/temperature difference table above with the more widely published traditional heater recommendations below (which vary between books and manufacturers) it will immediately become evident that the former are considerably lower. Many aquarists therefore still believe that it is better to stick to the traditional values, since these appear to provide a wider safety margin in case of emergencies. During a power cut, it makes no difference, of course whether a heater is rated at 10 watts or 1,000 watts. However, where higher-wattage models can help is in the speed with which normal water temperature can be restored after the power is back on (always bearing in mind that rapid temperature changes are distressing or dangerous to most fish).

RANGE OF TRADITIONAL HEATER RECOMMENDATIONS

AQUARIUM CAPACITY IN LITERS (APPROX. GAL/IMP GAL)	APPROX. WATTAGE
45 (12/10)	50–70
60 (16/13)	70–100
80 (21/18)	100–125
100 (26/22)	125–150
150 (40/33)	150–175
200 (53/44)	175–200
250 (66/55)	200–250
300 (79/66)	Up to 300

Aquarium Lighting

There are two approaches to aquarium lighting. The first uses the type of lighting itself as the starting point: the lighting is chosen before everything else. For example, after seeing an aquarium setup incorporating spotlights, some may well be tempted to incorporate them in their own plans. This is fine, of course, but there are limits: a 24 × 12 × 12in (60 × 30 × 30cm) tank is far from ideal for spotlights, whereas a tastefully arranged 60 × 18 × 18in (150 × 45 × 45cm) one can be absolutely magnificent. This is especially so if the larger aquarium includes submerged light-loving plants, such as *Cabomba*, *Hygrophila*, *Vallisneria* and *Ludwigia*, with some *Riccia* or *Salvinia* on the surface.

The second approach uses the fish, invertebrates and plants as the starting point, which means establishing the requirements of the various species involved (details of which are given in the Fish and Plant sections respectively) and then choosing the most appropriate lighting, or combination lighting, for them.

For instance, if a species tank is being set up for Blind Cave Fish (*Astyanax mexicanus*) there really is no need for lighting of any sort. In fact, providing these fish with a brightly lit and well-planted tank, albeit harmless, rather misses the point. Nothing shows these fish up better than a dim, reddish spotlight strategically placed off-center in relation to the tank surface. This will not only enhance the appearance of the fish themselves, but can create a most attractive cave-like arrangement of light and shadow, particularly if the bottom of the tank is adorned with lengths of stalagmite.

FOR AN UNUSUAL AQUARIUM LIKE THIS *100GAL (380 LITER)* ONE, DESIGNED TO GIVE A FEELING OF LOOKING IN ON A SECRET UNDERWATER WORLD, GOOD LIGHTING IS AN ESSENTIAL PART OF THE EXPERIENCE.

For crepuscular (twilight) species, brightly lit tanks housing light-loving species of plant are, again, not the most appropriate setup. It is much better to tone down the light, choose shade-loving plants, such as various species of *Cryptocoryne* and Java Moss,

Vesicularia dubyana, and provide a light/dark regime of approximately 10 hours on/14 hours off. (This, incidentally, also cuts down the risk of excessive algal growth.) Some species of fish that do well under these conditions (provided a vegetable/algal supplement is made available where necessary) are the Elephant-nose (*Gnathonemus petersii*), bristle-nosed catfish (*Ancistrus* spp.), spiny eels (*Mastacembelus* and *Macrognathus* spp.) and some knife fishes (e.g. *Notopterus* spp.).

Gouramis and closely related fishes, for their part, generally spawn at the water surface. Therefore, a tank housing these species should not be provided with high-heat-generating bulbs which will destroy the nest, the eggs and the newly hatched fry. Tungsten bulbs, spots and high-pressure bulbs are, therefore, best avoided. For these species, fluorescent lighting is more suitable.

Whatever the approach, one will still be faced with weighing up the pros and cons of the different types of lighting before making a final decision. For ease of reference, some of the main advantages and disadvantages are listed in the table (*left*).

Matching species and lighting is not the easiest of jobs, but with a thoughtful approach, paying due attention to the needs and characteristics of both the species and the various systems involved, most problems—including excessive algal growth—can be brought under control. If you have any doubts, consult your supplier or manufacturer, who will have literature in addition to the guidelines provided on the product packaging, which will prove invaluable in helping you to make a final decision.

The accompanying table (*below*) lists the approximate lighting requirements for a range of tank sizes. The figures shown apply broadly to well planted aquaria housing the more common species and varieties of

TYPE OF LIGHTING	SOME ADVANTAGES	SOME DISADVANTAGES
Daylight	The least expensive.	Unpredictable and difficult to control.
Tungsten (Incandescent) Bulbs and Tubes	Cheap to install. Reasonable lifespan. Can stimulate good plant growth.	Relatively expensive to run. Risk of implosion. Generate a great deal of heat. Unsuitable for most surface nesting species of fish. Bulky—may not fit inside some modern hoods.
Fluorescent Tubes	Cheap to run. Variety of light available to suit different needs, including "daylight" and "moonlight" tubes. Fit inside most aquarium hoods. Emit light at relatively low temperature.	Require starter unit. Expensive to install. Relatively expensive to replace.
Spotlights	Penetrate deeply—therefore good for large aquaria. "Cool" spots emit light at moderate temperatures compared to "normal" spotlights. Reasonably priced.	Bulky—do not fit inside conventional hoods. Generate a great deal of heat. Expensive to run.
High-pressure Mercury/ Metal Halide Bulbs	Brilliant penetrating light, suitable for deep tanks. Inexpensive to run. Long-lasting.	Bulky—do not fit inside conventional hoods. Generate a great deal of heat. Expensive to install. Require starter unit. Expensive to replace.

APPROXIMATE LIGHTING REQUIREMENTS

LENGTH OF TANK (in/cm)	TUNGSTEN BULBS	SPOTLIGHTS	FLUORESCENT TUBES	HIGH-PRESSURE MERCURY BULBS*
18/45	1 × 40W	Not suitable	1 × 8W	Not suitable
24/60	2 × 40W	Not suitable	1 × 15W	Not suitable
30/75	2 × 60W	2 × 60W	1 × 20W	Not suitable
35/90	3 × 40W	3 × 60W	2 × 20W	1 × 80W
47/120	3 × 60W	4 × 60W	2 × 30W	1 × 80W
59/150	5 × 40W	5 × 60W	2 × 40W	1 or 2 × 80W
71/180	5 × 60W	6 × 60W	2 × 50W	2 × 80W

NOTE

*Wattages for metal halides are a little lower than those recommended for mercury bulbs

plants and fish available. What this chart, like all others, cannot show are some of the hidden snags.

For example, spotlights, metal halide, and high-pressure mercury bulbs, have bright, penetrating light and can, therefore, be a better choice for deep tanks than some of the other types of lighting. However, hand-in-hand with this tremendous advantage are several significant disadvantages, such as the intense heat generated by the bulbs and their large size, which makes their installation under standard aquarium hoods impossible, and requires that a space of 12in (30cm) or more be left between the bulbs and the water surface. In the case of high-pressure mercury and metal halide bulbs, it is also difficult to calculate the exact number required because of the spread of the light (approx. 24in/60cm at a height of around 8in/20cm) and its intensity (an 80W mercury bulb is assumed to equal two 150W spotlights in terms of output). Clearly, these parameters will vary according to how the bulbs are placed above the tank.

Water Chemistry

Good water quality is not just a matter of cleanliness, adequate oxygenation, and appropriate temperature, and lighting control. It also involves water chemistry. In particular, as aquarists, we need to concern ourselves primarily with three aspects of water chemistry (though the more aspects one becomes familiar with, the better this will be for both fish and plants):

a) tapwater chemistry
b) acidity/alkalinity
c) hardness.

Water that comes out of a faucet (tap) is a very different compound from that found in a tropical stream. Tropical waters are often heavily loaded with iron taken from iron-rich soils (laterite) over (and through) which water flows on its course downstream. Tapwater, on the other hand, often has little or no iron. Conversely, tropical stream water contains no chlorine or chloramine, disinfecting substances used to render tapwater safe to drink. Other compounds added to water during its treatment can also affect acidity/alkalinity, as well as hardness. In nature, these attributes tend to be constant in any area, unless a major external factor such as pollution dictates otherwise. We therefore find, for example, that the majority of tropical jungle streams in South America and the Far East are soft and acid. In fact, some Amazonian waters where *Discus* are found can have a pH value as low as 4.0, which is extremely acidic. The African Rift

A MULTIPLE WATER-TESTING KIT: PH, AMMONIA, NITRATE LEVELS, ETC.

Lakes, on the other hand, contain hard water with pH values that can exceed 9.0, remarkably alkaline. There are other differences between tapwater and natural water, such as oxygen and carbon dioxide content.

CHLORINE AND CHLORAMINE

In making tapwater safe for humans to drink, not only do we lose some "natural" components (or find them in reduced quantities), but we also "gain" substances—such as chlorine and chloramine—which can actually kill fish (and not just in high concentrations). A chlorine concentration as low as 0.5mg/l (parts per million) can be harmful to some fish species.

When chlorine is bubbled through water, the two react to form hydrogen chloride, or hydrochloric acid (HCl) and hypochlorous acid (HOCl). It is the latter that is believed to be the main killer. Matters become more complicated when chlorine is bubbled through water containing ammonia: another compound, chloramine, is formed and, while chloramine itself may not pose a direct threat to fish health, the hypochlorous acid that it forms when it "breaks down" (dissociates) certainly does.

Chloramine takes a long time to break down. Chlorine is quite volatile and will dissipate within a few hours if the water is adequately aerated. Chloramine, however, can take up to a week to dissociate completely. Therefore, if an aquarium is not adequately filtered, with the result that there is a permanent background level of ammonia in the water, the addition of chlorinated tapwater can result in an equivalent background level of chloramine and, hence, toxic hypochlorous acid. By making tapwater safe for us, we render it quite unsuitable for aquatic life.

The actual amount of hypochlorous acid present in water is not determined just by the amount of chlorine added, but by temperature and pH. At lower temperatures, a lower percentage of the added chlorine ends up as hypochlorous acid than at higher temperatures, although the differences are relatively slight. With regard to pH, however, the differences are quite dramatic. For example, at pH 5.0, nearly 100 percent of the available chlorine occurs as hypochlorous acid, while at pH 7.0 (i.e. neutral water), the percentage is around 70 percent. At pH 8.0, only about 26 percent of the chlorine occurs as hypochlorous acid, reducing further at pH 9.0 where the concentration is only 3 percent.

The obvious conclusion is that the higher the pH, the lower the risk of chlorine toxicity, owing to the reduced levels of hypochlorous acid produced. In terms of actual levels of toxicity, 0.004mg/l (parts per million) of hypochlorous acid has been recommended as the maximum long-term level for sensitive fish like salmon. For short exposure, levels as high as 0.1mg/l (parts per million) can be tolerated by most fish species. However, even a concentration as low as 1.0mg/l (parts per million) can prove fatal after a short exposure. Fortunately, chlorine is easy to remove from aquarium water and, while chloramine is more resistant, it, too, can be neutralized. Traditionally, activated carbon placed within a filter has been used to reduce chlorine and chloramine concentrations. Chlorine can also (as mentioned earlier) be eliminated within a few hours under vigorous aeration; chloramine can take up to a week. Recently, the efficiency of activated filter carbon has been questioned but it still appears to do quite a good job. An alternative, probably more effective and certainly more expensive technique uses ultraviolet irradiation (via a UV sterilizer—see Fish Health).

There are also commercially available dechlorinating and dechloraminating agents and these should be used in all cases where major water changes or additions are made, especially in the absence of other control methods. Where minor water changes or topping up is concerned, amounting to around 10 percent or less of the total volume, it is generally safe to proceed without the aid of detoxifying agents or UV, but, even so, safety measures—such as aeration—should be adopted. Test kits are now available for measuring chlorine and chloramines, and these should be deemed essential by every aquarist.

ACIDITY AND ALKALINITY

We are all familiar with acid substances (from lemons and vinegar to battery acid) and alkaline, or basic, ones (such as caustic soda). But there are countless substances that do not have a neutral pH value. If any of these substances are dissolved in water, they will convey their acidic or alkalinic properties to the resulting solution.

Aquarium water, being a complex solution consisting not just of pure water but a whole host of dissolved substances, will have acidic/alkalinic (basic) properties, and these need to be matched with those of the natural water from which our fish originate and in which they have evolved. Thus fish from the Amazon will have evolved in acid waters, while those from the African Rift Lakes or many Mexican waters will come from alkalinic environments. Most aquarium fish come from waters ranging in pH values from 6 to 8 (with notable exceptions) and most will exhibit greater or lesser tolerance to conditions other than their native ones. However, for longterm peak health, every effort should be made to match aquarium water conditions with those that the fish in question experience in their natural habitat.

Acidity/alkalinity is measured in terms of pH (from 0 to 14), which is an indication of the hydrogen ion concentration of the solution being measured. The abbreviation pH actually stands for pondus hydrogenii, i.e. the "weight" or concentration of hydrogen. Hydrogen ions are positively charged hydrogen atoms that react readily with other substances. Therefore, the higher the number of such ions, the higher the reactivity of the solution. At first sight, this might suggest that the higher the pH of a water sample, the higher the concentration of hydrogen ions and therefore the more reactive it will be. However, the exact opposite is the case, because the pH scale actually represents the "negative log10 hydrogen ion concentration" of the solution being measured. This may sound complicated, but it can be "translated" into everyday language.

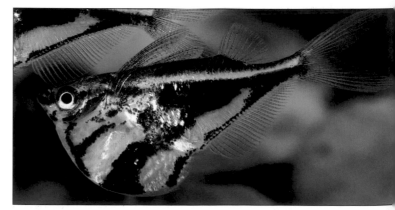

MARBLED HATCHETFISH (CARNEGIELLA STRIGATA) PREFER SOFT, ACID WATER—SEE PAGE 218.

Avoid hard water for the Diamond Tetra (Moenkhausia pittieri)—see page 206.

A "log10" scale is one in which each unit represents a tenfold increase or decrease. Therefore, a pH value of 8 represents a level of alkalinity that is ten times as high as a neutral solution with a pH value of 7. Equally, a solution with a pH value of 6 is ten times more acid than one with a pH value of 7 and 100 times more acid than one with a pH value of 8. In terms of hydrogen ion concentration, since the scale is a "negative log10" one, a solution with a pH value of 8 actually has 10 times fewer hydrogen ions than one with a pH value of 7 and 100 times fewer hydrogen ion than one with a pH value of 6.

This helps explain why, for instance, ammonia is less toxic in acid aquaria than in alkaline ones. There are many more highly reactive hydrogen ions available in acid-water aquaria to "bind up" toxic ammonia and render it safer. The reverse, of course, applies in alkaline-water systems.

The tenfold increases per pH unit explain why what appears to be a modest change on that 0–14 scale can be stressful, or even fatal, to fish. All pH changes must therefore be carried out gradually in order to ease fish from one set of chemical conditions to another.

Nowadays, there are numerous pH test kits available, ranging from electronic ones to color-chart types. Prices and levels of sophistication and accuracy vary, but all reputable makes are reliable. A pH test kit is absolutely essential, especially where the more delicate and challenging species of fish are concerned.

HARD AND SOFT WATER

Everyone can tell whether water is soft or hard. If it quickly forms a good lather, it is soft; if it doesn't, it is hard. We need to be rather more accurate when it comes to aquarium keeping. Without a more thorough understanding it is quite impossible to match fish with appropriate water conditions and, although many species and varieties will be able to adapt, others will not. Even those species that adapt quite readily to inappropriate hardness conditions may fail to breed. Cardinal Tetras (*Paracheirodon axelrodi*), and barbs such as the Tiger Barb (*Barbus tetrazona*), for example, can be acclimatized (gradually!) to survive perfectly adequately in water that is as hard as 300mg/l (parts per million). Under these conditions, though, egg fertilization is almost impossible.

Despite the importance of water hardness, some aquarists choose to ignore it, or pretend that it doesn't exist. The confusing terminology may well play a part in this: labels such as General, Total, Carbonate, Permanent, and Temporary Hardness do not help matters. Neither does the existence of different scales and units of measurement. Aquarium books, particularly some of the earlier works, are littered with terms such as Clark or English degrees of hardness, or American, or German degrees, which cannot easily or directly be compared.

Modern literature (thankfully) tends to adopt a more standardized or international approach that bases hardness on milligrams per liter (mg/l), which works out the same as parts per million (ppm). However, in order to make sense of any "nonstandard" units that may be encountered, the following are suitable conversion factors:

1 Clark or English Degree × 0.8 = 1 German Degree
1 Clark or English Degree × 0.84 = 1 American Degree

To convert these to mg/l or ppm, multiply:

1 Clark or English Degree × 14.3
1 German Degree × 17.9
1 American Degree × 17.1

It may be worth noting how the various degrees are calculated. Clark or English degrees of hardness are based on the number of grains—a grain = 64.7989mg, or 1/7000lb—of calcium carbonate ($CaCO_3$) per Imperial Gallon, while American degrees are an indication of grains of $CaCO_3$ per 1 million parts of water. German degrees represent parts of calcium oxide (CaO) per 100,000 parts of water.

Moving on to the terms used, Total Hardness refers, as its name implies, to the sum total of the hardness created by the various salts of calcium and magnesium present. Total Hardness includes:

1. General or Permanent Hardness produced by calcium and magnesium salts, primarily sulphates, nitrates and chlorides. This type of hardness is usually indicated as GH. Confusingly, "GH" is also used in many books to indicate Total Hardness.

2. Carbonate, Bicarbonate or Temporary Hardness produced by calcium and magnesium bicarbonates. This type of hardness is usually indicated as KH.

As the terms "Permanent" and "Temporary" indicate, the latter can be eliminated (by boiling, which results in an insoluble substance, the "fur" of kettles and other heating appliances) while the former will not be affected.

Both types are relevant to fishkeepers. A certain amount of Temporary/Carbonate/Bicarbonate Hardness (KH), for instance, helps to buffer or "cushion" water against abrupt fluctuations in pH. Bearing in mind the logarithmic nature of the pH scale (see previous section) and the potentially fatal consequences of abrupt changes, the importance of an appropriate KH becomes self-evident. General/Permanent Hardness (GH), on the other hand, needs to be low for some delicate species such as Discus and other fish from nutrient-poor, soft and acid waters, and high for fish from the other end of the spectrum, such as African Rift Lake cichlids.

If water is hard in any way, it may be softened through dilution either with rainwater or distilled water. Alternatively, proprietary products or ion-exchange units can achieve the same results. Temporary Hardness may be raised by gradually adding sodium bicarbonate ($NaHCO_3$) to water, while Permanent Hardness may be increased gradually through the use of limestone or other calcareous rocks as aquarium decorations, or through the use of coral sand or gravel, or limestone or marble pebbles, either as a substrate or enclosed in fine mesh within a filter. Alternatively, special salt mixes may be used.

When the hardness of a water sample is quoted, this usually refers to the Total Hardness, i.e. Temporary/Bicarbonate/Carbonate Hardness, plus Permanent/General Hardness. Water can be classified from very soft to very hard, depending on its total content of magnesium and calcium salts. Interpretation of where to draw the dividing line between one level of hardness and the next varies between books, so classifications must be regarded as guidelines only. Bearing in mind that most fish have a degree of hardness tolerance and that the crucial factor is the actual level of dissolved salts (and not how one splits them into categories) a workable hardness chart can be provided (see table p.41).

Although there is general agreement between the accompanying chart and most others at the "soft" end

THE FAIRY CICHLID (NEOLAMPROLOGUS BRICHARDI), "STAR" OF THE AFRICAN RIFT LAKES CICHLIDS, NEEDS MEDIUM-HARD, ALKALINE WATER—SEE PAGE 108.

WATER HARDNESS

WATER TYPE/CATEGORY	APPROX. TOTAL HARDNESS (mg/l—ppm)
Very soft	0–50
Moderately soft	50–100
Slightly hard	100–150
Moderately hard	150–200
Hard	200–300
Very hard	300+

ANUBIAS NANA *PLANTS BEING PLANTED INTO POCKETS OF A BOGWOOD DECOR PIECE.*
TANNINS THAT INITIALLY LEACH FROM BOGWOOD ARE ACTUALLY BENEFICIAL TO SOFT,
ACIDIC WATER SYSTEMS.

of the spectrum, some charts tend to have progressively higher values the further up the scale one moves toward the "hard" end of the range. I find the accompanying version particularly valuable in that it is a little "safer" than some other scales. The reason for this is that, while hardwater species can generally cope quite adequately with softer conditions, the more delicate softwater species can find hard conditions more challenging. By classifying the "harder" categories at lower values, the accompanying scale therefore tends to encourage the use of softer water. Three further points are worth considering before leaving the subject of water hardness:

1. It is important to know what type of hardness a test kit is actually designed to measure.
2. When measuring Temporary/Carbonate/ Bicarbonate Hardness, it is also important to appreciate that test kits designed to measure carbonate concentration do not always distinguish between calcium and magnesium salts and,

say, sodium carbonate (this last compound is particularly abundant in some African Lakes). As a result, Temporary Hardness readings can appear to be excessively high in such instances.
3. The term Total Dissolved Solids/Salts (T.D.S.) is sometimes used when referring to water hardness. In practical terms, it can be regarded as being equivalent to Total Hardness.

SETTING UP AN AQUARIUM

Aquaria can be set up to meet some very specific needs of fish: still or gently flowing, dimly lit, tannin-stained, soft, acid, brightly lit, clear, rockstrewn, hard or alkaline environments, according to species. Yet, despite specific differences, all aquaria share a number of basic characteristics. It is therefore possible to provide some general guidelines on setting up aquaria to suit a wide range of species, but which can be adapted accordingly to cater for more specialized requirements.

What follows is a series of easy-to-follow steps for setting up a general tropical community aquarium. Several versions of this setting up procedure exist, but all—in the end—achieve the same purpose.

1. Choose a site for the aquarium that is away from direct sunlight, drafts, banging doors, areas of high activity and other disturbances, making sure that the furniture or shelving on which the tank is to rest is capable of supporting the weight (water weighs about 10lb/gal (1kg/liter). Alternatively, buy a professional aquarium cabinet or stand.
2. Ensure that the chosen site has a sound, strong floor and—very importantly—that it is absolutely level.
3. Cushion the surface on which the base of the aquarium is to rest with appropriate material, e.g. strips or sheets of styrofoam.
4. Having rinsed the aquarium with clean water, *not* with detergents, to eliminate dust and other impurities, lay it on the styrofoam.
5. If an undergravel filter is being used, assemble it and rest the filter plate directly on the base of the aquarium.
6. To prevent the undergravel plate from becoming clogged with substrate, it is worth considering the use of a "gravel tidy." This is a meshlike sheet that can be laid on top of filter plates and prevents substrate grains being in direct physical contact with the slits or openings in the plate. This accessory is particularly useful when using fine-grained substrates.

7. Wash the gravel or other chosen substrate thoroughly in clean tapwater. Do *not* use detergents—they are highly toxic to all forms of aquatic life.

8. Add the substrate and arrange terracing or "integrated" decorations to give an attractive (preferably nonsymmetrical) effect. If undergravel filters are being used, it is important to provide a sufficiently thick layer of substrate for optimal biological filter activity; a thickness of some 2–3in (5–8cm) should be regarded as the minimum.

9. If the terracing being installed is commercially produced, then simply rinse it thoroughly prior to installation. If rocks and/or bogwood are being used, these may be glued together with silicone sealant, which must be allowed to set and "cure" before installation. To prevent bogwood or cork from floating, it is a good idea to stick the chosen pieces to slate, which can then be covered up with substrate. Make sure that rocks and/or bogwood or cork pieces are safely bedded into the substrate, avoiding the risk of their toppling over. This is particularly important in aquaria that will house bottom-rooting or burrowing/nesting species.

10. Position heaters, thermostats, internal filters (if these are being used) and air stone (and air line) strategically and, preferably, hidden from view. It is particularly important to ensure that there is no direct contact between the heater and either the decor or the substrate, since this will cause "hotspots." There are special mesh-type heater protectors (which, in reality, should be called fish protectors) and these may be used to eliminate the risk of causing burns to fish that like to rest close to the warmest spot in the aquarium. For optimal positioning the heater should be horizontal (or nearly so), approximately halfway along the back pane of the aquarium and as close to the substrate as possible. Do not plug in any electrical appliances at this stage! Whenever possible, air pumps should be positioned above water level (external to the aquarium, of course!). This minimizes the power needed in order to pump air along the air line and through the air or diffuser stone. It also eliminates the risk of water being siphoned into the pump when it is switched off. If it is not possible to locate the air pump as suggested, fit a non-return valve somewhere along the air line.

YELLOW SANDSTONE IS USED TO GOOD EFFECT IN THIS SETUP, PROVIDING LIGHTNESS AND HEIGHT.

11. To fill the aquarium with water, pour gently from a bucket or other suitable container, onto a plate or saucer, or into a jar stood on the plate or saucer, allowing the water to overflow gently onto the substrate, thus preventing any unnecessary disruption to the substrate or decor. If desired, the water can be warmed slightly before adding, speeding up the tank-warming process and protecting the plants against cold-temperature shock.

12. Once the aquarium is half-full, the plants can be installed or this can be delayed until the filling process has been completed. Both approaches have their advantages. The former makes the plants easier to position, while the latter provides a better idea of the overall effect from the outset.

13. The condensation tray—a clear plastic or glass cover designed to prevent excessive evaporation of aquarium water, as well as a means of protecting electrical connections from getting wet—can now be installed.

14. The lighting unit, starters, etc. can now also be fitted into the hood and the wiring appropriately arranged and connected. A cable tidy—a box that allows several pieces of electrical equipment to be wired centrally, with a single lead extending from the connection block to the mains—will help keep wiring neat and easy to manage. The one drawback of these devices is that every piece of equipment connected to them is then dependent on a single line of supply, with a single fuse (in those countries that use a fused plug/socket arrangement). The installation of a circuit breaker—a safety device that will cut off the electrical supply in case of

malfunction—is essential. If in any doubt whatsoever, consult a qualified electrician.

15. Put the thermometer in place and carry out water tests for pH and (if necessary) hardness. If these are outside the range required for the species that will be maintained, adjust accordingly. At this initial stage, proprietary adjusters (since they will produce results quickly) will be found particularly helpful.

16. Switch all the electrical equipment on and check that everything is working properly. Adjust the air flow, filter flow, temperature, etc., over the next few days while the aquarium is settling down.

17. Run the system on a 12–15 hours/day illumination period for about a week. Some aquarists do not deem this necessary, since proprietary water maturation products will speed up this initial settling-in phase. However, this first week is also valuable as a "training period" for the new aquarist.

18. The water may turn cloudy during this initial phase. However, resist the temptation to carry out a major water change. The cloudiness is caused by a bacterial bloom, which is characteristic of new aquatic systems. It will clear up of its own accord after a few days.

OTHER TYPES OF AQUARIA

While the guidelines given in the previous section will result in a well-setup freshwater tropical community aquarium, it will not (and cannot) cater for the needs of all types of freshwater aquarium fish. The basic principles will need modification in order to match the environmental and behavioral characteristics of the species in question. The following paragraphs provide a few pointers that should prove helpful in the design of some of these other types of systems.

Goldfish and Related Species

The most obvious difference between goldfish and fish that would qualify as tropical community species—in the general sense of the term—is that goldfish do not require the provision of supplementary heat. Therefore, when setting up an aquarium for goldfish, this stage does not apply. Among several other factors relating to goldfish aquaria, the following deserve special consideration:

1. Goldfish spend a great deal of time rooting among the gravel for morsels of food. In so doing, they very soon uncover the plates of an undergravel filter or, if this is protected by a gravel tidy, the mesh of the "tidy" itself. It is therefore sensible to avoid both undergravel filters and gravel tidies when designing goldfish aquaria.

2. Because of their almost incessant rooting, goldfish will mouth not just the substrate, but the surfaces of any submerged objects as well, including, of course, the rockwork. It is therefore particularly important to avoid the use of sharp-edged rocks or synthetic decorations in goldfish aquaria. (In any case, sharp-edged decor should be avoided in all types of aquaria).

3. Again, owing to their digging, bottom-feeding activities, goldfish will uproot most aquarium plants sooner or later. To prevent this, arrange plants in plastic pots or other suitable non-toxic containers and bury these in the substrate or hide them with rocks or other decorations. A layer of pebbles that are too large to be removed by the fish should be laid on the surface of the planting medium. Alternatively, surround any plants that are bedded directly into the substrate with large smooth pebbles to prevent direct access by the fish.

4. Goldfish and many related cyprinids are largely herbivorous in eating habits. They will therefore devour any delicate, succulent plants included in the aquarium decor. Only tough plants should therefore be used in such systems. Alternatively (or additionally), consider some of the excellent artificial plants currently available.

5. Continuing with the "artificial" theme, goldfish aquaria—particularly those housing the more fancy varieties—can be very effectively decorated

RED ORANDA (CARASSIUS AURATUS VAR.) NEED SPECIAL CONSIDERATION WHEN DESIGNING AN AQUARIUM.

with artificial "gravel" and "rocks" of differing colors. Jet-black or snow-white gravel make for particularly spectacular arrangements.

6. Goldfish aquaria should be well lit to show off the colors of the fish to maximum effect.
7. Efficient power filtration (but without excessive turbulence) with good mechanical facilities to remove the copious solid wastes produced by goldfish should be considered essential.
8. Owing to their substantial body size, goldfish should not be housed in aquaria measuring anything less than 24 × 12 × 12in (60 × 30 × 30cm). Even such an aquarium will only house a few medium-sized specimens.

Nowadays, it's not just goldfish that are kept in aquaria. Koi—particularly the newer, long-finned Butterfly or Fairy Koi—are now increasingly regarded as suitable aquarium choices. Some of the newer color varieties of tench (*Tinca tinca*) are also receiving attention.

In such cases, aquarium size is of course even more important. Koi can grow to 36in (90cm) or more in length. Tench can attain lengths of around 28in (70cm), although most specimens remain at around the 12–16in (30–40cm) mark. The implications are quite obvious: large aquaria, ultra-efficient filtration, especially close attention to water quality, etc..

African Rift Lake Cichlids

Many species of African Rift Lake cichlid grow to substantial sizes, with specimens in the region of 6–8in (15–20cm) quite common. Aquaria for these fish

A TYPICAL AFRICAN RIFT LAKE SETUP IS REQUIRED FOR THE LABIDOCHROMIS ELECTRIC YELLOW TANGANICAE; SEE PAGE 102.

therefore require very efficient filtration, which should not be of the undergravel type, owing to the digging behavior of many species. These aquaria should also be well-lit and water chemistry should (must) be on the hard, alkaline side (*see* relevant entries in the Fish section for details).

Aquarium backgrounds are important in all systems, whether to hide the wall against which the tank is sited, or trailing wires from view, or—for some internally positioned models—to provide shelter for fish as well as a natural-looking underwater scene. In African Rift Lake cichlid aquaria, though, it could be said that the aquarium background is even more important in the list of special decor requirements. Backgrounds are deemed so important in these setups that some specialists recommend their extension down one side (end) of the aquarium in addition to the back.

There are several related reasons why appropriate backgrounds in African Rift Lake cichlid aquaria are important. One is stress reduction, for example between competing, displaying, or territorial males. In addition, properly constructed backgrounds provide boltholes for fish, either to escape from tankmates, or from potential predators. (An aquarist approaching the front of a tank is, in effect, a potential predator, from the fishes' point of view!) Backgrounds for these aquaria should reach up to the water surface or nearly so. They should also be liberally supplied with caves and escape routes. If such a background is being constructed, great care must be taken to ensure that the resulting "cliff" is safe and cannot topple over. Some useful tips to help to achieve this:

1. Glue the individual pieces together with silicone sealant.
2. Make the cliff considerably wider at the base than at the top.
3. Make absolutely certain that the base is well-bedded into the substrate so that it cannot wobble.

Alternatively, some excellent synthetic backgrounds have appeared on the market. The best of these are so realistic that even experienced aquarists cannot tell the difference between them and natural rock. Among the many other advantages presented by these backgrounds are their ease of installation and their light weight. Not all African Rift Lake species are rock-dwellers or nesters; many occupy the sandy stretches between rocky outcrops. A sandy area must therefore also be provided for these fish.

Finally, these aquaria are traditionally stocked more heavily than general community or goldfish aquaria (up to 50 percent higher density of fish). Remarkably, the heavy stocking tends to reduce the level of aggression that any particular individual fish is subjected to. This is yet another reason why adequate shelter and efficient filtration are such central features of an African Rift Lake cichlid aquarium.

Amazonian/Soft Water Species

In sharp contrast to the clear, hard alkaline waters of the African Rift Lakes are the soft, acid waters of many Far East tropical regions and the Amazon itself. These waters, which often flow over iron-rich soils and have large accumulations of leaves, twigs, branches and tree trunks that continually fall into the water from the surrounding jungles, are also, very often, tannin-stained. This gives them the appearance of tea, which—particularly if the body of water in question is surrounded by jungle—produces dimly lit underwater conditions.

All these conditions can be imitated in home aquaria. Whenever possible, therefore, an attempt should be made to provide soft-water species with such an environment, especially since many of these fish show off their colors best in brown-stained, dimly lit water with little overall turbulence.

The tannin effect can be obtained in several ways. Firstly, there are proprietary water additives specifically for this purpose; these are the so-called "blackwater" treatments. Alternatively, or in addition, pieces of natural bogwood will create these conditions over a period of time, with the added bonuses that they contain lignin—the hard or "woody" material found in plants that forms part of the natural diet of some fish species, such as whiptail catfish (for example *Loricaria* spp); and they provide shelter for species that like to hide among submerged branches in the wild. Introducing a "peat sandwich"—a layer of peat wrapped in, for example, muslin—in a power filter can also help.

Dimly lit conditions can be created in several ways. One obvious method is to use low-wattage lights. Another, and probably better, alternative is to use tall-growing plants such as some of the *Cryptocoryne* species and allow their leaves to grow up to and across the water surface. This option has the added advantage that it can create a very attractive "dappled sunlight" effect that makes some fish, such as Lemon Tetras (*Hyphessobrycon pulchripinnis*) and especially Cardinal Tetras (*Paracheirodon axelrodi*), look particularly spectacular as they swim between "sun" and shade.

Many fish that come from this type of environment do not enjoy turbulent conditions. For these, vigorous power filtration should therefore be avoided. However,

Compare this picture of a Lemon Tetra (Hyphessobrycon pulchripinnis) with the one on page 202. The optimum aquarium setup can produce a striking improvement in color.

efficient filtration is still necessary to maintain good water quality, low in toxins such as ammonia and nitrites. It is still perfectly possible to use power filters for these aquaria, perhaps returning the flow to the tank via a fine spraybar with the jets of water being directed either horizontally onto the back pane of the aquarium, or onto the surface leaves of plants such as those mentioned earlier. Undergravel filters are generally good choices for the more sedate conditions found in most soft-water, acid communities; with some notable exceptions, such as aquaria housing large species such as Oscars (*Astronotus ocellatus*).

Another thing to avoid in soft-water, acid aquaria is the use of calcareous rocks as part of the decor. These will, over time, harden the water and make it alkaline. Many fish can tolerate this if the increases in hardness and alkalinity occur gradually. However, few species will be able to breed successfully in conditions that are so alien to those under which they have evolved.

Brackish Water Species

Some species of notionally freshwater fish actually live in brackish water habitats such as estuaries and mangrove swamps. Some—such as scats (*Scatophagus* spp.) and monos (*Monodactylus* spp.)—can occur either in freshwater or brackish habitats during their juvenile stages, migrating to fully marine conditions as they mature. Others, such as the Orange Chromide (*Etroplus maculatus*) are found in brackish water throughout their lives.

Although many brackish water species will tolerate genuinely freshwater conditions, even on a permanent basis, given the choice one should always attempt to provide brackish conditions, at least during the critical stages of such species' development.

Brackish water is water that contains a concentration of salt (particularly sodium chloride) that is higher than

IN BRACKISH-WATER AQUARIA, A MORE CALCAREOUS SUBSTRATE CAN BE USED.

that found in freshwater, but lower than in seawater. Since seawater contains around 30 parts of sodium chloride (NaCl) per 1000 parts of water—expressed as 30‰—and pure water contains no sodium chloride, the range of water chemistry that qualifies as brackish is quite wide. Another way of expressing salinity is in terms of specific gravity (or "weight"). Pure water has a specific gravity (SG) of 1.000, while the SG of seawater is around 1.020. (This value is pretty constant, but can vary. There are areas where salinity is higher, the most extreme example being the Red Sea.)

As a consequence of the range of salinity conditions that qualify as brackish, numerous types of setups can be devised for fish that come from such environments. The closer the conditions are to freshwater, the wider the range of species of both fish and plants that may be kept. At this end of the spectrum, the layout and design of the aquarium should be closer to a freshwater system than to a marine one. A mangrove-type setup in which the decor includes a fine substrate, submerged or partially immersed (and safely treated) roots or driftwood looks particularly effective for aquaria that fall on either side of the halfway point between freshwater and seawater. Further up the saline scale, the substrate can be a calcareous, coarser one consisting of coral gravel, calcareous rocks and other forms of decor usually associated with marine aquaria (refer to a marine aquarium book for details, *see* Bibliography).

If species such as archers (*Toxotes* spp.), four-eyed fish (*Anableps* spp.) or mudskippers (e.g. *Periophthalmus* spp.) are to be kept, it is advisable to lower the water level in order to observe the above-water activities of these fish (*see* individual entries in the Fish section for details). In the case of the last two, it is also advisable (necessary, in the case of mudskippers) to provide a "beach" or some other terrestrial, but moist, area onto which the fish can climb. Mudskippers will use such an area on a regular basis, while four-eyed fish

may use it, or may learn to use it, if food is provided for them some distance away from the water's edge.

Brackish systems that are closer to their freshwater than their marine counterparts are easier to manage and stock. The further up the scale one goes, the greater the significance of potential problems such as metal toxicity becomes. Guidance on how to avoid these will be found in any good marine aquarium book (*see* Bibliography). Specific gravity is easily measured using a hydrometer, which should be regarded as an essential piece of equipment by anyone contemplating setting up a brackish aquarium.

Large Fish

As husbandry techniques and aquarium technology have improved, the demand for large "companion" fish has also increased. One of these, Koi, has already been referred to earlier. This section deals with broad requirements for tropical equivalents in general. Since these large fish can be as varied as Red-tail Catfish (*Phractocephalus hemioliopterus*), Giant Gouramis (*Osphronemus goramy*); Dragon Fish (*Scleropages formosus*) or snakeheads (*Channa* spp.), precise guidelines cannot, obviously, be given here; fuller details may be found in the relevant entries in the Aquarium Fish section. All large fish are effective water polluters, especially in the confines of an aquarium. So their tank must be:

- very effectively filtered;
- conscientiously maintained;
- decorated in a way that facilitates cleaning.

Keep the decor simple, avoiding nooks and crannies in which debris can accumulate. In general, live aquatic plants and large fish are not compatible, most plants either being destroyed or consumed in a very short time. If greenery is desired, it may be better to consider using some of the more robust artificial types, along with "distasteful" natural plants, such as some of the aquatic ferns like Java Fern (*Microsorum pteropus*).

In terms of substrate, this should be coarse, except in those cases where the fish either bury themselves, as do some of the spiny eels such as the Fire Eel (*Mastacembelus erythrotaenia*), or sift the substrate in search of food such as the Dolphin Catfish or Black Doradid (*Pseudodoras niger*) or the Giraffe Catfish (*Auchenoglanis occidentalis*). Finer substrate suits these fish better, but it should not be so fine as to remain in suspension for any length of time when it is disturbed. Sand sold for use in water treatment plants that supply us with our drinking water, or for use in

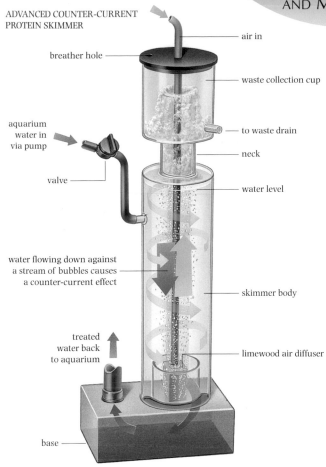

ADVANCED COUNTER-CURRENT
PROTEIN SKIMMER

air in

breather hole

waste collection cup

aquarium
water in
via pump

to waste drain

neck

valve

water level

water flowing down against
a stream of bubbles causes
a counter-current effect

skimmer body

treated
water back
to aquarium

limewood air diffuser

base

ADVANCED COUNTER-CURRENT PROTEIN SKIMMERS ARE INVARIABLY MADE FROM CLEAR ACRYLIC, ENABLING THE HOBBYIST TO MONITOR THE DENSITY OF BUBBLES AND THE CORRECT WATER LEVEL. A WIDE, FIRM BASE IS ESSENTIAL TO KEEP THE WHOLE STRUCTURE STABLE. THE BIGGER THE FISH, THE BIGGER THE AQUARIUM; AND AN ADVANCED PROTEIN SKIMMER THAT REMOVES ORGANIC (AND SOME INORGANIC) WASTE BY ATTRACTING SURFACTANTS—SEE GLOSSARY—BECOMES AN ATTRACTIVE INVESTMENT.

pond sand filters, is available in a range of grain sizes, all of which are suitable.

For particularly easy maintenance, some aquarists who keep large fish do so in bare aquaria with neither decor nor substrate. This undoubtedly makes for very easy cleaning. Whether it results in an attractive aquarium, or one with stress-free fish, is open to debate. Many territorial fish, for example, use rocks, bogwood or other submerged objects as markers of their home territory and/or for breeding purposes. It is only fair, therefore, to cater for these needs.

Many, but certainly not all, large fish prefer subdued lighting conditions. Since live plants are not a major consideration in such setups, lighting can be toned down. Even species that don't seem to be bothered by high illumination, such as Arowana (*Osteoglossum* spp.) are perfectly at home under low-wattage lights. Owing to their size, large fish can damage equipment that is located inside an aquarium. Heater/stats in particular can be easily broken if left unprotected. It is obviously advisable either to enclose such units within

a protector (models are available on the market) or take other steps, such as "fencing" the units in with rocks or decor. Alternatively, if the filtration system being used is a multi-chambered external one (which is well worth considering), the heater/stat may be placed within one of the filtration chambers. Other approaches are to dispense with a traditional heater/stat arrangement and use an external heating mat laid under the aquarium, or else use an external power filter with inbuilt heater.

The aquarium itself obviously needs to be substantial, which means that it will be very heavy. Strong supports are absolutely essential. It might even be necessary to build special brick supports or strengthen the floor of the room itself; remember this before embarking on a large-fish project.

The aquarium must be big enough in all directions to allow the fish to swim and—very importantly—turn around with ample space to spare. Large fish in cramped conditions look "wrong," but this should not be the main concern: it's quite simply unfair to keep fish under such conditions.

CHOOSING AND INTRODUCING FISH

What types of fish should you buy—and how many?

The first question should have been answered a long time ago, before the aquarium was set up. As the preceding section will have shown, different types of fish have different aquarium layout and water chemistry requirements. Therefore, unless these have been decided in advance, the risk of a mismatch, or having to compromise with regard to species selection and stocking density, is very real.

Safe Stocking

Irrespective of the type of fish chosen—with the exception of large companion fish—most aquaria will be able to house a reasonable number of specimens. Just how many will depend on numerous factors, including size, temperament, habits (shoaling or solitary), sex (male Bettas, *Betta splendens* for instance, will not tolerate other males in the same aquarium, but will tolerate females), water surface area, shelter availability, type and size of filtration system, etc. Ultimately, and assuming that the fish selected are compatible with each other and the water chemistry, the total number of fish will be determined by the aquarium system's capacity for maintaining adequate water quality.

In good aquatic shops, for example, aquaria are more heavily stocked than their average domestic counterparts. However, such shops possess staff with the expertise to monitor and maintain good water quality. They also enjoy the benefits of large, efficient water management systems, often incorporating such features as ultraviolet sterilization, fluid bed filtration, protein skimmers, substantial water reservoirs connected to centralized circulation/filtration, and facilities for isolating individual aquaria when necessary.

Few aquarists, if any, can boast such facilities at home. Nevertheless, the same principle of water quality as the key factor in determining stocking density should be applied. With this approach, the starting point is not the traditional one of using a guidance chart (like the accompanying one) for determining stocking levels, but the water itself. The great advantage using this method is that (always allowing for specific factors, such as temperament and compatibility), stocking levels are always kept within the tolerance limits of the aquarium support system. The potential disadvantage is that, in order not to exceed this limit, initial stocking can be a relatively slow process. This is a good thing, but new aquarists can find it difficult to keep to the longer stocking-time schedule, which involves regular testing of the water for the key environmental parameters discussed earlier. For coldwater and tropical freshwater fish, the recommended values for four key chemical parameters are given below. Specific requirements for delicate species may fall outside these limits.

Male Betta (Betta splendens var.) displaying to a female. Male Bettas will not live peacefully together.

The more traditional method of calculating stocking levels is based on unit lengths of fish (minus tail) in relation to surface area. For freshwater tropical species, this works out at around 12.5 sq. in (80 sq. cm) per 1–2in (2.5–5cm) fish, just over 17 sq. in (110 sq. cm) per 5–7.5cm (2–3in) fish and nearly 20 sq. in (130 sq. cm) per 3–4in (7.5–10cm) fish. For coldwater species, such as goldfish, the figures work out (again, very approximately) at 55 sq. in (360 sq. cm) per 2–3in (5–7.5cm) fish, and 93 sq. in (600 sq. cm) for fish measuring 3–4in (7.5–10cm). Using these formulae, we can arrive at approximately safe stocking levels (*see* chart below).

It must be stressed that the figures are rough guidelines only. They represent total stocking levels and relate to fish that are fully grown and are neither over-aggressive nor excessively territorial.

When stocking an aquarium, it is advisable to begin with at most 50 percent of the eventual stocks. Although even this relatively light stocking density will place some stress on the aquarium's raw filtration

DISSOLVED OXYGEN:	6mg/l (ppm)	MINIMUM
FREE AMMONIA:	0.02mg/l (ppm)	MAXIMUM
NITRITE:	0–0.2mg/l (ppm)	MAXIMUM
NITRATE:	50mg/l (ppm)	MAXIMUM

APPROXIMATE AQUARIUM STOCKING LEVELS

SURFACE DIMENSIONS OF AQUARIUM (in/cm)	NUMBER OF FISH				
	COLDWATER SPECIES/VARIETIES		TROPICAL SPECIES/VARIETIES		
	2–3in (5–7.5cm)	3–4in (7.5–10cm)	Up to 2in (5cm)	2–3in (5–7.5cm)	3–4in (7.5–10cm)
18 × 10 (45 × 25)	3	2	14	10	Not advisable
24 × 12 (60 × 30)	5	3	22	16	14
36 × 12 (90 × 30)	7	5	33	24	21
48 × 12 (120 × 30)	10	7	44	32	29
60 × 18 (150 × 45)	18	13	83	80	54

NOTE:

For African Rift Lake cichlids, the minimum size of aquarium recommended is one having surface dimensions of 90 × 30cm. In addition, stocking levels approximately 50% above those quoted in the chart are recommended (*see* earlier section for details)

system, it should be able to cope, as long as other parameters are satisfactory and the fish are not of the more delicate and demanding types. Once the fish have been introduced (*see* Safe Introductions below), water chemistry parameters should be monitored regularly and no further fish added until favorable conditions are being maintained without any significant fluctuations. Subsequent stocking can then be undertaken, with eventual numbers being reached gradually over a period of at least several weeks.

Selecting Fish

No one can give you a cast-iron guarantee that any fish you buy—however healthy they may look—are 100 percent disease/parasite-free. Indeed, as every living thing carries a natural safe "load" of parasites, it could be said that if a fish is completely free of parasites, it is dead! The reason why pathogenic (disease-causing) organisms don't normally cause epidemics is that if the fish carrying the load is strong, the microorganisms just can't secure a good enough foothold, or hookhold, or whatever, to multiply in sufficient numbers to cause disease. Despite the fact that it is quite impossible to give 100 percent health guarantees, there are a few signs that one can look for when buying fish. If, for example, several fish in a shop aquarium look decidedly unhealthy, it is best to forget buying any of the other fish, however healthy they may appear, from the same batch. It is not worth taking the risk.

A COCKATOO DWARF CICHLID (APISTOGRAMMA CACATUOIDES) WITH GOOD STRONG ERECT FINS AND CLEARLY IN GOOD HEALTH.

Look for raised scales (dropsy), swollen abdomens (possibly fluid retention), protruding eyes (pop-eye or exophthalmia, but in certain varieties of goldfish, such as telescope-eye moors, protruding eyes are quite normal), ulcers (bacterial lesions), "overlarge" heads (possibly a sign of what is usually referred to as "consump-

WHAT TO LOOK FOR IN A HEALTHY FISH

1. ERECT FINS. A lively fish will tend to carry its fins well extended. The dorsal (back) fin is often flicked open and shut, usually as the fish hovers or changes direction, and is generally held down as a fish allows a flick of the caudal fin (tail) to propel it over short distances. If, however, you are buying a long-tailed variety such as Sarassa Comet or a Fancy Guppy or Betta, the caudal will not be carried by such fish in as fully extended a state as in shorter-finned varieties.

2. LIVELY DISPOSITION. Fish that "hang" in midwater, or float on the surface, or lie on the bottom with little visible movement, are best avoided (unless, of course, you are buying a bottom dweller, like a Tench, or a surface swimmer, like a Halfbeak, which just happens to be resting). These exceptions aside, healthy fish are constantly on the move and exhibit quick reactions.

3. BRIGHT EYES. These are not always easy to spot, particularly from above, or where small and/or bottom-hugging fish are concerned. Take your time nevertheless and look out for signs of cloudiness. Healthy eyes are clear, injured or unhealthy ones tend to be "milky" in appearance.

4. BRIGHT COLORS. This can be a little difficult for the untrained or inexperienced buyer. What is meant by "bright" is the absence of a milky or cloudy covering of excess mucus on the body. Excess mucus creates a dull overall effect that, once recognized—and that presupposes knowledge of the "true" color—is unmistakable.

5. BALANCED SWIMMING. Healthy fish don't normally "roll around" or lose their balance when swimming; neither do they float or sink. However, immediately after a meal perfectly healthy fish, particularly larger types, will often hover and can sometimes rock gently as they chew their food. It is important to bear this in mind.

6. FULL BODY. This must not be taken to mean a full-looking belly. It is the flesh or muscle that we are talking about here. A healthy fish will look "solid." With the exception of naturally large-headed fish—fancy goldfish varieties such as Orandas, for example—healthy fish don't have oversize heads. In particular, look immediately behind the head; it should not look pinched. In other words, the "neck" area should either be about as wide as, or (in some species and varieties) even slightly wider than the head itself.

7. GOOD APPETITE. Tread carefully with this one! Without a doubt, healthy fish have healthy appetites. Consequently, aquarists are sometimes advised to ask to see the fish they want to buy actually feeding. Simple enough? Well, not quite. For a start, if the fish have already been fed, they may not be as voraciously hungry as you might wish them to be. You are going to have to time your visit. Then, suppose they are hungry and devour the food offered. Happy that you are buying healthy fish, you ask for your chosen specimens to be netted and bagged up for the journey home. The stress of being netted—especially immediately after a meal—soon results in the fish excreting in the bag water during the journey home. This is hardly the ideal way to undertake a journey, particularly a long one. Perhaps, therefore, it's best to forget about asking for a demonstration of healthy appetite and concentrate on the other factors, as well as relying on your dealer or an experienced aquarist for advice.

tion"), listless swimming or little visible movement. Damaged fins and missing scales are not always signs of poor health, though. Fin tears and scale loss can happen as a result of physical injury and are usually regenerated without any outbreak of infection. However, should the missing scales or torn fins exhibit blood spots, or streaks, or fungal growth, then caution should be exercised. Good pointers to look for in healthy fish are shown in the box on page 49.

Safe Introductions

The main thing to aim for (assuming that compatibility factors have been catered for) from the point at which a fish is selected to the time when it is released in the home aquarium is stress reduction at every stage.

This begins with the actual netting of fish in the shop. Experienced, well-trained staff will net a fish with deceptive ease (it's not easy!) and will appear to carry out the operation smoothly and without having to chase a fish throughout a tank. Transfer of the fish from the net to a suitable temporary receptacle, prior to pouring it gently into the bag in which it will be handed over to the customer is also done smoothly and with as little disruption to the fish as possible, though some disruption and stress is, of course, inevitable.

The polyethylene bags can, themselves, cause or minimize stress by their design. For example, some companies produce bags that have the bottom quarter or so colored and translucent, but not transparent. This means that, once a fish is bagged, it cannot see through the bag to the outside and is thus placed in a stress-reduced environment. In others, the corners are rounded, thus eliminating the risk of small fish being trapped (and stressed) during transportation. If the bags are shaped normally, the corners can be easily rounded by tying them up with rubber bands or sticking them down with adhesive tape.

The best shops will place the transparent polythene bag containing the fish inside a paper bag that will keep the fish in a semi-dark environment (which feels restful) and prevent them from seeing the potentially stressful scenes going on around them as they are taken from the aquarium to the cash register and thence to the aquarist's home. In a growing number of outlets, the paper bags are more than just thin paper wrappers, they are also partially insulated to prevent temperature loss. Do not assume that every shop offers this additional safeguard. To be on the safe side, it's worth taking with you an insulated box, one lined with styrofoam sheets or containing styrofoam chips.

SELECTING FISH SUMMARY

POSITIVE SIGNS	THINGS TO AVOID
Erect fins	Raised scales
Lively disposition	Swollen abdomen (if this is not a feature of the species or variety)
Bright eyes	
Bright colors	Protruding eyes (if these are not a characteristic of the fish, e.g. Telescope-eye Moors)
Balanced swimming	
Full body	Ulcers
Absence of fin tears, missing scales, injuries.	Overlarge head on undersized body
	Listless swimming and/or loss of balance
	Physical damage to fins, scales and/or body
	Fungal ("cottonwool") growths, blood spots, and/or streaks

COMMON GOLDFISH WITH DROPSY (TYPIFIED BY BLOATED BODY AND DISTENDED SCALES).

Alternatively, a padded/insulated bag, such as those used to keep frozen or chilled food cool, will do perfectly well. Or at least take an ordinary bag and plenty of newspaper and wrap the fish bags in several layers of newspaper. Temperature loss can of course be a major health-threatening stressor for tropical species and varieties.

During the journey home, avoid violent jolts or unnecessary noise. Remember that the fish cannot see where they are going, they are quite literally in the dark. While this may be restful, jolts and bangs coming out of the darkness are not. On arrival home, switch off all the aquarium lights. If it's already late evening, switch on a low-wattage room light, but not the main room lights. Do this before unpacking the fish, since abrupt transfer from darkness to full light is yet another stressor. In fact, this is deemed so important by professionals that in many commercial outlets (particularly importing establishments), unpacking of fish takes place either under subdued lighting conditions, or under red lights to which fish are not sensitive.

What now follows is a step-by-step guide to introducing newly bought fish into their aquarium. Just as there are several ways of setting up aquaria, there are various techniques for introducing fish, but all share the same "minimum-stress-philosophy."

1. Remove the fish bag from the insulating box or bag, and untie it. Do not pop it open!
2. Roll down the open end to form a "collar." This serves two purposes: it helps keep the top of the bag open and acts as a flotation ring.
3. Float the bag inside the aquarium and leave it for ten minutes until the temperature of the bag water is about the same as that of the aquarium water.
4. Pour some aquarium water into the bag (an amount equivalent to about one quarter of the volume of the bag water) and leave for another ten minutes or so. This introduces the new fish gradually to their aquarium water.
5. Repeat Step 4 at least once more, preferably twice.
6. Gently tip the fish out into the aquarium. The best way of doing this is by lowering the bag below the surface of the water, tipping it over and allowing the fish to swim out of their own accord. Do not pour the fish out, doing this will increase stress levels, which all the previous steps are designed to minimize.

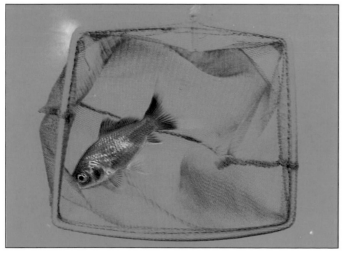

A STANDARD CATCHING NET FOR AQUARIUM FISH.

7. Do not switch the aquarium lights on and, if the introductions are being made in the evening, wait for a while before switching the main room lights on. This gives the fish a chance to explore their new surroundings under subdued lighting conditions. If the release has occurred during the evening, do not switch the aquarium lights on until the following day; otherwise, wait a while (until the fish appear settled) before switching the aquarium lights on.
8. Do not feed evening introductions until the following day; daytime introductions may be fed after they appear settled (preferably, after an hour or so). Feed very sparingly.

Quarantining New Fish

Whenever new fish are bought, they should be kept under observation for a time to monitor their health status. In the case of the very first batch of fish, the newly set up (but settled) aquarium will serve this purpose perfectly adequately. However, subsequent purchases should be kept elsewhere until all risk of accidentally introducing a disease into the established community has been eliminated.

This period of isolation (usually one to two or more weeks) in a separate tank is generally referred to as quarantine. To be absolutely precise, the period should be of 40 days' duration to "qualify" as quarantine, but the term has become so widely accepted that it is now used quite independently of the duration of the period of isolation.

During this time, the new fish should be observed closely for any signs of ill health and appropriate steps taken as necessary. Only when it can be ascertained that the fish are either not harboring a disease, or have completely overcome it, can they be safely introduced into the main community. At that point, the introduction procedures given in the previous section should be followed and adapted accordingly.

The quarantine tank itself need not be as elaborate a setup as the main aquarium, but it must, nevertheless, cater for all the fishes' basic needs, from shelter, to temperature, to appropriate water conditions. Once the quarantine period has been completed, the aquarium should be maintained in the normal way, not just awaiting future purchases, but also in readiness to be used as a hospital tank for any fish that may need to be separated from their tankmates for treatment.

If, either during the quarantine period, or subsequently, the tank is to be used for treatment purposes, it should be emptied once treatment has been completed and be set up from scratch again.

GENERAL AQUARIUM MAINTENANCE

Once an aquarium has been set up and stocked—even at its initial, reduced level—it needs regular maintenance to keep it operating smoothly. This is one of those instances where prevention is certainly better than cure. By establishing and adhering to a good maintenance program, most problems can be prevented and, even those that can arise quickly—like pollution from an accidental overfeed—can be corrected before they develop into crises.

One of the many major pluses of regular maintenance is that it keeps water quality on an even keel. Without this, some conditions would change at such a slow rate that they may go undetected until it's too late, or until the change needed to redress the anomaly is too large to be undertaken safely in a single step. Maintenance jobs range from those that need to be carried out on a daily basis, to those that only need attention once or twice a year. They are all, however, equally important in their own ways.

Daily Maintenance

1. Switch aquarium lights on either after daybreak, or after the room lights have been on for a little while, thus avoiding an abrupt (and stressful) dark-to-light change.
2. Check health status of all fish and take appropriate action if necessary (see Health Management, p.62).
3. Feed fish. For community fish and most other types, two feeds, one in the morning and one in the evening should suffice, but fish with specialist needs or behavior, such as crepuscular or nocturnal feeders, need their own feeding schedule and diet.
4. Check for breeding activity and remove pair to a separate aquarium if required; some fish become over-aggressive at breeding time. Removal is also necessary if fry are to be reared subsequently. In the case of livebearers, it might be easier to remove the fry, although removing the female gently (not lifting her physically from the water, but guiding her into a bowl) is preferable.
5. Check the water temperature.
6. Check all equipment to ensure that it is working properly and replace or repair if necessary.
7. Toward evening, check the health status of crepuscular and/or nocturnal species which will have been resting under cover during the day.
8. At the end of the day, turn off the aquarium lights some minutes before the room lights, thus avoiding an abrupt light-to-dark change.

Weekly Maintenance

1. Check ammonia, nitrite and pH levels and adjust accordingly or take remedial action, e.g. a partial water change (see earlier sections on these topics for details). It is essential to carry out changes gradually. Remember, one unit of difference in pH value represents a tenfold increase or decrease in acidity or alkalinity.
2. Carry out a more thorough check on aquarium equipment than that carried out on a daily basis.
3. Except in those cases where fish are being conditioned for breeding, or fry are being reared, do not feed the fish for one whole day. This will help counteract the effects of small-scale overfeeding that can take place over the week.
4. Check on stocks of foods, medications, water treatments, test kit reagents, etc., and replace as necessary.

Two-weekly Maintenance

1. Switch off air pump or power filter.
2. Gently stir up the surface of the substratum, taking care not to disturb plant roots.
3. Scrape encrusting algae off the front pane of the aquarium and sides if necessary (if the sides are in full view, encrusting algae may look unsightly). If possible, leave the back pane untreated, thus providing a fresh food supply for algal feeders.
4. Trim plants as necessary, removing all dead or dying leaves.
5. Allow the algae and debris to settle on the bottom.
6. Siphon off about a quarter of the total aquarium water, taking in the accumulated debris. (Use a

PHOSPHATE TEST KIT. PHOSPHATE LEVELS ARE INCREASING IN MANY DOMESTIC WATER SUPPLIES. DURING THE MATURATION OF THE AQUARIUM WATER IT IS ADVISABLE TO CHECK PHOSPHATE LEVELS FORTNIGHTLY. WHEN THE AQUARIUM IS ESTABLISHED THEY MAY OCCASIONALLY BE WORTH CHECKING, ESPECIALLY IF NUISANCE ALGAE ARE PREVAILING.

syphon bulb. NEVER suck water by mouth!) If weekly ammonia or nitrite readings are above safe levels, weekly partial water changes may be necessary until the underlying cause is remedied.

7. Replace removed water with tap or rainwater brought up to temperature (with boiled water) in a bucket or other suitable receptacle. Add dechlorinator or dechloraminator if the water change is larger than around 20–25 percent. Replacement water should match the aquarium water for hardness and pH.

8. Clean condensation tray or cover glass if necessary and reposition. Check and change activated carbon filter medium if necessary or as recommended by the manufacturer.

9. Switch on air pump or power filter.

Monthly Maintenance

1. Change or clean mechanical and chemical filter media.

2. Wash out biological filter media, in aquarium water if possible, to maintain full bacterial viability. Never use any form of detergent, despite thorough rinsing, since this will kill off the filter microfauna/flora and is toxic to fish, even in small concentrations. Boiling and sterilization of biological filter media will, likewise, kill off the micro-organisms and must also be avoided.

3. In the case of undergravel filters, insert a siphon tube down the airlift and suck out (not by mouth!) a small amount of the debris accumulation from under the filter plates.

4. Check all lighting equipment terminals and connections.

5. Clean out all filter pipes and spray bar attachments.

6. Check air pump diaphragm and replace if necessary.

7. Clean air (diffuser) stones.

8. Clean condensation tray and cover glass if this was not necessary at the two-weekly check.

9. Replace poor plant specimens and generally tidy up the aquascape.

Biannual/Occasional Maintenance

1. If a UV sterilizer is being employed, replace the radiation-emitting tube after six months.

2. Check fluorescent lighting levels and replace tube if necessary, or if plant growth is suffering. If several tubes are being used, replace one or more, and the remaining ones on a six-month rotation.

ACTIVATED CARBON MADE FROM COCONUT SHELLS HAS NOW REPLACED CHARCOAL AS A METHOD OF EXTRACTION OF DISSOLVED ORGANIC MATTER AND SOME METALS. IT SHOULD BE REPLACED—ACCORDING TO AQUARIUM SIZE AND STOCKING LEVELS—EVERY TWO TO THREE WEEKS.

3. Replace the air filter in the air pump, which, by now, will be partly blocked with trapped airborne particles.

4. Service power filter or powerhead motors. If you do not possess the necessary skills, your local shop, or an experienced aquarist, may be able to do this for you. Either way, use a replacement filter if the job is going to take longer than a day or so. Otherwise, ensure that aeration is strong enough to help counterbalance the temporary absence of the filter.

Pre-vacation Maintenance

1. A properly maintained aquarium should not present any significant problems to family vacations. Leading up to the vacation, though, check that all equipment is operating as it should and replace any for which there is some doubt. It is very important not to leave these checks, cleanouts and replacements until the last minute. Allow yourself 10–14 days to ensure that serviced or new equipment is functioning properly and has had ample opportunity to "settle down."

2. Lighting should be controlled by a timer. Alternatively, if friends are looking after things, brief them on the light/dark regime you operate, so that your plants don't suffer during your absence.

3. Feeding may be carried out via an automatic feeder that dispenses pre-determined amounts of dry food (flake or pellets) at set times. Most people, though, place this responsibility in the hands of friends. Ideally, these should be versed in aquarium keeping, but if they are not, take them through your feeding routine, as well as through the operation of your equipment. Leave food prepared in daily "doses," suitably labeled with the date, thus ensuring that the fish are not overfed, a real danger with temporary foster parents! There are also commercially produced vacation blocks that contain food in a slow-release matrix, and these may be worth considering. Finally, if fish have been fed properly throughout the rest of the year, and particularly if the aquarium is well planted, they will have built up adequate reserves to take them through several weeks without any undue hardship.

NUTRITION AND FEEDING

Whether a fish is a predator or a grazer, or even a parasite (like some catfishes), the biological aim of feeding is the same in all: to obtain adequate sustenance in the form of all the basic nutritional requirements for growth, survival and reproduction. Just as in humans, fish require proteins, fats or oils (referred to as lipids), carbohydrates, vitamins and minerals or trace elements.

Each of these components plays a range of roles in nutrition. Proteins, for instance, are the main compounds used in the "building" of tissues and, therefore, growth. They also perform important enzymatic functions in digestion, respiration, reproduction and other metabolic processes.

Lipids act as the main sources of energy, although carbohydrates also fill this role. They also facilitate the utilization of proteins and can be stored as energy reserves. Excess fats, however, can lead to problems, particularly since they end up being deposited around some of the vital organs such as the heart, kidneys and liver.

Carbohydrates constitute the primary "fuels" which can be oxidized quickly during respiration, with the subsequent release of energy that is then available to metabolize other dietary components such as proteins.

Vitamins, although only required in relatively low doses, are absolutely vital for health. Without them, serious problems will arise even if the diet is otherwise perfectly adequate. Without vitamin B6, for example,

protein and lipid metabolism will be significantly impaired, while lack of vitamin B2 will affect carbohydrate metabolism.

Minerals, too—as their alternative label, trace elements, indicates—are only required in small quantities. Detailed knowledge of all the roles that they play is lacking. One of the complicating factors is that fish actually absorb some minerals from the water they live in, over and above those they absorb via their food. Therefore, while we know that, say, iodine is essential for balanced hormonal activity, that calcium and phosphorus are important in bone formation, or that iron is vital for oxygen transport and the formation of haemoglobin (the red blood pigment) itself, there is still a great deal left to learn.

COMMERCIAL FOODS

From the earliest days of the aquarium hobby, fish have been fed on foods that they never encounter in their natural state. Yet not only do they survive, they also thrive and reproduce on many of these unnatural foods.

The reason for this is that proteins and other dietary components are first broken down during digestion, some of them subsequently being "reassembled" into the relevant compounds required. Therefore whether protein "X" comes from a pea or a string of algal cells, as long as it is protein "X" it will be exactly the same in composition and will therefore be utilized just as effectively by a fish. Armed with practical experience gained over many decades and the knowledge obtained from scientific studies and laboratory tests, manufacturers have been producing ever better foods for many years. The result is that we now have foods tailored to meet the needs of the vast majority of aquarium fish.

Commercial foods come in four main forms: as dry formulations, liquid diets (suspensions), frozen formulations and cultured live foods. Among the dry types there are powders (for fry), grains or granules of various sizes, flakes, sticks, tablets and freeze-dried livefoods. Different formulae are available for different types of fish, as well as for different purposes. For example, high-protein foods are ideal for actively growing fish, while conditioning foods are valuable when preparing fish for breeding. Herbivore and carnivore diets are self-explanatory, although herbivores will accept many carnivore foods and vice-versa.

THE HORSE-FACED LOACH (ACANTHOPSIS CHOIORHYNCHUS) WILL SPEND MUCH OF ITS TIME BURIED IN THE SUBSTRATUM. SINKING FOODS ARE RECOMMENDED, INCLUDING LIVEFOODS.

BLOODWORMS (CHIRONOMUS SP.) ARE JUST ONE OF SEVERAL PREPARATIONS THAT CAN BE BOUGHT FREEZE-DRIED.

You may either stick tablets onto the front pane of the aquarium, thus bringing the feeding fish into full view, or drop them into the tank and allow them to sink to the bottom. This is a good way of feeding bottom dwellers or crepuscular/nocturnal species, especially (in the latter cases) if the tablets are dropped in shortly before lights out.

Granules and sticks usually float (but some granular formulations also sink) and—with the exception of the finer grades of granules—are particularly suitable for larger fish. Freeze-dried livefoods come either loose or in small compressed blocks. The former are simply sprinkled on the surface, while the latter are either allowed to float or stuck onto the front pane of the aquarium. The range includes such traditional foods as *Daphnia* (waterfleas), brine shrimp *(Artemia salina)* of varying sizes, bloodworm *(Chironomus)*, Tubifex worms, *Mysis* shrimps and several types of mosquito larvae, as well as larger shrimps and other invertebrates for heavier feeders. One of the several advantages of freeze-dried livefoods is that the process employed in their preparation retains most of the nutrients of the live organism. Another is that, owing to their very low moisture content, they have a long shelf life. What they lack, of course, is the movement of the live animal (*see* below, Livefoods).

Liquid foods consisting largely of suspensions are not as wide-ranging in formulae or use as the other main types. For very young fry of both egglayers and livebearers, there are liquid foods which derive much of their benefit from their ability to stimulate growth of waterborne microorganisms that the fry can then feed on (in addition to the liquid food itself). For larger or adult fish, suspensions consisting of highly nutritious

eggs in a solution are, perhaps, the most widely used and available. Certainly, they are accepted with great gusto by the majority of fish.

Deep-frozen foods first made their appearance as "wet" frozen versions of freeze-dried livefoods. The range therefore included most of the same food organisms. Very soon, though, other types were added, including lancefish, mussel, squid and many others, which were particularly useful for feeding to marine fish and gross-feeding invertebrates. As technology and knowledge advanced, further developments took place, most notably, the introduction of complete diets which included a range of both animal and plant components. These newer foods proved especially valuable, once more, to the marine hobbyist, making the feeding of many hitherto challenging fish, such as certain butterfly and angel species, not just possible, but relatively easy.

As to livefood, traditional foods like *Daphnia* and Tubifex worms which were once collected from the wild, or *Artemia*, which needed to be hatched in salt solutions, have now long been widely available over the counter in many countries. Dedicated aquarists still collect and culture these and other livefoods but, as the commercial range continues to expand to include adult *Artemia* and live crickets *(Gryllus domesticus)* at every stage of their life cycle, collections from the wild are beginning to decline. There are very few books dealing with the fascinating subject of collecting and culturing livefoods, one of the best still being an encyclopedia on the subject published in 1975 (*see* Bibliography).

The ethics of feeding livefoods is something that each aquarist needs to ponder for him or herself. There are those who abhor the idea of feeding one live creature to another, but accept the feeding of a dead creature, freeze-dried or frozen, without any difficulty. Others will not wish to feed any creature, live or dead, but will use flakes. It's a personal choice.

Livefoods consist largely of water (from around 70 percent upward of the total body weight). Relatively large quantities need therefore to be consumed to match the nutritional content of the dry formulations. Further, the vast majority of today's dry commercial preparations are of such high quality that no fish is likely to suffer a dietary deficiency, even if fed exclusively on these foods. Difficult feeders however, which may be reluctant to accept dry, freeze-dried or deep-frozen foods, will normally take a moving livefood. Livefoods may be worth considering even if you feel uneasy about them, at least as a means of introducing difficult feeders to more traditional aquarium fare over a period of several weeks.

HOME-PRODUCED FOODS

Many aquarists produce their own foods or offer individual items, not usually as complete replacements for commercial formulations, but in addition. Breadcrumbs are particularly popular for most types of fish and peas, lettuce or spinach leaves, or slices of raw potato, cucumber or zucchini are also frequently offered to herbivorous fishes. For carnivores, minced or chopped ox heart or liver are widely used, along with mussels, shrimp (without the shells, except for large predators such as Dragon Fish or Arowana), raw (or cooked) fish, fish roe, chicken and other meats. Some hobbyists also devise composite diets consisting of both animal and vegetable components, either simply mixed together in chunks, or blended into a paste that is then frozen in individual-feed portions and used over a period of weeks. Among livefoods, all the commercially available species are also collected or cultured by dedicated hobbyists, along with other uncommercial types such as whiteworms, grindal worms, mealworms, earthworms, vinegar eels, woodlice, aphids, mosquito larvae and pupae, fly maggots, cockroaches, grasshoppers and locusts; even surplus or deformed live fish.

Undoubtedly, these feeds are both nutritious and well accepted by the appropriate fish. They also constitute useful dietary supplements. However, they must be fed in moderation. In particular, meat can cause fish digestive problems if fed to excess; ox heart and liver can also cause water pollution, while whiteworms, maggots, and some other types, have a very high fat content.

CORRECT FEEDING

Correct feeding is not just a question of dropping food into a tank and forgetting about it. Food has to be of the right type and be presented in an appropriate manner or, in some cases, at appropriate times of the day.

For the vast majority of fish, two feeds per day, preferably of different types, perhaps flakes and freeze-dried, given in the morning and some time before lights out in the evening, will be perfectly adequate. The quantity should be no more than will be completely consumed within five minutes or so. Ideally, any food left after this period should be removed. However, if the leftover quantity is small, it is probably easier to leave it for a while, especially if the fish are still actively feeding, but reduce the size of feeds from that point onward. In the case of tablets or freeze-dried blocks pushed onto the front pane or left to float or sink, it may well take longer than five minutes for the total amount to be consumed—not because the fish are not hungry, but because it is harder to get at than flakes, granules or sticks, which spread over the surface or sink individually. Common sense is obviously required.

Night-feeding fish can easily go hungry if food is only offered during the hours of daylight. Also, since most such aquarium species are bottom feeders, offering a floating formulation, even at the appropriate time, could still result in under-feeding. The best way to feed such fish is to use a suitable sinking formulation and offer it shortly before the aquarium lights are switched off, or even later.

With major predatory species, daily feeding is often not required. In the wild, these fish tend to take one large meal, followed by one or more days of fasting. Experience will soon demonstrate which particular feeding habits individual predatory species have, since they will tend to leave food untouched if they feel satiated. The feeding regime will then need to be adapted accordingly.

Herbivores, on the other hand, need to consume large quantities of plants in order to obtain adequate nourishment. As a result, they tend to graze or browse over long periods (like cattle) rather than obtain all their food in one single go. Such continual feeding has evolved in tune with the relatively low nourishment level of most plants when compared with animal-based foods and must be recognized when devising a feeding regime for these fish. This is also the reason why it is recommended that the back pane of an aquarium be left unscraped if possible, allowing it (and the rocks and other decorations) to develop a thin coating of encrusting algae.

Aquarium fish exhibit a wide diversity of dietary preferences and feeding habits and their needs must be checked in advance. If you can provide adequately for these, then there should be no problems. If, however, you cannot provide for their needs, it is preferable to give the species in question a miss.

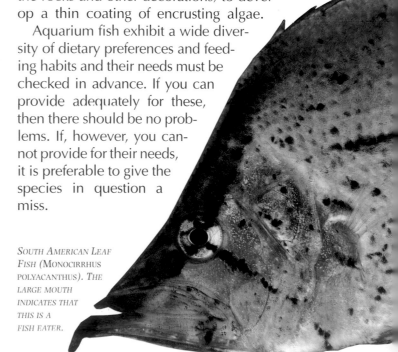

SOUTH AMERICAN LEAF FISH (MONOCIRRHUS POLYACANTHUS). THE LARGE MOUTH INDICATES THAT THIS IS A FISH EATER.

BREEDING FISH

Given adequate food and accommodation, many aquarium fish will breed, or attempt to do so, sooner or later. In fact, in the case of most of the popular livebearers, it is virtually impossible to prevent them from doing so.

In the confines of a community aquarium, however, the chances of achieving success—not just in breeding, but in at least some fry surviving—are generally small. Even fish that exhibit parental protection over their eggs and fry (such as cichlids) will usually fail to raise a full brood to the point where the young fish can fend for themselves and are no longer regarded as food items by some of the other tank inhabitants. Such species also exhibit intensified territorial behavior during courtship and breeding and can, as a result, totally disrupt an otherwise peaceful community. If breeding success is therefore sought, special provision must be made.

In terms of breeding strategies, aquarium fish are usually split into two main types: egglayers (oviparous species) and livebearers (viviparous species). These labels appear self-explanatory and—in the majority of cases—they are. Egglayers lay eggs, and livebearers give birth to live young—they produce small fish rather than eggs. In practice, though, the dividing line between the two is not clear-cut and even within the egglayer category there is a range of subcategories. While these two main labels apply most of the time, it is worth bearing in mind that within and across the two subsets lies a spectrum of reproductive strategies.

EGGLAYERS

Strict egglayers are distinguished by the release of eggs and sperm into the water, where fertilization takes place. Intimate contact between the mating fish may be exhibited, creating the impression that fertilization is internal, but it is not. Tight spawning embraces, as in gouramis, or the pressing together of anal and other fins, as in some killifish, are just different ways of optimizing the chances of external fertilization.

The range of techniques used by egglayers to optimize not just fertilization but survival of their eggs and subsequent fry is vast. The following are a few of these and include those that are most often encountered among aquarium fish.

Egg Scatterers

As the name implies, egg-scattering species disperse their gametes (eggs and sperm) into the surrounding water. They may do this in single pairs or mass spawnings and may release their gametes either into the water column (after which the fertilized eggs may float or sink) or hidden from view, such as among plant thickets or along the bottom.

These species rely for their survival on the sheer numbers of eggs produced (a female Koi can release upward of a quarter of a million eggs), the transparency of the eggs (making them difficult to see), or the terrain and vegetation among which the often-adhesive eggs are laid, which hides the eggs from predators. The

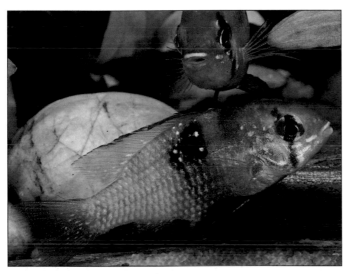

▲ *BUTTERFLY CICHLID FEMALE, RISING FROM NEST WITH EGG TUBE EXTENDED.*

▼ *A MARBLE SUBSTRATE BREEDING TANK FOR EGG SCATTERERS LETS THE EGGS FALL THROUGH, SO THE PARENTS CANNOT EAT THEM. AFTER SPAWNING, REMOVE THE PARENTS, AND TAKE AWAY THE MARBLES TO STOP FOOD DECOMPOSING BETWEEN THEM.*

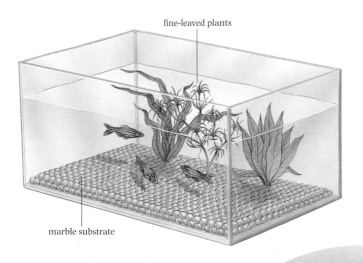

fine-leaved plants

marble substrate

numerous aquarium species that exhibit this breeding strategy include goldfish (and their much larger "cousins," the Koi), tetras, and barbs.

Substrate Spawners

If eggs can be positioned carefully in such a way that the batch is well hidden from view, then obviously the chances of survival of each egg are enhanced. This is what substrate spawners do, with or without parental protection of eggs and fry. If the eggs are also defended by one or both parents, survival possibilities are even better.

Although some egg scatterers may also deposit their eggs among vegetation or over the substratum, the deposition is haphazard, rather than closely coordinated. Their eggs are spread out over a relatively large area, while in substrate spawners, they are confined to a small patch like the underside of a single leaf, the roof of a cave or the top surface of a smooth rock. Numerous egglayers are substrate spawners, perhaps the best known being the Central and South American cichlids, but even some rasboras, like the Harlequin (*Rasbora [Trigonostigma] heteromorpha*) and catfish such as *Sturisoma* spp. employ this strategy.

Some fish do not bother with the preparation of a nest site but hide their eggs from view instead, either within the substrate itself or even inside a host. Among aquarium fish, the best known "substrate" hiders are those killifish species which deposit their eggs in the soft bottom layers of their pools (in aquaria, peat often serves as a suitable medium). By far the most widely kept examples of fish which use a host for the incubation of their eggs are the bitterlings (e.g. *Rhodeus* spp.) which lay their eggs inside the inhalant siphon of a freshwater mussel (e.g. *Anodonta* sp.).

Mouthbrooders

Mouthbrooding is a form of "egg-hiding" in that the eggs are kept out of view. In this case, though, they are hidden inside the mouth of one or other of the parents. The most famous of all the mouthbrooders are found among the African Rift Lake species. In these fish, the eggs are normally laid in a depression, or directly on the substratum, and are then picked up by the female, either as they are being fertilized, or even slightly before (in which case, fertilization may occur inside the female's mouth). The female then retains the eggs in her mouth until they hatch and will subsequently take in the fry whenever a threat is detected. This type of maternal protective behavior may last for several weeks. The most frequently encountered paternal mouthbrooders

in the hobby are the fascinating Arowana (*Osteoglossum* spp.), the Dragon Fish or Asian Bonytongue (*Scleropages formosus*) and their relatives. Mouthbrooding is also exhibited by some Betta species, as well as the Chocolate Gouramis (*Sphaerichthys* spp.).

Nestbuilders

Whether digging a depression in the substratum for the sole purpose of attracting females just for the duration of the act of spawning—as in the maternal mouthbrooders of the African Rift Lakes—is true nestbuilding is open to debate. However, there are many other types of fish that build a true nest, not just for spawning purposes, but also as an incubation site for the eggs. The most notable nest builders among aquarium fish are undoubtedly the bubblenesting gouramis and their closest relatives—*Colisa, Trichogaster, Trichopsis, Belontia, Macropodus* and *Pseudosphromenus*, along with some *Betta* and *Parosphromenus* species. Some catfish, too, e.g. *Hoplosternum* and its closest relatives, build bubble nests.

Among other nest builders, we find the delightful sticklebacks which build nests out of fine vegetation stuck together with kidney secretions into the form of a tunnel. In *Gasterosteus*, the nest is built on the substratum, while in *Pungitius*, it is constructed among vegetation well away from the bottom of the riverbed or aquarium.

Egg Carriers

Mouthbrooding is by definition a form of egg-carrying. However, this term is usually reserved for species that carry their eggs attached to their body for a time. Some male loricariid catfish (Whiptails), for example, carry

PARADISE FISH (MACROPODUS OPERCULARIS) MALE TENDING EGGS IN THE BUBBLE-NEST.

their eggs attached to their lower lip, while, in other species, such as the Rice Fish or Medaka (*Oryzias latipes*) and the unusual *Xenopoecilus*, females carry their fertilized eggs attached to their anal (belly) fin.

Internal Fertilization

The last two egglaying examples point up the problem of clear definition. Egg fertilization may in some instances be internal. Are these to be regarded as cases of true egglaying, or a "halfway house" between egglaying and livebearing, one of the defining characteristics of which is internal fertilization?

A few killifish, such as *Cynolebias brucei* and *C. melanotaenia*, as well as the rare *Horaichthys setnai*, the poeciliid *Tomeurus gracilis* (a member of the same family as the guppy) and even a characin, *Stevardia (Corynopoma) riisei*, also employ internal fertilization with subsequent release of eggs by the female. Many sharks and rays, too, exhibit this reproductive strategy, which leaves us with a problem in defining oviparity and viviparity, Although the debate regarding definitions of the various "degrees" of egglaying and livebearing has been a long-running one and is likely to continue to resurface from time to time, the modern trend is to divide reproductive strategies thus:

1. Oviparity is any form of egglaying, irrespective of whether fertilization is internal or external
2. Viviparity is any form of livebearing rather than the release/deposition of eggs. All viviparous species exhibit internal fertilization.

As a result, the fish mentioned in the previous paragraph would all be regarded as oviparous, even the poeciliid *Tomeurus gracilis*. However, since it belongs to the family *Poeciliidae*, which includes the guppy, swordtail and relatives — all of which are viviparous— it is sometimes referred to in scientific literature as being "facultatively viviparous," which means no more than "a bit of both." Another term that may be used (but only rarely these days, fortunately) to describe such fish is "ovi-ovoviviparous."

LIVEBEARERS

These were traditionally subdivided into two subcategories:

1. Ovoviviparous species, in which most of the nourishment for the developing embryos comes from the egg yolk. In these species, the resulting

AMARILLO GOODEID (GIRARDINICHTHYS VIVIPARUS) GIVING BIRTH; SEE PAGE 285.

fry weigh about the same, or even less than the fertilized egg.
2. Viviparous species, those in which nourishment for the developing embryos comes from both the yolk and secretions produced by the female. In these species, the resulting fry weigh considerably more than the fertilized egg (sometimes many thousands of times more).

As in previous examples, these categorizations are challenged by many exceptions which make clear-cut subdivisions impossible. This potential confusion has led to the current trend of referring to all species which exhibit internal fertilization and retention of the eggs within the female's body up to the point of birth as being viviparous. I refer to the former subdivisions simply because they still exist in aquarium literature (including some of my earlier books).

At one end of the livebearing spectrum then, is the type of viviparity where all or most of the embryos' nourishment comes from their egg yolk, even though there is intimate contact between the embryos' tissues and those of the mother. In these livebearers, the whole of the development of the embryos occurs within the egg sacs (ovarian follicles) embedded within the female's ovarian tissues. Yet, even here, there are gradations. In some species there is insufficient yolk in each egg to take the embryos through to full development. Where this is the case, as in some *Poeciliopsis* species, the mother contributes nutrients in addition to those contained in the yolk. As a result, the embryos gain weight during gestation and are born much heavier than the fertilized eggs. In a few species, such as the Mosquito Fish (*Heterandria formosa*), this strategy is supplemented by another in which a female is able to carry small numbers of embryos at different stages of development (a strategy referred to as superfetation).

Going "up" the viviparity scale, species such as the One-sided Livebearer *(Jenynsia)* not only nourish their embryos—in this case by outgrowths of ovarian tissue known as trophonemata—but by ovulating so that the embryos develop within the ovarian cavity or lumen, rather than within the egg sacs (ovarian follicles). In the livebearing members of the family Goodeidae, the embryos themselves (rather than the females) develop tissues through which they absorb nutrients as they develop within the ovarian cavity. These extensions, known as trophotaeniae, grow out of the vent area and are lost once the fry are born, or just before.

The end result of all these refinements on the basic "formula" is a significant increase in weight of the fry at birth, ranging from an increase of around 2,000 percent in the case of *Poeciliopsis turneri*, to nearly 4,000 percent in *Heterandria formosa* and many times more than this in *Jenynsia*, its close relatives, the various species of four-eyed fish *(Anableps spp.)* and the Goodeidae. Further details regarding reproductive characteristics are included under the main family introduction sections.

BREEDING TANK SUGGESTIONS

While it is not possible to provide specific guidance here on provisions for breeding every major type of aquarium fish, some broad guidelines should assist in highlighting the main requirements.

Egg Scatterers

If the species in question scatters its eggs among vegetation, including many barbs, tetras and killifishes, then an aquarium that provides, both open areas and thickets of fine-leaved plants would constitute an acceptable setup. Alternatively, "spawning mops" consisting of fine strands of undyed wool attached to a piece of cork or styrofoam will also prove adequate, as will (of course) commercially produced spawning media.

If the species scatters its eggs over the substratum—danios and some characins for example—large-grained gravel, or even marbles will help remove the eggs from the attentions of the spawning fish (which appear to have an almost-insatiable appetite for eggs). A mesh that is raised off the bottom of the tank will also allow the eggs through to the space below while preventing the spawners from doing so. Alternatively, the spawners may be confined inside a mesh basket suspended inside the aquarium.

Substrate Spawners

Some substrate spawners, such as Angels *(Pterophyllum spp.)* tend to spawn on vertical or near-vertical surfaces. These can be provided either by upright-growing broad-leaved plants like Amazon Swords *(Echinodorus spp.)* or pieces of slate.

Other Central and South American cichlids like to spawn on horizontal surfaces and for these, either pieces of slate laid flat on the substratum or smooth large pebbles should be provided. These should be positioned in an easily defended spot.

Substrate spawners that lay their eggs in caves, such as many dwarf cichlids do, or, as in the case of other species, inside shells (e.g. Bumblebee, *Brachygobius* spp. or some of the smaller *Lamprologus* species from Lake Tanganyika) must also be provided with appropriate sites. Half-coconut shells or flowerpots are found acceptable by most cave spawners.

Egg Hiders

Species that bury their eggs in the substratum, such as many of the killifishes—which originate from regions where ponds dry up during the summer—should be given a tank with a soft substrate, such as loose peat, of sufficient depth to allow the fish to bury themselves almost completely.

Bitterlings, e.g. *Rhodeus* spp., which deposit their eggs inside the inhalant siphon of a freshwater mussel, should, obviously, be provided with at least one such mussel in the spawning aquarium.

Mouthbrooders

Most mouthbrooders require an area where the male can establish his territory and to which he can attract a

CAVE-SPAWNING FISH (FOR EXAMPLE, MANY SPECIES OF DWARF CICHLIDS) REQUIRE A NUMBER OF DIFFERENT RETREATS, WHICH CAN BE CONSTRUCTED FROM VARIOUS MATERIALS.

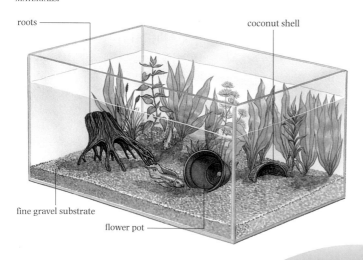

roots

coconut shell

fine gravel substrate

flower pot

number of females. Some males will use a rock as the spawning site, but in other species, like some Lake Malawi cichlids, large circular depressions may be constructed. Either way, suitable sites which can be easily defended should be made available to these species.

Females may brood their eggs either in the open, or in caves. Depending on species, therefore, adequate shelter must be provided.

Nestbuilders

Nestbuilding anabantoids will construct their bubblenests either at the water surface, as in all the *Colisa, Trichogaster* and nest-building *Betta* species, or under a leaf or other horizontal submerged surface, as in, for example, the Dwarf Croaking Gourami *(Trichopsis pumilus)*. For the former, there should be little or no water surface turbulence. The air above the surface should be moist (simply ensured by a suitable aquarium cover) and some floating vegetation around which the nest can be built, or which can be incorporated within the nest, should be provided. Where no floating vegetation is available, a small piece of styrofoam sheeting will act as the "nucleus" around which the nest will be built. Similar conditions will also be found acceptable by bubblenesting catfish.

In the case of species like sticklebacks, which cement vegetation into the form of a tunnel-shaped nest with kidney secretions, fineleaved submerged vegetation should be provided.

Egg Carriers

Egg-carrying *Oryzias* species will transfer their fertilized eggs onto submerged fine-leaved vegetation. There should therefore be several clumps of such plants, e.g., *Cabomba, Myriophyllum, Vesicularia*, in the aquarium.

In the case of *Xenopoecilus* species and egg-carrying loricariid catfish species, the eggs are carried around by the female until they hatch. No special provision need therefore be made for these eggs, although hiding places for the fry should be present.

Livebearers

Commercial breeding traps are widely available for confining livebearer females while giving birth. These traps can be floated inside a community aquarium and may be used as rearing mini-tanks for the fry until they are large enough to be released into the main aquarium. All models are designed to separate the female from her offspring (most livebearer females are cannibalistic) and, although the method employed may vary, the overall effectiveness is pretty good.

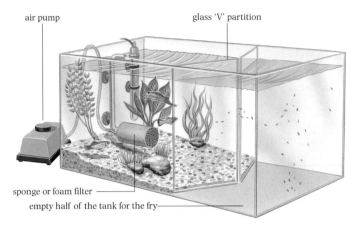

TANK SET-UP FOR LIVEBEARERS WITH A "V"-SHAPED INSERT THAT HAS A GAP TO LET THE FRY SWIM THROUGH. YOU CAN ALSO SPLIT THE TANK WITH A WIDE MESH OR PERFORATED DIVIDER.

FLOATING BREEDING TRAP IN USE. THE FEMALE GUPPY IS CONFINED TO THE "V" TRAP, WITH THE FRY DROPPING INTO THE BOX BODY BELOW.

One of the main difficulties with breeding traps is that they need to be small. As a result, the volume of water they contain can become polluted quite rapidly (although some models do have small holes through which at least some water circulation can occur).

In view of this, many experienced aquarists adopt a number of alternative approaches which allow the female the benefits of a larger volume of water. One technique uses a mesh basket like the one employed for egg scatterers. Another is the design of a special aquarium in which one half is planted out and serviced to act as a "normal" aquarium for the female or females. A V-shaped glass partition isolates the other section of the aquarium, with the apex of the "V" consisting of a vertical slit and pointing toward the bare half, where the fry gather by swimming "down" the "V" and through the slit to safety. If it is not possible to construct such an aquarium: a perforated tank divider (available commercially) or a mesh partition may be used.

HEALTH MANAGEMENT

A positive approach to health management aims at preventing problems from arising rather than waiting for them to occur and having to take steps to rectify them. In earlier sections, the importance of good water quality, quarantine and nutrition have been highlighted as essential to correct aquarium management, and their significance is emphasized here. Good water and dietary management programs, along with adequate quarantining of new stocks, are at the heart of every healthy aquarium.

In recent years, a number of research programs have begun to make significant progress in the development of vaccines and other forms of preventative medicine. These studies have resulted in the implementation of several antiviral, antibacterial and antiparasitic immunization treatments of fish during the period leading up to their export from some producing countries. The health of these fish before, during and after transportation is therefore improved, enhancing not only their overall quality but their ability to acclimatize during the period between purchase and release into home aquaria. This trend will undoubtedly continue over the coming years.

ULTRAVIOLET STERILIZATION

One preventative health measure that is well worth considering by all aquarists is the use of an ultraviolet sterilizer. In the past, the use of UV sterilizers was restricted almost exclusively to marine aquaria. From the mid-1980s, they were taken up by the pondkeeping sector of the hobby, largely because of their algae-clearing qualities. While their use in freshwater aquaria has lagged behind both the marine and pond sectors, they are beginning to be seen as a good idea, partly because of the growing popularity of keeping large companion fish, such as Koi, in aquaria.

One thing that needs to be stressed at the outset is that ultraviolet sterilizers are precisely what their name states: sterilizers; they are not filters, as some aquarium and pond literature would suggest. Their value lies in their ability to sterilize water as it flows past the UV-emitting lamp that is housed within the unit's casing. They sterilize water by destroying the nucleic material of many free-floating micropathogens (disease-causing organisms). They also cause free-floating algal cells to flocculate (clump together), making it possible for a mechanical filter medium (housed separately within the aquarium filter) to trap these algal aggregations. It is this last property that has led to the wide use of UV sterilizers within the pondkeeping hobby (where they are often referred to as clarifiers) to clear green-water problems.

Some aquarists believe that the use of a UV sterilizer will result in a sterile aquarium; this is not so. Since sterilization occurs only as water flows through the unit, filter bacteria are not affected by the use of a UV unit.

SOME PRECAUTIONS

Despite every effort to prevent it, disease will strike fish at some time. This will not necessarily be the result of new fish introductions or the inadvertent introduction of pathogens with, say, new plants. Sometimes, disease will affect a fish simply as a result of loss of condition arising from one or other of numerous factors such as an injury, post-spawning debility, or even old age.

When a disease outbreak or an obvious problem such as abnormal swimming occurs, the temptation is to treat the fish or aquarium without delay. Yet rushing in can actually cause more problems than it solves. Immediate action is necessary, but this should consist of identifying the disease or problem and the underlying cause. Environmental parameters such as pH, ammonia, oxygen and nitrite levels should be checked immediately and adjusted (safely) if necessary.

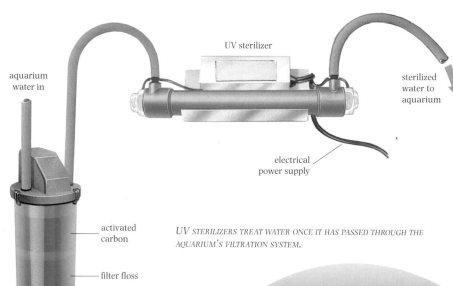

aquarium water in

UV sterilizer

sterilized water to aquarium

electrical power supply

activated carbon

filter floss

canister filter

UV STERILIZERS TREAT WATER ONCE IT HAS PASSED THROUGH THE AQUARIUM'S FILTRATION SYSTEM.

Only once a disease has been diagnosed correctly should treatment with medications begin.

Medications can stress fish, particularly if an overdose is administered. Underdosing will not have the desired effect. It is therefore essential to read all instructions carefully and adhere closely to dosage levels and any precautionary advice provided (*see* pp.66–7). It is also extremely important to ensure good hygiene if infection is not to spread or reoccur.

While antibiotics and organophosphates may be very effective against certain pathogenic organisms, their use and/or availability is restricted in many countries. In such instances, supplies may be obtained only by veterinary prescription. Nowadays, the number of veterinarians with in depth knowledge of aquarium and pond fish diseases is much greater than it used to be. Expert professional fish health advice is much more widely available and should be sought not just when a prescription is required but whenever there is any uncertainty regarding either correct diagnosis or treatment. Experienced aquarists and shop staff are also, of course, well placed to advise on health matters, so seek their assistance if in doubt.

COMMON DISEASES

Fish pathology is an extensive and complex subject. The following list of diseases, their diagnosis and treatments represents only a small fraction of the wide range of health problems that can affect fish. For more detailed information, consult specific literature (see Bibliography), experienced aquarists or shop staff, and/or a vet who specializes in fish diseases.

———— VIRAL INFECTIONS ————

CARP, OR FISH, POX

SYMPTOMS Hard, whitish or cream-colored, waxlike patches on the body; these may merge to cover substantial areas of the skin.

TREATMENTS At the moment, viral infections cannot be treated effectively (but some vaccinations have been used and others are under development). Usually, though, viruses are not lethal (but *see* SVC), and symptoms often disappear spontaneously, particularly if water temperatures increase. Improved all-round water quality will help overcome this problem which, owing to the relatively warm temperatures of tropical aquaria, is only rarely encountered in this sector of the hobby.

LYMPHOCYSTIS

SYMPTOMS Large cauliflower-like growths (sometimes referred to as tumors), or small, isolated, pearl-shaped nodules or warts distributed on fins or body. These are caused by enlargement—to as many as 100,000 times their normal size—of affected cells.

TREATMENTS As for carp or fish pox.

SPRING VIREMIA OF CARP (SVC)

SYMPTOMS *External:* bloated body, blood spots and bleeding under the skin and around the anal area; pale gills. *Internal:* enlarged spleen and liver; accumulations of fluid; damaged blood vessels.

TREATMENTS This is a highly infectious disease that in some countries is notifiable (the relevant authorities must be notified of an outbreak). There is no known cure, and affected fish must be humanely destroyed. Good hygiene and water quality control will help prevent outbreaks. Fish that survive SVC may become immune, but will be potential carriers of the disease. As with carp or fish pox, symptoms disappear as temperatures rise.

———— BACTERIAL INFECTIONS ————

FIN, TAIL OR BODY ROT (COLUMNARIS DISEASE), CAUSATIVE AGENT: *Flexibacter columnaris* and (occasionally) other bacteria

SYMPTOMS Localized or more general attack on body or fins, leading to ulcers or shredding of fin rays. Blood streaks in fin rays usually develop.

CARP, OR FISH, POX

LYMPHOCYSTIS

FIN ROT

TREATMENTS Acriflavine, Chloramphenicol and other antibiotics (*see* Note 1). Furan, Nifurpyrinol and related compounds are also effective, but may be dangerous to humans if use is prolonged (check with your vet, both for dosage levels of antibiotics and correct use of Furan and related products). Some proprietary remedies are available. Follow instructions to the letter.

MOUTH FUNGUS, CAUSATIVE AGENT: *Flexibacter columnaris* and, possibly, other bacteria (a misleading name because this is clearly not a fungus)

SYMPTOMS Whitish growths around the mouth, gradually progressing into the jaw bones and anterior cheek area, resulting in erosion of tissues.

TREATMENTS As for fin rot.

BACTEREMIA (milder form), Septicemia (more acute form), CAUSATIVE AGENT: *Aeromonas hydrophila*

SYMPTOMS Frayed fins, blood spots, ulcers, exophthalmia (pop-eye), individually or in combination.

TREATMENTS Chloramphenicol, Tetracycline, Oxolinic Acid (available in medicated flake or granule form). Some proprietary remedies are available. Chances of a cure are

▲ MOUTH FUNGUS
HOLE-IN-THE-HEAD ▶
▼ DROPSY

variable, depending on severity of infection. If treatment is being administered by injection (as antibiotics often are in the case of large fish), ask a vet to carry this out.

HOLE-IN-THE-HEAD/BODY; ULCER DISEASE or FURUNCOLOSIS, CAUSATIVE AGENT: primarily *Aeromonas salmoncida*, but *A. hydrophila* may act as a secondary agent

SYMPTOMS Ulcers (often circular) in head region and/or body.

TREATMENTS Chloramphenicol, Tetracycline, Sulphonamides, e.g. Furan-based remedy (*see* fin rot). Some proprietary remedies are available. After treatment, dress large ulcers with an oil-based antiseptic cream to protect the wound and prevent excessive intake of water through the lesions. Adding salt to the aquarium water to give a 3 percent solution will also help affected fish to control their water intake.

FISH TB, PRIMARY CAUSATIVE AGENT: *Mycobacterium* spp.

SYMPTOMS Any one or combination of: loss of color/condition, raised scales, exophthalmia, loss of appetite, emaciation, ulceration, frayed fins.

TREATMENTS No reliably effective treatment. Some antibiotics, e.g. Terramycin, may effect a cure when infection is not too severe. Fish TB can cause painful localized infected areas in humans, which can prove slow to cure. Always observe good personal hygiene procedures: wear rubber gloves, and avoid immersing your hands in water or handling fish if you have open or fresh cuts (*see* Risks to Humans, p.67).

DROPSY (BACTERIAL HEMORRHAGIC SEPTICEMIA), CAUSATIVE AGENT: *Aeromonas liquefaciens* (*ascitae* and/or *typica*) and, possibly, other bacteria

SYMPTOMS Swollen abdomen and raised scales, giving the body a "pine-cone" appearance.

TREATMENTS Usually no cure, but Chloramphenicol (see vet for instructions) may help. Humane destruction of affected specimens, plus good hygiene, are the most effective methods of eradicating the disease and preventing its recurrence.

—————— FUNGAL INFECTIONS ——————

COTTONWOOL DISEASE OR FUNGUS, CAUSATIVE AGENT: *Saprolegnia* and *Achyla* species; usually occurs on fish that are already weakened in some way, or on damaged tissues

SYMPTOMS White or cream-colored fluffy patches on fins and/or body.

TREATMENTS Proprietary remedies are widely available, usually based on Phenoxethol, Malachite Green (*see* Note 2), Copper Sulfate, Potassium Permanganate or Methylene Blue. Salt bath: 2–5 percent solution for 10–15 minutes.

▲ WHITE SPOT   ▼ FUNGAL INFECTION

PROTOZOAN INFECTIONS

WHITE SPOT (ICHTHYOPHTHIRIASIS, OR "ICH"), CAUSATIVE AGENT: *Ichthyophthirius multifiliis*; often occurs in fish that are already weakened or are subjected to chilling

SYMPTOMS   Body and fins covered in small white spots; in severe infestations, the spots may appear to join up; fins carried close to the body; violent swimming action or shimmying; scratching against stones, plants and pond equipment.

TREATMENTS   Numerous proprietary remedies are available, many based on Malachite Green (*see* Note 2), Methylene Blue or Copper Sulfate. Repeat treatment is often necessary to attack free-swimming stages of the parasite.

COSTIASIS (infectious turbidity of gills and skin), CAUSATIVE AGENT: *Ichthyobodo (Costia) necatrix*

SYMPTOMS   Slimy, bluish-white coloration of the skin and gills; badly affected areas may show blood spots; awkward swimming movements with fins carried closed to body; scratching, as in white spot.

TREATMENTS   Acriflavine (10ml of 0.001 percent stock solution/5 liters of water); salt (approx. 5g/liter): Formalin (approx. 15ml of 10 percent stock solution/5 liters for 15–20 minutes). Since free-swimming stages can survive only for

about one hour away from a host, affected aquaria can be disinfected by removing fish and treating them elsewhere.

CHILODONELLIASIS, CAUSATIVE AGENT: *Chilodonella cyprini*

SYMPTOMS   Similar to costiasis; in addition, the skin in the neck to dorsal fin region may develop a lumpy texture; respiration may be impaired.

TREATMENTS   A combination of Acriflavine (1g/100ml of water) at a temperature of 82°F (28°C) for 10 hours is normally effective; Malachite Green, *see* Note 2 (0.15mg/liter) for an indefinite period. Salt (25g/liter for 10–15 minutes or 10–15g/liter for 20 minutes); Potassium Permanganate (1g/100 liters) for 90 minutes; Methylene Blue (30ml of 1 percent solution/100 liters) for an indefinite period.

TRICHODINIASIS, CAUSATIVE AGENT: *Trichodina* spp.

SYMPTOMS   Similar to costiasis, but usually less severe. Microscopic examination is necessary for definite diagnosis.

TREATMENTS   As for *Ichthyobodo (Costia)* and *Chilodonella*.

WORM INFECTIONS

GILL FLUKE INFECTION by *Dactylogyrus* spp.—monogenetic trematodes

SYMPTOMS   Inflamed gills; excessive secretion of mucus on gills; accelerated respiration; gill covers may be held open; scratching of gill covers on aquarium sides, bottom and equipment.

TREATMENTS   Some proprietary remedies are available. These are based on a range of compounds, e.g. Copper Sulfate; salt bath (10–15g/liter for 20 minutes or 25g/liter for 10–15 minutes); Formalin (20ml commercial formalin/100 liters) for 30–35 minutes; Methylene Blue (30ml of 1 percent stock solution/100 liters) indefinitely.

SKIN FLUKE INFECTION (may also affect the gills) by *Gyrodactylus* spp.—monogenetic trematodes

SYMPTOMS   Inflamed patches on the skin and fins; erratic swimming; excessive secretion of body slime; accelerated respiration (if gills are affected); some loss of color; scratching on aquarium sides, bottom and equipment.

TREATMENTS   As for *Dactylogyrus*.

CRUSTACEAN INFECTIONS

FISH LOUSE INFECTION, CAUSATIVE AGENT: *Argulus*—usually *A. foliaceus*

SYMPTOMS   Nervous swimming and jumpiness, frequent, vigorous scratching, often resulting in loss of scales; heavy infestations are accompanied by anaemia and loss of color; the almost-transparent parasites can be seen attached to the body, mainly along the fin bases (adult parasites can be nearly ⅓in/1cm long).

TREATMENTS Organophosphate (Dichlorvos) bath (*see* Note 3). This treatment is recommended only for large fish: 1ppm for less than 1 hour, accompanied by very vigorous aeration, as Dichlorvos reduces oxygen levels; Potassium Permanganate (1g/liter for 30–45 seconds or 1g/10 liters for 5–10 minutes); physical removal of individual parasites with forceps followed by disinfection with a proprietary disinfectant, e.g. an Acriflavine-based compound.

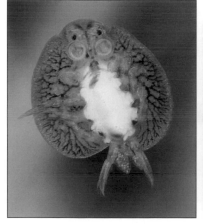

◀ FISH LOUSE   ▼ ANCHOR WORM

ANCHOR WORM INFECTION, CAUSATIVE AGENT: *Lernaea* spp.

SYMPTOMS Long, thin, white, wormlike parasites (up to ¾in/2cm in length) attached to the body and/or fins; two white egg-sacs at the posterior end are usually visible.

TREATMENTS Some proprietary remedies are available, e.g. based on Copper Sulfate; Potassium Permanganate—as for *Argulus*. Salt bath (10–15g/liter for 20 minutes or 25g/liter for 10–15 minutes); Trichlorphon has been used (but *see* Note 3) at 1mg/liter as an indefinite bath, during which the parasite may become dislodged.

Several important questions that arise quite regularly in discussions regarding fish health management include the dangers of over/underdosing fish, how to dispose of terminally sick fish humanely, possible effects of medications on filters, and health implications for humans. These are briefly addressed in this section.

In addition to consulting some of the specialized texts recommended in the Bibliography, check aquarium magazines and the worldwide web for features on health management, as well as for information about short courses at academic institutions and (as happens from time to time) those sponsored by some of the leading aquatic industry manufacturers.

NOTES
1. Whenever antibiotics are being considered, it is wise to check with a vet for accurate dosage levels, even in countries where such products are legally available without prescription.
2. Malachite Green is currently widely available, but this situation may change owing to its possessing carcinogenic properties (although, at the levels used to treat ornamental fish, there appears to be no evidence that it poses any danger either to humans or fish).
3. It is vitally important to check on the legality of using organophosphates. For instance, the only such product that is licensed for use on fish in the U.K. (and even then,

not on ornamentals) is Dichlorvos. It is now illegal to sell, or even give away, Trichlorphon products in Britain. (Trichlorphon breaks down into Dichlorvos, the active ingredient, after a longer or shorter time, depending on ambient conditions). However, it is legal to import it for use on one's own animals.

ADMINISTERING MEDICATION

When administering medications, it may prove necessary or desirable to treat an individual fish rather than a whole community. In such cases, the affected fish must be removed, either to a temporary bowl or bucket (if the treatment is designed to last for only a few minutes), or to a separate aquarium (quarantine tanks are particularly useful for this). Either way, the transfer should be carried out with as little stress to the fish as possible. Remember that the fish is already stressed as a result of its problems. Sick fish should be coaxed into a bowl or jar for transfer, rather than lifted physically from the water in a net. In any case, large fish, such as Koi, Dragon Fish, Arapaima or Pacus, should never be lifted in a net as their considerable weight means that—in the absence of supporting water—delicate internal organs can become damaged. Nets and receptacles used during transfer and treatment must be disinfected thoroughly after use.

Incorrect Dosage

Overdosing can kill not just the pathogens but the patient as well. It is therefore essential to know the exact capacity of the aquarium into which a medication is being introduced and to follow the recommended dosage levels to the letter. It is also vitally important to take the characteristics of the fish into consideration, since some types—scaleless species and varieties, such as some loaches, for example—

can be oversensitive to certain medications. Where relevant, such risks are normally pointed out by the medication's manufacturers.

Underdosing can be doubly injurious. In the short term, an inadequate dose will not kill the pathogenic organism, thus prolonging the treatment period and making it necessary to administer additional medication. In the long term, repeated use, particularly of antibiotics in low doses, can lead to a buildup of resistance.

If a fish exhibits any signs of distress while being subjected to medication, treatment must be stopped and the fish allowed to recover sufficiently before a revised dosage level is administered.

Filters, UV Sterilizers and Medications

Some filter media, such as ammonia-adsorbers, have only minor effects on medications. Other adsorbing media, such as activated carbon, can, however, remove at least some of the dosage. It is therefore advisable to switch off the aquarium filter during treatment or, alternatively, remove such media from the filter until treatment has been completed. Antibiotics do not generally distinguish between "good" and "bad" bacteria: they destroy both. As a result, filter bacteria will suffer if a biological filter is left in operation during antibiotic treatment.

Ultraviolet sterilizers can also neutralize or reduce the effects of certain medications, so they too should be switched off while the fish in an aquarium are undergoing treatment.

HUMANE DISPOSAL

This is a subject that causes great distress to many aquarists. However, it is one that must be faced, since some fish will become so ill that recovery is highly unlikely or out of the question. Several methods have been recommended over the years and, while some may be especially efficient in that death is virtually immediate, the mere fact that they involve inflicting physical damage on the fish rules them out for some. Two of the gentler forms of euthanasia appear not to cause undue distress and are therefore generally found to be acceptable.

Gradual Chilling

The fish is placed in a bag or bowl containing water with several tablespoonfuls of salt dissolved in it (this appears to calm the fish down). The bag or bowl is then placed in a freezer and allowed to cool gradually for several hours or overnight. As the temperature

drops, the metabolism of the fish slows down until it eventually ceases.

Anesthesia

Fish anesthetics, when used at higher than normal concentrations, will take fish beyond anesthesia to the point at which their metabolism stops (some time after they slip into unconsciousness). Anesthetics may be available with or without a vet's prescription, but, either way, professional advice should be sought when using this method of euthanasia.

RISKS TO HUMANS

Despite the occasional alarming headlines and distressing incidents of humans picking up disease organisms from aquatic animals (zoonoses), the risks are, in reality, very low and can be reduced even further with suitable precautions. Personal hygiene and protection measures adopted during aquarium maintenance should ensure that—barring an unforeseen circumstance—no contamination of any kind will occur.

ALWAYS ENSURE THAT YOU:

Use surgical gloves while carrying out maintenance or handling fish; particularly unhealthy specimens.

Avoid consuming food and drink while carrying out aquarium maintenance or handling sick fish.

Avoid exposing cuts or abrasions to aquarium water.

Wash hands thoroughly after carrying out aquarium maintenance or handling sick fish.

Never—but *never*—suck water via a siphon tube out of an aquarium by mouth.

The two pathogenic organisms that are associated with aquaria and, from time to time, cited as potentially harmful to humans are Salmonella (which can be contracted from many other sources, such as family pets, probably more easily than from aquarium water) and fish TB. Although the fish TB bacteria (at least two species of mycobacterium) are not ideally suited to survival within mammalian tissues, they can, on occasion, infect humans (usually via cuts or abrasions) and can cause localized and sometimes painful skin lesions that may require antibiotic treatment or chemotherapy and may prove slow to clear. Should any form of infection be suspected, medical advice should be sought promptly.

AQUARIUM PLANTS

The vast majority of freshwater fish species live on or within reach of the bottom of lakes, pools, rivers or streams. They therefore live associated with submerged vegetation, rocks and branches, without which they would be placed under stress. This can result in altered behavior patterns, subdued or pale coloration, susceptibility to disease, and other undesirable consequences. It therefore follows that aquaria should try to emulate the natural environment as closely as possible.

Aquascaping, whether this means providing cliffs and caves (as in African Rift Lake cichlid setups), or pieces of bogwood or other submerged shelters, is important in reducing stress on aquarium fish. Aquarium plants can provide not just shelter, food, breeding sites and nest-building materials, but can also act as territory markers, or even "gathering" points. For us, plants also immeasurably enhance the appearance of an aquarium. Although from the fishes' viewpoint attractiveness is irrelevant, due attention should be paid to this aspect of aquarium keeping, especially if the tank in question is located in a main living area.

PHOTOSYNTHESIS

Plants perform several important functions. Foremost among these is their part in photosynthesis, which synthesizes carbohydrate. Carbohydrates are food compounds made up of carbon (C), hydrogen (H), and oxygen (O), with the hydrogen and oxygen always occurring in the ratio of two atoms of hydrogen to every one of oxygen (as in water, H_2O). The best-known carbohydrate, which is also the one formed during photosynthesis, is glucose. (Other well-known carbohydrates include fructose, lactose, sucrose, starch and glycogen.)

The complex process of photosynthesis requires both light and the green pigment chlorophyll, which is found inside the tiny "granules" or organelles, known as chloroplasts, that give green plants their characteristic color. The raw materials for the process are carbon, hydrogen and oxygen, which are provided by carbon dioxide (CO_2) and water (H_2O). By putting these together, we end up with a crude form of chemical equation:

$$CO_2 + H_2O + \text{chlorophyll \& light} \rightarrow CH_2O + O_2$$

This "equation" presents the necessary compounds and their products in their basic relationship. CH_2O is not an actual carbohydrate; just an indication of the ratios of the three elements in carbohydrate synthesis. Glucose, the real carbohydrate formed, contains 6

atoms of carbon, 12 of hydrogen and 6 of oxygen, i.e. $C_6H_{12}O_6$. Reassembling the formula with this detail included, we arrive at the basic form of the standard summary equation for photosynthesis:

$$6CO_2 + 6H_2O + \text{chlorophyll \& light} \rightarrow C_6H_{12}O_6 + 6O_2$$

As this equation shows, the formation of glucose in the presence of chlorophyll and light results in the production of oxygen, as well as the consumption of carbon dioxide. This has led to the common misapprehension that green plants "breathe in carbon dioxide and breathe out oxygen" during the day and reverse the process at night. In fact, green plants breathe (respire) all the time, day and night. In so doing, they consume oxygen and produce carbon dioxide. However, during the hours of daylight, they also photosynthesize (in addition to, and not instead of, their respiratory activities). Both processes run alongside each other during the day. While this is going on, and if light conditions are sufficiently high, the consumption of carbon dioxide and the production of oxygen during photosynthesis are both higher than the consumption of oxygen and production of carbon dioxide during respiration. The net result is a drop in carbon dioxide levels in the water and a corresponding rise in oxygen concentration.

As darkness falls (or when aquarium lights are switched off), photosynthesis stops. However, respiration carries on, just as it has done during the daylight hours. Since no carbon dioxide is now being used up or oxygen being generated by photosynthetic processes, the result during the night is a drop in dissolved oxygen concentrations and a corresponding increase in carbon dioxide levels, until day breaks and photosynthesis begins once more.

In any case, plants cannot be regarded as the sole providers of oxygen in most home aquaria. This applies particularly to well-planted systems, where the dissolved oxygen concentration may drop to dangerously low levels during the night. Irrespective of how well or sparsely an aquarium is planted, additional aeration should be provided.

AQUARIUM PLANTS AFFECT THE BALANCE OF OXYGEN AND CARBON DIOXIDE DISSOLVED IN THE WATER. WITH THE TANK LIGHTING ON, THE NET RESULT IS THE RELEASE OF OXYGEN INTO THE WATER AND THE ABSORPTION OF CARBON DIOXIDE FROM IT (IF PHOTOSYNTHESIS EXCEEDS RESPIRATION). WITH THE LIGHTING OFF, OXYGEN IS REMOVED FROM THE WATER AND CARBON DIOXIDE IS RELEASED, SINCE RESPIRATION IS OCCURRING, BUT NOT PHOTOSYNTHESIS.

Water-enhancing Qualities

While oxygen production as a result of photosynthesis is the best-known beneficial effect of aquarium plants, plants also perform other desirable functions. It has been observed that—all else being equal—fish kept in well-planted aquaria are generally less prone to health problems than those kept in poorly planted or bare tanks. It is believed that this is because plants are able to remove not just certain mineral salts from the water, but also significant quantities of organic carbon compounds and even phenols. Some experiments have also shown that aquatic plants can actually reduce population densities of certain bacteria associated with health problems. Some plants, such as Duckweed (*Lemna* spp.) have even been shown to produce antibiotics.

Tropical freshwater aquarium with rainbow rock and natural plants.

Owing to their mineral-absorbing qualities, both floating and anchored plants can be used to keep some potentially damaging salts such as nitrates and phosphates under control, not just in aquaria and ponds, but in commercial establishments as well. The result is healthy water and luxuriant plant growth.

Aquarium, Aquatic and Terrestrial Plants

Many aquarists buy plants and are then disappointed at their lack of success with certain types. While in some cases failure can be easily tracked down to, say, lack of illumination or the plant-eating habits of particular fish, in other cases the plants simply rot and die for no apparent reason. In such instances, the "culprit" is often the plant itself in that it may not be a truly aquatic species.

There are three main types of plant sold for aquaria: genuinely aquatic species, marsh or marginal species, and terrestrial species that will survive (but not grow) for varying periods of time underwater.

Of the three types, the first, of course, provides the best choice if the plant is to be permanently submerged or floating. The second—marsh or marginal species—can also provide good aquarium plants, since many, e.g. swordplants (*Echinodorus* spp.) can grow perfectly well underwater, protruding above surface level only as the flowering season approaches.

Among the terrestrial species, the range is quite extensive and includes dwarf palms (e.g. *Chamaedorea elegans*), the spider plant (*Chlorophytym brichetii*), some dracaenas (such as *Dracaena sandeniana*), dumb cane (*Diffenbachia* spp.), the aluminum plants (*Fittonia* spp.), various *Hemigraphis* species, and many others. If only one or a few of these plants are kept, they will not cause any water pollution problems providing leaves are removed as soon as they begin to rot, with the whole plant being discarded well before it disintegrates. However, large concentrations of terrestrial plants should be avoided, since they may cause some disruption of the water chemistry balance, particularly once they begin to break down.

Artificial Plants

When these first appeared many years ago, they tended to be rather poor imitations of their natural counterparts. While some of these are still on offer—and some are intentionally artificial-looking in their shape and coloration—modern versions can appear very realistic. Purists sometimes dismiss such plants as compromises adopted by aquarists who cannot grow the real thing. Although this may sometimes be true, artificial plants are useful for providing welcome greenery in aquaria housing plant-eating or plant-destroying fish species. In such cases, artificial plants may represent the only means of making an aquarium attractive to the eye, while at the same time exerting a stress-reducing influence on the fish themselves.

Other advantages of artificial plants are their near indestructibility (they can be moved repeatedly without suffering damage), the ease with which they can be cleaned when they become encrusted with algae, and the way in which they can be combined with natural plants into spectacular displays. On the downside of course, they cannot contribute photosynthetically or in any other bioactive way to the aquarium community.

PLANT SUPPLIES

Aquarium plants are grown in vast numbers to supply an ever-increasing global demand. Although tropical regions are the prime producers and exporters, some countries in temperate and subtropical regions, including Denmark, Germany, Holland, the United Kingdom, Florida and Israel, now contribute significantly and increasingly to the plants available to aquarists. As the aquarium plant-growing industry has expanded, and as technology has improved, so has the range of plants and the various ways in which they are offered for sale.

Bunched Plants

At the least expensive end are the so-called "bunch plants." These are unrooted cuttings that are bunched together, either with elastic bands, or with lead or aluminum strips or wire. Numerous species and varieties are sold as bunch plants, which, owing to the uncomplicated, no-nonsense way in which they are

offered for sale, allow a good display to be made at very reasonable cost.

The simplest way of planting bunches is to press the base of each clump of cuttings gently into the substratum until the elastic band or metal strip is hidden from view. While this may work quite well, there are risks, not from metal toxicity (there's generally too little metal to cause any problems) but from damage the plants may already have suffered. When such plants are clipped together—especially since many of the species have delicate stems and leaves—some damage, including bruising, can result. This can subsequently lead to rotting of the tissues, with the plant shoots eventually breaking off. It is therefore advisable to remove the band or strip, cut off any damaged tissues, and then plant each cutting separately. Providing a little space between individual shoots also helps further reduce the risk of fungal infection.

Loose- or Barerooted Plants

One stage up, as it were, from unrooted, bunched cuttings are specimen (single) plants sold with roots, but not planted in pots. Many species may be sold in this form, but the main ones are the various types of Amazon swordplant (*Echinodorus* spp. and varieties), cryptos (*Cryptocoryne* spp.), onion plants (*Crinum* spp.), some *Aponogeton* and *Anubias* species, tape grass or vallis (*Vallisneria* spp.—also sometimes sold in bunches) and some sags (*Sagittaria* spp.).

Before planting, roots, stems and leaves should be examined carefully and damaged tissues removed. The roots should then be spread out and buried in the aquarium substrate, making sure that the growing points (crowns) are not covered up.

Potted Plants

Unlike their terrestrial garden equivalents, these pots do not contain soil or organic medium, but inert material such as rockwool. The pots, too, are different in that, besides being very small, they have slits or holes all round, allowing free entry of water around the bases of the plant stems.

Potted plants can be of any type (usually rooted). Truly aquatic stemmed plants, such as *Elodea*, *Cabomba* and the like, are often potted up as unrooted cuttings and allowed to root before being offered for sale. Specimen plants such as *Echinodorus* species and others that are sometimes also sold in loose-rooted form, are usually similarly allowed to settle down for a time before being sold. Stemmed terrestrial and marginal plants are often planted as unrooted cuttings and then encouraged to

ANUBIAS NANA *PLANTS UNDER CULTIVATION AT A PLANT FARM IN THAILAND.*

ECHINODORUS PANICULATUS

in the case of mosses and liverworts). Owing to the higher labor costs and lead times associated with the production of attached plants, expect to pay a little more for them.

Attached plants have advantages in addition to their attractiveness as decorative features. Being "self-contained," in that the piece of wood or rock holds the whole plant, including its roots, they can be moved around the aquarium at will without causing damage to any growing tissues. This is particularly useful where planted vegetation can hinder the netting of fish, resulting in stress for the fish. Attached plants can be removed from the aquarium before netting, making the fish more easily accessible.

Tissue-cultured Plants

Like attached plants, these are a relatively recent introduction to the aquarium scene. Small pieces of selected plant tissue are "sown" in a sealed flask or test tube containing a nutrient-rich soup. After a few weeks of culture under carefully controlled conditions, the initial mass of tissue will have replicated many times over and can be split, either into further tissue blocks, or into individual tiny plants that can then be grown on. This next stage can be laboratory-based, with the small plants being grown on for a time in a nutritious gel, or they can be transplanted into pots containing a rooting medium (such as mineral or rockwool) and cultivated in the normal way in a greenhouse. In tropical regions, these plants can subsequently be placed in outdoor ponds for their final period of growth before being offered for sale.

The sterile environment in which tissue-cultured plants begin their existence, along with the highly nutritious nature of the growth medium itself, ensures robust, healthy baby plants that stand an excellent chance of continuing to grow strongly when they are transferred to aquaria. Another bonus is that tissue culture makes the development of new types of plant a much more rapid process than do traditional methods. The reason for this is that if a mutation is spotted in a traditionally grown plant, the specimen can be used to obtain mother tissue, which, within a few weeks, will result in thousands of identical offspring. The commercial potential of such a situation is self-evident. What may not be so self-evident is the enormous and exciting potential that tissue culture has for propagating endangered species of plants or for reducing pressure on wild populations of desirable plants. The downside for the aquarium hobby at the moment is that tissue culture is expensive. As a result, tissue-produced aquarium

root by keeping the pots covered in water but the leaves exposed to the air.

Although potted plants can be simply pressed into the substrate, covered up and left to their own devices, many experienced aquarists actually remove them from the pots and plant them as if they were bare-rooted specimens. This is not essential, since many of these plants will produce runners (a horizontally spreading stem with an embryonic plant at its tip) and will therefore still reproduce despite the pot or rooting medium. However, removing this potential obstacle may help some plants in the initial stages.

Attached Plants

Some plants, most notably aquatic ferns, such as the Java Fern (*Microsorum pteropus*) or the African Water Fern or Congo Fern (*Bolbitis heudelotii*), mosses, such as Java Moss (*Vesicularia dubyana*), and recently a liverwort, *Riccia fluitans* (traditionally sold as a floating plant) plus the various types of *Anubias* are now sold growing attached to a piece of bogwood or rock.

At first, the plants are attached by means of an elastic band or short length of fishing line but as they begin to spread, they attach themselves by their "roots" (which are not true roots, but specially modified cells

plants currently account for only a small (but growing) fraction of the total aquarium plant market.

Floating Plants

Some plants that float on the surface of the water are not in fact floating plants, but surface plants. The distinction is quite simple: in floating plants, the leaves, stems and blooms are all found either on or above the surface of the water, while the roots hang freely underwater, not attached to the substrate; in surface plants, leaves, shoots and blooms may also lie on the surface or protrude above it, but the roots are anchored in the substrate. Water Hyacinth (*Eichhornia crassipes*) is a true floater but waterlilies (*Nymphaea* spp. and varieties) are surface plants.

FLOWERS OF THE AMAZON SWORDPLANT
(ECHINODORUS SP.)

Floating plants may be offered for sale loose, as single specimens (larger species) or as "portions" (smaller ones), or pre-bagged with a small amount of water. The latter are definitely easier to handle for buyer and seller and are therefore becoming progressively more popular. Many established aquarists, however, still prefer buying their floaters loose in the belief that the quality of plants that are bagged for any length of time may not be as good, even though there does not appear to be any conclusive evidence of this at the moment.

Bulbs, Tubers and Rhizomes

Some plants may also be offered for sale without any leaves or with just the initial stages of leaf. Bulbs of the various onion plants (*Crinum* spp.), for example, may be sold without any leaves, just as daffodil or hyacinth bulbs are sold for planting in pots or gardens. Spatterdocks (*Nuphar* spp.) and tropical lilies (*Nymphaea* spp.) may be sold as sections of a rhizome, or a complete rhizome, while species of *Aponogeton* may be available as individual tubers. Sometimes, ferns, with or without small developing fronds (leaves), are sold as lengths of rhizome with some roots already growing. *Anubias* plants may also be sold in this way. (*See* Glossary for distinction between tubers and rhizomes.)

Bulbs should be either buried in the substrate or planted in a pot, with the tip showing above the medium. The rhizomes and tubers of lilies, *Anubias* species and *Aponogeton* species may be partially buried. Ferns

should be planted with their rhizomes exposed and, preferably, attached to a piece of bogwood or a rock by means of an elastic band or short length of fishing line. (*Anubias* species may also be planted in this way.)

PLANTING AND MAINTENANCE

When planning a planting scheme, it is always better to opt for an asymmetrical layout: a symmetrical design invariably looks unnatural. This term is of course relative, since all aquarium planting schemes are by definition unnatural. Nevertheless, the best planting schemes are always those that have asymmetry built into them.

Generally speaking, low plants should be used along the front of the aquascape, with taller ones at the back. This, however, is not an inflexible rule. Setting a tall specimen plant relatively close to the front (but to the side of the display) can create a very interesting effect, as can low plants in specially created spaces among taller vegetation about halfway into a scheme (provided, of course, that these spaces can be seen from the front of the aquarium).

Protecting Plants

If an aquarium is to house plant-eating fish or species that constantly root around the substrate, or other types that pose a direct threat to plants, several approaches may be adopted. In the first instance, avoid delicate, "tasty" plants. This, unfortunately, includes many of the commonly available species. However, there are species that are either exceptionally tough or that are distasteful to fish. Prominent among these are the aquatic ferns, but many marsh/marginal plants and nonaquatic plants offered for aquaria will tend to be left alone by fish. Even some of the tougher or deep-rooted aquatic plants such as *Vallisneria americana* (also known as *V. gigantea*), some swordplants, e.g. *Echinodorus osiris* and the onion plants (*Crinum* spp.) tend not to be eaten by herbivorous species.

One of the best ways of protecting plants from rooting fish is by making the area around the bases of the stems inaccessible. Placing a few pebbles around clumps of plants is often sufficient, or specimen plants can be potted up and the surface of the rooting medium covered with pebbles. To make the latter arrangement attractive, pots should be either fully (often not possible) or at least partially buried, or hidden by aquarium decorations such as bogwood or rockwork.

Air-grown Plant Adaptation

Aquarists are understandably disappointed when, shortly after buying a luxuriant plant, its leaves begin to rot. When this happens, the temptation is to throw the plant away. But if the plant is a nonaquatic type, then—as explained earlier—it will die sooner or later, irrespective of what remedial action is taken. So simply remove the decaying leaves as they develop, discarding the plant finally when it begins to look unattractive.

In marginals and true aquatics, the reason for leaf degeneration often depends on how the plant was grown. Many aquarium plants, including Amazon swordplants (*Eichinodorus* spp.), Water Wisteria (*Hygrophila difformis*), *Bacopa* species and others, are often cultivated under marsh conditions with their roots in water and their leaves exposed to the air. This type of culture allows for ease of management and low labor costs and can result in robust and attractive plants. In fact, such plants are so robust that they have rigid or semirigid stems that will hold the aerial parts erect above the substratum. Specimens cultivated underwater will flop over if exposed, having developed in conditions where they are buoyed up by the water itself. One difficulty with air-grown plants is that when they are planted underwater the aerial leaves may begin to rot away. This does not, however, mean that the plant has died. It is readapting. Such plants should be left to reestablish themselves, which they will tend to do over a period of weeks.

GROWTH AIDS

Generally speaking, the more luxuriantly rooted a plant is, the more likely it is to belong to a species or variety that derives a significant amount of its mineral salts and trace elements via its roots. Even so, all truly aquatic plants also take in dissolved nutrients from the water via their leaves.

In well-planted aquaria, neither the substrate itself (often consisting of gravel, which does not release mineral nutrients) nor the water is likely to be able to cater adequately for these needs. Appropriate proprietary fertilizers, either in dissolved, tablet, or "pack," form should therefore be provided. These should be administered only in the recommended doses, since an excess of nutrients can lead to a burst of growth not just among the desirable aquatic plants but also in the less desirable ones, such as algae.

In the earlier section dealing with photosynthesis, the importance of carbon dioxide was highlighted. Clearly, if levels of carbon dioxide are too low then photosynthesis cannot function optimally and plant growth will suffer. Plants grown in aquaria that house large fish collections and that thus generate significant quantities of carbon dioxide will not usually suffer carbon dioxide deficiency. However, if the number of plants is particularly high, or if fish stocks are low, the addition of carbon dioxide via a diffuser (commercially produced models are widely available) will be found beneficial. Indeed, the use of a carbon dioxide diffuser will produce visible effects even in well-balanced aquaria, especially those containing fast-growing plant species.

◄ GREEN CABOMBA (CABOMBA AQUATICA) WITH MALE GUPPIES (POECILIA RETICULATA VAR.)

ALGAE

Algae are nonflowering plants, which, though primitive, are so well adapted to survive in such an array of environments that it is virtually impossible to find any body of water that does not contain at least some algal cells or spores. Traditionally, algae are regarded as problem plants in aquaria and ponds. Certainly, they can create problems, or can indicate that some environmental parameters are unfavorable, notably excessive levels of nitrates. However, to consider all algae as undesirables is wrong.

Algae will grow wherever conditions are appropriate for other plants to grow. They can therefore be seen as competitors for nutrients and space but also as a favorable "litmus test" on growing conditions. While we should provide conditions that favor the growth of higher plants and limit the growth of algae, there are only a few types of algae that are associated with problems in aquaria.

Blue-green Algae

These distinctive mat-forming algae are not, strictly speaking, true algae, but cyanobacteria, having characteristics of both bacteria and algae. Mats can form extremely rapidly and can cover plants and decorations to such an extent that the plants can die. Blue-green algae are particularly frequent in new aquaria that contain "raw" water, are thinly planted, excessively illuminated and contain some water pollutants, perhaps from overfeeding.

Physical removal, increasing planting density, reducing light and feeding levels, and a partial water change, allied to the addition of a proprietary algicide, will help to control these cyanobacteria and minimize risks of reinfestation. Rather than resort to chemical treatments, the aim is to create conditions that will not favor the growth of these pests.

Green Algae

Some authors divide green algae into several subcategories, depending on whether they are free-floating, single-celled or attached filamentous/encrusting types. For practical purposes, they can be grouped together; given high illumination and nitrates, these algae will proliferate in the absence of strong competition from higher plants.

The free-floating types will cause green-water problems if their population is allowed to explode. Filamentous types will, given appropriate conditions, produce tuftlike growths on plants, decorations and even the substratum, while the encrusting types will simply spread as a thin layer, mainly on plants, tank panes and decorations.

Light reduction and nitrate/phosphate control—along with physical removal—will reduce populations to manageable levels, but a water change is also desirable (particularly in the case of free-floating types) followed by algicide treatment to reduce risks of reinfestation while natural control measures are figured out and implemented.

In the case of attached green algae, whether of the filamentous or encrusting types, total elimination is often intentionally avoided by experienced fishkeepers, since these growths can act as food sources for some fish species, such as the Sucking Loach (*Gyrinocheilus aymonieri*), Siamese Flying Fox (*Crossocheilus siamensis*), and many sucker-mouthed catfish, such as *Ancistrus, Hypostomus, Pterygoplichthys, Otocinclus*, and others. Many popular aquarium species such as the Swordtail (*Xiphophorus helleri*), platies (*Xiphophorus maculatus* and *X. variatus*), mollies (*Poecilia sphenops, P. velifera*, etc.), and African Rift Lake cichlids will also graze off encrusting algae and the microorganisms they may harbor, in the process helping to keep plants free of excessive infestation.

Red Algae

Despite their name, the red algae encountered in aquaria do not appear red, but a dull greenish-brown. Most often, these algae form tufts on leaves and decorations, leading to the alternative names of beard, fir or brush algae.

These tough invaders can prove difficult to control. However, as in the case of other types of algae, balanced aquarium conditions will help limit their growth. This should be accompanied by physical removal and the addition of an algicide as a short-term measure until the underlying cause has been rectified. For biological control of red algae, one of the best fish to use is the Siamese Flying Fox (*Crossocheilus siamensis*).

Brown Algae

These algae generally form characteristic brown encrustations on aquarium panes, decorations and plant leaves. Brown algae usually appear in conjunction with poor growth of other plants, indicating that illumination levels are inadequate. Their elimination is therefore easily achieved by increasing light intensity above the aquarium. No algicide treatment is likely to be necessary, although scraping of the growths from the aquarium panes, rocks, etc., should be carried out.

PLANTS LISTING

The following is a selection of plant species that are available for use in freshwater aquaria (availability will vary between countries and between seasons). Some species are also suitable for brackish water systems that are closer to the freshwater end of the salinity spectrum than the marine one.

In each case, recommended light level, water type and temperature range are given. Temperature ranges are defined as coldwater or tropical. Division of coldwater and tropical temperature is at 72°F (22°C).

Specific characteristics are indicated as follows:

- Plants that will tolerate some salt in the water.
- Plants that, while being able to produce aerial leaves (leaves exposed above water), are also suitable for cultivation underwater.
- Nonaquatic plants that may be used for decorative purposes but that will not grow underwater and will die after a shorter or longer period of immersion.

PENNYWORT

Hydrocotyle verticillata ■
(May be cultivated as a rooted plant)

WATER PREFERENCES:	*Soft to medium hard*
LIGHTING:	*High to very high*
TEMPERATURE RANGE:	*Coldwater/tropical*

HYGRORHIZA ARISTATA

WATER PREFERENCES:	*Not critical*
LIGHTING:	*High to very high*
TEMPERATURE RANGE:	*Tropical*

▲ *FAIRY MOSS (AZOLLA CAROLINIANA)*
INDIAN FERN (CERATOPTERIS SP.) ▶

FLOATING SPECIES

FAIRY MOSS, AZOLLA

Azolla caroliniana

WATER PREFERENCES:	*Medium hard*
LIGHTING:	*High*
TEMPERATURE RANGE:	*Coldwater/tropical*

INDIAN FERN, WATER SPRITE

Ceratopteris thalictroides ● ■ (Also grows as a rooted plant)

WATER PREFERENCES:	*Soft to medium hard*
LIGHTING:	*High*
TEMPERATURE RANGE:	*Coldwater/tropical*

WATER HYACINTH

Eichhornia crassipes

WATER PREFERENCES:	*Not critical*
LIGHTING:	*High to very high*
TEMPERATURE RANGE:	*Tropical*

FROGBIT

Hydrocharis morsus-ranae

WATER PREFERENCES:	*Not critical*
LIGHTING:	*High*
TEMPERATURE RANGE:	*Coldwater*

DUCKWEED

Lemna spp.

WATER PREFERENCES: *Not critical*

LIGHTING: *High to very high*

TEMPERATURE RANGE: *Coldwater/tropical*

AMAZON FROGBIT

Limnobium laevigatum

WATER PREFERENCES: *Not critical*

LIGHTING: *High to very high*

TEMPERATURE RANGE: *Coldwater (upper end)/tropical*

▲ ALTERNANTHERA REINECKII, *"ROSEAFOLIA" VAR.*
▼ APONOGETON ULVACEUS

WATER LETTUCE, NILE CABBAGE

Pistia stratiotes

WATER PREFERENCES: *Not critical*

LIGHTING: *High to very high*

TEMPERATURE RANGE: *Tropical*

PHYLLANTHUS FLUITANS

WATER PREFERENCES: *Soft to medium hard*

LIGHTING: *High to very high*

TEMPERATURE RANGE: *Tropical*

RICCIA, CRYSTALWORT

Riccia fluitans

WATER PREFERENCES: *Medium hard*

LIGHTING: *High*

TEMPERATURE RANGE: *Coldwater/tropical*

SALVINIA, BUTTERFLY FERN

Salvinia spp.

WATER PREFERENCES: *Medium hard*

LIGHTING: *High*

TEMPERATURE RANGE: *Tropical*

WATER CHESTNUT

Trapa natans

WATER PREFERENCES: *Not critical*

LIGHTING: *High*

TEMPERATURE RANGE: *Coldwater/tropical*

SUBMERGED SPECIES

ACORUS, SWEET FLAG, JAPANESE "RUSH," and others

Acorus spp. ▲

WATER PREFERENCES: *Not critical*

LIGHTING: *Not critical, but will last longer under high illumination*

TEMPERATURE RANGE: *Coldwater*

ALTERNANTHERA, TELANTHERA

Alternanthera spp. and varieties ■

WATER PREFERENCES: *Soft to medium hard*

LIGHTING: *High to very high*

TEMPERATURE RANGE: *Coldwater (upper end)/tropical*

AMMANIA

Ammania senegalensis ● ■

WATER PREFERENCES: *Not critical*

LIGHTING: *High*

TEMPERATURE RANGE: *Coldwater (upper end)/tropical*

ANUBIAS

Anubias spp. ■

WATER PREFERENCES: *Not critical*

LIGHTING: *Generally low to medium*

TEMPERATURE RANGE: *Coldwater (upper end)/tropical*

APONOGETON

Aponogeton spp.

WATER PREFERENCES: *Not critical*

LIGHTING: *Medium to high*

TEMPERATURE RANGE: *Coldwater (upper end)/tropical*

BACOPA (numerous types)

Bacopa spp. ■

WATER PREFERENCES: *Not critical*

LIGHTING: *Medium to high*

TEMPERATURE RANGE: *Coldwater (upper end)/tropical*

BARCLAYA, ORCHID LILY

Barclaya longifolia

WATER PREFERENCES: *Not critical*

LIGHTING: *Medium to high*

TEMPERATURE RANGE: *Tropical*

BAMBOO PLANT

Blyxa japonica

WATER PREFERENCES: *Not critical*

LIGHTING: *Medium to high*

TEMPERATURE RANGE: *Tropical*

AFRICAN WATER FERN

Bolbitis heudelotii ■

WATER PREFERENCES: *Soft to medium hard*

LIGHTING: *Not critical*

TEMPERATURE RANGE: *Tropical*

CABOMBA

Cabomba spp.

WATER PREFERENCES: *Soft to medium hard*

LIGHTING: *I ligh*

TEMPERATURE RANGE: *Tropical (C. caroliniana will tolerate coldwater range)*

JAPANESE CRESS

Cardamine lyrata ■

WATER PREFERENCES: *Not critical*

LIGHTING: *Medium to high*

TEMPERATURE RANGE: *Coldwater/tropical*

HORNWORT

Ceratophyllum demersum ●, *C. submersum*

WATER PREFERENCES: *Not critical*

LIGHTING: *Not critical*

TEMPERATURE RANGE: *Coldwater/tropical (C. submersum is better adapted than* C. demersum *to tropical conditions)*

PARLOUR PALM

Chamaedorea elegans ▲

WATER PREFERENCES: *Not critical*

LIGHTING: *Not critical*

TEMPERATURE RANGE: *Coldwater/tropical*

SPIDER PLANT, PONGOL SWORD

Chlorophytum spp. ▲

WATER PREFERENCES: *Not critical*

LIGHTING: *Not critical*

TEMPERATURE RANGE: *Coldwater/tropical*

CROTON

Codiaeum variegatum ▲

WATER PREFERENCES: *Not critical*

LIGHTING: *Medium to high*

TEMPERATURE RANGE: *Coldwater/tropical*

CORDYLINE

Cordyline terminalis ▲

WATER PREFERENCES: *Not critical*

LIGHTING: *High*

TEMPERATURE RANGE: *Coldwater/tropical*

▼ CRYPTO (CRYPTOCORYNE SP.)

SWORDPLANT "MARBLE QUEEN" (ECHINODORUS SP.) ▶

ONION PLANT

Crinum spp. ■

WATER PREFERENCES: *Not critical*

LIGHTING: *Medium to very high*

TEMPERATURE RANGE: *Coldwater/tropical (C. thaianum is the most cold-resistant species)*

CRYPTO (numerous species)

Cryptocoryne spp., mostly ■ (*C. ciliata* ●)

WATER PREFERENCES: *Not critical*

LIGHTING: *Low to high (depending on species)*

TEMPERATURE RANGE: *Coldwater (only upper end)/ tropical*

UMBRELLA PLANT

Cyperus alternifolius ▲ and *C. helferi* ■

WATER PREFERENCES: *Not critical*

LIGHTING: *Medium to high*

TEMPERATURE RANGE: *Coldwater/tropical (C. helferi)*

WATER HEDGE

Didiplis diandra ■

WATER PREFERENCES: *Soft to medium hard*

LIGHTING: *Medium to very high*

TEMPERATURE RANGE: *Coldwater (upper end)/ tropical*

DRAGON PLANT

Dracaena sp. ▲

WATER PREFERENCES: *Not critical*

LIGHTING: *Medium to high*

TEMPERATURE RANGE: *Coldwater/tropical*

SWORDPLANT

NUMEROUS SPECIES AND CULTIVARS

Echinodorus spp. and varieties ■
(*E. tenellus* ●)

WATER PREFERENCES: *Not critical*

LIGHTING: *Low to very high (depending on type, but most tolerate a range of intensities)*

TEMPERATURE RANGE: *Coldwater/tropical*

DENSA, ARGENTINE WATER WEED, GIANT ELODEA

Egeria densa ●

WATER PREFERENCES: *Not critical*

LIGHTING: *Medium to very high*

TEMPERATURE RANGE: *Coldwater/tropical (lower end)*

BLUE WATER HYACINTH

Eichhornia azurea and *E. diversifolia* ■

WATER PREFERENCES: *Not critical*

LIGHTING: *High to very high*

TEMPERATURE RANGE: *Coldwater/tropical*

HAIR GRASS

Eleocharis spp. ■

WATER PREFERENCES: *Not critical*

LIGHTING: *Medium to high*

TEMPERATURE RANGE: *Coldwater/tropical (lower end)*

CANADIAN PONDWEED

Elodea canadensis

WATER PREFERENCES: *Not critical*

LIGHTING: *High*

TEMPERATURE RANGE: *Coldwater/tropical (lower end)*

EUSTERALIS STELLATA ■

WATER PREFERENCES: *Soft to medium hard*

LIGHTING: *High to very high*

TEMPERATURE RANGE: *Tropical*

WILLOW MOSS

Fontinalis antipyretica

WATER PREFERENCES: *Not critical*

LIGHTING: *Medium to high*

TEMPERATURE RANGE: *Coldwater*

GLOSSOSTIGMA ELATINOIDES

WATER PREFERENCES: *Soft to medium hard*

LIGHTING: *High to very high*

TEMPERATURE RANGE: *Coldwater/tropical (lower end)*

VARIEGATED HYGROPHILA (HYGROPHILA SPP.)

SPADE LEAF PLANT

Gymnocoronis spp. ■

WATER PREFERENCES: *Not critical*

LIGHTING: *Medium to very high*

TEMPERATURE RANGE: *Coldwater/tropical*

HEMIANTHUS MICRANTHEMOIDES ■

WATER PREFERENCES: *Not critical*

LIGHTING: *Medium to very high*

TEMPERATURE RANGE: *Coldwater/tropical*

HEMIGRAPHIS SPP. ▲

WATER PREFERENCES: *Not critical*

LIGHTING: *Medium to high*

TEMPERATURE RANGE: *Coldwater/tropical*

WATER STARGRASS

Heteranthera zosterifolia

WATER PREFERENCES: *Not critical*

LIGHTING: *High to very high*

TEMPERATURE RANGE: *Coldwater/tropical*

WATER VIOLET

Hottonia inflata and H. palustris

WATER PREFERENCES: *Soft to medium hard*

LIGHTING: *High to very high*

TEMPERATURE RANGE: *Coldwater/tropical (lower end)*

HYDRILLA

Hydrilla verticillata

WATER PREFERENCES: *Not critical*

LIGHTING: *High*

TEMPERATURE RANGE: *Tropical*

NUMEROUS TYPES, e.g. HYGROPHILA, WATER WISTERIA, WATER STAR

Hygrophila spp. and varieties ■
(H. polysperma ●)

WATER PREFERENCES: *Not critical*

LIGHTING: *Low to high, depending on type*

TEMPERATURE RANGE: *Coldwater (upper end)/ tropical*

CRISPA

Lagarosiphon major

WATER PREFERENCES: *Not critical*

LIGHTING: *High*

TEMPERATURE RANGE: *Coldwater*

FALSE TENELLUS

Lilaeopsis brasiliensis, L. novaezelandiae

WATER PREFERENCES: *Not critical*

LIGHTING: *Medium to very high*

TEMPERATURE RANGE: *Coldwater/tropical (lower end)*

AMBULIA

Limnophila spp.

WATER PREFERENCES: *Soft to medium hard*

LIGHTING: *Medium to very high*

TEMPERATURE RANGE: *Tropical (L. aquatica tolerant of slightly lower temperatures)*

LOBELIA

Lobelia cardinalis ■

WATER PREFERENCES: *Not critical*

LIGHTING: *Medium to very high*

TEMPERATURE RANGE: *Coldwater/tropical (lower end)*

LUDWIGIA

Ludwigia spp. ■

WATER PREFERENCES: *Not critical for most species (notable exception: L. inclinata—soft to medium)*

LIGHTING: *Medium to high*

TEMPERATURE RANGE: *Coldwater/tropical for most species. Notable exceptions: L. arcuata and L. glandulosa ("perennis")—only upper end of coldwater range; L. inclinata—only tropical*

MONEYWORT, CREEPING JENNY

Lysmachia nummularia ■

WATER PREFERENCES: *Not critical*

LIGHTING: *High to very high*

TEMPERATURE RANGE: *Coldwater/tropical (lower end)*

FALSE TENELLUS (LILAEOPSIS BRASILIENSIS)

MARCH TREFOIL, CLOVER

Marsilea crenata

WATER PREFERENCES: *Soft to medium*

LIGHTING: *Medium to high*

TEMPERATURE RANGE: *Coldwater*

JAVA FERN

Microsorum pteropus and varieties ● ■

WATER PREFERENCES: *Not critical*

LIGHTING: *Not critical*

JAVA FERN
(MICROSORUM
PTEROPUS) ▶

TEMPERATURE RANGE: *Coldwater/tropical*

MILFOIL

Myriophyllum spp. ■ *some species*

WATER PREFERENCES: *Not critical*

LIGHTING: *High to very high*

TEMPERATURE RANGE: *Coldwater/tropical*

INDIAN NAJAD

Najas indica ●

WATER PREFERENCES: *Soft to medium hard*

LIGHTING: *Medium to high*

TEMPERATURE RANGE: *Tropical*

GIANT HYGROPHILA

Nomaphila stricta ● ■

WATER PREFERENCES: *Not critical*

LIGHTING: *High*

TEMPERATURE RANGE: *Coldwater (upper end)/ tropical*

JAPANESE SPATTERDOCK

Nuphar japonica

WATER PREFERENCES: *Not critical*

LIGHTING: *Not critical*

TEMPERATURE RANGE: *Coldwater/tropical*

AFRICAN TIGER LOTUS

Nymphaea maculata

WATER PREFERENCES: *Not critical*

LIGHTING: *High*

TEMPERATURE RANGE: *Coldwater (upper end)/ tropical*

BANANA PLANT

Nymphoides aquatica

WATER PREFERENCES: *Not critical*

LIGHTING: *High*

TEMPERATURE RANGE: *Coldwater (upper end)/ tropical*

JAPANESE FOUNTAIN PLANT

Ophiopogon japonicus ▲

WATER PREFERENCES: *Not critical*

LIGHTING: *Medium to very high*

TEMPERATURE RANGE: *Coldwater/tropical*

ALUMINUM PLANT

Pilea cadieri ▲

WATER PREFERENCES: *Not critical*

LIGHTING: *Not critical*

TEMPERATURE RANGE: *Coldwater/tropical*

FLORIDA CRYPTO

Physostegia leptophylla ■

WATER PREFERENCES: *Not critical*

LIGHTING: *Medium to high*

TEMPERATURE RANGE: *Coldwater (upper end)/ tropical*

CURLED PONDWEED

Potamogeton crispus

WATER PREFERENCES: *Not critical*

LIGHTING: *High*

TEMPERATURE RANGE: *Coldwater*

ROTALA

Rotala spp. and varieties ■

WATER PREFERENCES: *Not critical, but some exceptions, e.g. R. wallichii—soft to medium hard*

LIGHTING: *High to very high*

TEMPERATURE RANGE: *Coldwater/tropical, but some exceptions, e.g. R. macrandra—tropical*

SAG or SAGITTARIA

Sagittaria spp. ● (some species) and ■

WATER PREFERENCES: *Not critical*

LIGHTING: *Not critical*

TEMPERATURE RANGE: *Coldwater/tropical*

WATER CABBAGE, WATER ROSE

Samolus spp. ■ (*S. parviflorus* ●)

WATER PREFERENCES: *Not critical*

LIGHTING: *High to very high*

TEMPERATURE RANGE: *Coldwater/tropical*

LIZARD'S TAIL

Saururus cernuus ■

WATER PREFERENCES: *Not critical*

LIGHTING: *High to very high*

TEMPERATURE RANGE: *Coldwater/tropical*

MEXICAN OAK LEAF

Shinnersia rivularis ■

WATER PREFERENCES: *Not critical*

LIGHTING: *Medium to high*

TEMPERATURE RANGE: *Coldwater/tropical*

SPATHIPHYLLUM

Spathiphyllum wallisii ■

WATER PREFERENCES: *Soft to medium hard*

LIGHTING: *Not critical*

TEMPERATURE RANGE: *Tropical*

SYNGONIUM, IVY LEAF

Syngonium podophyllum ▲

WATER PREFERENCES: *Not critical*

LIGHTING: *Not critical*

TEMPERATURE RANGE: *Coldwater/tropical*

BLADDERWORT

Utricularia spp.

WATER PREFERENCES: *Not critical*

LIGHTING: *Medium to high*

TEMPERATURE RANGE: *Coldwater/tropical*

VALLIS, TAPE GRASS

Vallisneria spp. and varieties ●

WATER PREFERENCES: *Not critical*

LIGHTING: *Not critical*

TEMPERATURE RANGE: *Coldwater/tropical*

JAVA MOSS

Vesicularia dubyana ● ■

WATER PREFERENCES: *Not critical*

LIGHTING: *Not critical*

TEMPERATURE RANGE: *Coldwater/tropical*

STRAIGHT VALLIS (VALLISNERIA SPP.) ▶

AQUARIUM FISH

THE SECTION THAT FOLLOWS CONTAINS AN EXTENSIVE selection of species and varieties of fish that are available for aquaria. As both popularity and availability vary from country to country, the selection includes species that may be virtually unknown, or which might only be occasionally encountered, in some regions. Every attempt has been made to use the latest scientific names for all species. However, level of acceptance or frequency of use of scientific names also vary between countries and alternatives have been indicated where they might help identification: *Barbus conchonius*, for example, the Rosy Barb, is also frequently referred to as *Puntius conchonius*. Hopefully, this double reference will help aquarists in different countries identify the fish in question without any difficulty.

All the major fish families carry an introductory section highlighting their main characteristics. However, space limitations dictate that this is not possible for every family. The Bibliography lists works that will allow interested readers to obtain such information.

CICHLIDS

WHEN NEW AQUARISTS SEE FISH THAT LOOK AS different from each other as angels (*Pterophyllum* spp.), pike cichlids (*Crenicichla* spp.), zebras (*Metriaclima zebra*), rams (*Microgeophagus ramirezi*) and discus (*Symphysodon* spp.), they often wonder what it is that enables us to classify them all as cichlids. The answer is that despite their apparently large differences they share a number of important fundamental characteristics, most notably in the position of the nostrils: cichlids have only one nostril on each side of the head, rather than the usual two. In addition, they usually have a "split" lateral line, the front (longer) section being located higher up the body, and most species have brown-tipped teeth. The dorsal fin is divided into a spiny, unbranched (hard) anterior section and a branched (soft) posterior one supported by rays.

The Cichlidae constitute a very large family, which, according to some estimates, contains some 2,000 species. In fact, some authors believe that, depending on how a species is defined, Lake Malawi alone could account for up to 1,600 species.

Cichlids are numerous and widely distributed, which is why they exhibit a wide range of body shape, color, behavior and size. They occur mainly in freshwater (although there are some brackish species, e.g. *Etroplus*), in Central and South America, the West Indies, Africa, Madagascar, Syria, the coastal areas of the southern half of the Indian subcontinent and Sri Lanka. The northernmost species is the Texas Cichlid (*Herichthys cyanoguttatus*). The largest species is *Boulengerochromis microlepis*, which is found in Lake Tanganyika. At a maximum length of 36in (90cm), it is, not surprisingly, hardly ever seen in aquaria. At the other extreme, some of the dwarf cichlids belonging to the genus *Apistogramma* grow no bigger than 1½in (3.5cm).

Spawning behavior is extremely varied, although parental care is characteristic. Spawning strategies include substrate spawning, i.e. deposition of eggs on rocks, leaves and so on, as in many of the acaras (*Aequidens* spp.), angelfish (*Pterophyllum* spp.), and the famous Oscar (*Astronotus ocellatus*). In many African Rift Lake species, the eggs are incubated orally (a method called mouthbrooding) by females. Mouthbrooders include the Golden Lake Malawi Cichlid (*Melanochromis auratus*) and the many *Aulonocara*, *Labeotropheus* and *Pseudotropheus* species. Others (admittedly only a few), such as discus (*Symphysodon* spp.), angels (*Pterophyllum* spp.), pike cichlids (*Crenicichla* spp.) and the Uaru *(Uaru amphiacanthoides)*, go a stage further and feed their young on body secretion ("milk") during the first few weeks of life.

On the whole, cichlids will eat a wide range of foods and are, therefore, not generally difficult to keep. There are so many species of cichlid available within the hobby that, once the basics of aquarium keeping have been mastered, most aquarists interested in cichlids begin to specialize. The specialization can be as broad as New World or Old World species, or as narrow as varieties of a single species, e.g. Scalare Angelfish (*Pterophyllum scalare*). Among the Old World (African species) specialists, you have those who stick to Rift Lake species (or those of a specific Rift Lake), or those who stick to the non-Rift species, such as *Hemichromis*, *Pelvicachromis*, and *Pseudocrenilabrus*. Among the New World (American species) specialists, there are those who restrict their main focus to the dwarf cichlids, such as *Nannacara, Dicrossus* or *Apistogramma* species, or the eartheaters, such as *Geophagus* and their relatives, or to a single genus, such as *Symphysodon* (two species, several subspecies, and countless wild morphs and commercially developed varieties), or the larger types such as *Astronotus, Cichla, Crenicichla* and so on.

The pages that follow include all the well-known species, plus a wide selection of lesser-known ones, listed in alphabetical order (by scientific name). Specialist texts should be consulted for further detailed information of particular groups, such as Lake Malawi and Lake Tanganyika species.

BLUE ACARA
BLUE-SPOT CICHLID

Aequidens pulcher

SYNONYMS: *Aequidens latifrons,*
A. cf. latifrons, A. caeruleopunctatus

DESPITE THE BLUE ACARA'S LONG HISTORY IN THE hobby (it was first introduced into Europe in 1906), there is still considerable debate regarding its correct scientific name. As a result, the various names given above are often used interchangeably, with some authorities regarding the Colombian Blue Acaras as valid species in their own rights—*A. latifrons, A. cf. latifrons* or *A. caeruleopunctatus*—and the others as *A. pulcher*. There are certainly observable differences between these, but some other authorities believe them to be insufficiently significant to warrant separation.

DISTRIBUTION: *A. pulcher: Panama, Trinidad and Venezuela; A. latifrons and A. caeruleopunctatus: Colombia*

SIZE: *Up to 8in (20cm) reported; usually smaller*

BEHAVIOR: *Relatively peaceful, except during breeding. Although this species burrows, it does not eat plants. Roots should nevertheless be protected*

DIET: *All commercial and livefoods accepted*

AQUARIUM: *Open areas, hiding places, and some flat or smooth, rounded rocks. Plants must be robust and/or artificial. Water chemistry not critical but quality must be good. Temperature range: 64–77°F (18–25°C); slightly higher for breeding*

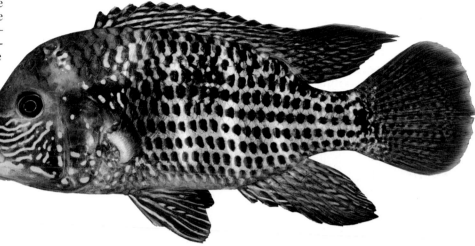

GREEN TERROR (AEQUIDENS RIVULATUS)

BREEDING: *Eggs are laid on a precleaned rock, and they and the fry are guarded by both parents. Hatching takes two to five days*

GREEN TERROR
SILVER SEAM, SILVER SAUM, GOLD SEAM, or GOLD SAUM

Aequidens rivulatus

THIS RELATIVELY LARGE FISH HAS DISTINCTIVE cheek markings that are similar to those found in the Blue Acara. However, the head, particularly in males, is considerably larger, with a noticeable "forehead." The Gold Saum and Silver Saum have golden/reddish and whitish/silvery edges to the dorsal and caudal fins respectively.

DISTRIBUTION: *Green Terror and Gold Saum: Ecuador; Silver Saum: Peru*

SIZE: *Up to 10½in (27cm) reported; usually smaller*

BEHAVIOR: *Territorial and aggressive, particularly at breeding time. Only equally large, robust tankmates recommended*

DIET: *Substantial commercial foods, e.g. granules, tablets and, particularly, livefoods*

AQUARIUM: *Large and as for A. pulcher, but temperature range: 68–75°F (20–24°C); slightly higher for breeding*

BREEDING: *As for A. pulcher*

PEARLY COMPRESSICEPS

Altolamprologus calvus

SYNONYM: *Lamprologus calvus*

ALTOLAMPROLOGUS SPECIES ARE EASILY DISTINguished from the related genus *Neolamprologus*—including *N. brichardi* (the Fairy Cichlid), *see* p.108—by their deeper (higher, i.e. "altum") body and dorsal fin. These fin characteristics make *Altolamprologus* appear considerably more robust and

OTHER *AEQUIDENS* SPECIES AND MORPHS

In recent years, a number of "new" Aequidens have been appearing in specialized outlets both in the U.S. and Europe. In addition, there are other, older, species that are still readily available. All require the same basic treatment outlined for A. pulcher and A. rivulatus. Check specialist literature for specific details (see Bibliography).

SCIENTIFIC NAME(S)	COMMON NAME(S)	SIZE
A. biseriatus	Choco Aequidens/Acara	5in (13cm)
A. diadema	Diadem Cichlid	8in (20cm)
A. epae	–	8in (20cm)
A. hoehnei (Nannacara hoehnei)	Hoehne's Nannacara	4in (10cm)
A. metae	Twin-Spot Flag Cichlid, Meta Aequidens/Acara	8in (20cm)
A. metae "Venezuela"	–	8¾in (22cm)
A. michaeli	Michael's Cichlid	12in (30cm)
A. pallidus	Río Negro Aequidens or Pale Flag Cichlid	10in (25cm)
A. patricki	Patrick's Cichlid	6¼in (16cm)
A. plagiozonatus	Oblique-band Cichlid	5½in (14cm)
A. pataroensis	Guyana Aequidens/Acara	8in (20cm)
A. rondoni	Mato Grosso Aequidens/Acara	8in (20cm)
A. sapayensis	Black-spot Flag Cichlid, Sapaya Aequidens/Acara	6¼in (16cm)
A. species (several morphs: e.g. "Atabapo," "Colombia," "Jenaro Herrera," "Vaupes")	–	6–8in (15–20cm)
A. tetramerus (several morphs: e.g. "Ecuador," "Río Tambopata," "Brazil")	Saddle Cichlid or Blue-scale Flag Cichlid	20cm (8in)

◄ *Pearly Compressiceps (Altolamprologus calvus)*
▲ *Midas Cichlid (Amphilophus citrinellus)*

predatory. Other *Altolamprologus* regularly available are: *A. compressiceps*, 6¼in (16cm); and the much smaller *A.* "Compressiceps Shell," maximum length 3in (8cm). Females of both species are smaller than the males.

DISTRIBUTION: *Lake Tanganyika, between Kapampa (Zaire) and Cape Chaitika (Zambia)*

SIZE: *Males 6in (15cm); females 4in (10cm)*

BEHAVIOR: *Should be kept with equally robust species. Has been reported to "steal" eggs from mouthbrooders (see Bibliography: Konings). Intolerant of its own and other* Altolamprologus *species*

DIET: *Livefoods preferred*

AQUARIUM: *Typical African Rift Lake aquarium (see Aquarium Set-up), with at least one sandy area and one large snail shell or small cave for female. Water should be hard and alkaline (pH 7.5–9.5), and well-filtered and oxygenated. Temperature range: 73–81°F (23–27°C)*

BREEDING: *Eggs are laid in a cave or shell that should be too small for male to enter. Female undertakes most brood-guarding responsibilities, with male predominantly responsible for guarding territory*

MIDAS CICHLID

Amphilophus citrinellus

THIS LARGE FISH IS AVAILABLE IN SEVERAL COLOR forms. In addition to the wild type (not often seen these days), there are "Gold," "Marble," "Red-head" and "Tiger" naturally occurring morphs, as well as some commercially produced varieties. In all, mature males develop a distinctive "bump" (nuchal hump) on the forehead.

DISTRIBUTION: *Nicaragua and Costa Rica*

SIZE: *13¾in (35cm); usually smaller*

BEHAVIOR: *Territorial and aggressive, particularly during breeding time; likes burrowing*

DIET: *Wide range of substantial commercial foods and livefoods accepted*

Red Devil (Amphilophus labiatus)

AQUARIUM: *Large, with well-protected, robust plants, shelters (caves or bogwood), and some flat or rounded rocks. Rocks should be well bedded to prevent them from being toppled over. Water chemistry not critical. Temperature range: 70–77°F (21–25°C)*

BREEDING: *Basically, as for A. pulcher*

RED DEVIL
THICK-LIPPED CICHLID

Amphilophus labiatus

AS ONE OF THE COMMON NAMES FOR THIS SPECIES indicates, one of the main characteristics is the thick lips possessed, particularly, by adult males. While red specimens occur in nature, this is, by no means, the only naturally occurring morph of this variable species. Several cultivated color varieties are also available.

DISTRIBUTION: *Nicaragua*

SIZE: *13¾in (35cm); usually smaller*

BEHAVIOR: *Aggressive, territorial; active burrower*

DIET: *All large foods accepted, e.g. tablets, granules*

AQUARIUM: *As for A. citrinellum*

BREEDING: *As for A. citrinellum, but female takes greater responsibility for the fry*

AFRICAN BUTTERFLY CICHLID
DWARF JEWEL FISH

Anomalochromis thomasi

THE SECOND OF THE ABOVE COMMON NAMES IS rarely encountered these days, but it reflects the fact that this beautifully marked species was once considered a *Hemichromis*, the genus to which the "true" Jewel Cichlids belong (*see* p.99).

Distribution: *Coastal freshwater habitats in Sierra Leone, Guinea and Liberia*

SIZE: *Male: 10cm (4in); females considerably smaller*

BEHAVIOR: *Territorial, but tolerant of other species*

DIET: *Wide range of foods accepted; both vegetable and livefood component recommended*

AQUARIUM: *Well-planted, with hiding places and flat-topped or smoothly rounded pebbles. Water chemistry not critical, but soft, slightly acid conditions are best for breeding. Temperature range: 73–81°F (23–27°C)*

BREEDING: *Eggs are laid on a precleaned broad leaf, or on a flat or rounded pebble. Both parents guard the eggs and fry. Hatching takes about two days*

AGASSIZ'S DWARF CICHLID

Apistogramma agassizii

THIS IS AN EXCEPTIONALLY BEAUTIFUL DWARF cichlid, although "dwarf" is in this case somewhat misleading since the fully mature males can attain considerable size. This old favorite (it was first imported into Europe in 1909) is available in numerous naturally occurring color morphs, as well as in some commercially developed ones.

DISTRIBUTION: *Wide distribution in southern tributaries of the Amazon*

SIZE: *Up to 4in (10cm) reported; usually smaller; males considerably larger than females*

BEHAVIOR: *Peaceful toward other species, but intolerant of its own in a confined space*

DIET: *Most commercial formulations accepted, but livefoods preferred*

AQUARIUM: *Thick planting, plus other forms of shelter, e.g. caves. Dark, fine-grained substratum*

AGASSIZ'S DWARF CICHLID (APISTOGRAMMA AGASSIZII)

recommended. Soft, acid water required. Temperature range: 72–77°F (22–25°C)

BREEDING: *Eggs are (usually) laid on the roof of a cave. Female takes on main responsibility for guarding both eggs and fry, with male defending territory. Hatching takes three to five days. If several females are kept in a sufficiently spacious aquarium with well-spaced-out caves, each will establish its own territory and may spawn with the same male*

BORELLI'S DWARF CICHLID
UMBRELLA DWARF CICHLID

Apistogramma borellii

SYNONYM: *Apistogramma reitzigi*

THIS IS A SLIGHTLY DEEPER-BODIED SPECIES THAN *A. agassizii*. Several naturally occurring color forms exist. In all forms, mature males have some blue coloration and quite splendid dorsal fins when expanded.

DISTRIBUTION: *Mainly Mato Grosso, Pantanal and Paraguay*

SIZE: *Males up to 3in (8cm); females considerably smaller*

BEHAVIOR: *Similar to A. agassizii*

DIET: *Will accept some commercial preparations, but prefers livefoods*

AQUARIUM: *As for A. agassizii, but water chemistry can be a little more flexible. Temperature range: 72–77°F (22–25°C); slightly higher for breeding*

BREEDING: *As for A. agassizii, but males may be more involved in fry protection. Hatching takes four to five days*

COCKATOO DWARF CICHLID
CRESTED DWARF CICHLID

Apistogramma cacatuoides

MALES OF THIS SPECIES ARE PARTICULARLY striking when in full color. As with the other species described above, numerous naturally occurring color forms are known, the most spectacular being those in which males in full breeding regalia exhibit deep-red coloration, mainly on the dorsal, caudal and anal fins.

DISTRIBUTION: *Peruvian sections of the Rio Amazonas (Solimoes) and Rio Ucayali (Peru); Upper Rio Amazonas (Solimoes) basin up to the Peru/Colombia/Brazil "triangle"*

SIZE: *Males up to 3½in (9cm); females considerably smaller*

BEHAVIOR: *Typical Apistogramma (see A. agassizii)*

DIET: *Livefoods preferred, but some commercial preparations also accepted*

BORELLI'S DWARF CICHLID (APISTOGRAMMA BORELLII)

AQUARIUM: *As for A. borellii*

BREEDING: *As for A. agassizii. Hatching takes about two-and-a-half days*

MACMASTER'S DWARF CICHLID

RED-TAILED DWARF CICHLID or VILLAVICENCIO APISTOGRAMMA

Apistogramma macmasteri

SYNONYM: *Apistogramma ornatipinnis*

ALTHOUGH THE ALTERNATIVE NAME, *A. ornatipinnis*, was most frequently used during the 1970s, it is still encountered from time to time today. To confuse matters further, *A. ornatipinnis* is considered a synonym of *A. steindachneri* (*see* below).

DISTRIBUTION: *Mainly Rio Meta drainage system, Colombia*

SIZE: *Males up to 4in (10cm); females considerably smaller*

BEHAVIOR: *Typical* Apistogramma

DIET: *Strong preference for livefoods; sometimes difficult to wean off livefoods and on to commercial diets*

AQUARIUM: *As for other* Apistogramma *species, but very soft, acid water recommended. Temperature range: 73–86°F (23–30°C)*

BREEDING: *As for other* Apistogramma *species. Hatching takes upward of two-and-a-half days, depending on temperature*

PANDA DWARF CICHLID

Apistogramma nijsseni

ONE OF THE MOST IMMEDIATELY RECOGNIZABLE features of this species is the rounded caudal fin of the vast majority of males (in most other species, there are upper and lower fin-ray extensions). As in many other *Apistogramma*, several naturally occurring color forms of this species—whose sex is influenced by both temperature and pH (*see* below)—exist.

DISTRIBUTION: *Mainly Rio Ucayali and Rio Yavari, west of Iquitos, Peru*

SIZE: *Males up to 3½in (9cm); females somewhat smaller*

BEHAVIOR: *Typical* Apistogramma

DIET: *Distinct preference for livefoods, but may also accept commercial preparations*

AQUARIUM: *Layout as for other* Apistogramma *species. A. nijsenni is less demanding than most of its closest relatives in its water chemistry requirements. Temperature range: 75–82°F (24–28°C); slightly higher for breeding*

BREEDING: *A challenging species that breeds in typical* Apistogramma *fashion. Peat filtration and soft, acid water recommended. Hatching takes three to four days. Experiments have shown that at 68–73°F (20–23°C) all eggs develop into females; the ratio of males begins to increase from 73.6°F (23.1°C), with 100 percent male offspring being produced at 84.4–89.6°F (29.1–32°C). Effects of pH on sex determination are less pronounced. Hatching rates are low in hard water (around 16 percent), rising to around 83 percent in soft water. Hatching takes about four days*

STEINDACHNER'S DWARF CICHLID

Apistogramma steindachneri

SYNONYMS: *Apistogramma ornatipinnis, A. wickleri*

THIS IS ANOTHER OF THE LARGER SPECIES IN THE genus although, in practice, few specimens grow to full size. In some males the turquoise-like, thin streaks under the eye make these fish look a little like an Acara (*see Aequidens pulcher*).

DISTRIBUTION: *Suriname, Guyana and eastern Venezuela*

SIZE: *Some males reported up to 4in (10cm); females considerably smaller*

BEHAVIOR: *As with many* Apistogramma *species, a single male can be kept with a number of females in a sufficiently spacious aquarium*

DIET: *Distinct preference for livefoods; sometimes difficult to feed on commercial preparations*

AQUARIUM: *As for other* Apistogramma *species. Temperature range: 73–77°F (23–25°C)*

BREEDING: *Typical* Apistogramma. *Hatching takes several days*

CONVICT CICHLID

ZEBRA CICHLID

Archocentrus nigrofasciatus

SYNONYMS: *Heros nigrofasciatus, Cichlasoma nigrofasciatum*

THIS STUNNINGLY PATTERNED FISH HAS BEEN popular within the aquarium hobby for nearly 70 years. This is, perhaps, a little surprising given that its strong territorial instincts make it somewhat aggressive toward many of its tankmates. However, the pleasure of keeping a well-matched pair housed in a sufficiently spacious, well-designed aquarium, stocked with robust species, more than makes up for the disadvantages in the behavioral aspects of the species. An albino variety is occasionally available.

DISTRIBUTION: *Widely distributed in Central America*

SIZE: *Males up to 6in (15cm); females smaller*

BEHAVIOR: *Highly territorial; will damage tender plants*

DIET: *All foods accepted; vegetable component essential*

AQUARIUM: *Spacious, with easily defended shelters, robust and/or unpalatable plants, and rounded or flat-topped pebbles. Water chemistry not critical. Temperature range: 68–77°F (20–25°C)*

▲ PANDA DWARF CICHLID (APISTOGRAMMA NIJSSENI)
MACMASTER'S DWARF CICHLID (APISTOGRAMMA MACMASTERI) ▶

OTHER *APISTOGRAMMA* SPECIES

There are numerous other species in this genus, detailed information on which will be found in specialist literature (*see* Bibliography). All basically exhibit the same behavior and characteristics, and they require the same general conditions outlined for the individual entries described in this book. Among the available *Apistogramma* are:

SCIENTIFIC NAME(S)	COMMON NAME(S)	SIZE (MALES)	SCIENTIFIC NAME(S)	COMMON NAME(S)	SIZE (MALES)
A. bitaeniata	Banded Dwarf Cichlid	2½in (6cm)	A. luelingi	Golden, or Lueling's, Dwarf Cichlid/Apistogramma	2¾in (7cm)
A. caetei	Caete, or Kullander's, Dwarf Cichlid	2½in (6cm)	A. meinkeni	Meinken's Dwarf Cichlid	2¾in (7cm)
A. commbrae	Commbrae Dwarf Cichlid	2in (5cm)	A. mendezi	Mendez's Dwarf Cichlid	4in (10cm)
A. diplotaenia	Double-banded Dwarf Cichlid or Apistogramma	2½in (6cm)	A. moae	Moae Dwarf Cichlid	2½in (6cm)
A. elizabethae	Elizabeth's Dwarf Cichlid	3in (8cm)	A. norberti	Thick-lipped Apistogramma	2¾in (7cm)
A. eunotus	Blue-cheek, or Eunotus, Dwarf Cichlid	3½in (9cm)	A. ortmanni	Ortmann's Dwarf Cichlid	2¾in (7cm)
A. geisleri	Geisler's Dwarf Cichlid	2¾in (7cm)	A. pertenensis	Amazon, or Pertensis, Dwarf Cichlid	2in (5cm)
A. gephyra	Mottled, or Gephyra, Dwarf Cichlid	2½in (6cm)	A. pulchra	Pulchra Dwarf Cichlid	2in (5cm)
A. gibbiceps	Yellow-cheeked Dwarf Cichlid	3in (8cm)	A. resticulosa	Resti Dwarf Cichlid	2in (5cm)
A. gossei	Brilliant, or Gosse's, Dwarf Cichlid	3in (8cm)	A. spp. (numerous types with common/trade names)	Examples: Alenquer, Alto Negro, Belem, Chao, Opal, Puerto-Narino, Red Spot, Red Wedge, Río Branco, Smaragd	2–3in (5–8cm)
A. hoignei	Hoignei Dwarf Cichlid	3in (8cm)			
A. hongsloi	Hongsloi Dwarf Cichlid	2¾in (7cm)	A. taeniata	Taenia or Banded Dwarf Cichlid	2¾in (7cm)
A. iniridae	Inirida Dwarf Cichlid	2¾in (7cm)	A. trifasciata	Three-Striped Dwarf Cichlid or Blue Apistogramma	2½in (6cm)
A. juruensis	Jurua Dwarf Cichlid	4in (10cm)	A. uaupesi	Uape Dwarf Cichlid	2½in (6cm)
A. linkei	Linke's Dwarf Cichlid	2½in (6cm)	A. viejita	Viejita Dwarf Cichlid	3in (8cm)

▼ *VIEJITA DWARF CICHLID* (*APISTOGRAMMA VIEJITA*)

PULCHRA DWARF CICHLID (*APISTOGRAMMA PULCHRA*) ▶

BREEDING: *Eggs are laid either in caves or in the open, and they and the fry are protected by both parents. Hatching takes a few days.*

T-BAR CICHLID

SAJICA'S CICHLID

Archocentrus sajica

SYNONYM: *Cichlasoma sajica*

ALTHOUGH THE SECOND OF THE ABOVE SCIENTIFIC names is now ceasing to be used, it is included here because it still appears in print from time to time, particularly in

T-BAR CICHLID (*ARCHOCENTRUS SAJICA*)

OSCAR (ASTRONOTUS OCELLATUS)

articles. Several naturally occurring forms of this species are available, the color and patterning depending on locality. Sajica's Cichlid is sometimes confused with the less colorful *A. spilurus*.

DISTRIBUTION: *Costa Rica*

SIZE: *Males up to 4¾in (12cm); females smaller*

BEHAVIOR: *Territorial, but generally more tolerant of other fish than some similar-sized cichlids, except during breeding*

DIET: *All foods accepted*

AQUARIUM: *Spacious, well planted, with hiding places, shelters, and caves. Water chemistry not critical. Temperature range: 72–77°F (22–25°C)*

BREEDING: *Eggs may be laid either in caves or in the open. Female generally cares for eggs and young (which hatch out in several days), with male guarding territory*

BURTON'S MOUTHBROODER

Astatotilapia burtoni

SYNONYM: *Haplochromis burtoni*

THIS SPECIES WAS AMONG THE EARLY MOUTH-brooders to be kept by aquarists, at a time when "eggspots" or "egg dummies" (*see* below) were still a novelty. It is perhaps not kept as widely these days owing to the numerous, more colorful, mouthbrooders that are now available.

DISTRIBUTION: *Lake Tanganyika basin*

SIZE: *Males up to 4¾in (12cm), but usually smaller; females around 2¾in (7cm)*

BEHAVIOR: *Males are aggressive toward each other, although juvenile males may be kept together in a sufficiently large aquarium. Several females may be kept with a single male*

DIET: *All foods accepted; vegetable component recommended*

AQUARIUM: *Numerous hiding places, plus an open swimming space and a fine-grained substratum should be provided. Plants must be protected (see Aquarium Plants) against the digging activities of males. Medium-hard alkaline water preferred. Temperature range: 68–77°F (20–25°C); slightly higher for breeding*

BREEDING: *Maternal mouthbrooder. Males dig large pits to which they attract females. Once a few eggs are laid, the female takes them into her mouth and pecks at the egg dummies on the male's anal fin as if these, too, were eggs. This is believed to stimulate the male to release sperm, thus ensuring egg fertilization. Hatching can take over one week. For a time after this, the female will guard her offspring, taking them into her mouth when danger threatens and rereleasing them later*

OSCAR
PEACOCK-EYE or VELVET CICHLID

Astronotus ocellatus

FIRST IMPORTED INTO THE EUROPEAN HOBBY IN the late 1920s, the Oscar is still going as strongly as ever. Indeed, with modern-day technology making it ever easier to keep large fish in aquaria, this species—which is available in numerous color forms and even in a long-finned variety—could be on its way to becoming even more popular.

DISTRIBUTION: *Amazon, Orinoco and Paraguay River basins*

SIZE: *Up to 13¾in (35cm) reported, but usually smaller*

BEHAVIOR: *Territorial, especially when paired up for breeding. At other times, relatively tolerant of other equally robust species*

DIET: *All large foods accepted*

AQUARIUM: *Large, with good cover and ample, open swimming areas. Plants must be robust and protected (see Aquarium Plants), or artificial. Large rounded/smooth stones and bogwood should make up most of the decor. Water chemistry not critical, but water must be well filtered. Temperature range: 68–77°F (20–25°C)*

BREEDING: *A strong bond is established between the pair as a result of numerous "trials of strength." From that point onward, the pair remains loyal. Broods of around 1,000 eggs are laid on a precleaned site. Both eggs and young are protected by the parents*

YELLOW PEACOCK
SUNSHINE/NKHOMO-BENGA/ BAENSCH'S PEACOCK, or AULONOCARA BENGA

Aulonocara baenschi

TWO OF THIS SPECIES' COMMON NAMES, YELLOW Peacock and Sunshine Peacock, accurately describe the resplendent colors of males in full breeding condition. Females are relatively drab.

DISTRIBUTION: *Around Nkhomo Reef in Lake Malawi*

SIZE: *Males around 3½in (9cm) in the wild, but can grow larger in aquaria; females smaller*

BEHAVIOR: *Territorial, but relatively peaceful toward other fishes*

DIET: *Livefoods and commercial diets accepted*

AQUARIUM: *Typical African Rift Lake layout (see Aquarium Set-up). Medium-hard, alkaline water required. Temperature range: 72–77°F (22–25°C)*

BREEDING: *Typical maternal mouthbrooder (see Astatotilapia burtoni)*

BUTTERFLY PEACOCK
MALAWI BUTTERFLY

Aulonocara jacobfreibergi

ALTHOUGH THE BASE BODY COLOR OF MALES IS blue, individuals differ in patterning and fin coloration, depending on locality. However, all are brilliantly colored when in full breeding regalia.

DISTRIBUTION: *Widely distributed in Lake Malawi*

SIZE: *Males up to 5in (13cm) in the wild, but can grow larger in aquaria; females considerably smaller*

BEHAVIOR: *Territorial and aggressive toward other conspecific males (i.e. males of the same species); more tolerant of other species*

DIET: *Predominantly livefood-based, but will also take some commercial formulations, particularly deep-frozen diets*

AQUARIUM: *As for A. baenschi*

BREEDING: *Maternal mouthbrooder, but male does not dig a pit; attracts females to his cave instead*

REGAL PEACOCK
FLAVESCENT PEACOCK, or AULONOCARA RED FLUSH/BLUE, NEON
Aulonocara stuartgranti

OWING TO ITS WIDE DISTRIBUTION, THIS SPECIES is available in a number of color morphs, most of which have their own trade or common name. Some are so distinctly colored or patterned that they appear to constitute separate species.

DISTRIBUTION: *The whole of the northwestern coastline of Lake Malawi and down the eastern side as far south as Makanjila Point*

SIZE: *Males up to 4¾in (12cm) in the wild, but slightly larger in aquaria, females somewhat smaller*

BEHAVIOR: *Generally as for A. jacobfreibergi*

DIET: *Livefoods preferred, but other diets—particularly deep-frozen ones—also accepted*

AQUARIUM: *As for other Aulonocara species*

BREEDING: *Typical maternal mouthbrooder*

YELLOW PERCH
Boulengerochromis microlepis

THIS IS THE GIANT OF THE AFRICAN RIFT LAKE species. It is an inhabitant of open, sandy areas and, despite its size, is often found in shallow water. This species is strictly for owners of very large aquaria.

DISTRIBUTION: *Throughout Lake Tanganyika*

SIZE: *Wild specimens up to 27½in (70cm); some aquarium specimens can grow to 36in (90cm)*

BEHAVIOR: *Although predatory, can be kept in small shoals (but only in extremely large aquaria)*

DIET: *In the wild, mainly fish; in aquaria, large meat-based commercial formulations (freeze-dried, deep frozen, pellets, etc.) accepted, along with fish filets and chunks*

BUTTERFLY PEACOCK (AULONOCARA JACOBFREIBERGI)

AQUARIUM: *Very large, well-covered, well-filtered aquaria essential. Medium-hard, alkaline water recommended. Temperature range: 73–77° (23–25°C)*

BREEDING: *A substrate-spawner. Both parents guard eggs and fry. Up to 12,000 eggs may be laid*

CALLOCHROMIS GRESHAKEI
Callochromis pleurospilus

THIS INTERESTING AND ATTRACTIVE SLENDER FISH is one of the sand-sifting African Rift Lake cichlids that have become progressively

OTHER *AULONOCARA* SPECIES

Several other *Aulonocara* species are available with varying degrees of regularity. Nomenclature is sometimes a little "loose" owing to the existence of many local morphs, as well as to doubts about correct scientific identities. All require the same basic conditions described in the main text for the three featured *Aulonocara* species.

SCIENTIFIC NAME	COMMON NAME(S)	SIZE**
A. ethelwynae	Northern, or Chitande, Aulonocara/Peacock	3in (8.5cm)
A. gertrudae	Jumbo, Lipingu, or Multispot, Aulonocara/Peacock	6¼in (16cm)
A. huesseri	Night, or White-top, Aulonocara/Peacock	3¾in (9.5cm)
A. kandeense	Blue Orchid	4in (10cm)
A. korneliae	Blue-gold, or Chizumulu, Aulonocara/Peacock	4in (10cm)
A. maylandi	Sulphur/Sulfur-head Aulonocara/Peacock	4in (10cm)
A. nyassae*	African or Nyassa Peacock	7in (18cm)
A. rostratum	Longnosed Aulonocara/ Peacock	8in (20cm)
A. spp	Numerous, e.g. Chitande (type Likoma, Mara, Mozambique Nkhomo), Iwanda (Red Top), Stuartgranti Malawi (Orange Aulonocara), Stuartgranti Mbenji (Mbenji Peacock) and others	3–5in (8–13cm)

▼ SULPHUR PEACOCK (A. MAYLANDI)

Notes

* Some authors believe that *A. nyassae* has never been exported from Lake Malawi and that the fish available under this name is probably *A. hansbaenschi*. This is not itself regarded as a valid species by others, who refer to it as *A. sp. hansbaenschi*.

** The size quoted is for wild-caught males. Aquarium-reared specimens usually grow a little larger. Females are somewhat smaller.

CALLOCHROMIS GRESHAKEI (CALLOCHROMIS PLEUROSPILUS)

more widely available from the early
1990s onward.

DISTRIBUTION: *Shallow water throughout Lake
Tanganyika*

SIZE: *Around 4in (10cm)*

BEHAVIOR: *Active shoaler and digger that should
be kept in small groups*

DIET: *Sinking formulations and livefoods preferred*

AQUARIUM: *Shelter, plus ample sandy areas, must
be provided. Medium-hard, alkaline, well-filtered
water recommended. Temperature range:
73–77°F (23–25°C)*

BREEDING: *Maternal mouthbrooder. Males
excavate pits to which they attract females*

▲▲ PEACOCK CICHLID (CICHLA OCELLARIS)   ▲ CICHLA TEMENSIS

GUNTHER'S KRIB
MOUTHBROODING KRIB
Chromidotilapia guentheri

SYNONYM: *Chromidotilapia guntheri*

ALTHOUGH IT IS NOT AS WIDELY AVAILABLE AS ITS
early importation into Europe (1913) might
suggest, this interesting species is well worth
seeking out if appropriate accommodations
can be provided. It has the ability to change
color rapidly, according to mood. Two subspecies are generally recognized: *C. guentheri guentheri* and *C. g. loennbergi*

DISTRIBUTION: *Coastal waters from Sierra Leone
to Cameroon*

SIZE: *Males reported up to 8in (20cm), but usually smaller; females smaller*

BEHAVIOR: *Territorial burrower; preys on small fishes*

DIET: *Wide range of foods accepted*

AQUARIUM: *Spacious, with adequate shelters/covers and fine-grained substratum. Plants need protection (see Aquarium Plants). Neutral, medium-hard water recommended. Temperature range: 73–77°F (23–25°C)*

BREEDING: *Paternal mouthbrooder, with fry being released after about one week. Both parents defend brood*

PEACOCK CICHLID
PEACOCK BASS, EYESPOT CICHLID, EYESPOT BASS or TUCUNARÉ
Cichla ocellaris

ALTHOUGH IT LOOKS SUPERFICIALLY LIKE A BASS, *C. ocellaris* is a true cichlid in every sense. It is a variable species, particularly attractive during its juvenile phase. It soon outgrows most aquaria. A closely related species, *C. temensis*, which is even larger, is also occasionally available.

DISTRIBUTION: *Central and northern South America*

SIZE: *Up to 24in (60cm); may be slightly larger in the wild*

BEHAVIOR: *Aggressive predator*

DIET: *Large livefoods and commercial diets (freeze-dried, deep frozen, pellets, etc.)*

AQUARIUM: *Large, with ample open spaces, bogwood, and large, robust plants. Water chemistry not critical, but water must be well filtered. Temperature range: 75–82°F (24–28°C)*

BREEDING: *Difficult in aquaria. This is a substrate-spawning species with typical parental protection*

BOLIVIAN CICHLASOMA
Cichlasoma boliviense

THIS INFREQUENTLY ENCOUNTERED SPECIES IS ONE of the few remaining within the once species-rich *Cichlasoma* genus. Superficially, it resembles *C. portalegrense (see below)* and may have been incorrectly offered for sale as *Aequidens portalegrensis*.

DISTRIBUTION: *Bolivian Amazon*

SIZE: *Up to 5in (13cm)*

BEHAVIOR: *Generally peaceful and hardy*

DIET: *Wide range of foods accepted*

AQUARIUM: *Well planted (with robust plants), with open spaces and flat-topped or smooth-rounded pebbles. Water chemistry not critical, but soft to medium-hard, slightly acid water preferred. Temperature range: 72–77°F (22–25°C)*

BREEDING: *No accurate reports, but likely to be similar to C. portalegrense (see below)*

BROWN CICHLID
BROWN ACARA, PORT CICHLID, or PORT ACARA
Cichlasoma portalegrense

SYNONYMS: *Cichlasoma portalegrensis, Aequidens portalegrensis*

THERE IS STILL SOME DEBATE ABOUT THE IDENTITY, as well as the correct spelling, of the species name of this relatively subtly colored but lovely cichlid. The "Acara" part of one of the common names reflects the fact that this fish is still also referred to as *Aequidens portalegrensis* in some quarters.

DISTRIBUTION: *Argentina, Bolivia, Brazil, the Guianas, Paraguay and Venezuela. However, owing to confusion regarding some lookalikes, e.g. C. bimaculatum, C. dimerus and C. boliviense, distribution details may be inaccurate.*

SIZE: *Up to 6in (15cm), but usually smaller*

BEHAVIOR: *Peaceful and hardy*

DIET: *All foods accepted*

AQUARIUM: *As for C. boliviense, but temperature range: 66–79°F (19–26°C)*

BREEDING: *Eggs laid on precleaned site and guarded by both parents who also share in the defense of the fry*

PARROT CICHLID
RED, or BLOOD-RED, PARROT CICHLID
"Cichlasoma" Red Parrot

WHEN THE PARROT (SEE PHOTO P.44) APPEARED during the early 1990s, it immediately caused a great deal of interest owing to its unusual shape and coloration. Its ancestry was not known with absolute certainty. Some believed it to be a *Heros* hybrid, others a mutant form of the Severum Cichlid (*Heros severus*), while yet others considered it to be an *Amphilophus* and listed it as such in books. The Parrot—which is in fact a hybrid between *Amphilophus citrinellus* and *Vieja synspilum*—is widely available in a range of colors from yellow through to blood-red.

DISTRIBUTION: *Nonexistent in the wild*

SIZE: *Up to 8in (20cm)*

BEHAVIOR: *Generally peaceful; may be kept as a group*

DIET: *All foods accepted*

AQUARIUM: *Spacious, with open spaces, plant thickets, shelter, e.g. bogwood, and at least one flat-topped or smooth-rounded rock. Water chemistry not critical. Temperature range: 75–82°F (24–28°C)*

BREEDING: *Can be difficult. Eggs laid on a precleaned site and defended (as are the fry) by both parents*

KEYHOLE CICHLID
Cleithracara maronii

SYNONYM: *Aequidens maronii*

THE MOST DISTINCTIVE FEATURE OF THIS SPECIES is the "keyhole" marking that is present

BROWN CICHLID (CICHLASOMA PORTALEGRENSE)

two-thirds of the way down the body, hence the common name. Unfortunately, the keyhole is not always complete, its intensity varying from fish to fish and in tune with the individual's mood.

DISTRIBUTION: *Guyana, Suriname and French Guiana*

SIZE: *Males up to 6in (15cm), but usually smaller; females smaller*

BEHAVIOR: *Peaceful and tolerant of other species*

DIET: *All foods accepted*

AQUARIUM: *As for the Parrot Cichlid. Temperature range: 72–79°F (22–26°C)*

BREEDING: *Eggs are laid on a precleaned site and defended by both parents. In many cases, fry may be left to grow in the same aquarium as the parents for several months*

HAPLOCHROMIS BORLEYI
HAPLOCHROMIS GOLDFIN, or RED KADANGO

Copadichromis borleyi

MALES OF THIS WIDESPREAD SPECIES DIFFER IN coloration depending on locality. Females are drab by comparison. In the wild, it is often found near large boulders or rocky islets in sandy areas—points worth bearing in mind when arranging the aquarium layout.

DISTRIBUTION: *Throughout Lake Malawi*

SIZE: *Males up to 6in (15cm); females smaller*

BEHAVIOR: *Relatively peaceful and tolerant of other similar-sized species*

DIET: *Wide range of foods accepted, but livefoods preferred*

AQUARIUM: *Large, typical African Rift Lake layout (see Aquarium Set-up), with large, well-bedded rocks. Medium-hard to hard, alkaline water essential. Temperature range: 75–79°F (24–26°C)*

BREEDING: *Males establish territories alongside rocks to which they attract females; female broods eggs orally*

HAPLOCHROMIS QUADS
HAPLOCHROMIS QUADRIMACULATUS

Copadichromis mbenjii

DESPITE ITS COMMON NAME, C. MBENJII IS A totally separate species from C. *quadrimaculatus* (whose common name is Haplochromis Mbarule). Unlike the latter, C. *mbenjii* does not migrate and is confined to a very specific area of Lake Malawi. It is also considerably smaller than C. *quadrimaculatus* (which can grow to over 8in/20cm).

DISTRIBUTION: *Mbenji Island in Lake Malawi*

SIZE: *Males up to 6in (15cm); females smaller*

BEHAVIOR: *Males territorial, while females and juveniles tend to shoal*

DIET: *Wide range of foods accepted, but livefoods preferred*

AQUARIUM: *Typical African Rift Lake layout (see Aquarium Set-up). Water conditions as for C. borleyi*

BREEDING: *Males construct semicircular sand nests to which they attract females; female broods eggs orally*

NICARAGUA CICHLID
Copora nicaraguense

SYNONYMS: *Cichlasoma nicaraguense, Copora nicaraguensis, Herichthys nicaraguense, Hypsophrys nicaraguensis*

THE TWO MAIN ATTRACTIONS OF THIS SPECIES are its rounded head and the body patterning or coloration of both male and female. Its disadvantages are its large size and its tendency to eat succulent plants.

HAPLOCHROMIS QUADS (COPADICHROMIS MBENJII)

OTHER *COPADICHROMIS* SPECIES

There are several other *Copadichromis* species currently available, some of which have not yet been scientifically described but, nevertheless, have common names. All require the same basic conditions. Aquarium sizes may be larger than those quoted below, which apply to wild-caught males.

NGUWA (COPADICHROMIS JACKSONI)

SCIENTIFIC NAME	COMMON NAME(S)	SIZE
C. azureus	Chrysonotus Mbenji or Haplochromis Chrysonotus	6in (15cm)
C. chrysonotus	Haplochromis Jacksoni (*see below**)	6¼in (16cm)
C. cyaneus	Haplochromis Munnae	7½in (19cm)
C. jacksoni* (see C. chrysonotus above)	Nguwa	8in (20cm)
C. spp.	Numerous, e.g. Haplochromis Kawanga, Midnight Mloto, Mloto Likoma, Verduyni Blueface, Verduyni Dwarf, Virginalis Gold	4–6¼in (10–16cm)
C. verduyni	Haplochromis Borleyi Eastern	4¼in (11cm)

SIZE: *Up to 15in (38cm)*

BEHAVIOR: *As for* C. lepidota

DIET: *As for* C. lepidota

AQUARIUM: *As for* C. lepidota, *except that an even larger aquarium is required*

BREEDING: *Not reported in aquaria, but likely to follow similar pattern to* C. lepidota

STRIPED PIKE CICHLID

Crenicichla strigata

SYNONYM: *Crenichla lugubris*

IN THIS SPECIES, IT IS THE BODY PATTERNING IN juveniles that is particularly interesting and gives a most striking appearance: in addition to the red and black coloration of the dorsal, caudal and anal fins, and set against a fawn-colored background, the juvenile has several thin, black lines running the length of the body.

DISTRIBUTION: *Brazil*

SIZE: *Up to 15in (38cm)*

BEHAVIOR: *As for* C. marmorata

DIET: *As for* C. marmorata

AQUARIUM: *As for* C. marmorata

BREEDING: *As for* C. marmorata

RED TOP AFRA

WHITE TOP AFRA or
DOGTOOTH CICHLID

Cynotilapia afra

MALES OF THIS SPECIES ARE BEAUTIFULLY MARKED, possessing bright-blue bodies with deep-blue stripes and strongly contrasting dorsal fins, usually yellow. Eggspots are not particularly numerous on the anal fin of the males.

DISTRIBUTION: *Northern coasts of Lake Malawi*

DISTRIBUTION: *Nicaragua and Costa Rica*

SIZE: *Males up to 10in (25cm); females somewhat smaller*

BEHAVIOR: *Territorial digger, but not overaggressive in sufficiently large aquaria*

DIET: *All foods accepted*

AQUARIUM: *Large, with adequate shelter and robust or unpalatable plants (both of which must be protected—see Aquarium Plants). Water chemistry not critical, but quality must be good. Temperature range: 73–79°F (23–26°C)*

BREEDING: *Eggs are laid in deep pits or in a cave. Egg and fry care usually performed by female, with male guarding territory*

TWO-SPOT CICHLID

COMB PIKE CICHLID

Crenicichla lepidota

THE GENUS *CRENICICHLA* PROBABLY CONTAINS around 175 or more species. Some of these have yet to be described scientifically, but many are available under a variety of trade names. *C. lepidota* is one of the most widely encountered species within the hobby, though not the most spectacularly colored.

DISTRIBUTION: *Brazil and Bolivia*

SIZE: *Occasionally reported up to 18in (45cm), but usually 6–8in (15–20cm)*

BEHAVIOR: *A predator that stalks its prey; can only be kept with fish too large for it to swallow*

DIET: *Mainly meat-based, i.e. large livefoods, deep frozen, freeze-dried, etc.*

AQUARIUM: *Large, well covered, with open areas and adequate shelter. Water chemistry not critical, but quality must be good. Temperature range: 73–80°F (23–27°C)*

BREEDING: *Quite difficult in aquaria. Eggs, laid on the roof of a cave, are guarded by female while male defends territory*

MARBLED PIKE CICHLID

Crenicichla marmorata

SYNONYM: Probably *Crenicichla minuano*

THIS IS ONE OF THE LARGER PIKE CICHLIDS WHOSE full coloration does not develop until the fish approach maturity. When in full regalia, this is a magnificent species.

DISTRIBUTION: *Rio Amazonas basin*

OTHER *CRENICICHLA* SPECIES

Crenicichla classification is in a confused state. As a result, many of the 175 or so species are poorly known, while numerous others have not even been scientifically described. For a good selection of the many pike cichlids currently available, consult specialist literature, including *South American Cichlids I* (see Bibliography).

All *Crenicichla* are predatory and require the conditions outlined for the three species featured here. Since they can be kept only in large aquaria, aquarists who cannot provide such accommodations should avoid these fish. Despite their apparent size and behavior disadvantages, many species are much sought after for their stunning coloration and interesting body patterning.

Blue Flash (Cyprichromis leptosoma)

SIZE: *Wild-caught males around 3½in (9cm); aquarium specimens grow larger*

BEHAVIOR: *Males aggressive toward each other, but may be kept with a number of females in an African Rift Lake fish community*

DIET: *Livefoods preferred*

AQUARIUM: *Typical African Rift Lake aquarium layout (see Aquarium Set-up). Medium-hard, alkaline water. Temperature range: 73–79°F (23–26°C)*

BREEDING: *Spawns inside caves; female incubates eggs orally*

FRONTOSA

TANGANYIKA HUMPHEAD

Cyphotilapia frontosa

THIS IMPRESSIVE DEEPWATER FISH IS ONE OF THE larger African Rift Lake species, which, despite its size, is very popular with specialist hobbyists. Markings vary depending on locality, but all adults possess the characteristic "humphead."

DISTRIBUTION: *Throughout Lake Tanganyika*

SIZE: *Up to 16in (40cm) reported; usually smaller*

BEHAVIOR: *Relatively tolerant for its size, but should not be kept with small fish. Should be kept in small groups*

DIET: *Selection of commercial formulations accepted, but livefoods preferred*

AQUARIUM: *Large and deep, African Rift Lake layout (see Aquarium Set-up). Medium-hard, alkaline water. Temperature range: 75–79°F (24–26°C)*

BREEDING: *Eggs normally laid in a cave; female incubates eggs orally for several weeks*

BLUE FLASH

Cyprichromis leptosoma

THERE ARE SEVERAL CYPRICHROMIS SPECIES available. All are slender-bodied and most contain some blue and yellow on their fins and/or bodies. These active fish look at their best when kept in a shoal.

DISTRIBUTION: *Throughout Lake Tanganyika, except the extreme north*

SIZE: *Wild-caught specimens around 3in (8cm); aquarium specimens can grow considerably larger*

BEHAVIOR: *A generally peaceful, active species, but males show some aggression toward each other*

DIET: *Wide range of foods accepted, but livefoods preferred*

AQUARIUM: *Large, open swimming areas in an otherwise African Rift Lake layout (see Aquarium Set-up). Medium-hard, alkaline water. Temperature range: 73–77°F (23–25°C)*

BREEDING: *Unusually, spawning takes place in midwater or just under the surface, with female picking up eggs as they begin to sink. Mouthbrooding females will tend to ignore fry once they are released some three weeks after spawning*

MALAWI BLUE DOLPHIN

BLUE LUMPHEAD or MOORII

Cyrtocara moorii

THE PRONOUNCED "LUMPHEAD" (NUCHAL HUMP) of mature males makes this popular species immediately recognizable. Females also develop this lump, but it may not be quite as pronounced as it is in older males.

DISTRIBUTION: *Throughout Lake Malawi*

SIZE: *Up to 9in (23cm) reported, but usually smaller*

BEHAVIOR: *Usually follows sand-sifting species around; while males show territorial behavior—in that they defend the space around their host—this "territory" is not fixed in the traditional sense*

DIET: *Some commercial formulations, e.g. tablets, accepted, but prefers livefoods*

AQUARIUM: *Spacious African Rift Lake System (see Aquarium Set-up). Medium-hard, alkaline water. Temperature range: 72–79°F (22–26°C)*

BREEDING: *Typical maternal mouthbrooder*

CHECKERBOARD CICHLID

LYRETAIL CHECKERBOARD CICHLID or CHESSBOARD CICHLID

Dicrossus filamentosus

SYNONYM: *Crenicara filamentosa*

ALTHOUGH THIS DELIGHTFUL SPECIES HAS BEEN officially known as *Dicrossus filamentosus* since 1990, it is still frequently referred to by its former name in aquarium literature. For this species to be at its best, careful attention must be paid to aquarium conditions.

DISTRIBUTION: *Rio Negro (Brazil) and Rio Orinoco (Colombia) basins*

SIZE: *Males up to 3½in (9cm); females considerably smaller*

Malawi Blue Dolphin (Cyrtocara moorii)

BEHAVIOR: *Territorial, but generally peaceful and timid except during breeding season. Best kept in a trio of one male and two females*

DIET: *Many commercial foods accepted, but small livefoods preferred*

AQUARIUM: *Well planted, with fine-grained substratum, numerous shelters, and at least one flat-topped or smooth-rounded pebble. Excellent-quality, soft, acid water is best, preferably peat-filtered (or with special proprietary "blackwater" or tannin extracts added); regular partial water changes are recommended. Temperature range: 73–77°F (23–25°C); slightly higher for breeding*

BREEDING: *Can be challenging. Very soft, acid, tannin-stained water required. Eggs are laid on broad leaves or stones and are guarded by female*

MALAWI EYE-BITER
COMPRESSICEPS

Dimidiochromis compressiceps

THERE'S NO MISTAKING THE FEEDING HABITS OF this large cichlid, whose whole body shape and head profile belie its predatory lifestyle. One of its common names derives from reports that it has been seen biting other fishes' eyes.

DISTRIBUTION: *Throughout Lake Malawi and Lake Malombe*

SIZE: *Wild-caught males about 9in (23cm); aquarium-reared specimens slightly larger*

BEHAVIOR: *Predatory, particularly on small fishes; may be housed with other large species*

DIET: *Predominantly carnivorous, requiring livefoods or deep-frozen/freeze-dried formulations*

AQUARIUM: *Large, well-covered, African Rift Lake system (see Aquarium Set-up), with open sandy areas and robust plants. Medium-hard,*

alkaline water. Temperature range: 72–80°F (22–27°C)*

BREEDING: *Maternal mouthbrooder; male attracts females to a shallow sand depression*

STRIPED GOBY CICHLID
HORSEFACE CICHLID

Eretmodus cyanosticus

THIS IS A CHALLENGING, BOTTOM-DWELLING species that is best left to the experienced aquarist. At first sight, the downslung mouth, elongated body form, and swimming manner make this fish appear more like a goby than a cichlid, hence one of the common names.

DISTRIBUTION: *Throughout Lake Tanganyika*

SIZE: *Around 3in (8cm)*

BEHAVIOR: *Males, in particular, are highly intolerant of their own species, but form a strong pair bond with a female*

DIET: *Almost exclusively livefoods*

AQUARIUM: *African Rift Lake scheme (see Aquarium Set-up), with numerous rocky shelters. Medium-hard to hard, alkaline, excellent-quality, well-oxygenated water essential. Temperature range: 75–79°F (24–26°C)*

BREEDING: *Biparental mouthbrooder; the male takes over from the female after approximately 10–12 days*

ORANGE CHROMIDE

Etroplus maculatus

ALTHOUGH A GOLDEN-ORANGE VARIETY OF THIS species exists, the common name refers to the numerous orange spots that are distributed all over the body of the wild type.

A blue-bodied form is also available. Unusually for a cichlid, the Orange Chromide is often found in brackish water in the wild.

DISTRIBUTION: *Western India and Sri Lanka*

SIZE: *Up to 4in (10cm), but usually smaller*

BEHAVIOR: *Generally peaceful*

DIET: *All foods accepted; vegetable component recommended*

AQUARIUM: *Well planted, but with open areas and a flat or rounded rock. Although medium-hard, neutral to alkaline freshwater is acceptable, the addition of a teaspoonful of good-quality marine salt to every 1 gallon (4.5 liters) is beneficial for fungus-free egg development, though not for general maintenance. Temperature range: 68–79°F (20–26°C); slightly higher for breeding*

BREEDING: *Eggs are laid on a precleaned site and defended by both parents who also care for fry and transfer them between pits excavated in the substratum*

GREEN CHROMIDE
BANDED CHROMIDE

Etroplus suratensis

THIS IS A CONSIDERABLY LARGER FISH THAN THE Orange Chromide. In its native waters, it is regarded as a food fish. Although it is usually reported as inhabiting brackish water, the Green Chromide also occurs in freshwater habitats.

DISTRIBUTION: *India and Sri Lanka*

SIZE: *Up to 18in (45cm) reported, but usually considerably smaller*

BEHAVIOR: *Somewhat intolerant of its own species especially during the breeding season. May eat succulent aquarium plants*

◀ *MALAWI EYE-BITER (DIMIDIOCHROMIS COMPRESSICEPS)*
▲ *ORANGE CHROMIDE (ETROPLUS MACULATUS)*

DIET: *As for* E. maculatus

AQUARIUM: *Spacious, basically as for* E. maculatus, *but with sturdy, unpalatable plants. Addition of salt (optional for* E. maculatus*) recommended for* E. suratensis, *particularly for breeding purposes. Acclimatization of specimens to freshwater is not difficult. Temperature range: 73–79°F (23–26°C)*

BREEDING: *As in* E. maculatus

PEARL CICHLID

Geophagus brasiliensis

GEOPHAGUS MEANS "EARTHEATER," AND THIS species lives up to its name tag, spending much of its time rooting around the substratum and generally burrowing. It is tolerant of a wide range of water conditions, and has even been collected in oxygen-deficient, algae-laden, partially polluted water.

DISTRIBUTION: *Atlantic coastal strip of Brazil, southward to the Rio de la Plata, Argentina*

SIZE: *Up to 11in (28cm) reported; usually considerably smaller*

BEHAVIOR: *Territorial, but somewhat more tolerant than most of its close relatives, particularly of similar-sized tankmates*

DIET: *All foods accepted*

AQUARIUM: *Grain size of substratum should be sufficiently fine—at least in some areas—to allow for burrowing. Plants must be protected (see Aquarium Plants). At least one large flat-topped or smoothly rounded rock should be provided. Water chemistry not critical, but soft-to-medium-hard, slightly acid water recommended. Temperature range: 68–81°F (20–27°C)*

BREEDING: *Eggs are laid on precleaned site, and both they and the fry are defended by the pair*

▲ GREEN CHROMIDE (ETROPLUS SURATENSIS)   ▼ PEARL CICHLID (GEOPHAGUS BRASILIENSIS)

RED-HUMP GEOPHAGUS

Geophagus hondae-steindachneri

SYNONYMS: *Geophagus hondae, G. steindachneri*

THERE HAVE LONG BEEN DIFFERENCES OF OPINION regarding the correct scientific name of this species, with all three above-mentioned names being used almost interchangeably. The most distinctive feature of the species is the pronounced hump on top of the head (nuchal/cranial hump) in mature males.

DISTRIBUTION: *Colombia*

SIZE: *Up to 10in (25cm) reported, but usually smaller*

BEHAVIOR: *Generally tolerant and hardly territorial, except at breeding time*

DIET: *All foods accepted*

AQUARIUM: *As for* G. brasiliensis. *Temperature range: 75–79°F (24–26°C); slightly higher for breeding*

BREEDING: *Eggs are laid on a precleaned site and are picked up by female in her mouth; female incubates eggs away from male for about 20 days*

SURINAME GEOPHAGUS

Geophagus surinamensis

THIS IS ONE OF SEVERAL SIMILAR-LOOKING SPECIES. Of these, the Flag-tailed Surinamensis (*G. proximus*) from Brazil is most often confused with it—as indicated by its common name. However, there are other "lookalikes" making precise identification (and distribution data) difficult.

DISTRIBUTION: *Suriname. However, at least one other possible species—often referred to as* G. cf.

surinamensis *(but which may turn out to be* G. surinamensis*)—is found in neighboring countries such as Guyana*

SIZE: *Up to 12in (30cm) reported, but usually smaller*

BEHAVIOR: *Territorial, intolerant, digging/burrowing species*

DIET: *All foods accepted*

AQUARIUM: *As for other* Geophagus *species*

BREEDING: *Eggs are laid on a precleaned site and are picked up orally by both parents at hatching time or slightly earlier*

BALZANI CICHLID
PARAGUAY EARTHEATER

Gymnogeophagus balzanii

THIS IS ONE OF THE MOST TOLERANT OF THE "EARTH-eaters." The main distinguishing feature is the pronounced "forehead" hump (nuchal/cranial hump) in fully mature males.

DISTRIBUTION: *Argentina and Paraguay*

SIZE: *Males up to 8in (20cm); females smaller*

BEHAVIOR: *Territorial, but relatively tolerant of other species. Active burrower*

DIET: *All foods accepted*

AQUARIUM: *As for* Geophagus

BREEDING: *Eggs are laid on a precleaned site and taken into the mouth by female some 24 hours after laying. Care of the young is also carried out by female*

SQUAREHEAD GEOPHAGUS

Gymnogeophagus gymnogenys

IN THIS SPECIES, THE "FOREHEAD" HUMP (NUCHAL/cranial hump) developed by males is quite distinct from that developed by *G. balzanii* in that it is squarish (hence the common name) rather than rounded. The reflective spangling of the body scales adds to the great beauty of this fish.

DISTRIBUTION: *Argentina, south Brazil and Uruguay*

SIZE: *Males reported up to 10in (25cm), but usually smaller; females smaller*

BEHAVIOR: *Basically as in G. balzanii*

DIET: *All foods accepted*

AQUARIUM: *As for* Geophagus

BREEDING: *Not widely reported, but appears to be a "delayed" mouthbrooder*

BROWN'S HAPLOCHROMIS

Haplochromis brownae

THIS IS ONE OF ONLY A FEW *HAPLOCHROMIS* species from Lake Victoria currently available within the hobby. Of the others, only *H. obliquidens* is available with any regularity, although others are gradually beginning to appear (largely as the result of captive-breeding by specialist hobbyists). The eggspots on the anal fin of *Haplochromis* males are usually very well marked.

DISTRIBUTION: *Lake Victoria*

SIZE: *Around 3in (8cm)*

BEHAVIOR: *Territorial*

DIET: *Livefoods preferred, but other formulations may be accepted*

AQUARIUM: *Open spaces, plus shelters, should be provided. Medium-hard, alkaline, well-filtered water recommended. Temperature range: 70–75°F (21–24°C); slightly higher for breeding*

BREEDING: *Maternal mouthbrooder. Eggs are fertilized when the male is stimulated to release sperm partly by the female's mouthing of the eggspots on his anal fin*

JEWEL CICHLID

Hemichromis bimaculatus

FIRST IMPORTED INTO EUROPE BEFORE 1910, THIS species immediately created interest owing to the intense reddish coloration of the males when in full breeding condition. Although it has subsequently been outshone in terms of color by its close relative *H. lifalili (see* below), it still remains popular.

DISTRIBUTION: *Southern Guinea to central Liberia*

SIZE: *Up to 6in (15cm) reported, but usually smaller*

BEHAVIOR: *Highly territorial, particularly during breeding. At other times, it will tolerate other similar-sized tankmates*

DIET: *Wide range of foods accepted*

AQUARIUM: *Well planted, with numerous shelters and at least one flat-topped or smoothly rounded rock. Some plants may need protection (see Aquarium Plants). Water chemistry not critical but should be well filtered. Temperature range: 70–77°F (21–25°C); higher for breeding*

BREEDING: *Eggs are laid on a precleaned site and are defended vigorously by both parents who then guard the fry, moving them to previously dug pits*

LIFALILI CICHLID
BLOOD-RED JEWEL CICHLID

Hemichromis lifalili

THIS IS A SLIGHTLY SMALLER SPECIES THAN ITS close relative *H. bimaculatus (see* above). However, what it may lack in size it more than makes up for in the intense coloration of the fully mature male in breeding regalia.

DISTRIBUTION: *Zaire River basin*

SIZE: *Around 4in (10cm)*

BEHAVIOR: *As for* H. bimaculatus

DIET: *Wide range of foods accepted*

AQUARIUM: *As for* H. bimaculatus*, but bottom end of maintenance temperature range should be just slightly higher*

BREEDING: *As for* H. bimaculatus

TEXAS CICHLID
PEARL CICHLID or
RIO GRANDE PERCH
Herichthys cyanoguttatus

SYNONYM: *Herichthys cyanoguttatum*

BESIDES ITS UNDOUBTED BEAUTY, THE TEXAS Cichlid is also famous for two other, totally

---

OTHER *GEOPHAGUS* SPECIES

At one time, numerous species were recognized as Geophagus. Today, many of these have been transferred to other genera, most notably *Satanoperca* (see under this genus). In addition to the three *Geophagus* featured above, only the following are now left within the genus: *G. altifrons* (several forms), *G. argyrostictus, G. australis, G. crassilabris, G. grammepareius, G. pelligrini, G. taeniopareius,* plus a number referred to as *G.* sp. plus a trade/hobby name, e.g. *G.* sp. Caqueta/Caroni/Maraba/Pindare, and others. Of these, *G. argyrostictus, G. grammepareius,* and *G. taeniopereius* exhibit straightforward substrate spawning. The remainder exhibit mouthbrooding to varying degrees.

JEWEL CICHLID (HEMICHROMIS BIMACULATUS)

unrelated, reasons. It was one of the first cichlids to be imported into Europe (1902), and it is the northernmost cichlid species known. A similar-looking species, the Blue or Green Texas Cichlid (*H. carpinte*), from Mexico (not Texas!) is sometimes confused with *H. cyanoguttatus*. Other *Herichthys* species are only infrequently encountered in the hobby.

DISTRIBUTION: *Texas and northern Mexico*

SIZE: *Up to 12in (30cm), but usually smaller*

BEHAVIOR: *Aggressive and territorial burrower that will uproot plants*

DIET: *Wide range of large foods accepted*

AQUARIUM: *Only stout, protected plants are suitable (see Aquarium Plants). Large open spaces with shelters should be provided. Water chemistry not critical but well-filtered water important. Temperature range: 59–77°F (15–25°C)*

BREEDING: *Eggs are laid on a precleaned site. Parental care is not as pronounced in this species as in most other cichlids*

SEVERUM CICHLID
EYESPOT, or BANDED, CICHLID

Heros severus

THE SEVERUM IS ANOTHER OLD FAVORITE (FIRST imported in 1909) that has held its own against strong competition from other species. Undoubtedly, the cultivated golden form of the species has played a large part in this.

DISTRIBUTION: *Northern South America, down to the Amazon basin*

SIZE: *Some wild-caught specimens reported up to 12in (30cm), but usually smaller*

BEHAVIOR: *Territorial but not overaggressive toward other medium-size or large tankmates, except during breeding*

DIET: *Wide range of foods accepted*

AQUARIUM: *Spacious, with substantial plants, shelters, and at least one flat-topped or smoothly rounded rock. Water chemistry not critical, but soft, acid, well-filtered water recommended. Temperature range: 73–77°F (23–25°C); slightly higher for breeding*

BREEDING: *Eggs are laid on a precleaned site and are defended—as are the fry—by both parents. This species is sometimes reported as showing some signs of mouthbrooding*

PARROT CICHLID

Hoplarchus psittacus

DESPITE ITS COMMON NAME, THIS SPECIES IS quite distinct from the Red Parrot Cichlid

TEXAS CICHLID (HERICHTHYS CYANOGUTTATUS)

featured elsewhere (*see* "Cichlasoma" Red Parrot, p.93). It is a large species in which fully adult males have a well-rounded head.

DISTRIBUTION: *Rio Negro and Rio Orinoco*

SIZE: *Fully mature males reported up to 16in (40cm); usually smaller*

BEHAVIOR: *Territorial, but can be kept with other large species in roomy aquaria*

DIET: *All large foods accepted; vegetable component recommended*

AQUARIUM: *Large tank with stout vegetation and sizable rocks (without sharp edges!) and/or bogwood. Water chemistry not critical, but soft, acid, well-filtered water is best. Temperature range: 75–81°F (24–27°C); slightly higher for breeding*

BREEDING: *Infrequent in aquaria. Eggs are laid on a precleaned site (often vertically oriented) and protected by both parents*

CHOCOLATE CICHLID

Hypselacara coryphaenoides

SYNONYM: *Hypselacara temporalis*

THE COMMON NAME CHOCOLATE CICHLID IS sometimes used for *Hypselacara temporalis* as well as for *H. coryphaenoides*. This has

led to frequent confusion and the misuse of the scientific names for the two "Chocolate Cichlids." It is for this reason that *H. temporalis*, which originates in the Brazilian and Peruvian Amazon, is listed above.

DISTRIBUTION: *Rio Orinoco basin*

SIZE: *Males up to 12in (30cm), but usually smaller*

BEHAVIOR: *Territorial, particularly during breeding*

DIET: *All large foods*

AQUARIUM: *Large, deep, with numerous shelters and stout plants. Water chemistry not critical, but soft, slightly acid, well-filtered water preferred. Temperature range: 75–82°F (24–28°C)*

BREEDING: *Eggs are laid on a precleaned site and protected by both parents*

RUSTY CICHLID
PETROTILAPIA TRIDENTIGER

Iodotropheus sprengerae

ALTHOUGH SOME COLOR MORPHS OF THIS SPECIES undoubtedly have a "rusty" element to their body coloration, *I. sprengerae* is, nevertheless, more colorful and variable than its name suggests. This is one of the easier species of African Rift Lake cichlids to keep and breed, and it is therefore often recommended for those entering this branch of the hobby for the first time. A few other *Iodotropheus* species are available but, generally, not as widely as the Rusty Cichlid.

DISTRIBUTION: *Southeastern arm of Lake Malawi*

SIZE: *Around 4in (10cm)*

BEHAVIOR: *Relatively tolerant, even of its own species (in a sufficiently roomy aquarium)*

DIET: *Wide range of foods accepted*

AQUARIUM: *Typical African Rift Lake layout (see Aquarium Set-up). Medium-hard, alkaline, well-filtered water important. Temperature range: 72–77°F (22–25°C); slightly higher for breeding*

BREEDING: *Typical maternal mouthbrooder; will breed even when quite small and relatively young (at around three-and-a-half months)*

DICKFELD'S JULIE
BROWN JULIE

Julidochromis dickfeldi

UNUSUALLY FOR AN AFRICAN RIFT LAKE SPECIES, the various Julies, including *J. dickfeldi*, are not mouthbrooders. This species, the Yellow or Ornate Julie (*J. ornatus*), and the Masked or Black-and-white Julie (*J. transcriptus*), are often referred to as the "dwarf" Julies, although the size difference between them and the other two species is not always as large as their "labels" might suggest.

DISTRIBUTION: *Southwestern part of Lake Tanganyika*

SIZE: *Up to 4in (10cm), but often smaller*

BEHAVIOR: *Intolerant toward its own species*

DIET: *Wide range of foods accepted*

AQUARIUM: *African Rift Lake layout (see Aquarium Set-up) with numerous rock shelters and open sandy areas. Medium-hard, alkaline, well-filtered water important. Temperature range: 72–77°F (22–25°C); slightly higher for breeding*

BREEDING: *Eggs are laid in a cave, and they and the fry are cared for by both parents*

MARLIER'S JULIE

Julidochromis marlieri

ALONG WITH THE STRIPED OR REGAN'S JULIE (*J. regani*), this variably patterned species is regarded as one of the "large" Julies. Some authors believe that the two groups should be regarded as separate subgenera, but the majority opinion still favors the current status quo.

DISTRIBUTION: *Discontinuous, occurring both in the northern and southeastern parts of Lake Tanganyika*

SIZE: *Up to 6in (15cm) reported, but usually smaller*

BEHAVIOR: *As for J. dickfeldi*

DIET: *As for J. dickfeldi*

AQUARIUM: *As for J. dickfeldi*

BREEDING: *As in J. dickfeldi, but may hybridize with J. ornatus. Egg care may be undertaken more by female than by male*

FUELLEBORN'S CICHLID

Labeotropheus fuelleborni

VIRTUALLY INDISTINGUISHABLE PHYSICALLY FROM *L. trewavassae* (*see* p.102), this exceptionally variable species is restricted to shallow, wave-washed habitats. Many morphs are available, both wild-caught and captive-bred ones.

DISTRIBUTION: *Throughout Lake Malawi*

RUSTY CICHLID (IODOTROPHEUS SPRENGERAE)

DICKFELD'S JULIE (JULIDOCHROMIS DICKFELDI)

SIZE: *Male, wild-caught specimens reported up to 7in (18cm), but usually smaller; females smaller*

BEHAVIOR: *Males are territorial and aggressive toward both sexes, particularly other males*

DIET: *Wide range of foods accepted*

AQUARIUM: *Roomy African Rift Lake layout (see Aquarium Set-up) with numerous caves and shelters. Robust plants may be added, as well as at least one flat-topped rock. Medium-hard, alkaline, well-filtered water important. Temperature range: 70–77°F (21–25°C); slightly higher for breeding*

BREEDING: *Eggs are laid on a flat surface or inside a cave and are incubated orally by female*

FUELLEBORN'S CICHLID (LABEOTROPHEUS FUELLEBORNI)

TREWAVAS' CICHLID
RED-FINNED, or RED-TOPPED, CICHLID

Labeotropheus trewavasae

UNLIKE FUELLEBORN'S CICHLID, THIS SPECIES IS found in water over 130ft (up to 40m) deep. It is also slimmer and smaller than *L. fuelleborni*. Otherwise, both species are very similar to each other. Numerous color morphs of this species are available.

DISTRIBUTION: *Throughout Lake Malawi*

SIZE: *Wild-caught specimens reported up to 6in (15cm), but usually smaller; females smaller*

BEHAVIOR: *As for* L. fuelleborni

DIET: *As for* L. fuelleborni

AQUARIUM: *As for* L. fuelleborni

BREEDING: *As for* L. fuelleborni

LABIDOCHROMIS ELECTRIC YELLOW
LABIDOCHROMIS YELLOW/WHITE/BLUE/TANGANICAE

Labidochromis caeruleus

THIS IS YET ANOTHER VARIABLE, ROCK-DWELLING cichlid (mbuna), the actual coloration and body patterning depending on locality. Some specimens (e.g. from Kakusa), have brilliant-yellow bodies, while others (e.g. from Nkata Bay), are blue, making them appear to be distinct species. However, both, have a characteristic black band running the whole length of the dorsal fin.

DISTRIBUTION: *Eastern and western coasts of Lake Malawi*

SIZE: *About 4in (10cm)*

BEHAVIOR: *Nonterritorial, not aggressive*

DIET: *Wide range of foods accepted, particularly livefoods*

AQUARIUM: *Typical African Rift Lake layout (see Aquarium Set-up). Medium-hard, alkaline, well-filtered water. Temperature range: 72–77°F (22–25°C)*

BREEDING: *Typical maternal mouthbrooder; females tend to incubate their eggs in caves*

FLAG CICHLID

Laetacara curviceps

SYNONYM: *Aequidens curviceps*

ALTHOUGH THE FLAG CICHLID WAS RENAMED before 1986, it still appears under the old (and now invalid) name, *A. curviceps*, in some books. First imported into Europe in 1909, this desirable and variable fish is still popular, and deservedly so. A somewhat similar species, the Red-breasted Flag Cichlid (*L. dorsigera*) from Bolivia is also available.

DISTRIBUTION: *Amazon basin*

SIZE: *Up to 4in (10cm), but usually smaller; females smaller than males*

BEHAVIOR: *Generally peaceful except at breeding time when the pair becomes territorial*

DIET: *Wide range of foods accepted*

AQUARIUM: *Well planted, with adequate shelter and open spaces, at least one flat-topped or smoothly rounded rock, and a fine-grained substratum. Soft to medium-hard, neutral or slightly acid water recommended. Temperature range: 72–79°F (22–26°C)*

BREEDING: *Eggs are laid on a precleaned site (which could be a broadleaved plant), and both they and the fry are protected by the parents*

GOLDEN LAMPROLOGUS
RED LAMPROLOGUS

Lamprologus ocellatus

THIS IS ONE OF THE SMALLER AFRICAN RIFT LAKE cichlids, which, along with some of its closest relatives, has become popular

LABIDOCHROMIS ELECTRIC YELLOW (LABIDOCHROMIS CAERULEUS)

GOLDEN LAMPROLOGUS (LAMPROLOGUS OCELLATUS)

owing, largely, to its interesting breeding habits (*see* below).

DISTRIBUTION: *Throughout Lake Tanganyika*

SIZE: *Around 2½in (6cm)*

BEHAVIOR: *Territorial, but—owing to the relatively small area defended (around an empty snail shell)—may be kept with conspecifics in a roomy aquarium*

DIET: *Livefoods preferred*

AQUARIUM: *Sandy areas and snail shells in an otherwise typical African Rift Lake layout (see Aquarium Set-up). Medium-hard, alkaline water important. Temperature range: 73–77°F (23–25°C)*

BREEDING: *Eggs are laid inside female's snail shell. Both eggs and fry are protected by the parents*

LAMPROLOGUS NKAMBAE

Lepidolamprologus kendalli

IN CONTRAST TO THE PREVIOUS SPECIES, THIS IS A large cichlid that has predatory habits. It is beautifully marked, and this, despite its size and habits, makes it a good candidate for a spacious aquarium stocked with appropriate tankmates.

DISTRIBUTION: *Southern part of Lake Tanganyika*

SIZE: *Around 8¾in (22cm)*

BEHAVIOR: *Predatory, but perhaps not quite as aggressive as some of its closest relatives*

DIET: *Large livefoods preferred*

AQUARIUM: *Medium-hard, alkaline water important. Temperature range: 73–77°F (23–25°C)*

BREEDING: *Eggs are laid inside a cave, and both they and the fry are protected by the pair*

AURATUS CICHLID
MALAWI GOLDEN CICHLID

Melanochromis auratus

THIS WAS ONE OF THE EARLY RIFT LAKE CICHLIDS to become established within the hobby. It still remains popular today, particularly owing to the attractive coloration of both males and females. At least two other "Auratus" are available: *M.* sp. "auratus dwarf" and *M.* sp. "auratus elongate," both from the eastern coast of the Lake.

DISTRIBUTION: *Southern part of Lake Malawi*

SIZE: *Males around 4in (10cm); females a little smaller*

BEHAVIOR: *Territorial. Males are intolerant of rivals*

DIET: *Wide range of commercial diets accepted, but livefoods preferred*

AQUARIUM: *Typical African Rift Lake layout (see Aquarium Set-up). Medium-hard, neutral to alkaline water important. Temperature range: 72–79°F (22–26°C); slightly higher for breeding*

BREEDING: *Eggs are often laid inside a cave and are incubated orally by female, who also protects the fry*

PEARL OF LIKOMA

Melanochromis joanjohnsoni

SYNONYMS: *Melanochromis exasperatus, M. textilis*

AS IN *MELANOCHROMIS AURATUS*, BOTH MALE and female *M. joanjohnsoni* are very attractively (though differently) marked. Coloration also varies according to locality.

DISTRIBUTION: *Native to Likoma Island near the east coast of Lake Malawi, but has been introduced around Thumbi West Island, located in the southwestern arm of the Lake*

SIZE: *Males around 4in (10cm); females a little smaller*

BEHAVIOR: *As for M. auratus*

DIET: *As for M. auratus*

AQUARIUM: *As for M. auratus*

BREEDING: *As for M. auratus, but spawning may occur in the open*

JOHANNI MBUNA

Melanochromis johanni

ALTHOUGH MALE JOHANNIS DIFFER IN coloration according to locality, they are all, basically, deep blue with lighter-colored bands. Females, in contrast, have varying degrees of orange pigmentation.

DISTRIBUTION: *From Makanjila Point to Metangula, Lake Malawi*

SIZE: *Up to 4¾in (12cm) reported; females slightly smaller*

BEHAVIOR: *As for M. auratus*

DIET: *As for M. auratus*

AQUARIUM: *As for M. auratus*

BREEDING: *As for M. auratus, but eggs are often laid either on sand or a flat rock, and are picked up by female*

FLAG CICHLID
FESTIVE CICHLID
Mesonauta festivus

SYNONYM: *Mesonauta festiva*

THIS IS AN OLD FAVORITE, FIRST INTRODUCED INTO Europe in 1908 and bred in captivity a year later. Despite this, there is still some

OTHER *MELANOCHROMIS* SPECIES

Several other described *Melanochromis* species (all from Lake Malawi), as well as some undescribed ones (but with trade names), are available with varying degrees of regularity. The same basic maintenance and breeding guidelines apply to all. Those most likely to be encountered include the following:

SCIENTIFIC NAME	COMMON NAME(S)	SIZE
M. chipokae (see M. parallelus)	Chipokae Mbuna	6in (15cm)
M. dialeptos	Dwarf Auratus (may be equivalent to M. sp. "auratus dwarf")	3in (8cm)
M. interruptus	Chizumulu Johanni or Melanochromis Red	4in (10cm)
M. labrosus*	Haplochromis Labrosus	6¾in (17cm)
M. loriae	–	6in (15cm)
M. melanopterus	Black Mbuna	5in (13cm)
M. parallelus (may be the same as M. chipokae)	Parallel-striped Mbuna	5in (13cm)
M. robustus	–	6in (15cm)
M. simulans	Longsnout Mbuna	4¾in (12cm)
M. sp.	Numerous, e.g. Black-white Johanni, Blotch, Maingano, Northern Blue, Double Spot, Tumbi, Matema, and others	3¼–6¾in (8.5–17cm)
M. vermivorus	Purple Mbuna	6in (15cm)
M. xanthodigma	–	6in (15cm)

* Some authorities believe that *M. labrosus* is not a *Melanochromis* at all and needs to be reassigned to another genus

▲ *Flag Cichlid (Mesonauta festivus)* ▼ *Zebra Cichlid (Metriaclima zebra)*

doubt regarding the true identity of the species, with a school of thought leaning toward the "festivus" from the Río Negro being renamed *M. insignis* and those from other areas being regarded as the "true" *M. festivus*.

DISTRIBUTION: *Amazon basin, but may exist elsewhere, e.g. Guyana*

SIZE: *Up to 8in (20cm) reported, but usually smaller*

BEHAVIOR: *Territorial at breeding time, but otherwise can be timid*

DIET: *All foods accepted*

AQUARIUM: *Spacious and well planted, with adequate shelter and at least one flat-topped or smooth, rounded rock. Water chemistry not critical, but soft, slightly acid conditions preferred. Temperature range: 72–77°F (22–25°C); slightly higher for breeding*

BREEDING: *Eggs are laid on a precleaned site, which can be a broadleaved plant or a rock. Eggs and fry are protected by both parents*

ZEBRA CICHLID
NYASA BLUE CICHLID
Metriaclima zebra

SYNONYM: *Pseudotropheus zebra*

THIS IS ONE OF THE "KEYSTONE" SPECIES OF THE African Rift Lake cichlid hobby. Numerous morphs occur in the wild, and male coloration is very different to that of the female. Some of the types are incapable of interbreeding, and this has given rise to the belief that they may constitute separate species, rather than morphs. As a result, the collection of all these intimately related species/morphs are referred to as the "zebra complex." The new name, *Metriaclima*, was erected in 1997 and now includes several new species that would formerly have been regarded as *Pseudotropheus*.

DISTRIBUTION: *Widely distributed in Lake Malawi*

SIZE: *Up to 6in (15cm) reported, but usually smaller*

BEHAVIOR: *Territorial and aggressive, particularly toward its own kind*

DIET: *Wide range of foods accepted*

AQUARIUM: *Typical African Rift Lake layout (see Aquarium Set-up). Medium-hard to hard, alkaline, well-filtered water important. Temperature range: 72–82°F (22–28°C)*

BREEDING: *Typical maternal mouthbrooder*

ALTISPINOSA BUTTERFLY CICHLID
BOLIVIAN BUTTERFLY CICHLID
Microgeophagus altispinosus

SYNONYM: *Papiliochromis altispinosus*

SLIGHTLY LARGER THAN ITS BETTER-KNOWN closest relative, the Ram (*M. ramirezi, see below*), this beautiful and variable species also has a particularly striking dorsal fin when it is fully extended. Males have extended top and bottom caudal fin rays and, generally speaking, brilliantly colored pelvic and anal fins.

DISTRIBUTION: *Eastern Bolivia and Mato Grosso, Brazil*

SIZE: *Males around 3in (8cm); females slightly smaller*

BEHAVIOR: *Peaceful and tolerant of other tankmates; territorial during breeding*

DIET: *Wide range of foods accepted, but livefoods preferred*

AQUARIUM: *Well planted, with adequate shelter, fine-grained substratum, and a flat-topped or rounded rock. Soft, slightly acid to slightly alkaline water recommended. Raw water should be avoided. Temperature range: 72–77°F (22–25°C); slightly higher for breeding*

BREEDING: *Eggs are laid on a precleaned site and are protected primarily by female. Care of fry (which are often transferred between pits dug by male) is undertaken by both parents*

RAM
BUTTERFLY, or RAMIREZ'S, DWARF CICHLID
Microgeophagus ramirezi

SYNONYM: *Papiliochromis ramirezi*

THIS SPECTACULAR DWARF CICHLID HAS BEEN popular in the hobby for over 50 years, and with good reason. The wild type, in particular, is one of the "jewels" of the aquarium, although many of the cultivated forms, especially the gold, are also extremely attractive. In the late 1990s, a "Jumbo" form of the Ram was introduced. Whether it ever replaces its smaller counterparts, though, only time will tell.

▲ RAM (MICROGEOPHAGUS RAMIREZI)
FRIEDRICHSTHAL'S CICHLID (NANDOPSIS FRIEDRICHSTHALII) ▶

DISTRIBUTION: *Colombia and Venezuela*

SIZE: *Wild-caught specimens and most cultivated forms up to 2¾in (7cm), but usually smaller; Jumbos somewhat larger*

BEHAVIOR: *As for M. altispinosus*

DIET: *As for M. altispinosus*

AQUARIUM: *As for M. altispinosus*

BREEDING: *Eggs are laid on a precleaned site or in a depression in the substratum, and they and the fry are cared for by both parents*

RED TERROR
FESTA'S, OR TIGER, CICHLID
Nandopsis festae

SYNONYMS: *Cichlasoma festae, Herichthys festae*

SOME OF THE COLOR FORMS OF THIS LARGE SPECIES are truly stunning, particularly during breeding. Orange-bodied, black- or blue-banded types with iridescent scales are especially striking.

DISTRIBUTION: *Ecuador*

SIZE: *Fully mature males reported up to 20in (50cm), but usually somewhat smaller; females smaller*

BEHAVIOR: *Aggressive and territorial; should be kept only with equally large, robust tankmates*

DIET: *Large commercial formulations and livefoods accepted*

AQUARIUM: *Spacious, with open spaces and substantial shelters. Rocks and other decor should be well bedded. Plants need to be protected (see Aquarium Plants). Water chemistry not critical, but well-filtered, soft, neutral water recommended. Temperature range: 77–82°F (25–28°C)*

BREEDING: *Eggs are laid on a precleaned site (usually a rock). Female guards eggs while male defends territory. Fry are initially moved between predug pits by both parents*

FRIEDRICHSTHAL'S CICHLID
Nandopsis friedrichsthalii

SYNONYMS: *Cichlasoma friedrichsthalii, Herichthys friedrichsthalii, Parachromis friedrichsthalii*

A LITTLE SMALLER BUT SOMEWHAT MORE ELONGATE than N. *festae*. This is another well-marked species whose beauty is best appreciated in fully mature specimens.

DISTRIBUTION: *Widely distributed in Central America*

SIZE: *Up to 13¾in (35cm), but usually smaller; females smaller than males*

BEHAVIOR: *As for N. festae*

DIET: *As for N. festae*

AQUARIUM: *As for N. festae, but temperature range: 72–81°F (22–27°C)*

BREEDING: *As for N. festae*

MANAGUA CICHLID
JAGUAR CICHLID
Nandopsis managuense

SYNONYMS: *Cichlasoma managuense, Heros managuense, Herichthys managuensis, Parachromis managuense*

THE SECOND COMMON NAME OF THIS SPECIES APTLY describes both the coloration and patterning

MANAGUA CICHLID
(NANDOPSIS MANAGUENSE)

of this impressive cichlid which, like other widely distributed species, occurs in several forms, depending on locality.

DISTRIBUTION: *Central America*

SIZE: *Some fully mature males reported over ca.18in (45cm), but usually smaller; females smaller than males*

BEHAVIOR: *As for N. festae*

DIET: *As for N. festae*

AQUARIUM: *As for N. festae, but temperature range: 73–77°F (23–25°C)*

BREEDING: *Basically, as for N. festae, but female often takes on the major share of fry care*

JACK DEMPSEY

Nandopsis octofasciatus

SYNONYMS: *Cichlasoma octofasciatum, Cichlasoma biocellatum, Heros octofasciatus*

NAMED AFTER LEGENDARY BOXER, JACK DEMPSEY, this pugnacious cichlid lives up to its name. However, it is a most attractively marked species that despite its temperament is still much sought after.

DISTRIBUTION: *Belize, Guatemala, Honduras and southern Mexico*

SIZE: *Males to over 8in (20cm); females smaller*

BEHAVIOR: *Territorial, aggressive burrower; will damage plants*

DIET: *As for N. festae*

AQUARIUM: *As for N. festae, but temperature range: 72–77°F (22–25°C)*

BREEDING: *As for N. festae*

SALVIN'S CICHLID

TRICOLOR CICHLID

Nandopsis salvini

SYNONYMS: *Cichlasoma salvini, Heros salvini, Herichthys salvini*

THIS IS ANOTHER SPECTACULARLY COLORED MEMber of the genus. Although it is a substantial fish, the adult coloration begins to develop (particularly in males) while the fish are still modestly sized (i.e. about half the full size).

DISTRIBUTION: *Guatemala, Honduras and southern Mexico*

SIZE: *Fully mature males reported over 8in (20cm), but usually smaller; females smaller*

BEHAVIOR: *Territorial and intolerant of rivals, but may be kept with similar-sized fish. Unlike other members of the genus, does not uproot plants*

DIET: *As for N. festae*

AQUARIUM: *As for N. festae, but temperature range: 72–79°F (22–26°C)*

BREEDING: *As for N. festae*

GOLDEN DWARF ACARA

GOLDEN-EYED DWARF CICHLID

Nannacara anomala

THIS IS A HIGHLY VARIABLE SPECIES WHOSE coloration and patterning both differ between localities. This has led to some doubt regarding its possible presence in French Guiana, with some authorities believing that the fish that are found in this region belong to a separate species, the Goldhead Nannacara (*N. aureocephalus*). A third species, the Adok Nannacara (*N. adoketa*) from the Río Negro in Brazil is also sometimes available to aquarists.

DISTRIBUTION: *Northern South America and, possibly, French Guiana (see above)*

SIZE: *Males up to 3½in (9cm); females much smaller*

BEHAVIOR: *A peaceful, tolerant species, except during breeding*

DIET: *Most commercial formulations accepted, but livefoods preferred*

AQUARIUM: *Heavily planted, with ample shelter and fine-grained substratum recommended. Soft to moderately hard, slightly acid water is best. Temperature range: 72–77°F (22–25°C); slightly higher for breeding*

BREEDING: *Eggs are laid in a cave, and both they and the fry are guarded by female, which develops distinctive coloration at this time*

CONGO DWARF CICHLID

NUDICEPS

Nanochromis parilus

SYNONYMS: *Nanochromis parilius, N. nudiceps*

THIS SPECIES, ALONG WITH TWO OF ITS CLOSEST relatives, *N. dimidiatus* and *N. transvestitus*, is one of the relatively few dwarf cichlids from Africa (excluding the Rift Lake dwarves) that is fairly widely available in the hobby. Both sexes are beautifully, though differently, colored. Females appear to be full of eggs all the time and possess a pinkish belly flush,

▲ JACK DEMPSEY (NANDOPSIS OCTOFASCIATUS)   ▼ SALVIN'S CICHLID (NANDOPSIS SALVINI)

OTHER *NANDOPSIS* SPECIES

Despite the obvious drawbacks that their large size and generally territorial and aggressive behavior pose, *Nandopsis* species are quite popular. In addition to the featured species, the following are also available with varying regularity. The sizes given below are for fully mature males; females are smaller.

SCIENTIFIC NAME	COMMON NAME(S)	SIZE
N. bartoni	Barton's Cichlid	8¾in (22cm)
N. beani	Bean's Cichlid	10in (25cm)
N. dovii	Dow's, or Wolf, Cichlid	20in (50cm)
N. facetum	Chancito Cichlid	10in (25cm)
N. grammodes	Sieve, or Many-pointed, Cichlid	10in (25cm)
N. haitiensis	Haiti Cichlid	10in (25cm)
N. istlanum	Rio Ixtla Cichlid or Istlanum	12in (30cm)
N. labridens	Tooth-lipped Cichlid	10in (25cm)
N. loisellei	Loiselle's Cichlid	12in (30cm)
N. motaguense	Motagua Cichlid	12in (30cm)
N. ornatus	Ornament Cichlid	10in (25cm)
N. ramsdeni	Ramsden's Cichlid	13¾in (35cm)
N. steindachneri	Steindachner's Cichlid	10in (25cm)
N. tetracanthus	Cuban Cichlid	13¾in (35cm)
N. umbriferus	Dark, or Blue-speckled, Cichlid	24in (60cm)
N. urophthalmus	Tail-spot Tiger, or Eight-barred, Cichlid	16in (40cm)
N. vombergae	Mia's Cichlid	8in (20cm)

GOLDEN DWARF ACARA (NANNACARA ANOMALA)

CONGO DWARF CICHLID (NANOCHROMIS PARILUS)

DOW'S CICHLID (N. DOVII)

which reveals the relationship of this species with the other African dwarves commonly referred to as Kribs (see *Pelvicachromis pulcher*, p.111).

DISTRIBUTION: *Zaire basin, particularly Stanley Pool*

SIZE: *Males up to 3in (8cm); females a little smaller*

BEHAVIOR: *Males are aggressive toward rivals and often toward unreceptive females as well*

DIET: *Commercial formulations accepted but livefoods preferred*

AQUARIUM: *Well planted, with numerous shelters and caves. Soft, slightly acid water (preferably filtered through peat or containing a "blackwater"* commercial additive) is best. Temperature range: 72–77°F (22–25°C); slightly higher for breeding

BREEDING: *Eggs are laid in a cave, and both they and the fry are guarded by female while male generally defends territory*

LITTLE LAKE CICHLID
PYGMY GREEN-EYED CICHLID

Neetroplus nematopus

SYNONYMS: *Neetroplus fluviatilis, N. nematopsis*

THIS MODESTLY SIZED SPECIES IS NOT SEEN AS often as it should be. One particularly interesting feature is that a breeding pair will reverse their color pattern once spawning is over. The female is first to change, with her body darkening and the dark body bar lightening; the male follows once the eggs hatch and fry care begins. An even more geographically variable species, *N. panamensis* (from Panama), is also available.

DISTRIBUTION: *Costa Rica and Nicaragua*

SIZE: *Up to 5½in (14cm)*

BEHAVIOR: *Can become very aggressive and territorial, particularly during breeding*

DIET: *All foods accepted; vegetable component recommended*

AQUARIUM: *Well planted, with at least one cave. Medium-hard to hard, alkaline water preferred. Temperature range: 75–81°F (24–27°C); slightly higher for breeding*

BREEDING: *Eggs are laid in a cave, and they and the fry are guarded by both parents*

BREVIS

Neolamprologus brevis

SYNONYM: *Lamprologus brevis*

THIS IS ONE OF THE SMALLEST AFRICAN RIFT LAKE cichlids in the hobby. In the wild, it occurs over a sandy substratum and lives in and around an empty snail shell. While not being spectacularly colored, males are very attractive.

DISTRIBUTION: *Throughout Lake Tanganyika*

SIZE: *Males up to 2in (5cm); females smaller*

BEHAVIOR: *Peaceful snail-shell dweller; tolerant of other species*

DIET: *Prefers livefoods but will accept other formulations, particularly deep-frozen ones*

AQUARIUM: *African Rift Lake layout (see Aquarium Set-up), with sandy areas and one cave and/or large empty snail shell per adult. Medium-hard, alkaline water important. Temperature range: 73–79°F (23–26°C)*

BREEDING: *Eggs are laid in a snail shell. Both parents care for the brood*

FAIRY CICHLID

LYRETAIL LAMPROLOGUS or
PRINCESS OF BURUNDI
Neolamprologus brichardi

SYNONYMS: *Lamprologus brichardi, Lamprologus elongatus*

THIS IS THE MOST WIDELY AVAILABLE AND MOST commercially bred member of the genus (*see* photo p.40). Several cultivated varieties, including an albino, have been produced, and these now out-sell wild-caught specimens. *N. brichardi* is a "must" for anyone interested in African Rift Lake cichlids.

DISTRIBUTION: *Throughout Lake Tanganyika*

SIZE: *Around 4in (10cm)*

BEHAVIOR: *Peaceful shoaler; can therefore be kept in a group*

DIET: *Wide range of commercial formulations accepted, but livefoods preferred*

AQUARIUM: *African Rift Lake layout (see Aquarium Set-up). Well-filtered, medium-hard, alkaline water important. Temperature range: 73–79°F (23–26°C)*

BREEDING: *Eggs are laid inside a cave. Brood care is undertaken largely by female*

TERETE LAMPROLOGUS

Neolamprologus cylindricus

SYNONYM: *Lamprologus cylindricus*

BESIDES ITS ELONGATE, "CYLINDER" BODY (HENCE its scientific name), this species is notable for its numerous, vertical, dark body bands and blue-edged fins. This is a very attractive fish which, unfortunately, cannot be kept in groups.

DISTRIBUTION: *Southeastern coast of Lake Tanganyika*

SIZE: *Around 4¼in (11cm)*

BEHAVIOR: *Tends to be a loner in the wild, but single pairs may be kept in a spacious aquarium*

DIET: *As for* N. brichardi

AQUARIUM: *As for* N. brichardi

BREEDING: *This is a cave-spawning and brooding species*

GRACEFUL LAMPROLOGUS

Neolamprologus gracilis

SYNONYMS: *Lamprologus gracilis, L. palmeri*

THIS ELEGANT SPECIES BEAUTIFULLY LIVES UP TO ITS name. Although it is superficially similar to *N. brichardi*, it does not possess the distinctive facial markings of its close relative.

DISTRIBUTION: *Central and western coasts of Lake Tanganyika*

SIZE: *Around 4in (10cm)*

BEHAVIOR: *As for* N. brichardi

DIET: *As for* N. brichardi

AQUARIUM: *As for* N. brichardi

BREEDING: *As for* N. brichardi

LEMON CICHLID

Neolamprologus leleupi

SYNONYMS: *Lamprologus leleupi, L. longior*

IN TERMS OF COLOR, NO OTHER *NEOLAMPROLOGUS* can match the Lemon Cichlid. The intensity of the yellow coloration can vary between "true" lemon-yellow, through more golden shades to almost goldish brown or burnished gold.

NOTE: This species must not be confused with the similarly named, but differently colored (i.e. non-yellow) Pearlscale Lamprologus (*N. leloupi*). *N. leloupi* is also smaller (3in/8cm) and altogether more peaceful.

DISTRIBUTION: *Unevenly distributed along northwestern, western, and eastern coasts of Lake Tanganyika*

SIZE: *Around 4¼in (11cm)*

BEHAVIOR: *May be aggressive toward members of its own species*

DIET: *As for* N. brichardi

AQUARIUM: *As for* N. brichardi

BREEDING: *As for* N. brichardi, *but it is advisable to remove male after spawning, leaving female to care for her brood in peace*

PRINCESS OF ZAMBIA

DAFFODIL
Neolamprologus pulcher

SYNONYM: *Lamprologus pulcher*

THIS IS ANOTHER *N. BRICHARDI* LOOKALIKE (*SEE N. brichardi* and *N. gracilis* above). The Daffodil morph of this species, which has yellow tinges in its dorsal and anal fins, and a distinctive yellow blotch at the base of the pectoral fins, may even be occasionally (and erroneously) labeled as *N. brichardi*

GRACEFUL LAMPROLOGUS (NEOLAMPROLOGUS GRACILIS)

Lemon Cichlid (Neolamprologus leleupi)

"Daffodil." *N. pulcher* does not, however, exhibit the distinctive face and cheek markings of its better-known relative.

DISTRIBUTION: *Unevenly distributed along southeastern coasts of Lake Tanganyika*

SIZE: *Around 4in (10cm)*

BEHAVIOR: *As for N. brichardi*

DIET: *As for N. brichardi*

AQUARIUM: *As for N. brichardi*

BREEDING: *As for N. brichardi*

MULTIFASCIATUS BIG EYE

Neolamprologus similis

SYNONYM: *Lamprologus similis*

AS SUGGESTED BY THE COMMON NAME, THIS species has a relatively large eye, but the most distinctive feature of this small attractive fish are the numerous, thin, vertical, light bands (as implied by the Multifasciatus part of the common name).

DISTRIBUTION: *Most of the southern half of Lake Tanganyika*

SIZE: *Around 1½in (4cm)*

BEHAVIOR: *Peaceful species; may be kept as a group*

DIET: *Livefoods preferred*

AQUARIUM: *African Rift Lake layout (see Aquarium Set-up) with sandy areas and empty snail shells. Medium-hard, alkaline water important. Temperature range: 73–79°F (23–26°C)*

BREEDING: *Eggs are laid inside a cave (empty snail shell), and both they and the fry are protected*

FIVE-BARRED LAMPROLOGUS

Neolamprologus tretocephalus

SYNONYM: *Lamprologus tretocephalus*

THIS SPECIES IS SUPERFICIALLY SIMILAR TO *N. sexfasciatus*, but possesses one fewer body bar. Both are spectacular fish in their own right, particularly during their juvenile and subadult stages.

DISTRIBUTION: *Northern half of Lake Tanganyika* (N. sexfasciatus *is found in the southern half*)

SIZE: *Around 5½in (14cm)*

OTHER *NEOLAMPROLOGUS* SPECIES

In addition to the featured species, several others are available. Some are small, usually peaceful, snail-shell dwellers and brooders; others fit the graceful *N. brichardi* image (in shape, though not necessarily in habits), with elegant finnage; a third group consists of more robust, more predatory species. Individual requirements should therefore be sought in specialist literature and from specialist dealers, although the overall characteristics and maintenance guidelines given for the featured species of each of these three main types will generally apply.

SCIENTIFIC NAME	COMMON NAME(S)	SIZE	SCIENTIFIC NAME	COMMON NAME(S)	SIZE
N. bifasciatus	Lamprologus Zambia	4in (10cm)	N. multifasciatus	Many-banded Dwarf Lamprologus	1½in (4cm)
N. boulengeri	Boulenger's Snail Dweller	3in (8cm)	N. mustax	Mustax	3½in (9cm)
N. buescheri	Striped Lamprologus	4in (10cm)	N. niger	Muddy Lamprologus	2¾in (7cm)
N. calliurus	Magara Shell Dweller	4in (10cm)	N. nigriventris	–	4in (10cm)
N. caudopunctatus	Checkerboard-tailed Lamprologus	3in (8cm)	N. obscurus	Mottley Lamprologus	3in (8cm)
N. christyi	Christy's Lamprologus	5½in (14cm)	N. olivaceus	Olive Lamprologus	3in (8cm)
N. crassus	–	3in (8cm)	N. pectoralis	–	4in (10cm)
N. falcicula	Long-finned Lamprologus	3in (8cm)	N. petricola	Petricola	5in (13cm)
N. fasciatus	Barred Lamprologus	6in (15cm)	N. savoryi	Savoryi	3in (8cm)
N. furcifer	Fork-tailed Lamprologus	6in (15cm)	N. schreyeni	Schreyen's Lamprologus	3in (8cm)
N. hecqui	Spotfin Lamprologus	3in (8cm)	N. speciosus	–	2in (5cm)
N. longicaudatus	Lamprologus "Kavala," Ubwari Buescheri	6in (15cm)	N. splendens	–	3in (8cm)
			N. tetracanthus	Pearl-lined Lamprologus	7½in (19cm)
N. meleagris	–	2½in (6cm)	N. toae	Toa Lamprologus	4in (10cm)
N. modestus	Modest Lamprologus	5in (13cm)	N. variostigma	–	4in (10cm)
N. mondabu	Mondabu Lamprologus	4¾in (12cm)	N. ventralis	Lamprologus Finalimus	2¾in (7cm)
N. moorii	Moore's Lamprologus	4¼in (11cm)	N. wauthioni	Wauthion's Lamprologus Zambia	2¼in (5.5cm)

BEHAVIOR: *Aggressive toward its own species; only one pair should be kept*

DIET: *Livefoods preferred*

AQUARIUM: *Typical African Rift Lake layout (see Aquarium Set-up). Well-filtered, medium-hard, alkaline water important. Temperature range: 73–79°F (23–26°C)*

BREEDING: *Eggs are laid inside a cave and are protected*

LIVINGSTONI

Nimbochromis livingstonii

SYNONYMS: *Haplochromis livingstonii, Cyrtocara livingstonii*

THIS RELATIVELY LARGE CICHLID SPECIES IS exceptionally marked. In particular, the brown body patches on a light-colored base, coupled with the red tinge of the anal fin of males, make it a striking fish even among more spectacularly colored species.

DISTRIBUTION: *Throughout Lake Malawi*

SIZE: *Up to 10in (25cm)*

BEHAVIOR: *Predatory; lies on the bottom feigning death, and lunges at any swallowable fish that swims up to investigate*

DIET: *Large commercial formulations accepted, but prefers livefood*

AQUARIUM: *Well-filtered, African Rift Lake layout (see Aquarium Set-up), with sandy areas. Medium-hard, alkaline water required. Temperature range: 73–79°F (23–26°C)*

BREEDING: *Maternal mouthbrooder*

VENUSTUS

Nimbochromis venustus

SYNONYMS: *Haplochromis venustus, Cyrtocara venusta*

WHILE VENUSTUS POSSESSES SOME DARK BODY patches, they are usually less pronounced than in *N. livingstonii*. The head is blue with or without yellow on the top. There is also yellow on the top of the caudal peduncle and elsewhere on the body.

DISTRIBUTION: *Throughout Lake Malawi*

SIZE: *Up to 9in (22.5cm) recorded in the wild*

BEHAVIOR: *Territorial and intolerant burrower*

DIET: *Commercial diets accepted, but livefoods preferred*

AQUARIUM: *As for* N. livingstonii

BREEDING: *As for* N. livingstonii

VENTRALIS CICHLID
BLUE GOLD-TIP CICHLID
Ophthalmotilapia ventralis

SYNONYM: *Ophthalmochromis ventralis*

THE MOST IMMEDIATELY DISTINGUISHABLE CHARacteristic of the four available *Opthalmotilapia* species are the extremely long pelvic fins of the males, each with a distinctively marked thickening of the tip. These act in the same way as the eggspots on the anal fin of other Rift Lake cichlids.

DISTRIBUTION: *Most of Lake Tanganyika, but not north of the Ubwari Peninsula*

SIZE: *About 6in (15cm)*

BEHAVIOR: *Territorial during breeding; may burrow while spawning; males aggressive toward each other*

DIET: *Wide range of foods accepted, but livefoods preferred; vegetable component recommended*

AQUARIUM: *African Rift Lake layout (see Aquarium Set-up), with sandy areas. Medium-hard, alkaline water required. Temperature range: 73–79°F (23–26°C)*

BREEDING: *Maternal mouthbrooder*

OTHER *NIMBOCHROMIS* SPECIES

Three other *Nimbochromis* are regularly available. All are predatory and have the same basic requirements as the two featured species.

SCIENTIFIC NAME	COMMON NAME(S)	SIZE
N. fuscotaeniatus	Fuscotaeniatus	10in (25cm)
N. linni	Elephant-nosed Cichlid	10in+ (25cm+)
N. polystigma	Polystigma	9in (23cm)

◄ LIVINGSTONI (NIMBOCHROMIS LIVINGSTONII)
▼ VENUSTUS (NIMBOCHROMIS VENUSTUS)

OTHER
OPHTHALMOTILAPIA SPECIES

In addition to *O. ventralis*, the three following species, which have similar requirements, are often available.

SCIENTIFIC NAME	COMMON NAME(S)	SIZE
O. boops	Dusty Gold-tip Cichlid	6in (15cm)
O. heterodonta	Gold-tip Cichlid	5½in (14cm)
O. nasuta	Nasutus, or Long-nosed, Cichlid	8in (20cm)

MOZAMBIQUE MOUTHBROODER

Oreochromis mossambicus

SYNONYMS: *Sarotherodon mossambicus, Tilapia mossambica*

THIS IS A LARGE, TOUGH FISH THAT IS ABLE TO tolerate a wide range of conditions (even fully marine ones) and will reproduce with great facility and regularity in aquaria. A "red" variety, which is more pink than red, plus several mottled ones, are available. It hybridizes with its close relatives and is widely used as a food fish, as are the two other *Oreochromis* species that are occasionally encountered in the hobby: *O. (Sarotherodon) galileus* and *O. niloticus.*

DISTRIBUTION: *Eastern Africa, but widely introduced elsewhere*

SIZE: *Fully mature males up to 16in (40cm); females much smaller*

BEHAVIOR: *Aggressive burrower that destroys (and eats) plants; highly territorial during breeding*

DIET: *All large foods accepted; vegetable supplement recommended*

AQUARIUM: *Large, with well-bedded decor or rocks. Well-filtered water. Water chemistry not critical and can range from soft to brackish. Temperature range: 68–74°F (20–24°C); slightly higher for breeding*

BREEDING: *Male excavates large pit to which he attracts females. After spawning, female incubates the eggs orally and subsequently cares for the fry*

POLLENI
MARAKELY

Paratilapia polleni

THIS IS AN IMPRESSIVE DARK-BROWN SPECIES with numerous, small, white, or cream-colored spots. During breeding, males turn almost blue-black, making them even more attractive. Being a large fish, the Marakely is primarily regarded as a food fish in wild.

DISTRIBUTION: *Madagascar*

SIZE: *Up to 12in (30cm)*

BEHAVIOR: *Territorial; should only be housed with similar-sized fish*

DIET: *Wide range of foods accepted, but livefoods preferred*

AQUARIUM: *Spacious, with appropriately large shelters. Plants need protection (see Aquarium Plants). Well-filtered water, avoiding extremes of pH and hardness, is recommended, as is*

YELLOW KRIB (PELVICACHROMIS HUMILIS)

the addition of a little salt (one teaspoonful per 1 Imp. gal/4 5 liters). Temperature range: 77–82°F (25–28°C); slightly higher for breeding

BREEDING: *Male excavates a simple nest to which he attracts the female. Egg care is usually undertaken by female; fry are protected by both parents*

YELLOW KRIB

Pelvicachromis humilis

SYNONYM: *Pelmatochromis humilis*

THE YELLOW PIGMENTATION INDICATED IN the common name is restricted to the cheek, chest, or belly in males. Females lack this distinctive coloration, but have violet or reddish bellies. At least three naturally occurring color morphs exist.

DISTRIBUTION: *Guinea, Liberia and Sierra Leone*

SIZE: *Males reported up to 5in (13cm), but usually smaller; females smaller*

BEHAVIOR: *Generally peaceful, but territorial during breeding*

DIET: *Wide range of foods accepted*

AQUARIUM: *Well matured and well planted, with shelters (caves). Soft, acid water recommended. Temperature range: 75–79°F (24–26°C); slightly higher for breeding*

BREEDING: *Eggs are laid in a cave, and both they and the fry are protected*

KRIB
KRIBENSIS, or PURPLE, CICHLID

Pelvicachromis pulcher

SYNONYM: *Pelmatochromis pulcher*

THIS OLD FAVORITE IS PERHAPS THE MOST POPULAR of all the African cichlids, with the possible exception of some of the Rift Lake species. It is a colorful, though variable, species in which the females always appear to be full of eggs and exhibit a particularly striking, reddish belly patch (not so pronounced in males). A well-matched pair make excellent parents. A large morph (possibly a separate species) usually referred to as *Pelvicachromis* cf. *pulcher* (Giant), is also available.

DISTRIBUTION: *Nigeria, often in brackish water*

SIZE: *Males up to 4in (10cm), but usually smaller; females smaller*

KRIB (PELVICACHROMIS PULCHER)

BEHAVIOR: *Territorial at breeding time, but usually peaceful toward other species*

DIET: *Wide range of foods accepted*

AQUARIUM: *Well planted, with adequate shelters (caves) and an open swimming area. Good-quality water important; medium-hard, slightly acid water recommended. Temperature range: 75–79°F (24–26°C); slightly higher for breeding*

BREEDING: *Eggs are laid on the roof of a cave, and both they and the fry are guarded by female; male defends territory, though he will also participate in fry care*

ROLOFF'S KRIB

Pelvicachromis roloffi

SYNONYM: *Pelmatochromis roloffi*

THIS IS ANOTHER BEAUTIFUL AND NATURALLY variable Krib in which females are particularly well patterned and colored.

DISTRIBUTION: *Guinea, Liberia and Sierra Leone*

SIZE: *Up to 3½in (9cm), but usually smaller; females smaller than males*

BEHAVIOR: *As for P. humilis*

DIET: *As for P. humilis*

AQUARIUM: *As for P. humilis*

BREEDING: *As for P. humilis*

EYESPOT KRIB

Pelvicachromis subocellatus

SYNONYM: *Pelmatochromis subocellatus*

THIS SPECIES IS HIGHLY VARIABLE, DEPENDING on locality, and it is found in a range of naturally occurring conditions, including brackish water. Despite the "ocellatus" part of its name, some specimens—particularly males—may lack ocelli ("eyespots") altogether.

DISTRIBUTION: *Widely distributed in western Africa*

SIZE: *Males up to 4in (10cm); females smaller*

BEHAVIOR: *As for P. pulcher*

DIET: *As for P. pulcher*

AQUARIUM: *As for P. pulcher*

BREEDING: *As for P. pulcher*

STRIPED DWARF CICHLID

STRIPED KRIB

Pelvicachromis taeniatus

SYNONYM: *Pelmatochromis taeniatus*

DESPITE BEING IMPORTED INTO EUROPE AS EARLY as 1911, and despite appearing in numerous aquarium books, this species is relatively rare in the hobby in comparison with, say, *P. pulcher*. Like the other members of the genus, it is a variable species with numerous naturally existing morphs.

DISTRIBUTION: *Widely distributed within southern Nigeria, Liberia and Cameroon*

SIZE: *Males up to 3½in (9cm); females smaller*

BEHAVIOR: *As for P. pulcher*

DIET: *As for P. pulcher*

AQUARIUM: *As for P. pulcher*

BREEDING: *As for P. pulcher*

PETEN CICHLID

GIANT CICHLID, or BAY/RED SNOOK

Petenia splendida

JUVENILES OF THIS SPECIES, WHICH IS ONE OF THE larger cichlids, are occasionally available in the hobby. While these specimens may appear attractive, the real beauty of the Peten Cichlid is fully appreciated only in mature fish.

DISTRIBUTION: *Belize, Guatemala, Nicaragua and southern Mexico*

SIZE: *Up to 20in (50cm) reported, usually smaller; females smaller than males*

BEHAVIOR: *Adults territorial and aggressive; should be kept only with similar species*

Diet: *Large commercial formulations accepted, but livefoods preferred*

AQUARIUM: *Spacious, with robust, well-bedded decor, caves and large rocks. Well-filtered, medium-hard, slightly alkaline water advisable. Temperature range: 71–77°F (22–25°C); slightly higher for breeding*

BREEDING: *Large numbers of eggs are laid on a precleaned site, and both they and the fry are protected by the parents*

LAVENDER MBUNA

Petrotilapia tridentiger

THERE IS CONSIDERABLE DEBATE REGARDING THE classification of *Petrotilapia* species, with many still awaiting scientific description. In the end, it may be that the fish available as

P. tridentiger belong to an, as yet, undescribed species, *P. sp.* "Yellow Chin" from a relatively wide area extending from Makanjila Point to Metangula, and around the Maleri, Mbenji and Namalenje islands. If so, it is also possible that the "true" *P. tridentiger* is the fish found around Boadzulu Island and Chia Lagoon.

DISTRIBUTION: *If the above applies, the species occurs in the southernmost area of Lake Malawi. Otherwise, the distribution area extends further northward along the east coast of the lake*

SIZE: *Up to 10in (25cm) reported, but usually smaller*

BEHAVIOR: *Intolerant and territorial*

DIET: *Wide range of foods accepted, but livefoods preferred; vegetable component recommended*

AQUARIUM: *African Rift Lake layout (see Aquarium Set-up). Well-filtered, medium-hard, alkaline water important. Temperature range: 75–81°F (24–27°C)*

BREEDING: *Typical maternal mouthbrooder*

DEEPWATER HAP

Placidochromis electra

SYNONYMS: *Haplochromis electra, H. jahni*

THIS SPECIES IS RELATIVELY EASY TO DISTINGUISH from other blue Rift Lake cichlid species by its two dark patches, one extending from the eye down to the throat area, and the other located on the "shoulder."

DISTRIBUTION: *Eastern coast of Lake Malawi, from Hai Reef southward to Makanjila Point, taking in Likoma Island*

SIZE: *Around 6¾in (17cm)*

BEHAVIOR: *More peaceful and less territorial than many of its closest relatives*

DIET: *Wide range of commercial formulations*

AQUARIUM: *Typical African Rift Lake layout (see Aquarium Set-up), with sandy areas. Medium-hard, alkaline water important. Temperature range: 75–79°F (24–26°C)*

BREEDING: *Spawning tubes, i.e. lengths of plastic piping, placed either on sand or on a rock, with female subsequently picking up eggs and incubating them orally*

FENESTRATUS

Protomelas fenestratus

SYNONYM: *Haplochromis fenestratus*

ALSO KNOWN IN THE TRADE AS *HAPLOCHROMIS steveni* "Thick Bars," this is one of several *Protomelas* species available, some of which are still awaiting scientific description.

DISTRIBUTION: *Throughout Lake Malawi*

SIZE: *Around 6in (15cm)*

PETEN CICHLID (*PETENIA SPLENDIDA*)

▲ DEEPWATER HAP (*PLACIDOCHROMIS ELECTRA*)　　▼ FENESTRATUS (*PROTOMELAS FENESTRATUS*)

BEHAVIOR: *Territorial but not overaggressive*

DIET: *Wide range of foods accepted, but livefoods preferred*

AQUARIUM: *Typical African Rift Lake layout (see Aquarium Set-up), with sandy areas. Well-filtered, medium-hard, alkaline water important. Temperature range: 75–79°F (24–26°C)*

OTHER *PROTOMELAS* SPECIES

Several other *Protomelas* species are available. Those listed below are among the most commonly encountered. All have the same basic requirements, although the degree of territorial behavior varies.

SCIENTIFIC NAME	COMMON NAME(S)	SIZE
P. annectens	Chunky Hap	8in (20cm)
P. ornatus	Ornate Hap	10in (25cm)
P. similis	Gorgeous Hap or Haplochromis Sunset	7in (18cm)
P. spilonotus	Two-bar Hap	8in (20cm)
P. taeniolatus	Spindle Hap, Haplochromis Fire Blue or Red Empress	7½in (19cm)

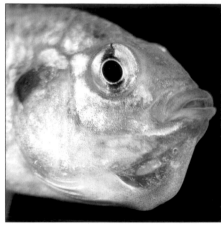

EGYPTIAN MOUTHBROODER
(PSEUDOCRENILABRUS MULTICOLOR)

BREEDING: *Males construct sand nests to which they attract females; female incubates eggs orally*

EGYPTIAN MOUTHBROODER

Pseudocrenilabrus multicolor

SYNONYMS: *Haplochromis multicolor, Hemihaplochromis multicolor*

THIS INTERESTING SPECIES WAS FIRST IMPORTED into Europe as far back as 1902. It once enjoyed enormous popularity owing to its breeding habits, but has since been overtaken by more colorful species, particularly from the African Rift Lakes.

DISTRIBUTION: *From Lower Nile basin southward to Uganda and Tanzania (as far as Lake Victoria)*

SIZE: *Up to 3in (8cm); females smaller than males*

BEHAVIOR: *Generally (but not invariably) peaceful and tolerant; territorial during breeding*

DIET: *All foods accepted*

AQUARIUM: *Well planted, with sandy bottom, swimming areas, and adequate shelter (caves). Turbulent water conditions should be avoided. Floating plants recommended to provide subdued lighting conditions underwater. Water chemistry not critical as long as extremes are avoided. Temperature range: 68–79°F (20–26°C)*

BREEDING: *Eggs are laid either in a depression dug by male, or on a rock, and are picked up by female; female incubates eggs orally and subsequently protects the fry*

SOUTH AFRICAN MOUTHBROODER

DWARF COPPER MOUTHBROODER

Pseudocrenilabrus philander

SYNONYM: *Hemihaplochromis philander*

THREE SUBSPECIES OF *P. PHILANDER* ARE GENERALLY recognized, with two—*P. p. dispersus* and *P. p. philander*—being more regularly available than the third, *P. p. luebberti*. All require the same aquarium conditions, and all are well worth keeping. However, to avoid crossbreeding, the three subspecies should not be kept not together.

DISTRIBUTION: *From southern Africa northward to Mozambique*

SIZE: *Up to 4¼in (11cm)*

BEHAVIOR: *Territorial and aggressive, particularly toward its own kind during breeding, when burrowing activities increase*

DIET: *As for P. multicolor*

AQUARIUM: *As for P. multicolor*

BREEDING: *As for P. multicolor*

AURORA CICHLID

Pseudoctropheus aurora

SYNONYMS: *Maylandia aurora, Metriaclima aurora*

AT THE PRESENT TIME, ALL THREE SCIENTIFIC names above are in use for species that, like the impressive Aurora Cichlid, form part of the so-called zebra complex (*see Metriaclima zebra*, p.104). Until the matter is resolved, and for some time subsequent to this, both the Aurora Cichlid and the other members of the complex will therefore appear under a variety of names in aquarium literature.

DISTRIBUTION: *Lake Malawi: originally around Likoma Island and a short stretch of the eastern coast (between Mara Point and Tumbi Point). Subsequently introduced around Thumbi West Island and Otter Point*

SIZE: *Around 4¼in (11cm)*

BEHAVIOR: *Territorial and aggressive*

DIET: *Wide range of foods accepted*

AQUARIUM: *Typical African Rift Lake layout (see Aquarium Set-up). Medium-hard, alkaline water important. Temperature range: 75–79°F (24–26°C)*

BREEDING: *Maternal mouthbrooder*

HORNET CICHLID

Pseudotropheus crabro

THIS SPECIES, BEAUTIFULLY MARKED IN BROWN and yellow, is not a member of the zebra complex and is thus not included in the *Pseudotropheus/Maylandia/Metriaclima* debate.

DISTRIBUTION: *Most of Lake Malawi*

SIZE: *Wild specimens reported up to 4¾in (12cm); aquarium specimens may be larger*

BEHAVIOR: *In the wild, this species is usually associated with the large catfish, Bagrus meridionalis, which it "serves" as a cleaner. P. crabro also feeds on catfish eggs and fry. In the aquarium, males are territorial, but not overaggressive*

DIET: *As for P. aurora*

AQUARIUM: *As for P. aurora*

BREEDING: *As for P. aurora*

KENNYI MBUNA

Pseudotropheus lombardoi

SYNONYMS: *Maylandia lombardoi, Metriaclima lombardoi*

IN THIS ZEBRA COMPLEX SPECIES, MALES, WHILE varying in coloration, are orangy/yellow, with or without vertical dark bands. Females are pale metallic blue with dark vertical bands.

DISTRIBUTION: *Mbenji Island and Nkhomo Reef in Lake Malawi*

SIZE: *Around 4¼in (11cm)*

BEHAVIOR: *As for P. aurora*

DIET: *As for P. aurora*

AQUARIUM: *As for P. aurora*

BREEDING: *As for P. aurora*

South African Mouthbrooder (Pseudocrenilabrus philander)

Aurora Cichlid (Pseudoctropheus aurora)

Hornet Cichlid (Pseudotropheus crabro)

Kennyi Mbuna (Pseudotropheus lombardoi)

TROPHEOPS BRIGHT YELLOW

Pseudotropheus macrophthalmus

SYNONYM: *Tropheops macrophthalmus*

THIS IS YET ANOTHER SPECIES FOR WHICH scientific names are not fully standardized or agreed. As the common name indicates, it is a stunningly colored fish, particularly the males

DISTRIBUTION: *The eastern coastline of Lake Malawi*

SIZE: *Wild-caught specimens reach about 4¾in (12cm) in length; aquarium specimens may attain 6in (15cm)*

BEHAVIOR: *Territorial, but less aggressive than its closest relatives*

DIET: *As for P. aurora*

AQUARIUM: *As for P. aurora*

BREEDING: *As for P. aurora*

MINUTUS

Pseudotropheus minutus

THIS IS ONE OF THE SMALLER SPECIES IN THE genus. Superficially, it looks like a smaller

Different morph of Pseudotropheus macrophthalmus but just as attractive, Orange Cheek Cichlid

version of a blue/black morph of *Metriaclima zebra.*

DISTRIBUTION: *Mainly found in Nkata Bay in Lake Malawi*

SIZE: *Up to 3½in (9cm)*

BEHAVIOR: *Territorial males aggressive, particularly toward rivals*

DIET: *As for P. aurora*

AQUARIUM: *As for P. aurora*

BREEDING: *As for P. aurora*

EDUARD'S MBUNA

Pseudotropheus socolofi

THIS IS ONE OF THE VERY FEW SPECIES THAT ARE named after someone, in this case Ross

LEOPOLD'S ANGEL

Pterophyllum leopoldi

THIS SPECIES, WHICH IS CONSIDERABLY SHORTER from dorsal to anal fin than *P. altum* and more closely resembles *P. scalare*, is only rarely seen in the hobby. It is generally smaller all round than its two other relatives, and the body often carries rusty-reddish spots.

DISTRIBUTION: *Believed to be restricted to an area extending about 56 miles (90km) upriver from Manacapurú (Colombia)*

SIZE: *Around 6in (15cm)*

BEHAVIOR: *As for P. altum*

DIET: *As for P. altum*

AQUARIUM: *As for P. altum*

BREEDING: *No reports of aquarium breeding available*

ANGEL
SCALARE

Pterophyllum scalare

THIS IS, BY FAR, THE BEST KNOWN OF THE ANGEL species. It is also one of the most popular of all aquarium fish. It was first imported into Europe in 1909 and, since then, has been bred extensively in captivity, which has led to the development of numerous fin and color varieties. The vast majority of specimens available in shops come from this source, with wild-caught specimens catering primarily for the specialist market.

DISTRIBUTION: *Widely distributed in the Amazon basin, from Peru down to the mouth of the River Amazon at Belem. Also found in many tributaries and in northeast South America*

SIZE: *Around 6in (15cm); usually smaller, but occasionally larger*

BEHAVIOR: *Territorial, but not aggressive, though very small fish may be regarded as food*

DIET: *Wide range of foods accepted, but livefoods preferred; vegetable supplement recommended*

AQUARIUM: *As for P. altum, but temperature range: 75–82°F (24–28°C)*

BREEDING: *Easy. Eggs are usually laid on a vertical surface, e.g. on an Amazon Swordplant (Echinodorus sp.) and are protected, as are fry, by both parents. After hatching, the fry feed on body mucus ("milk") secreted by the parents*

OTHER *PSEUDOTROPHEUS* SPECIES

Owing to the debate surrounding the genus *Pseudotropheus*, with some species being variously transferred to *Maylandia*, *Metriaclima*, and *Tropheops*, it is difficult to state with any certainty how many *Pseudotropheus* species and/or morphs are currently available in the hobby, although they are certainly numerous. This situation is likely to remain somewhat "fluid" for several years at least. For a review of the main issues, along with the assignations of the various species and morphs to the different genera, readers are advised to consult specialist literature. *African Cichlids I, Malawi Mbuna* (see Bibliography) will prove particularly useful in this respect. Specialist cichlid societies and dealers are also valuable sources of up-to-date information.

Socolof. However, some writers believe that the species itself is not valid and that the specimens collected from the wild are crosses between an undescribed species from Mozambique that was introduced into the area where "socolofi" is now found and one or more of the resident species.

DISTRIBUTION: *Central eastern coast of Lake Malawi from Tumbi Point to Cobue; fish reported from elsewhere, e.g. Thumbi West Island in the extreme southwest of the lake, are likely to be the result of the introductions that give rise to the doubt regarding the validity of the species*

SIZE: *Aquarium specimens up to 4¾in (12cm); wild-caught fish usually smaller*

BEHAVIOR: *Territorial, but one of the more peaceful Mbunas*

DIET: *As for P. aurora*

AQUARIUM: *As for P. aurora*

BREEDING: *As for P. aurora*

ALTUM ANGEL
DEEP-FINNED, or LONG-FINNED, ANGEL

Pterophyllum altum

WHILE THE SCALARE (*PTEROPHYLLUM SCALARE*) has been known for well over 100 years,

the Altum was imported into Europe for the first time only in 1950. Despite its overall similarity to its better-known relative, the Altum is easily distinguished by its much deeper (taller) size, especially when its dorsal and anal fins are extended. A further difference is that while *P. scalare* breeds with great ease in aquaria, *P. altum* is extremely challenging in this respect.

DISTRIBUTION: *Central Rio Orinoco, partly in Colombia and partly in Venezuela*

SIZE: *Up to ca.10in (25cm) reported, but usually smaller*

BEHAVIOR: *Territorial, but generally peaceful; will nevertheless consume very small fishes*

DIET: *A wide selection of foods accepted, but livefoods preferred; vegetable supplement recommended*

AQUARIUM: *Deep, with tall plants and non-calcareous rock decorations or, preferably, bogwood; subdued lighting advisable. Excellent water quality essential, but filtration should not cause excessive turbulence. Soft, acid water important. Temperature range: 75–84°F (24–29°C)*

BREEDING: *Challenging and only occasionally achieved in aquaria. Eggs are usually laid on a vertical service, e.g. on Amazon Swordplant (Echinodorus sp.), and both they and the fry are cared for by the pair*

◀ ALTUM ANGEL (PTEROPHYLLUM ALTUM)
▲ HALF-BLACK ANGEL (PTEROPHYLLUM SCALARE VAR.)

ALBINO GOLDEN DIAMOND ANGEL
(PTEROPHYLLUM SCALARE VAR.) ▶
▼ BLUE BLUSHING ANGEL (PTEROPHYLLUM SCALARE VAR.)

OTHER *PTEROPHYLLUM* "SPECIES"

The genus *Pterophyllum* is in great need of revision. For example, there is a distinct possibility that, being so widely distributed, the fish currently referred to as *Pterophyllum scalare* may consist of more than one species. It is also possible that there may be one or more species of *Pterophyllum* awaiting description (for example, I have collected large red-finned angels from a lake off the Río Cuiuni, itself a tributary of the Río Negro, which might, or might not, be *P. scalare*). The Sheepshead Angel, referred to as *P. dumerilii*, may also constitute a separate, as-yet undescribed species (the name *P. dumerilii* is regarded as a synonym of *P. scalare*). The so-called Peru Altum (a totally different fish from *P. altum*) is also currently believed to be *P. scalare*, but—as there is some doubt about this—it is being referred to as *P.* cf. *scalare*, while the Red-spotted Angel from Peru is, at present, being regarded as *P. scalare*. The same goes for the angel quoted as *P. eimekei*.

THREE-SPOT GEOPHAGUS (SATANOPERCA DAEMON)

SPARKLING GEOPHAGUS
FOUR-SPOT GEOPHAGUS

Satanoperca acuticeps

SYNONYM: *Geophagus acuticeps*

BOTH COMMON NAMES APPLY EQUALLY WELL TO this species, although the intensity of the body spots varies according to mood. The two main drawbacks of this otherwise desirable species are its burrowing/digging activities and relatively large size. However, if these can be catered for, this is an attractive species that is well worth keeping.

DISTRIBUTION: *Amazon basin*

SIZE: *Up to 10in (25cm) reported, but usually smaller*

OTHER *SATANOPERCA* SPECIES

Several other *Satanoperca* species are available from time to time. Some of these are still awaiting scientific description, while others may be naturally occurring morphs of already-described species. All require the same general conditions to the featured species. In the list that follows, one species is a substrate spawner (SS); the others are all delayed mouthbrooders (DMB).

SCIENTIFIC NAME	COMMON NAME	SIZE	BREEDING
S. sp. *jurupari*	—	8¾in (22cm)	DMB
S. leucosticta	"Jurupari"	10in (25cm)	DMB
S. sp. *leucostica*	Meta Satanoperca	10in (25cm)	DMB
S. sp. *leucostitca*	Pearl Satanoperca	8in (20cm)	DMB
S. lilith	One-spot Geophagus	10in (25cm)	SS
S. mapiritensis	Orinoco Geophagus	10in (25cm)	DMB
S. pappaterra	Pantanal Geophagus	8in (20cm)	DMB
S. sp. "Redlip"	Redlip Geophagus	8in (20cm)	DMB

BEHAVIOR: *Generally tolerant of other fish, despite its size. Constantly digs, so plants need protection*

DIET: *Wide range of foods accepted*

AQUARIUM: *Large, with adequate shelter and fine substratum. Protect plants (see Aquarium Plants) and use only robust types. Water chemistry not critical, but well-filtered, soft to medium-hard, slightly acid to neutral water recommended. Temperature range: 72–79°F (22–26°C)*

BREEDING: *Rare in aquaria. Scant details indicate spawning in the open with both parents guarding eggs and fry*

THREE-SPOT GEOPHAGUS
THREE-SPOT EARTHEATER or THREE-SPOT DEMONFISH

Satanoperca daemon

SYNONYM: *Geophagus daemon*

THIS IS A CHALLENGING SPECIES TO REAR FROM young, and even more challenging to breed. As in other members of the genus, the sexes are difficult to tell apart. The male is slightly slimmer and the genital papilla (a tiny projection from the genital aperture during breeding) is pointed, whereas, in the female, it is rounded.

DISTRIBUTION: *Rio Negro (Brazil), Orinoco (Venezuela), and extending into Colombia*

SIZE: *Around 10in (25cm) or even slightly larger*

BEHAVIOR: *As for P. acuticeps*

DIET: *As for P. acuticeps*

AQUARIUM: *As for P. acuticeps*

BREEDING: *Very rare in aquaria; believed to be a substrate spawner*

DEMONFISH

Satanoperca jurupari

SYNONYM: *Geophagus jurupari*

THIS IS THE MOST WIDELY AVAILABLE SPECIES IN the genus. One of the reasons may be its interesting breeding habits (*see* below). Although it lacks the distinct body spots of the two previous species, *S. jurupari* makes up for it with its beautifully reflective scales.

DISTRIBUTION: *Brazil and Guyana*

SIZE: *Around 10in (25cm)*

BEHAVIOR: *Perhaps the most peaceful in the genus, except during breeding; active burrower*

DIET: *As for S. acuticeps*

AQUARIUM: *As for S. acuticeps*

BREEDING: *A "delayed mouthbrooder," the eggs being picked up by the female about one day*

much less pronounced than in males. Like *Spathodus* (*see* separate entry), *Steatocranus* is a bottom dweller with limited swimming ability.

DISTRIBUTION: *Lower and central Democratic Republic of Congo (Zaire)*

SIZE: *Fully mature males reported up to 6½in (16.5cm), but usually much smaller; females smaller*

BEHAVIOR: *Intolerant, particularly of its own kind and other bottom dwellers. Pairs form very strong bond that may last for life*

DIET: *Most foods accepted, particularly sinking types*

AQUARIUM: *Numerous caves and other shelters, but with no sharp edges (the species' tends to rest on rocks or "hop" between them). Well-filtered, slightly acid to neutral, medium-hard water recommended. Temperature range: 75–82°F (24–28°C)*

BREEDING: *Eggs are laid in caves, and they and the fry are guarded by both parents*

AFRICAN BLOCKHEAD (STEATOCRANUS CASUARIUS)

after laying. From then on, mouthbrooding duties may be shared by both parents

AHLI
HAPLOCHROMIS ELECTRIC BLUE or POWDER BLUE HAP
Sciaenochromis fryeri

SYNONYMS: *Haplochromis ahli, Sciaenochromis ahli*

THE ELECTRIC-BLUE COLORATION OF MALES OF THIS species can take up to one year to develop. Juveniles therefore give little indication of the splendor that they will exhibit as adults.

DISTRIBUTION: *Throughout Lake Malawi*

SIZE: *Males reported up to 7in (18cm), but usually smaller; females slightly smaller*

BEHAVIOR: *A predator. Territorial, particularly at breeding time. Males aggressive toward each other and generally intolerant of similarly colored species*

DIET: *Prefers livefoods*

AQUARIUM: *Typical African Rift Lake layout (see Aquarium Set-up). Well-filtered, medium-hard, alkaline water important. Temperature range: 73–81°F (23–27°C)*

BREEDING: *Males court females vigorously, and may injure them in the confines of an aquarium. Females brood eggs orally*

GOBY CICHLID
Spathodus erythrodon

AS ITS COMMON NAME INDICATES, THIS SPECIES looks and behaves more like a goby than a cichlid. It is therefore not a fluent swimmer, spending much of its time on or near the bottom, swimming in short spurts. A second Goby Cichlid (*S. marlieri*) that is slightly larger and considerably more aggressive than *S. erythrodon*, but also much more plainly colored, is also available.

DISTRIBUTION: *Northern half of Lake Tanganyika*

SIZE: *Around 3in (8cm)*

BEHAVIOR: *Relatively tolerant of other species, but less so of its own*

DIET: *Wide range of foods accepted, but livefoods preferred; vegetable supplement recommended*

AQUARIUM: *African Rift Lake layout (see Aquarium Set-up) with numerous shelters and sandy areas Well-filtered, well-oxygenated, medium-hard, alkaline water important. Temperature range: 73–81°F (23–27°C)*

BREEDING: *Eggs and fry initially brooded orally by female for 10–12 days, after which male takes over for similar period*

AFRICAN BLOCKHEAD
AFRICAN BUMPHEAD, AFRICAN LUMPHEAD, or AFRICAN BUFFALOHEAD
Steatocranus casuarius

SYNONYM: *Steatocranus elongatus*

ALL THE COMMON NAMES OF THIS SPECIES—WHICH is the only *Steatocranus* frequently seen in the hobby—accurately describe the head shape of fully mature males. Females also possess the nuchal (head) hump, but it is

GREEN DISCUS AND BLUE DISCUS
Symphysodon aequifasciatus

SYNONYM: *Symphysodon aequifasciata*

TRADITIONALLY, *S. AEQUIFASCIATUS* HAS BEEN subdivided into three subspecies: *S. a. aequifasciatus* (Green Discus), *S. a. axelrodi* (Brown Discus), and *S. a. haraldi* (Blue Discus). This division still applies in most aquarium literature. However, Swedish ichthyologist, Sven Kullander concluded, in 1986, that there was no significant difference between *S. a. axelrodi* and *S. a. haraldi*, and that they should therefore be regarded as one and the same.

At the moment, though, no name has been given to this expanded subspecies. Accordingly, *S. aequifasciatus* is being regarded by many as a species consisting of two subspecies: *S. aequifasciatus aequifasciatus* (the Green Discus), and *S. aequifasciatus* ssp. (the Brown and the Blue Discus).

Captive breeding over many years, including countless crosses between the numerous naturally occurring forms of *S. aequifasciatus*, as well as between them and the cultivated types that have been developed, has resulted in a vast array of Discus varieties. Further, the pace of development is still as fast as ever, particularly in the Far East, where several new varieties are created every year.

DISTRIBUTION: *Widely distributed in tributaries of the Amazon basin*

SIZE: *Generally reported up to 6in (15cm), but many cultivated varieties can exceed this*

BEHAVIOR: *Territorial during breeding, but sedate and generally peaceful at other times*

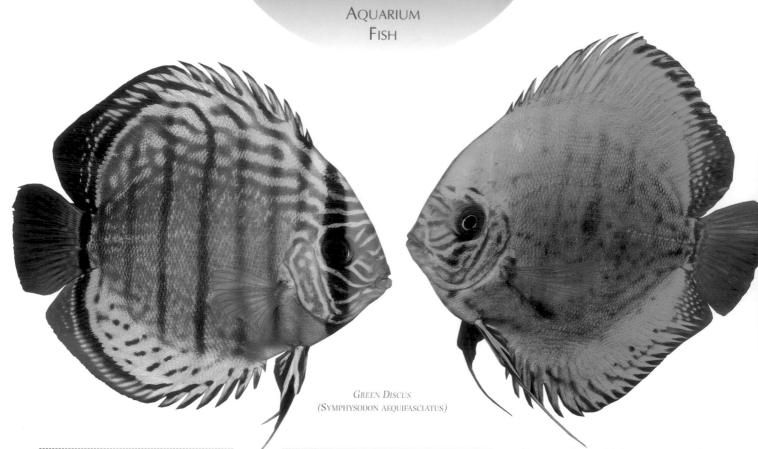

GREEN DISCUS
(SYMPHYSODON AEQUIFASCIATUS)

DIET: *Livefoods preferred, but deep-frozen, freeze-dried, and meat-based formulations, and some dry foods (e.g. flakes) accepted. Special, commercially produced Discus preparations are available*

AQUARIUM: *Large, thickly planted around sides and back, with open swimming area at front. Any rocks should be noncalcareous. Water soft and acid—preferably tannin-stained (bogwood will achieve this, as will a peat component in the filter and/or a proprietary "blackwater" preparation). Temperature range: 79–86°F (26–30°C); even slightly higher for breeding*

BREEDING: *Adhesive eggs are laid on precleaned site—usually vertical or nearly so: broadleaved plants, slates, tall rocks, special Discus-spawning earthenware cones, or even the aquarium panes. Both parents protect eggs, which take about two to three days to hatch. The fry subsequently feed for a time on body mucus ("Discus milk") secreted by parents. Some commercially produced Discus milk preparations are available.*

HECKEL DISCUS
POMPADOUR

Symphysodon discus

HECKEL DISCUS—WHATEVER THEIR PLACE OF origin and/or varying body coloration or patterning—can generally be easily distinguished from their *S. aequifasciatus* relatives by the central (fifth), vertical body band that extends from the base of the dorsal fin to the anal fin. In *S. discus*, this band is nearly always wider than the other bands and considerably more prominent, while, in *S. aequifasciatus*, all the body bands tend to be more-or-less equally wide and prominent. Some breeders have found the prominent band of *S. discus* "distracting," and as a result it has not been as widely bred or developed in captivity as has *S. aequifasciatus*.

HECKEL DISCUS
(SYMPHYSODON DISCUS)

A subspecies of the Heckel Discus, the so-called Pineapple Discus (*S. d. willischwartzi*) is sometimes cited. Most authorities, however, believe this fish to be a form of *S. discus* and not a valid subspecies.

DISTRIBUTION: *Rio Negro tributaries, Brazil*

SIZE: *Up to 8in (20cm)*

BEHAVIOR: *As for* S. aequifasciatus

DIET: *As for* S. aequifasciatus

AQUARIUM: *As for* S. aequifasciatus

BREEDING: *As for* S. aequifasciatus, *but successful spawning is more difficult to achieve in aquaria*

BLACK-STRIPED DWARF CICHLID
WEISE'S DWARF CICHLID
Taeniacara candidi

SYNONYM: *Apistogramma weisei*

THIS IS A SLIM-BODIED *APISTOGRAMMA*-LIKE species that is only occasionally seen within the hobby. It is the only representative of its genus. As in *Apistogramma*s, males are larger, have fin extensions, and are more brightly colored than the females. The black stripe is common to both sexes, but it varies in intensity according to the individual's mood.

DISTRIBUTION: *From Santarem, in the Rio Amazonas, upriver to Manaus, and on to the Rio Negro and its tributary, the Rio Branco*

SIZE: *Males up to 2¾in (7cm); females smaller*

BEHAVIOR: *Peaceful and generally retiring. Does best when single male kept with several females*

DIET: *Small livefoods preferred, but some commercial formulations accepted*

AQUARIUM: *Thickly planted, with numerous hiding places (caves) and pieces of bogwood. Subdued lighting and fine-grained substratum also recommended. Soft to medium-hard, acid to neutral water advisable. Frequent water changes also recommended, but these must be done gradually to avoid shock. Temperature range: around 79°F (26°C), slightly higher for breeding*

BREEDING: *Very soft, acidic water important. Eggs are laid on the roof of female's chosen cave. Eggs and brood care undertaken by female*

BRICHARD'S TELEO
Teleogramma brichardi

SYNONYM: *Telegramma brichardi*

THIS IS A VERY SLIM-BODIED SPECIES THAT PREFERS to stay close to the bottom of the aquarium. Despite their relatively modest size, pairs can command large territories in an aquarium.

DISTRIBUTION: *Lower reaches of the Zaire River*

SIZE: *Around 4¾in (12cm)*

BEHAVIOR: *Territorial and intolerant of its own kind*

DIET: *Wide range of foods accepted, but livefoods preferred*

AQUARIUM: *Spacious, with hiding places and caves; plants optional. Well-filtered, slightly acid to neutral, medium-hard water recommended. Temperature range: 68–77°F (20–25°C), the top end being suitable for breeding*

BREEDING: *Eggs are laid inside a cave and are cared for by female while male defends territory. Fry largely left to cater for themselves once they become free-swimming*

BRICHARD'S TELMAT
Telmatochromis brichardi

MEMBERS OF THIS GENUS ARE SUPERFICIALLY similar to the Julies (*Julidochromis, see* p.101)

with which they also share some of their breeding habits. Confusingly, *T. brichardi* is sometimes sold under the trade name of "Telmatochromis Bifrenatus," which is a closely related species—Two-banded Telmat (*T. bifrenatus*). This latter species is only rarely imported.

DISTRIBUTION: *Southern half of Lake Tanganyika and in the north, along the Burundi coast*

SIZE: *Around 2½in (6cm)*

BEHAVIOR: *Peaceful; does not require large aquaria*

DIET: *Range of commercial formulations accepted, but livefoods and deep-frozen diets preferred; vegetable component recommended*

AQUARIUM: *Typical African Rift Lake layout (see Aquarium Set-up). Medium-hard, alkaline water important. Temperature range: 75–79°F (24–26°C); slightly higher for breeding*

BREEDING: *Eggs are laid in a cave and guarded by female, while male largely defends territory. Fry protection is not intense*

OTHER *TELMATOCHROMIS* SPECIES

A few other members of this genus are available, some more frequently than others. Water requirements are as outlined for *T. brichardi*.

SCIENTIFIC NAME	COMMON NAME(S)	SIZE
T. burgeoni	Burgeon's Cichlid or Telmat	2¾in (7cm)
T. dhonti* (T. caninus)	Caninus Cichlid or Telmat	4¾in (12cm)
T. sp. "temporalis shell"**	Temporalis Telmat "Shell"	3in (8cm)
T. sp. "vittatus shell"**	Blunt-headed Telmat "Shell"	2¾in (7cm)
T. temporalis***	Temporalis Cichlid or Telmat	4in (10cm)
I. vittatus	Blunt-headed Cichlid or Telmat	4in (10cm)

NOTES:

*—this species is very aggressive
**—these fish require the provision of snail shells for breeding
***—this species may become very aggressive during breeding

TWO-BANDED TELMAT (TELMATOCHROMIS BIFRENATUS)

▲ PETEN CICHLID (THORICHTHYS AFFINIS)　　　▼ AUREUM GOLD CICHLID (THORICHTHYS AUREUS)

▼ FIREMOUTH (THORICHTHYS MEEKI)

PETEN CICHLID

PETEN THORICHTHYS

Thorichthys affinis

SYNONYM: *Herichthys affinis*

MUCH MORE RARELY SEEN THAN ITS CLOSE relative, the Firemouth (*T. meeki, see* below), the Peten Cichlid is well worth searching for. The golden chest of adult males, plus the pronounced black body spot and "sparkling" scales, make this a most attractive species indeed.

DISTRIBUTION: *Guatemala*

SIZE: *Males around 5½in (14cm); females smaller*

BEHAVIOR: *Territorial, particularly during breeding—but not overaggressive toward other similar-sized species*

DIET: *Wide range of foods accepted*

AQUARIUM: *Roomy, well planted, with ample shelter, open swimming area, and fine-grained substratum. A flat or rounded rock should be provided. Neutral or alkaline, medium-hard water recommended. Temperature range: 70–77°F (21–25°C); slightly higher for breeding*

BREEDING: *Eggs are laid on precleaned site, and both they and the fry are defended by the parents*

AUREUM CICHLID

GUATEMALA GOLD CICHLID

Thorichthys aureus

SYNONYM: *Herichthys aureus*

WHEN FULLY COLORED, MATURE MALES OF THIS species are, perhaps, the most beautiful of all *Thorichthys*, though they lack the brilliant red of *T. meeki*.

DISTRIBUTION: *Belize, Guatemala and Honduras*

SIZE: *Fully mature males over 6¼in (16cm); females smaller*

BEHAVIOR: *As for* T. affinis

DIET: *As for* T. affinis

AQUARIUM: *As for* T. affinis

BREEDING: *As for* T. affinis

FIREMOUTH

Thorichthys meeki

SYNONYM: *Herichthys meeki*

THE FIREMOUTH IS, BY FAR, THE BEST-KNOWN *Thorichthys* species in the hobby, having been first imported into Europe in 1937. The "fire" from which the common name derives is not restricted to the mouth, but extends to the throat, cheeks, and all along the lower area of the body, as far as the caudal fin, making this a most impressive species indeed.

OTHER *THORICHTHYS* SPECIES

A few other *Thorichthys* species are available in addition to the featured ones. They are all, basically, similar in body shape and requirements, but differ in coloration, particularly with regard to the chest/belly region in males. This is indicated in the accompanying list.

SCIENTIFIC NAME	COMMON NAME(S)	SIZE	CHEST/BELLY
T. callalepis	Malatengo Cichlid	6in (15cm)	Deep orange, with reddish tinge
T. ellioti	Elliot's Cichlid	6in (15cm)	Orange-red
T. helleri	Heller's Cichlid	6¼in (16cm)	Golden yellow, sometimes with a pinkish flush
T. pasionis	Passion Cichlid	7in (18cm)	Bright yellow, shading into orange
T. socolofi	Socolof's Cichlid	5½in (14cm)	Yellow, sometimes with a pinkish flush

ELLIOT'S CICHLID (THORICHTHYS ELLIOTI)

DISTRIBUTION: *Guatemala and Yucatán region in Mexico*

SIZE: *Males up to 6in (15cm); females smaller*

BEHAVIOR: *As for T. affinis*

DIET: *As for T. affinis*

AQUARIUM: *As for T. affinis*

BREEDING: *As for T. affinis*

ZEBRA TILAPIA

Tilapia buttikoferi

JUVENILE SPECIMENS OF THIS SPECIES LOOK stunning with their numerous vertical black and creamy white bands, especially when kept as a shoal. Unfortunately, this banding becomes considerably less distinct, and growth is rapid, with developing aggression keeping pace with body size. Eventually, this dictates that only one or two specimens can be kept in a spacious aquarium.

DISTRIBUTION: *West Africa, but introduced elsewhere as a food fish*

SIZE: *Up to 16in (40cm) reported*

BEHAVIOR: *Juveniles are relatively peaceful shoalers. Adults highly territorial and aggressive; may be kept only with similar-sized, robust tankmates*

DIET: *All substantial foods accepted*

AQUARIUM: *Spacious, with large shelters, open swimming space, and at least one large flat or smooth rock. Use only robust plants. Well-filtered water important, but water chemistry not critical. Temperature range: 72–77°F (22–25°C); slightly higher for breeding*

BREEDING: *Courtship may become violent. In such cases, spawning may be achieved by lowering a glass partition into the tank, leaving a gap along the bottom edge. The pair will then go through* the mating process physically separated from each other, with sperm passing through the gap and fertilizing the eggs. After this, male may be removed and female left to care for eggs and fry

FIVE-SPOT TILAPIA
TIGER TILAPIA

Tilapia mariae

AS IN *T. BUTTIKOFERI*, JUVENILE *T. MARIAE* ARE strikingly marked with vertical, dark and light bands; they also shoal. As they grow, though, the bands become reduced to blotches, which end up running as a horizontal line from behind the gill cover to the base of the caudal fin. Specimens also become progressively more aggressive as they mature.

DISTRIBUTION: *Benin, Cameroon, Ghana and Ivory Coast*

SIZE: *Up to 13¾in (35cm) reported*

BEHAVIOR: *As for T. buttikoferi*

DIET: *As for T. buttikoferi*

AQUARIUM: *Similar to T. buttikoferi, but use only unpalatable or artificial plants*

FIVE-SPOT TILAPIA (TILAPIA MARIAE)

BREEDING: *Eggs are laid on precleaned site and transferred to predug pits. Both parents guard eggs and fry*

ZILLI'S CICHLID

Tilapia zillii

MALES OF THIS SPECIES LOOK PARTICULARLY impressive when in breeding colors: then, they develop a deep-red flush on the chest and belly. Despite having been first imported into Europe as long ago as 1903, *T. zillii* is not frequently encountered in non-specialist aquatic shops.

DISTRIBUTION: *North Africa, extending eastward into Jordan and Syria*

SIZE: *Up to 12in (30cm)*

BEHAVIOR: *An aggressive, territorial burrower, with an appetite for succulent plants*

DIET: *As for T. buttikoferi and T. mariae*

AQUARIUM: *Similar to T. buttikoferi and T. mariae*

BREEDING: *Eggs are laid on precleaned site, and both they and the fry are cared for by the parents*

ELONGATUS MBUNA

SLENDER MBUNA

Tropheops elongatus

SYNONYM: *Pseudotropheus "elongatus"*

THERE ARE SO MANY DIFFERENT TYPES OF naturally occurring "elongatus" that it is difficult to identify any particular one as being the true "elongatus." Perhaps the specimens from around Mbamba Bay may eventually fill this niche. Similar "fluidity" applies to the generic name, with *Tropheops* becoming more widely accepted as a full genus (following the recommendation of Ethelwyn Trewavas back in 1984), rather than as a subgenus of *Pseudotropheus*. However, both names appear widely in aquarium literature.

DISTRIBUTION: *Probably Mbamba Bay in the Tanzanian section of Lake Malawi. Various "elongatus" occur elsewhere in the Lake*

SIZE: *Around 4¾in (12cm)*

BEHAVIOR: *Generally aggressive and territorial, but not always so*

DIET: *Wide range of foods accepted; vegetable component advisable*

AQUARIUM: *African Rift Lake layout (see Aquarium Set-up). Medium-hard, alkaline water important. Temperature range: 73–79°F (23–26°C)*

BREEDING: *Maternal mouthbrooder*

TROPHEOPS

Tropheops tropheops

SYNONYM: *Pseudotropheus tropheops*

THE NOMENCLATURE OF THIS SPECIES IS IN A similar state of ambiguity as described in the entry for *T. elongatus*. However, with more naturally occurring morphs of *T. tropheops* scattered throughout the Lake, the situation is even more complex.

DISTRIBUTION: *Probably centred around the southern area of Lake Malawi, e.g. Monkey Bay and Zimbabwe Rock. Various "tropheops" occur elsewhere in the Lake*

SIZE: *Around 5in (13cm)*

BEHAVIOR: *Aggressive and territorial*

DIET: *As for T. elongatus*

AQUARIUM: *As for T. elongatus*

BREEDING: *As for T. elongatus*

BLUE-EYED TROPHEUS

Tropheus brichardi

THIS VARIABLE SPECIES IS AVAILABLE UNDER A number of trade names, including Choco, Katonga, Green, Malagarasi and Kipili Moori, indicating that the Blue-eyed Tropheus is found in a range of color forms in the wild.

DISTRIBUTION: *Central coasts on both sides of Lake Tanganyika*

SIZE: *Around 5in (13cm)*

BEHAVIOR: *Not overaggressive or territorial, but males may harass females*

DIET: *Wide range of foods accepted; vegetable component recommended*

AQUARIUM: *African Rift Lake layout (see Aquarium Set-up), with sandy areas, and good illumination to encourage growth of encrusting green algae. Medium-hard, alkaline water important. Temperature range: 73–81°F (23–27°C)*

BREEDING: *Maternal mouthbrooder, with eggs being laid in the open and immediately picked up by female*

WHITE-SPOTTED CICHLID/DUBOISI

Tropheus duboisi

THE WHITE SPOTS REFERRED TO IN THE COMMON name of this popular species occur in juveniles, which carry the numerous spots on an almost-black background body color. Adults—which are very differently colored to the juveniles—occur in a number of color forms, a reflection of the discontinuous distribution of the species in its natural habitat.

DISTRIBUTION: *Discontinuous in the northern half of Lake Tanganyika*

SIZE: *Around 5in (13cm)*

BEHAVIOR: *Regarded as the most peaceful member of its genus, but can be territorial and sometimes aggressive toward rivals*

DIET: *As for T. brichardi*

AQUARIUM: *As for T. brichardi*

BREEDING: *As for T. brichardi*

MOORII

Tropheus moorii

THIS SPECIES IS VERY SIMILAR IN OVERALL BODY shape to *T. duboisi*. It is, however, even more variable and occurs in a different part of the Lake.

DISTRIBUTION: *Southern half of Lake Tanganyika*

SIZE: *Up to 6in (15cm) reported*

BEHAVIOR: *Similar to* T. duboisi, *but somewhat less peaceful*

DIET: *As for* T. brichardi

AQUARIUM: *As for* T. brichardi

BREEDING: *As for* T. brichardi

UARU CICHLID
WAROO, or TRIANGLE, CICHLID

Uaru amphiacanthoides

THE LAST OF THE COMMON NAMES DERIVES FROM the shape of this species' body patch, which is dark and roughly triangular, with the triangle's apex pointing toward the tail. The sharpness of the shape, as well as its "triangularity," varies between individuals. In its native waters, the Uaru is generally regarded as a food fish. Juveniles look quite different than adults, exhibiting numerous, light body spots.

DISTRIBUTION: *Northern Amazon and Guyana*

SIZE: *Up to 12in (30cm), but usually smaller*

BEHAVIOR: *Quite peaceful despite its size; likes to shoal*

DIET: *Some commercial dry foods accepted, but prefers livefoods and deep-frozen or freeze-dried diets; juveniles welcome a vegetable component*

AQUARIUM: *Roomy, with ample cover around sides and back, and with large, open swimming area at front, subdued lighting, and large shelters, e.g. bogwood. Use only robust aquarium plants. Soft, acid, tannin-stained water (bogwood, peat filtration, or commercial "blackwater" preparation will achieve this) recommended. Temperature range: 77–82°F (25–28°C); even slightly higher for breeding*

BREEDING: *Challenging to achieve in aquaria. Eggs are laid on precleaned site and are protected, as are the fry, by both parents. Both produce "body milk" (as in discus, angels and pike cichlids) on which the fry feed during their early stages of development*

HARTWEG'S CICHLID
TAIL-BAR CICHLID
Vieja hartwegi

SYNONYMS: *Cichlasoma hartwegi, Herichthys hartwegi*

LIKE SOME OF ITS CLOSER RELATIVES, *V. HARTWE-GI* is a species that becomes progressively more beautiful as it grows. The drawback is that, owing to its eventual large size, it is quite unsuitable for most home aquaria.

WHITE-SPOTTED CICHLID/DUBOISI (TROPHEUS DUBOISI)

UARU CICHLID (UARU AMPHIACANTHOIDES)

Distribution: *Southern Mexico and Guatemala*

SIZE: *Fully mature males around 11in (28cm); females smaller*

BEHAVIOR: *Not overaggressive given its territorial instincts and large size. Shows a distinct liking for succulent vegetation*

DIET: *Wide range of large aquarium foods accepted; vegetable component recommended*

AQUARIUM: *Large, with sizable shelters (caves, bogwood, etc.) and at least one flat or smooth rock. Well-filtered water important, but water chemistry not critical, as long as extremes are avoided. Use only unpalatable or artificial plants. Temperature range: 72–79°F (22–26°C)*

BREEDING: *Eggs are laid on precleaned site and are protected, as are the fry, by both parents*

BLACK-BELT CICHLID
Vieja maculicauda

SYNONYMS: *Cichlasoma maculicauda, Herichthys maculicauda, Heros maculicauda*

THE BLACK BELT IS AN OLD FAVORITE. IT IS EASILY distinguished by its prominent, vertical central-body band, from which the common name derives. This band runs from the center of the dorsal fin right down to the belly, although its breadth and sharpness vary from specimen to specimen and according to the individual's mood.

DISTRIBUTION: *Quite widely distributed in Central America*

SIZE: *Fully mature males reported up to 16in (40cm), but usually smaller; females smaller*

BEHAVIOR: *Similar to* V. hartwegi, *but may be more aggressive*

DIET: *As for* V. hartwegi

AQUARIUM: *As for* V. hartwegi

BREEDING: *As for* V. hartwegi

QUETZAL
FIREHEAD CICHLID

Vieja synspilum

SYNONYMS: *Cichlasoma synspilum, Herichthys synspilus, Heros synspilus, Paratheraps synspilum*

THIS IS A MULTICOLORED, LARGE CICHLID IN WHICH mature males develop a pronounced head (nuchal) hump; females possess a more modestly sized version. Spawning this species is not particularly difficult; obtaining a compatible pair is difficult. The usual advice given is to obtain about six juveniles and grow them on, allowing a natural pair to select themselves. Suitable alternative accommodations must, however, be found for the remaining unpaired fish as they are unlikely to be tolerated within the chosen pair's territory.

DISTRIBUTION: *Widely distributed in Central America*

SIZE: *Fully mature males up to 16in (40cm), but usually smaller; females smaller*

BEHAVIOR: *Relatively peaceful toward other similar-sized fish, but not its own kind. Territorial, particularly during breeding*

▲▲ BLACK-BELT CICHLID (VIEJA MACULICAUDA)
▲ QUETZAL (VIEJA SYNSPILUM)

DIET: *As for* V. hartwegi

AQUARIUM: *As for* V. hartwegi

Breeding: *As for* V. hartwegi

YELLOW-FINNED XENOTILAPIA

Xenotilapia flavipinnis

THIS SPECIES IS OFTEN AVAILABLE UNDER THE TRADE name Xenotilapia Boulengeri. Members of the genus prefer life close to the bottom, especially over sandy or muddy areas. They are active diggers, particularly at breeding time, and may be harassed by some of the more aggressive African Rift Lake Cichlid species.

DISTRIBUTION: *Throughout Lake Tanganyika*

OTHER *VIEJA* SPECIES

Vieja species appear under a variety of generic names in aquarium literature, the most frequently encountered ones being *Cichlasoma, Herichthys, Heros, Paratheraps*, and *Theraps*. Therefore, for specific details of the following list of the *Vieja* species that are available within the hobby, it is worth checking under the various generic names in specialist literature. All have similar characteristics and aquarium needs to the three featured species. The sizes given are for fully mature males.

SCIENTIFIC NAME	COMMON NAME(S)	SIZE
V. argentea	Silver Vieja	13¾in (35cm)
V. bifasciatus	Two-striped, or Red-spotted, Cichlid	13¾in (35cm)
V. breidohri	Breidohr's Cichlid	12in (30cm)
V. fenestratus	Window, or Mosaic, Cichlid	16in (40cm)
V. guttulatum	Red-tail, or Gold-cheeked, Theraps	16in (40cm)
V. heterospila	Marbled, or Black-flecked, Vieja	10in (25cm)
V. melanurus	Black-tailed Vieja, or Black-blotch, Cichlid	16in (40cm)
V. regani	Regan's Cichlid	13¾in (35cm)
V. tuyrensis	Tuyra, or Tuyre, Cichlid	13¾in (35cm)
V. zonatus	Belt, or Red-tailed, Cichlid	12in (30cm)

YELLOW-FINNED XENOTILAPIA (XENOTILAPIA FLAVIPINNIS)

SIZE: *Around 3½in (9cm)*

BEHAVIOR: *Peaceful, though males will defend spawning site; may be kept as a shoal in a roomy aquarium*

DIET: *Range of commercial diets, particularly sinking formulations, accepted, but livefood and deep-frozen/freeze-dried foods preferred*

AQUARIUM: *African Rift Lake layout (see Aquarium Set-up), with sandy areas. Well-filtered, well-oxygenated, medium-hard, alkaline water important. Temperature range: 73–81°F (23–27°C)*

BREEDING: *Mouthbrooding is shared by both parents, with female incubating eggs and fry for*

RED STRIPED XENOTILAPIA (XENOTILAPIA OCHROGENYS)

around nine days. Male then takes over mouthbrooding duties for a further five to six days. While the fry are in the open, both parents share protective duties

RED-STRIPED XENOTILAPIA

Xenotilapia ochrogenys

IN MOST SPECIMENS, THE "RED STRIPES" OF THE common name are varying shades of orange, rather than true red. They are nevertheless sufficiently striking to make this a very attractive member of the genus.

DISTRIBUTION: *Most of Lake Tanganyika except Cameron Bay*

SIZE: *Aquarium-reared males up to 6in (15cm), wild-caught ones smaller; females smaller than males*

BEHAVIOR: *As for X. flavipinnis*

OTHER *XENOTILAPIA* SPECIES

In addition to the two featured species, eight other *Xenotilapia* are available from time to time (although this figure is likely to increase with time). They are all generally peaceful and have similar requirements. Some are maternal mouthbrooders (MMB), while others are biparental mouthbrooders (B-PMB). This is indicated in the accompanying list. Sizes given are for wild-caught males; aquarium-reared specimens may be larger.

SCIENTIFIC NAME	COMMON NAME(S)	SIZE	BREEDING
X. bathyphilus	None	4¼in (11cm)	MMB
X. sp. "ochrogenys ndole"	None	4¾in (12cm)	MMB
X. ornatipinnis	None	5in (13cm)	MMB
X. papilio	None	4¼in (11cm)	B-PMB
X. sp. "papilio katete"	None	3in (8cm)	B-PMB
X. sp. "papilio sunflower"	Xenotilapia Chituta	3½in (9cm)	B-PMB
X. sima	Big-eyed Xenotilapia	6¾in (17cm)	MMB
X. spilopterus	Spot-finned Xenotilapia	4¾in (12cm)	B-PMB

DIET: *As for X. flavipinnis*

AQUARIUM: *As for X. flavipinnis, but groups should consist of one male and several females*

BREEDING: *Male digs a number of pits that he defends against rivals. Eggs are incubated orally by female*

CATFISHES

DESPITE THE DIVERSITY OF SIZE, BODY SHAPE AND habit that they exhibit, catfishes constitute one of the easiest groups of fish to identify since they all have the "whiskers" responsible for their group name. Yet, while barbels (as the whiskers are, more correctly, known) are a distinctive feature of catfishes, not all fish that possess barbels are catfish. Carp (*Cyprinus carpio*) and barbs (*Barbus* spp.) are just two of numerous examples of non-catfish species that possess barbels.

It is more a combination of features, rather than a single one, that identifies a species as a catfish. However, most of these features are skeletal and, as such, not directly observable in living specimens. Among these is the "Weberian apparatus," a remarkable bony structure that links the swimbladder with the inner ear.

The apparatus itself consists of small bones, or ossicles, which are able to transmit changes in the volume of the bladder to the inner ear. As this volume changes—as it does when, for example, it receives sound vibrations—it affects the internal pressure in the bladder which, in turn, sends information to the inner ear. The Weberian apparatus can therefore act as a means of accentuating sound waves, assisting catfish in picking up sound waves from their surrounding environment. This is particularly important for species that live in turbid water, which is often characteristic of many catfish habitats. Thus, by being able to combine the benefits rendered by the Weberian apparatus with the sensory information picked up via the barbels, many catfish can not only survive, but actually thrive, in low-visibility, silt-laden conditions that numerous other fish would find difficult or intolerable.

In some catfish, the swimbladder has an additional function: sound production. A structure known as the elastic spring mechanism can make the swimbladder vibrate and, thus, emit sounds. Some types of catfish use this, or alternative/additional sound-producing mechanisms to such an extent that they form one of the most distinctive features of such species, which are referred to in the hobby as talking, squeaking, or croaking catfishes, e.g. *Amblydoras hancocki*.

A further characteristic of many catfish is a two-spine locking mechanism on the dorsal fin. The first of these spines is sometimes so small as to be barely visible to the naked eye, but the second—irrespective of the size of the first one—is always prominent. When a catfish is disturbed, one of its instinctive reactions is to extend its dorsal fin, which causes the first spine to lock the second one into its upright position. This, combined with extended spines on other fins and the tough scales (scutes) or body armor that many species possess, acts as an effective defense strategy that makes many catfish difficult prey items for predators.

In a number of species, fin spines are not just physical defensive structures, but chemical (venomous) ones as well. In these species, it is the pectoral-fin spines that are (usually) particularly important. Generally speaking, catfish species that can inflict injury via their spines (some of which are serrated) are "passive stingers." In other words, they do not actively search out a victim but, rather, extend their protective spines if they are threatened, bitten (as by predators), picked up or stepped on. Careful handling of aquarium specimens is therefore absolutely essential.

In some of the madtoms (*Noturus* spp.)—generally regarded as passive stingers—toxicity produced by venomous glands adds to the dangers of being stung. Other species, including the Asian Stinging Catfish (*Heteropneustes fossilis*), are somewhat more aggressive and will actively seek out victims. The sting of such species is not just extremely painful, but may also have more serious consequences. Even more potent is the venom possessed by the marine catfish of the genus *Plotosus*, whose sting can be fatal. Most venomous species of catfish, such as the long-whiskered catfish or "pims" (family Pimelodidae) are only moderately potent, although they must nevertheless be treated with due respect.

Without doubt, it is the barbels that most people identify with catfish. Usually, there are four pairs of these sensory, whiskerlike structures: one on the head, one on the upper jaw, and two on the chin. Some types of catfish have reduced barbels; others may lack one or more pairs (but never all four).

As in characoids, most catfish possess an adipose fin, which, in some species, can be quite large, e.g. in the bagrids (family Bagridae) and the squeakers or upside-down catfishes (family Mochokidae). A notable exception is the family Siluridae, which includes the popular Glass Catfish (*Kryptopterus bicirrhis*).

In terms of size, catfishes probably vary more widely than any other major group of fish known to aquarists. At one extreme, there are giants like the Wels Catfish (*Silurus glanis*) which can frequently attain a length of about 10ft (3m)—and has reportedly been recorded at 16½ft (5m)—and the Giant or Mekong Catfish (*Pangasianodon gigas*), which can grow to over 6½ft (2m). At the other end of the scale, there are tiny species such as the Pygmy Catfish (*Corydoras pygmaeus*), which is fully mature at a mere 1½in (3.5cm).

According to Nelson (1994—*see* Bibliography), there are 34 families of catfish, together forming the order Siluriformes. More than 410 genera and 2,400 species are known. In the pages that follow, representatives of 19 families are featured:

Amphiliidae These are the African hillstream or loach catfishes, whose main, but few, aquarium representatives are from the genus *Phractura*.

Ariidae Although known as the sea catfishes, the Ariidae are represented in the freshwater

BANDED CORYDORAS (CORYDORAS BARBATUS)

hobby by the shark catfishes (*Arius jordani* and *A. seemani*).

Aspredinidae This family includes the famous and unusual banjo catfishes, such as *Bunocephalus* spp.

Auchenipteridae These are the driftwood catfishes, which include the Zamora or Midnight Catfish (*Auchenipterus thoracatus*).

Bagridae This family includes the large and popular Giraffe Catfish (*Auchenoglanis occidentalis*).

Callichthyidae In aquarium terms, the callichthyid armored catfishes represent what is, by far, the largest family, since it includes the numerous *Corydoras*, *Brochis* and related species.

Chacidae In sharp contrast, this family— known as the squarehead, angler or frog-mouth catfishes—is represented by a grand total of just three species, among which is the Frogmouth Catfish (*Chaca chaca*) itself.

Clariidae This family includes the air-breathing or walking catfishes, e.g. *Clarias* spp.

Doradidae The dorads or thorny catfishes have some very interesting aquarium representatives, including the Talking Catfish (*Amblydoras hancocki*).

Heteropneustidae The stinging or airsac catfishes are classified as the Saccobranchidae by some authors and include the potentially dangerous (venomous) species *Heteropneustes fossilis*.

Ictaluridae Relatively few ictalurids or North American freshwater catfishes are kept in aquaria; the Channel Catfish (*Ictalurus punctatus*) is among them.

Loricariidae These are the popular suckermouth armored catfishes such as the plecos (e.g. *Hypostomus*), the Stick or Twig Catfish (*Farlowella acus*) and the Bristle-nosed Catfish (*Ancistrus hoplogenys*).

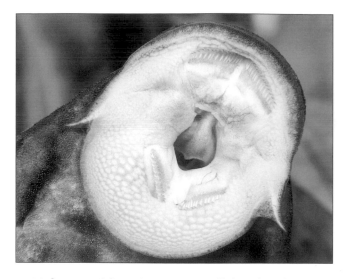

Pimelodidae These are the long-whiskered catfishes or pims, among which occur the popular *Pimelodus* species, as well as the Red-tailed Cat (*Phractocephalus hemioliopterus*) and the various shovelnoses (e.g. *Platystoma*, *Sorubim*, etc.).

Schilbeidae There are about 19 genera of schilbeid catfishes, but only a few are popular in the aquarium hobby, most notably the Striped Schilbe Catfish (*Schilbe mystus*).

Siluridae This family, known as the sheat-fishes or sheat catfishes, includes the "giants" referred to in the introductory text, as well as some interesting aquarium species such as the Glass Catfish (*Kryptopterus bicirrhis*).

Sisoridae Classified as the Bagariidae by some authors, these Asian hillstream or sisorid catfishes include some of the more recently introduced species to the hobby, such as the Butterfly Catfish (*Hara hara*) and the Clown Catfish (*Gagata cenia*).

Malapteruridae This very small family of electric catfishes includes the potentially dangerous species *Malapterurus electricus*.

Mochokidae The squeaking or upside-down catfishes include the members of the interesting genus *Synodontis* from Africa.

Pangasiidae These are shark catfish. Only one species, *Pangasius sutchi*, is popular within the hobby.

RED WHIPTAIL CATFISH
AFRICAN WHIPTAIL CATFISH

Phractura ansorgii
FAMILY: Amphiliidae

FEW AMPHILIIDAE (AFRICAN HILLSTREAM CAT-fishes) are ever found in aquaria. Their natural habitat is fast-flowing vegetated water, and this is reflected in their long, slim body shape.

DISTRIBUTION: *Nigeria and Congo*

SIZE: *Usually reported as around 2in (5cm), but occasionally larger*

BEHAVIOR: *Will spend much time resting on plants or aquarium decor*

DIET: *A range of foods accepted, including flakes and tablets*

AQUARIUM: *Well-planted, with some broadleaved species and pieces of bogwood recommended. Well-oxygenated water and a current (as produced by a power filter or powerhead) should*

RED WHIPTAIL CATFISH (PHRACTURA ANSORGII)

be provided. Water chemistry not critical, but extreme pH and hardness should be avoided. Temperature range: 72–77°F (22–25°C)

BREEDING: *No documented accounts currently available*

COLOMBIAN SHARK CATFISH

HIGH-FIN, BLACK-FIN, or SILVER, SHARK CATFISH

Arius jordani

FAMILY: Ariidae

THIS IS PREDOMINANTLY AN ESTUARINE SPECIES, but one that can adapt to freshwater conditions if the change is made gradually. Juveniles are more attractive than adults, which, owing to their relatively large size, are unsuitable for community aquaria.

DISTRIBUTION: *Coastal regions of (mainly) Colombia and Peru*

SIZE: *Around 13in (33cm)*

BEHAVIOR: *Not overaggressive, but will eat small fish*

DIET: *Wide range of foods accepted*

AQUARIUM: *Spacious, with ample swimming areas and water current. A small amount of sea salt (about 1 teaspoonful per gallon/4.5 liters) recommended. This can be reduced gradually over time, if desired. Water chemistry not critical. Temperature range: 72–82°F (22–28°C)*

BREEDING: *No documented accounts currently available. All members of the genus are believed to be mouthbrooders*

BANJO CATFISH

Bunocephalus hypsiurus

FAMILY: Aspredinidae
SUBFAMILY: Bunocephalinae

SPECIES OF THE GENUS *BUNOCEPHALUS* ARE generally so similar to each other that they can be difficult to differentiate from each other. In addition, some are now regarded as *Disichthys*, creating further confusion. Their main claim to fame is their unusual shape.

DISTRIBUTION: *Rio Branco (Brazil)*

SIZE: *Around 4in (10cm)*

BEHAVIOR: *A peaceful, sedentary species that spends most of the day resting on, or buried in, the substratum; becomes relatively active as night approaches*

DIET: *All sinking formulations, including bottom-dwelling livefoods, accepted*

AQUARIUM: *Numerous shelters (pieces of bogwood are ideal) and fine-grained substratum should be provided. Dry (as opposed to fresh), well-browned oak leaves—presoaked to allow them to sink—should cover at least past of the substratum (retailers may be able to supply some of the*

COLOMBIAN SHARK CATFISH (ARIUS JORDANI)

leaves that are usually placed in transportation bags by suppliers of these fish). Water chemistry not critical. Temperature range: 70–79°F (21–26°C)

BREEDING: *No documented accounts currently available*

BANJO CATFISH

FRYING PAN CATFISH

Disichthys coracoideus

SYNONYM: *Bunocephalus coracoideus*
FAMILY: Aspredinidae
SUBFAMILY: Bunocephalinae

THE OVERALL CONFUSION MENTIONED IN THE previous entry relating to the naming of *Bunocephalus* also applies to this species and its closest relatives.

DISTRIBUTION: *Amazon basin*

SIZE: *Up to 6in (15cm)*

BEHAVIOR: *As for* Bunocephalus hypsiurus

DIET: *As for* Bunocephalus hypsiurus

AQUARIUM: *As for* Bunocephalus hypsiurus

BREEDING: *Challenging in aquaria, with few reports available. Several thousand eggs are laid in a depression in the sandy substratum and guarded by male*

MIDNIGHT CATFISH

ZAMORA WOODCAT

Auchenipterichthys thoracatus

SYNONYMS: *Auchenipterus thoracatus, Zamora cunchi*
FAMILY: Auchenipteridae

THERE ARE ONLY TWO SPECIES IN THE GENUS *Auchenipterichthys*, with Midnight Catfish being the one seen more frequently in aquaria. It is able to produce a buzzing sound by rotating the pectoral-fin spines

BANJO CATFISH (BUNOCEPHALUS HYPSIURUS)

Midnight Catfish (Auchenipterichthys thoracatus)

in their sockets, this sound being amplified via the swimbladder (*see* introduction to catfishes).

DISTRIBUTION: *Upper Amazon*

SIZE: *Up to 5¼in (13.5cm)*

BEHAVIOR: *Nocturnal; not overaggressive, but predatory on small fishes*

DIET: *Livefoods preferred, but will accept other diets*

AQUARIUM: *Numerous shelters required as daytime hiding places. Water chemistry not critical, but extremes of pH and hardness should be avoided. Temperature range: 70–77°F (21–25°C)*

BREEDING: *Challenging in aquaria. Fertilization is internal and the sperm "plug" can remain potent for several months in, at least, some species of the family. Egg deposition can therefore occur some time after mating.*

SNOWFLAKE WOODCAT
DRIFTWOOD CATFISH
Tatia aulopygia

FAMILY: Auchenipteridae

THERE ARE SOME 14 SPECIES IN THIS GENUS, ALL of which are relatively small and easy to distinguish from each other. The Snowflake Woodcat is dark-bodied, with numerous small creamy-white flecks on its body (hence the "snowflake" part of the common name). In some mature specimens, which may be particularly dark, the "flakes" may almost disappear. The belly—in contrast— is white.

DISTRIBUTION: *Mainly Guaporé river, bordering Brazil*

SIZE: *Around 4in (10cm)*

BEHAVIOR: *Generally sedentary during the day*

DIET: *Livefoods preferred, but may accept other diets*

AQUARIUM: *Well-planted, with numerous shelters. The water should be well-oxygenated. Water chemistry not critical, but extremes should be avoided. Temperature range: 72–79°F (22–26°C)*

BREEDING: *No documented accounts currently available. In a closely related species, T. galaxias (Starry Woodcat), fertilization is internal, with the eggs being subsequently released by female and hatching taking three to four days at 72°F (22°C)*

GIRAFFE CATFISH
AFRICAN EYESPOT, or DUSKY VACUUM-MOUTHED CATFISH
Auchenoglanis occidentalis

FAMILY: Bagridae

THE GIRAFFE CATFISH—SO-CALLED BECAUSE OF the patchwork-like body patterning found in many specimens—was first imported into the hobby in 1909. Despite this long history, it has never been kept in large numbers, no doubt because of its large size. Modern aquarium technology and advances in husbandry techniques, however, bring the successful upkeep of this species within the reach of any aquarist who can provide adequate accommodations for this gentle giant.

DISTRIBUTION: *Widely distributed in tropical regions of Africa*

Giraffe Catfish (Auchenoglanis occidentalis)

SIZE: *Up to 24in (60cm)*

BEHAVIOR: *Peaceful despite its size*

DIET: *Wide range of chunky foods taken*

AQUARIUM: *Large, deep and efficiently filtered, with sandy substratum and large pieces of bogwood. Water chemistry not critical. Temperature range: 72–77°F (22–25°C)*

BREEDING: *No documented accounts currently available*

MOTTLED CATFISH
AFRICAN WOODCAT

Chrysichthys ornatus

FAMILY: Bagridae

WHILE THERE ARE AROUND 40 SPECIES IN THE genus *Chrysichthys*, few are ever seen in aquaria—*C. ornatus* being one of the exceptions. It is an attractively marked species with sharp dorsal- and pectoral-fin spines. Careful handling is therefore essential. It is ranked as one of the smaller members of the genus, with some of its larger relatives, such as *C. grandis*, attaining a size of ca6½ft (2m) and a weight of ca420lb (190kg).

OTHER *AUCHENOGLANIS* SPECIES

While *A. occidentalis** is the most popular species in the genus (which contains some 20 species), others are occasionally available. All, with one exception, are substantial fish requiring similar care as that described for *A. occidentalis*.

SCIENTIFIC NAME	COMMON NAME(S)	SIZE
A. biscutatus	Nile Vacuum-mouthed Catfish	25½in (65cm)
A. ngamensis	Ngami Vacuum-mouthed Catfish, Bigmouth Spiny Catfish	9¾in (25cm)
A. pantherinus	Panther Vacuum-mouthed Catfish	26¾in (68cm)
A. punctatus **	African Spotted Spiny Catfish	3in (8cm)

NOTES:

* At least three naturally occurring morphs of *A. occidentalis* are known: the dark, "basic" one, a lighter, well-marked type ("Variant A") and a second light-colored morph with less sharply demarcated patterning ("Barmoi").

** A species from Zimbabwe, referred to as *A. cf. punctatus*, but with the same common name—African Spotted Spiny Catfish—is reported to grow to 9¾in (25cm).

NGAMI VACUUM-MOUTHED CATFISH (AUCHENOGLANIS NGAMENSIS)

DISTRIBUTION: *Widely distributed in tropical regions of West Africa*

SIZE: *Up to ca8in (20cm)*

BEHAVIOR: *Lively; increasingly predatory on small fishes as full size is attained*

DIET: *Livefoods preferred; may be weaned on to chunky commercial preparations*

AQUARIUM: *Spacious, with suitable cover (bogwood or equivalent) recommended. Provide efficient filtration and protect any plants against uprooting (see Aquarium Plants). Water chemistry not critical. Temperature range: 68–79°F (20–26°C)*

BREEDING: *No documented accounts currently available.*

ASIAN BUMBLEBEE CATFISH
BARRED SIAMESE CATFISH

Leiocassis siamensis

FAMILY: Bagridae

THIS IS THE MOST POPULAR AND WIDELY AVAILABLE species in the genus. Its striking body patterning contrasts sharply with its white caudal fin, which bears two rather faint black blotches—one on each lobe.

DISTRIBUTION: *Widely distributed in Thailand, sometimes even occurring near estuaries and, hence, in brackish conditions*

SIZE: *Around 7in (18cm)*

ASIAN BUMBLEBEE CATFISH (LEIOCASSIS SIAMENSIS)

BEHAVIOR: *Largely nocturnal. Not excessively predatory, but may take small fishes; progressively intolerant of its own species*

DIET: *Livefoods preferred, but may become accustomed to deep-frozen, freeze-dried and other commercial preparations*

AQUARIUM: *Adequate bogwood or rock shelters and subdued lighting required. Efficient filtration recommended but water chemistry not critical. Temperature range: 72–77°F (22–25°C)*

BREEDING: *No documented accounts currently available.*

BAR-TAILED BAGRID
TWO-SPOT PINK BAGRID

Mystus micracanthus

FAMILY: Bagridae

BOTH COMMON NAMES APPLY EQUALLY WELL TO this attractive, modest-sized catfish. Owing to a golden anterior border, the black body spot, in particular, stands out beautifully against the pink body color.

DISTRIBUTION: *Borneo, Java, Sumatra and Thailand*

SIZE: *Around 6in (15cm)*

BEHAVIOR: *Does well with similar-sized tankmates, but may prey on small fish*

DIET: *Some commercial formulations accepted, but livefoods preferred*

AQUARIUM: *Spacious, well-filtered, with open swimming areas and hiding places. Water chemistry not critical. Temperature range: 68–79°F (20–26°C)*

BREEDING: *No documented accounts currently available*

BANDED MYSTUS
STRIPED CATFISH

Mystus vittatus

FAMILY: Bagridae

THIS SPECIES HAS A SIMILAR BODY COLOR TO *M. micracanthus* but this is overlaid with two distinct darker bands that run from behind a body spot (similar in color to that possessed by *M. micracanthus*, but smaller) to the base of the caudal fin. A fainter band is also discernible above the main one.

DISTRIBUTION: *Myanmar (Burma), India, Sri Lanka, Nepal, Malaysia and Thailand*

SIZE: *Around 8in (20cm)*

BEHAVIOR: *As for* M. micracanthus

DIET: *As for* M. micracanthus

AQUARIUM: *As for* M. micracanthus. *Temperature range: 72–82°F (22–28°C)*

BREEDING: *Although it is known that an active courtship, accompanied by "tweeting" noises, culminates in eggs being released among roots or plants, there are no known breeding successes in aquaria*

AFRICAN SPOTTED CATFISH

Parauchenoglanis macrostoma

FAMILY: Bagridae

ONE OF JUST FOUR SPECIES IN THE GENUS, THE African Spotted Catfish is the only one seen on a reasonably regular basis in specialist outlets. Owing to the fin-locking mechanisms in the dorsal and pectoral fins, this fish needs to be handled with care to avoid injury to both fish and aquarist.

DISTRIBUTION: *Niger delta*

SIZE: *Around 9¾in (25cm)*

BEHAVIOR: *A territorial loner, and crepuscular and nocturnal predator. It is also an active digger*

DIET: *Livefoods preferred, but wide range of other items also accepted*

AQUARIUM: *Large, with open areas, several shelters, subdued lighting, and efficient filtration. Plants should be protected against digging (see Aquarium Plants). Water chemistry not critical. Temperature range: 68–81°F (20–27°C)*

BREEDING: *No documented accounts currently available*

AMUR DRAGON CATFISH
TAWNY DRAGON CATFISH

Pelteobagrus fluvidraco

FAMILY: Bagridae

AS WITH THE OTHER BAGRID GENERA FEATURED, few *Pelteobagrus* species are encountered in the hobby. Though not frequently seen, this species is included here largely because of its low-temperature tolerance, which makes it one of the few catfish species that can be housed in coldwater aquaria. The species needs careful handling since its spines can inflict painful injuries.

DISTRIBUTION: *China, Siberia, and Amur River basin (Russia)*

SIZE: *Up to 13¾in (35cm) reported, but usually considerably smaller*

BEHAVIOR: *Not overly aggressive, but will prey on small, slow-moving tankmates*

DIET: *Livefoods preferred, but chunky commercial formulations also accepted*

BANDED MYSTUS (MYSTUS VITTATUS)

OTHER *MYSTUS* SPECIES

Although nearly 40 species of *Mystus* are known, few—other than those featured—are available with anything approaching regularity. The following four are among the most frequently encountered.

SCIENTIFIC NAME	COMMON NAME(S)	SIZE
M. montanus	Mountain Asian Bagrid	8¾in (22cm)
M. nemurus	Asian Red-tailed Bagrid	24in (60cm)
M. tengara	None	7in (18cm)
M. wyckii	None	28in (70cm)

◄ MYSTUS TENGARA

AQUARIUM: *Large, unheated, with open areas and hiding places. Water well-filtered, but water chemistry not critical. Temperature range: from around 50–75°F (10°–24°C)*

BREEDING: *Eggs are laid in shallow nest excavated in substratum and guarded by male. Hatching takes about two days*

DWARF ORNATE BAGRID

Pelteobagrus ornatus

FAMILY: Bagridae

IN SHARP CONTRAST TO *P. FLUVIDRACO* (SEE previous entry), the Dwarf Ornate Bagrid is—as its name indicates—a small fish. It is also much more tropical in its requirements and very different from its much larger relative in terms of demeanor and breeding habits.

DISTRIBUTION: *Indonesia and Malaysia*

SIZE: *Around 1½in (4cm)*

BEHAVIOR: *Can be kept with other similar-sized (i.e. small) fish, including other members of its species*

DIET: *Livefoods preferred, but some commercial formulations accepted*

AQUARIUM: *Well-planted. Water chemistry not critical, but extremes of pH and hardness should be avoided. Temperature range: 72–77°F (22–25°C)*

BREEDING: *Eggs are deposited among fine-leaved vegetation such as Java Moss (Vesicularia dubyana)*

FALSE CORYDORAS

BLOTCH-FIN ASPIDORAS

Aspidoras pauciradiatus

SYNONYM: *Corydoras pauciradiatus*
FAMILY: Callichthyidae
SUBFAMILY: Corydoradinae

BOTH THE FIRST COMMON NAME AND THE synonym for this species indicate just how closely *Aspidoras* and *Corydoras* catfish are related to each other. The main distinguishing skeletal feature between the two—but one that cannot be observed in living specimens—is the number of cranial fontanels (skull pores, openings or "holes"): *Aspidoras* has two, while *Corydoras* (and *Brochis*) have one. The False Corydoras is a delightful species, liberally speckled in black and with a distinctive black blotch on the dorsal fin.

DISTRIBUTION: *Mainly Araguaia River (Brazil), but also reported from the Rio Negro*

SIZE: *Up to 1½in (4cm) reported, but usually no larger than 1¼in (3cm)*

BEHAVIOR: *A (sometimes) retiring shoaler that should not be kept with boisterous tankmates*

DIET: *Wide range of foods accepted*

AQUARIUM: *Well-planted, with numerous shelters and fine-grained substratum. Avoid excessive water turbulence but use efficient filtration and well-oxygenated water. Slightly acid to neutral, softish water preferred. Temperature range: 72–79°F (22–26°C)*

BREEDING: *No documented accounts currently available*

FALSE CORYDORAS (ASPIDORAS PAUCIRADIATUS)

GIANT BROCHIS

BRITSKI'S CATFISH

Brochis britskii

FAMILY: Callichthyidae
SUBFAMILY: Corydoradinae

BROCHIS ARE VERY SIMILAR, OVERALL, TO *Corydoras* species. However, they can be easily distinguished by their much higher

OTHER *ASPIDORAS* SPECIES

Aspidoras species are much less widely available than their better-known relatives *Brochis* and *Corydoras*. Nevertheless, some species are being more frequently imported than they were in the past. All require the same basic aquarium conditions outlined for *A. pauciradiatus*.

SCIENTIFIC NAME	COMMON NAME(S)	SIZE
A. albater	–	1½in (4cm)
A. fuscoguttatus	Spotted Aspidoras	1¼in (3.5cm)
A. lakoi	Spot-line Aspidoras	1½in (4cm)
A. maculosus	Rio Paiaia Aspidoras	2in (5cm)
A. menezesi	–	2in (5cm)

SPOT-LINE ASPIDORAS (ASPIDORAS LAKOI) ▼

NOTE:

In addition to the above, there are several species over which there is some doubt regarding their identity, e.g. *A.* cf. *eurycephalus* (1¼in/3.5cm), *A.* cf. *poecilus* (1½in/4cm), or which have not yet been officially described, e.g. *A.* sp. "Black Phantom" (1¾in/4.5cm).

number of dorsal-fin rays. *Brochis* have 11 or more rays (Giant Brochis possesses 15–18), while, in *Corydoras*, the number rarely exceeds seven. The Giant Brochis is a relatively new addition to the hobby, first making its appearance in significant numbers during the last decade and a half of the 20th century.

DISTRIBUTION: *Mainly Mato Grosso, Brazil*

SIZE: *Up to 5in (13cm) reported, but usually a little smaller*

BEHAVIOR: *Peaceful shoaler that, despite its size, can be kept with small tankmates*

DIET: *Wide range of foods accepted*

AQUARIUM: *Roomy, well-planted, with open areas, as well as hiding places. Substratum fine-grained, with no sharp edges on which the fish could damage their mouths and/or barbels. Water chemistry not critical, but quality must be good. Temperature range: 72–77°F (22–25°C)*

BREEDING: *No documented accounts currently available, but probably as for* Corydoras

HOG-NOSED BROCHIS
LONG-FINNED BROCHIS
Brochis multiradiatus

FAMILY: Callichthyidae
SUBFAMILY: Corydoradinae

AS ITS SCIENTIFIC NAME IMPLIES, HOG-NOSED Brochis has many dorsal-fin rays (around 17). Although it is slightly outdone in this department by *B. britskii* (*see* previous entry), the latter had not yet been discovered when Hog-nosed Brochis was first described. Both species are similar-looking

overall, but this one lacks the bony plate that covers the underside of the head in its close relative. It also possesses a much longer snout and is a little smaller.

DISTRIBUTION: *Madeira River region (Brazil); Rio Lagarto/Upper Napo (Ecuador), and Ucayali and Nanay (Peru)*

SIZE: *Up to 4in (10cm)*

BEHAVIOR: *As for* B. britskii

DIET: *As for* B. britskii

AQUARIUM: *As for* B. britskii

BREEDING: *As for* B. britskii

COMMON BROCHIS
EMERALD, SHORT-BODIED or SAIL-FIN, BROCHIS/CORYDORAS/CATFISH
Brochis splendens

SYNONYM: *Brochis coeruleus*
FAMILY: Callichthyidae
SUBFAMILY: Corydoradinae

OF ALL ITS COMMON NAMES, THE ONE THAT FITS this species best is Emerald Brochis. It is a truly beautiful species, which can be found in, at least, two (named) naturally occurring color forms—spotted and

▲ HOG-NOSED BROCHIS (BROCHIS MULTIRADIATUS)
◄ COMMON BROCHIS (BROCHIS SPLENDENS)

black—in addition to the more usual emerald one. Of the three *Brochis* species, this is the one that has been in the hobby longest, having first been imported in the late 1930s.

DISTRIBUTION: *Brazil, Ecuador and Peru*

SIZE: *Up to 3in (8cm)*

BEHAVIOR: *As for* B. britskii

DIET: *As for* B. britskii

AQUARIUM: *As for* B. britskii. *Temperature range: 70–82°F (21–28°C)*

BREEDING: *Challenging in aquaria. Eggs are deposited on the underside of broadleaved plants (egg deposition among floating plants has also been reported). No parental care is exhibited, and hatching takes about four days*

ARMORED CATFISH

Callichthys callichthys

FAMILY: Callichthyidae
SUBFAMILY: Callichthyinae

THE FEATURE THAT BEST DISTINGUISHES THIS subfamily from that containing *Corydoras* and its relatives (Corydoradinae) is the snout. In the Callichthyinae, it is depressed, i.e. "flattened" to a certain extent, while in the Corydoradinae it is considerably more rounded. The Armored Catfish—after which the family was named—has been known in the hobby for over a century, having first been imported into Europe in 1897.

DISTRIBUTION: *Widely distributed in tropical regions of South America*

SIZE: *Up to 8in (20cm) reported, but usually smaller*

BEHAVIOR: *Relatively inactive during daylight hours. May consume very small tankmates, but generally peaceful. Surfaces periodically to gulp in air, which it passes down into its hindgut, where oxygen is absorbed into the bloodstream*

DIET: *Wide range of chunky foods accepted, particularly sinking formulations like granules and tablets. Food should be administered during the evening, i.e. shortly before tank lights are switched off*

AQUARIUM: *Thickly planted, with numerous shelters. Water chemistry not critical. Temperature range: 64–82°F (18–28°C)*

BREEDING: *A cover of floating plants must be provided. The male will build a nest of mucus-covered bubbles among the floating plants. Spawning takes place beneath this raft and the eggs are deposited among the bubbles. The male will then vigorously defend the nest against all comers*

BRONZE CORYDORAS

BRONZE CATFISH

Corydoras aeneus

FAMILY: Callichthyidae
SUBFAMILY: Corydoradinae

CORYDORAS SPECIES ARE, BY FAR, THE MOST popular of all the catfish kept in aquaria, and justifiably so. Most are hardy, adaptable, peaceful shoalers, and they have a habit that humans find particularly appealing: they "wink" at their owners. In reality, of course, they don't wink at all; rather, it is an effect created when a fish rotates its eyes quickly—as *Corydoras* species can do. As the eye is rotated downward, the pupil and iris disappear briefly from view, with the surrounding reflective tissues becoming momentarily visible. As the eye rotates back into its more normal orientation, the illusion of a wink is created. Of all the *Corydoras* species, Bronze Corydoras is the best known and still one of the most popular. Several naturally occurring color forms are known, e.g. Belem, Peru Gold Shoulder Red, Gold Shoulder Green, Peru Green Stripe, Peru Gold Stripe and even Aeneus Black. In addition, a cultivated albino form is regularly available.

DISTRIBUTION: *Bolivia, Brazil, Colombia, Ecuador, Peru, Suriname, Trinidad and Venezuela*

SIZE: *Around 2¾in (7cm); occasionally a little larger*

BEHAVIOR: *Peaceful shoaler that looks impressive in a group*

DIET: *Wide range of foods accepted, particularly bottom-dwelling livefoods and sinking commercial formulations*

AQUARIUM: *Well-planted, with open swimming areas, and fine-grained substratum. Water*

BRONZE CORYDORAS (CORYDORAS AENEUS)

Juvenile Arched Corydoras (Corydoras arcuatus)

chemistry not critical, but excessively acid conditions (which are said to cause damage to the barbels) must be avoided. Temperature range: 64–79°F (18–26°C), but exposure to lower temperatures should not be prolonged

BREEDING: *Best results are often obtained after a water change and using a trio consisting of a single female and two males. The critical stage in the spawning process is characterized by the so-called "T-position" in which the female aligns her body at right angles to the chosen male and will nuzzle his vent. When in this position, the male will clasp the female's barbels with his pectoral fin spine, thus holding her at the appropriate angle. Sperm are released at this point and are actually swallowed by the female. These then pass rapidly and undamaged through the female's gut and are released onto the female's cupped pelvic fins into which she has previously released a few eggs. The female will subsequently deposit these adhesive eggs on a surface, e.g. broad leaf, rocks or even an aquarium pane, where they will hatch some five or six days later, depending on temperature*

ARCHED CORYDORAS
SKUNK CORYDORAS
Corydoras arcuatus

FAMILY: Callichthyidae
SUBFAMILY: Corydoradinae

THIS IS A PREDOMINANTLY PINK-BODIED SPECIES with an elegant black "arch" extending from the snout, backward and upward through the eye, to the front of the dorsal fin and then along the back (but just below the top edge), all the way to the lower edge of the caudal fin base. The Arched Corydoras is one of several similarly patterned species which can easily be confused with each other.

DISTRIBUTION: *Brazil, Ecuador and Peru*

SIZE: *Up to 3in (8cm) reported for the 'Super Arcuatus' morph, but usually around 2in (5cm)*

BEHAVIOR: *As for C. aeneus*

DIET: *As for C. aeneus*

AQUARIUM: *As for C. aeneus. Temperature range: 72–79°F (22–26°C)*

BREEDING: *As for C. aeneus*

BANDED CORYDORAS
FILIGREE CORY or BARBATUS CATFISH
Corydoras barbatus

FAMILY: Callichthyidae
SUBFAMILY: Corydoradinae

THIS—THE LARGEST OF THE CORYDORAS—IS A slender-looking species (*see* photo p.129) often found in flowing waters in its natural habitat. It is a very distinctly marked corydoras which, despite its relatively restricted geographical distribution, occurs in at least two forms, the one from around Rio being darker and containing more yellow in the body pattern.

DISTRIBUTION: *Regions around Rio de Janeiro and São Paulo, Brazil*

SIZE: *Up to 5in (13cm) reported, but usually considerably smaller*

BEHAVIOR: *As for C. aeneus*

DIET: *As for C. aeneus*

AQUARIUM: *As for C. aeneus. Temperature range: 68–77°F (20–25°C). Water chemistry should be slightly on the acid side*

BREEDING: *Basically, as for C. aeneus. Aquarium breeding is somewhat more challenging and less frequently achieved than in C. aeneus*

DELPHAX CORYDORAS
FALSE BLOCHI CATFISH
Corydoras delphax

FAMILY: Callichthyidae
SUBFAMILY: Corydoradinae

THIS IS A BOLDLY SPOTTED SPECIES WITH A BLACK blotch in the anterior half of the dorsal fin and another over and above the eye. The space between these black areas—known as the "saddle"—is light in color, but variably so, ranging from golden to pinkish hues.

DISTRIBUTION: *Mainly Inírida river system (Colombia)*

SIZE: *Up to 3in (7.5cm) reported, but usually smaller*

BEHAVIOR: *As for C. aeneus*

DIET: *As for C. aeneus*

AQUARIUM: *As for C. aeneus. Temperature range: 70–79°F (21–26°C)*

BREEDING: *As for C. aeneus*

ELEGANT CORYDORAS
Corydoras elegans

FAMILY: Callichthyidae
SUBFAMILY: Corydoradinae

WHILE UNDOUBTEDLY A BEAUTIFUL SPECIES, THE claim made by this species' common name seems somewhat excessive since there are numerous *Corydoras* species that could embody the label of "elegant" every bit as well as—or better than—this one. Several naturally occurring morphs of this widely distributed species are known.

DISTRIBUTION: *Tefé River region (Brazil), Aguarico system (Ecuador) and Napo River system (Peru)*

DELPHAX CORYDORAS (CORYDORAS DELPHAX)

SIZE:	*Around 2in (5cm)*

BEHAVIOR:	*One of relatively few Corydoras species that frequently swim in midwater*

DIET:	*As for C. aeneus*

AQUARIUM:	*As for C. aeneus. Temperature range: 70–79°F (21–26°C)*

BREEDING:	*As for C. aeneus*

SALT-AND-PEPPER CORYDORAS

RIO SALINAS CORY

Corydoras habrosus

FAMILY: Callichthyidae
SUBFAMILY: Corydoradinae

THIS IS ONE OF THE SO-CALLED "DWARF" corydoras. It is a distinctly patterned species which must be kept in a sizable shoal for best effect. Owing to its small size, it should not be housed with larger or aggressive species. It is not totally defenseless, though, as its strong dorsal and pectoral spines will prove to any would-be predator. This species is sometimes confused with the even smaller *C. cochui* from the Araguaia river in Brazil.

DISTRIBUTION:	*Originally reported from the Salinas river in Venezuela. Now also known from several rivers in Suriname*

SIZE:	*Up to 1½in (4cm), but usually a little smaller*

BEHAVIOR:	*This peaceful species likes to swim in midwater*

DIET:	*As for C. aeneus*

AQUARIUM:	*As for C. aeneus. Temperature range: 70–77°F (21–25°C)*

BREEDING:	*As for C. aeneus*

DWARF CORYDORAS

SPOTLIGHT MINI CORY

Corydoras hastatus

FAMILY: Callichthyidae
SUBFAMILY: Corydoradinae

THE DWARF CORYDORAS AND *C. COCHUI* ARE THE smallest members of the genus. They are closely followed by *C. habrosus* (*see* previous entry) and *C. pygmaeus* (Pygmy Corydoras)—from Guyana, Suriname and, possibly, Peru—with which it is sometimes confused. However, Dwarf Corydoras has a black spot on the caudal peduncle, while *C. pygmaeus* has a black longitudinal line that runs from the snout to the tail.

DISTRIBUTION:	*Mato Grosso (Brazil) and Paraguay*

SIZE:	*Around 1¼in (3cm)*

BEHAVIOR:	*As for C. habrosus*

DIET:	*As for C. habrosus*

AQUARIUM:	*As for C. habrosus*

BREEDING:	*As for C. habrosus*

BLACK SAIL CORYDORAS

BLACK-SPOTTED CORYDORAS

Corydoras melanistius

FAMILY: Callichthyidae
SUBFAMILY: Corydoradinae

BOTH COMMON NAMES ARE, TO A GREATER OR lesser extent, descriptive of this highly variable species. There is such variety in the degree of spotting on the body, and the size and intensity of the black blotch on the dorsal fin, that the species is subdivided into two subspecies and these, in turn, into "variants" and/or "intergrades." *C. melanistius brevirostris*—as its name indicates—has a shorter snout (or rostrum) than *C. m. melanistius.*

DISTRIBUTION:	*C. m. brevirostris: reported from the Orinoco (Venezuela), Mato Grosso (Brazil) and the Brokoponda District of Suriname; C. m. melanistius: as for C. m. brevirostris, but also reported from Essequibo River (Guyana)*

SIZE:	*Up to 2¼in (6cm)*

BEHAVIOR:	*As for C. aeneus*

DIET:	*As for C. aeneus*

AQUARIUM:	*As for C. aeneus. Temperature range: 68–75°F (20–24°C)*

BREEDING:	*As for C. aeneus*

BANDIT CORYDORAS

RIO META CORYDORAS

Corydoras metae

FAMILY: Callichthyidae
SUBFAMILY: Corydoradinae

THIS PINK AND BLACK CORYDORAS HAS A BLACK "mask" that extends from the top of the head, through the eye, to the bottom edge of the gill covers—hence the "Bandit" part of the name. The front of the dorsal fin is also black, this pigmentation running, in a single, central band, along the back to the top front edge of the caudal fin and then down to the bottom front edge of the fin. From the side, it can easily be confused with *C. melini* (Diagonal Stripe, or False Bandit, Corydoras) from the state of Amazonas in Brazil. However, from above,

DWARF CORYDORAS (CORYDORAS HASTATUS)

the single dorsal black band of Bandit Corydoras splits into two separate, narrower bands in *C. melini*; these extend diagonally toward the caudal peduncle (base of the tail fin).

DISTRIBUTION: *Meta River (Colombia)*

SIZE: *Around 2½in (6cm), but usually a little smaller*

BEHAVIOR: *As for* C. aeneus

DIET: *As for* C. aeneus

AQUARIUM: *As for* C. aeneus. *Temperature range: 70–79°F (21–26°C)*

BREEDING: *As for* C. aeneus

PEPPERED CORYDORAS

Corydoras paleatus

FAMILY: Callichthyidae
SUBFAMILY: Corydoradinae

DISCOVERED BY CHARLES DARWIN OVER 150 years ago, the Peppered Corydoras (*see* photo p.7)—along with *C. aeneus* (*see* above)—is the most popular member of its genus in the hobby. It is widely distributed and, consequently, exhibits considerable variation, with some populations having larger irregular body spots and others possessing an exceptionally long dorsal fin. There are also, at least, two cultivated varieties: an albino and one (Golden Paleatus) with a golden/pinkish base color and a liberal "dusting" of fine black dots.

DISTRIBUTION: *Argentina, Southern Brazil, (possibly) Paraguay, Suriname and around Montevideo in Uruguay*

SIZE: *Around 3in (7.5cm)*

BEHAVIOR: *As for* C. aeneus

BANDIT CORYDORAS (CORYDORAS METAE)

DIET: *As for* C. aeneus

AQUARIUM: *As for* C. aeneus. *Temperature range: 64–79°F (18–26°C), but lower end best avoided for albino and golden varieties; top end should always be avoided*

BREEDING: *As for* C. aeneus

PANDA CORYDORAS

Corydoras panda

FAMILY: Callichthyidae
SUBFAMILY: Corydoradinae

THE PANDA IS A PINK-BODIED FISH WITH THREE black blotches: one extends from the top of the head, through the eye and on to the cheek; the second occupies most of the dorsal fin; and the third is located on the caudal peduncle. Two naturally occurring morphs are recognized, depending on the size of this last blotch: Big-spot and Small-spot.

DISTRIBUTION: *Ucayali River system (Peru)*

SIZE: *Up to 2in (5cm) reported, but usually smaller*

BEHAVIOR: *As for* C. aeneus

DIET: *As for* C. aeneus

AQUARIUM: *As for* C. aeneus. *Temperature range: 72–79°F (22–26°C)*

BREEDING: *As for* C. aeneus. *More challenging than* C. aeneus

PANDA CORYDORAS (CORYDORAS PANDA)

RETICULATED CORYDORAS
NETWORK CORYDORAS
Corydoras reticulatus

FAMILY: Callichthyidae
SUBFAMILY: Corydoradinae

THE RETICULATED DARK PATTERNING ON A LIGHT background possessed by this species makes a shoal a most striking sight indeed. *C. reticulatus* may be distinguished from the similar-looking Netted Corydoras (*C.*

sodalis) by the black patch that *C. reticulatus* possesses on the dorsal fin; this is absent in *C. sodalis*.

DISTRIBUTION: *Amazon basin—mainly in the state of Pará (Brazil); also found in Loreto (Peru)*

SIZE: *Around 2½in (6cm)*

BEHAVIOR: *As for C. aeneus*

DIET: *As for C. aeneus*

AQUARIUM: *As for C. aeneus. Temperature range: 72–77°F (22–25°C)*

BREEDING: *As for C. aeneus*

OTHER *CORYDORAS* SPECIES

There are around 140 species of *Corydoras* known, with new ones being discovered or described on an ongoing basis. Some have been imported only once, or very occasionally, while others are regularly available. Specialist literature (*see* Bibliography) should be consulted for detailed information, but, generally speaking, most species have similar behavioral characteristics and maintenance requirements to those outlined for *Corydoras aeneus*, although a temperature range between 72–79°F (22–26°C) is more appropriate for the majority of species. Of the numerous *Corydoras* available to hobbyists, the following (in addition to the species featured and mentioned in the accompanying entries) are among the ones most frequently encountered.

SCIENTIFIC NAME	COMMON NAME(S)	SIZE:
C. acutus	Blacktop Corydoras	2¾in (7cm)
C. adolfoi	Adolfo's Corydoras	2¾in (7cm)
C. axelrodi	Axelrod's Corydoras	2in (5cm)
C. burgessi	Burgess' Corydoras	2½in (6cm)
C. caudimaculatus	Tail-spot, or Big-blotch, Corydoras	2½in (6cm)
C. garbei	Garbe's Corydoras	2in (5cm)
C. haraldschultzi	Harald Schultz's Corydoras	3in (8cm)
C. imitator	Imitator Corydoras	2¾in (7cm)
C. julii	Julii Corydoras	2in (5cm)
C. latus	Iridescent Corydoras	2in (5cm)
C. leopardus	Leopard Corydoras	2½in (6cm)
C. leucomelas	Blackfin Corydoras	2½in (6cm)
C. nattereri	Blue, or Natterer's, Corydoras	2½in (6cm)
C. nijsseni	Nijssen's Corydoras	2in (5cm)
C. polysticus	Many-spotted Corydoras	1¾in (4.5cm)
C. rabauti	Rabaut's Corydoras	2½in (6cm)
C. robinae	Robina's, or Flag-tailed, Corydoras	2¾in (7cm)
C. schwartzi	Schwartz's Corydoras	2½in (6cm)
C. septerionalis	Dusky, or Southern Green, Corydoras	2in (5cm)
C. zigatus	Zygatus Corydoras	2¾in (7cm)

NOTE:

In addition to these, there is a considerable number of as-yet undescribed species which are available under their trade names, e.g. *Corydoras* sp. "Correa", *C.* sp. "Pereira", *C.* sp. "Rio Tapajos", *C.* sp. "Long-nose".

RABAUT'S CORYDORAS
(CORYDORAS RABAUTI)

STERBA'S CORYDORAS
Corydoras sterbai

FAMILY: Callichthyidae
SUBFAMILY: Corydoradinae

THIS IS A PARTICULARLY BEAUTIFUL SPECIES IN which the rich speckling of the anterior half of the body merges into a number of thin, irregular, dark bands that run on to the caudal peduncle. The lower cheek area and, particularly, the pectoral-fin spine can be a rich golden yellow. Some of these golden hues extend into the pelvic fins. The anal, caudal, and dorsal fins are also liberally speckled.

DISTRIBUTION: *Upper Guaporé River system (Bolivia/Brazil), Ucayali River system (Peru)*

SIZE: *Up to 3in (8cm) reported, but usually considerably smaller*

BEHAVIOR: *As for C. aeneus*

DIET: *As for C. aeneus*

AQUARIUM: *As for C. aeneus. Temperature range: 70–79°F (21–26°C)*

BREEDING: *As for C. aeneus*

THREE-LINED CORYDORAS
Corydoras trilineatus

FAMILY: Callichthyidae
SUBFAMILY: Corydoradinae

THE THREE LINES REFERRED TO IN THE NAME OF this species consist of a bold central black line that runs from behind the gill cover to the caudal peduncle bordered, above and below, by two white-silvery bands that separate it from the body speckles. The dorsal fin has a white base and a black tip.

DISTRIBUTION: *Maranhão (Brazil), Pastaza River system (Ecuador), Loreto and Ucayali River system (Peru)*

SIZE: *Around 2in (5cm)*

BEHAVIOR: *As for C. aeneus*

DIET: *As for C. aeneus*

AQUARIUM: *As for C. aeneus. Temperature range: 72–77°F (22–25°C)*

BREEDING: *As for C. aeneus*

PORTHOLE CATFISH
Dianema longibarbis

FAMILY: Callichthyidae
SUBFAMILY: Callichthyinae

AS THE SCIENTIFIC NAME FOR THIS SPECIES indicates, the mouth is adorned with long barbels, the two longest of which (the top ones) are generally held out horizontally and pointing forward. The relatively light body armor helps distinguish the two *Dianema* species from their closest relatives in the subfamily, *Callichthys* and *Hoplosternum*.

DISTRIBUTION: *Ambyiac and Pacaya rivers (Peru)*

SIZE: *Up to 4in (10cm)*

BEHAVIOR: *Peaceful shoaler; can be kept with smaller tankmates except, perhaps, very small fry. Becomes progressively more active as evening falls*

DIET: *Wide range of foods accepted*

AQUARIUM: *Spacious, containing clumps of vegetation, open swimming areas, and resting and hiding places (e.g. pieces of bogwood). Water chemistry not critical, but softish, slightly acid conditions preferred. Temperature range: 72–79°F (22–26°C)*

BREEDING: *Challenging in aquaria. Males build bubble nests into which the eggs are deposited. Shallow water and raised temperature (82°F/28°C) recommended*

FLAG-TAILED CATFISH
STRIPE-TAILED CATFISH
Dianema urostriata

FAMILY: Callichthyidae
SUBFAMILY: Callichthyinae

THIS SPECIES IS VERY SIMILAR TO *D. LONGIBARBIS* (*see* previous entry). However, it can be immediately distinguished by its boldly striped caudal fin (in *D. longibarbis*, the tail is plain). Occasionally, specimens without any body speckling appear in shipments of this attractive species.

DISTRIBUTION: *Manáus area of the Rio Negro (Brazil)*

SIZE: *Females reported up to 4¾in (12cm); males about ¾in (2cm) shorter*

BEHAVIOR: *As for D. longibarbis*

DIET: *As for D. longibarbis*

AQUARIUM: *As for D. longibarbis*

BREEDING: *As for D. longibarbis*

CASCUDO HOPLO
Hoplosternum littorale

FAMILY: Callichthyidae
SUBFAMILY: Callichthyinae

THIS IS ONE OF THREE SIMILAR-LOOKING SPECIES that have traditionally been regarded as members of the genus *Hoplosternum*. In 1997, a review of these resulted in their being split into three distinct genera (*see Lethoplosternum* and *Megalechis*). Of the three, Cascudo Hoplo was the only species left within its original genus. It is the largest of the three species and may also be distinguished by its lightly forked caudal fin. Owing to its wide distribution, a number of variants are known, but whether these are morphs or separate species remains to be decided.

DISTRIBUTION: *Widely distributed in tropical South America*

SIZE: *Up to 8¾in (22cm)*

BEHAVIOR: *Generally peaceful except at spawning time*

DIET: *Wide range of foods accepted*

AQUARIUM: *Roomy, well-covered, with plenty of resting and hiding places, and subdued lighting. Water chemistry not critical. Temperature range: 70–79°F (21–26°C); slightly higher for breeding*

BREEDING: *Male builds bubble nest at the water surface. Eggs are deposited among the bubbles and are guarded by male. Hatching takes three to four days*

DWARF HOPLO
SPOTTED HOPLO
Lethoplosternum pectorale

SYNONYM: *Hoplosternum pectorale*
FAMILY: Callichthyidae
SUBFAMILY: Callichthyinae

AS ONE OF ITS COMMON NAME IMPLIES, THIS IS THE smallest of the three *Hoplo* species featured.

▲ FLAG-TAILED CATFISH (DIANEMA UROSTRIATA)

▼ PORTHOLE CATFISH (DIANEMA LONGIBARBIS)

PORT HOPLO (MEGALECHIS THORACATA)

Its base color is yellowish brown (though this can vary), liberally covered in small dark spots (hence its other common name). A further distinguishing characteristic is that the caudal fin is gently rounded (it is slightly forked in *Hoplosternum littorale* and truncated in *Megalechis thoracata*). A naturally occurring "dwarf" of this species—attaining only 3½in (9cm)—is occasionally seen. A fourth Hoplo, referred to as *Hoplosternum magdalenae*, may turn out to be *L. pectorale*, but differences of opinion exist. A long-barbeled form of unknown origin is also known to exist, but is only rarely imported.

DISTRIBUTION: H. (Lethoplosternum) pectorale (magdalenae?) is reported from the Magdalena River in Brazil; the fish definitely identified as L. pectorale is found mainly in Paraguay

SIZE: Up to 6in (15cm) reported, but usually smaller

BEHAVIOR: As for Hoplosternum littorale

DIET: As for Hoplosternum littorale

AQUARIUM: As for Hoplosternum littorale

BREEDING: As for Hoplosternum littorale

PORT HOPLO

Megalechis thoracata

SYNONYM: *Hoplosternum thoracatum*
FAMILY: Callichthyidae
SUBFAMILY: Callichthyinae

THIS IS THE MOST VARIABLE OF THE THREE HOPlos, so much so that some of the naturally occurring morphs may eventually turn out to be valid species in their own right. The one easily discernible feature that all possess—and that distinguishes them from the other hoplos—is the sharply truncated caudal fin (see *Lethoplosternum pectorale*, p.142). Port Hoplo males can also be distinguished from their *H. littorale* counterparts in that Port Hoplo's main pectoral fin spine does not turn up at the tip with advancing age (as it does in *H. littorale*). Further, during the breeding season, this ray turns orange in Port Hoplo and deep-red to maroon in *H. littorale*.

DISTRIBUTION: Widely distributed in northern South America

SIZE: Up to 7in (18cm)

BEHAVIOR: As for Hoplosternum littorale

DIET: As for Hoplosternum littorale

AQUARIUM: As for Hoplosternum littorale. Temperature range: 64–82°F (18–28°C)

BREEDING: As for Hoplosternum littorale, but Port Hoplo is perhaps the easiest of the three hoplos to breed in aquaria

FROGMOUTH CATFISH
ANGLER CATFISH

Chaca chaca

FAMILY: Chacidae

THE FROGMOUTH IS INACTIVE DURING THE DAY, lying perfectly camouflaged among the leaf litter that accumulates on the bottom of its native streams. In this position, it both rests and waits for suitable prey to come its way. When this happens, it wiggles its short, upper-jaw barbels to lure the potential victim into range of its cavernous mouth. Most feeding and higher levels of activity are, however, reserved for the hours of darkness. A very similar species, *C. bankanensis* (Chocolate Frogmouth Catfish), from peninsular Malaysia and Indonesia, is also available.

DISTRIBUTION: *Reported from Bangladesh, India, Myanmar (Burma), Borneo and Sumatra*

SIZE: *Up to 8in (20cm)*

BEHAVIOR: *Lone, predominantly nocturnal predator; should not be housed with tankmates that may be small enough to be swallowed*

DIET: *Live fish and crustacea preferred (a factor that needs to be considered prior to purchase). May be weaned off these and on to chunky foods, such as tablets*

AQUARIUM: *Appropriate hiding places (e.g. bogwood, rocks) and subdued lighting recommended. Water chemistry not critical. Temperature range: 72–75°F (22–24°C)*

BREEDING: *No documented accounts currently available*

WALKING CATFISH
CLARIAS CATFISH
Clarias batrachus

FAMILY: Clariidae

SO CALLED BECAUSE OF ITS REPORTED ABILITY TO "walk" out of water (e.g. during storms or humid weather), the Walking Catfish is, first and foremost, a food fish. The main reason that it has become known in the hobby is that albinos, which are produced primarily for human consumption, are particularly attractive and are therefore of interest to some aquarists. However, owing to the large size that specimens can attain, the species is suitable only for the specialist who can cater adequately for its needs.

DISTRIBUTION: *Widespread in tropical regions of Asia*

SIZE: *Up to ca20in (50cm) reported*

BEHAVIOR: *Predatory species; must not be kept with tankmates that are small enough to be swallowed*

DIET: *Wide range of live and chunky commercial foods accepted*

AQUARIUM: *Large, well-covered, and well-filtered. Decoration and shelters should consist of large pieces of bogwood, smooth rocks or equivalent. Large, robust (or artificial) plants may be provided. Water chemistry not critical. Temperature range: 68–77°F (20–25°C) adequate, but wider range tolerated*

BREEDING: *Not reported in aquaria. In the wild (or commercial farms), eggs are laid in burrows excavated in the banks of rivers and ponds*

PAINTED TALKING CATFISH
Acanthodoras cataphractus

FAMILY: Doradidae

OF THE THREE SPECIES IN THE GENUS, TWO— Painted Talking Catfish and *A. spinosissimus* (Talking Catfish) from Ecuador or eastern Peru—are frequently encountered in the hobby, while the third, *A. calderonensis*, is only rarely available. Both talking catfish species are often confused. However, the "granules" on the skull are much sharper in *A. spinosissimus*; and the gill cover in Painted Talking Catfish has fine grooves, while in *A. spinosissimus* it is granular in texture.

DISTRIBUTION: *Lower Amazon*

SIZE: *4in (10cm)*

BEHAVIOR: *Peaceful species that becomes more active during the night and likes to rest partly buried or in hollows during the day. Avoid keeping with small tankmates*

DIET: *Wide range of foods accepted. Feed just before aquarium lights are switched off in the evening*

AQUARIUM: *Adequate shelters, ample planting and soft substratum required. Water chemistry not critical. Temperature range: 72–80°F (22–27°C)*

BREEDING: *Challenging in aquaria. Eggs are laid in a depression and guarded by both parents. Hatching take four to five days*

SPOTTED DORADID
WHITE-SPOTTED DORADID or SPOTTED TALKING CATFISH
Agamyxis pectinifrons

FAMILY: Doradidae

AS IN THE OTHER TALKING CATFISHES (SEE introduction to catfishes), Spotted Doradid is able to produce sounds by rotating its pectoral-fin spines and amplifying this via its swimbladder. The overall color is

▲ *WALKING CATFISH (CLARIAS BATRACHUS)*
◀ *SPOTTED DORADID (AGAMYXIS PECTINIFRONS)*

almost black, overlaid with numerous white or cream spots.

DISTRIBUTION: *Ecuador*

SIZE: *Up to 5½in (14cm) reported*

BEHAVIOR: *As for* Acanthodoras cataphractus

DIET: *As for* Acanthodoras cataphractus

AQUARIUM: *As for* Acanthodoras cataphractus. *Temperature range: 70–79°F (21–26°C)*

BREEDING: *No documented accounts currently available*

HANCOCK'S CATFISH
TALKING CATFISH
Amblydoras hancocki

FAMILY: Doradidae

THIS IS, PERHAPS, THE MOST WIDELY AVAILABLE of all the talking catfishes. It is an attractively marked species that tends to "talk" more than most other members of the family (*see* previous entry, as well as introduction to catfishes).

DISTRIBUTION: *Widely distributed from Brazil and Colombia to Guyana*

SIZE: *Up to 6in (15cm) reported, but usually smaller*

BEHAVIOR: *May be more active than some of its relatives during the day*

DIET: *As for* Acanthodoras cataphractus

AQUARIUM: *As for* Acanthodoras cataphractus. *Temperature range: 70–82°F (21–28°C)*

BREEDING: *No accounts of aquarium spawnings available. In the wild, it is reported that eggs are laid on the bottom, covered up with leaves, and guarded by both parents*

STAR-GAZING DORADID
STARRY GROWLER
Astrodoras asterifrons

FAMILY: Doradidae

SIMILARLY COLORED TO *AMBLYDORAS HANCOCKI*, Star-gazing Doradid is the only species in its genus. It can be distinguished from its

---

closest relatives, such as *Acanthodoras* and *Amblydoras* in that its dorsal-fin spine is serrated only along the front edge and not along the sides and back as well.

DISTRIBUTION: *Reported from Bolivia and the Brazilian Amazon*

SIZE: *Up to 4¾in (12cm), but usually smaller*

BEHAVIOR: *As for* Acanthodoras cataphractus

DIET: *As for* Acanthodoras cataphractus

AQUARIUM: *As for* Acanthodoras cataphractus. *Temperature range: 70–77°F (21–25°C)*

BREEDING: *No documented accounts currently available*

JAGUAR CATFISH
Liosomadoras oncinus

FAMILY: Doradidae (but *see* below)

THIS IS A BOLDLY MARKED SPECIES THAT LIVES UP to its name of Jaguar Catfish. It has been (and still is) the subject of some controversy with regard to its classification, since it possesses characteristics of two distinct families. Following Nelson (1994—*see* Bibliography), it is listed as a doradid here, but it frequently appears as a member of the Auchenipteridae (the driftwood catfish family) in some other publications.

DISTRIBUTION: *Reported from Brazil and Peru, but may also occur elsewhere*

SIZE: *Up to 8in (20cm)*

BEHAVIOR: *Mostly sedentary during daylight hours, hiding in caves or holes in bogwood*

DIET: *Large livefoods preferred, but chunky meat- or fish-based foods will also be accepted. It may also be accustomed to granular and tablet formulations*

AQUARIUM: *Spacious, well-filtered, with ample supply of shelters important. Soft, slightly acid water. Temperature range: 70–77°F (21–25°C)*

BREEDING: *Not reported in aquaria, but known to be as in driftwood catfishes, i.e. eggs are fertilized internally and subsequently released*

SNAIL-EATING DORADID

Megalodoras irwini
FAMILY: Doradidae

THIS IS ONE OF THE LARGEST SPECIES IN THE genus—a factor that requires careful consideration before purchase, although growth in aquaria is slow. Due care must also be taken with regard to the numerous spines that develop on the tough body plates, as well as to the serrations on the dorsal- and pectoral-fin spines.

DISTRIBUTION: *Reported from the Brazilian Amazon and northeast South America*

SIZE: *Up to 24in (60cm), or even slightly larger*

BEHAVIOR: *Mostly sedentary during daylight hours*

DIET: *Chunky meat- and fish-based diets accepted. Once acclimatized, granular and tablet formulations are also taken*

AQUARIUM: *Large, well-filtered, with roomy hiding places, essential. Water chemistry not critical, but extremes must be avoided. Temperature range: 72–79°F (22–26°C)*

BREEDING: *No documented accounts currently available*

CHOCOLATE DORADID

HUMBUG CATFISH

Platydoras costatus

FAMILY: Doradidae

THIS IS A BEAUTIFULLY MARKED SPECIES IN WHICH the base chocolate (or almost black) color of the body contrasts sharply with the white or creamy bands. Its only significant drawback for many aquaria is its eventual size.

DISTRIBUTION: *Widespread in the Brazilian Amazon and Peru*

SIZE: *Up to 8¾in (22cm)*

BEHAVIOR: *Sedentary and peaceful toward other species, but territorial toward its own. Likes to burrow*

DIET: *Wide range of foods accepted*

AQUARIUM: *Spacious, with adequate shelter and fine substratum. Protect plants against burrowing (see Aquarium Plants). Water chemistry not critical, but extremes must be avoided. Temperature range: 74–86°F (24–30°C)*

BREEDING: *No documented accounts currently available*

BLACK DORADID

Pseudodoras niger
FAMILY: Doradidae

THIS IS A VERY LARGE SPECIES. WHICH SHOULD BE purchased only by aquarists who can provide it with appropriate accommodations. The strong thorny spines on its body plates and powerful fin spines also mean that it must be handled with care.

DISTRIBUTION: *Widely distributed in the Amazon basin*

SIZE: *Up to 39in (100cm) reported*

BEHAVIOR: *Peaceful despite its size. Likes the company of its own species*

▼ CHOCOLATE DORADID (PLATYDORAS COSTATUS)
▼▼ BLACK DORADID (PSEUDODORAS NIGER)

Brown Bullhead (Ictalurus nebulosus)

DIET: *Wide range of chunky foods accepted*

AQUARIUM: *Large, well-filtered, with fine- or medium-grained substratum. Water chemistry not critical. Temperature range: 70–75°F (21–24°C)*

BREEDING: *No documented accounts currently available*

ASIAN STINGING CATFISH

LIVER CATFISH

Heteropneustes fossilis

FAMILY: Heteropneustidae

THIS IS ONE OF THE MOST POTENTIALLY DANGEROUS catfish species. Its venomous spines have, reportedly, caused deaths among rice-paddy workers. It is also said to be aggressive, actively seeking out and attacking victims. While reports of this behavior may be exaggerated, careful consideration must be given to this prior to purchase.

DISTRIBUTION: *Widely distributed in tropical Asia*

SIZE: *Up to 20in (50cm) reported, but usually smaller*

BEHAVIOR: *Can be aggressive; potentially very dangerous*

DIET: *Wide range of chunky foods accepted*

AQUARIUM: *Large, well-covered and with bogwood or rocks. Water chemistry not critical. Temperature range: 72–80°F (22–27°C)*

BREEDING: *Eggs are laid in a depression and guarded by both parents, as are the fry for a short time after hatching*

BLACK BULLHEAD

Ictalurus melas

SYNONYM: *Ameiurus melas*
FAMILY: Ictaluridae

MANY OF THE BULLHEAD CATFISHES, INCLUDING this one, are considered primarily as food or bait fishes, although several species—again, including the Black Bullhead—are also popular in the hobby among catfish specialists. Small or moderate-sized specimens may be housed in unheated aquaria, although its wide temperature tolerance also makes it suitable for appropriately large tropical setups.

DISTRIBUTION: *Widely distributed in North America and introduced into many locations outside its range*

SIZE: *Up to 24½in (62cm), but usually much smaller*

BEHAVIOR: *Predatory; must not be housed with tankmates that are small enough to be swallowed*

DIET: *Live fish preferred (a factor that requires consideration prior to purchase), but other chunky livefoods and commercial diets may be accepted*

AQUARIUM: *Large, well-filtered, with substantial decor, e.g. bogwood, must be provided. Water chemistry not critical. Temperature range: from 50–86°F (10–30°C)*

BREEDING: *Challenging. Eggs are laid in a depression and guarded by the spawners, which also care for the fry for a short time after hatching*

BROWN BULLHEAD

Ictalurus nebulosus

SYNONYM: *Ameiurus nebulosus*
FAMILY: Ictaluridae

THIS IS A SLIGHTLY SMALLER SPECIES THAN *I. melas*, but it is even hardier in terms of water-quality tolerance. In the wild, it can even, reportedly, survive in wet mud when its pond dries up.

DISTRIBUTION: *Widely distributed in North America, and introduced into a large number of other countries*

SIZE: *Around 20in (50cm)*

BEHAVIOR: *As for* I. melas

DIET: *As for* I. melas

AQUARIUM: *As for* I. melas

BREEDING: *As for* I. melas. *Eggs may be guarded by just one parent, or both*

GRACEFUL CATFISH

STINGING, SPOTTED, or CHANNEL, CATFISH

Ictalurus punctatus

FAMILY: Ictaluridae

THIS IS THE MOST COMMONLY SEEN SPECIES OF ITS genus, probably as a result of the produc-

tion of albino specimens (primarily for the food fish industry).

DISTRIBUTION: *Widely distributed in North America, and introduced elsewhere*

SIZE: *Up to 47¼in (120cm), but usually considerably smaller*

BEHAVIOR: *As for* I. melas

DIET: *As for* I. melas

AQUARIUM: *As for* I. melas

BREEDING: *As for* I. melas. *Eggs may be laid in caves or under rocks and are guarded by male*

ADONIS CATFISH

Acanthicus adonis

FAMILY: Loricariidae
SUBFAMILY: Ancistrinae

THIS SPECIES IS A RELATIVE NEWCOMER TO THE hobby, having been described as recently as 1988. In most features, it is very similar to *A. hystrix* (*see* next entry). However, the Adonis Catfish has white or cream-colored spots on its body.

DISTRIBUTION: *Tocantins river (Brazil)*

SIZE: *Up to 15¾in (40cm) reported, but usually smaller*

BEHAVIOR: *Generally sedentary, although territorial toward its own species and with a distinct appetite for plants*

DIET: *Almost exclusively vegetarian. Slices of potato or cucumber, plus lettuce leaves, may be provided on a regular basis*

AQUARIUM: *Spacious, well-filtered, with shelters and unpalatable/robust plants. A water current (created by, e.g., the outflow from a powerhead) recommended. Softish, slightly acid to neutral water preferred. Temperature range: 70–75°F (21–24°C)*

BREEDING: *No documented accounts available*

▲ *Adonis Catfish (Acanthicus adonis)*

BLACK ADONIS CATFISH

Acanthicus hystrix

FAMILY: Loricariidae
SUBFAMILY: Ancistrinae

FOR NEARLY 150 YEARS, THIS SPECIES WAS believed to be the sole representative of its genus until *A. adonis* was discovered and described (*see* previous entry). Black Adonis Catfish can be distinguished from its relative by its black body coloration and the absence of spots.

DISTRIBUTION: *Amazon and (possibly) Guyana*

SIZE: *Around 18in (45cm)*

BEHAVIOR: *As for A. adonis*

DIET: *As for A. adonis*

AQUARIUM: *As for A. adonis*

BREEDING: *As for A. adonis*

BIG-FINNED BRISTLENOSE

BLUE CHIN ANCISTRUS

Ancistrus dolichopterus

FAMILY: Loricariidae
SUBFAMILY: Ancistrinae

THERE ARE AROUND 50 DESCRIBED SPECIES OF *Ancistrus*, plus an almost equal number of undescribed ones referred to by their "L" number, or their "Loricariid Number," e.g. *Ancistrus* sp. Orange Spot (L110). For detailed information on this genus, it is therefore advisable to consult specialist literature (*see* Bibliography). In all species, mature males exhibit the characteristic, filament-like outgrowths of the snout—the "bristlenose"—from which one of its common names is derived.

DISTRIBUTION: *Widespread in tropical South America*

SIZE: *Around 5in (13cm)*

BEHAVIOR: *Peaceful toward other tankmates, but males territorial and aggressive toward other Ancistrus. Exhibits distinct appetite for succulent plants*

DIET: *Predominantly vegetarian, but commercial formulations accepted. A slice of potato or cucumber, or lettuce leaves will be appreciated*

AQUARIUM: *Spacious, with ample bogwood shelters. Water well-filtered and flowing (such as produced by powerhead outlet). Water chemistry not critical. Temperature range: 73–81°F (23–27°C)*

BREEDING: *Eggs are laid in hollows in bogwood or roots, and they and the fry are guarded by male. Soft, acid water appears to enhance chances of success. Hatching takes about five days*

SPOTTED BRISTLENOSE

SNOWFLAKE BRISTLENOSE

Ancistrus hoplogenys

FAMILY: Loricariidae
SUBFAMILY: Ancistrinae

VARIOUS WHITE-SPOTTED, BLACK-BASED SPECIES are available under the *A. hoplogenys* label. Some are, undoubtedly, correctly identified as this species; some of the others either belong to closely related species, such as *A. cirrhosus*, or are, as yet, undescribed and belong to species that at the moment can be referred to only by their "L" numbers, e.g. L107, L125 and others.

DISTRIBUTION: *Amazon basin*

SIZE: *Around 6in (15cm)*

FEMALE BIG-FINNED BRISTLENOSE (ANCISTRUS DOLICHOPTERUS); SEE MALE PHOTO P. 5

WHITE-SPOTTED CHAETOSTOMA (CHAETOSTOMA SP.); SEE TEXT, BELOW

BEHAVIOR: *As for* A. dolichopterus

DIET: *As for* A. dolichopterus

AQUARIUM: *As for* A. dolichopterus

BREEDING: *As for* A. dolichopterus

"REAL/TRUE" THOMASI

Chaetostoma thomasi

FAMILY: Loricariidae
SUBFAMILY: Ancistrinae

THE FISH NORMALLY AVAILABLE AS *C. THOMASI* has a tan or brownish base color with white spots, and is referred to as the White-Spotted Chaetostoma (*Chaetostoma* sp., probably L188). However, according to some authorities, the "Real" or "True" Thomasi has a tan or brownish base color with black spots. Considerable confusion therefore exists about the identity of this species.

DISTRIBUTION: *Both types occur in Colombia*

SIZE: *"Real/True" Thomasi: around 4¾in (12cm); White-Spotted Chaetostoma: up to 6in (15cm)*

BEHAVIOR: *Generally peaceful toward other species, but territorial toward conspecifics*

DIET: *Will accept a variety of (particularly) sinking formulations and livefoods*

AQUARIUM: *Well-planted, with numerous bogwood and other shelters. A water current (as produced by powerhead outlet) recommended. Slightly acid or neutral, soft to medium-hard water preferred. Temperature range: 68–75°F (20–24°C)*

BREEDING: *No documented accounts currently available*

STICK CATFISH
TWIG CATFISH

Farlowella acus

FAMILY: Loricariidae
SUBFAMILY: Loricariinae

TRUE TO ITS NAME, THIS SLENDER SPECIES LOOKS like a stick or twig, both in shape and coloration. Owing to its vegetarian habits, it is not the easiest of loricariids to keep and is better suited to experienced aquarists than to newcomers to the hobby. *F. gracilis* (also Twig Catfish), from Colombia, which has long, slender extensions to the caudal fin, is also regularly available.

DISTRIBUTION: *Venezuela and southern tributaries of the Amazon*

SIZE: *Around 6in (15cm)*

BEHAVIOR: *Peaceful, generally retiring; should not be kept with boisterous tankmates*

DIET: *Largely herbivorous; vegetable dietary component, such as peas, lettuce, vegetable flake, etc., is therefore essential*

AQUARIUM: *Well-planted, with hiding places and clean, well-oxygenated, flowing, soft, slightly acid water recommended. Temperature range: 70–79°F (21–26°C)*

BREEDING: *Adhesive eggs are laid, often in flowing water, and are guarded by male or by both parents*

STICK CATFISH (FARLOWELLA ACUS)

SPOTTED PLECO
SAILFIN SUCKERMOUTH CATFISH
Glyptoperichthys gibbiceps

SYNONYM: *Pterygoplichthys gibbiceps*
FAMILY: Loricariidae
SUBFAMILY: Hypostominae

THIS SPECIES STILL APPEARS UNDER ITS FORMER name in many aquarium books. However, the genus *Pterygoplichthys* is no longer valid, having been replaced by two genera, *Glyptoperichthys* and *Liposarcus* (*see* p.151). The common name of Pleco is also applied to species of the genus *Hypostomus* (*see* below), from which *Glyptoperichthys* is easily distinguished by its dorsal fin, which has more than ten rays; *Hypostomus* has only seven.

DISTRIBUTION: *Peru*

SIZE: *Up to 24in (60cm), but usually smaller*

BEHAVIOR: *Predominantly nocturnal and peaceful, even toward smaller tankmates*

DIET: *Almost exclusively vegetarian; offer plant-based sinking formulations, slices of potato or cucumber, lettuce, spinach or peas*

AQUARIUM: *Large, well-planted, well-filtered, with numerous shelters. Water chemistry not critical. A "moonlight" fluorescent tube to facilitate night viewing is advisable. Temperature range: 68–81°F (22–27°C)*

SPOTTED PLECO
(GLYPTOPERICHTHYS GIBBICEPS)

BREEDING: *No documented accounts of aquarium breeding currently available*

ZEBRA PECKOLTIA
ZEBRA PLECO
Hypancistrus zebra

FAMILY: Loricariidae
SUBFAMILY: Ancistrinae

THIS SPECIES, SPECTACULARLY PATTERNED IN BLACK and white (as indicated by its name) is a relatively recent introduction into the hobby. For a time, it was known only by its "L" number (L46) until it was officially described and named in 1991. Although rare at first, the Zebra Peckoltia is now quite readily available.

DISTRIBUTION: *Reported upriver of Altamira on the Xingu River (Brazil)*

SIZE: *Up to 4¾in (12cm) reported, but usually smaller*

BEHAVIOR: *Peaceful and sometimes retiring*

DIET: *Considerably less herbivorous than many of its relatives; will accept a range of (primarily) sinking formulations*

AQUARIUM: *Well-planted, with hiding places and subdued lighting recommended. Softish, slightly acid water preferred. Temperature range: 72–77°F (22–25°C)*

BREEDING: *No documented accounts of aquarium breeding currently available*

DWARF SUCKER CATFISH
Hypoptopoma thoracatum

FAMILY: Loricariidae
SUBFAMILY: Hypoptopomatinae

THE 12 OR SO SPECIES OF THIS GENUS ARE ALL referred to as dwarf sucker catfish. However, the real dwarves are the members of

the genera *Parotocinclus* and *Otocinclus* (*see* pp.152). All *Hypoptopoma* species are distinguished by a long snout, large, laterally placed eyes, and a much reduced adipose fin (represented by a single spine in some species); in some cases, even this single spine is missing.

DISTRIBUTION: *Amazon up to the mouth of the Rio Negro (Brazil); also reported from the Mato Grosso*

SIZE: *3in (8cm)*

BEHAVIOR: *A peaceful loner; generally more active at dusk and during the night*

DIET: *Predominantly herbivorous (algae, vegetable flakes/pellets/tablets)*

AQUARIUM: *Well-planted, with hiding places and subdued lighting recommended. Softish, acid to slightly alkaline water preferred. Temperature range: 73–81°F (23–27°C)*

BREEDING: *No documented accounts currently available*

PLECO
PLEC
Hypostomus plecostomus

SYNONYM: *Plecostomus plecostomus*
FAMILY: Loricariidae
SUBFAMILY: Hypostominae

EVEN TODAY, OVER 240 YEARS AFTER THIS SPECIES was first described (as *Plecostomus*, rather than *Hypostomus*), confusion still exists about its name, or even the correct identity of plecos available to aquarists under the name *Hypostomus plecostomus*. The generic name *Hypostomus* did not appear until 1803, yet—for reasons that are unclear—it replaced *Plecostomus*. Despite this, aquarists around the world have traditionally referred to *H. plecostomus* and the other *Hypostomus* species as plecos or plecs, thus heightening the confusion. *Hypostomus* species—of which there are more than 100—are distinguished from their closest relatives in the genera *Glyptoperichthys* and *Liposarcus* in several ways. The most distinguishable feature is the small number of dorsal fin rays (seven) possessed by *Hypostomus* (cf *Glyptoperichthys gibbiceps*, above). Of the numerous species in the genus, very few are ever available within the hobby; *H. plecostomus* is one of these. At least two commercially produced varieties—an albino and a piebald—are occasionally available.

DISTRIBUTION: *Suriname*

SIZE: *Up to 24in (60cm) reported*

BEHAVIOR: *Peaceful despite its large size; most active at dusk and during the night*

DIET: *Herbivorous (algae, vegetable flakes/pellets/tablets, lettuce, spinach, peas, potato, cucumber slices, etc.)*

AQUARIUM: *Large, well-planted, with numerous sizable shelters. Water chemistry not critical, but quality must be good. Temperature range: 72–82°F (22–28°C)*

BREEDING: *No documented accounts of aquarium breeding currently available. In the wild and in commercial ornamental fisheries, the species breeds in deep burrows excavated in riverbanks.*

The male guards the eggs, and the fry feed off the body mucus—as in Symphysodon spp. (Discus), see pp.119–20

SPOTTED HYPOSTOMUS

SPOTTED PLECO

Hypostomus punctatus

SYNONYM: *Plecostomus punctatus*
FAMILY: Loricariidae
SUBFAMILY: Hypostominae

THIS BEAUTIFULLY SPOTTED SPECIES IS ONE OF THE few species of *Hypostomus* (other than *H. plecostomus—see* previous entry) regularly available in shops. It is somewhat smaller than *H. plecostomus* making it a little easier to accommodate.

DISTRIBUTION: *Southern and southeastern Brazil*

SIZE: *Around 12in (30cm)*

BEHAVIOR: *As for* H. plecostomus

DIET: *As for* H. plecostomus

AQUARIUM: *As for* H. plecostomus

BREEDING: *As for* H. plecostomus

SNOW KING PLEC

SNOW KING PLECO

Liposarcus anisisti

SYNONYMS: *Pterygoplichthys anisisti, Glyptoperichthys anisisti*
FAMILY: Loricariidae
SUBFAMILY: Hypostominae

ALONG WITH THE BLACK-SPOTTED *LIPOSARCUS multiradiatus* from the Amazon basin, Bolivia, Paraguay and Peru, the white-spotted Snow King Plec is the most widely available species in the genus. This is largely as a result of large-scale breeding

▲ *ZEBRA PECKOLTIA* (HYPANCISTRUS ZEBRA) ▼ *SPOTTED HYPOSTOMUS* (HYPOSTOMUS PUNCTATUS)

▼ *PLECO* (HYPOSTOMUS PLECOSTOMUS) ▼ *SNOW KING PLEC* (LIPOSARCUS ANISISTI)

of the species (predominantly in Florida ornamental fish farms).

DISTRIBUTION: *Brazil and Paraguay*

SIZE: *Over 15¾in (40cm)*

BEHAVIOR: *As for* Hypostomus plecostomus

DIET: *As for* Hypostomus plecostomus

AQUARIUM: *As for* Hypostomus plecostomus

BREEDING: *As for* Hypostomus plecostomus

DWARF OTOCINCLUS

GOLDEN OTOCINCLUS or MIDGET SUCKER CATFISH

Otocinclus affinis

FAMILY: Loricariidae
SUBFAMILY: Hypoptopomatinae

DESPITE ITS COMMON NAMES, DWARF OTOCINCLUS is only slightly smaller than its close relative, *O. vestitus* (Ampiyacu Dwarf Sucker Catfish), from Rio de Janeiro in Brazil. It is also about the same size as *O. paulinus* (Marbled Otocinclus) from São Paulo, Brazil. Of the 20 or so species in the genus, these three are the ones most frequently seen in the hobby. All have the same basic requirements.

DISTRIBUTION: *Southeastern Brazil*

SIZE: *Up to 2in (5cm) reported, but usually smaller*

BEHAVIOR: *Peaceful; should not be housed with boisterous tankmates*

DIET: *Predominantly herbivorous: algae and vegetable flakes, plus lettuce or spinach leaves, peas, etc.*

AQUARIUM: *Well-planted, with numerous hiding and resting places. Good filtration and fine-grained substratum recommended. At first, the water should be soft and acid; both values can be raised gradually once fish are acclimatized. Temperature range: 68–79°F (20–26°C)*

BREEDING: *Adhesive eggs are deposited on broad leaves. Hatching takes about three days*

EMPEROR PANAQUE

PIN-STRIPED, or ROYAL, PANAQUE

Panaque nigrolineatus

FAMILY: Loricariidae
SUBFAMILY: Ancistrinae

THERE ARE ONLY SOME HALF-A-DOZEN SPECIES IN the genus *Panaque*, of which two—Emperor Panaque and the black-bodied *P. suttoni* (Blue-Eyed Plec, Pleco or Panaque) from northern South America—are regularly available. Distinguished by their large heads, sloping foreheads and beautiful eyes, panaques make interesting additions to appropriately furnished and maintained aquaria.

DISTRIBUTION: *Southern Colombia*

SIZE: *Up to 12in (30cm) reported, but usually smaller*

BEHAVIOR: *Generally peaceful toward other tankmates, but strongly territorial toward its own species*

DIET: *Predominantly herbivorous: sinking plant-based formulations (e.g. vegetable tablets/granules/flakes), lettuce or spinach leaves, peas, etc.*

AQUARIUM: *Spacious, well-filtered, with flowing water (as produced by powerhead outlet), along with adequate plant and bogwood or rock cover. Softish, slightly acid water preferred, though some deviation tolerated. Temperature range: 72–79°F (22–26°C)*

BREEDING: *No documented accounts currently available*

REDFIN OTOCINCLUS

Parotocinclus maculicauda

FAMILY: Loricariidae
SUBFAMILY: Hypoptopomatinae

THIS LIBERALLY SPOTTED SPECIES HAS RED EDGES on its dorsal, pectoral and caudal fins (*see* photo p.1). The genus itself can be distinguished from its close relative, *Otocinclus*, by the adipose fin (absent in *Otocinclus*). Of the 13 or so other species, only *P. amazonensis* (False Sucker), from coastal areas of southern Brazil, is seen with any regularity.

DISTRIBUTION: *Southern Brazil*

SIZE: *Around 1¾in (4.5cm)*

EMPEROR PANAQUE (PANAQUE NIGROLINEATUS)

Spiny Plec (Pseudacanthicus spinosus)

BEHAVIOR: *As for* Otocinclus affinis

DIET: *As for* Otocinclus affinis

AQUARIUM: *As for* Otocinclus affinis. *Temperature range: 72–77°F (22–25°C)*

BREEDING: *No documented accounts currently available*

PRETTY PECKOLTIA

Peckoltia pulcher

SYNONYM: *Hemiancistrus pulcher*
FAMILY: Loricariidae
SUBFAMILY: Ancistrinae

ALTHOUGH, AS ITS NAME IMPLIES, THIS SPECIES IS pretty, the same could be said of the 18 or so other species in the genus. Of these, *P. arenaria* (Clown Plec) from Peru and *P. vittata* (Broad-Banded Peckoltia) from the Amazon are, perhaps, the two most frequently encountered species, other than Pretty Peckoltia. All have the same basic requirements.

DISTRIBUTION: *Rio Negro (Brazil)*

SIZE: *Around 2½in (6cm)*

BEHAVIOR: *Peaceful toward other tankmates, but territorial toward its own species*

DIET: *Predominantly herbivorous (algae, vegetable tablet/granules/flakes, lettuce, peas, etc.), but may also accept some livefoods*

AQUARIUM: *Well-planted, well-filtered, with adequate bogwood or rock cover. Softish, slightly*

acid to neutral water recommended. *Temperature range: 75–82°F (24–28°C)*

BREEDING: *No documented accounts currently available*

SPINY PLEC
SPINY PLECO

Pseudacanthicus spinosus

FAMILY: Loricariidae
SUBFAMILY: Ancistrinae

AS THE NAME IMPLIES, THIS IS A SPINY FISH, BUT it also possesses serrations on the scales. All members of this genus are spiny by nature, making them difficult to handle. There are probably about 12 species in the genus (the number is unclear, as some have not been described and are currently referred to only by their "L" numbers). Of the described species, *P. leopardus* (Leopard Plec), from the Rio Negro area in Brazil, is one of the few other *Pseudacanthicus* that are fairly regularly available.

DISTRIBUTION: *Brazilian Amazon basin*

SIZE: *Around 9¾in (25cm)*

BEHAVIOR: *Highly territorial, particularly toward its own species*

DIET: *Wide range of sinking foods accepted*

AQUARIUM: *Large, well-filtered, with flowing water (as produced by powerhead outlet), recommended. Provide large bogwood or rock shelters. Softish, slightly acid to slightly alkaline*

water advisable. *Temperature range: 72–79°F (22–26°C)*

BREEDING: *No documented accounts currently available*

DELICATE WHIPTAIL LORICARIA

Rineloricaria fallax

SYNONYMS: *Rineloricaria parva, Loricaria parva*
FAMILY: Loricariidae
SUBFAMILY: Loricariinae

OF THE 40 OR SO SPECIES IN THIS GENUS (SOME OF which are difficult to distinguish from one another), few clearly identified species are imported regularly. Delicate Whiptail Loricaria and *R. lanceolata* (Lanceolate Whiptail Catfish) are notable exceptions. Both have similar requirements, although the latter has a more restricted temperature range (70–77°F/21–25°C).

DISTRIBUTION: *Rio de la Plata region (Paraguay)*

SIZE: *Around 4¾in (12cm)*

BEHAVIOR: *Peaceful; most active at dusk and at night*

DIET: *Predominantly herbivorous, but will accept a range of commercial formulations and livefoods*

AQUARIUM: *Well-planted, well-filtered, well-oxygenated, with fine substratum and adequate shelters. Slow-flowing water (as produced by suitably adjusted powerhead outlet) also* recommended. Soft, acid water preferred. Temperature range: 59–77°F (15–25°C)

BREEDING: *Soft, acid conditions, and slightly higher temperature, recommended. Adhesive eggs are laid in caves or hollows and are protected by male. Hatching takes 9 to 12 days, depending on temperature*

HI-FIN WHIPTAIL
ROYAL WHIPTAIL, ROYAL FAR-LOWELLA, or STURGEON CATFISH
Sturisoma panamense

FAMILY: Loricariidae
SUBFAMILY: Loricariinae

OF THE 15 OR SO SPECIES IN THIS GENUS, ONLY TWO (or possibly three) are imported regularly. Of these, Hi-Fin Whiptail is, perhaps, the one most frequently seen, followed by *S. aureum* (Giant Whiptail, from Colombia, synonymized with Hi-Fin Whiptail by

this species more easily observable. Soft to medium hard, slightly acid to neutral water preferred. Temperature range: 72–81°F (22–27°C)

BREEDING: *Adhesive eggs are guarded by male. Hatching takes eight to ten days, depending on temperature*

ELECTRIC CATFISH
Melapterurus electricus

FAMILY: Malapteruridae

A FISH THAT CAN GENERATE AN ELECTRICAL current of up to 400 volts is most certainly one for the specialist who knows and respects its amazing qualities. High-voltage discharges are emitted only by the largest specimens, but even modest-sized individuals pack quite a punch. In addition to this species, one other electric catfish is known: *M. microstoma* (Smallmouth Electric Catfish) from the Congo basin. Of the two, Elec-

BREEDING: *No documented accounts of aquarium breeding currently available*

MOUSTACHE SYNODONTIS
Hemisynodontis membranaceus

FAMILY: Mochokidae

THE MOUSTACHE SYNODONTIS—THE ONLY SPECIES in its genus—has the typical Mochokidae pointed head and bony headshield (bony plate) sloping up to a dorsal fin with a prominent front spine and a large, well-developed adipose fin. Its mouth barbels are also well-developed, with one pair carrying the characteristic membrane responsible for its name. Some authors believe this genus to be synonymous with *Synodontis*.

DISTRIBUTION: *Widely distributed from west Africa to the Nile*

ELECTRIC CATFISH (*MELAPTERURUS ELECTRICUS*)

some authors), and *S. barbatum* (Long-Nosed Whiptail) from Cujaba-Fluss. The male Hi-fin Whiptail is distinguished from the female by his cheek bristles.

DISTRIBUTION: *Panama*

SIZE: *Up to 9¾in (25cm) reported, but often smaller*

BEHAVIOR: *Peaceful and tolerant despite its size; most active at dusk and during the night*

DIET: *Predominantly herbivorous, but will accept other foods*

AQUARIUM: *Spacious, well-planted, well-filtered, and with flowing water (as produced by powerhead outlet); numerous shelters and hiding places, and subdued lighting, recommended. A "moonlight" fluorescent tube makes the nighttime forages of*

tric Catfish is the one more commonly encountered, and it is seen both in its wild type and in its mottled or albino form.

DISTRIBUTION: *Widely distributed in central Africa*

SIZE: *Up to 39in (1m) reported, but usually much smaller*

BEHAVIOR: *Lone, nocturnal predator that stuns its prey*

DIET: *Chunks of meat, large livefoods, e.g. earthworms and live fish (a factor that demands consideration prior to purchase)*

AQUARIUM: *Large, well-filtered, with large shelters. Use only robust plants. Water chemistry not critical. Temperature range: 72–86°F (22–30°C)*

SIZE: *Up to approximately 20in (50cm), but usually smaller*

BEHAVIOR: *Relatively peaceful despite its size; prefers to be kept in groups. Tends to feed in an upside-down position, as the common name for the family (upside-down catfish) implies (although few species actually exhibit this behavior)*

DIET: *Floating livefoods and other formulations (including pellets) preferred*

AQUARIUM: *Large, with substantial shelters. Use only robust, well-protected plants. Water chemistry not critical. Temperature range: 72–77°F (22–25°C)*

BREEDING: *No documented accounts currently available*

PAYNE'S SYNODONTIS

Mochokiella paynei

FAMILY: Mochokidae

PAYNE'S SYNODONTIS IS ONE OF THE SMALLER species and the only representative of its genus. Atypically for a mochokid catfish, it has a somewhat blunt snout. Its attractive mottled patterning and its small size make it more suitable for community aquaria than the majority of its relatives.

DISTRIBUTION: *Sierra Leone*

SIZE: *Around 2in (5cm), but often smaller*

BEHAVIOR: *A peaceful species; most active at dusk and during the night*

DIET: *Livefoods preferred, but other formulations also accepted*

AQUARIUM: *Well-planted, with adequate shelter and some open swimming areas. Softish, slightly acid to slightly alkaline water preferred. Temperature range: 72–77°F (22–25°C)*

BREEDING: *No documented accounts currently available*

PAYNE'S SYNODONTIS (MOCHOKIELLA PAYNEI)

ANGEL CATFISH

ANGEL or POLKA DOT SYNODONTIS

Synodontis angelicus

FAMILY: Mochokidae

THIS IS A DARK, CHOCOLATE-BROWN FISH WITH numerous cream-colored spots. The intensity of the dark coloration, as well as the number, color and size of the spots, can vary considerably, but all variants are impressively patterned.

DISTRIBUTION: *Stanley Pool (Zaire) and Cameroon*

SIZE: *Up to 7in (20cm) reported, but usually smaller*

BEHAVIOR: *Territorial toward its own species, with open aggression sometimes displayed in confined spaces. Swims upside-down only occasionally; most activity occurs at dusk and during the night*

DIET: *Livefoods are preferred, but some commercial formulations also accepted*

AQUARIUM: *Spacious, well-planted, with adequate shelter, fine-grained substratum and subdued lighting. A "moonlight" fluorescent tube will make nighttime activity of the species easily observable. Soft to moderately hard, slightly acid to slightly alkaline water preferred. Temperature range: 72–82°F (22–28°C).*

BREEDING: *No documented accounts currently available*

BRICHARD'S SYNODONTIS

BANDED SYNODONTIS

Synodontis brichardi

FAMILY: Mochokidae

THIS IS A SLIM-BODIED SPECIES, ATTRACTIVELY marked with dark, vertical body bands separated by light-colored stripes.

DISTRIBUTION: *Congo River*

SIZE: *Up to 7in (18cm) reported, but usually smaller*

ANGEL CATFISH (SYNODONTIS ANGELICUS)

FEATHERFIN SYNODONTIS (SYNODONTIS EUPTERUS)

BEHAVIOR: *Generally peaceful, but may prey on very small fish; will occasionally swim upside-down*

DIET: *As for* S. angelicus

AQUARIUM: *As for* S. angelicus *but requires vigorous water flow (as produced by powerhead outlet). Temperature range: 72–77°F (22–25°C)*

BREEDING: *As for* S. angelicus

DECORATED SYNODONTIS

CLOWN SYNODONTIS

Synodontis decorus

FAMILY: Mochokidae

THIS IS A SPECTACULAR SPECIES, NOTABLE NOT just for its large, black blotches on a pinky-white base, but especially for the long, delicate extension of the dorsal fin in adult specimens.

DISTRIBUTION: *Upper Zaire and Cameroon*

SIZE: *Up to 12in (30cm) reported, but usually smaller*

BEHAVIOR: *Peaceful; swims upside-down only occasionally*

DIET: *As for* S. angelicus

AQUARIUM: *As for* S. angelicus. *Temperature range: 73–81°F (23–27°C)*

BREEDING: *As for* S. angelicus

FEATHERFIN SYNODONTIS

Synodontis eupterus

FAMILY: Mochokidae

AS ITS COMMON NAME SUGGESTS, THIS SPECIES— like *S. decorus*—develops a dorsal fin extension. This, and its numerous, small, dark body spots, make it a much-sought-after *Synodontis*.

DISTRIBUTION: *Widely distributed from west Africa to the White Nile*

SIZE: *Around 6in (15cm)*

BEHAVIOR: *Peaceful, even toward smaller tankmates. Swims upside-down only occasionally*

DIET: *As for* S. angelicus

AQUARIUM: *Basically, as for* S. angelicus. *Temperature range: 72–79°F (22–26°C)*

BREEDING: *As for* S. angelicus

STRIPED SYNODONTIS

PYJAMA SYNODONTIS

Synodontis flavitaeniatus

FAMILY: Mochokidae

THIS IS ONE OF THE MOST BEAUTIFUL OF ALL *Synodontis*. Its unusual body patterning includes narrow, yellowish to orange, longitudinal stripes on a dark background. It

is not, however, seen as frequently as some of its relatives.

DISTRIBUTION: *Stanley Pool region (Zaire)*

SIZE: *Up to 8in (20cm)*

BEHAVIOR: *As for* S. brichardi

DIET: *As for* S. angelicus

AQUARIUM: *Basically, as for* S. angelicus. *Temperature range: 73–79°F (23–26°C)*

BREEDING: *As for* S. angelicus

CUCKOO SYNODONTIS

MANY-SPOTTED SYNODONTIS

Synodontis multipunctatus

FAMILY: Mochokidae

THIS SPECIES IS OFTEN CONFUSED WITH OTHER similarly patterned species. Its white base color is overlaid with black spots that increase in size from the head to the tail. The Cuckoo Synodontis is of special interest because of its breeding habits.

DISTRIBUTION: *Lake Tanganyika*

SIZE: *Reported up to 12in (30cm), but almost always considerably smaller*

BEHAVIOR: *Can be territorial toward its own species; breeding behavior unusual (see below)*

DIET: *As for* S. angelicus

AQUARIUM: *Typical African Rift Lake cichlid layout suits this species well (see Aquarium Set-up). Neutral to alkaline water preferred. Temperature range: 70–77°F (21–25°C)*

BREEDING: *Pairs spawn among mouthbrooding cichlids that are, themselves, spawning. The female cichlids therefore pick up the Cuckoo's eggs along with their own and incubate them orally. They will also protect the catfish fry as if they were their own offspring*

BLACK-SPOTTED UPSIDE-DOWN CATFISH

COMMON UPSIDE-DOWN CATFISH

Synodontis nigriventris

FAMILY: Mochokidae

OF ALL THE *SYNODONTIS* KNOWN IN THE HOBBY, this is the species that spends most time in an inverted swimming position. The habit is so highly developed in this fish that it has actually evolved reversed body shading, i.e. in some species, the belly is darker than the back—the complete opposite to the shading pattern exhibited by other fishes, including other members of the Mochokidae. Despite its upside-down habit, the Black-Spotted Upside-Down Catfish is perfectly capable of swimming the "right way up," and occasionally does so. Interestingly, young fish do not adopt the upside-down orientation until they are about two months old.

DISTRIBUTION: *Congo basin*

SIZE: *Up to 4in (10cm) or larger reported, but often smaller*

BEHAVIOR: *A peaceful fish that can be kept in groups; spends most of its time in an upside-down position; most activity occurs at dusk and during the night*

DIET: *Floating livefoods, freeze-dried or deep-frozen diets are preferred; other foods accepted more reluctantly*

AQUARIUM: *As for* S. angelicus

BREEDING: *Challenging, but achievable, in aquaria. Eggs are laid in a depression, hollow or on the roof of a cave. There may be some degree of parental care. Hatching takes about seven days*

ONE-SPOT SYNODONTIS

Synodontis notatus

FAMILY: Mochokidae

THIS IS ONE OF THE MOST FREQUENTLY SEEN species of *Synodontis*. It is easily identified by its single central body spot (although some specimens may exhibit more than one) on a pinkish, grayish or silvery background.

DISTRIBUTION: *Zaire*

SIZE: *Up to 8in (20cm) reported, but usually smaller*

BEHAVIOR: *Peaceful toward tankmates, but adults can be boisterous*

DIET: *As for* S. angelicus

AQUARIUM: *As for* S. angelicus. *Temperature range: 72–79°F (22–26°C)*

BREEDING: *As for* S. angelicus

ASIAN SHARK CATFISH
SIAMESE or IRIDESCENT SHARK

Pangasius sutchi

FAMILY: Pangasiidae

THE PANGASIIDAE CONTAINS *PANGASIANODON GIGAS* (Giant Catfish), which can grow to over 6½ft (2m) and weigh over 240lb (110kg). The genus *Pangasius* is the only one of the pangasiids encountered with any frequency in the hobby, with the Asian Shark Catfish being the species most often seen, either in its wild type or albino forms. Most specimens offered are juveniles, but these will soon grow into large fish. This is therefore a species that is suitable only for aquarists who can provide appropriate accommodations. It is widely bred commercially as a food fish as well as an ornamental.

DISTRIBUTION: *Around Bangkok, Thailand*

BLACK-SPOTTED UPSIDE-DOWN CATFISH (SYNODONTIS NIGRIVENTRIS)

OTHER *SYNODONTIS* SPECIES

There are more than 100 species in the genus *Synodontis*. Although not all are available within the hobby, a wide selection, in addition to the ones featured in the previous pages, may be found with varying degrees of regularity. Of these, most are capable of swimming upside down from time to time, but relatively few habitually exhibit this behavior. Sizes within the genus can vary between some 2½in (6cm) and 28in (70cm). Most species offered for home aquaria, however, are 12in (30cm) or less. Even so, these are sizable catfish, so adequate accommodations must be provided (*see*, for example, *S. angelicus*). Although temperature requirements may vary a little between species, most are happy between 72°F (22°C) and 79°F (26°C). The following are some of the most frequently available species. The sizes quoted are indicative of approximate maximum lengths; most individuals are somewhat smaller.

SCIENTIFIC NAME	COMMON NAME(S)	SIZE
S. alberti	Albert's or Congo Hi-Fin Synodontis	8in (20cm)
S. batesii	Bate's Synodontis	6in (15cm)
S. budgeti	Brown Synodontis	8¾in (22cm)
S. came;opardalis	Ruki Synodontis	6in (15cm)
S. congicus	Congo Synodontis	6in (15cm)
S. longirostris	Long-Nosed Synodontis	24in (60cm)
S. nigrita	Dark-Spotted or False Upside-Down Synodontis	8in (20cm)
S. njassae	Nyassa Synodontis	8in (20cm)
S. ornatipinnis	White-Barred Synodontis	12in (30cm)
S. petricola	Pygmy Leopard or Even-Spotted Synodontis	5½in (14cm)
S. pleurops	Big-Eyed Synodontis	8in (20cm)
S. schoutedeni	Vermiculated Synodontis	5½in (14cm)
S. victoriae	Victoria Synodontis	12in (30cm)

SIZE: *Up to 39in (1m) reported, but usually smaller*

BEHAVIOR: *Large shoals are encountered in the wild; in aquaria, however, only single specimens should be kept, except during the juvenile phase; a nervous, predatory species that can disrupt aquarium decor*

DIET: *Substantial, chunky livefoods and commercial preparations accepted*

AQUARIUM: *Spacious, well-covered, with ample swimming space, efficient filtration, and water current (as produced by power filter or powerhead outlet). Neutral, soft to medium-hard water preferred. Temperature range: 72–79°F (22–26°C)*

BREEDING: *No documented accounts currently available*

BANDED SHOVELNOSED CATFISH

DOURADA, or GOLDEN, ZEBRA

Brachyplatystoma juruense

FAMILY: Pimelodidae

THIS PREDATORY SPECIES IS USUALLY AVAILABLE in its boldly patterned juvenile phase. It will eventually grow into a large fish with an equally large appetite and exacting demands. It is undoubtedly a species best reserved for the specialist, as are the few other species of this genus that are occasionally encountered.

DISTRIBUTION: *Jurua River (Brazil)*

SIZE: *Up to 31½in (80cm)*

BEHAVIOR: *Highly predatory*

DIET: *Large livefoods—including fish—accepted (a factor that demands consideration prior to purchase)*

AQUARIUM: *Large, well-covered, well-filtered, with water current (as produced by power filter or powerhead outlet) essential. Provide large shelters. Water chemistry not critical, but extremes must be avoided. Temperature range: 72–81°F (22–27°C)*

BREEDING: *No documented accounts currently available*

SPOTTED SHOVEL-NOSED CATFISH

PORTHOLE, or FLAT-NOSED, ANTENNA CATFISH

Hemisorubim platyrhynchos

FAMILY: Pimelodidae

THIS ATTRACTIVELY SPOTTED CATFISH IS considerably more manageable than *Brachyplatystoma juruense* in home aquaria. It is smaller and more flexible in its dietary habits than *B. juruense*, although it is still a substantial fish.

DISTRIBUTION: *Northern and eastern South America*

SIZE: *Up to 20in (50cm), but usually smaller*

BEHAVIOR: *Predatory*

DIET: *Chunky livefoods and meat-based diets accepted, as well as tablets and granules*

AQUARIUM: *As for Brachyplatystoma juruense, but subdued lighting and soft substratum also recommended*

BREEDING: *Unknown in aquaria*

SAILFIN MARBLED CATFISH

SAILFIN PIM

Leiarius pictus

FAMILY: Pimelodidae

THIS SPECTACULAR SPECIES IS DISTINGUISHED BY its large, sail-like dorsal fin and bold chocolate-brown and creamy-pink body patterning. Its most obvious disadvantages as an aquarium fish are its large size and feeding habit, which make it suitable only for those specialist hobbyists who can cater for its needs. A mottled species, *L.*

▲ SPOTTED SHOVELNOSED CATFISH (HEMISORUBIM PLATYRHYNCHOS)

◄ SAILFIN MARBLED CATFISH (LEIARIUS PICTUS)

marmoratus (False Perrunichthys), from the Brazilian and Peruvian Amazon, is also occasionally available.

DISTRIBUTION: *Amazon basin*

SIZE: *Up to 24in (60cm)*

BEHAVIOR: *As for Brachyplatystoma juruense*

DIET: *As for Brachyplatystoma juruense*

AQUARIUM: *As for Brachyplatystoma juruense*

RED-TAILED CATFISH (*PHRACTOCEPHALUS HEMIOLIOPTERUS*)

BREEDING: *As for* Brachyplatystoma juruense

BUMBLEBEE CATFISH

Microglanis iheringi

FAMILY: Pimelodidae

OF THE EIGHT OR SO SPECIES IN THIS GENUS, ONLY two are encountered on a regular basis: this one and the smaller, equally beautifully marked *M. poecilus* (Dwarf Marbled Catfish) from Suriname.

DISTRIBUTION: *Widely distributed in northern South America*

SIZE: *Up to 4in (10cm) reported, but usually about half this size*

BEHAVIOR: *Sedentary; nocturnal; peaceful toward tankmates of a similar size; small fish may be treated as prey*

DIET: *Livefoods preferred, but commercial formulations also accepted*

AQUARIUM: *Well-planted, with adequate shelter, fine-grained substratum, and some water movement (as produced by powerhead outlet) recommended. A "moonlight" fluorescent tube will facilitate nighttime viewing. Water chemistry not critical, but extremes should be avoided. Temperature range: 70–79°F (21–26°C)*

BREEDING: *No documented accounts currently available*

RED-TAILED CATFISH

Phractocephalus hemioliopterus

FAMILY: Pimelodidae

THIS CATFISH IS EXCEPTIONAL IN THAT ITS coloration remains bright and distinct, even in large specimens. It is, undoubtedly, one of the most attractive of all large catfish, and offers the extra advantage that it can become very tame. On the downside is its eventual large size—an important factor that needs careful consideration. The small, commercially bred juveniles that are generally available will, in appropriate conditions, grow into giants in a relatively short period of time.

DISTRIBUTION: *Widely distributed in the Amazon basin*

SIZE: *Up to 4ft (1.2m)*

BEHAVIOR: *Highly predatory*

DIET: *Large livefoods, including fish, preferred (a factor that requires consideration prior to purchase). Chunky meat-/fish-based foods and commercial formulations may also be accepted*

AQUARIUM: *Large, well-covered, well-filtered, with some large pieces of decor. Water chemistry not critical, but quality must be good. Temperature range: 70–81°F (21–27°C)*

BREEDING: *No documented accounts of aquarium breeding currently available, although the species has been bred commercially*

GRACEFUL PIM

Pimelodella gracilis

SYNONYMS: *Pimelodella cristata, P. geryi*

FAMILY: Pimelodidae

THE CURRENT STATE OF *PIMELODELLA* AND *Pimelodus* classification is highly confused. The main difference between the two is based, largely, on the shape of one of the skull bones (the postoccipital process). This variable factor, plus the close similarity between species, makes correct identification extremely difficult. It also means that a particular fish may appear as a *Pimelodella* in one book and as a *Pimelodus* in another. Graceful Pim—as its name suggests—is a graceful species, with scattered body spots on a silvery base color and a black longitudinal band running the whole length of the body. Note that this, and other pimelodids, possess powerful dorsal- and pectoral-fin spines that can inflict painful injuries and cause allergic reactions in some people.

DISTRIBUTION: *Widely distributed in tropical South America*

SIZE: *Up to 12in (30cm) reported, but usually considerably smaller*

BEHAVIOR: *May prey on small tankmates, but generally peaceful toward similarly sized fish; most active in the evening and during the night*

DIET: *Livefoods preferred, but will accept some commercial formulations*

AQUARIUM: *Sufficiently large to accommodate a group, and with open swimming spaces and adequate shelter. Well-filtered, soft, slightly acid water preferred. Temperature range: 72–77°F (22–25°C)*

BREEDING: *No documented accounts available*

ORNATE PIM

Pimelodus ornatus

FAMILY: Pimelodidae

THIS UNUSUALLY MARKED SPECIES HAS A GREY, broad, vertical band in the "shoulder" region, behind which are two similarly colored, but longitudinal, bands that run all along the body and into the caudal fin. The whitish dorsal fin has a distinct black spot.

DISTRIBUTION: *Tropical South America*

SIZE: *Around 9¾in (25cm)*

BEHAVIOR: *As for* Pimelodella gracilis

DIET: *As for* Pimelodella gracilis

AQUARIUM: *As for* Pimelodella gracilis

BREEDING: *As for* Pimelodella gracilis

ANGELICUS PIM

Pimelodus pictus

SYNONYM: *Pimelodella pictus*
FAMILY: Pimelodidae

THIS STRIKING FISH IS ONE OF THE MOST frequently seen pims in the hobby. It is also one of the most peaceful, though care must be taken not to house it with small tankmates.

DISTRIBUTION: *Colombia and Peru*

SIZE: *Up to 6in (15cm) reported, but usually smaller*

BEHAVIOR: *As for* Pimelodella gracilis

DIET: *As for* Pimelodella gracilis

AQUARIUM: *As for* Pimelodella gracilis

BREEDING: *As for* Pimelodella gracilis

STURGEON CATFISH

Platystomatichthys sturio

FAMILY: Pimelodidae

THE COMMON NAME OF THIS SPECIES DERIVES FROM the long snout, which may be upturned at the tip and thus look very similar to the snout possessed by many *Acipenser* (sturgeon) species. Another notable feature of this species is the extremely long maxillary barbels, which can extend beyond the tip of the caudal fin.

DISTRIBUTION: *Amazon basin*

ANGELICUS PIM (PIMELODUS PICTUS)

OTHER *PIMELODID* SPECIES

Owing to the considerable confusion that exists between the genera *Pimelodella* and *Pimelodus*, as well as the difficulties with the correct identification of many of the similar-looking species, pims are found under a variety of names, some accurate, some less so. In general, *Pimelodella* is regarded as containing more than 60 species, while *Pimelodus* may contain around 20. Of these, it is unclear just how many are actually available on a regular basis. In addition to the featured species, though, the following are, at least, reasonably well known in the hobby.

SCIENTIFIC NAME	COMMON NAME(S)	SIZE
Pimelodella dorseyi	Dorsey's Pim	8¾in (22cm)
Pimelodella laticeps	Flat-Headed Pim	6in (15cm)
Pimelodella linami	Linam's Pim Pim	4¾in (12cm)
Pimelodus albofasciatus	White-Spotted, or White-Striped, Pim	9¾in (25cm)
Pimelodus blochi	Dusky Pim	9¾in (25cm)
Pimelodus maculatus	Spotted Pim	9¾in (25cm)

SIZE: *Up to 24in (60cm) reported*

BEHAVIOR: *As for* Brachyplatystoma juruense

DIET: *As for* Brachyplatystoma juruense

AQUARIUM: *As for Brachyplatystoma juruense,* although Sturgeon Catfish may be somewhat more difficult to acclimatize to aquarium conditions

BREEDING: *As for* Brachyplatystoma juruense

TIGER SHOVELNOSED CATFISH

Pseudoplatystoma fasciatum

FAMILY: Pimelodidae

SEVERAL SIMILAR SHOVELNOSES ARE KNOWN, giving rise to the possibility that at least two—Tiger Shovelnosed Catfish and *P. tigrinum*—are either closely related species or subspecies, or even variants of one species. As many as five subspecies of Tiger Shovelnosed Catfish are generally recognized.

DISTRIBUTION: *Eastern South America, from east of the Andes to the Panamá/Rio de la Plata basin*

SIZE: *Up to 39in (1m) reported*

BEHAVIOUR: *As for* Brachyplatystoma juruense

DIET: *As for* Brachyplatystoma juruense

AQUARIUM: *As for* Brachyplatystoma juruense

BREEDING: *As for* Brachyplatystoma juruense

DUCKBEAK SHOVEL-NOSED CATFISH

Sorubim lima

FAMILY: Pimelodidae

THIS SPECIES IS EASILY DISTINGUISHED FROM ITS relatives by the broad, black band that runs from the snout to the caudal fin, dipping "down" into the lower lobe of the fin. The area of the body below the band is silvery white.

DISTRIBUTION: *Amazon basin*

SIZE: *Up to 24in (60cm) reported*

BEHAVIOR: *As for* Brachyplatystoma juruense

DIET: *As for* Brachyplatystoma juruense

AQUARIUM: *As for* Brachyplatystoma juruense. *Temperature range: 73–86°F (23–30°C)*

BREEDING: *As for* Brachyplatystoma juruense

AFRICAN GLASS CATFISH

Eutropiellus debauwi

FAMILY: Schilbeidae

AFRICAN GLASS CATFISH IS AN UNUSUALLY patterned species that likes to swim in midwater. It is often confused with *E. vanderweyeri* from the Niger River system.

*STURGEON CATFISH (*PLATYSTOMATICHTHYS STURIO*)*

However, the latter has black streaks on both lobes of the caudal fin.

DISTRIBUTION: *Congo and Gabon*

SIZE: *Around 3in (8cm)*

BEHAVIOR: *A peaceful shoaler, active during the day*

DIET: *Will accept a range of commercial diets*

AQUARIUM: *Ample swimming areas should be provided, along with some shelter, surface cover*

EUTROPIELLUS VANDERWEYERI; *SEE TEXT, ABOVE*

(floating plants) and a water current (as produced by powerhead outlet). A dark substratum and peat filtration (or tannin-stained water, see Aquarium Set-up) also desirable. Soft to medium-hard, acid to slightly alkaline water suitable. Temperature range: 75–81°F (24–27°C)

BREEDING: *No documented accounts currently available*

STRIPED SCHILBE
BUTTER CATFISH
Schilbe mystus
FAMILY: Schilbeidae

GENERALLY AVAILABLE AS SMALL SPECIMENS, THIS active species can grow to a relatively large size, making it unsuitable for community aquaria (other than those housing equally sized tankmates). At slightly less than half the size, *S. marmoratus* (African Shoulder-Spot Catfish) is easier to accommodate but is not seen as frequently.

DISTRIBUTION: *From west Africa to the Nile Lakes; Chad and Victoria*

SIZE: *Up to 13¾in (35cm)*

BEHAVIOR: *Active shoaler; may eat small fish*

DIET: *Larger livefoods, although chunky commercial preparations also accepted*

AQUARIUM: *Large, well-filtered, with soft, dark substratum and ample swimming space recommended. Water chemistry not critical. Temperature range: 73–81°F (23–27°C)*

BREEDING: *No documented accounts available*

GLASS CATFISH
GHOST CATFISH
Kryptopterus bicirrhis
FAMILY: Siluridae

THE GLASS CATFISH BELONGS TO THE SAME family as the gigantic *Silurus glanis* (Wels Catfish), which can attain lengths of around 10ft (3m), and *Wallago attu*, which can grow to over 6½ft (2m); both are most unsuitable aquarium fish despite being occasionally available. Unusually for a catfish, the Glass Catfish is a midwater swimmer that looks absolutely stunning when kept—as it should be—in a shoal. A second, less transparent, species, from the same general area—*K. macrocephalus* (the so-called Poor Man's Glass Catfish)—is also available, along with a smaller, highly transparent species, *K. minor*, and a species from Borneo, *K. cryptopterus*. All have the same basic requirements.

DISTRIBUTION: *Eastern India and southeast Asia*

SIZE: *Up to 6in (15cm), but usually smaller*

BEHAVIOR: *Peaceful, midwater shoaler; must be kept in a group*

DIET: *Swimming livefoods preferred, but deep-frozen, freeze-dried and other formulations may be accepted, especially if distributed via a current (as produced by a powerhead)*

AQUARIUM: *Well-planted, with ample open swimming areas. Water chemistry not critical, but soft, slightly acid water preferred. Temperature*

range: 70–79°F (21–26°C)

BREEDING: *No documented accounts currently available*

GLASS CATFISH
Ompok bimaculatus
FAMILY: Siluridae

DESPITE ITS COMMON NAME, THIS GLASS CATFISH is nowhere as transparent as its better-known, smaller relative, *Kryptopterus bicirrhis* (the "true" glass catfish)—*see* previous entry. This species is characterized by two spots, one behind the gill cover and the other on the caudal peduncle. Another species, *O. eugeniatus* (Vaillant's Butter Catfish), which is smaller, is also occasionally available.

DISTRIBUTION: *Widely distributed in tropical Asia*

SIZE: *Up to 18in (45cm), but usually about half this size*

BEHAVIOR: *Relatively peaceful shoaler, which is active during the day; adults may become quarrelsome*

DIET: *Chunky meat-/fish-based foods and commercial formulations accepted*

AQUARIUM: *Well-lit, well-planted, well-filtered, with ample open swimming space for a group, recommended. Water chemistry not critical. Temperature range: 68–79°F (20–26°C)*

BREEDING: *Aquarium spawnings have not been reported, but spawning in tropical ponds has occurred*

GLASS CATFISH (KRYPTOPTERUS BICIRRHIS)

Vaillant's Butter Catfish (Ompok eugeniatus)

CLOWN CATFISH

Gagata cenia

FAMILY: Sisoridae

SO CALLED (LIKE MANY OTHER SIMILARLY PAT-
terned species) because of its black spots
on a light background, the Clown Catfish
has been known since 1822—although it
did not begin to appear with much frequency until the 1990s. An albino form is
occasionally available.

DISTRIBUTION: *Mainly from north and northeast
India*

SIZE: *Around 6in (15cm)*

BEHAVIOR: *Generally peaceful, active shoaler*

DIET: *Livefoods preferred, but other foods also
accepted*

AQUARIUM: *Plants not vital, but well-lit, well-planted
aquarium with gravelly bottom and some flat or
smoothly rounded resting places recommended.
Provide a water current (as produced by power
filter or powerhead outlet). Hard alkaline water
preferred. Temperature range: 64–72°F (18–22°C)*

BREEDING: *No documented accounts available*

BUTTERFLY CATFISH

Hara hara

FAMILY: Sisoridae

TWO SPECIES OF *HARA* ARE OCCASIONALLY AVAIL-
able—the Butterfly Catfish and its smaller
relative, *H. jerdoni* (Dwarf Anchor Catfish). The two other species in the genus
are only rarely seen in aquaria. All species
have the same basic requirements.

DISTRIBUTION: *Indian subcontinent*

▲ CLOWN CATFISH (GAGATA CENIA)　　　▼ BUTTERFLY CATFISH (HARA HARA)

SIZE: *Up to 1½in (4cm)*

BEHAVIOR: *Peaceful, retiring; may be kept in
groups*

DIET: *Sinking livefoods preferred, but commercial
formulations also accepted*

AQUARIUM: *Well-filtered, with numerous shelters
and subdued lighting recommended. Soft, acid
water preferred. Temperature range: 64–72°F
(18–22°C)*

BREEDING: *No documented accounts available*

CYPRINIDS

THE FAMILY CYPRINIDAE IS THE LARGEST OF THE exclusively freshwater families of fishes and, with the possible exception of the freshwater/brackish/marine family, the Gobiidae, it is also the largest family of vertebrates. Indeed, the family as we currently recognize it is deemed by some authorities to be artificially large.

Not surprisingly, therefore, opinions vary as to how the family should be subdivided. The following listing of subfamilies follows that of Nelson (1994)—*see* Bibliography.

Cyprininae (about 700 species). These fish usually (but not invariably) possess anterior and posterior barbels. The three *Carassius* species (including the Goldfish—*C. auratus*), for instance, don't possess barbels, while the Common Carp and, therefore, Koi (*Cyprinus carpio*), *Barbus* and relatives, *Labeo* and *Epalzeorhynchus* ("Sharks" and Flying Foxes) and numerous other species, have barbels.

Gobioninae, which includes the European Gudgeon (*Gobio gobio*).

Rasborinae (= Danioninae), which—as the name implies—includes all the popular tropical aquarium rasboras and danios.

Acheilognathinae, which includes the amazing bitterlings (*Rhodeus* and *Tanakia*).

Leuciscinae, the intra-subfamilial relationships of which are, perhaps, debatable, but that—as things stand—includes the minnows (*Phoxinus*), the Ide or Orfe (*Leuciscus*), the Roach (*Rutilus*), the Rudd (*Scardinius*) and the Tench (*Tinca*).

Cultrinae, consisting of Eastern Asian genera like *Parabramis*.

Alburninae, including the Bleak (*Alburnus*).

Psilorhynchinae, with only two genera from Nepal, India and parts of Myanmar (Burma): *Psilorhynchoides* and *Psilorhynchus*.

There are about 2,010 species in the family spread among some 210–220 genera in Eurasia, North America and Africa. With such a high number of species and such wide distribution, it is to be expected that cyprinids will exhibit great diversity of shape, size and characteristics.

There are giant species, such as *Catlocarpio siamensis* from Thailand and *Tor putitora*, the Large-scaled Barb or Mahseer, from the Bhramaputra, in Eastern India, both of which are known to grow to lengths in excess of 8ft (2.5m). In contrast, the largest specimen of *Danionella translucida*, from Burma so far found is a mere ½in (1.2cm) in length. It is hardly surprising, therefore, that the debate regarding the actual composition of the family and its subdivision into subfamilies is so complex and still apparently so far from being resolved. Even selecting characteristics that are shared by all members of the family and which distinguish them from other families is fraught with difficulty. Cyprinids have a protrusile, or extendible, mouth and jaws without teeth. However, they possess pharyngeal ("throat") bones with teeth. They also exhibit a number of skull bone and muscle modifications, along with two pairs of mouth barbels (but not in all species) and a scaleless head. They lack an adipose ("second dorsal") fin.

The difficulty with using these features to identify a fish as belonging to the family Cyprinidae is that none of these characteristics is unique to cyprinids. Furthermore, all of them, plus others, are shared with the other families which together constitute the order Cypriniformes.

Yet, despite this sharing of characteristics with fish belonging to related families, there is a general consensus as to what constitutes a cyprinid. The selection of species that follows can be safely regarded as consisting of noncontroversial, universally accepted members of the family Cyprinidae.

SILVER SHARK
BALA, MALAYSIAN or
TRI-COLOR SHARK
Balantiocheilos melanopterus

SYNONYM: *Balantiocheilus melanopterus*
SUBFAMILY: Cyprininae

SHARK IN NAME AND, SUPERFICIALLY, IN OVERALL shape—but certainly not in demeanour—the Silver Shark is a predominantly herbivorous species which has been popular for many years. This is, perhaps, a little surprising, since this species can attain a substantial size (*see* details below) and can outgrow most home aquaria. However, with the improvements in aquarium technology that are being seen in recent times, and as the keeping of larger setups becomes more feasible, the Silver Shark is likely to continue enjoying popularity among aquarists. It may even be possible to breed this attractive and active fish in aquaria before long.

The Silver Shark is a shoaling species and should therefore be kept in groups. However, the average home aquarium will only be able to house a shoal of juveniles, which, provided with an appropriate diet, will soon outgrow their quarters. In the past, Silver Sharks used to be collected in large numbers from the wild. Today, this species is bred commercially in the Far East and it is these captive-bred stocks that meet most of the demand.

DISTRIBUTION: *Southeast Asia; Kalimantan (Borneo), Thailand, Sumatra and Peninsular Malaysia*

SIZE: *Usually sold as juveniles measuring 4in (10cm) or less, but can grow to around 14in (35cm) in roomy aquaria with good water quality and an appropriate diet*

BEHAVIOR: *Nonaggressive, even toward smaller fishes, despite its size; active shoaler*

DIET: *Will accept a wide range of livefoods and commercial diets, which should include vegetable matter. Delicate plants are likely to suffer in an aquarium housing this species*

AQUARIUM: *Roomy with ample swimming space and a well-fitting cover to prevent specimens from jumping out. Will tolerate a wide range of hardness and pH—although the latter should, ideally, be kept between slightly acid and neutral. Temperature range: 72–82°F (22–28°C)*

BREEDING: *This has not been reported in home aquaria. However, the species is commercially bred in large numbers*

ARULIUS BARB
FOUR-SPOT or LONGFIN BARB
Barbus arulius

SYNONYMS: *Puntius arulius, Capoeta arulius*
SUBFAMILY: Cyprininae

ACCORDING TO SOME AUTHORS, THE GENERIC name *Barbus* should only be used in connection with African and European species of barb. If this recommendation is accepted, the Arulius Barb, which originates in India, should be known as *Puntius arulius*, rather than *Barbus arulius*. However, difficulties in barb taxonomy, which embraces not just variations between species, but even within individual species, has—so far—meant that the recommendation has not found universal acceptance. In this book, therefore, for the sake of simplicity, all the barbs will be referred to as *Barbus*, with alternative names indicated as in this entry.

The Arulius Barb is an active shoaler in which males are slow to develop their full adult characteristics, consisting of extended dorsal ray fins. This relative slowness (it can take over a year) is one of the main reasons why this species has not become more popular. Although mature males can grow quite large (*see* below) for a community fish, this barb is relatively peaceful and can be kept with tankmates smaller than itself. In reflected light, the white/silvery areas between the black body bands have an iridescent sheen—particularly attractive in mature males.

DISTRIBUTION: *Southern and southeast India*

SIZE: *Up to 4¾in (12cm)*

BEHAVIOR: *Sociable fish which is tolerant of other species and should be kept in a shoal*

DIET: *Wide range of foods accepted; vegetable matter should be included*

AQUARIUM: *Roomy with plenty of swimming space and clumps of vegetation. Although tolerant of a range of conditions, soft, slightly acid water is recommended. Temperature range: 66–77°F (19–25°C)*

BREEDING: *This is an egg-scattering species which releases its spawn among vegetation. Relatively few eggs are laid*

TWO-SPOT BARB
REDSIDE BARB
Barbus bimaculatus

SYNONYM: *Puntius bimaculatus*
SUBFAMILY: Cyprininae

THIS IS A SLIM-BODIED BARB IN WHICH MATURE specimens sport a red line running the length of the body, originating in the top half of the eye and ending at the posterior edge of the fork in the caudal fin. In some wild populations, such as the one from Ginigathena in Sri Lanka, this line is either missing or very faint. The dorsal fin in all types is reddish and carries a black spot halfway along its base. The second spot responsible for one of the common names for this species is located on the caudal peduncle. Albino specimens are

SILVER SHARK (BALANTIOCHEILOS MELANOPTERUS)

ARULIUS BARB (BARBUS ARULIUS)

ROSY BARB (BARBUS CONCHONIUS)

occasionally encountered. It is a hardy species suitable for beginners.

DISTRIBUTION: *Sri Lanka and Mysore (southern India)*

SIZE: *Up to 2¾in (7cm), but usually smaller*

BEHAVIOR: *This is a shoaling species that prefers to stay close to the bottom; it is tolerant of other fish*

DIET: *Accepts most aquarium foods, but should receive a vegetable supplement*

AQUARIUM: *A medium-sized aquarium will prove adequate for a small shoal which should be provided with both open swimming spaces and shelter. Although the species does not have strict water chemistry requirements, extremes of both acidity/alkalinity and hardness should be avoided. Temperature range: 72–77°F (22–25°C)*

BREEDING: *Typical egg-scattering species that can produce several batches of eggs in a single season. Hatching takes about 48 hours.*

ROSY BARB

Barbus conchonius

SYNONYM: *Puntius conchonius*
SUBFAMILY: Cyprininae

THIS IS ONE OF THE MOST FAMOUS AND POPULAR species in the aquarium hobby. As the name implies, the basic body color is rosy—but only really pronounced in males, particularly during the breeding season. Over the years, many varieties of this attractive fish have been produced by commercial breeders, most notably long-finned, red and copper/bronze types in which the females are also more deeply pigmented than their wild or basic counterparts. The Rosy Barb can tolerate relatively low temperatures (*see* below), making them suitable for some

coldwater aquaria—but not in areas that experience severe winter weather.

DISTRIBUTION: *Northern India*

SIZE: *Up to 6in (15cm) reported, but usually much smaller*

BEHAVIOR: *An active shoaling species which is tolerant of others*

DIET: *All livefoods and commercial diets are accepted*

AQUARIUM: *Open swimming areas, along with plant thickets should be provided. Although a wide range of water chemistry conditions are tolerated, extremes of pH and hardness should be avoided. Temperature range: as low as 59°F (15°C) can be tolerated during the winter season*

without trouble (I have kept this species in outdoor ponds in Southern Spain for many years without the slightest difficulty). At other times of the year, 64–77°F (18–25°C)

BREEDING: *A typical egg scatterer among fine-leaved vegetation. As with all other scatterers, the parents will consume their eggs, given the opportunity. Hatching takes about 30 hours at the higher end of the temperature range*

CUMING'S BARB

Barbus cumingi

SYNONYM: *Puntius cumingii*
SUBFAMILY: Cyprininae

CUMING'S BARB SHOULD REALLY BE FAR MORE popular than it is, for it is a delightful little fish that does well in aquaria. A possible reason for its relatively low demand among aquarists could be the deeper colors and longer finnage found in cultivated varieties of *B. nigrofasciatus* (*see* p.168) (with which it shares certain physical characteristics) and *B. conchonius*.

Two different color variants are found in the species' native waters in Sri Lanka: a red-finned variety from the Kelani River catchment and northward from there, and a yellow-finned variety from the Kalu River and the areas to the south. Speckled red and speckled yellow specimens are also encountered in the wild.

While in the past all the Cuming's Barbs available were wild-caught, recent years have seen the development of very successful captive breeding programmes. Today, all

CUMING'S BARB, RED FINNED (BARBUS CUMINGI)

Cuming's Barbs exported from Sri Lanka are bred in farms.

The close similarity between Cuming's Barb and its closest relatives, particularly *B. bandula* and *B. nigrofasciatus*, allied to the possibility of hybridization occurring between all three, means that the status of the species is a little debatable. Cuming's Barb has also been considered as a possible "parental" species of the Odessa Barb (*Barbus "odessa"*)—*see* p.168.

DISTRIBUTION: *Mountain streams in southwest Sri Lanka*

SIZE: *Up to 2in (5cm)*

BEHAVIOR: *Peaceful shoaling species*

DIET: *Wide range of natural and commercial foods accepted*

AQUARIUM: *Medium-sized aquarium with open swimming spaces and shaded areas. Neutral, slightly soft water suits this species best. Temperature range: 72–81°F (22–27°C)*

BREEDING: *Typical egg-scattering barb. Not one of the easiest species to breed. Hatching takes just over 1 day at the higher end of the temperature range*

CLOWN BARB

Barbus everetti

SYNONYM: *Puntius everetti*
SUBFAMILY: Cyprininae

FISH THAT HAVE EITHER BLACK BANDS OR SPOTS separated by golden/orange patches, are often given the name "Clown" and this species is no exception. When fully colored, this is a truly beautiful fish. It is not always as widely available as some other species but when it is—and when it is displayed as a sizable shoal of fully mature fish—it almost sells itself. Unfortunately, males can take up to 18 months to mature and show their full colors, so the majority of specimens that are offered for sale are not quite as attractive as they will eventually become. It is therefore worth bearing this in mind when on the lookout for fish to buy and investing in the future by obtaining a small shoal of specimens, whatever their size.

DISTRIBUTION: *Southeast Asia: Singapore, Kalimantan, Sarawak*

SIZE: *Up to 5in (13cm) reported, but generally smaller than this*

BEHAVIOR: *Peaceful shoaler, but older (and larger) specimens may be a little aggressive toward small fish. This species prefers the lower reaches of the aquarium and has a tendency to nibble tender plants*

DIET: *A wide range of livefoods and commercial diets is accepted; a vegetable supplement should be provided*

CLOWN BARB (BARBUS EVERETTI)

AQUARIUM: *Roomy with open swimming spaces and heavily planted areas. Soft, slightly acid water is preferred, with regular partial water changes. Temperature range: 75–86°F (24–30°C)*

BREEDING: *Not an easy egg-scattering species to breed. Chances of success are improved if the potential, fully mature breeders are kept apart for several weeks and conditioned well with both livefoods and vegetable matter. Positioning the roomy breeding tank where it will catch the rays of the morning sun also seems to help*

BLACK-SPOT BARB

FILAMENT BARB

Barbus filamentosus

SYNONYM: *Puntius filamentosus*
SUBFAMILY: Cyprininae

THE BLACK-SPOT BARB IS ANOTHER SPECIES THAT only exhibits its full characteristics once it matures fully. Even then, it is only the males that develop the extended dorsal fin rays responsible for one of the common names, the Filament Barb. Immature specimens, which account for the majority of those offered for sale, are very attractive in their own right but do not give a true indication of the full beauty and elegance of this fish. This, allied to the fact that some specimens can reportedly grow to a substantial size (*see* below) means that the Black-spot Barb is not always widely available.

DISTRIBUTION: *Sri Lanka and southern India*

SIZE: *Up to 6in (15cm) reported, but usually remains considerably smaller, rarely exceeding 4–4¾in (10–12cm)*

BEHAVIOR: *A lively, sociable species which should be kept in a shoal*

DIET: *Wide range of foods accepted; vegetable supplement recommended*

AQUARIUM: *Owing to its relatively large size, a spacious aquarium is required, with ample swimming space. Subdued lighting shows off its iridescence to good effect. Soft, slightly acid water is recommended. Temperature range: 68–75°F (20–24°C)—slightly higher for breeding purposes*

BREEDING: *Large numbers of eggs (up to 1,000) are laid by this egg-scattering, egg-eating species. Hatching takes 36 hours at the top end of the temperature range*

GOLDEN DWARF BARB

Barbus gelius

SYNONYM: *Puntius gelius*
SUBFAMILY: Cyprininae

DESPITE ITS SMALL SIZE AND APPARENTLY DELICATE appearance, the Golden Dwarf Barb is quite hardy and easy to keep. It should, however, only be kept with other small species. Markings vary between individuals, but all specimens are attractive, particularly under lighting conditions that allow the golden body sheen to glisten.

DISTRIBUTION: *Widely reported as from central India, but Tekriwal and Rao (see Bibliography) report it from eastern and northeastern India*

SIZE: *Up to 1½in (4cm), but often smaller*

BEHAVIOR: *A sociable shoaling species which should never be kept either as single specimens or pairs (males are slimmer)*

DIET: *Large selection of small livefoods and commercial diets accepted; vegetable supplement recommended*

AQUARIUM: *May be kept in smaller aquaria, but also does well in larger ones, provided tankmates are compatible and both open swimming areas and plant thickets is recommended. Softish, slightly acid to neutral water is recommended. Temperature range: as low as 61°F (16°C) during winter; up to 72°F (22°C) at other times and slightly higher for breeding*

BREEDING: *Atypically for a barb, this species lays its eggs on the underside of a broad leaf (when such plants are available). Hatching takes about 1 day*

SPANNER BARB

Barbus lateristriga

SYNONYM: *Puntius lateristriga*
SUBFAMILY: Cyprininae

THE SPANNER BARB IS ONE OF THE LARGER SPECIES of barb available: at least in theory. In practice, most specimens remain well below their maximum potential size, making it possible to keep this unusually marked species in medium-sized aquaria. Owing to its wide distribution in the wild, the Spanner Barb occurs in a number of forms.

DISTRIBUTION: *Widely distributed in southeast Asia*

SIZE: *Up to 7in (18cm) reported for some wild specimens; usually up to 4in (10cm) in aquaria*

BEHAVIOR: *Juveniles shoal, while adults tend to be more solitary*

DIET: *All foods accepted; vegetable supplement recommended*

AQUARIUM: *Roomy with open swimming spaces and plant thickets. Water chemistry is*

not critical, but softish slightly acid to neutral conditions are preferred. Temperature range: as low as 66°F (19°C) in winter, but, generally, 72–79°F (22–26°C)

BREEDING: *A prolific egg scatterer. Hatching takes about 1 day*

RUBY BARB
BLACK RUBY or
PURPLE-HEADED BARB
Barbus nigrofasciatus

SYNONYM: *Puntius nigrofasciatus*
SUBFAMILY: Cyprininae

ONCE WIDELY REGARDED AS SRI LANKA'S MOST popular freshwater fish, the Ruby Barb is now bred commercially in large numbers (*see* photo p.1), both in its native country as well as in all other aquarium fish breeding regions. Several cultivated varieties have as a result been produced over the years, some consisting of color variations on the basic wild type, with some of these having fin modifications as well. Ruby Barbs can be susceptible to shock if transfer from one type of water to another, or introduction into a new aquarium, is undertaken without due care.

DISTRIBUTION: *Southwest Sri Lanka*

SIZE: *Up to 2½in (6.5cm), but often a little smaller*

BEHAVIOR: *A sociable shoaling species which looks best when kept in groups of six or more individuals*

DIET: *All livefoods and commercial diets accepted; vegetable supplement recommended*

AQUARIUM: *As with many other Sri Lankan barbs, this species looks at its best in subdued lighting in an aquarium that provides swimming space and*

plant thickets. Soft, slightly acid water is preferred. Temperature range: 72–79°F (22–26°C); slightly higher for breeding

BREEDING: *A typical egg-scattering, egg-eating species. Hatching takes about 1 day*

ODESSA BARB
Barbus "odessa"

SYNONYMS: *Barbus ticto, Puntius ticto*
SUBFAMILY: Cyprininae

THE ODESSA BARB IS SOMETHING OF A MYSTERY; no-one really knows its true identity. In some books, it is actually referred to as a color variety of the Ticto Barb (*B. ticto*). However, most reports refer to its discovery in a fish bazaar in the Ukrainian city of Odessa in 1971/72. There are several known species of barb that are similar to the Odessa: *B. ticto* (or *B. ticto ticto*), *B. stolickzkanus* (or *B. ticto stolickzkanus*), *B. cumingi* and *B. conchonius*, but no Odessas have ever been collected from the wild. *Barbus "odessa"* is therefore not a valid scientific name.

DISTRIBUTION: *Not known in the wild*

SIZE: *Around 2½in (6cm)*

BEHAVIOR: *A very active shoaling fish*

DIET: *All livefoods and commercial diets accepted*

AQUARIUM: *Should be provided with ample swimming space owing to its very active nature. Water chemistry is not critical, but softish, slightly acid water suits Odessas well. Temperature range: very wide range tolerated, from around 68°F (20°C) to 86°F (30°C)*

BREEDING: *An erratic breeder; typical egg scatterer and egg eater. Hatching takes about 36 hours*

◄ GOLDEN DWARF BARB (BARBUS GELIUS)
▼ SPANNER BARB (BARBUS LATERISTRIGA)

TINFOIL BARB
GOLDFOIL or SCHWANENFELD'S BARB

Barbus schwanenfeldi

SYNONYMS: *Barbus schwanefeldi, Puntius schwanenfeldi*
SUBFAMILY: Cyprininae

THIS IS THE LARGEST BARB SPECIES USUALLY KEPT in home aquaria (*see* below), but usually as juveniles, since adults will outgrow most setups. As specimens grow, they can become aggressive, particularly toward small fish. This, added to the species' plant-eating habits, makes the Tinfoil less suitable than many other barb species. A very attractive gold-bodied, red-finned variety is now available.

DISTRIBUTION: *Widely distributed in southeast Asia*

SIZE: *Up to 14in (35cm) for fully mature wild specimens; smaller than this in aquaria*

BEHAVIOR: *An active shoaler which should only be kept with similarly sized fish*

DIET: *All foods accepted; vegetable component, e.g. lettuce leaves, essential*

AQUARIUM: *Spacious aquarium with well-fitting cover, lots of swimming space and robust or unpalatable plants (see Aquarium Plants). Water chemistry is not critical, but raw water should be avoided. Temperature range: 72–77°F (22–25°C)*

BREEDING: *Widely bred commercially, but not in home aquaria. Eggs are scattered over the substratum or among plants. Hatching takes about 1 day*

GOLDEN BARB
SCHUBERT'S, HALF-STRIPED, or GREEN, BARB

Barbus semifasciolatus

SYNONYMS: *Puntius semifasciolatus, Capoeta semifasciolatus, Barbus schuberti, "Barbus schuberti", Barbus "schuberti"*
SUBFAMILY: Cyprininae

THE BURNISHED YELLOW BODY COLORATION OF mature wild males has been developed by specialist breeders over the years into the widely available and very popular Golden or Schubert's Barb, to such an extent that the true, wild type of this species is now rarely found in shops. As this fish matures, the back can darken into a deep orangey-red in some specimens, particularly in males. None of the names incorporating "schuberti" is a valid scientific name.

DISTRIBUTION: *Southern China*

SIZE: *Up to 4in (10cm) reported, but usually smaller*

BEHAVIOR: *Peaceful shoaler*

TINFOIL BARB (BARBUS SCHWANENFELDII)

DIET: *All types of food accepted; vegetable supplement recommended*

AQUARIUM: *Swimming space with planted areas recommended. Water chemistry is not critical, but raw water should be avoided. Temperature range: 64–75°F (18–24°C); slightly higher for breeding*

BREEDING: *Typical egg-scattering, egg-eating species. Hatching takes about 30 hours*

TIGER BARB
SUMATRA BARB

Barbus tetrazona

SYNONYMS: *Puntius tetrazona, Capoeta tetrazona*
SUBFAMILY: Cyprininae

THIS IS THE MOST WIDELY AVAILABLE AND popular of the barbs kept in home aquaria (*see* photo p.25). It has a long aquarium history, having been introduced

GOLDEN BARB (BARBUS SEMIFASCIOLATUS)

in the mid-1930s and has been bred in vast numbers by both aquarists and commercial breeders. Many color varieties are currently available, with new ones continuing to appear from time to time.

DISTRIBUTION: *Indonesia (particularly Sumatra) and Borneo, including Kalimantan. Reports of the species being found in Thailand are dubious and may refer to a fish often called B. tetrazona partipentazona*

SIZE: *Up to 2¾in (7cm), but usually a little smaller*

BEHAVIOR: *Extremely active shoaler which will nip fins of other fish if kept singly or in pairs. A minimum number of six specimens should be kept*

DIET: *All foods accepted; vegetable component recommended*

AQUARIUM: *Ample open swimming area surrounded by plant thickets should be provided. Will accept a wide range of water chemistry conditions (as long as the water quality is good) but will not breed successfully*

Cherry Barb (*Barbus titteya*)

unless conditions are soft and slightly acid.
Temperature range: 68–79°F (20–26°C); a little
higher for breeding

BREEDING: *Typical egg scatterer, egg eater.
Hatching takes about 36 hours. Mated pairs are
recommended for optimal results*

CHERRY BARB
Barbus titteya

SYNONYM: *Puntius titteya*
SUBFAMILY: Cyprininae

THIS IS A STUNNINGLY BEAUTIFUL FISH WHEN IN peak condition. In particular, fully mature males exhibit the cherry coloration to perfection. Wild-caught specimens are variable in their coloration, with at least three varieties known from different localities. Virtually all aquarium specimens are now commercially bred, in Sri

OTHER BARB SPECIES

The genus *Barbus sensu lato*—in the broadest sense, including those fish variously referred to as *Capoeta* and *Puntius*—contains more than 100 species. Of these, a considerable number over and above those featured here are available. Generally, all do well under the same basic conditions, but check individual requirements elsewhere if in doubt, beginning with experienced aquarists and your local dealer. The following is a selection of some of the species that are most commonly encountered.

SCIENTIFIC NAME	COMMON NAME	SIZE	TEMPERATURE
B. bariloides	Orange Barb	2in (5cm)	73–79°F (23–26°C)
B. binotatus	Spotted Barb	4¾in (12cm) but 7in (18cm) reported	75–79°F (24–26°C)
B. callipterus	Clipper Barb	3½in (9cm)	72–77°F (22–25°C)
B. denisoni (umangii)	Red Line Torpedo Fish	6in (15cm)	72–77°F (22–25°C)
B. fasciatus*	Striped, Banded or Melon Barb	c.2½in (6cm)	72–77°F (22–25°C)
B. holotaenia	—	4¾in (12cm)	75–86°F (24–30°C)
B. hulstaerti	Butterfly Barb	1½in (3.5cm)	75°F (c.24°C)
B. lineatus	Striped Barb	4¾in (12cm)	70–75°F (21–24°C)
B. oligolepis	Checkered or Island Barb	6in (15cm)	68–75°F (20–24°C)
B. pentazona**	Five-banded Barb	2in (5cm)	68–79°F (20–26°C)
B. rhomboocellatus	Round-banded Barb	2in (5cm)	73–82°F (23–28°C)
B. stoliczkanus (B. ticto stoliczkanus)	Stoliczk's or Stoliczka's Barb	c.2½in (6cm)	72–75°F (22–24°C)
B. ticto (B. ticto ticto)	Ticto or Tic-Tac-Toe Barb	2in (5cm) but 4in (10cm) reported	57–72°F (14–22°C)
B. viviparus***	Livebearing Barb	2½in (6.5cm)	72–75°F (22–24°C)

NOTES:

* Two different species are variously referred to as *B. fasciatus*: the Striped or Banded Barb, from Malaysia, Sumatra and Borneo, and the Melon Barb from India

** *B. pentazona* is often divided into subspecies: *B. pentazona pentazona, B. p. tetrazona* and *B. p. hexazona*

*** *B. viviparus* is not a livebearer, despite its name

SPOTTED BARB (BARBUS BINOTATUS) ▲▲▲
FIVE-BANDED BARB (BARBUS PENTAZONA) ▲▲
TICTO BARB (BARBUS TICTO) ▲

Lanka or elsewhere. An albino variety is occasionally available.

DISTRIBUTION: *Southwest Sri Lanka*

SIZE: *Up to 2in (5cm) widely reported; usually smaller*

BEHAVIOR: *Not as active or as prone to shoaling as many other species. It is nevertheless a peaceful fish which should be kept in groups*

DIET: *Most small foods are accepted; vegetable component recommended*

AQUARIUM: *This species is a little more retiring than most other barbs. Therefore, large open areas should be avoided. Some swimming space should, nevertheless, be provided, with ample shelter around. Soft, slightly acid water is best. Temperature range: 72–75°F (22–24°C) is adequate for normal maintenance, but should be raised to around 79°F (26°C) for breeding*

BREEDING: *Typical egg-scattering, egg-eating species. Hatching takes about 1 day*

DWARF RASBORA
PYGMY OR SPOTTED RASBORA
Borarus maculata

SYNONYMS: *Rasbora maculata. Microrasbora maculata*
SUBFAMILY: Rasborinae (Danioninae)

AT ONE TIME, ADULT DWARF RASBORA WERE thought to be juvenile *Rasbora kalochroma*, being similar but smaller. However, *B. maculata* is a species in its own right, and a particularly striking one at that. It is also one of the smallest fish kept in aquaria.

DISTRIBUTION: *Western Malaysia, Singapore, Sumatra*

SIZE: *Up to 1in (2.5cm), but often smaller*

BEHAVIOR: *A peaceful shoaler*

DIET: *Wide range of small-sized foods accepted*

AQUARIUM: *As for R. heteromorpha (see p. 184) but slightly lower temperature*

BREEDING: *Small breeding tank with soft, slightly acid, shallow water. Eggs are scattered among plants. Hatching takes about 1-1½ days*

PEARL DANIO
Brachydanio albolineatus

SUBFAMILY: Rasborinae (Danioninae)

THE DANIOS (*BRACHYDANIO* AND *DANIO* SPECIES) are all active shoalers and have been part of the hobby for many years. The Pearl Danio was first imported into Europe in 1911 and is still very popular today. This is despite the fact that it is not often displayed to maximum effect and therefore does not always show off its best colors. Two forms of the Pearl Danio are generally available (though several more exist): the wild type and, more infrequently, a yellow morph usually referred to as the Yellow Danio.

DISTRIBUTION: *Southeast Asia*

SIZE: *Up to 2½in (6cm); usually smaller*

BEHAVIOR: *Very active shoaler that prefers the upper layers of the water column, but will swim at all levels*

DIET: *Most livefoods and commercial diets are accepted*

AQUARIUM: *A well-covered aquarium with ample swimming areas should be provided, with no tall plants obstructing this space (tall plants are best arranged around the sides and back of the aquarium). Water chemistry is not critical, but*

overall quality must be good. Temperature range: *68–77°F (20–25°C); a little higher for breeding*

BREEDING: *Chances of success are enhanced if two males and a female are introduced into the breeding tank placed in a sunny position. This is an egg-scattering, egg-eating species. Hatching takes in about 36-48 hours*

KERR'S DANIO
BLUE DANIO
Brachydanio kerri

SUBFAMILY: Rasborinae (Danioninae)

THIS IS A MUCH MORE RECENT INTRODUCTION THAN the Pearl Danio, first making its appearance in the mid-1950s. Although quite widely available, this danio is not kept as often as some of its nearest relatives. Like them, it is a beautiful, active jumper.

DISTRIBUTION: *Restricted to two islands in Thailand*

SIZE: *Up to 2in (5cm)*

BEHAVIOR: *Active shoaler; excellent jumper*

DIET: *Most foods accepted*

AQUARIUM: *As for B. albolineatus. Temperature range: 72–77°F (22–25°C)*

BREEDING: *Eggs are scattered, primarily, over the substratum. Hatching can take up to 4 days. Will hybridize with its closest relatives*

SPOTTED DANIO
Brachydanio nigrofasciatus

SUBFAMILY: Rasborinae (Danioninae)

LIKE *B. ALBOLINEATUS*, THE SPOTTED DANIO HAS been around since 1911 and, while it is not now kept by as many aquarists as it

▲ SPOTTED DANIO (BRACHYDANIO NIGROFASCIATUS)

ZEBRA DANIO
LEOPARD DANIO

Brachydanio rerio

SYNONYMS: *Brachydanio frankei, B. "frankei"*

THIS IS BY FAR THE MOST POPULAR OF ALL THE danios. It is widely available in several forms, including wild, golden and long-finned types in different combinations. Of these, the wild type is the most robust. The Leopard Danio—also available as a long-finned variant—has traditionally been regarded as a separate species: *B. frankei*. However, genetic analysis of crosses between Leopards and Zebras have now confirmed that the Leopard is a Zebra morph and therefore belongs to the same species.

DISTRIBUTION: *Zebra—from Eastern India; Leopard—not encountered in the wild*

SIZE: *2⅓in (6cm) including extended fins; short-finned varieties generally only attain around 1¾in (4.5cm)*

BEHAVIOR: *Extremely active shoaler which may nip fin extensions of fancy varieties of Guppies, Swordtails, Angels, etc.*

DIET: *Most foods accepted*

AQUARIUM: *Open spaces surrounded by plant thickets. Water chemistry is not critical, but soft, slightly acid water is preferred. Temperature range: 64–75°F (18–24°C)—short-finned wild-type specimens can tolerate slightly lower temperatures in winter*

BREEDING: *Egg-scattering, egg-eating species. Eggs may be released over the substratum, as well as among plants. Best results are obtained with pairs that select themselves from a shoal; these will tend to stay together. Hatching takes about 2 days*

INDIAN GLASS BARB
INDIAN GLASS HATCHET, or BLUE LAUBUCA

Chela laubuca

SUBFAMILY: Rasborinae (Danioninae)

THERE ARE SEVERAL SPECIES OF *CHELA* occasionally available: *C. laubuca* (the most common), *C. cachuis* (Neon Hatchet), *C. dadyburjori* (Burjor's Brilliance or Orange Chela), *C. fasciata* (Striped Chela) and—perhaps the most colorful of all—*C. auropurpurens* (Orange False Barilius).

All are small, with the exception of the last species which is reported to attain 4in (10cm) in length. Despite two of its common names, *C. laubuca* is neither a barb nor a hatchet fish. Chelas can prove delicate during the initial phases of acclimatisation.

DISTRIBUTION: *Southeast Asia (widely distributed)*

▲▲ ZEBRA DANIO (BRACHYDANIO RERIO)

▲ GOLDEN ZEBRA DANIO (BRACHYDANIO RERIO VAR.)

once was, it remains a firm favorite, especially among experienced hobbyists who appreciate its beauty, despite its small size.

DISTRIBUTION: *Myanmar (Burma)*

SIZE: *Around 1½in (4cm)*

BEHAVIOR: *A peaceful shoaler which is not quite as active as some of its closest relatives*

DIET: *Most foods accepted*

AQUARIUM: *As for other Brachydanio species. Temperature range: 74–82°F (24–28°C)*

BREEDING: *As for B. albolineatus, but at around 77–82°F (25–28°C). B. nigrofasciatus can hybridize with, at least, B. albolineatus, possibly other danios*

GOLDFISH
Carassius auratus

SYNONYM: *Carassius auratus auratus*
SUBFAMILY: Cyprininae

THE GOLDFISH IS BELIEVED TO BE NOT JUST THE MOST WIDELY KEPT ornamental fish in the world, but the most popular of all pets. Virtually every aquarist and pondkeeper in the world has kept a goldfish at one time or other. Although there is documentary evidence of the goldfish having been kept as a pet in ponds in China as far back as the Sung Dynasty (AD 960–1279), there are indications that its history could stretch back to the Western Jin Dynasty (AD 262–315), which would make the goldfish–human association at least 1,700 years old. Over the centuries, countless varieties of the goldfish have been developed in numerous countries. Today, there are over 100 officially recognized varieties, and an unknown number of "unofficial" ones.

A few of the best-known varieties are listed here. However, as variants are continually combined to select color or fin features, the rate at which new goldfish varieties become available shows no sign of slowing down. While some of the old favorites will remain so well into the future, every few years will most likely see the establishment of new favorites.

The alternative scientific name cited, *Carassius auratus auratus*, indicates that the goldfish was until quite recently regarded as a subspecies of the species *C. auratus*, the other one being *C. auratus gibelius*, the Gibel or Prussian Carp. Today though, both are regarded as valid species in their own right.

DISTRIBUTION: *China and parts of Siberia. However, widely introduced in numerous tropical, subtropical and temperate regions worldwide*

SIZE: *Up to around 12in (30cm) for slim-bodied types; round-bodied varieties tend to be considerably smaller, but some types of Orandas, for example, can also grow to substantial sizes*

BEHAVIOR: *Generally peaceful, although some specimens—and in particular mature males during the breeding season—can harass other fish. All varieties will eat soft, succulent plants and will constantly root around the bottom of the tank*

DIET: *All foods accepted; vegetable component important*

AQUARIUM: *This should be roomy with wide open areas that allow full view of the fish. Robust and/or unpalatable plants should be used, perhaps supplemented with artificial types. Roots should be protected (see Aquarium Plants). Water chemistry is not critical, but quality must be good. Efficient filtration and aeration are essential. Temperature range: from well below 50°F (10°C) to above 86°F (30°C); higher temperatures should not be maintained on a long-term basis*

COMMON GOLDFISH *THE "CLASSIC" SHORT-FINNED VARIETY, USUALLY ORANGE-COLORED (TOP), BUT ALSO AVAILABLE IN OTHER SINGLE COLORS AND COMBINATIONS (ABOVE: BLOOD-RED VARIETY).*

COMET *SLIMMER THAN A BRISTOL SHUBUNKIN AND WITH A LONGER TAIL, PREFERABLY POINTED. THE MOST POPULAR TYPE IS RED AND WHITE IS KNOWN AS THE SARASA (LEFT).*

FANTAIL *OVAL-BODIED, DOUBLE-TAILED VARIETY WITH RELATIVELY SHORT FINS (BELOW: CALICO).*

BREEDING: *Persistent chasing (driving) by the male—which develops white pimple-like tubercles on its snout and gill covers during the breeding season—will eventually result in the pair (or a shoal) spawning among fine-leaved vegetation. Goldfish are egg scatterers/eaters, so, either they, or the eggs, should be removed after spawning (which tends to occur at temperatures above 68°F (20°C)). Hatching can take up to 1 week, but generally takes less*

RYUKIN *SUPERFICIALLY SIMILAR TO THE FANTAIL BUT WITH HIGH DORSAL (BACK) FIN AND VERY DEEP BODY.*

VEILTAIL *SIMILAR TO THE FANTAIL, BUT WITH LONG FLOWING FINS (ABOVE: CALICO; RIGHT: RED AND WHITE—ORIENTAL STYLE; BLOOD STREAKS IN TAIL SUGGEST POOR CONDITION).*

ORANDA *SIMILAR TO VEILTAIL, BUT WITH RASPBERRY-LIKE GROWTH (KNOWN AS A HOOD) ON THE HEAD (ABOVE LEFT: RED POM-POM; ABOVE: BICOLOR—CHOCOLATE AND SILVER; LEFT: BRONZE POM-POM AND RED CAP).*

MOOR *DOUBLE-TAILED, BUT WITHOUT A HOOD. THE EYE MAY PROTRUDE. BODY COLOR: BLACK.*

BUTTERFLY MOOR *LIKE THE MOOR, BUT WITH A SHORTER DOUBLE TAIL WHICH IS OFTEN SPLAYED OUT AND HAS THE APPEARANCE OF A BUTTERFLY (ABOVE: BLUE BUTTERFLY MOOR).*

HAMANISHIKI *OVAL-BODIED, SHORT-FINNED, DOUBLE-TAILED VARIETY WITH DOMED SCALES THAT LOOK LIKE PEARLS. TWO "BUBBLES" ON TOP OF THE HEAD. ALSO KNOWN AS THE HIGH-HEAD PEARLSCALE (ABOVE).*

LIONHEAD *SIMILAR TO AN ORANDA, BUT WITHOUT A DORSAL (BACK) FIN. THE DORSAL PROFILE IS RELATIVELY STRAIGHT (FAR LEFT: BLUE LIONHEAD; LEFT: RED-EYED LIONHEAD).*

RANCHU *LIKE THE LIONHEAD, BUT WITH A CURVED BACK PROFILE (BELOW LEFT: RED AND WHITE RANCHU; BELOW: BLACK RANCHU).*

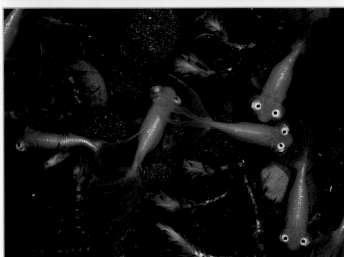

CELESTIAL *SIMILAR BODY SHAPE CHARACTERISTICS TO THE LIONHEAD, BUT WITHOUT A HOOD AND WITH UPWARD-LOOKING EYES.*

BUBBLE-EYE *SIMILAR TO THE CELESTIAL BUT, WITH LARGE FLUID-FILLED EYE SACS (ABOVE: RED BUBBLE-EYE).*

SIZE: *Up to 2⅓in (6cm)*

BEHAVIOR: *A peaceful shoaler which has a strong preference for the surface layers of the aquarium*

DIET: *Wide range of (predominantly) floating foods accepted; will not feed off the bottom*

AQUARIUM: *Open swimming areas surrounded by vegetation. Frequent partial water changes recommended, as well as soft, slightly acid water. Temperature range: 75–79°F (24–26°C)*

BREEDING: *Eggs laid among fine-leaved vegetation. Hatching takes about 1 day*

SIAMESE FLYING FOX
SIAMESE ALGAE EATER
Crossocheilus siamensis

SUBFAMILY: Cyprininae (classified as Garrinae by some authors)

WHAT THE SIAMESE FLYING FOX MAY LACK IN brilliant coloration, it more than makes up for with its other attributes. In particular, it is one of the few aquarium fish that actually eats thread algae. Its only potential drawback for many home aquaria is that it can grow to a substantial size.

DISTRIBUTION: *Thailand, Peninsular Malaysia*

SIZE: *Up to 6in (15cm) reported, but usually smaller*

BEHAVIOR: *Tolerant of other species, but less so of its own*

DIET: *Wide range of foods accepted; vegetable component essential. Reported to eat planarian worms (flatworms) which are sometimes introduced accidentally with some livefoods*

AQUARIUM: *Roomy tank with thickets of vegetation (Siamese Flying Foxes will eat algae, but do not generally harm other plants). Hiding places should be provided. Well-oxygenated, soft, slightly acid water is recommended, though harder, more alkaline conditions are also tolerated. Temperature range: 73–79°F (23–26°C)*

BREEDING: *No details are available*

RED SHINER
SANDPAPER SHINER, RED HORSE MINNOW, or RAINBOW DACE
Cyprinella lutrensis

SYNONYM: *Notropis lutrensis*
SUBFAMILY: Leuciscinae

TWO OF THE COMMON NAMES REFER TO THE RED patches that mature males develop on top of and behind the head, as well as on all the fins. This contrasts beautifully with the grayish blue of the rest of the body,

KOI, HAND-FEEDING (CYPRINUS CARPIO)

making the Red Shiner a most attractive choice for the coldwater aquarium. While the Red Shiner (wild type or albino) is by far the most common shiner, other *Cyprinella* and *Notropis* species are beginning to appear with greater regularity.

DISTRIBUTION: *Mississippi River Basin (US) and Gulf drainages west of the Mississippi. Widely introduced elsewhere in the US; also in northern Mexico*

SIZE: *3½in (9cm)*

BEHAVIOR: *A very active shoaler*

DIET: *All foods accepted*

AQUARIUM: *Roomy with ample swimming space; well-filtered, well-oxygenated water and frequent partial water changes recommended. Water chemistry not critical. Temperature range: 50–77°F (10–25°C)*

BREEDING: *Eggs laid in a depression on a sandy/silty bottom. Hatching takes several days*

KOI
BROCADED CARP
Cyprinus carpio

SUBFAMILY: Cyprininae

IN THE PAST THESE HIGHLY DEVELOPED VARIETIES OF the Common Carp have only been kept in ponds but improvements in aquarium technology, along with the rise in interest in "companion pets", have led to some types of Koi being introduced into large aquaria.

Fairy or Butterfly (long-finned) Koi are the most popular of the "aquarium" varieties, but even the more traditional pond varieties are now being sought after by aquarists, many of whom also keep Koi in ponds.

The history of the Koi, though considerably shorter than that of the goldfish (the first recognized Koi being associated with developments during the early 19th century in Niigata Prefecture on the Japanese island of Honshu) is long enough to have produced numerous color and scale modifications. The result is a bewildering array of fish bred in vast quantities in Japan, Israel, Italy, the UK, the US, the Far East and virtually every other region with an interest in coldwater fishkeeping. However, Japan still leads the way in terms of pedigree fish production.

DISTRIBUTION: *Originally from the Danube and other freshwaters of the Black Sea Basin. Now found throughout Europe (except the extreme north) and numerous other regions*

SIZE: *Up to 40in (1m) for fully grown wild C. carpio; usually a little smaller for Koi, even "jumbo" specimens*

BEHAVIOR: *Generally peaceful, even toward smaller fish, but some males may become somewhat aggressive during the breeding season. All types will eat soft, succulent plants and will spend much of the time rooting around the bottom of the aquarium*

DIET: *All foods accepted; vegetable component important. Treats can include items like shrimp,*

SOME KOI VARIETIES

Nonmetallic Varieties

KOHAKU
White base color with red markings.

TANCHO SANKE (or SANKE)
White base color with superimposed red and black markings.

SHOWA SANSHOKU (usually referred to as SHOWA)
Black base color with red and white markings.

BEKKO
Black markings on a white, red or yellow base color.

UTSURIMONO
White, red or yellow markings on a black base.

ASAGI
Blue base with red on the belly, fins and sides of head; top of head is light grayish-blue.

TANCHO
Single, red marking on the top of the head; this classification is reserved for Kohaku, Sanke and Showa Koi that bear this very distinctive head spot.

Metallic Varieties

HIKARIMONO (or OGON)
Single-colored fish.

HIKARI-UTSURIMONO
Metallic versions of Utsuri and Showa.

HIKARIMONO-MONO
Term embracing all other types of metallic Koi.

Other Categories

KINGINRIN
Fish having 20 or more reflective/sparkling scales; previously, judging of this category at Koi shows embraced fish of any variety, provided they had the appropriate scalation. Nowadays, only Kohaku, Sanke and Showa are included.

▼ *SILVER OGON KOI (CYPRINUS CARPIO VAR.)*
▼▼ *BLUE MIRROR KOI (CYPRINUS CARPIO VAR.)*

GOSHIKI
Five-colored Koi classified within the Kawarimono in countries other than Japan.

DOITSU
Doitsu-scaled fish (almost scale-less, but with a few rows of large, reflective scales, as found in the Mirror Carp) are generally classified under their color variety. However, in Japan, Doitsu fish of any variety are classified separately, except for Shusui.

GOLD GHOST KOI (CYPRINUS CARPIO VAR.)

HANA SHUSUI KOI (CYPRINUS CARPIO VAR.)

SHUSUI
Similar to the Asagi, but with dark blue coloration restricted to the large Doitsu scales (*see* OTHER CATEGORIES, below); naked areas are light blue, except for the head, which is light grayish-blue.

KOROMO
White base color with red markings that are overlaid with darker patterning.

KAWARIMONO
A catch-all term for all other types of nonmetallic Koi, including single-colored fish, e.g. Ki-goi (yellow fish), almost single-colored fish, e.g. Hajiro (black fish with white fin edges) and Goshiki (five-colored fish, but *see* OTHER CATEGORIES below).

peas, lettuce and brown bread, but not as major components of the diet

AQUARIUM: *Only large and deep aquaria which are efficiently filtered can be considered suitable. Use robust and unpalatable plants, perhaps combined with artificial types. Protect plant roots (see Aquarium Plants). Water chemistry not critical. Temperature range: from well below 50°F (10°C) to above 86°F (30°C); higher temperatures should not be maintained for long periods*

BREEDING: *This is difficult to achieve in most aquaria owing to the lack of space. Eggs are scattered among vegetation when the temperature rises above 63°F (17°C). Injuries may result during the vigorous chasing (driving) that occurs. Spawning brushes/mats are recommended, to be subsequently removed to another aquarium for hatching, which takes 3–4 days at 68–72°F (20–22°C).*

▲ GIANT DANIO (DANIO AEQUIPINNATUS)   ▼ BARRED DANIO (DANIO PATHIRANA)

GIANT DANIO

Danio aequipinnatus

SYNONYM: *Danio malabaricus*
SUBFAMILY: Rasborinae (Danioninae)

THE GENUS DANIO IS VERY SIMILAR TO BRACHY-danio, differing only in details relating to fin ray and lateral line features. More obvious is the larger size attained by *Danio* species.

There is still considerable debate as to whether *D. aequipinnatus* and *D. malabaricus* are one and the same species or whether, at least in Sri Lanka, they constitute two very closely related species. Most authorities believe them to be the same fish. Several color varieties, including a golden one, are available.

DISTRIBUTION: *Southwest India and Sri Lanka*

SIZE: *Up to 6in (15cm) reported, but usually considerably smaller*

BEHAVIOR: *Very active, peaceful shoaler which prefers the upper layers of the water column*

DIET: *Wide range of foods accepted*

AQUARIUM: *Roomy with well-fitting cover, open swimming spaces and plant thickets. Water chemistry not critical but quality must be good. Temperature range: 72–75°F (22–24°C); slightly higher for breeding*

BREEDING: *Eggs are scattered among fine-leaved vegetation. Hatching takes about 1 day*

BENGAL DANIO

TURQUOISE DANIO

Danio devario

SUBFAMILY: Rasborinae (Danioninae)

THIS SPECIES IS THE LEAST STREAMLINED OF THE danios. The females in particular, have a relatively deep body. It is also the most subtly colored member of the genus, its colors best exhibited in reflected light and when kept as a shoal.

DISTRIBUTION: *Northern and eastern India, Bangladesh and Pakistan*

SIZE: *Up to 6in (15cm) reported, but generally significantly smaller*

BEHAVIOR: *An active shoaling species which can be a bit timid. It prefers the top layers*

DIET: *Wide range of foods accepted*

AQUARIUM: *A dark substratum helps to show off this species to good effect. Ample spaces surrounded by plant thickets should be provided. Water chemistry not critical. Temperature range: 59–79°F (15–26°C) considered by some*

to be adequate, but 68–79°F (20–26°C) is recommended

BREEDING: *This is a typical egg-scatterer. Hatching takes about 1 day*

BARRED DANIO

Danio pathirana

SUBFAMILY: Rasborinae (Danioninae)

THIS IS THE MOST RECENTLY DISCOVERED AND KEPT of the *Danio* species (officially described in 1990) and in the opinion of some, the most beautiful. Within its restricted range it has been found in both still and flowing waters.

Although bred in captivity, this species is not yet available in large numbers. It is, however, an adaptable fish which is likely to become progressively more popular.

DISTRIBUTION: *Southwest Sri Lanka*

SIZE: *About 2½in (6cm)*

BEHAVIOR: *Not as active as some of its closest relatives. Tends to form small groups, rather than large shoals, in the wild and exhibits fin-nipping behavior at times*

DIET: *Wide range of foods accepted*

AQUARIUM: *Basically as for D. aequipinnatus*

BREEDING: *Egg-scattering species, but details are unavailable*

RED-TAILED BLACK SHARK
RED-TAILED LABEO
Epalzeorhynchus bicolor

SYNONYM: *Labeo bicolor*
SUBFAMILY: Cyprininae (classified as Garrinae by some authors)

THIS IS BY FAR THE MOST STRIKINGLY COLORED OF all the aquarium "sharks"—which are only sharklike in their overall body shape and even then, only superficially. Unless water conditions are to its liking, this species will not show off its best colors, becoming darkish gray and faint red, rather than jet black and bright red. Due

attention must therefore be paid to aquarium layout and conditions.

DISTRIBUTION: *Thailand*

SIZE: *Up to 4¾in (12cm)*

BEHAVIOR: *A loner which stakes out its own territory and will become aggressive toward other members of its species. This intolerance can be extended to other species as well, particularly by older specimens*

DIET: *Wide range of foods accepted; sinking formulations and a vegetable component are recommended*

AQUARIUM: *Spacious, with shelters or caves provided. A fine-grained substratum is recommended, as is soft to medium-hard water. Temperature range: 72–79°F (22–26°C); higher for breeding*

BREEDING: *Infrequent in aquaria. Eggs are reported to be laid in a depression in the substratum. Hatching takes about 2 days*

RUBY SHARK
RAINBOW, or RED-FINNED, SHARK
Epalzeorhynchus frenatus

SYNONYMS: *Labeo frenatus, Labeo erythrurus*
SUBFAMILY: Cyprininae (classified as Garrinae by some authors)

THIS IS A SLIMMER SPECIES THAN E. BICOLOR. Specimens offered as *L. erythrurus* are generally believed to be either mature *E. frena-*

tus, or a local variety. A commercially produced albino morph is widely available.

DISTRIBUTION: *Thailand*

SIZE: *Up to 6in (15cm), but usually quite a bit smaller*

BEHAVIOR: *As for E. bicolor*

DIET: *As for E. bicolor*

AQUARIUM: *As for E. bicolor*

BREEDING: *Infrequent in aquaria; no documented accounts appear to be available*

FLYING FOX
Epalzeorhynchus kallopterus

SUBFAMILY: Cyprininae (classified as Garrinae by some authors)

THIS SPECIES IS SIMILAR IN APPEARANCE TO *Crossocheilus siamensis* (Siamese Flying Fox)—see p.176. At close quarters, the Flying Fox can be seen to possess two pairs of barbels on the upper lip, while *C. siamensis* only has one.

DISTRIBUTION: *Indonesia: Sumatra, Java, Kalimantan; also variously reported from Thailand and northern India*

SIZE: *Up to 6in (15cm) reported, but usually smaller*

BEHAVIOR: *Rests on the tips of its pectoral (chest) fins. Territorial, but otherwise generally peaceful*

DIET: *Grazes on algae; therefore wide-ranging diet must include a vegetable component*

AQUARIUM: *Hiding places and broad-leaved plants should be provided. Soft, slightly acid water and frequent partial changes recommended. Temperature range: 75–79°F (24–26°C), with some flexibility*

BREEDING: *No documented reports available*

FLYING BARB
Esomus thermoicos

SYNONYM: *Esomus danrica*
SUBFAMILY: Rasborinae (Danioninae)

MOST BOOKS WILL REFER TO THE FLYING BARB AS *E. danrica*, rather than *E. thermoicos*. However, comparative work carried out on Indian and Sri Lankan collections indicates that both nominal species are more closely related than first thought; they may be subspecies or even just normally varying populations. Further work is awaited. The most unusual feature of this attractive species is its very long, filament-like barbels responsible for its common name, although it is not a barb. It does, however, jump ("fly").

DISTRIBUTION: *India, Sri Lanka and Thailand*

SIZE: *Up to 6in (15cm) reported, but usually much smaller. About 2½in (6cm) common in wild-caught specimens*

RED-TAILED BLACK SHARK (EPALZEORHYNCHUS BICOLOR)

BEHAVIOR: *Very active fish with a tendency to leap out of the water. Prefers the top layers of the aquarium*

DIET: *Wide range of foods accepted*

AQUARIUM: *Roomy, well-covered tank with ample surface swimming space surrounded by plants. Water chemistry not critical but quality must be good. Temperature range: 72–75°F (22–24°C); higher (around 81°F—27°C) for breeding*

BREEDING: *Eggs are scattered among plants. Hatching takes 1–2 days, depending on temperature*

SIAMESE STONE-LAPPING SUCKER

Garra taeniatia

SUBFAMILY: Cyprininae

OVER RECENT YEARS, A NUMBER OF *GARRA* SPECIES have begun appearing in the hobby with increasing regularity. All are, basically, bottom-dwelling species from flowing-water habitats and are not difficult to keep. The Siamese Stone-lapping Sucker is the most commonly encountered species.

DISTRIBUTION: *Thailand*

SIZE: *Up to 6in (15cm)*

BEHAVIOR: *Generally tolerant of other species, but may disrupt the substratum, particularly when kept in groups*

DIET: *Most foods accepted, especially sinking formulations*

AQUARIUM: *Roomy, with ample resting/hiding places and robust plants, with roots protected (see Aquarium Plants). Water should be well*

SIAMESE STONE-LAPPING SUCKER (GARRA TAENIATIA)

aerated and filtered. Temperature range: 75–79°F (24–26°C)

BREEDING: *No details are available*

GUDGEON

Gobio gobio

SUBFAMILY: Gobioninae

THE GUDGEON IS PREDOMINANTLY A BOTTOM-dwelling species that has traditionally been regarded as a pondfish by (mostly) European hobbyists. However, as cold-water aquarium keeping has expanded, so has the gudgeon gained greater popularity.

DISTRIBUTION: *Europe, except most of Italy, northern Finland, Sweden and the Adriatic coast. Spanish, Scottish and Northern Irish populations are introduced, rather than native*

SIZE: *Up to 8in (20cm), but usually smaller*

BEHAVIOR: *Peaceful bottom-dweller that will learn to take food from the surface*

DIET: *Most foods accepted, particularly sinking formulations and livefoods*

GUDGEON (GOBIO GOBIO)

AQUARIUM: *Well-filtered, well-oxygenated water essential (this species is sensitive to pollution). Substratum should be fine-grained and shelters should be provided. Neutral to slightly alkaline, medium-hard water is preferred. Temperature range: 50–68°F (10–20°C)*

BREEDING: *Infrequent in aquaria. Adhesive eggs laid on substratum in flowing water. Hatching takes 10–30 days, depending on temperature*

BLACK SHARK

BLACK LABEO

Labeo chrysophekadion

SUBFAMILY: Cyprininae

THIS IS THE LARGEST "SHARK" SPECIES KEPT IN aquaria. Most specimens offered are around 4in (10cm) or smaller, but will grow quickly and are therefore not suitable for average aquaria. However, if sufficiently spacious accommodation is available, a lone large specimen will prove a long-lived and impressive companion. Two other *Labeo* species (both smaller, but still substantial) are also available: *L. forskalli* (Plain Shark) and *L. variegatus* (Harlequin or Variegated Shark).

DISTRIBUTION: *Southwest Asia (widely distributed)*

SIZE: *Up to 24in (60cm) reported*

BEHAVIOR: *A loner which is aggressive toward members of its own species*

DIET: *All foods accepted; vegetable component important*

AQUARIUM: *Roomy, well-filtered, well-aerated aquarium with large shelters, e.g. caves or bogwood. Water chemistry not critical. Temperature range: 75–81°F (24–27°C)*

BREEDING: *No reports available*

MODERLIESCHEN

BELLICA or OPALINE

Leucaspius delineatus

SUBFAMILY: Leuciscinae (classified as Abraminae by some authors)

THIS PREDOMINANTLY SILVER-BODIED FISH, WITH a bluish line running from head to tail, gained considerable popularity, mainly in Europe, during the 1980s and early 1990s. Although it is still available, it is not so popular now and has not experienced a global demand.

DISTRIBUTION: *Mostly central and eastern Europe*

SIZE: *Up to 4¾in (12cm); usually smaller*

BEHAVIOR: *Active, peaceful shoaler*

DIET: *Wide range of diets accepted, but livefoods preferred*

AQUARIUM: *Roomy with ample swimming spaces and plant thickets. Water chemistry not critical, but medium-hard neutral water is recommended. Temperature range: 50–72°F (10–22°C)*

BREEDING: *Egg strips are looped around plants and are guarded by the male. Hatching takes several days*

GOLDEN ORFE

IDE

Leuciscus idus

SYNONYM: *Idus idus*

SUBFAMILY: Leuciscinae

LEUCISCUS IDUS IS USUALLY AVAILABLE AS A GOLD morph—known as the Golden Orfe—and is one of the most popular pondfish kept in Europe. However, growing numbers are now also kept in aquaria, either temporarily (for subsequent release into a garden pond) or on a permanent basis. In addition to the gold morph, there is the wild type (silver) morph and a blue variety which looks particularly attractive in aquaria.

DISTRIBUTION: *Most of Europe*

SIZE: *Up to 39in (1m) in the wild; cultivated varieties do not normally exceed 24in (60cm), even in large ponds*

BEHAVIOR: *Active shoaler that prefers the upper layers*

DIET: *All foods accepted, but livefoods preferred*

AQUARIUM: *Very spacious aquarium with open swimming areas and well-fitting cover. Well-oxygenated, well-filtered water—very important. Water chemistry not critical. Temperature range: from near-freezing to over 86°F (30°C), but higher temperatures should be short-lived*

BREEDING: *Infrequent in aquaria. Egg scattering species. Hatching may take up to 20 days at cool temperatures*

SOUTHERN RED-BELLY DACE

Phoxinus erythrogaster

SUBFAMILY: Leuciscinae

THIS DACE OR MINNOW STARTED GAINING IN popularity during the late 1980s and has become a great favorite among coldwater hobbyists. It is the spectacular red belly of mature males that is the most distinctive feature. The European Minnow (*P. phoxinus*) is also available, but is not as colorful. It has similar requirements.

DISTRIBUTION: *New York State and westward to Minnesota, including the Great Lakes and Mississippi River basins*

SIZE: *Up to 3½in (9cm)*

BEHAVIOR: *Peaceful shoaler*

DIET: *Most foods accepted, but livefoods preferred*

AQUARIUM: *Open swimming spaces, as well as adequate shelter. Water chemistry not critical, but quality must be good. Temperature range: 50–77°F (10–25°C)*

BREEDING: *Eggs scattered over the substratum. Hatching takes over 1 week at cooler temperatures*

FATHEAD MINNOW

GOLDEN MINNOW or ROSY RED

Pimephales promelas

SUBFAMILY: Leuciscinae

THE FATHEAD WAS ORIGINALLY CULTIVATED commercially in the United States as a bait fish. However, the attractive coloration of the golden morph, added to its interesting breeding habits, soon created a demand among aquarists. Today, virtually all the Fathead Minnows in the hobby are of the golden variety.

DISTRIBUTION: *Most of North America; introduced into many exotic locations as far south as Mexico*

SIZE: *Up to 4in (10cm); usually considerably smaller*

BEHAVIOR: *Active shoaler; males become territorial during breeding*

DIET: *All foods accepted*

AQUARIUM: *Caves and broad-leaved floating plants should be provided. Water chemistry not critical. Temperature range: 50–77°F (10–25°C)*

BREEDING: *Eggs are attached to the undersurface of floating plants or the roof of a cave and are guarded by the male. Hatching takes around a week*

HARD-LIPPED BARB

Osteochilus hasselti

SUBFAMILY: Cyprininae

THIS IS A SUBSTANTIAL FISH WHICH GROWS TOO large for many aquaria. However, juveniles, which are more brightly marked than adults, make good subjects for mixed collections, always assuming that larger accommodation can be provided in due course. In addition to the normally colored morph,

there is a pink-bodied, black-eyed variety which is occasionally available.

DISTRIBUTION: *Southeast Asia*

SIZE: *Up to 12½in (32cm) reported*

BEHAVIOR: *A peaceful shoaler which will, nevertheless, damage succulent plants and will also root around the bottom of the aquarium*

DIET: *All foods; vegetable component essential*

AQUARIUM: *Roomy, with stout and/or unpalatable plants, whose roots should be protected (see Aquarium Plants). Well-filtered water; chemistry is not critical, but soft, slightly acid water is recommended. Temperature range: 72–77°F (22–25°C)*

BREEDING: *Not recorded in home aquaria*

RED-TAILED RASBORA

Rasbora borapetensis

SUBFAMILY: Rasborinae (Danioninae)

THIS IS A SLENDER FISH WHICH ONLY LOOKS ITS best when water and tank conditions are right (*see* below). At other times, the red coloration responsible for the common name, and which makes a shoal of these rasboras an absolute delight, fades significantly.

DISTRIBUTION: *Thailand and western Malaysia*

SIZE: *2in (5cm)*

BEHAVIOR: *A peaceful shoaler*

DIET: *Most small foods accepted, but livefoods preferred*

AQUARIUM: *For best effect, lighting should not be too bright (floating plants will help diffuse it). Open swimming spaces and abundant vegetation should be provided. Soft, slightly acid water (perhaps filtered through peat) recommended. Temperature range: 72–79°F (22–26°C)*

BREEDING: *Egg-scattering/eating species. Shallow water recommended. Hatching takes about 1½ days*

GREATER SCISSORTAIL

GIANT, or SPOT-TAILED, SCISSORTAIL

Rasbora caudimaculata

SUBFAMILY: Rasborinae (Danioninae)

DESPITE TWO OF ITS COMMON NAMES, *R. caudimaculata* is no larger than its more widely available close relative *R. trilineata* (the Scissortail–*see* p.185). Both are very attractive fish when conditions are to their liking.

DISTRIBUTION: *Southeast Asia*

SIZE: *Up to 4¾in (12cm) reported, but usually smaller*

BEHAVIOR: *An active shoaler with excellent jumping ability*

DIET: *All foods accepted, particularly livefoods*

AQUARIUM: *Roomy, well-covered tank with ample swimming areas and plant thickets. Water chemistry not critical. Temperature range: 68–77°F (20–25°C); slightly higher for breeding*

BREEDING: *Egg-scattering species; breeding infrequent in aquaria*

EYE-SPOT RASBORA

HI-SPOT RASBORA

Rasbora dorsiocellata

SUBFAMILY: Rasborinae (Danioninae)

TWO SUBSPECIES OF *R. DORSIOCELLATA* ARE frequently referred to in aquarium literature: *R. d. dorsiocellata* and *R. d. macrophthalma*, in which the eyes (as the specific name indicates) are larger, although the fish itself is smaller. The former is more usually available and is generally referred to by its species, rather than subspecies, name.

DISTRIBUTION: *Southeast Asia: mainly Peninsular Malaysia and Sumatra*

SIZE: *Up to 2½in (6.5cm)*

RED-TAILED RASBORA (RASBORA BORAPETENSIS)

or one sometimes being almost diamond-shaped. The black line that runs along the base of the anal fin is also very distinctive.

DISTRIBUTION: *Southeast Asia*

SIZE: *Up to 8in (20cm) reported, but usually much smaller*

BEHAVIOR: *A peaceful shoaler despite its size*

DIET: *All foods accepted*

AQUARIUM: *Roomy with a well-fitting cover, ample swimming areas and plant thickets; a dark substratum is recommended. Soft, slightly acid water and regular partial changes preferred. Temperature range: 72–77°F (22–25°C)*

BREEDING: *As for* R. dorsiocellata. *Hatching takes about 1½ days*

SLIM HARLEQUIN
NARROW-WEDGED, GLOWLIGHT, or ESPE'S, RASBORA

Rasbora espei

SYNONYMS: *Rasbora heteromorpha espei, Trigonostigma espei*

SUBFAMILY: Rasboriniae (Danioninae)

(AS FROM 1999, THIS SPECIES, ALONG WITH *R. hengeli* and *R. heteromorpha*, was transferred to a new genus, *Trigonostigma*. While accepting this revision, all three species are included under *Rasbora* in this book for ease of access, until the new

BEHAVIOR: *A peaceful shoaler*

DIET: *All foods accepted*

AQUARIUM: *Ample swimming area and abundant plant thickets should be provided. Soft, slightly acid water is preferred. Temperature range: 68–77°F (20–25°C)*

BREEDING: *Low water level recommended for this egg-scattering/eating species. Introducing the female a day or so before the male may help. Hatching takes about 1 day*

ELEGANT RASBORA
TWO-SPOT RASBORA

Rasbora elegans

SUBFAMILY: Rasborinae (Danioninae)

WHILE THE ELEGANT RASBORA IS, UNDOUBTEDLY, an "elegant" fish, it is no more so than its close relatives. The most striking features about this attractive fish are its body spots which can vary in shape, the posteri-

name becomes more widely distributed in aquarium literature.)

The Slim Harlequin can be easily distinguished from its better-known relative *R. heteromorpha* (the Harlequin): the most distinctive feature of both, the dark body cone pattern, is much narrower in the Slim Harlequin. In this, it resembles the other closely related species, *R. hengeli*, the Glass or Hengel's Harlequin from Sumatra, which is rarely kept (most "*hengeli*" are probably *espei*). Further work is required to establish differences between the two.

DISTRIBUTION: *Thailand*

SIZE: *Up to 2in (5cm) reported, but usually smaller*

BEHAVIOR: *A peaceful shoaler*

DIET: *All small commercial and live foods*

AQUARIUM: *Subdued lighting and a dark substratum shows this species off to best effect. Soft, slightly acid water is recommended. Temperature range: 73–82°F (22–28°C)*

BREEDING: *Infrequent in aquaria. Shallow, mature water and trio (one female/two males) recommended. Eggs laid on underside of broad-leaved plants. Hatching takes about 1 day*

HARLEQUIN
RED RASBORA
Rasbora heteromorpha, Trigonostigma heteromorpha: see Rasbora espei

SUBFAMILY: Rasborinae (Danioninae)

THE HARLEQUIN IS ONE OF THE OLD AQUARIUM favorites, having first been imported into Europe way back in 1906. It is still very popular today, largely owing to its striking coloration and dark body cone. Of the three "harlequins", this species possesses the widest body cone, making it immediately identifiable. A dark or blue variety is now also widely available.

DISTRIBUTION: *Peninsular Malaysia, Singapore, Sumatra and probably Thailand*

SIZE: *Up to 1¾in (4.5cm)*

BEHAVIOR: *A peaceful shoaler*

DIET: *Most foods accepted*

AQUARIUM: *As for R. espei, but slightly lower top temperature recommended*

BREEDING: *As for R. espei*

CLOWN RASBORA
TWO-SPOT, or THREE-SPOT, RASBORA
Rasbora kalochroma

SUBFAMILY: Rasborinae (Danioninae)

THIS IS ONE OF THE LARGER RASBORAS (*SEE BELOW*) which is seen less often than it deserves, since it is a truly beautiful fish when in peak condition. It is a little more sensitive than some other species. Particular care should therefore be given to water chemistry and quality.

DISTRIBUTION: *Malaysia, Borneo and Sumatra*

SIZE: *Up to 4in (10cm)*

BEHAVIOR: *Although it should be kept as a group, this species does not exhibit the strong shoaling instincts of its close relatives*

DIET: *Most foods accepted, particularly livefoods*

AQUARIUM: *Ample swimming space, plus plant thickets should be provided. Mature, soft, slightly acid water is best. Subdued lighting and a dark substratum also recommended. Temperature range: 77–82°F (25–28°C)*

BREEDING: *No documented reports available, but almost certainly an egg-scattering/eating species*

GLOWLIGHT RASBORA
RED-STRIPED, or RED-LINE, RASBORA
Rasbora pauciperforata

SUBFAMILY: Rasborinae (Danioninae)

UNDER APPROPRIATE CONDITIONS THE GLOWLIGHT Rasbora really lives up to its name. Unlike other rasboras, though, this species can tolerate relatively low temperatures during the winter, something that may improve the chances of achieving breeding success, particularly if pairs are allowed to select themselves from a shoal.

DISTRIBUTION: *Western Malaysia, Sumatra*

SIZE: *Up to 2¾in (7cm) reported; usually smaller*

BEHAVIOR: *A rather timid species which prefers the lower reaches of the aquarium, especially among vegetation*

DIET: *Will take a range of commercial formulations, but prefers livefoods*

AQUARIUM: *Subdued illumination and ample vegetation recommended. Soft, slightly acid water with regular partial water changes and filtration through peat is preferred. Temperature range: 66–70°F (19–21°C) during winter, rising to 73–77°F (23–25°C) at other times and slightly higher for breeding*

BREEDING: *A challenging species which scatters eggs among fine-leaved vegetation. Hatching takes about 1–1½ days*

▲ SLIM HARLEQUIN (RASBORA ESPEI VAR.)　　　▼ HARLEQUIN (RASBORA HETEROMORPHA)

▲ *Glowlight Rasbora (Rasbora pauciperforata)*
Fire Rasbora (Rasbora vaterifloris) ▶

SCISSORTAIL
THREE-LINED RASBORA
Rasbora trilineata

SUBFAMILY: Rasborinae (Danioninae)

THIS IS ANOTHER OF THE LARGER RASBORAS (although the maximum size is rarely attained, either in aquaria or in the wild). It is a species that only looks at its best when kept in a shoal. It prefers the middle and upper reaches of the aquarium but will also venture farther down.

DISTRIBUTION: *Malaysia, Borneo and Sumatra*

SIZE: *Up to 6in (15cm) reported; almost always considerably smaller*

BEHAVIOR: *An active shoaling species*

DIET: *Wide range accepted, but livefoods preferred*

AQUARIUM: *Ample swimming areas surrounded by plant thickets. Dark substratum and soft, slightly acid water with regular partial changes recommended. Temperature range: 72–77°F (22–25°C); slightly higher for breeding*

BREEDING: *Shallow water required with plenty of fine-leaved vegetation. Challenging egg-scattering/ eating species. Hatching takes about 1 day.*

FIRE RASBORA
GOLDEN, or PEARLY RASBORA, FIRE or ORANGE-FINNED BARB
Rasbora vaterifloris

SUBFAMILY: Rasborinae (Danioninae)

WITHOUT BEING ONE OF THE MOST COLORFUL OF the rasboras, this species is one of the most beautiful when in peak condition and under appropriate lighting. It is a challenging fish best avoided by less-experienced aquarists.

DISTRIBUTION: *Sri Lanka*

SIZE: *Up to 1½in (4cm); usually a little smaller*

BEHAVIOR: *A shy, peaceful shoaler that avoids bright lights*

DIET: *Wide range of foods accepted, particularly livefoods; will not generally feed off the bottom*

AQUARIUM: *Subdued lighting and a dark substratum recommended. Sensitive to water*

OTHER *RASBORA* SPECIES

In addition to the *Rasbora* species featured, there are others which are available with greater or lesser regularity. Although individual requirements may need checking out, basic aquarium needs are generally similar for all: soft, slightly acid, good-quality water, swimming space/plant thickets, etc.

SCIENTIFIC NAME	COMMON NAME	SIZE	TEMPERATURE
R. argyrotaenia	Silver Rasbora	6¾in (17cm)	64–77°F (18–25°C)
R. cephalotaenia	—	5in (13cm)	60–75°F (20–24°C)
R. daniconius	Striped Rasbora	4in (10cm)	75–79°F (24–26°C)
R. einthovenii	Brilliant, or Long-banded, Rasbora	3½in (9cm)	72–77°F (22–25°C)
R. reticulata	Net Rasbora	2½in (6cm)	72–79°F (22–26°C)
R. somphongsi (Trigonostigma somphongsi)	—	1in (3cm)	73–77°F (23–25°C)
R. taeniata	Black-striped or Black-lined Rasbora	2¾in (7cm)	72–75°F (22–24°C)
R. urophthalma	—	1¼in (3.5cm)	73–77°F (23–25°C)

Striped Rasbora (R. daniconius)

Brilliant, or Long-Banded, Rasbora (R. einthovenii)

conditions which should be mature, soft, slightly acid and well-filtered. Some swimming areas with ample planting should be provided. Temperature range: 75–82°F (24–28°C)

BREEDING: Challenging. Prolific in the wild, but not in aquaria. Shallow, mature, well-planted conditions recommended. Egg-scattering species. Hatching takes about 1½ days

BITTERLING

Rhodeus sericeus

SYNONYMS: *Rhodeus amarus, R. amarus sericeus, R. sericeus amarus*
SUBFAMILY: Acheilognathinae (sometimes classified as Rhodeinae)

DESPITE IT BEING A LONG-ESTABLISHED AQUARIUM fish, there is still debate regarding the correct scientific name of this species, with the weight of opinion tending toward *R. sericeus*. Males look particularly attractive during the breeding season (April to August) and when subjected to side lighting.

DISTRIBUTION: Most of Europe north of the Alps, but excluding Scandinavia and most of the British Isles (although there are introduced populations)

SIZE: 4in (10cm)

BEHAVIOR: An active fish which may be kept in pairs or small groups

DIET: All foods accepted, particularly livefoods; vegetable component recommended

AQUARIUM: Roomy and well planted. At least part of the substratum should be fine-grained to accommodate Freshwater Mussels (e.g. Anodonta or Unio) if breeding is required. Water chemistry not critical but quality must be good. Temperature range: 64–70°F (18–21°C); cold spell at around 50°F (10°C) during winter improves chances of breeding success

BREEDING: Egg are laid and fertilized inside breathing tube (inhalant siphon) of Mussel. Hatching can take up to 3 weeks

RUDD (SCARDINIUS ERYTHROPHTHALMUS)

RUDD
RED-EYE
Scardinius erythrophthalmus

SUBFAMILY: Leuciscinae

THE RUDD IS AVAILABLE IN TWO COLOR FORMS: the silvery wild type and a cultivated golden form. It is the latter which is kept, primarily by pondkeepers, but to an increasing extent by aquarists as well.

DISTRIBUTION: Europe, north of the Pyrenees, but absent from the extreme north; introduced into numerous exotic locations

SIZE: Up to 18in (45cm); usually considerably smaller

BEHAVIOR: An active peaceful shoaler which prefers the upper layers of the water column

DIET: Wide range of foods accepted

AQUARIUM: Roomy, well oxygenated and well filtered. Water chemistry not critical. Temperature range: from close to freezing up to tropical temperatures, but 50–68°F (10–20°C) recommended

BREEDING: Only feasible in large aquaria. Up to 200,000 eggs may be released by a large female. Hatching takes 8–15 days

WHITE CLOUD MOUNTAIN MINNOW

Tanichthys albonubes

SUBFAMILY: Rasborinae (Danioninae)

TWO COLOR TYPES OF THIS POPULAR FISH ARE available: one with light-colored anal and dorsal fin edges and one with red edges. A long-finned variety which almost disappeared during the early 1990s is now found with greater frequency once more.

DISTRIBUTION: White Cloud Mountain region near Canton, China (type with light-colored fin edges); "red" type found around Hong Kong, probably from aquarium-bred escapes

SIZE: 1¾in (4.5cm)

BEHAVIOR: A peaceful shoaler

DIET: All foods accepted

AQUARIUM: A dark substratum in a well-planted tank that offers some swimming spaces is recommended. Water chemistry not critical. Temperature range: 50°F (15°C) during winter to 64–77°F (18–25°C) at other times

BREEDING: Eggs are scattered among fine-leaved vegetation. Hatching takes about 1½ days

TENCH
DOCTOR FISH
Tinca tinca

SUBFAMILY: Leuciscinae (sometimes classified as Cyprininae)

THE TENCH IS ANOTHER TRADITIONAL PONDFISH that is gradually making a transition to (large) aquaria. To the mid-1990s, two color forms were available: the green (or wild type) and a golden (sometimes mottled)

WHITE CLOUD MOUNTAIN MINNOW (TANICHTHYS ALBONUBES)

▲ RED AND WHITE TENCH (TINCA TINCA VAR.)
▼ RED TENCH (TINCA TINCA VAR.)   ▼▼ GOLDEN TENCH (TINCA TINCA VAR.)

variety. Since then, at least two other colors have become available: a deep orange (sometimes referred to as red) and an orange/red and white type.

DISTRIBUTION: *Widespread in Europe and stretching eastward to Russia; absent from northern Scandinavia, possibly Scotland, Ireland, Iberia and the Adriatic coastline; widely introduced into exotic locations, including the United States*

SIZE: *Up to 28in (70cm) reported in the wild; usually much smaller*

BEHAVIOR: *Bottom dweller that will rise to the surface for food. Juveniles may be kept as a shoal*

DIET: *All foods accepted*

AQUARIUM: *Large, well-filtered (for water clarity purposes) aquaria with robust vegetation. Water chemistry not critical. Temperature range: from near freezing to over 86°F (30°C), but 68–77°F (20–25°C) is perfectly adequate*

BREEDING: *Difficult in aquaria. Huge numbers of eggs (up to 900,000) laid among plants in late spring/early summer. Hatching takes 6–8 days*

ZACCO

PALE CHUB

Zacco platypus

SUBFAMILY: Rasborinae (Danioninae)

THIS IS A BEAUTIFUL FISH WHICH SHOULD BE SEEN more often. In addition to their unusual and attractive body coloring and patterning, males also possess an interesting extension of the anal (belly) fin.

DISTRIBUTION: *Far East; mainly imported from Japan*

SIZE: *Up to 7in (18cm); usually smaller*

BEHAVIOR: *Undemanding; excellent jumping ability; not suitable for keeping with small tankmates*

DIET: *All foods accepted*

AQUARIUM: *Spacious and well-covered aquaria, with well-oxygenated, well-filtered water. Water chemistry not critical. Temperature range: wide tolerance, but 68–77°F (20–25°C) is adequate*

BREEDING: *No details available*

CHARACOIDS

Although members of the Characidae can be very different from each other (the piranha and the Neon Tetra are examples), they share a sufficiently large number of similarities for most authorities to believe that they are members of one and the same family. Despite this general acceptance, though, the assemblage of characid species is so diverse that, pending a detailed review, they are grouped by some authors, including Nelson, whose classification is followed here (*see* Bibliography), into a number of subfamilies.

Broadening the issue further, there are many other fish species that share some characteristics with the members of the family Characidae; however, they also exhibit significant differences. Therefore, they are not, strictly speaking, characids, but are definitely characid-like. These other fish species are grouped together into a number of distinct families, which, together with the Characidae, form the order Characiformes, the so-called characiforms or characoids (as opposed to characids).

The Characiformes usually have well-developed teeth—even tiny species such as the Neon Tetra (*Paracheirodon innesi*) and Cardinal Tetra (*P. axelrodi*) have excellent dentition—and an adipose fin (a second, small, fleshy, rayless dorsal fin). In a few Characiformes, e.g. the Silver-tipped or Copper Tetra (*Hasemania nana*), the adipose fin is not present, but in such fish other characteristics place them firmly in one or other of the characoid families. These other characteristics include a (usually) decurved lateral line, i.e. it curves downward to a greater or lesser extent (with some exceptions), and pharyngeal ("throat") teeth. Characoids lack barbels, and the upper jaw is not usually protractile, i.e. extensible. There are also several skeletal features relating to the tail bones, fin rays, and so on, which identify fish as characoids.

Within this broad framework, ten families can be identified. Within these, there is a total of about 240 genera and 1,350 species, of which around 210 genera occur in Africa; the remainder are largely distributed in Central or South America, with a relatively small number in Mexico and southwestern U.S.A. Representatives of all ten families are featured here. Where relevant, the subfamilies will also be indicated. As with the families themselves, there are considerable differences of opinion between taxonomists regarding both the number and the actual status of some of the subfamilies. Again, the subfamilial classification followed here is that published in Nelson, 1994 (*see* Bibliography), while accepting that, at some stage in the future, there will undoubtedly be changes both to the characoid subfamilies and to the families themselves.

In alphabetical order, the ten characoid families containing, in total, around 170 genera and 900 species, are:

Anostomidae (subfamilies: Anostominae, Chilodontinae) This family includes the fish commonly referred to as headstanders and leporins.

Characidae This is the largest and most controversial characoid assemblage, consisting (according to Nelson) of no fewer than nine subfamilies: Alestiinae (African tetras), Characinae ("true" characins), Tetragonopterinae (South American tetras), Iguanodectinae (slender tetras), Glandulocaudinae (croaking and bristly mouthed tetras), Serrasalminae (pacus, piranhas, and silver dollars), Rhoadsiinae (*Carlana*, *Parastremma*, and *Rhoadsia* species—no common name), Crenuchinae (darter and sailfin tetras), and Characidiinae (South American "darters"). In addition to these subfamilies, there are several South American genera, which, in Nelson's opinion, cannot be assigned to any specific subfamily but nevertheless belong within the Characidae, e.g. *Aphyocharax* and *Brycon*.

Citharinidae (subfamilies: Distichodontinae, Citharininae) The fish making up this family are often referred to as distichodids or citharinids, and include genera such as *Distichodus* and *Neolebias*.

Ctenolucidae These are the pike characins.

Curimatidae (subfamilies: Curimatinae, Prochilodontinae) These are often called the curimatas.

Erythrinidae The trahiras include predatory species, such as *Hoplias malabaricus*, occasionally available for aquaria.

Gasteropelecidae This small, but famous, family, is known universally as the hatchetfishes.

Hemiodontidae (subfamilies: Paradontinae, Hemiodontinae, the latter being further subdivided into four tribes) These fish are collectively referred to as hemiodids.

Hepsetidae This consists of just one species, the African Pike Characin (*Hepsetus odoe*).

Lebiasinidae (subfamilies: Lebiasininae, Pyrrhulininae) This family includes the popular and interesting pencilfishes.

This section of the book differs from some others in that it deals with an order (Characiformes, consisting of a number of families) rather than with a family. Two of the previous sections each dealt with a single family: Cyprinidae (cyprinids) and Cichlidae (cichlids). In the Cyprinidae, the featured species were listed in alphabetical order, with each entry including details of the subfamily to which the cyprinid in question belonged. In the Cichlidae, no distinction was made between the major "groups," i.e. Central, South American, Asian, African, and African Rift Lake cichlids, simply because no subfamilial divisions exist.

In this section, the characoid families will be featured alphabetically (*see* above list). Within each family, species will be dealt with alphabetically. Where relevant, the name of the subfamily will be entered. For example, the entry for the Cardinal Tetra will read:

CARDINAL TETRA

Paracheirodon axelrodi

FAMILY: Characidae
SUBFAMILY: Tetragonopterinae

In those few cases where a species belonging to the family Characidae cannot be assigned to a particular subfamily, this will be indicated as follows:

BLOODFIN

Aphyocarax anisitsi

FAMILY: Characidae
SUBFAMILY: Uncertain

Where no subfamily exists, this line of the entry will be deleted, as in:

AFRICAN PIKE CHARACIN

Hepsetus odoe

FAMILY: Hepsetidae

HIGH-BACKED HEADSTANDER

Abramites hypselonotus

SYNONYM: *Abramites microcephalus*
FAMILY: Anostomidae
SUBFAMILY: Anostominae

MEMBERS OF THIS SPECIES ARE SOMETIMES split into two subspecies: *A. hypselonotus hypselonotus*, from the Amazon, and *A. h. ternetzi*, from the Paraguay River basin. The former is said to have its dorsal fin set farther forward and to possess a narrower caudal peduncle (the base from which the caudal fin originates). Juveniles do not have the characteristic high backs of mature specimens.

DISTRIBUTION: *Amazon, and Orinoco and Paraguay River basins*

SIZE: *Up to 5½in (14cm)*

BEHAVIOR: *Progressively more intolerant of their own species as they mature, at least in aquaria*

HIGH-BACKED HEADSTANDER (*ABRAMITES HYPSELONOTUS*)

(found in shoals in the wild). Appetite for tender succulent plants. Excellent jumpers

DIET: A range of commercial foods, as well as livefoods, accepted; vegetable component important

AQUARIUM: Well-covered (essential to prevent jumping out), and with bogwood or large rocks; no succulent plants—use only unpalatable and/or artificial plants. Medium-hard, neutral to slightly alkaline water recommended. Temperature range: 73–81°F (23–27°C)

BREEDING: No documented reports of aquarium breeding currently available

STRIPED ANOSTOMUS
STRIPED HEADSTANDER
Anostomus anostomus

FAMILY: Anostomidae
SUBFAMILY: Anostominae

IN OVERALL BODY SHAPE, *ANOSTOMUS* SPECIES ARE somewhat slenderer than *Abramites*. They also lack the broad, vertical banding, having (in most cases) longitudinal stripes, and they possess a distinctively upturned mouth. Striped Anostomus is the most commonly seen species of its genus.

DISTRIBUTION: Amazon (upriver from Manáus), Orinoco, Colombia, and Guyana

SIZE: Up to 7in (18cm), but generally smaller

BEHAVIOR: Large shoals tend to get along, but small groups will scrap. Single specimens generally tolerate other species. Individuals like to shelter in vertical crevices

DIET: As for Abramites hyselonotus

AQUARIUM: Roomy, well-planted, well-covered, with adequate bogwood and other shelters, including vertical hiding places, and with good aeration and filtration (power filtration recommended to create water current). Soft, slightly acid water preferred. Temperature range: 72–82°F (22–28°C)

STRIPED ANOSTOMUS (ANOSTOMUS ANOSTOMUS)

BREEDING: Very rare in aquaria; no details currently available

TERNETZ'S ANOSTOMUS
TERNETZ'S HEADSTANDER
Anostomus ternetzi

FAMILY: Anostomidae
SUBFAMILY: Anostominae

THIS SPECIES IS SUPERFICIALLY SIMILAR TO *A. anostomus*, but it is somewhat smaller, slimmer, and less colorful, particularly in the red dorsal- and caudal-fin coloration. Its major advantages for mixed aquaria are its smaller size and peaceful nature.

DISTRIBUTION: Orinoco basin (Venezuela); Xingu, and Araguaia Rivers (Brazil)

SIZE: Sometimes reported up to 7in (18cm), i.e. same size as A. anostomus, but usually at least ¾in (2cm) smaller

BEHAVIOR: More peaceful toward its own species than A. anostomus

DIET: As for A. anostomus

AQUARIUM: As for A. anostomus

BREEDING: No reports of aquarium breeding currently available

THREE-SPOT ANOSTOMUS
THREE-SPOT HEADSTANDER
Anostomus trimaculatus

SYNONYM: *Anostomus plicatus*
FAMILY: Anostomidae
SUBFAMILY: Anostominae

TWO OF THE THREE SPOTS INDICATED IN THE common name are a central, round body spot and a smaller one at the base of the tail. The third spot is the eye itself. This species is also adorned with thin, vertical bands, making it appear very different to the two aforementioned headstanders.

DISTRIBUTION: Guyana and Amazon region (Brazil)

SIZE: Around 4¾in (12cm), but up to 8in (20cm) reported

BEHAVIOR: Peaceful, shoaler, with an appetite for tender succulent plants

DIET: As for Abramites hypselonotus

AQUARIUM: As for Anostomus anostomus, but use only unpalatable/robust/artificial plants

TERNETZ'S ANOSTOMUS (ANOSTOMUS TERNETZI)

OTHER *ANOSTOMUS* SPECIES

A few other *Anostomus* species are available in addition to the featured ones. The general guidelines described for the featured species, as well as for *Abramites hypselonotus*, apply.

SCIENTIFIC NAME	COMMON NAME(S)	SIZE
A. garmani	Gray-lined Anostomus/Headstander	7in (18cm)
A. gracilis	Four-spot Anostomus/Headstander	7in (18cm)
A. spiloclistron	False Three-spot Anostomus/Headstander	8in (20cm)
A. taeniatus	Lisa	8in (20cm)
A. varius	Checkerboard Anostomus/Headstander	9¾in (25cm)

LISA (ANOSTOMUS TAENIATUS)

BREEDING: *No reports of aquarium breeding currently available*

SPOTTED HEADSTANDER

Chilodus punctatus

FAMILY: Anostomidae
SUBFAMILY: Chilodontinae

THIS IS A VARIABLE SPECIES IN WHICH THE BODY spotting, as well as the length, intensity and sharpness of the longitudinal black line (which begins at the tip of the snout and extends backward through the eye onto the gill cover and then into the body), can differ considerably. There is a possibility that specimens in which this line is well-pronounced and extends to the base of the caudal fin may constitute a separate species, *C. gracilis* (Black-banded Headstander).

DISTRIBUTION: *Widely distributed in northeastern South America*

SIZE: *Around 4¾in (12cm)*

BEHAVIOR: *Peaceful, timid shoaler*

DIET: *Livefoods preferred to dry formulations; vegetable component important*

AQUARIUM: *Well-planted, with subdued lighting. Tannin-stained water (see Aquarium Set-up) preferred. Softish, slightly acid water recommended. Temperature range: 75–82°F (24–28°C)*

BREEDING: *Mating takes place just below the surface, and eggs are released among plants. Parents or eggs should be removed to separate accommodations after spawning. Hatching takes about four days*

MANY-BANDED LEPORINUS

Leporinus affinis

SYNONYM: *Leporinus fasciatus affinis*
FAMILY: Anostomidae
SUBFAMILY: Anostominae

THERE ARE TWO VIRTUALLY IDENTICAL *LEPORINUS* with black body bands: this species and *L. fasciatus* (Black-banded Leporinus). Many-banded Leporinus has nine bands, while *L. fasciatus* has ten. Many-banded Leporinus also has somewhat more rounded tips to the caudal fin and *L. fasciatus* has an orange/reddish tinge along its throat. In many books, these two fish are regarded as subspecies of *L. fasciatus*.

DISTRIBUTION: *South America. L. affinis: down to the Paraguay River; L. fasciatus: Rio de la Plata*

SIZE: *L. affinis: around 9¾in (25cm); L. fasciatus: up to 12in (30cm)*

BEHAVIOR: *Generally peaceful toward other species; may scrap with members of their own species, but not overaggressive. Both species have an appetite for succulent plants*

DIET: *Predominantly vegetable-based, but will also take livefoods and some commercial formulations*

AQUARIUM: *Spacious, well-covered, and with bogwood, non-calcareous rocks, and tough/unpalatable or artificial plants. Power filtration to create a current also advisable. Water chemistry not critical, but medium-hard, slightly acid to slightly alkaline water, preferably tannin-stained (see Aquarium Set-up) suits these fish well. Temperature range: 72–82°F (22–28°C)*

BREEDING: *No documented reports currently available*

STRIPED LEPORINUS

Leporinus striatus

FAMILY: Anostomidae
SUBFAMILY: Anostominae

TWO "STRIPED" *LEPORINUS* ARE KNOWN: this species, which has four prominent dark stripes running from nose to tail; and

MANY-BANDED LEPORINUS (LEPORINUS AFFINIS)

L. arcus (Lipstick Leporinus), which has three. Both have similar characteristics and requirements.

DISTRIBUTION: L. striatus: *widely distributed in northern South America;* L. arcus: *reportedly restricted to Venezuela*

SIZE: L. striatus: *reported up to 16in (40cm), but usually smaller;* L. fasciatus: *reported up to 12in (30cm), but usually remaining smaller*

BEHAVIOR: *Generally peaceful shoaler, with an appetite for succulent plants*

DIET: *As for* L. affinis

AQUARIUM: *As for* L. affinis, *but temperature range: 72–79°F (22–26°C)*

BREEDING: *As for* L. affinis

SPOTTED CACHORRO

Acestorhynchus falcatus

FAMILY: Characidae
SUBFAMILY: Characinae

PIKE-LIKE CHARACINS, INCLUDING THE SPOTTED Cachorro, are grouped together according to certain body characteristics—usually the depth of the body in relation to its length. The *A. falcatus* group or complex is distinguished by its body depth being 4.0 to 4.75 times shorter than its body length. Members of other groups are hardly ever encountered in the hobby, while the Spotted Cachorro itself is only occasionally imported.

DISTRIBUTION: *Guiana, Amazon and Orinoco basins*

SIZE: *Up to 12in (30cm)*

BEHAVIOR: *Highly aggressive and predatory*

DIET: *Feeds almost exclusively on other fishes, thus raising ethical questions about its maintenance in aquaria*

AQUARIUM: *Large, well-filtered, well-covered, and with open spaces. Soft, acid water preferred. Temperature range: 73–81°F (23–27°C)*

BREEDING: *Unknown in aquaria*

FALSE FLAME-TAILED TETRA

Aphyocharax alburnus

SYNONYM: *Aphyocharax erythrurus (but see below)*
FAMILY: Characidae
SUBFAMILY: Uncertain

THERE ARE ABOUT 20 SPECIES OF *APHYOCHARAX* known, but only a few are available to hobbyists. All are slender fish, most with varying degrees of red in their fins, particularly the pelvic and anal fins, and the lower lobe of the caudal fin. This has given rise to their common names of flamed-tailed tetras or bloodfins. The False Flame-tailed Tetra does not possess the intense col-oration of some of its closest relatives but, nevertheless, makes an impressive sight when kept as a shoal. The almost-identical *A. erythrurus* (from the Guianas), is regarded as a separate species by some ichthyologists, and as a geographical variant of the False Flame-tailed Tetra by others.

OTHER *LEPORINUS* SPECIES *

Several other *Leporinus*** species are available from time to time. All require the same basic conditions described for the featured species. These elegant fish are usually sold as juveniles and will soon outgrow most home aquaria. Sizes given below are approximate only.

SCIENTIFIC NAME	COMMON NAME(S)	SIZE
L. agassizi	Half-striped Leporinus	4¾in (12cm)
L. desmotes	Black/Yellow Leporinus	8¾in (22cm)
L. friderici***	Frideric's Leporinus	8in (20cm)
L. granti	Grant's Leporinus	6in (15cm)
L. maculatus	Spotted Leporinus	8in (20cm)
L. megalepis	Big-scaled Leporinus	9¾in (25cm)
L. melanopleura	Spot-tailed Leporinus	10½in (27cm)
L. melanosticus	Silver Leporinus	4in (10cm)
L. moralesi	Faded Leporinus	5in (12.5cm)
L. nigrotaeniatus	Black-lined Leporinus	15¾in (40cm)
L. octofasciatus	Eight-banded Leporinus	6¼in (16cm)
L. pellegrini	Belted Leporinus	4¾in (12cm)
L. spp.****	Golden Leporinus	9¾in (25cm)
L. spp.****	Reticulated Leporinus	12in (30cm)

NOTES:

*The genus *Leporinus* is still one of the least known of the characoid genera. As a result, the names given in the chart are likely to vary between publications and are likely to change with time. There is doubt even regarding the validity of some of the listed species, e.g. the fish known in aquarium literature as *L. maculatus* may, in fact, be synonymous with *L. pellegrini*. The situation regarding *L. granti* and *L. megalepis* is similarly confused.

***Leporinus* translates as "young or little hare" and is used for this genus because of its snout, which bears a characteristic cleft in the center creating a "hare lip" type of mouth. Two prominent teeth help complete the hare lip effect.

***This species is also encountered in aquarium literature as *L. frederici* (Frederic's Leporinus).

****Several *Leporinus* species are awaiting scientific description.

SPOTTED LEPORINUS (LEPORINUS MACULATUS)

DISTRIBUTION: *Reported from southern Brazil, Bolivia, Argentina, Paraguay, Peru and, possibly, the Guianas*

SIZE: *Up to 2¾in (7cm), but often smaller*

BEHAVIOR: *Peaceful, shoaler*

DIET: *Wide range of commercial diets and livefoods accepted*

AQUARIUM: *Well-planted, with some open spaces recommended. A dark substratum helps show these fish to good effect. Water chemistry not critical, but pH values above 7.5 should be avoided. Temperature range: 68–82°F (20–28°C)*

BREEDING: *Soft, acid water recommended. Eggs are scattered, either in the open or among vegetation (usually in the morning), and may be eaten by the parents. Hatching takes about one-and-a-half days*

BLOODFIN
ARGENTINIAN BLOODFIN

Aphyocharax anisitsi

SYNONYM: *Aphyocharax rubripinnis*
FAMILY: Characidae
SUBFAMILY: Uncertain (classified as Aphyocharacinae by some authors)

THIS IS THE FISH GENERALLY REGARDED WITHIN THE hobby as the "true" Bloodfin, although *A. rathbuni* (*see* below) can exhibit even deeper red coloration. Coming from an area a little distance from the genuinely tropical zones of South America, this species can tolerate coldwater aquarium temperatures, as long as these are not allowed to drop excessively. However, best coloration is exhibited when kept within a tropical regime. The species is long-lived, with some specimens reportedly attaining an age of ten years.

DISTRIBUTION: *Mainly Paraná River (Argentina)*

SIZE: *Up to 3in (7.5cm) reported, but usually smaller*

BEHAVIOR: *As for A. alburnus*

DIET: *As for A. alburnus*

AQUARIUM: *As for A. alburnus, but more tolerant of slightly higher pH (up to 8). Temperature range: 64–82°F (18–28°C)*

BREEDING: *As for A. alburnus*

RATHBUN'S BLOODFIN

Aphyocharax rathbuni

FAMILY: Characidae
SUBFAMILY: Uncertain (classified as Aphyocharacinae by some authors)

WHEN IN PEAK CONDITION, RATHBUN'S BLOODFIN is the most colorful *Aphyocharax* species generally available for aquaria. In *A. alburnus*, there is no red on the lower side of the body, while in *A. anisitsi*, the red pigmentation extends a little way into the body from the anal fin base. In Rathbun's Bloodfin, this can extend from the front edge of the anal fin, up to almost half the body width, and then back toward the caudal fin, creating a most impressive cone-like patch.

DISTRIBUTION: *Paraguay River basin*

SIZE: *Up to 2in (5cm)*

BEHAVIOR: *As for A. alburnus*

DIET: *As for A. alburnus*

AQUARIUM: *As for A. alburnus*

BREEDING: *As for A. alburnus*

RED-EYED TETRA
AFRICAN RED-EYED CHARACIN

Arnoldichthys spilopterus

FAMILY: Characidae
SUBFAMILY: Alestiinae

THIS SPECIES IS THE ONLY REPRESENTATIVE OF ITS genus. It was first imported into Europe in 1907; since then it has always been available but has never achieved the "greatness" of some other tetras, despite its undoubted beauty.

DISTRIBUTION: *From the Niger delta to Lagos in west Africa*

SIZE: *Up to 4¾in (12cm) reported, but usually smaller*

BEHAVIOR: *Peaceful, but active; should be kept as a shoal*

▲ *BLOODFIN (APHYOCHARAX ANISITSI)*
◀ *RATHBUN'S BLOODFIN (APHYOCHARAX RATHBUNI)*

DIET: *Range of commercial formulations accepted, but livefoods preferred*

AQUARIUM: *Spacious, with large, open swimming spaces, plants around sides and back, and dark substratum. Tannin-stained water advisable (see Aquarium Set-up). Water chemistry not critical, but raw water*

should be avoided. Temperature range: 73–82°F (23–28°C)

BREEDING: *Soft, acid water required. Eggs are scattered and hatch in about one-and-a-half days*

BLIND CAVEFISH
BLIND CAVE CHARACIN or MEXICAN TETRA

Astyanax mexicanus

SYNONYMS: *Astyanax fasciatus, Astyanax fasciatus mexicanus, Astyanax mexicanus jordani, Anoptichthys jordani*
FAMILY: Characidae
SUBFAMILY: Tetragonopterinae

THE BLIND CAVEFISH AND THE MEXICAN TETRA were once believed to belong not just to different species, but to different genera, as the former name of *Anoptichthys* shows. However, they were eventually shown to be very different-looking members of the same species, the Mexican Tetra being the form that inhabits above-ground watercourses, while the Blind Cavefish lives underground. There is still some debate as to whether the current name for the species is *A. fasciatus* or *A. mexicanus*. Not so long ago, *A. fasciatus* appeared to be the preferred name, but in recent years the balance has moved toward the latter.

DISTRIBUTION: *Blind Cavefish form: limestone caves in a 87-mile (140-km) area that includes Sierra del Abra, Sierra de Guatemala, and Sierra de Colmera, in the region of San Luis Potosi, Mexico; Mexican Tetra form: widely distributed through Texas, Mexico, and Central America, through to Panama*

▲ RED-EYED TETRA (ARNOLDICHTHYS SPILOPTERUS)   ▼ BLIND CAVEFISH (ASTYANAX MEXICANUS)

SIZE: *Around 3½in (9cm)*

BEHAVIOR: *Active but peaceful shoaler that likes to nibble succulent plants. Blind Cavefish may be harassed by aggressive tankmates*

DIET: *All foods accepted; vegetable component advisable*

AQUARIUM: *May be kept in well-lit aquarium, with standard decor, but best effects are created in plantless, darkened aquarium, with calcareous gravel and pieces of stalagmites or stalactites. Illumination can be provided by a "night" fluorescent tube (widely available for use in marine aquaria). Water chemistry not critical, as long as the quality is good, but medium-hard, alkaline conditions preferred. Temperature range: from 59–64°F (15–18°C) at the lower end, to 82–86°F (28–30°C), with 77°F (25°C) being adequate, both for maintenance and breeding*

BREEDING: *Eggs are scattered and may be eaten by the parents. Hatching takes one to three days, depending on temperature. The cave morph will hybridize easily with the sighted, fully colored Mexican Tetra*

PEPPER TETRA
WHITE-STAR TETRA

Axelrodia stigmatias

FAMILY: Characidae
SUBFAMILY: Tetragonopterinae

THIS TINY, GLORIOUS LITTLE FISH IS NOT SEEN AS frequently as it deserves to be. Kept in a shoal under appropriate conditions, the red, white, and silver are shown off to excellent effect. Since the 1970s, a similar, but slightly deeper-bodied species, *A. riesei*

(Ruby Tetra) from the Meta River in Colombia, has also been available.

DISTRIBUTION: *Amazon basin*

SIZE: *Up to 2in (5cm) reported, but usually smaller*

BEHAVIOR: *Peaceful shoaler*

DIET: *A range of small commercial formulations accepted, but livefoods preferred*

AQUARIUM: *Well-planted, but with subdued lighting and floating plants recommended, as well as dark substratum. Soft, slightly acid water required, preferably peat- or tannin-stained (see Aquarium Set-up). Temperature range: 72–79°F (22–26°C)*

BREEDING: *No documented accounts currently available*

LONG-FINNED CHARACIN

Brycinus longipinnis

SYNONYM: *Alestes longipinnis*
FAMILY: Characidae
SUBFAMILY: Alestiinae

SO CALLED BECAUSE OF THE EXTENDED DORSAL FIN rays of mature males, this species should be kept as a group, despite its relatively large size, for best effect. It is the most frequently encountered species of its genus, all of which are predominantly silvery-bodied fish with black bands originating in the fork of the caudal fin and extending to varying lengths into the body. Yellow-gold, reddish or white coloration usually accompanies the bands.

DISTRIBUTION: *Tropical west Africa*

SIZE: *Up to 5in (13cm)*

BEHAVIOR: *Peaceful shoaler*

DIET: *Wide range of foods accepted*

AQUARIUM: *Roomy, well-covered, well-filtered, with ample swimming space, planted along sides and back; dark substratum recommended. Soft to medium-hard, slightly acid to slightly alkaline water preferred. Temperature range: 72–79°F (22–26°C)*

BREEDING: *Soft, slightly acid water should be provided. Eggs are scattered among vegetation and take up to six days to hatch*

TAIL-LIGHT TETRA

Bryconops melanurus

FAMILY: Characidae
SUBFAMILY: Tetragonopterinae

THIS SPECIES HAS A LARGE HEAD AND EYE, attractive black edging on its body scales, and a black blotch in the fork of its caudal fin with a reddish orange/golden patch directly above it. Although it is the most commonly available species of its genus, it is one of the less frequently seen tetras.

DISTRIBUTION: *Amazon and the Guianas*

SIZE: *Up to 4in (10cm) reported, but usually grows to around 2½in (6cm)*

BEHAVIOR: *Peaceful when young, but progressively more intolerant with age*

DIET: *Wide range of commercial formulations accepted, but livefoods preferred*

AQUARIUM: *Spacious, well-filtered, well-oxygenated, well-planted, with ample swimming space recommended. Soft, acid water required. Temperature range: 73–79°F (23–26°C)*

BREEDING: *No documented accounts currently available, but likely to be an egg scatterer with an appetite for its own eggs*

PINK-TAILED CHARACIN

PINK-TAILED CHALCEUS

Chalceus macrolepidotus

FAMILY: Characidae
SUBFAMILY: Uncertain (*see* below)

THE GENUS *CHALCEUS* HAS A NUMBER OF characteristics that place it close to the genus *Brycon*. In addition, it seems to resemble some *Brycinus* (*Alestes*) species. As mentioned in the introductory section to characoids, Nelson (whose classification is followed here) does not allocate *Brycon* to any subfamily of the Characidae, while *Brycinus* belongs to the subfamily Alestiinae. As a result, the taxonomic position of these large-scaled, silvery-bodied tetras must be considered uncertain at this stage. The Pink-tailed Characin has pink/red fins, while the closely related *C. erythrurus* (Yellow-finned Characin) from the Amazon basin (believed, by some, to be a color form rather than a separate species) has yellow fins, except for the caudal fin, which contains some red.

DISTRIBUTION: *Amazon basin and Guianas*

SIZE: *Up to 9¾in (25cm)*

BEHAVIOR: *Predatory species; should be kept only with similar-sized tankmates*

DIET: *Can be weaned off livefoods and on to substantial deep-frozen or freeze-dried diets and tablet food. Juveniles will accept other formulations*

AQUARIUM: *Large, well covered, well-filtered, with ample swimming space and plants around sides and back. Water chemistry not critical. Temperature range: 73–82°F (23–28°C)*

BREEDING: *No documented accounts currently available*

BANDED CHARACIDIUM

Characidium fasciatum

FAMILY: Characidae
SUBFAMILY: Characidiinae

THIS SUBFAMILY IS GENERALLY KNOWN AS THE South American darters, indicating at least a passing similarity to the North American darters of the family Percidae. They share a generally elongated body shape and bottom-hugging habits, and are often found in flowing waters. Few

LONG-FINNED CHARACIN (BRYCINUS LONGIPINNIS)

PINK-TAILED CHARACIN (CHALCEUS MACROLEPIDOTUS)

Characidium are imported for the aquarium; Banded Characidium is the species most frequently encountered.

DISTRIBUTION: *Widely distributed in South America*

SIZE: *Up to 4in (10cm)*

BEHAVIOR: *Peaceful non-shoaling fish, tolerant of other species; may nibble succulent plants*

DIET: *Wide variety of sinking formulations and livefoods accepted*

AQUARIUM: *Well-oxygenated, soft, slightly acid, tannin-stained water (see Aquarium Set-up) recommended. Use only unpalatable or robust plants. Temperature range: 64–74°F (18–24°C); slightly higher for breeding*

BREEDING: *Eggs are scattered along the bottom or among plants, and may be eaten by the parents. Hatching takes one-and-a-half to two days*

THREE-SPOT TETRA

Cheirodon kriegi

FAMILY: Characidae
SUBFAMILY: Tetragonopterinae

THE THREE SPOTS INDICATED IN THE COMMON name consist of the eye, plus two body spots, one located at the base of the caudal fin and the other around the vent, i.e. just in front of the anal fin. While not being outstandingly colored, this tetra—one of the few imported from this genus—looks very impressive when kept as a shoal.

DISTRIBUTION: *Mainly northeastern Paraguay*

SIZE: *Around 2in (5cm)*

BEHAVIOR: *Peaceful shoaler*

DIET: *Wide range of foods accepted*

AQUARIUM: *Well-planted (including floating plants), with open swimming areas and dark substratum recommended. Soft, slightly acid to neutral water, which must be of good quality. Temperature range: 73–79°F (23–26°C)*

BREEDING: *Eggs are scattered among fine-leaved vegetation. Hatching may take five or six days*

BLUE TETRA

Coelurichthys microlepis

SYNONYM: *Mimagoniates microlepis*
FAMILY: Characidae
SUBFAMILY: Glandulocaudinae

THE BLUE TETRA, ALONG WITH ITS RELATIVE *C. tenuis* (Tenuis Tetra)—formerly known as *Mimagoniates barberi* from southern Brazil, Argentina, and Paraguay—and allied genera and species, are often referred to as croaking tetras because of the ability of some species to emit sounds. The males of all the species have a gland in the caudal fin (hence the name of the subfamily) which secretes substances believed to be effective in attracting females. *Coelurichthys* are gorgeous fish when kept under appropriate conditions, which can be a little challenging for new aquarists.

DISTRIBUTION: *Southern Brazil*

SIZE: *Around 2¼in (5.5cm)*

BEHAVIOR: *Active but peaceful shoaler*

DIET: *Wide range of commercial formulations accepted, but livefoods preferred*

AQUARIUM: *Plants should be arranged along sides and back, leaving large swimming area along front. Well-filtered, well-oxygenated water required, preferably with a current. Soft, slightly acid water recommended. Temperature range: 66–78°F (19–25°C)*

BREEDING: *Eggs are released and attached to vegetation by female following internal fertilization*

BLACK-FINNED PACU

Colossoma macropomum

FAMILY: Characidae
SUBFAMILY: Serrasalminae

ALTHOUGH THIS FISH SUPERFICIALLY RESEMBLES a piranha, and belongs to the same subfamily, the Pacu is a plant-eating species rather than a predator. It is a large fish that is bred commercially, both for aquaria and as a food fish, and is quite unsuitable for most home aquaria. However, in its proper setting, the species is long-lived and well-worth keeping.

DISTRIBUTION: *Widespread in the Amazon region*

SIZE: *Around 16in (40cm)*

BEHAVIOR: *Peaceful, despite its size; has a keen appetite for plants*

DIET: *Large commercial formulations, plus added vegetable component, e.g. lettuce leaves*

AQUARIUM: *Only large, deep aquaria are suitable. Use only unpalatable or artificial plants, plus large pieces of bogwood and other forms of decor. Water chemistry not critical, but water should be well-filtered. Temperature range: 72–82°F (22–28°C)*

BREEDING: *No accounts of successful aquarium breeding available*

BUCK-TOOTHED TETRA

Exodon paradoxus

FAMILY: Characidae
SUBFAMILY: Uncertain

THIS IS A SPECIES FOR MORE ADVANCED HOBBYISTS because its aggressive tendencies and relatively large size (for a tetra) make it quite unsuitable for the usual community aquarium setups. Under appropriate conditions, a shoal of Buck-toothed Tetra make an unforgettable sight, not just because of their coloration and bold patterning, but because of their high level of activity.

DISTRIBUTION: *Widely, but locally, distributed in the Amazon basin*

SIZE: *Up to 6in (15cm)*

BEHAVIOR: *Aggressive predator, always on the move. May be kept in a large shoal, but not as small groups of two or three individuals. May also be kept with similar-sized or larger, robust fish*

DIET: *Meat-based commercial formulations, deep-frozen, freeze-dried, and livefoods all accepted*

AQUARIUM: *Large, well-covered aquarium, with ample swimming space, essential. Efficient filtration, thickets of vegetation (including floating plants), and subdued lighting are also required. Temperature range: 72–82°F (22–28°C)*

BUCK-TOOTHED TETRA (EXODON PARADOXUS)

BLACK WIDOW (GYMNOCORYMBUS TERNETZI)

BREEDING: *Eggs are scattered among vegetation. Hatching takes about one-and-a-half days*

BLACK WIDOW
BLACK TETRA
Gymnocorymbus ternetzi

FAMILY: Characidae
SUBFAMILY: Tetragonopterinae

THIS SPECIES HAS BEEN POPULAR EVER SINCE ITS introduction into Europe in 1935. For many years, the basic—and very beautiful—wild type was the only form available. However, over time, several fin and color varieties have been developed, including a long-finned, large-bodied, white type, and a reddish/pinkish one. Two other species with the same basic requirements are also available, but not as frequently as the Black Widow: *G. socolofi* (Socolof's Tetra) from the Meta River in Colombia, and *G. thayeri* (Straight-finned Black Tetra) from the Amazon and Orinoco basins.

Distribution: *Paraguay River, Bolivian section of the Guaporé and the Brazilian Mato Grosso*

SIZE: *Wild type around 2¼in (5.5cm); larger for some cultivated varieties*

BEHAVIOR: *Peaceful shoaler*

DIET: *Most commercial formulations and livefoods accepted*

AQUARIUM: *Well-planted, with some open swimming spaces, and tannin-stained water (see Aquarium Set-up) recommended. Soft, acid water*

preferred; some deviation from this accepted, though raw water must be avoided. Temperature range: 68–82°F (20–28°C)

BREEDING: *Eggs are scattered among vegetation and may be eaten by the spawners. Hatching takes about one day*

SILVER-TIPPED TETRA
COPPER TETRA
Hasemania nana

SYNONYM: *Hasemania marginata, Hasemania melanura, Hemigrammus nanus*
FAMILY: Characidae
SUBFAMILY: Tetragonopterinae

UNUSUALLY FOR A CHARACIN, THE SILVER-TIPPED Tetra lacks an adipose fin. Under appropriate conditions, this tiny species lives up

beautifully to both its common names. It is a fish that—at one time or another—should form part of every aquarist's community setup.

DISTRIBUTION: *Eastern Brazil (São Francisco basin) and western Brazil (Purus tributaries)*

SIZE: *Up to 2in (5cm) reported, but often smaller*

BEHAVIOR: *Peaceful; should be kept in as large a shoal as possible*

DIET: *Most small foods accepted*

AQUARIUM: *Plant thickets, subdued light, and open swimming spaces required. Soft, slightly acid, well-oxygenated, tannin-stained water (see Aquarium Set-up) recommended. Temperature range: 72–82°F (22–28°C)*

BREEDING: *Eggs are scattered among fine-leaved vegetation and may be eaten by the spawners. Hatching takes about one day*

YELLOW-TAILED CONGO TETRA

Hemigrammopetersius caudalis

FAMILY: Characidae
SUBFAMILY: Alestiinae

THE MOST STRIKING FEATURE OF THIS TETRA IS its remarkably colored caudal fin (which is seen at its best only in specimens that are in peak condition), and the fin's central extension. The white edges to the other fins give it a further attractive touch which, allied to its suitability for community aquaria, makes the Yellow-tailed Congo Tetra a highly desirable fish to collectors.

DISTRIBUTION: *Zaire (Democratic Republic of Congo)*

SIZE: *Up to 4in (10cm) reported, but usually around 2¾in (7cm)*

BEHAVIOR: *Peaceful; best suited to being kept in groups of six or more specimens*

DIET: *Wide range of foods accepted*

SILVER-TIPPED TETRA (HASEMANIA NANA)

AQUARIUM: *Well-planted, with open swimming spaces. Medium-hard, slightly acid to slightly alkaline water recommended. Temperature range: 72–79°F (22–26°C)*

BREEDING: *Spawning may be stimulated by high levels of illumination. Eggs are scattered over plants or the substratum. Hatching can take up to five or six days*

BRILLIANT RUMMY-NOSED TETRA

Hemigrammus bleheri

FAMILY: Characidae
SUBFAMILY: Tetragonopterinae

THIS SPECIES (LARGELY EXPORTED FROM THE RÍO Negro, in Brazil, and the Vaupés, in Colombia, and first imported into Europe in 1965) was originally known simply as the Rummy Nose or Rummy-nosed Tetra (*see* photo p.1). However, a very similar species, *H. rhodostomus*, which had been imported for many years prior to this from around the Belém region in Brazil, was already known as the Rummy Nose. This, invariably, led to considerable confusion, with the Rio Negro Rummy Nose being frequently named *H. rhodostomus*, instead of *H. bleheri*. The distinction between the two was not settled—at least, ichthyologically—until 1986, but exports of *H. bleheri* from the Rio Negro are still often referred to as *H. rhodostomus*. Skeletal differences exist between the two but these are impossible to determine in living specimens. Fortunately, there are several other, more easily identified, distinguishing characteristics: in *H. bleheri*, the red coloration in the head region covers most of the head and extends some way into the body, while in *H. rhodostomus*—the "True" or Banded Rummy Nose—it is much more restricted; the tip of the snout is more rounded in *H. bleheri*; the black band that, in *H. rhodostomus*, extends along the base of the anal fin, is lacking in *H. bleheri*, as are any marks on the rays of the anal fin. A third species, *Petitella georgiae* (the False Rummy Nose) is similar to both these rummy noses but has a number of distinguishing features.

DISTRIBUTION: H. bleheri: *middle Rio Negro (Brazil); those from Colombia appear to be* H. bleheri *but formal confirmation of this is still awaited.* H. rhodostomus: *Belém region of Brazil; also reported from Venezuela*

SIZE: *Around 1¾in (4.5cm)*

BEHAVIOR: *Peaceful shoalers;* H. bleheri *is known to "parasitize" brooding pairs of* Uaru amphiacanthoides *by feeding on the "body milk" that the Uarus secrete and on which their fry feed during their early days*

DIET: *Most foods accepted*

AQUARIUM: *Well-planted, with swimming spaces. Soft, slightly acid, good-quality, tannin-stained water (see Aquarium Set-up) recommended. Temperature range: 72–79°F (22–26°C).* H. rhodostomus *is a little more tolerant of fluctuations*

BREEDING: *Very soft, acid water recommended. Eggs are scattered among vegetation or over the substratum. Hatching takes about one-and-a-half days*

BUENOS AIRES TETRA

Hemigrammus caudovittatus

FAMILY: Characidae
SUBFAMILY: Tetragonopterinae

THIS ACTIVE SPECIES HAS BEEN KNOWN IN THE hobby since 1922. It is often recommended as an ideal community fish, although its behavior does not always justify this (*see* below). Specimens in peak condition exhibit very attractive red coloration in the fins, except the pectoral fins. A variant, in which the caudal fin is predominantly yellow, is occasionally available.

DISTRIBUTION: *Argentina (mainly around Rio de la Plata), southeastern Brazil, and Paraguay*

SIZE: *Up to 4¾in (12cm) reported, but usually around 2¾–3in (7–8cm)*

BEHAVIOR: *Generally peaceful shoaler, but larger specimens can become progressively more aggressive with age. Has a distinct appetite for succulent plants*

DIET: *Wide variety of foods accepted*

AQUARIUM: *Plant thickets (not delicate succulent types) and open swimming spaces required. Water chemistry not critical, but quality must be good and oxygenation level high. Temperature range: 64–82°F (18–28°C)*

BREEDING: *Eggs are scattered among vegetation and may be eaten by the parents. Hatching takes about one day*

GLOWLIGHT TETRA

Hemigrammus erythrozonus

FAMILY: Characidae
SUBFAMILY: Tetragonopterinae

THE GLOWLIGHT IS ONE OF THE OLD FAVORITES OF the hobby and deservedly so. A shoal of these tiny fish kept under appropriate conditions makes a truly impressive sight. There is some doubt regarding the assignation of this species to the genus *Hemigrammus*, and studies may eventually result in its being assigned to the genus *Cheirodon*.

DISTRIBUTION: *Essequibo basin (Guyana)*

SIZE: *Around 1½in (4cm)*

BEHAVIOR: *Peaceful shoaler*

DIET: *Wide range of small foods accepted*

AQUARIUM: *Well-planted, with open swimming spaces, and tannin-stained water (see Aquarium Set-up). Soft, slightly acid water preferred, but some deviation accepted if adjustments are made gradually. Temperature range: 72–82°F (22–28°C)*

BUENOS AIRES TETRA (HEMIGRAMMUS CAUDOVITTATUS)

BREEDING: *Spawning may be achieved using either pairs or a shoal. Eggs are scattered among vegetation in soft, acid water. Hatching takes about one day*

HEAD-AND-TAIL LIGHT TETRA

BEACON FISH

Hemigrammus ocellifer

FAMILY: Characidae
SUBFAMILY: Tetragonopterinae

TWO SUBSPECIES ARE GENERALLY RECOGNIZED: *H. ocellifer falsus* (first imported into Europe in 1910, and the type most frequently encountered in aquaria); and *H. o. ocellifer* (introduced around 1960). Both are very similar, but *H. o. ocellifer* has a distinct, gold-bordered, black spot just behind the gill covers; in *H. o. falsus*, this feature is indistinct. In *H. o. ocellifer*, there are also two red patches on the top and bottom lobes of the caudal fin.

DISTRIBUTION: H. o. falsus: *the Amazon basin;* H. o. ocellifer: *the lower reaches of the Amazon and French Guiana*

SIZE: *Around 1¾in (4.5cm)*

BEHAVIOR: *Peaceful shoaler*

DIET: *Wide range of foods accepted*

AQUARIUM: *Basically, as for* H. erythrozonus. *Temperature range: 72–79°F (22–26°C) for* H. o. falsus*; 75–82°F (24–28°C) for* H. o. ocellifer

BREEDING: *As for* H. erythrozonus

PRETTY TETRA

BLACK WEDGE, OR GARNET, TETRA

Hemigrammus pulcher

FAMILY: Characidae
SUBFAMILY: Tetragonopterinae

THE PRETTY TETRA IS, INDEED, VERY PRETTY, BUT the second (less-often-used) common name is far more appropriate given the black, wedge-like patch that occupies the posterior lower section of the body. Two subspecies are generally recognized: *H. pulcher haraldi*, which is not frequently kept; and *H. p. pulcher*, the popular type.

DISTRIBUTION: H. p. haraldi: *the central Amazon around Manáus;* H. p. pulcher: *wider distribution, including the Peruvian Amazon*

SIZE: *Around 1¾in (4.5cm)*

BEHAVIOR: *As for* H. erythrozonus

DIET: *As for* H. erythrozonus

AQUARIUM: *Basically as for* H. erythrozonus. *Temperature range: 73–81°F (23–27°C)*

BREEDING: *Breeding is not difficult once a good pair has been established. Eggs are scattered*

▲ PRETTY TETRA (HEMIGRAMMUS PULCHER)

▼ ULREY'S TETRA (HEMIGRAMMUS ULREYI)

among vegetation and may be eaten by the parents. Hatching takes about one day

GOLDEN TETRA

Hemigrammus rodwayi

SYNONYM: *Hemigrammus armstrongi*
FAMILY: Characidae
SUBFAMILY: Tetragonopterinae

THE DEGREE OF GOLD COLORATION— KNOWN AS "gold dust"—varies between specimens. This variation may be related to the amount of guanin that is secreted as a protective measure against skin parasites. Specimens with little or no gold dust are occasionally available, but are not generally considered to be as attractive as their golden counterparts.

DISTRIBUTION: *Guyana*

SIZE: *Around 2¼in (5.5cm)*

BEHAVIOR: *Peaceful shoaler*

DIET: *Wide range of foods accepted*

AQUARIUM: *Basically, as for* H. erythrozonus. *Temperature range: 75–82°F (24–28°C)*

BREEDING: *As for* H. erythrozonus. *The gold sheen may disappear after one or more generations of aquarium breeding.*

ULREY'S TETRA

Hemigrammus ulreyi

FAMILY: Characidae
SUBFAMILY: Tetragonopterinae

THIS SPECIES, WHILE LACKING SOME OF THE MORE intense coloration of some other tetras is, nevertheless, every bit as beautiful when in good condition and kept in a shoal. In such circumstances, the bold, gold and black lines that run from the tip of the snout, through the eye, and on to the base of the tail, stand out to great effect. Ulrey's Tetra is sometimes confused with *Hyphessobrycon heterorhabdus* (Flag Tetra)—*see* p.202—from the southern tributaries of the central Amazon region, which has a reddish line, rather than a golden one, above the black body stripe.

DISTRIBUTION: *Paraguay River basin*

SIZE: *Up to 2in (5cm)*

BEHAVIOR: *Peaceful, sometimes shy, shoaler*

DIET: *Wide range of foods accepted*

AQUARIUM: *Well-planted aquarium, with open areas and a current (as produced by a power filter) suits this species well. Soft, slightly acid to neutral water preferred. Temperature range: 73–81°F (23–27°C)*

BREEDING: *No documented accounts currently available*

BENTOS TETRA

ROSY TETRA

Hyphessobrycon bentosi

SYNONYMS: *Hyphessobrycon bentosi bentosi, H. b. callistus, H. b. rosaceus, H. callistus, H. ornatus, H. rosaceus*
FAMILY: Characidae
SUBFAMILY: Tetragonopterinae

THE CORRECT IDENTITY, OR NAME, OF THIS POPU-LAR tetra is far from established with any certainty. There are several similarly named species (or subspecies, depending on the literature consulted), over which there is considerable debate and confusion. Variation in the intensity of the red coloration, black shoulder spots, and white fin edging, are all complicating factors, as are the changes brought about through commercial breeding. The result is that "Rosy" Tetras are encountered under a variety of scientific names, as shown above. In addition, the fish usually referred to as *Hyphessobrycon "robertsi"* (Robert's Tetra) may be a hybrid.

DISTRIBUTION: *Mainly Guyana and Lower Amazon*

SIZE: *Around 1½in (4cm)*

BEHAVIOR: *All "Rosy" Tetras are generally peaceful shoalers*

DIET: *Wide range of foods accepted*

AQUARIUM: *Well-planted, with ample swimming space. Tannin-stained water (see Aquarium Set-up) recommended. Dark substratum will also help. Soft, slightly acid to neutral water, preferably with gentle current. Temperature range: 75–82°F (24–28°C)*

BENTOS TETRA (HYPHESSOBRYCON BENTOSI)

OTHER *HEMIGRAMMUS* SPECIES

In total, there are about 40 species in the genus *Hemigrammus*. In overall characteristics and requirements, they are similar to the closely related genus *Hyphessobrycon* (see pp.200–2). However, *Hemigrammus* species can be distinguished by the scales on the caudal fin. Most species of *Hemigrammus* have similar basic behavioral characteristics and aquarium requirements. The following are among the most frequently encountered species.

SCIENTIFIC NAME	COMMON NAME(S)	SIZE
H. bellotti	Dash-dot Tetra	2in (5cm)
H. boesemani	Boeseman's Tetra	2in (5cm)
H. coeruleus	Coerulean Tetra	3in (7.5cm)
H. hyanuary	January, Costello, or Green Neon, Tetra	1½in (4cm)
H. levis	Golden Neon Tetra	2in (5cm)
H. luelingi	Lueling's Tetra	2in (5cm)
H. marginatus	Bassam Tetra	2¾in (7cm)
H. mininus	False Gold Tetra	2½in (6.5cm)
H. schmardae	Schmard Tetra	2in (5cm)
H. stictus	Red Base Tetra	2¼in (5.5cm)
H. unilineatus	Featherfin Tetra	2in (5cm)

DASH-DOT TETRA (HEMIGRAMMUS BELLOTTI)   *JANUARY TETRA* (HEMIGRAMMUS HYANUARY)

BREEDING: *Eggs are scattered among vegetation and may be eaten by the spawners. Hatching takes about one day*

BLEEDING HEART TETRA

Hyphessobrycon erythrostigma

SYNONYMS: *Hyphessobrycon rubrostigma, H. callistus rubrostigma*
FAMILY: Characidae
SUBFAMILY: Tetragonopterinae

BOTH THE "ERYTHRO" AND "RUBRO" PARTS OF THE current valid scientific name and the alternative that is still in use mean "red," while "stigma" means "spot." Both are beautifully descriptive of this impressive tetra. The only potential drawback of this species is the relatively large size that fully mature specimens can attain, making such fish better suited for medium and large community aquaria than for the smaller, more popular, versions.

DISTRIBUTION: *Upper Amazon basin*

SIZE: *Up to 4¾in (12cm) reported, but usually smaller*

BEHAVIOR: *Males may scrap among themselves, but little or no damage ever occurs. This behavior may be a necessary part of keeping them in peak reproductive condition. Otherwise tolerant of other species*

DIET: *Wide range of foods accepted*

AQUARIUM: *Spacious; setup as for* H. bentosi. *Temperature range: 75–82°F (23–28°C)*

BREEDING: *Challenging in aquaria. Eggs are scattered and may be eaten by the parents*

FLAME TETRA

Hyphessobrycon flammeus

SYNONYM: *Hyphessobrycon bifasciatus*
FAMILY: Characidae
SUBFAMILY: Tetragonopterinae

OVER THE YEARS, THE FLAME TETRA—WHOSE name derives from its red coloration—has lost ground to its other, more vividly colored, relatives, especially their cultivated forms. It is very similar overall to *H. bifasciatus* (Copper Bifasciatus) with which it is often confused to the extent that *H. bifasciatus* is often used as a synonym of *H. flammeus*. However, the true *H. bifasciatus* lacks the red coloration, has several skeletal differences, and is slightly larger. *H. griemi* (Griem's Tetra), from central Brazil, is also similar to Flame Tetra but has three, instead of two, shoulder patches.

DISTRIBUTION: *Southeastern Brazil (both* H. bifasciatus *and* H. flammeus)

SIZE: *1½in (4cm)*

BLEEDING HEART TETRA (HYPHESSOBRYCON ERYTHROSTIGMA)

BEHAVIOR: *As for* H. bentosi

DIET: *As for* H. bentosi

AQUARIUM: *As for* H. bentosi. *Subdued lighting shows this species off well*

BREEDING: *As for* H. bentosi

STRAWBERRY TETRA
GEORGETTE'S TETRA

Hyphessobrycon georgettae

FAMILY: Characidae
SUBFAMILY: Tetragonopterinae

THIS IS YET ANOTHER REDDISH-COLORED SPECIES closely related to *H. bentosi* (*see* p.201). However, the Strawberry Tetra does not possess a black shoulder spot, and unless it is kept in ideal conditions it is often pale in overall color intensity. It is also the smallest species in the group.

DISTRIBUTION: *Suriname*

SIZE: *Up to 2in (5cm) reported, but usually only half this size*

BEHAVIOR: *As for* H. bentosi

DIET: *As for* H. bentosi

AQUARIUM: *As for* H. bentosi

BREEDING: *As for* H. bentosi

BLACK NEON

Hyphessobrycon herbertaxelrodi

FAMILY: Characidae
SUBFAMILY: Tetragonopterinae

ALTHOUGH REFERRED TO AS A "NEON," THE BLACK Neon is quite distinct from the "true" Neon Tetra (*Paracheirodon innesi—see* p.208). It is, nevertheless, neon-like in that it possesses an iridescent golden-green line that runs all the way from the head to the base of the caudal fin. This contrasts sharply with the bold black line that runs below it. Such coloration makes a large shoal of Black Neons a truly impressive sight.

DISTRIBUTION: *Taquari River in the Mato Grosso (Brazil)*

SIZE: *Up to 2in (5cm), but usually smaller*

BLACK NEON (HYPHESSOBRYCON HERBERTAXELRODI)

BEHAVIOR: *As for* H. bentosi

DIET: *As for* H. bentosi

AQUARIUM: *As for* H. bentosi

BREEDING: *Very soft, acid water recommended. Eggs are scattered among plants. Hatching takes about one-and-a-half days*

FLAG TETRA

Hyphessobrycon heterorhabdus

FAMILY: Characidae
SUBFAMILY: Tetragonopterinae

ALTHOUGH THIS SPECIES HAS BEEN AROUND SINCE 1910, and belongs to a separate genus, it is still sometimes confused with *Hemigrammus ulreyi* (Ulrey's Tetra)—*see p.199*—first imported even earlier. The Flag Tetra, however, possesses a reddish line above the black body line, while, in *Hemigrammus ulreyi*, the red is replaced with gold. The Flag Tetra is also distinguishable—although less easily—by the lack of scales on its caudal fin (*H. ulreyi* has a scaled caudal fin).

DISTRIBUTION: *Southern tributaries of the central region of the Amazon*

SIZE: *Around 1¾in (4.5cm)*

BEHAVIOR: *Prefers to be kept in largish groups*

DIET: *As for* H. bentosi

AQUARIUM: *As for* H. bentosi

BREEDING: *As for* H. bentosi

LORETO TETRA
TETRA LORETO

Hyphessobrycon loretoensis

FAMILY: Characidae
SUBFAMILY: Tetragonopterinae

WHEN IN PEAK CONDITION, THIS IS AN attractively marked species. Unfortunately, it is not often seen in stores. A second "species," *H. metae* (Purple Tetra) from the Meta River in Colombia, which is also sometimes available, may be a geographical variety of the Loreto Tetra, rather than a distinct species.

DISTRIBUTION: *Peruvian Amazon (if* H. metae *is excluded)*

SIZE: *Around 1½in (4cm)*

BEHAVIOR: *Peaceful shoaler*

DIET: *Aquarium-adapted specimens will accept a wide range of the available foods from the outset; newly imported specimens may prove more challenging and may need to be started off on small livefoods*

AQUARIUM: *Basically, as for* H. bentosi. *Temperature range: 72–79°F (22–26°C)*

LEMON TETRA (HYPHESSOBRYCON PULCHRIPINNIS)

BREEDING: *No documented reports currently available*

LEMON TETRA

Hyphessobrycon pulchripinnis

FAMILY: Characidae
SUBFAMILY: Tetragonopterinae

THIS IS A TRULY OUTSTANDING TETRA, BUT ONLY when kept in appropriate conditions (*see* photo p.45). When these are not provided, the colors fade, making it a rather nondescript fish. Since the appropriate conditions cannot be easily provided in shop aquaria, the fish may appear pale even if healthy. Such fish will, however, soon begin to show their true colors—quite literally—once they are settled into an appropriate home-aquarium setup.

DISTRIBUTION: *Central Brazil*

SIZE: *Up to 2in (5cm)*

BEHAVIOR: *Active, peaceful shoaler*

DIET: *Wide range of foods accepted*

AQUARIUM: *Spacious, with plant thickets and ample swimming space required. Floating plants, or tall plants whose leaves or stems can extend along the water surface, subdued lighting, and dark substratum also recommended. Tannin-stained water (see Aquarium Set-up) will enhance the brilliant-lemon streaks in the fins, as well as the red of the eye. Soft, acid water usually recommended, but will tolerate harder, more alkaline conditions, as long as quality is high and any changes are carried out gradually. Temperature range: 73–82°F (23–28°C)*

BREEDING: *Only occasionally achieved in aquaria. This is an egg-scattering, egg-eating species*

BLACK-LINE TETRA

Hyphessobrycon scholzei

FAMILY: Characidae
SUBFAMILY: Tetragonopterinae

IN SOME WAYS, THE BLACK-LINE TETRA LOOKS LIKE *H. herbertaxelrodi* (Black Neon) but without the intense coloration. It is also much hardier, and therefore easier to keep, and it does well in community aquaria.

DISTRIBUTION: *Eastern Brazil and Paraguay*

SIZE: *Up to 2in (5cm)*

BEHAVIOR: *Peaceful shoaler, with an appetite for delicate plants*

DIET: *As for* H. bentosi

AQUARIUM: *As for* H. bentosi, *but higher pH values are tolerated. Delicate plants should be avoided. Temperature range: 72–82°F (22–28°C)*

BREEDING: *A prolific breeder. Eggs are scattered among vegetation or over the substratum, and may be eaten by the spawners. Hatching takes about one day*

SLENDER TETRA

Iguanodectes spilurus

SYNONYM: *Iguanodectes tenuis*
FAMILY: Characidae
SUBFAMILY: Tetragonopterinae

THIS LIVELY, SLIM-BODIED TETRA IS OFTEN OVERlooked in those stores where bright lights may be used to illuminate predominantly bare tanks. Such conditions are not to its liking, and as a result it loses much of its subtle brilliance. Under appropriate conditions, though, it is a useful addition to a community aquarium.

DISTRIBUTION: *Guyana, central Amazon and Madeira River (Brazil)*

SIZE: *Around 2½in (6cm)*

BEHAVIOR: *Active, but peaceful, shoaler*

DIET: *Wide range of foods accepted*

AQUARIUM: *Ample swimming areas, surrounded by plants, should be provided. Water chemistry not critical, but quality must be good and oxygenation level must be high; a water current is also advisable. Temperature range: 73–81°F (23–27°C)*

BREEDING: *Soft, slightly acid water recommended. Eggs are scattered and may be eaten by the spawners. Hatching can take up to 14 days*

BLUE EMPEROR

Inpaichthys kerri

FAMILY: Characidae
SUBFAMILY: Tetragonopterinae

THIS SMALL TETRA, IN WHICH THE MALE EXHIBITS a reflective blue sheen on the body, is a relatively new introduction when compared to most of the other tetras encountered in the hobby. It first appeared in Germany in 1977 and, since then, has been consistently available, though not in large numbers. It is a good choice for community aquaria that do not house robust, overactive species.

DISTRIBUTION: *Aripuanã River, Amazonia*

SIZE: *Up to 2in (5cm) reported, but usually smaller*

BEHAVIOR: *Peaceful shoaler*

DIET: *Wide range of foods accepted*

SLENDER TETRA (IGUANODECTES SPILURUS)

OTHER *HYPHESSOBRYCON* SPECIES

The genus *Hyphessobrycon* contains around 60 species, not all of which are available within the hobby. Many *Hyphessobrycon* species look similar to their close relatives, which belong to the genus *Hemigrammus*. However, in *Hyphessobrycon*, the caudal fin has no scales. All species in the selection that follows have, broadly speaking, similar behavioral characteristics and aquarium requirements.

SCIENTIFIC NAME	COMMON NAME(S)	SIZE
H. agulha	Red-tailed Flag Tetra	2in (5cm)
H. amandae	Ember Tetra	2in (5cm)
H. copelandi	Copeland's Tetra	1¾in (4.5cm)
H. peruvianus	Peruvian Tetra	2in (5cm)
H. reticulatus	Reticulated or Netted Tetra	3in (8cm)
H. saizi	Saiz's Tetra	2in (5cm)
H. socolofi	Lesser Bleeding Heart Tetra	1¾in (4.5cm)
H. takasei	Coffee Bean Tetra	1¼in (3cm)
H. vilmae	Vilma's Tetra	1½in (4cm)

VILMA'S TETRA (HYPHESSOBRYCON VILMAE)

◀ *BLUE EMPEROR* (INPAICHTHYS KERRI)   ▲ *JELLY BEAN TETRA* (LADIGESIA ROLOFFI)   ▼ *RED PHANTOM TETRA* (MEGALAMPHODUS SWEGLESI)

AQUARIUM: *Thickly planted, providing adequate shelter, and with open swimming areas. Subdued lighting and dark substratum recommended. Neutral, soft water preferred. Temperature range: 75–81°F (24–27°C)*

BREEDING: *Eggs are laid singly among fine-leaved vegetation and may be eaten by the spawners. Hatching takes one to two days*

JELLY BEAN TETRA
SIERRA LEONE DWARF CHARACIN

Ladigesia roloffi

FAMILY: Characidae
SUBFAMILY: Alestiinae

THIS IS A SMALL, BEAUTIFUL, BUT RARELY SEEN tetra. For long-term success, aquarium conditions must be given close attention (*see* below). In particular, the red coloration of the caudal fin will fade quickly in water which is of an inappropriate quality.

DISTRIBUTION: *Ivory Coast, Ghana, Liberia and Sierra Leone*

SIZE: *Up to 1½in (4cm)*

BEHAVIOR: *Retiring, peaceful shoaler (but with jumping ability); should not be kept with active or robust species*

DIET: *Wide range of small commercial and livefoods accepted*

AQUARIUM: *Well-covered, with subdued lighting, dark substratum, plant thickets and floating vegetation. Soft, acid, tannin-stained water (see Aquarium Set-up) required. Temperature range: 72–79°F (22–26°C)*

BREEDING: *Very soft, acid water recommended. Eggs are released over the substratum (which, ideally, should incorporate some peat)*

BLACK PHANTOM TETRA

Megalamphodus megalopterus

FAMILY: Characidae
SUBFAMILY: Tetragonopterinae

IN GOOD CONDITION, THIS SPECIES MAKES AN impressive sight, which is owed not just to its coloration but to the way in which it swims, with all its fins extended. Following its introduction into Europe in 1956, the species has received a great deal of attention from commercial breeders and is now available in a range of fin and color varieties.

DISTRIBUTION: *Guaporé basin*

SIZE: *Wild-caught specimens around 1¾in (4.5cm); some cultivated varieties larger*

BEHAVIOR: *Peaceful shoaler; males will nevertheless spar with each other (without causing any damage)*

DIET: *Wide range of foods accepted*

AQUARIUM: *Plant thickets, open spaces, and subdued lighting required. Water chemistry not critical, but quality must be good. Temperature range: 72–82°F (22–28°C)*

BREEDING: *Can be challenging in aquaria. Soft, acid water and subdued lighting recommended. Eggs are scattered over plants or the substratum*

RED PHANTOM TETRA
SWEGLES' TETRA

Megalamphodus sweglesi

FAMILY: Characidae
SUBFAMILY: Tetragonopterinae

THIS SPECIES, INTRODUCED INTO THE HOBBY IN the early 1960s, has bright-red coloration when in peak condition. It is, however, somewhat more demanding with regard to water conditions than its close relative, *M. melanopterus* (Black Phantom Tetra)— *see* above. Two other *Megalamphodus* species are also occasionally available: *M. axelrodi* (Calypso Tetra), from Trinidad;

and *M. roseus* (Golden Phantom Tetra), from the Guianas.

DISTRIBUTION: *Upper Amazon basin and, possibly, upper Orinoco basin*

SIZE: *Around 1½in (4cm)*

BEHAVIOR: *Peaceful shoaler*

DIET: *Wide range of foods accepted*

AQUARIUM: *Layout as for* M. melanopterus. *Soft, slightly acid water recommended, with adequate temperature and water chemistry equilibration (i.e. no temperature or water chemistry "shocks"), and with regular partial water changes. Temperature range: 68–73°F (20–23°C)*

BREEDING: *As for* M. melanopterus, *but temperature should be kept below 73°F (23°C)*

▲ SILVER DOLLAR (METYNNIS ARGENTIUS)   ▼ SILVER DOLLAR (METYNNIS HYPSAUCHEN)

SILVER DOLLAR
SILVER PACU
Metynnis argenteus

SYNONYMS: *Metynnis anisurus;* possibly *M. altidorsalis, M. snethlageae*
FAMILY: Characidae
SUBFAMILY: Serrasalminae

METYNNIS CLASSIFICATION IS PROBABLY THE MOST inconsistent among the characoids. The existence of naturally occurring forms that could be morphs, subspecies, or even species, adds to the confusion. Individual *Metynnis* species therefore appear under various names in both aquarium and scientific literature. A distinguishing feature of the genus, which separates it from all the other members of the subfamily, is the long-based adipose fin.

DISTRIBUTION: *Amazon basin and the Guianas*

SIZE: *Around 5½in (14cm)*

BEHAVIOR: *Peaceful shoaler, with a keen appetite for plants*

DIET: *Some commercial formulations, including vegetable flakes, tablets, pellets, livefoods, and freeze-dried foods, accepted. Fresh vegetable matter, e.g. lettuce leaves, should be provided daily*

AQUARIUM: *Large, with open swimming areas and unpalatable, robust, and/or artificial plants, as well as large shelters. Subdued lighting and dark substratum also recommended. Water chemistry not critical, but extremes must be avoided. Temperature range: 75–82°F (24–28°C)*

BREEDING: *Soft, acid, tannin-stained water (see Aquarium Set-up) recommended. Aquarium should be darkened at first, then gradually exposed to light. Provide some feathery-rooted floating plants, e.g. Water Hyacinth (Eichhornia crassipes), or submerged, unpalatable, fine-leaved or fine-fronded plants, e.g. Java Moss (Vesicularia dubyana) as a spawning medium. Spawning takes place among this vegetation, with the eggs dropping to the bottom of the tank, where they are ignored. Hatching takes about three days*

SILVER DOLLAR
PLAIN METYNNIS OR PACU
Metynnis hypsauchen

SYNONYMS: *Metynnis calichromus, M. ehrhardti, M. fasciatus, M. orinocensis, M. schreitmuelleri*
FAMILY: Characidae
SUBFAMILY: Serrasalminae

THE SAME NOMENCLATURAL CONFUSION OUTLINED for *M. argenteus* (*see* above) applies to this species, only more so. Both species have been known in the hobby since 1912–13, and both continue to be regularly available. They look particularly impressive when kept in a sizable shoal in a spacious aquarium.

DISTRIBUTION: *Western region of Amazon basin, Paraguay basin, Orinoco and Guyana*

SIZE: *Around 6in (15cm)*

BEHAVIOR: *As for* H. argenteus

DIET: *As for* H. argenteus

AQUARIUM: *As for* H. argenteus

BREEDING: *As for* H. argenteus

GLASSY TETRA
GLASS TETRA

Moenkhausia oligolepis

FAMILY: Characidae
SUBFAMILY: Tetragonopterinae

SUPERFICIALLY, THIS SPECIES LOOKS SIMILAR TO *M. sanctaefilomenae* (Yellow-banded Tetra), *see* below. However, the Glassy Tetra has no yellow band in front of the black tail band, and the black band at the base of the caudal fin is less distinct; it is also a deeper-bodied, larger fish.

DISTRIBUTION: *Upper Amazon and Guyana*

SIZE: *Up to 4¾in (12cm) reported*

BEHAVIOR: *Tolerant shoaler*

DIET: *Wide range of foods accepted*

AQUARIUM: *Spacious, planted, with large open swimming areas and dark substratum. Good-quality, mature water preferred, but wide range of water chemistry conditions tolerated. Temperature range: 68–77°F (20–25°C)*

BREEDING: *Eggs are scattered among the feathery roots of floating plants, such as Water Hyacinth (*Eichhornia crassipes*), or over fine-leaved vegetation. Soft, acid, tannin-stained water (see Aquarium Set-up) recommended. The spawners may eat their eggs. Hatching takes one to two days*

DIAMOND TETRA

Moenkhausia pittieri

FAMILY: Characidae
SUBFAMILY: Tetragonopterinae

THE MALE POSSESSES A VERY LONG DORSAL FIN, which, when extended at the same time as the anal fin, makes this fish look quite spectacular. The glistening body scales (the "diamonds" from which the name derives) add to this effect. However, juvenile specimens—which are the type most often available in stores—lack these features and can therefore be easily overlooked.

DISTRIBUTION: *Region of Lake Valencia (Venezuela)*

SIZE: *Up to 2½in (6cm)*

BEHAVIOR: *As for* M. oligolepis

DIET: *As for* M. oligolepis

AQUARIUM: *Basically, as for* M. oligolepis. *Hard water should be avoided. Temperature range: 75–82°F (24–28°C)*

BREEDING: *Eggs are scattered among fine-leaved vegetation and may be eaten by the parents. It is helpful to darken the aquarium during the initial prespawning stage so that the level of illumination can be gradually increased when the fish are ready to spawn. Hatching takes two to three days*

YELLOW-BANDED TETRA
RED-EYED TETRA

Moenkhausia sanctaefilomenae

FAMILY: Characidae
SUBFAMILY: Tetragonopterinae

OF THE TWO COMMON NAMES, THE RED-EYED Tetra more accurately describes this species because the intensity of the yellow band in front of the caudal fin can vary considerably. The species is superficially similar to *Moenkhausia oligolepis* (Glass Tetra), *see* above, but is generally more vividly colored and does not attain the same size.

DISTRIBUTION: *Eastern Bolivia, western Brazil, Paraguay and eastern Peru*

SIZE: *Up to 2¾in (7cm), but often smaller*

BEHAVIOR: *As for* M. oligolepis

DIET: *As for* M. oligolepis

AQUARIUM: *Basically, as for* M. oligolepis. *Temperature range: 72–79°F (23–26°C), but slightly higher and lower temperatures also tolerated*

BREEDING: *As for* M. oligolepis

REDHOOK PACU
REDHOOK METYNNIS

Myleus rubripinnis

SYNONYMS: *Mylopus rubripnnis,* possibly *Myleus asterias*
FAMILY: Characidae
SUBFAMILY: Serrasalminae

OWING TO ITS OVERALL SIMILARITY TO *METYNNIS* species (*see* p.205), this species is sometimes misleadingly referred to as the Redhook Metynnis. As both common names imply, a major characteristic of this fish is the large hook-like anal fin, which can be particularly distinctive in juvenile specimens. Two subspecies are generally recognized: *M. rubripinnis rubripinnis* and *M. r. luna*. Several other *Myleus* species are available (under a variety of scientific names owing to the confused state of the taxonomy of these fishes); all have basically similar requirements.

DISTRIBUTION: *M. r. rubripinnis: Suriname and, probably, Guyana; M. r. luna: Maroni River*

SIZE: *Some wild-caught specimens reported up to 10in (25cm); aquarium specimens usually slightly less than half this size*

BEHAVIOR: *Peaceful shoaler, with appetite for plants*

DIET: *As for* Metynnis argenteus

AQUARIUM: *As for* Metynnis argenteus

BREEDING: *Appears not to have bred in aquaria*

YELLOW-BANDED TETRA (MOENKHAUSIA SANCTAEFILOMENAE)

DIET: *As for* M. argenteus

AQUARIUM: *As for* M. argenteus

BREEDING: *Assumed to be similar to* M. argenteus

RAINBOW EMPEROR TETRA

Nematobrycon lecortei

SYNONYM: *Nematobrycon amphiloxus* (itself used as a synonym of *N. palmeri*)
FAMILY: Characidae
SUBFAMILY: Tetragonopterinae

ALTHOUGH THIS FISH IS LESS WELL KNOWN THAN *N. palmeri* (Emperor Tetra), *see* below, the Rainbow Emperor is just as beautiful. When kept in appropriate conditions, the iridescent blue marbling along the body, allied with the bright-red eye, makes a shoal of these fish quite an unforgettable sight.

DISTRIBUTION: *Atrato River (Western Colombia)*

SIZE: *Up to 2¼in (6cm), but usually a little smaller*

BEHAVIOR: *Quiet, peaceful fish; should he kept in small groups*

DIET: *Wide range of foods accepted*

AQUARIUM: *Well-planted, with ample swimming space, and dark substratum. Softish, acid to slightly alkaline water quite suitable. If possible, water should be tannin-stained (see Aquarium Set-up). Regular partial water changes should be carried out, but any alterations to water chemistry must be made gradually. Temperature range: 73–81°F (23–27°C)*

BREEDING: *Assumed to be similar to* N. palmeri *(see below)*

EMPEROR TETRA

Nematobrycon palmeri

SYNONYM: *Nematobrycon amphiloxus*
FAMILY: Characidae
SUBFAMILY: Tetragonopterinae

EMPEROR TETRAS ARE AMONG THE LONGEST-LIVED tetras: fish kept in appropriate conditions may live for around five years. This species does not possess the blue marbling of *N. lecortei*, and its eyes are greenish blue, rather than red. *N. amphiloxus* (sometimes written as *N.* "amphiloxus") is believed to be a smoky colored, naturally occurring morph of the Emperor Tetra.

DISTRIBUTION: *Western Colombia*

SIZE: *Up to 2¼in (6cm), but usually a little smaller*

BEHAVIOR: *As for* N. lecortei

DIET: *As for* N. lecortei

AQUARIUM: *As for* N. lecortei

▲ *REDHOOK PACU (MYLEUS RUBRIPINNIS)*

▼ *SILVER MYLOSSOMA (MYLOSSOMA DURIVENTRE)*

SILVER MYLOSSOMA

HARD-BELLIED SILVER DOLLAR

Mylossoma duriventre

SYNONYMS: *Myletes duriventris, Mylossoma argenteum, M. albiscopus, M. ocellatum*
FAMILY: Characidae
SUBFAMILY: Serrasalminae

THE MANY NAMES UNDER WHICH THIS FISH appears in aquarium and other literature is an indication of the difficulties encountered in correctly identifying individual species. Like its close relatives, it bears a close resemblance to the piranhas, but the mouth is neither as powerful nor is it armed with sharp teeth. Of the other four or so species in the genus, one of the silver dollars, *M. aureum*, from the Amazon basin, is the most frequently encountered.

DISTRIBUTION: *Amazon basin*

SIZE: *Up to 9in (23cm) reported, but usually smaller*

BEHAVIOR: *Tolerant shoaler, with a voracious appetite for plants*

EMPEROR TETRA (NEMATOBRYCON PALMERI)

BREEDING: *Can be challenging. Soft, acid water and darkened aquarium recommended. Eggs are laid singly among vegetation and may be eaten by the spawning pair. Hatching takes one to two days*

CARDINAL TETRA

Paracheirodon axelrodi

SYNONYMS: *Cheirodon axelrodi, Hyphesso-brycon cardinalis*
FAMILY: Characidae
SUBFAMILY: Tetragonopterinae

THE CARDINAL TETRA IS ONE OF THE MOST famous and popular species in the hobby. It is a truly magnificent fish, which forms the cornerstone of the Brazilian Amazon ornamental fishery. It is also bred commercially in several countries, most notably the Czech Republic. Several forms of the species are known within its natural range, and may represent several, rather than a single, species. A cultivated golden variety is occasionally available.

DISTRIBUTION: *From the Orinoco (Venezuela), through the northern tributaries of the Rio Negro (Brazil), on to western Colombia*

SIZE: *Up to 2in (5cm)*

BEHAVIOR: *Peaceful shoaler*

DIET: *Wide range of foods accepted*

AQUARIUM: *Well-planted, with some open spaces and subdued lighting (e.g. provided by floating plants), recommended. These fish are often, but not invariably, found in tannin-stained water (see Aquarium Set-up). Soft, acid water recommended, but harder, more alkaline conditions tolerated if adjustments carried out gradually. Temperature range: 73–81°F (23–27°C)*

BREEDING: *Challenging in aquaria. Subdued lighting and very soft, acid, tannin-stained water will enhance chances of success. Eggs are scattered among vegetation and may be eaten by the parents. Hatching takes about one day*

NEON TETRA

Paracheirodon innesi

SYNONYM: *Hyphessobrycon innesi*
FAMILY: Characidae
SUBFAMILY: Tetragonopterinae

AT FIRST SIGHT, THIS SPECIES MAY BE CONFUSED with *P. axelrodi*. However, in the Neon Tetra, the red body coloration occupies only the posterior half of the body, while, in *P. axelrodi* it extends from head to tail. Traditionally, there have been two major sources of neons: wild-caught specimens from South America, and captive-bred stocks from Hong Kong. However, other sources of captive-bred fish are becoming established, particularly in Sri Lanka. Several cultivated varieties of neon are available in addition to the wild type, including Diamondhead, Gold, Albino, Brilliant, and "Mon Cheri" (yellow).

DISTRIBUTION: *Putumayo river, eastern Peru*

SIZE: *Around 1½in (4cm)*

BEHAVIOR: *As for P. axelrodi*

DIET: *As for P. axelrodi*

AQUARIUM: *As for P. axelrodi. Temperature range: 68–79°F (20–26°C)*

BREEDING: *As for P. axelrodi*

FALSE NEON TETRA

GREEN NEON TETRA

Paracheirodon simulans

SYNONYM: *Hyphessobrycon simulans*
FAMILY: Characidae
SUBFAMILY: Tetragonopterinae

THIS IS THE LEAST FREQUENTLY ENCOUNTERED OF the three *Paracheirodon* species featured. In overall coloration, it falls somewhere in between *P. innesi* and *P. axelrodi*. Despite its relative rarity, at least two varieties are known in addition to the wild type: a White Green (or False) Neon and a Gold Green (or False) Neon.

DISTRIBUTION: *Jufaris or Tupari rivers in the area of the Rio Negro (Brazil)*

SIZE: *Up to 1½in (4cm), but usually a little smaller*

BEHAVIOR: *As for P. axelrodi*

DIET: *As for P. axelrodi*

FALSE NEON TETRA (PARACHEIRODON SIMULANS)

CARDINAL TETRA
(PARACHEIRODON AXELRODI) ▼

▲ CARDINAL TETRA (PARACHEIRODON AXELRODI)
NEON TETRA (PARACHEIRODON INNESI) ▼ ▶

AQUARIUM: *As for* P. axelrodi. *Avoid alkaline, hardwater conditions*

BREEDING: *Challenging in aquaria; conditions similar to those for* P. axelrodi *recommended*

FALSE RED-NOSED TETRA

FALSE RUMMY-NOSED TETRA

Petitella georgia

FAMILY: Characidae
SUBFAMILY: Tetragonopterinae

THIS SPECIES IS SUPERFICIALLY SIMILAR TO THE other rummy-nosed tetras (*Hemigrammus bleheri* and *H. rhodostomus*—*see* p.198). However, in *Petitella*, the central black band in the caudal fin extends forward somewhat into the body, and the black band along the base of the anal fin is wider than in *H. rhodostomus*. False Red-nosed Tetra is also a larger fish.

DISTRIBUTION: *Upper Amazon basin*

SIZE: *Up to 3in (8cm) reported, but usually around 5cm (2in)*

BEHAVIOR: *Peaceful shoaler*

DIET: *Most foods accepted*

AQUARIUM: *As for* Hemigrammus bleheri

BREEDING: *No documented reports currently available*

CONGO TETRA

Phenacogrammus interruptus

SYNONYM: *Micralestes interruptus*
FAMILY: Characidae
SUBFAMILY: Alestiinae

THE SCIENTIFIC NAME OF THIS SPECIES IS ONE OF the most "fluid" among the tetras, apparently changing in acceptance and popularity with time. During the early part of the last decade of the 20th century, for example, *Micralestes* gained ground over the former choice, *Phenacogrammus*. As the new millennium approached, though, *Phenacogrammus* seemed to come back into fashion. The main contributing factor to this confusion is the considerable overlap in certain characteristics between the two genera. The main distinguishing feature between the two is that, in *Phenacogrammus*, the lateral line is incomplete, while in *Micralestes* it is complete (although this distinction is not infallible since, in some *Micralestes*, the lateral line can also be incomplete). Whatever its true identity, the species is an elegant fish that looks splendid when kept in appropriate conditions and in a small shoal.

DISTRIBUTION: *Zaire (Republic of Congo)*

CONGO TETRA (PHENACOGRAMMUS INTERRUPTUS)

SIZE: *Fully mature males up to 3¼in (9cm); females somewhat smaller*

BEHAVIOR: *Peaceful and tolerant; may become timid in the presence of robust, hyperactive, or aggressive tankmates. May also nibble delicate or succulent plants*

DIET: *Wide range of foods accepted; vegetable component recommended*

AQUARIUM: *Spacious, well-planted, with ample swimming areas. Soft, slightly acid water, preferably tannin-stained (see Aquarium Set-up) recommended. Temperature range: 75–81°F (24–27°C)*

BREEDING: *Uncommon in aquaria. Bright illumination may act as a stimulus for well-matched pairs or shoals. Eggs are scattered over the substratum and take up to six days to hatch*

SAILFIN CHARACIN

SAILFIN TETRA

Crenuchus spilurus

FAMILY: Characidae
SUBFAMILY: Crenuchinae

THIS SPECIES HAS THE SAME CAVERNOUS MOUTH as its close relative, *Poecilocharax weitzmani* (Black Darter Tetra), *see* below. It is not quite as vividly colored but is, nonetheless, an impressive fish—the males, with their large expanded dorsal fins, more so than the females.

DISTRIBUTION: *Guyana and middle Amazon*

SIZE: *Up to 2¼in (6cm)*

BEHAVIOR: *Large specimens may prey on small fish; otherwise peaceful, if sometimes timid*

DIET: *Livefoods and deep-frozen diets preferred, but acclimatized specimens will also accept some commercial formulations*

AQUARIUM: *Dense vegetation, ample shelters, and subdued lighting. Soft, acid, tannin-stained water (see Aquarium Set-up) preferred. Temperature range: 75–81°F (24–27°C)*

BREEDING: *Very challenging in aquaria. Eggs may be laid on a flat or smooth rock, and may receive some parental care*

BLACK DARTER TETRA

WEITZMAN'S PREDATOR TETRA

Poecilocharax weitzmani

FAMILY: Characidae
SUBFAMILY: Crenuchinae

FOR A SMALL FISH, THIS SPECIES CAN BE absolutely stunning. Males, in particular, have large (relatively speaking) dorsal and anal fins, which, during displays, they spread out while at the same time opening the cavernous mouth to its full extent, thus creating the impression that they are much larger than they really are. This is a challenging species best suited to the experienced aquarist.

DISTRIBUTION: *Upper Solimões, Upper Rio Negro and Orinoco basins*

SIZE: *Up to 1½in (4cm), but often smaller*

BEHAVIOR: *A shoaler; males display to each other but do not generally cause any damage*

DIET: *Livefoods preferred; deep-frozen, freeze-dried diets may be accepted*

AQUARIUM: *Well-planted, with some open spaces and subdued lighting recommended. Soft, acid water, preferably tannin-stained (see Aquarium Set-up). Temperature range: 75–82°F (24–28°C)*

BREEDING: *No documented reports of aquarium breeding currently available*

GLASS BLOODFIN

TRANSLUCENT BLOODFIN or GLASS BLOODFISH

Prionobrama filigera

SYNONYMS: *Aphyocharax filigerus*, *Prionobrama madeirae*
FAMILY: Characidae
SUBFAMILY: Uncertain (classified as Paragoni-atinae by some authors)

CLOSELY RELATED TO *APHYOCHARAX ANISITSI* (Bloodfin), *see* p.193, this species is much less frequently seen in the hobby. This is a shame because it is an elegant, strikingly patterned fish, with the added attraction that the male's anal fin possesses a brilliant-white, curved extension along its front edge.

DISTRIBUTION: *Reported from central and southern Brazil, Madeira, Paraguay rivers, and Argentina*

SIZE: *Around 2½in (6cm)*

BEHAVIOR: *Peaceful shoaler*

DIET: *Wide range of foods accepted*

AQUARIUM: *Well-planted, with ample swimming space, recommended. Surface cover in the form of floating plants also advisable. Softish, slightly acid water appears to be preferred, but higher pH and hardness also tolerated. Temperature range: 72–86°F (22–30°C)*

BREEDING: *Soft, acid, tannin-stained water (see Aquarium Set-up) recommended. Sunlight will also help. Eggs are scattered among fine-leaved vegetation and hatch after about three days*

X-RAY TETRA

X-RAY FISH or WATER GOLDFINCH

Pristella maxillaris

SYNONYM: *Pristella riddlei*
FAMILY: Characidae
SUBFAMILY: Tetragonopterinae

THIS IS AN UNDEMANDING SPECIES THAT TOLER-ATES a range of aquarium conditions. However, for its colors to be seen to best effect, the overall water quality must be good. The somewhat intriguing common name of Water Goldfinch probably derives from the gold, white, black, and red coloration, which is shared with its feathered namesake.

DISTRIBUTION: *Lower Amazon, Guyana, and Venezuela*

SIZE: *Around 1¾in (4.5cm)*

BEHAVIOR: *Peaceful shoaler*

DIET: *Wide range of foods accepted*

AQUARIUM: *Well-planted, with ample swimming space, a dark substratum, and subdued lighting will show off a shoal to great effect. Water*

chemistry not critical (although soft, slightly acid conditions preferred), but quality must be good. Temperature range: 70–82°F (21–28°C)—low temperatures should not be maintained on a long-term basis*

BREEDING: *Sometimes difficult if pairs are not well matched; otherwise spawning is easy. Eggs are scattered and take about one day to hatch*

RED-BELLIED PIRANHA

Pygocentrus nattereri

SYNONYMS: *Serrasalmus nattereri, Pygocentrus altus*
FAMILY: Characidae
SUBFAMILY: Serrasalminae

AS IN THE CASE OF OTHER MEMBERS OF THE SUB-family Serrasalminae, such as the silver dollars (e.g. *Metynnis, Myleus*—*see* pp.205 and 206 respectively), piranha taxonomy is currently somewhat unsettled. The former subgeneric name, *Pygocentrus*, for example, is now becoming more widely accepted as a full generic name for some types of piranha, as indicated above. Despite its formidable reputation, the Red-bellied Piranha is not quite the indiscriminate killer it is made out to be. It is, nevertheless, a potentially dangerous species and even small specimens must be treated with due caution, particularly when cleaning their aquaria.

DISTRIBUTION: *Amazon and Orinoco basins*

SIZE: *Up to 12in (30cm)*

BEHAVIOR: *Aggressive, often toward subordinate tankmates of their own species, but can be timid when housed in bare, brightly lit aquaria*

DIET: *Meat/fish-based diet and large livefoods. Live fish will also be eaten, but the ethics of this practice need to be considered before providing such a diet*

GLASS BLOODFIN (PRIONOBRAMA FILIGERA)

RED-BELLIED PIRANHA (PYGOCENTRUS NATTERERI)

SWORDTAIL CHARACIN (STEVARDIA RIISEI)

AQUARIUM: *Large, deep, well-filtered, and with large pieces of bogwood laid out for shelter. Only robust and/or artificial plants suitable. Lighting should not be too bright. Soft, slightly acid water preferred, but not essential. Temperature range: 73–81°F (23–27°C)*

BREEDING: *Infrequent in aquaria. Eggs have been laid among the feathery roots of large floating plants such as Water Hyacinth (Eichhornia crassipes), but usually they are laid inside a depression dug in the substratum. Both parents, or one (usually the male), will defend the eggs until they hatch about two to three days later*

BLACK PIRANHA
WHITE, or SPOTTED, PIRANHA
Pygocenrus rhombeus

SYNONYMS: *Serrasalmus rhombeus, S. niger,* and several others
FAMILY: Characidae
SUBFAMILY: Serrasalminae

LIKE *P. NATTERERI*, THIS LARGE, PREDATORY species is regularly available, albeit under a variety of names. Other members of the genus, as well as related ones, are only occasionally encountered, with the possible exception of *Serrasalmus hollandi* (Holland's Piranha), which is found south of the Amazon basin and known not to be as aggressive as *P. nattereri* and Black Piranha.

DISTRIBUTION: *Amazon basin and Guyana*

SIZE: *Up to c.15in (38cm)*

BEHAVIOR: *As for P. nattereri*

DIET: *As for P. nattereri*

AQUARIUM: *As for P. nattereri*

BREEDING: *As for P. nattereri*

SWORDTAIL CHARACIN
Stevardia riisei

SYNONYM: *Corynopoma riisei*
FAMILY: Characidae
SUBFAMILY: Glandulocaudinae

THIS BASICALLY SILVER-COLORED FISH HAS RATHER unusual, and distinguishing, physical and reproductive characteristics. Mature males possess a long extension of the lower rays of the caudal fin—the "sword" that gives the species its common name. In addition, they have a long, filament-like extension on each gill cover, with a fleshy structure at the tip; it is believed that this "paddle" is used as a lure to attract a female into the appropriate breeding position.

DISTRIBUTION: *Meta river in Colombia and (possibly) Trinidad*

SIZE: *Up to 2¾in (7cm)*

BEHAVIOR: *Peaceful shoaler; should not be housed with fin-nipping species such as Barbus tetrazona (Tiger Barb)*

DIET: *Wide range of foods accepted*

AQUARIUM: *Well-planted, with ample swimming areas recommended. Water chemistry can range from slightly acid to slightly alkaline and from soft to medium-hard. Temperature range: 72–82°F (22–28°C)*

BREEDING: *Unusually for a characin, the eggs are fertilized internally (hence the need for the female to adopt a precise position for mating). The eggs are subsequently released and hatch in one to one-and a half days*

BOEHLKE'S PENGUIN FISH
BLACK-LINE THAYERIA
Thayeria boehlkei

FAMILY: Characidae
SUBFAMILY: Tetragonopterinae

THIS SPECIES LOOKS BEST WHEN KEPT IN A SHOAL, as this emphasizes the bold, black, gold-bordered body band, as well as the unusual way in which this band extends into the lower part of the caudal fin. The species also adopts a characteristic angled posture when at rest, with the head pointed slightly upward, and often with all the fish in a shoal facing in the same direction.

DISTRIBUTION: *Peruvian Amazon, and Araguaia (Brazil)*

BOEHLKE'S PENGUIN FISH (THAYERIA BOEHLKEI)

SIZE: *Up to 3in (8cm) reported, but usually smaller*

BEHAVIOR: *Peaceful shoaler*

DIET: *Wide range of foods accepted*

AQUARIUM: *Thickly planted, with some (but not necessarily ample) swimming space, recommended. Soft, slightly acid, well-oxygenated water preferred, but some deviation is tolerated, as long as changes are carried out gradually. Frequent water changes (observing this rule) also advisable. Temperature range: 72–82°F (22–28°C)*

BREEDING: *Eggs are scattered freely among fine-leaved vegetation. Hatching takes about one day*

PENGUIN FISH
SHORT-STRIPED THAYERIA

Thayeria obliqua

FAMILY: Characidae
SUBFAMILY: Tetragonopterinae

AT FIRST SIGHT, THIS SPECIES CAN BE CONFUSED with *T. boehlkei* (*see* above). However, in the Penguin Fish the black band extends forward from the tip of the lower lobe of the caudal fin at an upwardly directed angle to a point on the back just posterior to the dorsal fin. In *T. boehlkei*, the band extends all the way along the center of the body right up to the gill cover.

DISTRIBUTION: *Amazon basin*

SIZE: *Up to 3in (8cm) reported, but usually smaller*

BEHAVIOR: *As for* T. boehlkei

DIET: *As for* T. boehlkei

AQUARIUM: *As for* T. boehlkei

BREEDING: *No documented reports appear to be available, but breeding strategy likely to be as in* T. boehlkei

NARROW HATCHETFISH (TRIPORTHEUS ANGULATUS)

NARROW HATCHETFISH

Triportheus angulatus

FAMILY: Characidae
SUBFAMILY: Uncertain (classified as Bryconinae by some authors)

MEMBERS OF THIS GENUS (OF WHICH THIS SPECIES is the most frequently encountered in the hobby) have a keel-like chest that resembles that found in the "true" hatchetfishes (family Gasteropelecidae—*see* pp.218–19). This forms the anchor for powerful chest muscles that allow the fish to jump out of the water and—with the aid of wing-like pectoral fins—glide for short distances, thus escaping predators.

DISTRIBUTION: *Amazon basin*

SIZE: *Up to 8in (20cm) reported, but usually smaller*

BEHAVIOR: *Generally peaceful, but may attack small tankmates*

DIET: *Livefoods preferred, but will accept a range of commercial diets*

AQUARIUM: *Large, well-covered, well-illuminated, with ample swimming areas, recommended. Well-oxygenated water important, but composition may vary from slightly acid to slightly alkaline, and from soft to medium-hard. Temperature range: 72–82°F (22–28°C)*

BREEDING: *No documented reports currently available*

LINED CITHARINID

Citharinus citharus

FAMILY: Citharinidae
SUBFAMILY: Citharininae

THIS LARGE, PREDOMINANTLY SILVERY FISH HAS dusky dorsal, caudal, and anal fins, clear pectoral fins, and reddish pelvic fins. Only juveniles are suitable for average-sized aquaria. This species is therefore best avoided unless adequate accommodation can be provided for adults.

DISTRIBUTION: *From Senegal to the Nile basin*

SIZE: *Up to 20in (50cm) reported, but usually much smaller*

BEHAVIOR: *Not aggressive; may be kept in shoals, space permitting. Likes to dig in the substrate in search of food*

DIET: *Wide range of foods accepted*

AQUARIUM: *Large, deep, with ample swimming space and fine-grained substratum recommended. Neutral to alkaline, soft to medium-hard water preferred. Temperature range: 72–82°F (22–28°C)*

BREEDING: *Believed to be an egg scatterer, but no documented accounts currently available*

LINED CITHARINID (CITHARINUS CITHARUS)

SILVER DISTICHODUS (DISTICHODUS AFFINIS)

SILVER DISTICHODUS

Distichodus affinis

FAMILY: Citharinidae
SUBFAMILY: Distichodontinae

THE SILVER DISTICHODUS WAS FIRST IMPORTED into Europe in 1911 and has been available ever since, despite its plant-eating habits. Overall, it is similar to *D. noboli* (Nobol's Distichodus) from Upper Congo (Zaire) with which it is sometimes confused. All *Distichodus* are specialist feeders and are best suited to experienced aquarists.

DISTRIBUTION: *Congo (Zaire) basin*

SIZE: *Up to 5in (13cm)*

BEHAVIOR: *Peaceful, with a distinct liking for succulent plants*

DIET: *Some commercial foods accepted, particularly vegetable flakes; lettuce, spinach, watercress, and other plants, should form an important part of the diet*

AQUARIUM: *Roomy, with rock and bogwood decor, recommended. Use only unpalatable or artificial plants, and provide swimming space. Slightly acid to neutral, soft to medium-hard water. Temperature range: 73–81°F (23–27°C)*

BREEDING: *No documented accounts currently available*

LONG-NOSED DISTICHODUS

Distichodus lusosso

FAMILY: Citharinidae
SUBFAMILY: Distichodontinae

OWING TO THE LARGE SIZE ATTAINED BY ADULTS, only juveniles of this species are suitable for most aquaria. A similar-looking species, *D. sexfasciatus* (Six-lined Distichodus)—also from the Congo (Zaire) basin—can be confused with this species, although, as its name implies, the Long-nosed Distichodus has a somewhat longer and more pointed snout than its close relative.

DISTRIBUTION: *Congo (Zaire) basin, Angola, Cameroon*

SIZE: *Up to 16in (40cm) reported, but usually smaller*

BEHAVIOR: *Peaceful, with a strong appetite for plants*

DIET: *As for* D. affinis

AQUARIUM: *As for* D. affinis. *Temperature range: 72–79°F (22–26°C)*

BREEDING: *As for* D. affinis

OTHER *DISTICHODUS* SPECIES

In addition to the two featured species and the two others mentioned, several other *Distichodus* are available. All are plant eaters and require the same basic care and feeding.

SCIENTIFIC NAME	COMMON NAME(S):	SIZE
D. antonii	Antoni's Distichodus	8¼in (21cm)
D. atroventralis	Gray Distichodus	6in (15cm)
D. decemmaculatus	Dwarf Distichodus	3in (8cm)
D. fasciolatus	Shark-tailed Distichodus	12in (30cm)
D. maculatus	Many-spotted Distichodus	8in (20cm)*
D. notospilus	Red-finned, or African, Straight Distichodus	6in (15cm)*

Note

*Sizes up to 12in (30cm) have been reported but are not encountered in aquaria.

RED-FINNED DISTICHODUS (DISTICHODUS NOTOSPILUS)

▲ Long-nosed Distichodus (Distichodus lusosso)
Ansorge's Neolebias (Neolebias ansorgii) ▶

ONE-STRIPED AFRICAN CHARACIN

Nannaethiops unitaeniatus

FAMILY: Citharinidae
SUBFAMILY: Distichodontinae

ALTHOUGH IT LOOKS QUITE DIFFERENT TO THE other members of the family featured in the foregoing entries, the One-striped Characin possesses fin ray, skeletal, and tooth characteristics that identify it as a citharinid. Despite the subtle coloration of this species, it nevertheless makes an impressive display when kept in appropriate conditions. A gold-striped variety is also occasionally available.

DISTRIBUTION: *Widely distributed in tropical regions of Africa*

SIZE: *Around 2¾in (7cm)*

BEHAVIOR: *Peaceful shoaler best kept in a species aquarium, i.e. one set up specifically for it*

DIET: *Wide range of foods accepted once specimens have been adequately acclimatized*

AQUARIUM: *Brightly lit, with ample swimming space and fine-grained substratum recommended. Tannin-stained water (see Aquarium Set-up) advisable. Neutral, softish water preferred, but a little deviation accepted. Temperature range: 73–79°F (23–26°C)*

BREEDING: *Morning sunlight appears to stimulate spawning. Eggs are scattered, and hatch in a little over one day*

ANSORGE'S NEOLEBIAS

Neolebias ansorgii

SYNONYM: *Neolebias ansorgei*
FAMILY: Citharinidae
SUBFAMILY: Distichodontinae

THIS COLORFUL SPECIES (THE MOST COLORFUL OF ITS genus) has been available since the 1920s without ever attaining the high levels of popularity it deserves. It is, nevertheless, the most widely available *Neolebias* species. Unusually for characoids, *Neolebias* species lack an adipose fin.

DISTRIBUTION: *Widely distributed from Cameroon to Congo (Zaire)*

SIZE: *Around 1½in (3.5cm)*

BEHAVIOR: *Peaceful, timid; best kept in a species aquarium, i.e. one set up specifically for it*

DIET: *Livefoods preferred, but other foods accepted*

AQUARIUM: *Subdued lighting, dark substratum, and ample planting recommended, as is relatively shallow water (around 8in/20cm). Raw water must be avoided (add a good conditioner when carrying out partial changes). Slightly acid, softish water preferred. Temperature range: 73–82°F (23–28°C)*

BREEDING: *Peat or moss base recommended. Eggs are scattered, and hatch in about one day*

OTHER *NEOLEBIAS* SPECIES

Four other species of *Neolebias*, in addition to the one featured, are occasionally available.

SCIENTIFIC NAME	COMMON NAME(S)	SIZE
N. axelrodi*	Axelrod's Neolebias	1¼in (3cm)
N. trewavasae*	Three-lined**, or Trewavas', Neolebias	2in (5cm)
N. trilineatus	Three-lined**, Goldband, or Goldenline, Neolebias	2in (5cm)
N. unifasciatus	Schwarzer, or Black, Neolebias, One-banded African Tetra	2in (5cm)

Notes

*These species are more colorful than the others.

**Confusingly, the common name Three-lined Neolebias is sometimes used for both these species. The name seems to be more appropriate for N. trilineatus.

AFRICAN PIKE CHARACIN (PHAGO MACULATUS)

AFRICAN PIKE CHARACIN

Phago maculatus

FAMILY: Citharinidae
SUBFAMILY: Distichodontinae

THE THREE MEMBERS OF THIS GENUS (OR FOUR members according to some literature) look quite different from the other citharinids featured above. The body is long and slim, and the mouth is armed with a fearsome set of cutting teeth. The snout itself is elongated into a "beak" whose top half actually lifts when the mouth is opened. Since *Phago* species are known for eating small fishes and biting the fins of larger specimens, they are often referred to as the "fin-eaters."

DISTRIBUTION: *Niger basin in West Africa*

SIZE: *Around 5½in (14cm)*

BEHAVIOR: *Unsociable and highly predatory; despite this,* Phago *can be very timid in aquaria*

DIET: *May eat larger invertebrate livefoods, but exhibits a clear preference for live fish. This species should therefore be kept only after serious consideration of its dietary requirements*

AQUARIUM: *Roomy, with ample swimming space, and suitable shelters of bogwood or caves. Water chemistry not critical. Temperature range: 73–82°F (23–28°C)*

BREEDING: *No accounts of successful aquarium breeding currently available*

SPOTTED PIKE CHARACIN

Boulengerella maculata

FAMILY: Ctenoluciidae

BUILT IN A WAY THAT CLEARLY INDICATES ITS predatory habits, the Spotted Pike Characin is the most frequently encountered member of its genus. It is demanding in its requirements and is a fish for the specialist.

DISTRIBUTION: *Amazon basin*

HUJETA (CTENOLUCIUS HUJETA)

SIZE: *Up to 13¾in (35cm)*

BEHAVIOR: *May be extremely nervous in exposed aquaria and may injure itself as it dashes about in panic. Group specimens less likely to exhibit this behavior than solitary ones*

DIET: *Juveniles may accept commercial diets, but adults prefer livefoods, particularly small fish—a factor that needs to be taken into consideration before acquiring this species*

AQUARIUM: *Spacious, with large open areas on surface, plus some plant and/or bogwood shelters. Slightly acid to slightly alkaline, soft to medium-hard, well-oxygenated water recommended. Temperature range: 73–81°F (23–27°C)*

BREEDING: *No documented accounts currently available*

HUJETA

PIKE CHARACIN or GAR

Ctenolucius hujeta

Family: Ctenoluciidae

LIKE ITS RELATIVES IN THE GENUS *BOULENGERELLA* (*see* above), the Hujeta is a slim-line fish with a pointed snout in which the lower jaw is slightly shorter than the upper one. It, too, is a fish for the specialist aquarist. Three subspecies are generally recognized: *C. h. beani* (Panama and Colombia); *P. h. insculpus* (Colombia); and *C. h. hujeta* (Venezuela).

DISTRIBUTION: *Central and northwest South America*

SIZE: *Up to 28in (70cm) reported, but usually less than half this size*

BEHAVIOR: *As for* Boulengerella maculata

DIET: *As for* B. maculata

AQUARIUM: *As for* B. maculata, *but surface cover in the form of floating plants may be provided. Temperature range: 72–77°F (22–25°C)*

BREEDING: *Challenging in aquaria, but has been achieved. Chances of success may be improved by using two males to a single female. Eggs may hatch in just under one day*

DIAMOND SPOT CURIMATA

Curimata spilura

FAMILY: Curimatidae
SUBFAMILY: Curimatinae

THE DIAMOND SPOT CURIMATA BELONGS TO A group of some 80 to 90 species, sometimes referred to as the "small curimatas." (The "large curimatas" are distinguished, partly, by their large number (48–110) of lateral line scales.) The small curimatas are subdivided into several groups, sometimes making positive identification difficult. Diamond Spot Curimata belongs to a species complex that carries a more or less conspicuous black spot in the caudal part of the body.

DISTRIBUTION: *Widely distributed in South America*

SIZE: *Around 3½in (9cm)*

BEHAVIOR: *Peaceful shoaler, with distinct appetite for succulent plants and algae*

DIET: *Wide range of foods accepted; vegetable component essential*

AQUARIUM: *Roomy, with good illumination, fine-grained substratum and tough or unpalatable plants (or artificial equivalents), recommended. Water chemistry not critical, but good filtration advisable. Temperature range: 70–81°F (21–27°C)*

BREEDING: *No documented accounts of aquarium breeding currently available*

SILVER PROCHILODUS

Semaprochilodus taeniurus

SYNONYM: *Prochilodus taeniurus*
FAMILY: Curimatidae
SUBFAMILY: Prochilodontinae

WHEN IN PEAK CONDITION, THE SILVER Prochilodus (one of only a few prochilodontids seen with any regularity) is an extremely attractive fish in which the black-and-white markings of the dorsal and caudal fins contrast beautifully with the silvery body and the bright-red pelvic fins. Its main drawbacks as an aquarium fish are its plant-eating and burrowing habits, plus its relatively large size.

DISTRIBUTION: *Brazil and western Colombia*

SIZE: *Up to 12in (30cm)*

BEHAVIOR: *Peaceful, despite its size*

DIET: *As for Curimata spilura*

AQUARIUM: *As for C. spilura. Temperature range: 72–79°F (22–26°C)*

BREEDING: *As for C. spilura*

GOLDEN TRAHIRA

BLACKBAND PREDATOR CHARACIN

Hoplerythrinus unitaeniatus

SYNONYMS: *Erythrinus unitaeniatus, E. gronovii, E. kessleri, E. salvus, E. vittatus*
FAMILY: Erythrinidae

THE LARGE NUMBER OF NAMES BY WHICH THIS species has been referred to in scientific and other literature indicates the difficulty encountered when dealing with a widely distributed and variable species. It is unusual for a characoid in that it lacks an adipose fin. Other features include a thick layer of slippery body mucus and an ability to use its swimbladder as an auxiliary respiratory organ. The Golden Trahira is, most definitely, a fish for the specialist.

DISTRIBUTION: *Guyana, Paraguay, Trinidad and Venezuela*

SIZE: *Up to 40cm (16in)*

BEHAVIOR: *Solitary predator; can be kept with larger fish*

DIET: *Livefoods, including fish—a factor that needs to be considered prior to obtaining a specimen. May be weaned onto dead/frozen foods and some chunky commercial diets*

AQUARIUM: *Large, well-covered, well-filtered, with hiding places and robust plants, recommended. Water chemistry not critical. Temperature range: 72–81°F (22–27°C)*

BREEDING: *No documented accounts of aquarium breeding currently available*

WOLF FISH
SOUTH AMERICAN TIGER FISH

Hoplias malabaricus

FAMILY: Erythrinidae

THE WOLF FISH IS ONE OF THE BEST KNOWN OF all predatory characoids (other than the piranhas), although it is not seen with any great frequency. Like *Hoplerythrinus unitaeniatus* (*see* above), this species is widely distributed. One other species, *H. microlepis*, is very occasionally available: it is somewhat smaller and comes from southern Ecuador, Panama and Costa Rica.

DISTRIBUTION: *Widespread in Central America and northern South America*

SIZE: *Up to 20in (50cm)*

BEHAVIOR: *As for* Hoplerythrinus unitaeniatus

DIET: *As for* Hoplerythrinus unitaeniatus

AQUARIUM: *As for* Hoplerythrinus unitaeniatus

SILVER PROCHILODUS (SEMAPROCHILODUS TAENIURUS)

GOLDEN TRAHIRA (HOPLERYTHRINUS UNITAENIATUS)

WOLF FISH (HOPLIAS MALABARICUS)

BREEDING: *Has been achieved in aquaria, but details not currently available*

BLACK-WINGED HATCHETFISH

Carnegiella marthae

FAMILY: Gasteropelecidae

THIS IS ONE OF THREE *CARNEGIELLA* SPECIES, ALL of which are smaller than their closest relatives, *Gasteropelecus* (*see* below), from which they can also be distinguished by their lack of an adipose fin. The characteristic breast "keel" of hatchetfishes accommodates strong muscles that, allied to the wing-like pectoral fins, allow these fish to jump out of the water and glide (not fly!) for distances up to 50ft (15m), thus helping them escape from predators. All species are highly desirable aquarium fish. A former subspecies of Black-winged Hatchetfish, Scherer's Silver Hatchetfish (*C. m. schereri*) from Peru, is now generally regarded as a full species in its own right, *C. schereri*.

DISTRIBUTION: *Rio Negro area, Orinoco and Venezuela*

SIZE: *Up to 1½in (3.5cm)*

BEHAVIOR: *Peaceful shoaler; should not be kept with boisterous tankmates*

DIET: *Wide range of floating foods accepted; sinking foods usually ignored once they float down below top few centimeters of the water column*

AQUARIUM: *Well-covered and well-filtered, with some clear spaces on the surface, recommended. Plant thickets and some floating plants should be provided as shelter. Softish, slightly acid water*

preferred, *as is a water current (produced via the outlet of a power filter or power head). Temperature range: 73–81°F (23–27°C)*

BREEDING: *Challenging in aquaria. Spawning among the hanging roots of floating plants has been observed. The adhesive eggs stick to the feathery roots and hatch in one to one-and-a-half days*

MYER'S HATCHETFISH

PYGMY HATCHETFISH

Carnegiella myersi

FAMILY: Gasteropelecidae

THIS TINY HATCHETFISH IS NOT SEEN AS FREquently as its larger relatives although it is every bit as attractive. It should not be kept with larger, boisterous species.

DISTRIBUTION: *Peruvian Amazon, Ucayali river and Bolivia*

SIZE: *Around 1in (2.5cm)*

BEHAVIOR: *Very peaceful shoaler*

DIET: *As for C. marthae*

AQUARIUM: *As for C. marthae*

BREEDING: *No documented accounts currently available*

MARBLED HATCHETFISH

Carnegiella strigata

SYNONYM: *Carnegiella vesca*
FAMILY: Gasteropelecidae

TWO SUBSPECIES OF MARBLED HATCHETFISH (*SEE* photo p.38) are generally recognized: *C.*

strigata strigata, and *C. s. fasciata* (Dark Marbled Hatchetfish), which is found in the more southern regions of the range (although there is some overlap where "intermediate" specimens are known to occur). In *C. s. strigata,* the dark band that originates from the middle of the edge of the breast keel, and extends upward and backward through the body, is divided into two "sub-bands" almost from its point of origin. In *C. s. fasciata,* this dark band does not divide until it reaches the level of the pectoral fins. However, since this feature is variable, unequivocal identification can be difficult. A lutino morph of *C. s. strigata,* which lacks most of the body markings but (unlike albinos) possesses normal-colored eyes, is also occasionally available.

DISTRIBUTION: *Guianas and Amazon basin*

SIZE: *Around 1½in (4cm)*

BEHAVIOR: *As for C. marthae*

DIET: *As for C. marthae*

AQUARIUM: *As for C. marthae. Temperature range: 75–82°F (24–28°C)*

BREEDING: *Soft, acid, heavily tannin-stained water (see Aquarium Set-up) recommended, along with subdued lighting. Eggs are deposited among the feathery roots of floating plants, though not all will remain attached. Hatching takes just over one day*

SILVER HATCHETFISH

Gasteropelecus levis

FAMILY: Gasteropelecidae

THIS SPECIES IS VERY SIMILAR TO *G. STERNICLA* (Common Hatchetfish, *see* p.219), although its colors are somewhat more intense, particularly with regard to the black line that runs from behind the head to the base of the caudal fin.

DISTRIBUTION: *Lower Amazon*

SIZE: *Around 2½in (6cm)*

BEHAVIOR: *Peaceful, though active, shoaler*

DIET: *As for Carnegiella marthae*

AQUARIUM: *As for C. marthae. Temperature range: 75–86°F (24–30°C)*

BREEDING: *No documented reports currently available*

SPOTTED HATCHETFISH

Gasteropelecus maculatus

SYNONYM: *Thoracocharax maculatus*
FAMILY: Gasteropelecidae

THE SPECKLING ON THE BODY OF THIS SPECIES makes it immediately distinguishable from its closest relatives. It is also the largest member of the genus.

DISTRIBUTION:	*Colombia, Panama, Suriname and Venezuela*
SIZE:	*Up to 3½in (9cm) reported*
BEHAVIOR:	*As for* Carnegiella marthae
DIET:	*As for* C. marthae
AQUARIUM:	*Basically, as for* C. marthae. *Temperature range: 72–82°F (22–28°C)*
BREEDING:	*No documented reports available, but reproductive strategy assumed to be similar to that of* C. strigata

COMMON HATCHETFISH

BLACK-LINED, or BLACK-STROKE, HATCHETFISH

Gasteropelecus sternicla

FAMILY: Gasteropelecidae

WHILE SIMILAR TO *G. LEVIS* (SILVER HATCHETfish, *see* p.218), the coloration in the Common Hatchetfish is somewhat less pronounced, a feature that also makes it appear similar to the other Silver Hatchetfish (*Thoracocharax securis, see* below).

DISTRIBUTION:	*Peruvian Amazon, Guianas, Suriname, Trinidad and Mato Grosso (Brazil)*
SIZE:	*Around 2½in (6.5cm)*
BEHAVIOR:	*As for* Carnegiella marthae
DIET:	*As for* C. marthae
AQUARIUM:	*Basically, as for* C. marthae. *Temperature range: 73–82°F (23–28°C)*
BREEDING:	*No documented accounts currently available*

SILVER HATCHETFISH

PECTOROSUS HATCHETFISH

Thoracocharax securis

SYNONYMS: *Gasteropelecus securis, Thoracocharax stellatus, T. pectorosus*
FAMILY: Gasteropelecidae

DEPENDING ON THE LITERATURE CONSULTED, there is either just one species in this genus (*T. securis*) or two, if *T. stellatus* is accepted as a valid species. Both appear almost identical, although *T. stellatus* has a black spot on the base of the dorsal fin and two or three rows of almost-microscopic scales along the base of the anal fin. *T. securis* lacks the spot and has five to six rows of tiny scales. *Thoracocharax* can be distinguished from *Gasteropelecus* by the more pronounced chest profile, whose anterior edge is almost vertical in *Thoracocharax* and more gently sloping in *Gasteropelecus*.

DISTRIBUTION:	*If* T. stellatus *is regarded as synonymous with* T. securis: *widespread in central South America; if not,* T. securis: *middle/upper parts of the Amazon basin*

COMMON HATCHETFISH (GASTEROPELECUS STERNICLA)

SIZE:	*Around 3½in (9cm)*
BEHAVIOR:	*As for* Carnegiella marthae
DIET:	*As for* C. marthae
AQUARIUM:	*Basically, as for* C. marthae. *Temperature range: 73–86°F (23–30°C)*
BREEDING:	*No documented accounts currently available*

SLENDER HEMIODUS

Hemiodopsis gracilis

SYNONYM: *Hemiodus gracilis*
FAMILY: Hemiodontidae (referred to as Hemiodidae by some authors)
SUBFAMILY: Hemiodontinae

THE SYNONYM (*HEMIODUS*), CURRENT GENERIC name (*Hemiodopsis*) and the common name, all reflect the uncertainty that still exists regarding the classification of these characoids. The main feature quoted as distinguishing *Hemiodus* are the scales on the back of adult and semi-adult specimens, which are quite distinctly smaller than those above the pelvic fins.

DISTRIBUTION:	*Amazon and Guyana*
SIZE:	*Around 6in (15cm)*
BEHAVIOR:	*Shoaler, with distinct appetite for succulent plants*
DIET:	*Most foods accepted; vegetable component recommended*
AQUARIUM:	*Spacious, with ample swimming space and robust, unpalatable, or artificial plants. Well-oxygenated water important; water chemistry not critical, but soft, acid conditions preferred. Temperature range: 73–81°F (23–27°C)*
BREEDING:	*No documented accounts currently available*

SLENDER HEMIODUS (HEMIODOPSIS GRACILIS)

HALF-LINED HEMIODUS
BLACK-AND-WHITE TAILED HEMIODUS or SILVER HEMIODUS
Hemiodopsis semitaeniatus

SYNONYMS: *Hemiodus semitaeniatus;* (possibly) *Hemiodopsis argenteus*
FAMILY: Hemiodontidae (referred to as Hemiodidae by some authors)
SUBFAMILY: Hemiodontinae

THE HALF-LINED HEMIODUS IS QUITE SIMILAR TO the previous species, but lacks some of the intensity of *H. gracilis*, particularly the red streak in the lower lobe of the caudal fin. It is also a little larger and possesses more lateral line scales (around 64, as opposed to around 42).

DISTRIBUTION: *Guaporé river*

SIZE: *Up to 8in (20cm) reported, but usually smaller*

BEHAVIOR: *As for* H. gracilis

DIET: *As for* H. gracilis

AQUARIUM: *As for* H. gracilis

BREEDING: *As for* H. gracilis

ONE-SPOT HEMIODUS
YELLOW-TAILED HEMIODUS
Hemiodus unimaculatus

Synonyms: *Anisitsia notata, Hemiodus microcephalus*
FAMILY: Hemiodontidae (referred to as Hemiodidae by some authors)
SUBFAMILY: Hemiodontinae

THE ONE-SPOT HEMIODUS IS SIMILAR IN OVERALL features to *Hemiodopsis microlepis* (Red-tailed, or Feather, Hemiodus), possessing a distinct black body spot and a black- or cream-streaked caudal fin. At full size, it is also slightly larger. In the southern parts of the range, around the Río Paraguay, there is yet another similar-looking species, *Hemiodus orthonops* (which has a greater number of lateral line scales). *Hemiodus rudolphoi* (Rudolph's Hemiodus), the only other species in the genus, is occasionally seen.

DISTRIBUTION: *Rio Negro (Brazil), the Guianas and the Orinoco system*

SIZE: *Up to 7½in (19cm)*

BEHAVIOR: *As for* Hemiodopsis gracilis

DIET: *As for* Hemiodopsis gracilis

AQUARIUM: *As for* Hemiodopsis gracilis

BREEDING: *As for* Hemiodopsis gracilis

ONE-SPOT HEMIODUS (HEMIODUS UNIMACULATUS)

OTHER *HEMIODOPSIS* SPECIES

While the two featured species are the most frequently seen species of *Hemiodopsis*, several others are also occasionally available. All have the same basic characteristics and requirements. The following are the ones most likely to be encountered.

SCIENTIFIC NAME	COMMON NAME(S)	SIZE
H. argenteus*	One-spotted Hemiodus/Hemiodopsis	6in (15cm)
H. goeldii	Goeld's Hemiodus/Hemiodopsis	4¾in (12cm)
H. immaculatus	Silver Hemiodus/Hemiodopsis	8¾in (22cm)
H. microlepis	Red-tailed or Feather Hemiodus/Hemiodopsis	6in (15cm)
H. quadrimaculatus quadrimaculatus	Four-banded Hemiodus/Hemiodopsis	4in (10cm)
H. quadrimaculatus vorderwinkleri	Vorderwinkler's Hemiodus/Hemiodopsis, Torpedo Fish, or Barred Hemiodopsis	4in (10cm)
H. sterni	Stern's Hemiodus/Hemiodopsis	4in (10cm)

NOTE
* This species may be synonymous with *H. semitaeniatus*

▼ FEATHER HEMIODUS/HEMIODOPSIS (HEMIODOPSIS MICROLEPIS)

AFRICAN PIKE CHARACIN (HEPSETUS ODOE)

AFRICAN PIKE CHARACIN

Hepsetus odoe

SYNONYM: *Sarcodaces odoe*
FAMILY: Hepsetidae

THIS SPECIES IS THE ONLY MEMBER OF ITS GENUS and family. It is built like a pike (*Esox* spp.), as indicated by its common name, and hunts using similar techniques of stealth followed by a lightning-fast strike. This is, most definitely, a species for the specialist.

DISTRIBUTION: *Widely distributed in tropical regions of Africa, except the Nile basin*

SIZE: *Up to 26–28in (65–70cm) reported in the wild, but usually around half this size*

BEHAVIOR: *Solitary predator; can only be kept with tankmates that are far too large to swallow. Can be timid and nervous in bare aquaria*

DIET: *Young specimens can be accustomed to chunky meat- and fish-based foods; adults are considerably more difficult, preferring live fish—a factor that needs to be considered before obtaining a specimen*

AQUARIUM: *Large, well-covered, well-filtered aquarium essential. Use bogwood and rounded rocks to construct shelters—avoid sharp objects as fish may injure themselves during "panic attacks." Water chemistry not critical, but extremes must be avoided. Temperature range: 79–82°F (26–28°C)*

BREEDING: *No documented accounts of aquarium breeding available. In nature, this species is known to build a bubble nest on the surface of the water, into which eggs are deposited; eggs guarded by one or both spawners*

RED-SPOTTED COPEINA

RED-SPOTTED CHARACIN

Copeina guttata

FAMILY: Libiasinidae
SUBFAMILY: Pyrrhulininae

PRIMARILY DISTINGUISHED FROM THE CLOSELY related members of the genus *Copella* (*see below*) by its jawbone characteristics, Red-spotted Copeina is popular for its striking coloration. Specimens in peak condition have a shiny light-blue body overlaid with numerous red spots. The pelvic, anal and lower lobe of the caudal fin all have red borders as well.

DISTRIBUTION: *Amazon basin*

SIZE: *Up to 6in (15cm) reported, but usually only about half this size*

BEHAVIOR: *Peaceful, except during breeding, when males may become aggressive*

DIET: *Wide range of foods accepted*

AQUARIUM: *Large aquarium usually recommended, with fine-grained substratum. Plants not eaten but may be uprooted during nestbuilding. Tannin-stained water (see Aquarium Set-up). Water chemistry not critical, but softish, acid to neutral conditions preferred. Temperature range: 73–82°F (23–28°C)*

BREEDING: *Male hollows out a shallow depression in the substratum, and the pair spawn in it. The eggs are guarded by male until they hatch one-and-a-half to two days later. Recommended breeding temperature: 82–86°F (28–30°C)*

SPLASHING TETRA/CHARACIN

JUMPING, or SPRAYING, TETRA/CHARACIN

Copella arnoldi

SYNONYM: *Copeina arnoldi*
FAMILY: Lebiasinidae
SUBFAMILY: Pyrrhulininae

SPLASHING TETRA OWES ITS COMMON NAMES TO its breeding habits, which are quite unusual. All other members of the genus breed in more "traditional" ways (*see C. metae*).

DISTRIBUTION: *Lower Amazon basin*

SIZE: *Males up to 3¼in (8cm); females somewhat smaller*

RED-SPOTTED COPEINA (COPEINA GUTTATA)

FEMALE SPLASHING TETRA/CHARACIN (COPELLA ARNOLDI)

META TETRA (COPELLA METAE)

Behavior: Peaceful; may be kept in pairs or in a shoal

DIET: Wide range of foods accepted, particularly floating types

AQUARIUM: Well-covered aquarium essential. Surface vegetation and open swimming spaces required. Soft, slightly acid water, preferably tannin-stained (see Aquarium Set-up) recommended. Temperature range: 77–84°F (25–29°C)

BREEDING: Well-covered aquarium, with lowered water level to allow some broadleaved plants to project a few centimeters above surface. The spawning pair will jump out of the water and deposit their eggs on these leaves, or on the aquarium cover itself. The eggs are then kept moist by spraying or splashing by male until they hatch two or three days later

META TETRA
BROWN-BANDED COPELLA
Copella metae

SYNONYM: *Copeina metae*
FAMILY: Lebiasinidae
SUBFAMILY: Pyrrhulininae

DESPITE ONE OF THE COMMON NAMES, NOT ALL Meta Tetras exhibit the bold body band at all times. Well-banded specimens are particularly attractive when kept in a shoal under appropriate conditions (see below).

DISTRIBUTION: Meta river (Colombia) and Peruvian Amazon

SIZE: Up to 2¼in (6cm)

BEHAVIOR: Peaceful, active but timid; should be kept in shoals with other species of similar temperament

DIET: Wide range of foods accepted

AQUARIUM: Well-covered, with surface vegetation and subdued lighting. Submerged plants should include some broadleaved species, e.g. Echinodorus spp. Water chemistry can range from acid to slightly alkaline and from soft to medium-hard (adjustments must be carried out gradually). Temperature range: 73–81°F (23–27°C)

BREEDING: Soft water, preferably tannin-stained (see Aquarium Set-up). Eggs are laid on

OTHER *COPELLA* SPECIES

In addition to the two featured species, several others are available with varying degrees of regularity. In general, aquarium conditions should be similar to those provided for C. metae. The following are the species most likely to be encountered.

SCIENTIFIC NAME	COMMON NAME(S)	SIZE
C. callolepis	False Splashing Tetra	2in (5cm)
C. compta	Red-bellied Copella	2⅓in (6cm)
C. eigenmanni	Eigenman's Splashing Tetra	2⅓in (6cm)
C. nattereri	Beautiful Scaled or Plain Characin	2in (5cm)
C. nigrofasciata	Black-banded Copella	2⅓in (6cm)
C. vilmae	Rainbow Copella	c.2⅓in (6.5cm)

EIGENMAN'S SPLASHING TETRA (COPELLA EIGENMANNI)

submerged broadleaved plant and guarded by male. Hatching takes just over one day

COLOMBIAN DWARF PREDATORY TETRA
ELEGANT PENCILFISH
Lebiasina astrigata

SYNONYM: *Piabucina astrigata*
FAMILY: Lebiasinidae
SUBFAMILY: Lebiasininae

LEBIASINA SPECIES ARE DISTINGUISHED FROM THEIR close relatives, the Copella (see above), by their four (rather than three) branchiostegal rays (see Glossary) and a relatively long upper jawbone. Lebiasina are also considerably more resilient in terms of environmental tolerance and have a very different temperament. A few other species may be occasionally available, most notably, L. multipunctata (Multi-spotted Lebiasina), which is from northwest Colombia.

DISTRIBUTION: Colombia and northern South America

SIZE: Up to 3¼in (8cm)

BEHAVIOR: Predatory; must not be kept with small tankmates

DIET: Primarily livefoods and deep-frozen diets, although dried formulations may also be accepted after the fish have been acclimatized to aquarium conditions

AQUARIUM: *Thickly planted. Water chemistry not critical. Temperature range: 72–79°F (22–26°C)*

BREEDING: *No documented accounts currently available*

GOLDEN PENCILFISH

Nannostomus beckfordi

SYNONYMS: *Nannostomus anomalus, N. aripirangensis, N. simplex*
FAMILY: Lebiasinidae
SUBFAMILY: Pyrrhulininae

THREE GENERIC NAMES ARE OFTEN ENCOUNTERED in relation to the pencilfishes that form the "group" to which Golden Pencilfish belongs: *Poecilobrycon, Nannobrycon* and *Nannostomus*. Features, including the presence or absence of an adipose fin (Golden Pencilfish lacks this fin), presence or absence of a canal in one of the bones surrounding the eye (not directly observable in live specimens), relative length of the snout and angle of orientation when at rest or swimming (horizontal or angled upward, i.e. head-up) have all been cited as distinguishing characteristics. However, variability of some of these, e.g. presence/absence of an adipose fin, has led to considerable debate, with *Poecilobrycon* tending to be dropped and *Nannobrycon* being retained only by some ichthyologists for two species that exhibit the head-up

characteristic, along with an enlarged lower caudal fin lobe. Most authorities, however, tend to regard all the species concerned as members of a single genus, *Nannostomus*. Their peaceful nature and shoaling behavior make them attractive as aquarium fish, but pencilfishes are also desirable because of their two, very different color patterns: one reserved for the daylight hours and one for the night.

DISTRIBUTION: *Central Amazon, lower Rio Negro and Guyana*

SIZE: *Up to 2½in (6.5cm) reported, but usually smaller*

BEHAVIOR: *Peaceful shoaler; unusually for a pencilfish, it can be kept with lively tankmates as long as these are not predatory*

DIET: *Most small foods accepted, particularly livefoods*

AQUARIUM: *Well-planted (but not excessively so), with reasonable amount of cover recommended. Tolerant of a range of water and lighting conditions, but soft, acid water—preferably tannin-stained (see Aquarium Set-up)—and subdued illumination preferred. Temperature range: 75–82°F (24–28°C)*

BREEDING: *Subdued lighting, soft, acid water and fine-leaved vegetation required. Water temperature: around 86°F (30°C). Eggs are scattered among the vegetation and may be eaten by the spawners. Hatching takes one to three days*

TWO-LINED PENCILFISH

Nannostomus bifasciatus

FAMILY: Lebiasinidae
SUBFAMILY: Pyrrhulininae

ALTHOUGH THIS SPECIES LACKS THE RED BODY coloration of prime *N. beckfordi* specimens, it is nevertheless beautifully patterned with a broad, body-long, black band along the midline and a considerably narrower one above. This species lacks an adipose fin.

DISTRIBUTION: *Suriname and Guyana*

SIZE: *Up to 2in (5cm)*

BEHAVIOR: *Peaceful shoaler, somewhat more timid than N. beckfordi; should not be kept with lively tankmates*

DIET: *As for N. beckfordi*

AQUARIUM: *Thickly planted and with subdued lighting. Soft, slightly acid, nitrate-free water preferred (any changes in conditions must be carried out gradually), as is tannin-stained water (see Aquarium Set-up). Temperature range: 73–81°F (23–27°C)*

BREEDING: *As for N. beckfordi*

TWIN-STRIPED PENCILFISH

Nannostomus digrammus

FAMILY: Lebiasinidae
SUBFAMILY: Pyrrhulininae

THE TWO BODY STRIPES IN THIS SPECIES ARE somewhat less distinctly marked than in *N. bifasciatus*. In addition, the two stripes are more similar in size than they are in *N. bifasciatus* (although the upper stripe is still thinner than the lower one). This species lacks an adipose fin.

DISTRIBUTION: *Lower and middle Amazon, and Guyana*

SIZE: *Around 1½in (4cm)*

BEHAVIOR: *As for N. bifasciatus*

DIET: *As for N. bifasciatus*

AQUARIUM: *As for N. bifasciatus*

BREEDING: *As for N. bifasciatus*

THREE-STRIPED PENCILFISH

HOCKEY STICK PENCILFISH

Nannostomus eques

SYNONYM: *Nannobrycon eques*
FAMILY: Lebiasinidae
SUBFAMILY: Pyrrhulininae

THIS DISTINCTIVELY MARKED SPECIES IS ONE OF THE pencilfishes that exhibits the "head-up" posture and enlarged lower caudal-fin lobe

GOLDEN PENCILFISH (NANNOSTOMUS BECKFORDI)

that some authorities identify as *Nannobrycon* characteristics. This species lacks an adipose fin.

DISTRIBUTION: *Rio Negro, western Colombia and Guyana*

SIZE: *Around 2in (5cm)*

BEHAVIOR: *As for* N. bifasciatus

DIET: *As for* N. bifasciatus

AQUARIUM: *As for* N. bifasciatus

Breeding: *As for* N. bifasciatus

ESPE'S PENCILFISH
BARRED PENCILFISH
Nannostomus espei

SYNONYM: *Poecilobrycon espei*
FAMILY: Lebiasinidae
SUBFAMILY: Pyrrhulininae

THIS IS AN ATTRACTIVELY MARKED (THOUGH small) pencilfish in which the body is adorned with a row of black blotches running from head to tail. This species possesses an adipose fin.

DISTRIBUTION: *Southwestern Guyana*

SIZE: *1½in (3.5cm)*

BEHAVIOR: *As for* N. bifasciatus

DIET: *As for* N. bifasciatus

AQUARIUM: *As for* N. bifasciatus

BREEDING: *As for* N. bifasciatus

HARRISON'S PENCILFISH
Nannostomus harrisoni

SYNONYM: *Poecilobrycon harrisoni*
FAMILY: Lebiasinidae
SUBFAMILY: Pyrrhulininae

THIS PENCILFISH POSSESSES RED MARKINGS ON THE pelvic, anal and caudal fins. These, added to the snout-to-tail body band, make for an impressive show when the species is kept in a large shoal. This species possesses an adipose fin.

DISTRIBUTION: *Guyana*

SIZE: *Around 2⅜in (6cm)*

BEHAVIOR: *As for* N. bifasciatus

DIET: *As for* N. bifasciatus

AQUARIUM: *As for* N. bifasciatus

BREEDING: *As for* N. bifasciatus

DWARF PENCILFISH
Nannostomus marginatus

FAMILY: Lebiasinidae
SUBFAMILY: Pyrrhulininae

THIS IS A DELIGHTFUL SPECIES THAT, DESPITE ITS small size, creates a sparkling display. It has vivid red coloration on its fins (except the caudal fin), three prominent, dark-brown bands on its body, and a splash of several red scales along the midpoint of the central band. This species lacks an adipose fin.

DISTRIBUTION: *Guyana, Suriname and (possibly) lower reaches of the Amazon*

SIZE: *Around 1½in (3.5cm)*

BEHAVIOR: *As for* N. bifasciatus

DIET: *As for* N. bifasciatus

AQUARIUM: *As for* N. bifasciatus

BREEDING: *As for* N. bifasciatus

THREE-LINED PENCILFISH
Nannostomus trifasciatus

SYNONYMS: *Poecilobrycon trifasciatus, Nannostomus trilineatus*
FAMILY: Lebiasinidae
SUBFAMILY: Pyrrhulininae

THIS THREE-BANDED PENCILFISH CAN BE EASILY distinguished from *N. marginatus* by the two red patches at the base of its caudal fin. It is also a somewhat slimmer and longer species, and it possesses an adipose fin.

DISTRIBUTION: *Wide distribution in the Amazon basin*

SIZE: *Around 2¼in (5.5cm)*

BEHAVIOR: *As for* N. bifasciatus

DIET: *As for* N. bifasciatus

AQUARIUM: *As for* N. bifasciatus

BREEDING: *As for* N. bifasciatus

ONE-LINED PENCILFISH
Nannostomus unifasciatus

SYNONYM: *Nannobrycon unifasciatus*
FAMILY: Lebiasinidae
SUBFAMILY: Pyrrhulininae

THIS PENCILFISH IS ONE OF THE FEW THAT EXHIBIT the "head-up" orientation referred to under *N. beckfordi* (*see* p.223), as well as the enlarged lower caudal fin lobe—hence its synonym, *Nannobrycon*. The One-lined Pencilfish possesses an adipose fin.

DISTRIBUTION: *Middle and upper Amazon basin, Rio Negro, Upper Rio Orinoco and Guyana*

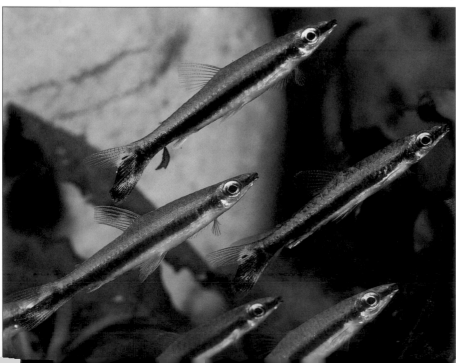

▲ DWARF PENCILFISH (NANNOSTOMUS MARGINATUS)   ▼ ONE-LINED PENCILFISH (NANNOSTOMUS UNIFASCIATUS)

SIZE:	Around 2¼in (6cm)
BEHAVIOR:	As for N. bifasciatus
DIET:	As for N. bifasciatus
AQUARIUM:	As for N. bifasciatus
BREEDING:	As for N. bifasciatus

SHORT-LINED PYRRHULINA
SCALEBLOTCH PYRRHULINA
Pyrrhulina brevis

FAMILY: Lebiasinidae
SUBFAMILY: Pyrrhulininae

SHORT-LINED PYRRHULINA (*PYRRHULINA BREVIS*)

SUPERFICIALLY, MEMBERS OF THIS SPECIES ARE difficult to distinguish from *Copeina* and *Copella* species. There are, however, several cranial and dental characteristics that allow distinctions to be made on close examination of preserved specimens. In live specimens, perhaps the most easily detectable of these features is that, in *Pyrrhulina*, the nostrils are very close to each other. Within the genus *Pyrrhulina* (which—like its close relatives—lacks an adipose fin) confusion still exists regarding the exact number of species or, in some cases, even the full characteristics of single species. The Short-lined Pyrrhulina is one of these, with some of the naturally existing variants possibly constituting subspecies, varieties or full species in their own right.

DISTRIBUTION: *Amazon basin, extending into Colombia (this applies to the Short-lined Pyrrhulina in its broadest sense)*

SIZE: *Up to 3¼in (8cm) reported, but usually around 2in (5cm)*

BEHAVIOR: *May react nervously to external disturbances; prefers to be kept in groups although it does not possess strong shoaling instincts*

DIET: *Predominantly livefoods, but may accept deep-frozen, freeze-dried, and other commercial formulations*

AQUARIUM: *Spacious, well-planted, with subdued lighting and dark substratum recommended. Slightly acid, medium-hard water preferred, particularly if tannin-stained (see Aquarium Set-up). Temperature range: 75–79°F (24–26°C)*

BREEDING: *No documented accounts currently available*

OTHER *PYRRHULINA* SPECIES

Several other *Pyrrhulina* species are available from time to time. They all have the same basic requirements. The sizes quoted are maximum sizes for fully mature males; females are generally smaller.

SCIENTIFIC NAME	COMMON NAME(S)	SIZE
P. eleanori	Elenor's Pyrrhulina	3¼in (8cm)
P. filamentosa	Longfin Pyrrhulina	4¾in (12cm)
P. laeta	Halfstroke or Half-striped Pyrrhulina	3¼in (8cm)
P. spilota	Blotched, or Whiteseam, Pyrrhulina	2⅜in (6cm)
P. vittata	Striped Pyrrhulina	2⅜in (6cm)
P. zigzag	Zig-zag or Black Pyrrhulina	3½in (9cm)

ZIG-ZAG PYRRHULINA VAR. "BLACK BLOTCHES" (*PYRRHULINA ZIGZAG*)

RED-SPOTTED RACHOW'S PYRRHULINA
EYESTROKE PYRRHULINA or FANNING CHARACIN
Pyrrhulina rachoviana

FAMILY: Lebiasinidae
SUBFAMILY: Pyrrhulininae

THIS ATTRACTIVELY MARKED SPECIES HAS A DARK band running from the tip of the snout to the base of the caudal fin and a golden band just above it. The dorsal fin carries a pronounced black blotch, and the body is covered in small red spots.

DISTRIBUTION: *Paraná and Rio de la Plata basins*

SIZE: *Up to 2⅜in (6cm)*

BEHAVIOR: *As for P. brevis. Males become aggressive toward each other if kept in a single-sex group*

DIET: *As for P. brevis*

AQUARIUM: *As for P. brevis*

BREEDING: *Soft, acid water at 79–81°F (26–27°C) recommended. Adhesive eggs are laid on broadleaved plant and are subsequently fanned and guarded by male. Hatching takes about one day*

LOACHES AND SUCKERS

Within the order Cypriniformes, which includes the family Cyprinidae (carps, minnows, rasboras, etc.), there are four closely related "groups" of fish, three of which are referred to as loaches and one as suckers. Together, these four families make up the subfamily Cobitoidea. Nelson (1994—*see* Bibliography), whose classification is followed here, divides the four families as follows (listed alphabetically).

Balitoridae Classified as Homalopteridae by some authors, these fish are commonly referred to as river loaches (an indication of their preferred habitat). They possess three or more pairs of barbels around the mouth. Within the family, two subfamilies are recognized:

   a) the Balitorinae, also known as hillstream or flat loaches, includes species such as the Saddled Hillstream Loach (*Homaloptera orthogoniata*)

   b) the Nemacheilinae includes species such as the Stone Loach (*Nemacheilus barbatulus*) and its closest relatives.

Catostomidae These are the suckers, distinguished by their thick, fleshy lips, usually with plicae (folds, membranes or wrinkles) or papillae (tiny conical protuberances). Three subfamilies are recognized. Two of these, the Ictiobinae and Catostominae, are little known within the aquarium hobby, although the latter does contain some North American species, belonging to the genus *Catostomus,* that may become better known among coldwater aquarists if this sector continues to expand. The best-known species among aquarists— the Chinese Sailfin Sucker (*Myxocyprinus asiaticus*)— is a member of the remaining subfamily, the Cycleptinae.

Cobitidae This family includes most of the aquarium species generally referred to as loaches. Among the distinguishing features is an erectile spine below the eye. The Cobitidae is subdivided into two subfamilies:

   a) the Botinae are distinguished from their nearest relatives by the two pairs of rostral (snout) barbels. The best-known members of this subfamily are the loaches belonging to the genus *Botia*, e.g., the Clown Loach (*Botia macracantha* or *macracanthus*)

   b) the Cobitinae usually possess one pair of rostral barbels (or occasionally none, but never two). The best-known representatives are the various "kuhli" loaches belonging to the genus *Pangio* (formerly known as *Acanthophthalmus*) and the weather loaches of the genus *Misgurnus*.

Gyrinocheilidae This family contains just one genus, *Gyrinocheilus*. Of the four species, only one, the Sucking Loach or Chinese Algae Eater (*G. aymonieri*), is known to aquarists.

The profiles that follow appear in alphabetical order of family. Within each family, any subfamilies that are included also appear in alphabetical order, as do the genera within these subfamilies.

CLOWN LOACH (BOTIA MACRACANTHA)

SADDLED HILLSTREAM LOACH

Homaloptera orthogoniata

FAMILY: Balitoridae (classified as Homalopteridae by some authors)
SUBFAMILY: Balitorinae

ONLY TWO SPECIES OF *HOMALOPTERA* ARE SEEN with any regularity in aquatic stores: the Saddled Hillstream Loach and *H. zollingeri* (Zollinger's Hillstream Loach). Of the two, the former is more attractively patterned and easier to maintain.

DISTRIBUTION: *Indonesia and Thailand*

SIZE: *Up to 4¾in (12cm) reported*

BEHAVIOR: *A bottom dweller, peaceful toward other species, but may be a little scrappy toward conspecifics*

DIET: *Wide range of foods accepted; algal or vegetable component recommended*

AQUARIUM: *Well-filtered, well-oxygenated, with water current (as produced by a powerhead outlet). Smoothly rounded rocks and other decor, including broadleaved plants, should also be included. Softish, neutral water preferred, but some deviation accepted. Temperature range: 68–75°F (20–24°C)*

BREEDING: *No documented accounts available*

MYER'S HILLSTREAM LOACH

ORNATE PSEUDOGASTOMYZON, BUTTERFLY PLECO, HONG KONG PLECO

Pseudogastromyzon myersi

FAMILY: Balitoridae (classified as Homalopteridae by some authors)
SUBFAMILY: Balitorinae

OF THE FOUR COMMON NAMES, THE LAST TWO are the ones most commonly used for this unusual-looking species, which began achieving popularity only during the last couple of decades of the 20th century. The commonly used names are, however, misleading labels because *P. myersi* is not a pleco (plecos are suckermouth catfish of the family Loricariidae).

DISTRIBUTION: *Southeast Asia*

SIZE: *Up to 2in (5cm)*

BEHAVIOR: *Peaceful toward tankmates of other species; territorial displays common between conspecifics, but no damage ever occurs; most active during the evening and at night*

DIET: *Predominantly encrusting algae, but some commercial formulations, e.g., tablets and livefoods, accepted*

SADDLED HILLSTREAM LOACH (HOMALOPTERA ORTHOGONIATA)

AQUARIUM: *Well-lit, well-planted, well-oxygenated and filtered, with suitable surfaces in open areas for algae to grow. Soft, slightly acid water preferred. Temperature range: 64–75°F (18–24°C)*

BREEDING: *No documented accounts currently available*

STONE LOACH
COMMON LOACH

Nemacheilus barbatulus

SYNONYM: *Noemacheilus barbatulus*
FAMILY: Balitoridae (classified as Homalopteridae by some authors)
SUBFAMILY: Nemacheilinae

ALTHOUGH ENCOUNTERED ON A REASONABLY regular basis, this species can prove challenging to keep in aquaria, not because of difficult dietary demands but because modern homes are often too warm for it. Therefore, unless the aquarium can be maintained within the temperature range given below, it is best to avoid this species.

DISTRIBUTION: *Most of Europe, excluding northernmost and southernmost regions*

SIZE: *Around 6in (15cm)*

BEHAVIOR: *Generally peaceful; mostly nocturnal*

DIET: *Livefoods preferred, but some commercial preparations may be accepted*

AQUARIUM: *Well-oxygenated, well-filtered, with a water current (as produced by a powerhead outlet), and substratum consisting of gravel, pebbles and rocks. Water chemistry not critical. Temperature range: around 50°F (10°C) to 64°F (18°C)*

BREEDING: *Eggs are laid on substratum and may be guarded by male. Hatching takes about seven days*

CHINESE SAILFIN SUCKER

CHINESE HIGH FIN, BANDED SHARK, HILSA HERRING, ROUGH FISH

Myxocyprinus asiaticus

FAMILY: Catostomidae
SUBFAMILY: Cycleptinae

THIS FISH OF MANY NAMES BEGAN APPEARING IN stores with considerable frequency during the last decade of the 20th century. However, the stunning juveniles grow to great length and depth of body, making this

CHINESE SAILFIN SUCKER (MYXOCYPRINUS ASIATICUS)

BANDED LOACH

Botia helodes

FAMILY: Cobitidae
SUBFAMILY: Botinae

THIS SPECIES IS SOMETIMES AVAILABLE AS *B. hymenophysa*, but the true *B. hymenophysa* has a different range (Borneo, southern Malaysia and Sumatra). Like some other *Botia* species, Banded Loach can produce clicking sounds when excited.

DISTRIBUTION: *Southeast Asia, but not overlapping B. hymenophysa*

SIZE: *Up to 8¾in (22cm), but usually smaller*

BEHAVIOR: *Very active and potentially aggressive, particularly toward conspecifics; most active in the evening and at night; likes to burrow*

DIET: *Wide range of foods accepted*

AQUARIUM: *A fine-grained substratum and shelters should be provided, but protect plants (see Aquarium Plants). Soft, slightly acid water and subdued lighting preferred. Temperature range: 75–86°F (24–30°C)*

BREEDING: *No documented accounts currently available*

PAKISTANI LOACH

Y-LOACH

Botia lohachata

FAMILY: Cobitidae
SUBFAMILY: Botinae

BOLDLY MARKED IN BLACK AND WHITE OR BLACK and cream (though the intensity of coloration can vary), this species can prove nervous and easily frightened during the initial stages of acclimatization to a new aquarium.

DISTRIBUTION: *Northern and northeastern India, and Bangladesh*

SIZE: *Up to 4¾in (12cm) reported, but usually much smaller*

BEHAVIOR: *As for B. helodes*

DIET: *As for B. helodes*

AQUARIUM: *As for B. helodes*

BREEDING: *As for B. helodes*

▲▲ BANDED LOACH (BOTIA HELODES) ▲ PAKISTANI LOACH (BOTIA LOHACHATA)

attractive species totally unsuitable for most home aquaria.

DISTRIBUTION: *Yangtze River (China)*

SIZE: *Up to 39in (1m)*

BEHAVIOR: *A peaceful bottom dweller*

DIET: *Wide range of foods accepted, but diet must include vegetable component*

AQUARIUM: *Large, deep aquarium essential once specimens are approximating even one quarter of their eventual size. Efficient filtration, high oxygenation, and water current (as produced by a powerhead outlet), also recommended. Water chemistry not critical. Temperature range: below 59°F (15°C) to around 72°F (22°C)*

BREEDING: *No documented accounts currently available*

CLOWN LOACH

TIGER LOACH

Botia macracantha

SYNONYM: *Botia macracanthus*
FAMILY: Cobitidae
SUBFAMILY: Botinae

THIS IS THE BEST-KNOWN AND PROBABLY THE MOST attractive of the *Botia* loaches (*see* photo p.226). Owing to its relatively large size, it is considered a food fish in its native waters.

DISTRIBUTION: *Borneo, Sumatra and Indonesia*

SIZE: *Up to 12in (30cm) reported, but usually smaller*

BEHAVIOR: *An active shoaler that should be kept in groups; less aggressive than some other* Botia

species and more active during the day. May lie on its side, seemingly dead or dying, for some time; such specimens are, however, perfectly healthy and appear to be resting or asleep (some other Botia species are also known to exhibit this behavior).

ORANGE-FINNED LOACH (BOTIA MODESTA)

OTHER *BOTIA* SPECIES

In addition to the featured species, other *Botia* loaches are available on a more or less regular basis. All have the same basic requirements, and some exhibit the unusual "lying-on-the-side" behavior of *B. macracantha* (see p.228). The following are among the most frequently imported species. Sizes quoted are approximate maximums for wild-caught specimens.

SCIENTIFIC NAME	COMMON NAME(S)	SIZE
B. beauforti *	Beaufort's Loach	8in (20cm)
B. berdmorei *	None	10in (25cm)
B. dario	Bengal Loach	4in (10cm)
B. morleti (formerly horae)	Hora's Loach	4in (10cm)
B. striata	Zebra Loach	4in (10cm)

NOTE

*It is possible that *B. berdmorei* and *B. beauforti* may be one and the same species. However, until this matter is decided, they are generally regarded as separate species.

BEAUFORT'S LOACH (BOTIA BEAUFORTI) ▼

DIET: *As for* B. helodes

AQUARIUM: *As for* B. helodes

BREEDING: *Has been bred commercially, but only rarely in aquaria*

ORANGE-FINNED LOACH
BLUE LOACH
Botia modesta

FAMILY: Cobitidae
SUBFAMILY: Botinae

THIS IS AN UNUSUALLY, BUT MOST ATTRACTIVELY, colored species. It is sometimes confused with *B. lecontei* (Leconte's Loach). However, in Orange-finned Loach, all the fins are orange to yellow, while in *B. lecontei*, the dorsal fin is grayish blue.

DISTRIBUTION: *Malaysia, Thailand and Vietnam*

SIZE: *Up to 9½in (24cm) reported, but usually much smaller*

BEHAVIOR: *Can be timid; may be kept in a group*

DIET: *As for* B. helodes

AQUARIUM: *As for* B. helodes

BREEDING: *As for* B. helodes

CHAIN LOACH
DWARF LOACH
Botia sidthimunki

FAMILY: Cobitidae
SUBFAMILY: Botinae

THIS SMALL GEM IS AVAILABLE MORE WIDELY THAN it was during the latter decades of the 20th century. For optimum effect, it is best to maintain a shoal of a minimum of six specimens.

DISTRIBUTION: *Northern India and northern Thailand*

SIZE: *Up to 2¼in (5.5cm)*

BEHAVIOR: *An active species that likes to rest on broadleaved plants in full view. Unlike some other* Botia *species, it does not avoid bright lights.*

DIET: *As for* B. helodes

AQUARIUM: *As for* B. helodes

BREEDING: *As for* B. helodes

HORSE-FACED LOACH
LONG-NOSED LOACH
Acanthopsis choirorhynchus

FAMILY: Cobitidae
SUBFAMILY: Cobitinae

THIS DELICATELY MARKED SPECIES IS A POOR swimmer, which spends most of its time on the bottom or actually buried in the

HORSE-FACED LOACH
(ACANTHOPSIS CHOIRORHYNCHUS)

substratum with only its eyes poking out of the surface. It is, however, capable of producing short spurts of lightning speed.

DISTRIBUTION: *Southeast Asia*

SIZE: *Up to 9in (22½cm) reported, but usually much smaller*

BEHAVIOR: *A peaceful, burrowing, crepuscular/nocturnal bottom dweller*

DIET: *All foods accepted, particularly sinking types, including livefoods*

AQUARIUM: *Soft, fine-grained substratum. Protect plants from being uprooted (see Aquarium Plants). Use a "moonlight" fluorescent tube for night viewing. Water chemistry not critical. Temperature range: 77–82°F (25–28°C)*

BREEDING: *No documented accounts currently available*

SPINED WEATHER LOACH
SPOTTED WEATHER LOACH

Cobitis taenia

FAMILY: Cobitidae
SUBFAMILY: Cobitinae

THERE ARE SEVERAL FORMS OF THIS LOACH (regarded as subspecies by some authors). It is quite sensitive to high temperatures, and is therefore strictly a species for the coldwater aquarium.

DISTRIBUTION: *Widely distributed in Europe and western Asia, but not in northern regions*

SIZE: *4¾in (12cm)*

BEHAVIOR: *Generally peaceful; most active during the evening and at night*

DIET: *Strong preference for bottom-dwelling livefoods; may be difficult to acclimatize to dry foods*

AQUARIUM: *Basically as for* Nemacheilus barbatulus

BREEDING: *Eggs are scattered among plants and/or over substratum*

LESSER LOACH
INDIAN STONEBITER

Lepidocephalus thermalis

SYNONYM: *Lepidocephalichthys thermalis*
FAMILY: Cobitidae
SUBFAMILY: Cobitinae

THIS SPECIES IS OFTEN FOUND IN QUIET, slow-flowing waters with a sandy bottom into which it sometimes burrows. It was originally found in an area of thermal springs, hence its scientific species name.

DISTRIBUTION: *India and Sri Lanka*

SIZE: *Around 3in (8cm)*

BEHAVIOR: *A sociable species that frequently burrows; most active during the evening and at night*

DIET: *Bottom-dwelling livefoods preferred, but other diets accepted*

AQUARIUM: *Well-filtered, well-oxygenated, with fine-grained substratum and some flat rocks and plants. Water chemistry not critical. Temperature range: 72–77°F (22–25°C), but higher temperatures accepted*

BREEDING: *No documented accounts currently available*

DOJO
CHINESE, or JAPANESE, WEATHER LOACH

Misgurnus anguillicaudatus

FAMILY: Cobitidae
SUBFAMILY: Cobitinae

WEATHER LOACHES ARE RENOWNED FOR THEIR sensitivity to barometric pressure. When this drops—as happens preceding a storm— the drop in gas pressure in the

DOJO (MISGURNUS ANGUILLICAUDATUS)

MYER'S LOACH (PANGIO MYERSI)

swimbladder makes these fish very active. Thus they are said to be able to "predict" stormy weather. If the pressure drop is excessive, weather loaches (both the Dojo and its European relative, *M. fossilis*, the Pond Loach) will "burp" or "break wind." Golden forms of the Dojo and of *M. fossilis* are also available.

DISTRIBUTION: *Dojo: widely distributed in northeast Asia;* M. fossilis: *widely distributed in central and eastern Europe*

SIZE: *Up to 8in (20cm) or even larger reported, but usually smaller*

BEHAVIOR: *Peaceful bottom dweller; most active during the evening and at night, and in the period preceding stormy weather*

DIET: *Wide range of foods accepted*

AQUARIUM: *Basically, as for* Lepidocephalus thermalis. *Temperature range: around 50°F (10°C)—or even lower for* M. fossilis—*to around 68°F (20°C) or a little higher*

BREEDING: *Infrequent in aquaria; the pair wrap their bodies around each other and scatter their eggs among vegetation*

CHINESE ALGAE EATER (GYRINOCHEILUS AYMONIERI)

MYER'S LOACH
SLIMY, or KUHLI, LOACH
Pangio myersi

SYNONYM: *Acanthophthalmus myersi*
FAMILY: Cobitidae
SUBFAMILY: Cobitinae

THIS IS A VARIABLY PATTERNED SPECIES, GIVING rise to speculation that the fish currently considered *P. myersi* may consist of more than just a single species, or may contain several subspecies. Similar doubts surround some of the other species in the genus, making a detailed review highly desirable. In addition to Myer's Loach, the following are the main species currently encountered in the hobby. All have similar behavioral characteristics and aquarium requirements: *P. semicinctus* (Half-banded Kuhli Loach), from Indonesia; *P. kuhli* ("True" Kuhli Loach), from Indonesia, Java, Malaysia, Singapore, Sumatra and Thailand; *P. shelfordi* (Shelford's Loach), from Borneo, Malaysia and Sarawak; and *P. javanicus* (Javanese Loach), from Java.

DISTRIBUTION: *Myer's Loach: Thailand*

SIZE: *Up to 3in (8cm)*

BEHAVIOR: *All "kuhli" loaches like to burrow; often active during the day, but most active during the evening and at night*

DIET: *Wide range of foods accepted, but sinking livefoods and other formulations preferred*

AQUARIUM: *Well-covered (kuhlis can squeeze through the tiniest openings), with fine-grained substratum, subdued lighting, floating vegetation, and shelters. A "moonlight" fluorescent tube will facilitate night viewing. Soft, slightly acid water preferred, but some deviation accepted. Temperature range: 75–86°F (24–30°C)*

BREEDING: *Infrequent in aquaria. Green eggs may be scattered among surface vegetation, plant stems, or roots*

CHINESE ALGAE EATER
SUCKING LOACH
Gyrinocheilus aymonieri

FAMILY: Gyrinocheilidae

BOTH THE COMMON NAMES FOR THIS SPECIES ARE misnomers, since this fish is not a "true" loach—as in the barbel-bearing Balitoridae and Cobitidae—and it does not occur in China. It does, however, eat algae and is able to attach itself to the substratum with its suckerlike mouth. It also has special adaptations, such as an aperture in the top corner of the gill cover that allows it to take in water for respiratory purposes while still clinging on to a surface with its mouth. A golden form of this species is now widely available.

DISTRIBUTION: *Thailand*

SIZE: *Up to 10½in (27cm), but usually much smaller*

BEHAVIOR: *Juveniles peaceful toward each other; progressively territorial as they grow. May also graze on thick skin mucus of other fish*

DIET: *Most foods accepted; vegetable component should be included*

AQUARIUM: *Well-planted, well-oxygenated and filtered, with adequate shelter. Water chemistry not critical. Temperature range: 70–82°F (21–28°C)*

BREEDING: *No reports of aquarium breeding available, although the species—particularly the golden form—has been bred commercially*

GOURAMIS AND RELATIVES

Gouramis, along with some of their close relatives, such as the Siamese Fighter (*Betta splendens*) and the Combtail (*Belontia signata*), have been strong favorites within the hobby for the best part of 100 years. For example, the Dwarf Gourami (*Colisa lalia*) was first imported into Europe in 1903, while the Paradise Fish (*Macropodus opercularis*) has been known even longer, being the first "tropical" fish to be imported into Europe way back in 1869.

Together, these fish, along with the Pikehead (*Luciocephalus pulcher*—family Luciocephalidae) constitute the suborder Anabantoidei, commonly referred to as the Labyrinthfishes (Nelson 1994—*see* Bibliography). Closely related to the Anabantoidei is the suborder Channoidei, with its single family, the Channidae (the snakeheads).

Other fish, such as the Chameleon Fish (*Badis badis*) and its relatives, the leaf fishes (*Monocirrhus,*

▲▲ *Kissing Gourami* (Helostoma temminckii)
▲ *Dwarf Gourami* (Colisa lalia) *building nest*

Polycentrus and others) constitute the family Nandidae (suborder Percoidei). The nandids are deemed by some authorities to have some affinity with the Anabantoidei, but this is not universally accepted. Nevertheless, taking note of the possible affinity of, particularly, *Badis* with the Anabantoidei, plus the fact that *Badis* is grouped within the Nandidae (albeit provisionally) by Nelson—whose classification is followed here—the pages that follow will feature entries for all the above families.

Anabantoids possess an auxiliary respiratory organ known as the labyrinth. This allows them to take in air at the water surface and thus survive in conditions in which the oxygen concentration fluctuates from time to time (and may even fall to dangerously low levels). The labyrinth is located in a special chamber just above and behind the gills, and consists of folds of tissue served by a rich blood supply. Air is gulped in at the water surface and passed into the labyrinth chamber, where the oxygen is extracted, enabling labyrinth-bearing fish to survive in oxygen-deficient waters that would be unbearable for many other fish. Most species of anabantoids have become so dependent on the labyrinth that they will actually drown if prevented from surfacing for air.

The labyrinth is also employed by many anabantoids to construct bubble nests, either at the water surface, or under a broad submerged leaf or other appropriate surface. In these species, spawning occurs under the nest and the eggs are deposited among the bubbles by one or both parents, one of whom (the male) subsequently mounts guard until the eggs hatch and the resulting fry are free swimming. Other species dispense with nests altogether, or else incubate their eggs orally until they hatch. Both types of anabantoids (nestbuilding and mouthbrooding) will be featured in this section.

Among these will be all the well-known species referred to as "gouramis." Although many of the best-known anabantoids are known as gouramis,

FISH CARRYING THE GOURAMI NAME TAG

Common Name(s)	Genus	Subfamily	Family
Kissing Gourami	Helostoma	None	Helostomatidae
Giant Gourami	Osphronemus	None	Osphronemidae
Three-spot Gourami and relatives	Trichogaster	Trichogasterinae	Belontiidae
Dwarf Gourami and relatives	Colisa	Trichogasterinae	Belontiidae
Chocolate Gourami	Sphaerichthys	Trichogasterinae	Belontiidae
False Chocolate Gourami	Parasphaerichthys	Trichogasterinae	Belontiidae
Croaking Gourami and relatives	Trichopsis	Macropodinae	Belontiidae
Licorice (Liquorice) Gourami and relatives	Parosphromenus	Macroprodinae	Belontiidae
Ornate Pointed-tail Gourami	Malpulutta	Macropodinae	Belontiidae
Noble Gourami	Ctenops	Macropodinae	Belontiidae

the term itself cannot be precisely defined. It is simply one that over the years has been applied to some species in a genus, but not others, some genera, but not others, and some families of anabantoids, but not others. If there is a "true" gourami at all, it is the Giant Gourami (*Osphronemus goramy*). It was the misspelling—intentional or otherwise—of *goramy* that originally gave rise to "gourami," a label that is applied to a number of other anabantoids. Fish carrying the gourami name tag occur in various genera, families and subfamilies (*see* table above).

Following the format of previous sections, the individual families constituting the Anabantoidei will be featured in alphabetical order, as will the subfamilies and the individual genera. This family will be followed by the Channidae. The Nandidae will be featured last, as they are not members of the Anabantoidae, despite their aforementioned possible affinities and are therefore more distantly related to the anabantoids than are the Channidae. Therefore, the species in this section will appear in the following sequence:

SUBORDER: Anabantoidei
Family: Anabantidae
Genera: *Anabas, Ctenopoma* (including species now being referred to as *Microctenopoma*)

Family: Belontiidae
Subfamily: Belontiinae
Genus: *Belontia*
Subfamily: Macropodinae
Genera: *Betta, Ctenops, Macropodus, Malpulutta, Parosphromenus, Pseudosphromenus, Trichopsis*
Subfamily: Trichogasterinae
Genera: *Colisa, Parasphaerichthys, Sphaerichthys, Trichogaster*
Family: Helostomatidae
Genus: *Helostoma*
Family: Luciocephalidae
Genus: *Luciocephalus*
Family: Osphronemidae
Genus: *Osphronemus*

SUBORDER: Channoidei
Family: Channidae
Genus: *Channa*

SUBORDER: Percoidei
Family: Nandidae
Subfamily: Badinae
Genus: *Badis*
Subfamily: Nandinae
Genera: *Monocirrhus, Nandus, Polycentrus*

CLIMBING PERCH

WALKING PERCH

Anabas testudineus
SYNONYMS: *A. elongatus, A. macrocephalus, A. scandens,* and others
FAMILY: Anabantidae

THIS TOUGH, DURABLE SPECIES WAS FIRST imported into Europe in 1891, making it one of the oldest tropical fish in the hobby.

It has been reported as being able to "walk" on land and even to climb trees. The former behavior is known to be within the species' capabilities, e.g., during wet weather and, perhaps, in moving from one pond to another, but its climbing powers are somewhat exaggerated. A yellow (xanthistic) form has been reported, but is rarely seen, as is a second species, the High-bodied Climbing Perch (*A. oligolepis*), from India and Bangladesh.

DISTRIBUTION: *Widely distributed in tropical Asia*

SIZE: *Up to 10in (25cm) reported, but usually smaller*

BEHAVIOR: *Retiring, but can be aggressive in the confines of an aquarium*

DIET: *Livefoods preferred, but other formulations may be accepted*

AQUARIUM: *Well-covered, with adequate shelter and surface vegetation. Water chemistry not*

critical. Temperature range: around 59°F (15°C)
to 86°F (30°C)

BREEDING: *Insignificant nest is built (or none at all).
The floating eggs receive very little or no
parental care. Hatching takes about one day at
the higher end of the temperature range*

LEOPARD CTENOPOMA
SPOTTED CTENOPOMA, BUSHFISH
OR CLIMBING PERCH
Ctenopoma acutirostre
FAMILY: Anabantidae

THE LEOPARD CTENOPOMA, ALONG WITH SOME
other members of its genus, is now encountered with greater regularity than in the
past, thanks to the efforts of specialist anabantoid societies in several countries. The
species belongs to the "larger" *Ctenopoma*—
a group of species that exceed 6in (15cm)
in length. A nonspotted and a violet morph
are occasionally available. *Sandelia*, a close
relation of both *Anabas* and *Ctenopoma*, is
hardly ever seen in the hobby.

DISTRIBUTION: *Lower and central Congo basin*

SIZE: *Up to 8in (20cm) reported, but usually smaller*

BEHAVIOR: *Generally shy and retiring, but predatory;
most active during the evening and at night*

DIET: *Livefoods and a range of commercial diets
accepted*

AQUARIUM: *Well-planted, with shelters and open
swimming spaces. Subdued lighting during the
day and a "moonlight" fluorescent tube for night
viewing recommended. Water chemistry not
critical. Temperature range: 73–82°F (23–28°C)*

BREEDING: *Eggs are laid in male-built bubble nest,
though nest quality is variable and may consist of
very few bubbles, if any. Little parental care occurs*

CLIMBING PERCH (ANABAS TESTUDINEUS)

ORANGE BUSHFISH

Ctenopoma ansorgii

SYNONYM: *Microctenopoma ansorgii*
FAMILY: Anabantidae

ONE OF THE SMALLER MEMBERS OF THE GENUS, THIS
is probably the most beautiful of all the
Ctenopoma species. Some variation in body
coloring and patterning occurs in wild-
caught specimens.

DISTRIBUTION: *Congo River basin*

SIZE: *Up to 3in (8cm), but often smaller*

BEHAVIOR: *One of the more peaceful* Ctenopoma
species

DIET: *A range of livefoods and commercial
formulations accepted*

AQUARIUM: *Basically, as for* C. acutirostre

BREEDING: *Male builds bubble nest and cares for
the eggs and newly hatched fry. Hatching takes
about one day*

TAILSPOT BUSHFISH

Ctenopoma kingsleyae

SYNONYM: Possibly *Ctenopoma argentoventer*
FAMILY: Anabantidae

THIS IS A PLAINLY COLORED SPECIES WITH A
distinct black spot on the caudal peduncle
and, often, a yellowish tinge on the anal
and pectoral fins. The tail spot is usually
ringed in gold in juvenile specimens. Several morphs are known to exist in the wild.

DISTRIBUTION: *West Africa, from Gambia to
Cameroon*

SIZE: *Up to 8in (20cm), but often smaller*

BEHAVIOR: *Placid, especially with similar-sized
tankmates*

DIET: *Wide range of foods accepted*

AQUARIUM: *As for* C. acutirostre

BREEDING: *Basically, as for* C. acutirostre, *i.e., this is
one of the free-spawning (non-nestbuilding)
species. Hatching takes about one day*

DWARF BUSHFISH
DWARF CLIMBING PERCH
Ctenopoma nanum

SYNONYM: *Microctenopoma nanum*
FAMILY: Anabantidae

AS ITS NAME IMPLIES, THIS IS A SMALL SPECIES. IT
was first imported into Europe in 1933, the
same year as its much larger relative, *C.
kingsleyae* (*see* previous entry). Males are

LEOPARD CTENOPOMA (CTENOPOMA ACUTIROSTRE)

particularly impressive when in spawning coloration, which can be almost black.

DISTRIBUTION: *Southern Cameroon, Gabon and Zaire*

SIZE: *Up to 3in (8cm), or smaller*

BEHAVIOR: *Shy, retiring; should not be kept with boisterous tankmates. Males (as in other nestbuilding* Ctenopoma) *are territorial during spawning*

DIET: *Wide range of foods accepted*

AQUARIUM: *As for* C. acutirostre

BREEDING: *As for* C. ansorgii

MOTTLED CTENOPOMA
MOTTLED BUSHFISH
Ctenopoma weeksii

SYNONYMS: *C. oxyrhynchum, C. oxyrhynchus*
FAMILY: Anabantidae

THIS IS A LATERALLY COMPRESSED SPECIES WITH mottled appearance. It may show a central body spot, and banding in the caudal fin.

DISTRIBUTION: *Zaire*

SIZE: *Up to 4¾in (12cm), but often a little smaller*

BEHAVIOR: *Generally peaceful toward similar-sized tankmates, but males become aggressive and territorial during breeding season*

DIET: *Wide range of foods accepted*

AQUARIUM: *As for* C. acutirostre

BREEDING: *Basically, as for* C. acutirostre: *no nest is built. Hatching takes three to four days*

JAVA COMBTAIL
HONEYCOMB COMBTAIL
Belontia hasselti

FAMILY: Belontiidae
SUBFAMILY: Belontiinae

THE SECOND, LESS FREQUENTLY USED, COMMON name of this species beautifully describes the delicate reticulated scale and fin patterns of this handsome fish.

DISTRIBUTION: *Borneo, Malaysia, Singapore and Sumatra; also said to occur in Java*

SIZE: *Up to 8in (20cm), but often smaller*

BEHAVIOR: *Relatively peaceful except during breeding when males become territorial and aggressive*

DIET: *Primarily livefoods and deep-frozen/freeze-dried formulations; other commercial preparations also accepted; vegetable component recommended*

AQUARIUM: *Large, well-planted, well-illuminated, with good (but not over-turbulent) water filtration. Water chemistry not critical, but alkaline, hardish conditions preferred. Temperature range: 77–86°F (25–30°C)*

MOTTLED CTENOPOMA (*CTENOPOMA WEEKSII*)

OTHER *CTENOPOMA* SPECIES

Several *Ctenopoma* species, other than those featured, are also available. They include representatives of both the large/small groups and the free-spawning/bubble-nesting ones. All have the same basic requirements, with the smaller species being considerably more suitable for mixed collections than the larger ones.

SCIENTIFIC NAME	COMMON NAME(S)	SIZE	BREEDING
C. argentoventer*	Dusky Bushfish	8in (20cm)	FS
C. congicum**	Congo Bushfish	3in (8cm)	BN
C. damasi**	Pearl Bushfish	2¾in (7cm)	BN
C. fasciolatum**	Banded Bushfish	3½in (9cm)	BN
C. intermedium**	Pale Bushfish	3in (8cm)	BN
C. maculatum	One-spot Bushfish	8in (20cm)	FS
C. multispinis	Many-spined Bushfish	6in (15cm)	FS
C. muriei	Small Tailspot Bushfish	3¾in (10cm)	FS
C. nebulosum	Fog Bushfish	6in (15cm)	FS
C. nigropannosum	Dark Bushfish	6¾in (17cm)	FS
C. ocellatum	Eye-spot Bushfish	6in (15cm)	FS
C. pellegrini	Pellegrin's Bushfish	6in (15cm)	FS
C. petherici	Petheric's Bushfish	6¼in (16cm)	FS

NOTES

a) In the list above, BN = bubble nester; FS = free-spawner

b) In the common names, the term Bushfish is used just as frequently as Ctenopoma or Climbing Perch

* *C. argentoventer* may be synonymous with *C. kingsleyae* (several morphs of *C. kingsleyae* are known to exist).

**Following a revision of the *Ctenopoma* genus in 1996, these species are now increasingly referred to as *Microctenopoma*.

BANDED BUSHFISH (*CTENOPOMA FASCIOLATUM*) ▼

BREEDING: *Shallow water preferred; a bubble nest is usually, but not invariably, built. Hatching takes one to two days*

COMBTAIL

Belontia signata

FAMILY: Belontiidae
SUBFAMILY: Belontiinae

ADULT SPECIMENS EXHIBIT THE EXTENDED RAYS in the caudal fin, which gives rise to the common name of this impressive species. Two subspecies are generally recognized: *B. s. signata* (the "traditional" Combtail), and *B. s. jonklaasi* (Pectoral Spot Combtail), also from Sri Lanka. There is also a dark-bodied morph named "Kottawa Forest."

DISTRIBUTION: *Sri Lanka*

SIZE: *Up to 6in (15cm) reported, but often smaller*

BEHAVIOR: *Can be quite aggressive, particularly at breeding time*

DIET: *As for B. hasselti*

AQUARIUM: *As for B. hasselti, but less alkaline conditions and slightly lower temperatures preferred*

BREEDING: *Basically, as for B. hasselti. Hatching takes about one-and-a-half days*

SLENDER BETTA

Betta bellica

FAMILY: Belontiidae
SUBFAMILY: Macropodinae

BOTH ADULT MALES AND FEMALES OF THIS SPECIES have a yellowish-brown anterior half, with bluish-green scales appearing pro-gressively down the body. The fins also have this bluish-green sheen. Males have longer, more pointed fins than do females.

DISTRIBUTION: *Mainly Perak region of peninsular Malaysia*

SIZE: *Around 4¼in (11cm)*

BEHAVIOR: *Relatively peaceful, despite its* bellica *("warlike") species name*

DIET: *Livefoods, deep-frozen and freeze-dried diets preferred, but other foods may also be accepted*

AQUARIUM: *Densely planted (including floating vegetation), with a number of shelters. Illumination not too bright. Soft, acid water. Temperature range: 75–82°F (24–28°C)*

BREEDING: *A challenging bubble-nesting species*

WINE RED FIGHTER
CLARET BETTA

Betta coccina

FAMILY: Belontiidae
SUBFAMILY: Macropodinae

THIS EXCEPTIONALLY MARKED SPECIES HAS A reddish-brown body with longitudinal bands and a central spot (not always visible). The dorsal and caudal fins are delicately edged in bluish white.

DISTRIBUTION: *Reported from southern peninsular Malaysia and central Sumatra*

SIZE: *Up to 2¼in (5.5cm) reported, but often smaller*

BEHAVIOR: *Timid, retiring; must not be kept with boisterous tankmates*

▲ COMBTAIL (BELONTIA SIGNATA)　　　　▼ SLENDER BETTA (BETTA BELLICA)

▲ *WINE RED FIGHTER (BETTA COCCINA)*
◄ *FEMALE CRESCENT BETTA (BETTA IMBELLIS)*

DISTRIBUTION: *Western Borneo, northeast Sumatra and Malaysia*

SIZE: *Around 2in (5cm)*

BEHAVIOR: *Relatively peaceful, except at breeding time or when a new specimen is introduced into the aquarium*

DIET: *As for* B. bellica

AQUARIUM: *As for* B. bellica

BREEDING: *Easier than* B. bellica *and* B. coccina. *Male builds bubble nest under floating or submerged leaves; spawning is nonviolent, and male guards the eggs and newly hatched fry. Hatching can take up to three days*

PENANG MOUTH-BROODING BETTA

Betta pugnax

FAMILY: Belontiidae
SUBFAMILY: Macropodina

THIS WAS ONE OF THE EARLY *BETTA* SPECIES TO BE imported, arriving in 1905. It has never become widespread in the hobby, having been overshadowed by its more spectacular relative, *B. splendens* (Siamese Fighter). It is nevertheless a delicately colored species worthy of greater recognition. Several naturally occurring color morphs are known.

DISTRIBUTION: *Malaysia*

SIZE: *Up to 4¾in (12cm), but usually smaller*

BEHAVIOR: *Relatively peaceful except during breeding*

DIET: *As for B. bellica*

AQUARIUM: *Basically, as for B. bellica, but slow water flow appreciated. Tannin-stained water (see Aquarium Set-up) advisable*

BREEDING: *A mouthbrooding species in which male retains the eggs and larvae in his mouth for about ten days*

EMERALD BETTA
SMARAGD BETTA/FIGHTER

Betta smaragdina

FAMILY: Belontiidae
SUBFAMILY: Macropodinae

ALTHOUGH INTRODUCED ONLY AROUND 1970, the Emerald Betta has become one of the more popular *Betta* species in the hobby. It is a truly magnificent species when in peak condition, rivaling both *B. imbellis* and *B. splendens* in beauty.

DISTRIBUTION: *Cambodia, Laos, northeastern and eastern Thailand*

SIZE: *Up to 2¾in (7cm)*

BEHAVIOR: *Males are aggressive toward each other, but will accept several females in the same aquarium; should not be kept with boisterous tankmates*

DIET: *As for B. bellica*

AQUARIUM: *As for B. bellica*

BREEDING: *A bubble-nester that can be relatively easily bred. Nests may be built at water surface, or under submerged leaf or other surface. Male guards the eggs and newly hatched fry*

SIAMESE FIGHTER

Betta splendens

FAMILY: Belontiidae
SUBFAMILY: Macropodinae

THIS FAMOUS OLD FAVORITE WAS IMPORTED INTO Europe during the last decade of the 19th century and has been popular ever since. It was originally renowned, not just for its coloration, but for its fighting qualities. As far as the aquarium hobby is concerned, though, the species' ongoing popularity is owed to the exceptionally colorful, long-finned varieties that have been developed over the years. This is a "must keep" fish for every aquarist at some stage.

DISTRIBUTION: *Southeast Asia, but some self-sustaining populations have become established in a number of nonnative locations in, e.g., Laos, Myanmar (Burma) and Colombia*

SIZE: *Up to 2½in (6cm)*

DIET: *As for* B. bellica

AQUARIUM: *Basically, as for* B. bellica; *lighting levels should be subdued*

BREEDING: *As for* B. bellica

CRESCENT BETTA
PEACEFUL BETTA

Betta imbellis

FAMILY: Belontiidae
SUBFAMILY: Macropodinae

THE CRESCENT FROM WHICH ONE OF THE COMMON names for this species is derived is particularly well-exhibited on the caudal fin of males in peak condition. The deep red of this crescent is also evident on the anal and pelvic fins.

Siamese Fighter (Betta splendens)

BEHAVIOR: *Males will fight, sometimes to the death; otherwise, a slow-moving, tolerant, retiring species that should not be kept with boisterous tankmates; males become territorial during breeding and aggressive toward females after spawning*

DIET: *Wide range of livefoods and commercial formulations accepted*

AQUARIUM: *As for B. bellica*

BREEDING: *Male builds beautiful bubble nest at water surface, and guards the eggs and newly hatched fry for several days. Hatching takes about one day*

OTHER *BETTA* SPECIES

During the 1980s and 1990s, there was a significant increase in the number of *Betta* species discovered, described, and introduced into the specialist sector of the aquarium hobby. Most of these species, while available through anabantoid societies, are rarely encountered in stores. However, as the numbers bred in captivity continue to increase, some will become better known and more widely available. Seek detailed advice before attempting to keep and breed these species (*see also* Bibliography). The list that follows includes many of the new *Betta* species, along with all the older ones that have not been featured in the main entries. Most require the same basic care outlined for the featured species.

SCIENTIFIC NAME	COMMON NAME(S)	SIZE	BREEDING
B. akarensis	Akara Betta	4¾in (12cm)	MB
B. albimarginata	Whiteseam Betta	2in (5cm)	MB?
B. anabatoides	Unspotted Betta	5in (13cm)	MB
B. balunga	Balunga Betta	5½in (14cm)	MB
B. brownorum	Brown's Red Dwarf Betta	1½in (4cm)	BN
B. chloropharynx	Greenthroat Betta	5½in (14cm)	MB
B. climacura	Ladder Betta	5½in (14cm)	MB
B. dimidiata	Dwarf Betta	2¾in (7cm)	MB
B. edithae	Edith's Betta	3½in (8.5cm)	MB
B. foerschi	Foersh's Betta	2¾in (7cm)	MB
B. fusca	Brown Betta	4¾in (12cm)	MB
B. livida	Selangor Red Betta	2in (5cm)	BN
B. macrostoma	Peacock Betta	5½in (14cm)	MB
B. ocellata	Eye-spot Betta	4¾in (12cm)	MB
B. persephone	Black Betta	1½in (4cm)	BN
B. picta	Javan Betta	2⅓in (6cm)	MB
B. rutilans	Red Dwarf Betta	2⅓in (6cm)	BN
B. simorum	Simor Betta	4¾in (12cm)	BN
B. taeniata	Striped Betta	3in (8cm)	MB
B. tussyae	Tussy's Betta	2⅓in (6cm)	BN

Notes:

a) In this list, BN = bubble-nester; MB = mouthbrooder

b) In the common names (which may vary from author to author), the term Betta is frequently used interchangeably with Fighter or—as in the case of oral brooders—with Mouthbrooder.

ONE-SPOT BETTA

ONE-SPOT FIGHTER

Betta unimaculata

FAMILY: Belontiidae
SUBFAMILY: Macropodinae

THIS IS A SLENDER-BODIED *BETTA* WITH THE characteristically large mouth of a mouth-brooding species. The anal and caudal fins of males exhibit intensified blue-green coloration at breeding time; a spot behind the gills becomes similarly colored.

DISTRIBUTION: *Kalimantan Timur and Sabah (Borneo)*

SIZE: *Up to 4¾in (12cm), but often smaller*

BEHAVIOR: *Generally peaceful toward conspecifics; peaceful and tolerant toward other species*

DIET: *Livefoods preferred, but other diets also accepted*

AQUARIUM: *As for B. bellica*

BREEDING: *Eggs are incubated orally by male. Hatching and subsequent release of fry takes about nine to ten days in total*

INDIAN GOURAMI
NOBLE GOURAMI, CTENOPS

Ctenops nobilis

FAMILY: Belontiidae
SUBFAMILY: Macropodinae

ALTHOUGH THE INDIAN GOURAMI WAS IMPORTED into Europe during the early decades of the 20th century, it never attained wide popularity owing to its "challenging" requirements and delicate nature. This is, undoubtedly, a species that should be kept only by experienced aquarists. Kept in appropriate conditions, it is a truly beautiful fish.

DISTRIBUTION: *Eastern India and Bangladesh*

SIZE: *Up to 4¾in (12cm), but usually smaller*

BEHAVIOR: *Shy, retiring; must not be kept with boisterous tankmates*

DIET: *Livefoods preferred, but deep-frozen, freeze-dried, and some other commercial diets, may be accepted*

AQUARIUM: *Heavily planted, tranquil, with subdued lighting and numerous bogwood shelters. Softish, neutral water advisable, with a little deviation tolerated. Temperature range: 77–86°F (25–30°C)*

BREEDING: *Very challenging and infrequent in aquaria. Small numbers of eggs are incubated orally by female who releases free-swimming fry 10–15 days after spawning*

BLACK PARADISE FISH

Macropodus concolor

SYNONYM: *Macropodus opercularis concolor*
FAMILY: Belontiidae
SUBFAMILY: Macropodinae

THERE HAS LONG BEEN CONTROVERSY REGARDING the status of this fish. Some believe it to be a subspecies of the better-known *M. opercularis* (Paradise Fish), while others see it merely as a naturally occurring morph. Most modern opinion, however, tends toward regarding it as a valid species in its own right, despite the ease with which it hybridizes with *M. opercularis* to produce the Dark Paradise Fish.

DISTRIBUTION: *Cambodia and Vietnam*

SIZE: *Males around 4¾in (12cm); females somewhat smaller*

BEHAVIOR: *Considerably less aggressive than* M. opercularis, *but territorial during breeding*

DIET: *Wide range of foods accepted*

AQUARIUM: *Spacious, well-planted, with some open areas and shelters. Water chemistry not critical. Temperature range: 68–79°F (20–26°C)*

BREEDING: *Male builds bubble nests and vigorously defends nest, eggs and subsequent fry until they are free-swimming. Hatching takes about one day*

CHINESE PARADISE FISH
ROUND-TAILED PARADISE FISH

Macropodus ocellatus

SYNONYM: *Macropodus chinensis*
FAMILY: Belontiidae
SUBFAMILY: Macropodinae

THIS EXCEPTIONALLY BEAUTIFUL SPECIES IS SEEN much less frequently than its two closest relatives. Despite one of its common names, the caudal fin of fully adult males tends to have a blunted-tip profile rather than a smoothly rounded one. This species is known to hybridize with *M. opercularis*: the hybrids are sometimes referred to as Matte's Paradise Fish.

DISTRIBUTION: *Southern China and (possibly) Korea*

SIZE: *Males around 3in (8cm); females smaller*

BEHAVIOR: *As for* M. concolor

DIET: *As for* M. concolor

AQUARIUM: *As for* M. concolor

BREEDING: *As for* M. concolor. *Temperature range: around 61°F (16°C) to 79°F (26°C)*

PARADISE FISH

Macropodus opercularis

FAMILY: Belontiidae
SUBFAMILY: Macropodinae

THIS WAS THE FIRST "TROPICAL" FISH TO BE imported into Europe (arriving in 1869). It soon became popular because of its hardiness, coloration and interesting breeding habits. Today, it is still widely available and popular in a range of colors, from the wild type, through a "blue," to an albino form. This species hybridizes easily with its two closest relatives (*see M. concolor* and *M. ocellatus*).

DISTRIBUTION: *Southern China, Vietnam, Korea, Taiwan and other islands in the region*

SIZE: *Males up to 4¾in (12cm); females smaller*

BEHAVIOR: *More aggressive and territorial than its relatives; keep only one male per aquarium*

DIET: *As for* M. concolor

AQUARIUM: *As for* M. concolor. *Temperature range: below 61°F (16°C) to 82°F (28°C)*

BREEDING: *As for* M. concolor

ORNATE GOURAMI
PARADISE FISH, MALPULUTTA, SPOTTED POINTED-TAIL GOURAMI

Malpulutta kretseri

FAMILY: Belontiidae
SUBFAMILY: Macropodinae

THIS IS A DELICATE-LOOKING SPECIES, CONSIDERED to be under some threat in the wild. It has never been available in large numbers, but captive-bred stocks from specialist aquarists, as well as from a long-term commercial government-approved project, may ensure a continued limited supply. Two subspecies are generally recognized: *M. k. kretseri* and, a bluer type, *M. k. minor*. There is also a violet-tinged morph.

DISTRIBUTION: *Sri Lanka*

PARADISE FISH (MACROPODUS OPERCULARIS)

SIZE: *Up to 3½in (9cm) reported, but most specimens less than 2⅜in (6cm) long*

BEHAVIOR: *Shy, retiring*

DIET: *Small livefoods preferred, but some commercial diets also accepted*

AQUARIUM: *Quiet, well-covered, well-planted, with surface plants, a number of shelters, subdued lighting, and dark substratum. Water soft and acid, though some deviation may be accepted. Temperature range: 75–82°F (24–28°C)*

BREEDING: *Male builds bubble nest under leaf or overhang, and guards the eggs and newly hatched fry. Hatching takes about two days*

LICORICE DWARF GOURAMI

LIQUORICE, or SPLENDID, DWARF GOURAMI

Parosphromenus deisneri

FAMILY: Belontiidae
SUBFAMILY: Macropodinae

THIS IS, BY FAR, THE MOST FREQUENTLY AVAILABLE of all the licorice gourami species. It has a long history in the hobby, having first been imported in 1914, but its rather demanding requirements mean that it is often not seen at its best in aquatic stores—a factor that has undoubtedly contributed to its somewhat limited occurrence in home aquaria.

DISTRIBUTION: *Banka (Indonesia), peninsular Malaysia and Sumatra*

SIZE: *Around 1½in (4cm), although 3in (7.5cm) reported*

BEHAVIOR: *Gentle, slow-moving; must not be kept with boisterous tankmates*

DIET: *Small livefoods preferred, but some commercial diets may also be accepted*

AQUARIUM: *As for Malpulutta kretseri*

BREEDING: *Male builds bubble nest (usually in a cave), often after egg release. Hatching can take three days. Male guards the eggs and newly hatched fry*

SPIKE-TAILED PARADISE FISH

RED-EYE SPIKETAIL

Pseudosphromenus cupanus

SYNONYM: *Macropodus cupanus*
FAMILY: Belontiidae
SUBFAMILY: Macropodinae

ALTHOUGH THE OLD NAME FOR THIS SPECIES IS NOW disappearing from aquarium literature, it is still encountered from time to time. It is a relic of the days when this species and *P. dayi* were believed to be more closely related to *Macropodus opercularis* than they

---

OTHER *PAROSPHROMENUS* SPECIES

The 1980s and 1990s saw a marked increase in the number of *Parosphromenus* species discovered and described. This increase mirrored, though on a more modest scale, the *Betta* "explosion" referred to in the OTHER *BETTA* SPECIES table (*see* p.238). Most of the "new" *Parosphromenus* are generally available through specialist anabantoid societies, though a few, such as the featured species and *P. filamentosus*, are also encountered from time to time in stores. The list that follows includes some of the newer species, as well as all the older ones. There are also, in addition, several species that are awaiting description. Most have similar requirements to *P. deisneri*, but specialist advice should be sought.

SCIENTIFIC NAME	COMMON NAME(S)	SIZE
P. allani	Allan's Licorice/Liquorice Gourami	1½in (4cm)
P. anjuganensis	Anjugan Licorice/Liquorice Gourami	1½in (4cm)
P. filamentosus	Filament-tailed Licorice/Liquorice Gourami	1½in (4cm)
P. harveyi	Harvey's Licorice/Liquorice Gourami	1½in (4cm)
P. linkei	Linke's Licorice/Liquorice Gourami	1½in (4cm)
P. nagyi	Nagy's Licorice/Liquorice Gourami	1½in (4cm)
P. ornaticauda	Red-tailed Licorice/Liquorice Gourami	1¼in (3cm)
P. paludicola	Swamp Licorice/Liquorice Gourami	1½in (4cm)
P. parvulus	Small Licorice/Liquorice Gourami	1¼in (3cm)

actually are. Both *Pseudosphromenus* were also once believed to be subspecies, rather than distinct valid species.

DISTRIBUTION: *Probably from southern India, originally; now found in Sri Lanka and (possibly) Bengal, Myanmar (Burma), Sumatra and Tonkin (north Vietnam)*

SIZE: *Around 2½in (6cm)*

BEHAVIOR: *Peaceful; should not be kept with boisterous tankmates*

DIET: *Wide range of foods accepted*

AQUARIUM: *Heavily planted, with caves or other shelters, and dark substratum. Water chemistry not critical. Temperature range: around 68°F (20°C) to 82°F (28°C)*

BREEDING: *Male builds bubble nest under broad leaf or in a cave. Egg care usually undertaken by male, but female may participate. Hatching takes about two days*

DAY'S SPIKE-TAILED PARADISE FISH

BROWN SPIKE-TAILED PARADISE FISH, DAY'S SPIKETAIL

Pseudosphromenus dayi

SYNONYM: *Macropodus dayi*
FAMILY: Belontiidae
SUBFAMILY: Macropodinae

ADULT MALES OF THIS SPECIES POSSESS FINE extensions on the central rays of the caudal fin, along with bright greenish-blue fin edges. There are also two dark bands on the body, which run all the way from the

head to the caudal peduncle. Hybridization between the two *Pseudosphromenus* species is known to occur, with the resulting hybrids being fertile.

DISTRIBUTION: *Range said to include southern and western India, Sri Lanka, Vietnam, Sumatra, Myanmar (Burma) and the Malabar Coast*

SIZE: *Up to 3in (7.5cm) reported, but usually smaller*

FEMALE SPIKE-TAILED PARADISE FISH (PSEUDOSPHROMENUS CUPANUS)

BEHAVIOR: *As for P. cupanus*

DIET: *As for P. cupanus*

AQUARIUM: *As for P. cupanus; temperature range may be even wider*

BREEDING: *Normally, a bubble-nester (like P. cupanus); but in colder parts of its range has been reported as spawning like cichlids.*

DWARF CROAKING GOURAMI
PYGMY CROAKING GOURAMI

Trichopsis pumilus

SYNONYM: *Trichopsis pumila*
FAMILY: Belontiidae
SUBFAMILY: Macropodinae

THE THREE SPECIES BELONGING TO THE GENUS *Trichopsis* are capable of producing croaking sounds, hence the common names of this species and *T. vittatus*. All three are slender species with pointed snouts resembling some of the *Parosphromenus* species, to which they are related. The Dwarf Croaking Gourami is, reportedly, capable of hybridizing with *T. schalleri*, with the resulting offspring being fertile.

DISTRIBUTION: *Indonesia, Malaysia and Thailand*

SIZE: *Up to 1½in (4cm)*

BEHAVIOR: *Peaceful; must not be kept with boisterous tankmates*

DIET: *Wide range of foods accepted*

AQUARIUM: *As for Pseudosphromenus cupanus, but water should be closer to soft, acid end of the chemistry spectrum. Temperature range: 77–82°F (25–28°C)*

BREEDING: *Bubble nest of variable quality is built, and the eggs and newly hatched fry are guarded by male. Hatching takes about two days*

SPARKLING GOURAMI
SCHALLER'S GOURAMI

Trichopsis schalleri

FAMILY: Belontiidae
SUBFAMILY: Macropodinae

THIS IS PERHAPS THE MOST BEAUTIFUL OF THE THREE *Trichopsis* species, with specimens in peak condition living up to the "sparkling" label. Sparkling Gourami is reported to produce fertile hybrids in crosses with its two close relatives.

DISTRIBUTION: *Southern Thailand*

SIZE: *Up to 2½in (6cm)*

BEHAVIOR: *As for T. pumilus*

DIET: *As for T. pumilus*

AQUARIUM: *As for T. pumilus*

BREEDING: *As for T. pumilus*

BANDED GOURAMI (COLISA FASCIATA)

CROAKING GOURAMI

Trichopsis vittatus

SYNONYM: *Trichopsis vittata*
FAMILY: Belontiidae
SUBFAMILY: Macropodinae

SEVERAL FORMS OF THIS SPECIES ARE KNOWN IN THE wild, including a two-spot type and a blue one (sometimes referred to as *T. harrisi*). Owing to its widespread distribution and variability, some doubts remain regarding the correct identification of the various types. The Croaking Gourami is known to interbreed with *T. schalleri*, with the resulting offspring being fertile.

DISTRIBUTION: *Widely distributed in southeast Asia*

SIZE: *Up to 2¾in (7cm), but often smaller*

BEHAVIOR: *As for T. pumilus*

DIET: *As for T. pumilus*

AQUARIUM: *As for T. pumilus. Temperature range: 72–82°F (22–28°C).*

BREEDING: *As for T. pumilus. Male may build more substantial bubble nest than his T. pumilus and T. schalleri counterparts. Hatching takes about one day*

HONEY GOURAMI
HONEY DWARF GOURAMI

Colisa chuna

SYNONYM: *Colisa sota*
FAMILY: Belontiidae
SUBFAMILY: Trichogasterinae (Trichogastrinae in *Nelson* 1994—*see* Bibliography)

THE SCIENTIFIC NAME OF THIS, THE SMALLEST member of the genus *Colisa*, has oscillated over time, with current opinion settling on *Colisa chuna*. The Honey Gourami is different from the other *Colisa* species in that it lacks oblique body bands. Males in nuptial coloration are particularly impressive, especially when they "stand on their tails" during courtship displays. Golden, peach and mottled varieties are frequently available.

DISTRIBUTION: *Northeastern India and Bangladesh*

SIZE: *Up to 2¾in (7cm), but generally smaller*

BEHAVIOR: *Peaceful, retiring; should not be kept with boisterous tankmates*

DIET: *Most foods accepted*

AQUARIUM: *Heavily planted, tranquil, with surface vegetation and adequate shelter. Water chemistry not critical. Temperature range: 72–82°F (22–28°C)*

BREEDING: *Male builds good bubble nest, and guards the eggs and newly hatched fry. Hatching takes about one day*

BANDED GOURAMI
STRIPED, INDIAN, or GIANT, GOURAMI

Colisa fasciata

FAMILY: Belontiidae
SUBFAMILY: Trichogasterinae (Trichogastrinae in *Nelson* 1994—*see* Bibliography)

THIS SPECIES HAS BEEN KNOWN IN THE HOBBY FOR over 100 years. However, unlike the three other members of the genus, it has never been developed into fin or color varieties. The Banded Gourami will interbreed with its closest relatives, *C. labiosa* and *C. lalia*; the resulting hybrids from *C. labiosa* crosses are fertile.

DISTRIBUTION: *Most of India, except south and southwest; also reported from Myanmar (Burma)*

SIZE: *Up to 4¾in (12cm) reported, but usually a little smaller*

BEHAVIOR: *Peaceful toward other species, except during breeding; males somewhat less peaceful toward each other*

DIET: *As for* C. chuna

AQUARIUM: *As for* C. chuna

BREEDING: *As for* C. chuna

THICK-LIPPED GOURAMI

THICKLIP GOURAMI

Colisa labiosa

FAMILY: Belontiidae
SUBFAMILY: Trichogasterinae (Trichogastrinae in *Nelson* 1994—*see* Bibliography)

CLOSELY RELATED TO C. FASCIATA, THE Thicklipped Gourami can be immediately recognized by its smaller head and (in fully mature males) the elegantly extended tip of the dorsal fin. C. *labiosa* x *fasciata* hybrids are fertile, while C. *labiosa* x *lalia* are not. A peach-colored variety is widely available.

DISTRIBUTION: *Irrawaddy River (Myanmar/Burma)*

SIZE: *Up to 4in (10cm) reported, but usually smaller*

BEHAVIOR: *As for* C. fasciata

DIET: *As for* C. chuna

AQUARIUM: *As for* C. chuna

BREEDING: *As for* C. chuna

DWARF GOURAMI

Colisa lalia

FAMILY: Belontiidae
SUBFAMILY: Trichogasterinae (Trichogastrinae in *Nelson* 1994—*see* Bibliography)

THIS IS THE MOST WIDELY KEPT *COLISA* SPECIES (*see* photo p.232). It has been developed into a number of color forms, the best known being the Sunset (Red), Rainbow, Blue, Neon, and Multicolored. C. *lalia* will hybridize with both C. *fasciata* and C. *labiosa*, although the hybrids are infertile.

DISTRIBUTION: *Northern India*

SIZE: *Up to 2½in (6cm), but usually smaller*

BEHAVIOR: *More tolerant of conspecific males than are* C. fasciata *and* C. labiosa

DIET: *As for* C. chuna

AQUARIUM: *As for* C. chuna

BREEDING: *As for* C. chuna; *male builds exceptional nest containing interwoven vegetation*

FALSE CHOCOLATE GOURAMI

Parasphaerichthys ocellatus

FAMILY: Belontiidae
SUBFAMILY: Trichogasterinae (Trichogastrinac in *Nelson* 1994—*see* Bibliography)

ALTHOUGH DESCRIBED AS LONG AGO AS 1929, this remains one of the rarely seen species. It is a somewhat more elongate fish than *Sphaerichthys osphromenoides* (Chocolate Gourami), with a rounded tail. Exacting in its demands, it is undoubtedly one for the specialist and best avoided by new aquarists.

DISTRIBUTION: *Mountain streams in northern Myanmar (Burma)*

SIZE: *Up to 2½in (6cm) reported, but usually smaller*

BEHAVIOR: *Shy, retiring; can be kept only with quiet tankmates*

DIET: *Small livefoods, although some deep-frozen/ freeze-dried foods may be accepted; dried formulations may be accepted only reluctantly*

AQUARIUM: *Well-planted, with surface vegetation and subdued lighting important. Soft, slightly acid to neutral water. Temperature range: 72–77°F (22–25°C)*

BREEDING: *No documented accounts available; may be a mouthbrooder like* Sphaerichthys *(see following entries)*

POINTED-MOUTHED GOURAMI

LARGE CHOCOLATE GOURAMI

Sphaerichthys acrostoma

FAMILY: Belontiidae
SUBFAMILY: Trichogasterinae (Trichogastrinae in *Nelson* 1994—*see* Bibliography)

IN ADDITION TO BEING LARGER AND POSSESSING a more pointed snout than other *Sphaerichthys* species, the Pointed-mouthed Gourami has a plainer-colored, i.e., less-patterned, body. It is also less frequently encountered than S. *osphromenoides* (*see* next entry).

DISTRIBUTION: *Borneo*

SIZE: *Up to 4in (10cm), but usually smaller*

BEHAVIOR: *Generally retiring; must not be kept with boisterous tankmates*

DIET: *As for* Parasphaerichthys ocellatus

AQUARIUM: *As for* Parasphaerichthys ocellatus, *but pH should be maintained within the acid part of the spectrum. Temperature range: 77–86°F (25–30°C)*

BREEDING: *Very challenging. Eggs are incubated orally by female*

CHOCOLATE GOURAMI

Sphaerichthys osphromenoides

FAMILY: Belontiidae
SUBFAMILY: Trichogasterinae (Trichogastrinae in *Nelson* 1994—*see* Bibliography)

THIS IS, BY FAR, THE MOST FAMOUS MEMBER OF ITS genus, having first been imported into Europe in 1905. In the late 1970s, a red-finned "Chocolate"—the Crossband Chocolate Gourami—was described and afforded subspecific status: S. o. selatanensis. At that point, S. *osphromenoides* became S. *o. osphromenoides*.

DISTRIBUTION: S. o. osphromenoides: *Indonesia and Malaysia;* S. o. selatanensis: *Borneo*

SIZE: *Up to 2½in (6cm), but usually smaller*

BEHAVIOR: *Retiring and peaceful; must not be kept with boisterous tankmates*

DIET: *As for* S. acrostoma

AQUARIUM: *As for* S. acrostoma

BREEDING: *Challenging in aquaria; female orally incubates the eggs and fry for up to two weeks*

VAILLANT'S CHOCOLATE GOURAMI
Sphaerichthys vaillanti

FAMILY: Belontiidae
SUBFAMILY: Trichogasterinae (Trichogastrinae in *Nelson* 1994—*see* Bibliography)

THOUGH NOT THE "YOUNGEST" OF THE *Sphaerichthys* species, Vaillant's Chocolate Gourami is, perhaps, the most recent one to appear with any degree of regularity. It is a beautifully marked species when in peak condition.

DISTRIBUTION: *Borneo*

SIZE: *Up to 3in (8cm), but usually smaller*

BEHAVIOR: *As for S. acrostoma and S. osphromenoides*

DIET: *As for S. acrostoma and S. osphromenoides*

AQUARIUM: *As for S. acrostoma and S. osphromenoides*

BREEDING: *As for S. acrostoma and S. osphromenoides. Some doubt exists regarding the sex of the mouthbrooding parent*

PEARL GOURAMI
LACE, LEERI, or MOSAIC, GOURAMI
Trichogaster leeri

FAMILY: Belontiidae
SUBFAMILY: Trichogasterinae (Trichogastrinae in *Nelson* 1994—*see* Bibliography)

ONCE SEEN, A LARGE, MATURE, MALE PEARL Gourami in full breeding regalia is never forgotten. This is another of those "must keep" fish. A golden form appeared in outdoor ponds in Florida in the early 1990s, but the colors faded and were replaced by normal wild-type coloration over a period of a few weeks once the fish were transferred to indoor aquaria.

DISTRIBUTION: *Peninsular Malaysia, Borneo, Sumatra, (possibly) Java and the area around Bangkok (Thailand)*

SIZE: *Up to 6in (15cm) reported, but usually considerably smaller*

BEHAVIOR: *Generally peaceful, except at breeding time when males become territorial*

DIET: *Most foods accepted*

AQUARIUM: *Large, covered, well-planted, with central open area. Surface vegetation also recommended, as well as subdued illumination. Water chemistry not critical. Temperature range: 73–82°F (23–28°C)*

BREEDING: *Substantial bubble nest may be built at water surface by male. The eggs and newly hatched fry are also guarded by male. Hatching takes about one day*

▲ *CHOCOLATE GOURAMI (SPHAERICHTHYS OSPHROMENOIDES)* ▼ *PEARL GOURAMI (TRICHOGASTER LEERI)*

MOONLIGHT GOURAMI
MOONBEAM, or THINLIP, GOURAMI
Trichogaster microlepis

FAMILY: Belontiidae
SUBFAMILY: Trichogasterinae (Trichogastrinae in *Nelson* 1994—*see* Bibliography)

THIS IS AN ELEGANT, SILVERY FISH WITH extremely long filament-like pelvic fins. Neither it, nor any of the other gouramis in its genus, or within *Colisa*, should be kept with fin-nipping species, such as *Barbus tetrazona* (Tiger Barb), which would—sooner or later—damage these delicate fins.

DISTRIBUTION: *Cambodia, Malaysia, Singapore and Thailand*

SIZE: *Up to 8in (20cm) reported, but usually considerably smaller*

BEHAVIOR: *As for T. leeri*

DIET: *As for T. leeri*

AQUARIUM: *As for T. leeri*

BREEDING: *Basically, as for T. leeri. Male may tear off bits of submerged vegetation for inclusion in bubble nest*

SNAKESKIN GOURAMI

Trichogaster pectoralis

FAMILY: Belontiidae
SUBFAMILY: Trichogasterinae (Trichogastrinae in *Nelson* 1994—*see* Bibliography)

WHILE NOT SPECTACULARLY COLORED, THE BROWN shades and patterns of the Snakeskin Gourami, suffused overall with a delicate purplish sheen, make it a very attractive fish. It is much loved by the anabantoid enthusiasts that have kept and bred it.

DISTRIBUTION: *Cambodia, Vietnam and Thailand, but also introduced elsewhere in southeast Asia and other regions, including Sri Lanka and Haiti*

SIZE: *Up to 8in (20cm)*

BEHAVIOR: *Very peaceful despite its size*

DIET: *As for T. leeri*

AQUARIUM: *As for T. leeri*

BREEDING: *Basically, as for T. leeri; bubble nests can be quite small*

SPOTTED GOURAMI

TWO-SPOT, THREE-SPOT, BLUE, COSBY, OPALINE, OPAL, PLATINUM, LAVENDER, GOLDEN, AMETHYST, or BROWN, GOURAMI, HAIRFIN

Trichogaster trichopterus

FAMILY: Belontiidae
SUBFAMILY: Trichogasterinae (Trichogastrinae in *Nelson* 1994—*see* Bibliography)

THIS SPECIES, IN ITS NUMEROUS COLOR VARIETIES, is, along with the Dwarf Gourami (*Colisa lalia*—*see* p.242) the most widely kept of all the gouramis. Two subspecies are generally recognized: *T. t. trichopterus*, which occurs in various (nonblue) natural forms, such as the Brown and Lavender Gourami; and *T. t. sumatranus*, a blue form found exclusively in Sumatra. According to some authorities, the blue "sumatranus" is no more than yet another color morph and not a distinct subspecies.

DISTRIBUTION: T. t. trichopterus: *widely distributed in Indochina, Malaysia, Indonesia, Thailand and neighboring regions;* T. t. sumatranus: *restricted to Sumatra*

SIZE: *Up to 6in (15cm), but often smaller*

BEHAVIOR: *Males more intolerant of each other than are those of related species*

DIET: *Basically, as for T. leeri*

AQUARIUM: *Basically, as for T. leeri*

▲ MOONLIGHT GOURAMI (TRICHOGASTER MICROLEPIS) ▼ SNAKESKIN GOURAMI (TRICHOGASTER PECTORALIS)

BREEDING: *Basically, as for T. leeri. Quality of nest may vary from small, single layer of bubbles to major construction*

KISSING GOURAMI

Helostoma temminckii

SYNONYM: *Helostoma rudolfi*
FAMILY: Helostomatidae

THIS LARGE SPECIES IS FAMOUS FOR ITS "KISSING" habit and fleshy lips (*see* photo p.232). The kissing, though, has little to do with affection and a great deal to do with gaining or maintaining territory; it is, in fact, a mouth-to-mouth trial of strength, which results in no damage to either party. There are three color forms available: the green or wild type, a pink-bodied version, and a mottled one.

DISTRIBUTION: *Widely distributed (and introduced) in southeast Asia*

SIZE: *Up to 12in (30cm), but usually only around half this size*

BEHAVIOR: *Generally peaceful, despite its size (and strength trials); exhibits strong appetite for delicate plants*

DIET: *All foods accepted; vegetable component recommended*

AQUARIUM: *Large, well-covered, and with a selection of hardy and/or unpalatable plants (see Aquarium Plants). A gravel substratum, with several large pieces of decor, e.g., rocks or bogwood, also recommended. Water chemistry not critical. Temperature range: 72–86°F (22–30°C)*

BREEDING: *Spawning may occur in the absence of bubble nest or in the presence of a token one. No strong egg/fry care exhibited. Hatching takes about one day, or slightly less at high temperatures*

PIKEHEAD
Luciocephalus pulcher

FAMILY: Luciocephalidae

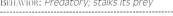

BUILT LIKE A TORPEDO AND ARMED WITH A LARGE mouth, the Pikehead is an efficient predator. It is a fish for the specialist who can cater to its needs. A second, as yet, unidentified species, the Spotted Pikehead, was collected in the late 1990s but has not become widespread.

DISTRIBUTION: *Southeast Asia*

SIZE: *Up to 8in (20cm)*

BEHAVIOR: *Predatory; stalks its prey*

DIET: *Almost exclusively livefoods—e.g., insects, but including fish—a factor that needs due consideration prior to purchase*

AQUARIUM: *Well-covered, with adequate shelter, open spaces, and subdued lighting. Soft, slightly acid water preferred. Temperature range: 72–84°F (22–29°C)*

BREEDING: *No documented accounts currently available; assumed to be a mouthbrooder*

GIANT GOURAMI
Osphronemus goramy

SYNONYM: *Osphronemus gorami*
FAMILY: Osphronemidae

AS ITS NAME IMPLIES, THIS IS A LARGE FISH THAT can be kept on a longterm basis only by aquarists who can accommodate it. It is usually available as juveniles of various colors, including (mainly) the wild type and a golden-bodied one. The Red-finned Giant Gourami, which began becoming available in the 1990s, is probably *O. laticlavus*, originally from Sabah. The *O. septemfasciatus* (Sevenstripe Giant Gourami) is only rarely seen. Both these last species were described only during the early 1990s.

DISTRIBUTION: *Widely distributed and introduced in tropical Asia, but probably originating in Borneo, Java and Sumatra*

SIZE: *Up to 24in (60cm) or slightly larger*

◀ SPOTTED GOURAMI (TRICHOGASTER TRICHOPTERUS)
▼ GIANT GOURAMI (OSPHRONEMUS GORAMY)

RED SNAKEHEAD
(CHANNA MICROPELTES)

BEHAVIOR: *Stealthy predator; can be kept only with tankmates that are too large to swallow*

DIET: *Chunky meat-/fish-based foods, plus live fish—a factor that needs due consideration prior to purchase*

AQUARIUM: *Large, well-covered, well-filtered, with coarse gravel, large decor and caves, e.g., lumps of bogwood. Subdued lighting recommended. Water chemistry not critical. Temperature range: 75–82°F (24–28°C)*

BREEDING: *Difficult to achieve. No bubble nest is built. Eggs float on water surface and are guarded by male. The young fish are cannibalistic*

RED SNAKEHEAD

Channa micropeltes

FAMILY: Channidae

THIS IS THE MOST WIDELY AVAILABLE *CHANNA* species, usually sold as strikingly marked, striped juveniles, with red areas around the caudal and pectoral fins. These markings are gradually lost until the fish becomes more irregularly marked, with little or no red. It is, nevertheless, a very attractive fish, even in its adult form. This is a "tempting" species that beginners would be wise to avoid (*see C. marulia*).

DISTRIBUTION: *Widely distributed in tropical Asia*

SIZE: *Up to 39in (1m)*

BEHAVIOR: *As for C. marulia*

DIET: *As for C. marulia*

AQUARIUM: *As for C. marulia*

BREEDING: *As for C. marulia*

DARK AFRICAN SNAKEHEAD

Channa obscura

FAMILY: Channidae

THIS IS ONE OF THE SMALLER SPECIES IN THE GENUS, and therefore easier to accommodate. Adult specimens exhibit excellent black body markings.

DISTRIBUTION: *Widely distributed in western Africa*

SIZE: *Around 13¾in (35cm)*

BEHAVIOR: *As for C. marulia*

DIET: *As for C. marulia*

AQUARIUM: *As for C. marulia*

BREEDING: *As for C. marulia*

BEHAVIOR: *Sedate and tolerant*

DIET: *Wide range of foods accepted; vegetable component recommended*

AQUARIUM: *Juveniles may be kept in community setup, but special provision must be made as they grow: a large, well-filtered, well-covered aquarium, with some large decorations (including large unpalatable or artificial plants), and adequately wide and deep swimming areas. Water chemistry not critical. Temperature range: 66–86°F (19–30°C)*

BREEDING: *Difficult to achieve in aquaria. Bubble nest built on water surface or below, with plant material incorporated. Eggs and fry are guarded by male. Hatching takes around two days*

INDIAN SNAKEHEAD

Channa marulia

FAMILY: Channidae

THERE ARE OVER 30 SPECIES OF *CHANNA* recognized, but very few are seen within the aquarium hobby. The Indian Snakehead is one of these. Like all its relatives in the genus and family, it is predatory and large. Snakeheads are, most definitely, not fishes for beginners.

DISTRIBUTION: *From southern China to India*

SIZE: *Up to 4ft (1.2m)*

OTHER *CHANNA* SPECIES

In addition to the featured species, some other snakeheads—including the following selection—are available. All have the same basic predatory instincts and aquarium requirements. Sizes given are approximate.

SCIENTIFIC NAME	COMMON NAME(S)	SIZE
C. africana	African Snakehead	16in (40cm)
C. argus	Eastern, or Spotted, Snakehead	39in (100cm)
C. asiatica	Chinese, or Northern, Green Snakehead	13¾in (35cm)
C. bleheri	Rainbow Snakehead	8in (20cm)
C. gachua	Frog, or Brown, Snakehead	6in (15cm)
C. lucia	Splendid Snakehead	16in (40cm)
C. orientalis	Bengal, Ceylon, or Smooth-breasted, Snakehead	16in (40cm)
C. pleurophthalma	Eyespot Snakehead	16in (40cm)
C. striata	Striped, or Chevron, Snakehead/Murrel	39in (100cm)

CHAMELEON FISH

BADIS

Badis badis

FAMILY: Nandidae
SUBFAMILY: Badinae (classified as Badidae by some authors)

THE CHAMELEON FISH IS SO NAMED BECAUSE OF its ability to change color rapidly according to mood. Two basic color forms have been known for a long time in the wild, usually regarded as separate subspecies: *B. b. badis* (Blue Dwarf), with bluish fins, and *B. b. burmanicus* (Burmese Chameleon Fish), a reddish form. More recently, a darker form: *B. b. siamensis* (Siamese Chameleon Fish) has begun appearing in the hobby. A less colorful, fourth Chameleon Fish (probably *B. b. assamensis*) has also been recorded.

DISTRIBUTION: B. b. badis: *India;* B. b. burmanicus: *Myanmar (Burma);* B. b. siamensis: *Phuket (Thailand);* B. b. assamensis: *Assam*

SIZE: *Males up to 3in (8cm); females a little smaller*

BEHAVIOR: *Generally peaceful, although males may become territorial*

DIET: *Wide range of foods accepted*

AQUARIUM: *Heavily planted, with sandy substratum and numerous shelters. Water chemistry not critical. Temperature range: 73–82°F (23–28°C)*

BREEDING: *Eggs are usually laid in caves. Male guards eggs and also cares for the fry until they are free swimming. Hatching takes about three days*

SOUTH AMERICAN LEAF FISH

Monocirrhus polyacanthus

FAMILY: Nandidae
SUBFAMILY: Nandinae

APTLY NAMED, THE SOUTH AMERICAN LEAF FISH floats in midwater, head angled downward, creating the perfect impression of a drifting leaf. The large mouth is a clear indication of the diet of this very challenging fish.

DISTRIBUTION: *Peruvian Amazon*

SIZE: *Up to 4in (10cm)*

BEHAVIOR: *Slow-moving, stalking predator; should be kept only with tankmates that are too large to swallow*

DIET: *Livefoods, including live fish—a factor that needs due consideration prior to purchase*

AQUARIUM: *Heavily planted, well-filtered (but with little water turbulence), with numerous shelters. Soft, acid water important. Temperature range: 72–77°F (22–25°C)*

BREEDING: *Challenging in aquaria. Eggs are laid on broad leaves or flat surfaces and are guarded by male. Hatching takes about four days*

COMMON NANDUS

Nandus nandus

FAMILY: Nandidae
SUBFAMILY: Nandinae

ALTHOUGH A LEAF FISH, COMMON NANDUS DOES not exhibit the head-down posture of *Monocirrhus polyacanthus* (see previous entry) and is not as leaflike. It exhibits more normal swimming activity, but has an equally large mouth and habits.

DISTRIBUTION: *India, Myanmar (Burma) and Thailand*

SIZE: *Up to 8in (20cm)*

BEHAVIOR: *Predatory, nocturnal loner*

DIET: *Livefoods, but more adaptable in its requirements than M. polyacanthus; may accept some commercial preparations*

AQUARIUM: *Basically, as for M. polyacanthus, but use neutral to alkaline, medium-hard water with 1 teaspoon salt per 1 Imp. gal (4.5 liters) added. Temperature range: 72–79°F (22–26°C)*

BREEDING: *Challenging. The water should not contain salt. Eggs are scattered over substratum; no parental care occurs. Hatching takes about two days*

SCHOMBURGK'S LEAF FISH

Polycentrus schomburgki

FAMILY: Nandidae
SUBFAMILY: Nandinae

ADULTS OF THIS SPECIES HAVE A SOMEWHAT MORE rounded head profile than *Monocirrhus polyacanthus* and *Nandus nandus*. Some specimens have very attractive dark mottling.

DISTRIBUTION: *Guyanas, Trinidad and Venezuela*

SIZE: *Around 4in (10cm)*

BEHAVIOR: *As for Nandus nandus*

DIET: *As for Monocirrhus polyacanthus*

AQUARIUM: *As for Nandus nandus*

BREEDING: *As for Monocirrhus polyacanthus. Hatching takes about three days*

SOUTH AMERICAN LEAF FISH (MONOCIRRHUS POLYACANTHUS)

RAINBOWS AND BLUE-EYES

The first rainbowfish was described in 1843 as *Atherina nigrans*. Some 20 years later, it was reassigned to a new genus, *Melanotaenia* and it is this genus that contains most of the species that have, over the years, become popular aquarium species.

Over time, these beautiful fish and their relatives have been well-studied and, gradually, their biology and relationships have been worked out. However, there remain doubts as to the exact status of the various recognized "groups"—all of which share certain characteristics, such as two dorsal fins, a long-based anal fin, a deeply forked mouth and large eyes.

One of the most widely accepted classifications and the one followed here (Nelson 1994; see Bibli-

ography), separates the rainbows and their relatives into the following families (in alphabetical order):

Atherinidae (silversides), Bedotiidae (Madagascan rainbows), Dentatherinidae (only one species), Melanotaeniidae (rainbowfishes), Nothocheiridae (Isonidae—exclusively marine), Phallostethidae (species with an exceptional copulatory appendage, the priapium), Pseudomugilidae (blue-eyes) and Telmatherinidae (Celebes rainbowfishes).

In the entries that follow, representatives of four of these families will be featured: Bedotiidae, Melanotaeniidae, Pseudomugilidae, and Telmatherinidae.

▲ BOWFISH (BEDOTIA MADAGASCARIENSIS)　　　▼ SALMON RED RAINBOWFISH (GLOSSOLEPIS INCISUS)

BOWFISH

Bedotia madagascariensis

SYNONYM: *Bedotia geayi*
FAMILY: Bedotiidae

THIS SLENDER-BODIED AQUARIUM FAVORITE IS THE only rainbowfish of African origin. A large shoal kept under appropriate conditions creates an unforgettable sight.

DISTRIBUTION: *Madagascar*

SIZE: *Up to 6in (15cm) reported, but usually smaller*

BEHAVIOR: *A peaceful shoaler*

DIET: *Wide range of (mainly) floating formulations accepted. Food that sinks to the bottom is ignored*

AQUARIUM: *Spacious, well-planted, with large, central, open swimming area. Water chemistry not critical, as long as quality is good, but neutral to slightly alkaline, medium-hard water preferred, with frequent partial water changes. Temperature range: 68–77°F (20–25°C)*

BREEDING: *Eggs are scattered among fine-leaved vegetation. Hatching can take around seven days*

SALMON RED RAINBOWFISH

Glossolepis incisus

FAMILY: Melanotaeniidae

THIS IS, BY FAR, THE MOST WIDELY AVAILABLE species in the genus. It first made its appearance in the hobby in 1973 and, since then, has been widely bred commercially. Some mature cultivated males have particularly deep coloration. There is also a marbled variety.

DISTRIBUTION: *Lake Sentani and surrounding areas in Irian Jaya (New Guinea)*

SIZE: *Up to 6in (15cm) reported, but usually smaller*

BEHAVIOR: *A peaceful, though active, shoaler*

DIET: *Livefoods preferred, but some commercial formulations also accepted*

AQUARIUM: *As for Bedotia madagascariensis, but slightly higher alkaline and hardness levels accepted*

BREEDING: *As for B. madagascariensis*

OTHER *GLOSSOLEPIS* SPECIES

In addition to the species featured, the genus contains a few others, although at least one of these is yet to be described and only three are generally available to the aquarist. Aquarium requirements are as for *G. incisus*. Sizes given are approximate.

SCIENTIFIC NAME	COMMON NAME(S)	SIZE
G. maculosus	Spotted Rainbowfish	2¾in (7cm)
G. multisquamatus	Sepik Rainbowfish	5½in (14cm)
G. wanamensis *	Lake Wanam Rainbowfish	5in (13cm)

SEPIK RAINBOWFISH
(GLOSSOLEPIS
MULTISQUAMATUS) ▼

NOTE

* During the mid-1990s, owing to the introduction of three nonnative species into Lake Wanam, this species was close to extinction in the wild. However, captive-bred stocks, plus the partial recovery of the lake population in the late 1990s, mean that the species is now somewhat more secure.

The genus *Chilatherina* is closely related to *Glossolepis*. Four species are occasionally available, all with the same basic requirements as *Glossolepis*.

SCIENTIFIC NAME	COMMON NAME(S)	SIZE
C. axelrodi	Axelrod's Rainbowfish	4¼in (11cm)
C. bleheri	Bleher's Rainbowfish	5in (13cm)
C. fasciata	Barred Rainbowfish	5in (13cm)
C. sentaniensis	Sentani Rainbowfish	4¾in (12cm)

THREADFIN RAINBOWFISH

Iriatherina werneri

FAMILY: Melanotaeniidae

THIS IS THE ONLY SPECIES IN ITS GENUS. It is distinguished from other members of the family by its slender body and thread-like fin extensions. Despite its delicate appearance, Threadfin Rainbowfish is relatively hardy. A light-bodied, dark-eyed form (Lutino) is also occasionally available. *Rhadinocentrus ornatus* (Ornate Rainbowfish)—a slim-bodied species from Queensland and Victoria (Australia)—can be easily distinguished from Threadfin Rainbowfish by its long-based anal fin, lack of fin extensions, and blunt snout.

DISTRIBUTION: *Irian Jaya (New Guinea) and northern Australia*

SIZE: *Up to 2in (5cm) reported*

BEHAVIOR: *A peaceful shoaler*

DIET: *Livefoods preferred, but many commercial diets also accepted*

AQUARIUM: *Well-planted, and with no fin-nipping tankmates—e.g., Tiger Barbs (Barbus tetrazona) or Mosquito Fish (Gambusia spp.)—present.*

THREADFIN RAINBOWFISH
(IRIATHERINA WERNERI)

BOESEMAN'S RAINBOWFISH (MELANOTAENIA BOESEMANI)

Subdued lighting. Relatively soft, slightly acid water preferred. Temperature range: 72–84°F (22–29°C)

BREEDING: *Eggs are scattered—over a period of several days—among fine-leaved vegetation. Hatching can take 10 to 12 days, depending on temperature*

BOESEMAN'S RAINBOWFISH

Melanotaenia boesemani

FAMILY: Melanotaeniidae

THIS SPLENDID FISH WAS FIRST IMPORTED INTO Europe in 1980. Its strikingly unusual coloration, best seen in mature males in peak condition, quickly made it popular with aquarists. The vast majority of specimens available for aquaria are now captive-bred.

DISTRIBUTION: *Ajamaru Lakes and surrounding areas in Irian Jaya (New Guinea)*

SIZE: *Up to 4¾in (12cm) reported, but usually smaller*

BEHAVIOR: *Generally peaceful, though active, shoaler*

DIET: *Wide range of foods accepted*

AQUARIUM: *Spacious, well-planted, with large open central area. Short, fine-leaved/fronded plants, such as Java Moss (Vesicularia dubyana), may be used along bottom of swimming area. Soft, slightly acid to neutral water recommended; well-filtered, but not turbulent. Temperature range: 77–86°F (25–30°C)*

Breeding: *Eggs are scattered—over a period of a few days—among fine-leaved vegetation, e.g., Java Moss. Hatching takes approximately seven days*

LAKE TEBERA RAINBOWFISH

Melanotaenia herbertaxelrodi

FAMILY: Melanotaeniidae

FULLY MATURE SPECIMENS OF THIS SPECIES ARE very impressive, owing not just to their coloration but in addition to the depth of the body. This species was first described in 1981 and has been popular ever since this time.

DISTRIBUTION: *Lake Tebera (Papua New Guinea)*

SIZE: *Up to 5in (13cm), but usually smaller*

BEHAVIOR: *Generally peaceful shoaler*

DIET: *As for M. boesemani.*

AQUARIUM: *As for M. boesemani, but slightly lower temperatures and slightly higher alkalinity and hardness recommended*

BREEDING: *As for M. boesemani*

LAKE TEBERA RAINBOWFISH (MELANOTAENIA HERBERTAXELRODI)

LAKE KUTUBU RAINBOWFISH

Melanotaenia lacustris

FAMILY: Melanotaeniidae

ALTHOUGH THIS MAGNIFICENT SPECIES WAS described in 1964, it was not until the 1980s—when commercially bred stocks became more widely available—that it began to be seen on a regular basis. Mature males make a truly impressive sight in their metallic-blue and silvery white livery.

DISTRIBUTION: *Lake Kutubu (Papua New Guinea)*

SIZE: *Up to 4¾in (12cm), but usually smaller*

BEHAVIOR: *As for* M. herbertaxelrodi

DIET: *As for* M. herbertaxelrodi

AQUARIUM: *As for* M. herbertaxelrodi

BREEDING: *As for* M. herbertaxelrodi

DISTRIBUTION: *Southeastern Papua New Guinea*

SIZE:: *Fully mature males reported up to 5½in (14cm)*

BEHAVIOR: *As for* M. herbertaxelrodi

DIET: *As for* M. herbertaxelrodi

AQUARIUM: *As for* M. herbertaxelrodi. *Temperature range: 77–84°F (25–29°C)*

BREEDING: *As for* M. herbertaxelrodi

LAKE KUTUBU RAINBOWFISH (MELANOTAENIA LACUSTRIS)

MacCULLOCH'S RAINBOWFISH

BLACK-LINED, DWARF, or AUSTRALIAN, RAINBOWFISH

Melanotaenia maccullochi

FAMILY: Melanotaeniidae

THIS IS ONE OF THE "EARLIER" RAINBOWS, FIRST imported into Europe in 1934. It is also one of the smaller species, whose popularity has gradually been eclipsed by the more recent and more colorful additions to the range of species that are available. At least two naturally occurring forms are known.

DISTRIBUTION: *Northeast Australia and southeast Papua New Guinea*

SIZE: *Up to 2¾in (7cm)*

BEHAVIOR: *As for* M. herbertaxelrodi

DIET: *As for* M. herbertaxelrodi

AQUARIUM: *As for* M. herbertaxelrodi. *Temperature range: 68–86°F (20–30°C)*

BREEDING: *As for* M. herbertaxelrodi

MacCULLOCH'S RAINBOWFISH (MELANOTAENIA MACCULLOCHI)

PARKINSON'S RAINBOWFISH

Melanotaenia parkinsoni

FAMILY: Melanotaeniidae

THIS IS AN UNUSUALLY COLORED AND PATTERNED fish in which a sparkling bluish base color is liberally mottled in yellow, gold and orange in the posterior half of the body. The same yellow, gold, orange coloration extends into the unpaired fins. A red form is also available.

PARKINSON'S RAINBOWFISH (MELANOTAENIA PARKINSONI)

SPLENDID RAINBOWFISH (MELANOTAENIA SPLENDIDA)

OTHER *MELANOTAENIA* SPECIES

Australian Rainbowfish of the genus *Melanotaenia* are relatively young in evolutionary terms, with the main "surge" in their evolution believed to have begun only some 10,000 years ago. It is also believed that the pace of these changes is still being maintained today, as evidenced by the large-scale variations observed in separate populations of individual species. Some of these may eventually be regarded as distinct subspecies or even species in their own right. The following are some of the species (subspecies excluded) that are more widely available. Most do well in soft to medium-hard, neutral to slightly alkaline water, with the harder/alkaline end of the spectrum being preferable as it is more resistant to chemical fluctuations. (Two exceptions are noted below.) Sizes given are approximate.

SCIENTIFIC NAME	COMMON NAME(S)	SIZE
M. affinis	Northern Rainbowfish	5½in (14cm)
M. duboulayi	Crimson-spotted Rainbowfish	4¼in (11cm)
M. exquisita	Exquisite Rainbowfish	2¾in (7cm)
M. fluviatilis	Murray River Rainbowfish	3½in (9cm)
M. goldei	Goldie River Rainbowfish	5½in (14cm)
M. gracilis	Slender Rainbowfish	2¾in (7cm)
*M. monticola**	Mountain Rainbowfish	4in (10cm)
M. nigrans	Black-banded Rainbowfish	3½in (9cm)
*M. praecox***	Dwarf Neon Rainbowfish	2⅜in (6cm)
M. sexlineata	Fly River Rainbowfish	3in (8cm)
*M. trifasciata****	Banded River Rainbowfish	5in (13cm)

DWARF NEON RAINBOWFISH (MELANOTAENIA PRAECOX)

NOTES

* *M. monticola* requires slightly lower temperatures, ranging from around 61°F (16°C) to 72°F (22°C).

** *M. praecox* requires soft, slightly acid water and should therefore not be kept in hard or alkaline conditions.

*** *M. trifasciata* is one of the most variable of all the *Melanotaenia* species, with individual rivers having their own distinctive form of the species. The Goyder River morph—known, appropriately, as the Goyder River Rainbowfish—requires harder, more alkaline water than many of the other naturally occurring forms.

SPLENDID RAINBOWFISH

Melanotaenia splendida

FAMILY: Melanotaeniidae

FOUR SUBSPECIES OF THIS POPULAR RAINBOW ARE known: *M. s. splendida* (Eastern Rainbowfish), *M. s. australis* (Western Rainbowfish), *M. s. inornata* (Chequered Rainbowfish) and *M. s. rubrostriata* (Red-striped Rainbowfish). All have the same basic requirements.

DISTRIBUTION: M. s. splendida: *Queensland*; M. s. australis: *Western Australia and Northern Territory*; M. s. inornata: *Daly River (Northern Territory)*; M. s. rubrostriata: *Aru Island and southern New Guinea*

SIZE: M. s. splendida: *5½in (14cm)*; M. s. australis: *4¼in (11cm)*; M. s. inornata: *4¾in (12cm)*; M. s. rubrostriata: *6in (15cm)*

BEHAVIOR: *As for* M. herbertaxelrodi

DIET: *As for* M. herbertaxelrodi

AQUARIUM: *As for* M. herbertaxelrodi. *Temperature range: 70–82°F (21–28°C)*

BREEDING: *As for* M. herbertaxelrodi

FORK-TAILED BLUE-EYE

FORK-TAILED RAINBOWFISH

Pseudomugil furcatus

SYNONYM: *Popondichthys furcatus*
FAMILY: Pseudomugilidae

OWING TO THEIR DIETARY PREFERENCES AND SMALL size, members of this genus can prove somewhat more challenging to keep than *Melanotaenia* rainbows. A good shoal in peak condition, however, is nothing short of magnificent. The Fork-tailed Blue-eye and *P. signifer* are the largest species in the genus.

DISTRIBUTION: *Eastern Papua New Guinea*

SIZE: *Up to 2¼in (6cm), but often smaller*

BEHAVIOR: *Peaceful, though active, shoaler; must not be kept with larger, more boisterous tankmates*

DIET: *Livefoods preferred, but deep-frozen, freeze-dried, and some dry formulations, may also be accepted*

AQUARIUM: *Heavily planted, with central open swimming area. Surface cover in the form of floating vegetation also recommended. Soft to medium-hard, neutral to slightly alkaline water preferred. Temperature range: 73–79°F (23–26°C)*

BREEDING: *Eggs are scattered (usually over several days) among feathery roots of floating plants or among fine-leaved vegetation. Hatching can take up to around 20 days, depending on temperature*

AUSTRALIAN BLUE-EYE (PSEUDOMUGIL SIGNIFER)

AUSTRALIAN BLUE-EYE
PACIFIC BLUE-EYE
Pseudomugil signifer

FAMILY: Pseudomugilidae

THIS SPECIES SHOWS CONSIDERABLE VARIATION throughout its range. Some populations are more colorful, or larger, or (as reported for some of the more northern ones) more aggressive than others.

DISTRIBUTION: *Queensland and Victoria (eastern Australia)*

SIZE: *Up to 2¼in (6cm) reported, but often smaller*

BEHAVIOR: *As for* P. furcatus, *although males from some populations can become a little aggressive*

DIET: *As for* P. furcatus

AQUARIUM: *As for* P. furcatus, *but slightly harder, more alkaline water accepted. Some salt (slightly less than 1oz per gal/500mg per liter) may be added to the water, but this is not essential. Temperature range: 73–82°F (23–28°C)*

BREEDING: *As for* P. furcatus

CELEBES RAINBOWFISH
SAILFISH
Marosatherina ladigesi

SYNONYM: *Telmatherina ladigesi*
FAMILY: Telmatherinidae

THIS SPECIES HAS BEEN AVAILABLE SINCE 1933, and although it has never achieved the popularity *of Melanotaenia* rainbows it has always been popular among specialist fishkeepers. It does well only in good-quality water and in the absence of larger, aggressive tankmates.

DISTRIBUTION: *Sulawesi (Indonesia)*

SIZE: *Up to 3in (7.5cm), but usually smaller*

BEHAVIOR: *Peaceful, though active, shoaler*

OTHER *PSEUDOMUGIL* SPECIES

Only one other species of *Pseudomugil*—*P. gertrudae*—has been widely available; others are on offer on a less regular basis. All have basically similar requirements to *P. signifer*, with two possible exceptions, noted below.

SCIENTIFIC NAME	COMMON NAME(S)	SIZE
P. connieae *	Popondetta Blue-eye	2in (5cm)
P. cyanodorsalis **	Blueback Blue-eye	1¼in (3cm)
P. gertrudae	Spotted Blue-eye	1½in (4cm)
P. mellis	Honey Blue-eye	1¼in (3cm)
P. tenellus	Delicate Blue-eye	1½in (4cm)

SPOTTED BLUE-EYE (PSEUDOMUGIL GERTRUDAE)

NOTES

* Provide tank conditions as for *P. furcatus*.

** This species requires salt in the water, i.e., it is essential rather than optional

DIET: *Wide range of livefoods and commercial diets accepted*

AQUARIUM: *Setup as for* Pseudomugil furcatus. *Softish, slightly acid conditions may be accepted, but seems to do better at higher pH and hardness values. Water quality must be good. Temperature range: 68–82°F (20–28°C)*

BREEDING: *Long breeding season lasting several months. Eggs are scattered among fine-leaved vegetation. Hatching takes 8 to 12 days, depending on temperature*

CELEBES RAINBOWFISH (MAROSATHERINA LADIGESI)

SUNFISH AND DARTERS

Within the sunfish, two "groups" have traditionally been recognized: the "normal" sunfish species, such as the Pumpkinseed (*Lepomis gibbosus*) and its relatives, on the one hand, and the pygmy or dwarf sunfishes like the Everglades Dwarf or Pygmy Sunfish (*Elassoma evergladei*).

At one time, both groups were deemed to be so closely related that they were regarded as subfamilies (Centrarchinae and Elassomatinae) of the family Centrarchidae. Currently, they are regarded as distinct families: Centrarchidae and Elassomatidae (referred to as Elassomidae by some authors). However, this is now being questioned as new evidence begins to indicate that they may not be even closely related. Indeed, some consider that pygmy sunfishes may be more closely related to sticklebacks (Gasterosteidae) and swamp eels (Synbranchidae) than to the Centrarchidae. Pending the resolution of this controversial matter, the classification followed here (Nelson, 1994—*see* Bibliography) assigns sunfishes to the Centrarchidae and pygmy sunfishes to the Elassomatidae.

No such controversy surrounds the darters, which belong to the family Percidae, although there is some debate regarding the splitting of this family into two subfamilies, one of which, the Percinae, is then subdivided into two tribes: Percini—including such species as the various perches (*Perca* spp.), and the Etheostomatini—which contains the darters, proper, e.g. *Etheostoma* spp.

BLUE-SPOTTED SUNFISH

Enneacanthus gloriosus

FAMILY: Centrarchidae

THIS SPARKLING SILVERY FISH WITH REFLECTIVE blue spots is probably the most attractive of the three species in its genus. It has been in the hobby since the early 1900s but, owing to its low temperature requirements, it has never acquired great popularity among tropical freshwater aquarists.

DISTRIBUTION: *Atlantic and Gulf Slope drainages of the United States, from New York in the north, southward to Florida*

SIZE: *Up to 3¾in (9.5cm)*

BEHAVIOR: *A shoaling species, except at breeding time when males become highly territorial and aggressive*

DIET: *Livefoods preferred, but deep-frozen, freeze-dried and other commercial formulations accepted*

AQUARIUM: *Spacious, heavily planted with cool-water species, and with numerous hiding places and a coarse sand or fine-gravel substratum. Neutral to slightly alkaline, medium-hard water preferred. Temperature range: 50–72°F (10–22°C)*

BREEDING: *Lowering water level to around 6in (15cm) seems to enhance chances of success. Eggs are laid in a depression dug by male, who also defends the brood*

PUMPKINSEED

Lepomis gibbosus

FAMILY: Centrarchidae

FIRST IMPORTED INTO EUROPE IN 1877, THIS stunning species, with its reflective blue speckling, is the most frequently kept of all the sunfish species. Tough and adaptable, it is capable of becoming established in most temperate habitats, so it is essential to ensure that it neither escapes nor is released into non-native waters. Such cautionary advice applies not just to the Pumpkinseed but to all other sunfishes and similarly adaptable species. Since the Pumpkinseed can attain a substantial size, it will outgrow most average-sized aquaria, a factor that requires consideration prior to purchase.

DISTRIBUTION: *Widely distributed along the Atlantic drainages of the United States; also introduced into other areas of North America, Canada and Europe where it has become established in a number of locations*

SIZE: *Up to 16in (40cm), but usually smaller*

BEHAVIOR: *Generally peaceful, but territorial and aggressive during breeding*

DIET: *As for* Enneacanthus gloriosus

AQUARIUM: *As for* E. gloriosus, *but with open swimming area. Temperature range: 39–72°F (4–22°C)*

BREEDING: *As for* E. gloriosus

LONGEAR SUNFISH

Lepomis megalotis

FAMILY: Centrarchidae

AS ITS COMMON NAME INDICATES, THIS SPECIES has long "ears"— fleshy extensions along the posterior edge of the gill cover (these extensions—but shorter—are characteristic of all *Lepomis* species). The spotted body patterning, incorporating both red and blue pigments, is striking.

DISTRIBUTION: *Widely distributed in broad band extending from the Great Lakes down to the Florida panhandle, southern Texas, New Mexico and northeast Mexico; also introduced outside its native range in the United States*

OTHER *ENNEACANTHUS* SPECIES

Two other species of *Enneacanthus* are also available. Their basic requirements are as for *E. gloriosus*, although one, *E. chaetodon* can tolerate even lower temperatures around 39°F (4°C).

SCIENTIFIC NAME	COMMON NAME(S)	SIZE
E. chaetodon	Black-banded Sunfish	3in (8cm)
E. obesus	Banded, Diamond, or Little, Sunfish	3¾in (9.5cm)

PUMPKINSEED (LEPOMIS GIBBOSUS)

SIZE: *Up to 9½in (24cm)*

BEHAVIOR: *Adults may be intolerant of each other, with males becoming territorial and aggressive at breeding time*

DIET: *As for* Lepomis gibbosus

AQUARIUM: *As for* Lepomis gibbosus

BREEDING: *As for* Lepomis gibbosus

EVERGLADES PYGMY SUNFISH

FLORIDA PYGMY SUNFISH

Elassoma evergladei

FAMILY: Elassomatidae (referred to as Elasso-midae by some authors)

THE EVERGLADES PYGMY SUNFISH IS THE BEST known of the six species in the genus. It has been available for nearly three quarters of a century and is still much sought after by coldwater aquarists. It is not, however, a community fish that can be kept with other, larger, cool-water fish such as goldfish.

DISTRIBUTION: *From North Carolina to Florida, including the Everglades*

OTHER *LEPOMIS* SPECIES

There are nine other species of *Lepomis*, of which two are more frequently encountered than the others. All have similar characteristics to those outlined for the featured species, and they have wide temperature tolerance, although excessively low temperatures should be avoided (around 50°F/10°C should be regarded as a safe minimum). Sizes quoted are approximate.

SCIENTIFIC NAME	COMMON NAME(S)	SIZE
L. auritus	Redbreast Sunfish	9½in (24cm)
L. cyanellus *	Green Sunfish	12¼in (31cm)
L. gulosus	Warmouth	12¼in (31cm)
L. humilis	Orange-spotted Sunfish	6in (15cm)
L. macrochirus *	Bluegill	16in (41cm)
L. marginatus	Dollar Sunfish	4¾in (12cm)
L. microlophus	Redear Sunfish	10in (25cm)
L. punctatus	Spotted Sunfish	8in (20cm)
L. symmetricus	Bantam Sunfish	3½in (9cm)

NOTE:

* These two species are usually more frequently available than the others

ORANGE-SPOTTED SUNFISH (LEPOMIS HUMILIS) ▲
BLUEGILL (LEPOMIS MACROCHIRUS) ▶

SIZE: *Around 1½in (3.5cm)*

BEHAVIOR: *Timid, sometimes retiring; best kept in a tank specifically set aside for it; males become territorial at breeding time*

DIET: *Livefoods preferred, but other diets also accepted*

AQUARIUM: *Heavily planted, with hiding places, open swimming area and sandy substratum. Mature, neutral to alkaline, medium-hard water preferred. Temperature range: 46–86°F (8–30°C)*

BREEDING: *Eggs are laid among fine-leaved vegetation. Hatching takes two to three days*

RAINBOW DARTER

Etheostoma caeruleum

FAMILY: Percidae

THIS BRILLIANTLY COLORED COOL-WATER SPECIES is, like many of its closest relatives, susceptible to deteriorating water quality. It is not suitable for beginners.

DISTRIBUTION: *Great Lakes and Mississippi River basin*

SIZE: *Up to 3in (7.7cm)*

BEHAVIOR: *Bottom dweller, with high oxygen demands*

DIET: *Predominantly livefood-based*

AQUARIUM: *Well-filtered, well-oxygenated, with a gravel bottom and scattered rocks. Slightly acid to slightly alkaline, medium-hard water preferred. Temperature range: 43–59°F (6–15°C)*

BREEDING: *Challenging in aquaria. Eggs are laid over gravel in fast-flowing water*

ORANGETHROAT DARTER (ETHEOSTOMA SPECTABILE)

OTHER *ELASSOMA* SPECIES

In addition to *Elassoma evergladei*, there are five other species in the genus, all with the same basic characteristics and requirements.

SCIENTIFIC NAME	COMMON NAME(S)	SIZE
E. alabamae	Spring Pygmy Sunfish	c. 1¼in (3cm)
E. boehlkei	Carolina Pygmy Sunfish	c. 1¼in (3.2cm)
E. okatie	Blue-barred Sunfish	c. 1¼in (3.4cm)
E. okefenokee	Okefenokee Pygmy Sunfish	c. 1¼in (3.4cm)
E. zonatum	Banded Pygmy Sunfish	2in (4.7cm)

ORANGETHROAT DARTER

Etheostoma spectabile

FAMILY: Percidae

THIS IS THE MOST VARIABLE OF ALL THE DARTER species. Five of these variants are regarded as subspecies: *E. s. spectabile*, *E. s. fragi*, *E. s. pulchellum*, *E. s. squamosum* and *E. s. uniporum*. All have varying degrees of orange on the throat area and on the two dorsal fins, with variations mostly occurring in the body patterning and/or coloration. *E. s. spectabile*, for example, has a row of thin dark stripes or spots on its body (depending on where in the range a particular population or race originates), while *E. s. fragi* has oblique blue-green bands. All have the same requirements in aquaria.

DISTRIBUTION: *Lake Erie and Mississippi river basins, and Gulf drainages (U.S.A)*

SIZE: *Up to 2¾in (7.2cm)*

BEHAVIOR: *As for E. caeruleum*

DIET: *As for E. caeruleum*

AQUARIUM: *As for E. caeruleum*

BREEDING: *As for E. caeruleum*

OTHER *ETHEOSTOMA* SPECIES

Although, in total, there are some 106 *Etheostoma* species, the two featured in the accompanying entries are the only ones seen with any regularity. The keeping of darters in aquaria is best reserved for specialists. Even where winter water temperatures in unheated aquaria may be tolerated, summer temperatures will often prove too high for these species, causing stress and making death likely. An aquarium water chiller/cooler is essential for keeping these fish in certain climates.

PERCH (PERCA FLUVIATILIS)

PERCH

Perca fluviatilis

FAMILY: Percidae

THIS BEAUTIFULLY MARKED SPECIES, WHILE belonging to the same subfamily (Percinae) and family as the darters, belongs to a separate tribe, the Percini. (Darters belong to the tribe Etheostomatini). Although the Perch has considerably wider temperature tolerance than darters, it is best reserved for the specialist.

DISTRIBUTION: *Europe, but also introduced elsewhere*

SIZE: *Up to 18in (45cm), but usually smaller*

BEHAVIOR: *Shoaling predator during juvenile phase, but tends to be a loner as it matures; can be kept only with tankmates too large to swallow*

DIET: *Almost exclusively livefoods (invertebrates and fish)*

AQUARIUM: *Large, well-filtered, well-oxygenated, with ample plant cover and gravel substratum. Neutral, soft to medium-hard water preferred, but some variation tolerated. Temperature range: 46–68°F (8–20°C)*

BREEDING: *Very large setup necessary. Eggs are laid among plants or rocks and may take up to three weeks to hatch*

OTHER PERCHES

Occasionally, other perch species become available in specialist "coldwater" outlets. All are predatory and none is suitable for beginners. While all will take live fish—a factor that requires serious consideration prior to purchase—most will also accept large invertebrate livefoods such as earthworms, river shrimp, etc. All require the same basic conditions listed for *Perca fluviatilis*. Sizes given are approximate for free living specimens; aquarium specimens are likely to be smaller.

SCIENTIFIC NAME	COMMON NAME(S)	SIZE
Gymnocephalus cernuus (cernua)	Ruffe	c.12in (30cm)
Perca flavescens	Yellow Perch	16in (40cm)
Percina caprodes (3 subspecies)	Logperch	7in (18cm)
Stizostedion lucioperca	Zander	51in (130cm)
Stizostedion vitreum	Walleye	c.36in (90cm)

ZANDER (STIZOSTEDION LUCIOPERCA)

SLEEPERS AND GOBIES

Traditionally, sleepers (also referred to as sleeper gobies) and gobies have been regarded as two distinct, albeit closely related, families: Eleotridae and Gobiidae, respectively, of the suborder Gobioidei. In 1993, Hoese and Gill (see Bibliography) defined three families of Gobioidei and divided the family Gobiidae into three subfamilies; Butinae, Eleotridinae and Gobiinae. This classification therefore assigns sleepers and gobies not to separate families but to subfamilies of Gobiidae.

Nelson, 1994 (see Bibliography) considered this arrangement "uncertain," so he retained the original separation of the sleepers and gobies. Nelson's classification is followed here, but the Hoese and Gill arrangement is mentioned because it illustrates the closeness of the relationship between sleepers and gobies and because it may become more widely adopted in the future.

The feature that most distinctly separates sleepers and gobies is the pelvic fin. In gobies, the fins are united to form a sucker; in sleepers, they are generally separate, although their bases may be fused (and the degree of fusion varies widely between species). Consequently, sleepers do not possess the sucker arrangement of the gobies.

The sleepers (Eleotridae) are made up of a relatively small family of around 35 genera and 150 species. In sharp contrast to this, there are in excess of 212 genera and some 1,900 species of goby (Gobiidae). It is the family with the most marine species, and is also often the one with most freshwater species on oceanic islands. If it is decided that the sleepers should be included within the family, the Gobiidae will, almost certainly, become the largest family of fishes known, outstripping even the Cyprinidae.

MARBLED SLEEPER

Oxyleotris marmoratus

FAMILY: Eleotridae (subfamily Eleotridinae—*sensu* Hoese and Gill)
SUBFAMILY: Butinae (*sensu* Nelson)

THE MARBLED SLEEPER IS ONE OF THE VERY FEW members of its subfamily encountered in aquaria. (*Butis butis*—the highly adaptable, so-called Crazy Fish—is another occasional find). Like its relatives, Marbled Sleeper is predominantly a bottom-dwelling predator. It can grow to a large size and is not suitable for beginners.

DISTRIBUTION: *Well distributed in Southeast Asia*

SIZE: *Up to 20in (50cm), but often smaller*

BEHAVIOR: *Sedentary, nocturnal predator; can be housed only with tankmates that are too large to swallow*

DIET: *Wide range of chunky foods accepted, but livefoods preferred*

AQUARIUM: *Spacious, well-planted, with a fine-grained substratum, large hiding places and subdued lighting. Neutral, medium-hard water recommended. Temperature range: 72–82°F (22–28°C)*

BREEDING: *No documented accounts currently available*

STRIPED SLEEPER GOBY

FAT SLEEPER GOBY, SPOTTED GOBY
Dormitator maculatus

FAMILY: Eleotridae (subfamily Eleotridinae—*sensu* Hoese and Gill)
SUBFAMILY: Eleotrinae or Eleotridinae (*sensu* Nelson)

THIS IS A STURDY SPECIES, WHICH, DESPITE ITS hardy appearance, is unable to adapt fully to pure freshwater conditions. It is, however, a good candidate for brackish water setups housing similar-sized tankmates. This is not a species for beginners.

DISTRIBUTION: *Atlantic coast of tropical South America*

SIZE: *Up to 10in (25cm) reported, but usually smaller*

FEMALE STRIPED SLEEPER GOBY (DORMITATOR MACULATUS). THE MALE HAS A BIGGER HEAD AND IS MORE FULL-BODIED.

BEHAVIOR: *A territorial predator; has a tendency to dig*

DIET: *Livefoods, including fish—a factor that requires consideration prior to purchase; invertebrate livefoods also taken, as well as (though more reluctantly) deep-frozen and freeze-dried preparations*

AQUARIUM: *Spacious, with large adequately spaced out shelters, e.g. caves, and a relatively fine-grained substratum. Salt-tolerant plants must be suitably protected (see Aquarium Plants) against digging activities. Well-filtered, alkaline, hardish water, with about two teaspoonfuls of salt to every 1 Imp. gal (4.5–5 liters). Temperature range: 72–77°F (22–25°C)*

BREEDING: *Challenging in aquaria. Eggs are laid on a pre-cleaned site, e.g. stone. Hatching takes about one day*

EMPIRE GOBY (*HYPSELEOTRIS COMPRESSA*)

EMPIRE GOBY

EMPIRE GUDGEON, CARP GUDGEON

Hypseleotris compressa

FAMILY: Eleotridae (subfamily Eleotridinae—*sensu* Hoese and Gill)
SUBFAMILY: Eleotrinae or Eleotridinae (*sensu* Nelson)

FULLY MATURE MALES OF THIS SPECIES ARE spectacular, especially when in breeding colors. The Empire Goby is somewhat more flexible than many other sleepers; it is also more tolerant of tankmates, making it a better choice for mixed collections.

DISTRIBUTION: *Australia and New Guinea*

SIZE: *Up to 4¼in (11cm), but often smaller*

BEHAVIOR: *Territorial and predatory, but less so than previously featured species*

DIET: *Livefoods preferred, but deep-frozen, freeze-dried and some other diets also accepted*

AQUARIUM: *Spacious, well-planted, with an open area containing some largish, smooth-rounded or flat stones. Neutral or slightly alkaline, moderately hard water with 1 teaspoonful of salt to each 1*

OTHER *HYPSELEOTRIS* SPECIES

Although *H. compressa* is the most frequently seen member of its genus, several other (smaller) species are available on a more occasional basis. All have the same basic aquarium requirements. *Hypseleotris* and other sleepers are often referred to as gudgeons, although there is no relationship to the Gudgeon (*Gobio gobio*), see p.180, which despite its scientific name is a member of the Cyprinidae, not Gobiidae. Sizes given are approximate.

SCIENTIFIC NAME	COMMON NAME(S)	SIZE
H. aureus (aurea)	Golden Sleeper Goby/Gudgeon	2⅜in (6cm)
H. cyprinoides	Minnow Sleeper Goby/Gudgeon	1½in (4cm)
H. ejuncida	Slender Sleeper Goby/Gudgeon	2in (5cm)
H. galii	Firetail Sleeper Goby/Gudgeon	2⅜in (6cm)
H. kimberleyensis	Barnett River Sleeper Goby/Gudgeon	2in (5cm)
H. klunzingeri	Western Carp Gudgeon	1¾in (4.5cm)
H. regalis	Prince Regent Sleeper Goby/Gudgeon	2in (5cm)

Imp. gal (4.5–5 liters) is advisable, although this species will also accept freshwater conditions (carry transitions out gradually). Temperature range: 54–82°F (12–28°C)

BREEDING: *Eggs are laid on a pre-cleaned stone and protected by male. Hatching takes one day or slightly less*

PURPLE-STRIPED SLEEPER GOBY

PURPLE-SPOTTED, or NORTHERN TROUT, SLEEPER GOBY/GUDGEON

Mogurnda mogurnda

FAMILY: Eleotridae (subfamily Eleotridinae—*sensu* Hoese and Gill)
SUBFAMILY: Eleotrinae or Eleotridinae (*sensu* Nelson)

OF THE SEVERAL COMMON NAMES FOR THIS beautifully marked species, the first two

PURPLE-STRIPED SLEEPER GOBY
(*MOGURNDA MOGURNDA*)

are the most appropriate; the connection with trout embodied in the third is misleading because there is none. The slightly smaller, but equally beautiful *M. adspersa*, also known as the Purple-spotted Gudgeon, from the eastern and southeastern parts of Australia, has similar requirements, but is less frequently available.

DISTRIBUTION: *Central and north Australia, New Guinea*

SIZE: *Up to 7in (17.5cm), but often smaller*

BEHAVIOR: *Males become aggressive and territorial during breeding; less so at other times*

DIET: *Livefoods preferred, but other diets accepted*

AQUARIUM: *Sufficiently spacious and planted, with open area, and with strategically placed caves or shelters around which several males can establish territories. Neutral to slightly alkaline, hardish water preferred. Temperature range: 72–86°F (22–30°C)*

BREEDING: *Eggs are laid in caves or on flat surfaces (including bogwood, or even the aquarium panes) and are guarded by male. Hatching can take five to nine days*

PEACOCK GOBY
PEACOCK GUDGEON

Tateurndina ocellicauda

FAMILY: Eleotridae (subfamily Eleotridinae—*sensu* Hoese and Gill)
SUBFAMILY: Eleotrinae or Eleotridinae (*sensu* Nelson)

THIS SPECIES, THE MOST COLORFUL OF ALL THE sleeper gobies, achieved great popularity during the mid-1980s and the 1990s. It has now been widely bred in captivity and is one of the most often seen eleotrids.

DISTRIBUTION: *New Guinea*

SIZE: *Up to 3in (7.5cm) reported, but usually smaller*

BEHAVIOR: *Peaceful; should not be kept with boisterous tankmates*

DIET: *Livefoods preferred, but a range of other diets accepted*

AQUARIUM: *Well-planted, with a number of hiding places or caves. Softish, slightly acid or neutral water preferred, though some deviation tolerated if adjustments are carried out gradually. Temperature range: 72–81°F (22–27°C)*

BREEDING: *Eggs are laid on the roof of cave or other hiding place (although spawning in the open also occurs). The eggs are guarded by male. Hatching takes about seven days*

BUMBLEBEE GOBY
GOLD-BANDED GOBY

Brachygobius nunus

SYNONYMS: *See* below
FAMILY: Gobiidae
SUBFAMILY: Gobiinae

THE GENUS *BRACHYGOBIUS* IS CLEARLY IN GREAT need of closer study, for several similar-looking species appear under a number of (often disputed) names. *B. nunus*, for example, is regarded by some as synonymous with *B. doriae*, while some doubt the validity of the most frequently encountered name, *B. xanthozona*. In addition, there is *B. aggregatus*. All species have the same basic requirements and characteristics.

DISTRIBUTION: *Southeast Asia*

SIZE: *Around 1¾in (4.5cm), but often smaller*

BEHAVIOR: *Peaceful and retiring toward other tankmates (which must be neither large nor boisterous), but territorial toward conspecifics*

◀ BUMBLEBEE GOBY (BRACHYGOBIUS NUNUS)
▼ PEACOCK GOBY (TATEURNDINA OCELLICAUDA)

DIET: *Livefoods preferred, but deep-frozen and (sometimes) waterlogged freeze-dried formulations may be accepted*

AQUARIUM: *Smallish, well-planted, with several small caves or snail shells. Hard, alkaline water with as much as one tablespoonful of salt per 1 Imp. gal (4.5–5 liters) preferred. Temperature range: 75–86°F (24–30°C)*

BREEDING: *Eggs are laid in caves or snail shells and are guarded by male. Hatching takes about four days*

KNIGHT GOBY

Stigmatogobius sadanundio

FAMILY: Gobiidae
SUBFAMILY: Gobionellinae

THIS IMPRESSIVE, STURDY LOOKING FISH IS regularly available. It can adapt to freshwater (it is often found in such habitats in the wild), but in aquaria it appears not to fare so well in the absence of salt.

DISTRIBUTION: *Indonesia and Philippines*

SIZE: *Up to 3½in (8.5cm)*

BEHAVIOR: *Males are territorial, especially toward their own species and (somewhat less so) toward other bottom-dwelling tankmates*

DIET: *Livefoods preferred, but deep-frozen, freeze-dried and other formulations may also be accepted; algal supplement recommended*

AQUARIUM: *Well-planted (with salt-tolerant species), and with a fine-grained substratum and several caves or shelters. Well-filtered, hard, alkaline water with one teaspoonful of salt per 1 Imp. gal (4.5–5 liters). Soft water must be avoided. Temperature range: 68–79°F (20–26°C)*

BREEDING: *Eggs are laid on roof of cave, and both they and the fry are protected by both parents*

BLOTCHED MUDSKIPPER

Periophthalmus barbarus

FAMILY: Gobiidae
SUBFAMILY: Oxudercinae

MUDSKIPPERS ARE FASCINATING FISH THAT LIVE in burrows on mangrove flats and spend a great deal of time out of water grazing the mud surface for microalgae and other tiny organisms. All species can prove challenging to keep and are not suitable for beginners. Male Blotched Mudskippers have spectacularly colored dorsal fins which they flick open and shut during displays. Two other species are also occasionally available: *P. papilio* (Butterfly Mudskipper) and *P. vulgaris* (Blue Flagfin); both have similar characteristics and requirements to *P. barbarus*.

DISTRIBUTION: *Widespread in estuaries in Africa, Red Sea, Madagascar, Southeast Asia, and Australia*

SIZE: *Up to 6in (15cm)*

BEHAVIOR: *Territorial; needs an exposed area on to which it can climb*

DIET: *Livefoods taken, especially from the surface of exposed substrates*

AQUARIUM: *Spacious, covered, with reduced water level and an exposed "beach" area or rocks and/or bogwood. Hard, alkaline water with a teaspoonful of salt per 1 Imp. gal (4.5–5 liters) is necessary. Ensure that a high level of humidity is maintained above the water surface. Temperature range: 77–86°F (25–30°C)*

BREEDING: *No documented accounts currently available*

EMERALD RIVER GOBY

Stiphodon elegans

FAMILY: Gobiidae
SUBFAMILY: Sicydiinae

THIS IS ONE OF THE MORE RECENT SPECIES OF goby to appear in the hobby. The lightish colored body has a few irregular dark bands extending from snout to tail, but fully mature males develop the shiny emerald coloration indicated by the name.

DISTRIBUTION: *Southeast Asia*

SIZE: *Around 1¾in (4.5cm)*

BEHAVIOR: *Active, but peaceful*

DIET: *Livefoods preferred, but other diets, including algae, accepted*

AQUARIUM: *Well-filtered, planted, with fine-grained substratum, some pebbles, and a water current (e.g. as produced by a powerhead outlet). Neutral, medium-hard water preferred, but some deviation (though not extreme) tolerated. Temperature range: 75–81°F (24–27°C)*

BREEDING: *Challenging, but achievable, in aquaria. However, no documented accounts currently available*

KNIGHT GOBY (STIGMATOGOBIUS SADANUNDIO)

KILLIFISHES

Although some killifishes have been known to aquarists for around 100 years, debate still continues regarding the overall classification of the group. Old classifications tended to lump all species within a single family, the Cyprinodontidae. With the acquisition of new information, various classifications have been put forward, all of them resulting in the splitting of the Cyprinodontidae into new families.

One of the most influential of these revisions was that of Lynne Parenti (1981—see Bibliography), which is largely adopted by Nelson (1994)—the classification that is being followed in this book. Nelson, however, does not adopt the Parenti classification with regard to the Old World Rivulines (to which he affords the status of subfamily: Aplochelinae) and the

New World Rivulines (which he regards as the subfamily Rivulinae); Parenti lists these as families. For comparison, both the Parenti and Nelson interpretations are indicated in the pages that follow.

Whatever their scientific "status," killifish are fascinating aquarium fish, which should be kept by every experienced aquarist at one time or other. Some species are annual, surviving for just one season, during which they lay eggs that survive buried in the dried-up substratum of the pond or ditch until the next rains arrive. Others live for several years and spawn among plants. Some species are highly territorial and aggressive; some are spectacularly colored. Some are extremely demanding in their aquarium requirements, while others are hardy.

LYRETAIL

CAPE LOPEZ LYRETAIL,
LYRETAILED PANCHAX

Aphyosemion australe

FAMILY: Aplocheilidae (*sensu* Parenti and Nelson)
SUBFAMILY: Aplocheilinae (*sensu* Nelson)

LYRETAIL (APHYOSEMION AUSTRALE)

THIS SPLENDID FISH first made its appearance in the hobby around 1913. It is one of the longer-lived killies, with a lifespan of around three years being common. Only mature males exhibit the characteristic lyretail. Several naturally occurring color forms, as well as some cultivated ones, are available.

DISTRIBUTION: *Western Africa, including Gabon, Cameroon and southern Congo (Zaire)*

SIZE: *Males around 2¹⁄₂in (6cm); females smaller*

BEHAVIOR: *Peaceful; should not be kept with boisterous tankmates*

DIET: *Livefoods preferred, but will accept other diets*

AQUARIUM: *"Quiet," heavily planted, with subdued lighting, dark substratum (incorporating some peat) and tannin-stained water (see Aquarium Setup). Soft, acid water important. Temperature range: 64–75°F (18–24°C); avoid prolonged exposure to the lower temperature*

BREEDING: *Eggs are scattered among fine-leaved vegetation or a spawning mop (strands of non-toxic wool attached to a cork that is floated on the water surface). Hatching takes about two weeks*

RED-SEAM KILLIFISH

BANNER LYRETAIL

Aphyosemion calliurum

FAMILY: Aplocheilidae (*sensu* Parenti and Nelson)
SUBFAMILY: Aplocheilinae (*sensu* Nelson)

THIS IS A STUMPIER SPECIES THAN *A. AUSTRALE*, lacking long extensions to the tail. Several naturally occurring color forms are known.

DISTRIBUTION: *West Africa, including Cameroon and Niger Delta*

SIZE: *Males around 1³⁄₄in (4.5cm); females smaller*

BEHAVIOR: *Quarrelsome and territorial toward rivals*

DIET: *As for A. australe*

AQUARIUM: *As for A. australe. Temperature range: 72–79°F (22–26°C); water may be slightly more alkaline and harder*

BREEDING: *As for A. australe*

BLUE KILLIFISH

PLUMED KILLIFISH

Aphyosemion filamentosum

SYNONYM: *Fundulopanchax filamentosum*

FAMILY: Aplocheilidae (*sensu* Parenti and Nelson)
SUBFAMILY: Aplocheilinae (*sensu* Nelson)

THE MALES OF SOME POPULATIONS OF THIS SPECIES, e.g. Southern Togo, possess a great deal of blue on their bodies, hence one of the common names. Confusingly, some other populations from this region are orange-red. Most populations from other locations contain varying amounts of blue, orange-red and reddish brown.

DISTRIBUTION: *Western Africa; mainly Togo, southern Benin and western Nigeria*

SIZE: *Around 2¼in (5.5cm) for males; females smaller*

BEHAVIOR: *Territorial during breeding; generally peaceful at other times*

DIET: *As for A. australe*

AQUARIUM: *As for A. australe but more adaptable in terms of water chemistry. Temperature range: 72–77°F (22–25°C)*

BREEDING: *Lowered water level, subdued lighting and a thick layer of peat on the bottom are necessary. One male and several females should be introduced. Eggs are buried in the peat. After spawning, the peat should be removed, gently squeezed to eliminate excess moisture and stored, e.g. in a small polythene bag or tub, at a moderate temperature (around 72°F/22°C) for about three months, ensuring that the peat does not dry out at any time. After this resting period (diapause) the eggs need to be covered with aquarium water. Hatching will occur over a number of days. (For fuller details on killifish breeding of this type, consult specialist literature—see Bibliography—and/or killifish specialist societies)*

STEEL-BLUE KILLIFISH
GARDNER'S KILLIFISH
Aphyosemion gardneri

SYNONYM: *Fundulopanchax gardneri*
FAMILY: Aplocheilidae (*sensu* Parenti and Nelson)
SUBFAMILY: Aplocheilinae (*sensu* Nelson)

THIS HUGELY VARIABLE SPECIES IS SPLIT INTO A number of subspecies. Even these subspecies exhibit variation, and some have their own common names, e.g. *A. g. gardneri* (Gardner's Killifish), *A. g. lacustre* (Ejagham Killifish), *A. g. mamfense* (Mamfe Killifish), *A. g. nigerianum* (Nigerian Killifish).

DISTRIBUTION: *West Africa, including western Cameroon and Nigeria*

SIZE: *Males around 2⅜in (6cm); females smaller*

BLUE KILLIFISH (APHYOSEMION FILAMENTOSUM)

OTHER *APHYOSEMION* SPECIES

There are about 115 species and subspecies of *Aphyosemion*, some of which are regarded by some authors as belonging to the genus *Fundulopanchax*. In addition, there are numerous naturally occurring variants, plus a number of cultivated varieties. The range of choice within the genus is therefore extremely wide, and availability may vary quite significantly from time to time and country to country. The small selection of species that are featured here have been chosen to illustrate some of the main aquarium requirements and characteristics of the genus. For detailed information on individual species, consult specialist literature (*see* Bibliography). Membership of a killifish society should be seriously considered by anyone wishing to keep these delightful but challenging fishes.

BEHAVIOR: *Males intolerant of each other and may be aggressive toward other tankmates*

DIET: *As for A. australe*

AQUARIUM: *As for A. australe. Temperature range: 72–77°F (22–25°C)*

BREEDING: *As for A. australe. Alternatively, the eggs may be removed and treated as for A. filamentosum for 28–30 days*

RED APHYOSEMION
GOLDEN PHEASANT, BLUE GULARIS
Aphyosemion sjoestedti

SYNONYM: *Fundulopanchax sjoestedti*
FAMILY: Aplocheilidae (*sensu* Parenti and Nelson)
SUBFAMILY: Aplocheilinae (*sensu* Nelson)

THIS IS ANOTHER VARIABLE SPECIES, BUT ONE THAT is not split into subspecies. While possessing some blue (as indicated by one of the common names), most forms of *A. sjoestedti* exhibit attractive red patches and stripes.

DISTRIBUTION: *West Africa, including southern Nigeria, western Cameroon and Ghana*

SIZE: *Males up to 4¾in (12cm); females somewhat smaller*

BEHAVIOR: *Active and generally aggressive, particularly toward conspecifics*

DIET: *Predominantly livefoods, including small fish—a factor that needs consideration prior to purchase; some other diets may also be accepted*

AQUARIUM: *Spacious setup, basically as for A. australe. Temperature range: 73–79°F (23–26°C)*

BREEDING: *As for A. filamentosum. Store eggs for four to six weeks at 64–68°F (18–20°C)*

CLOWN KILLIFISH
COMET, or ROCKET, PANCHAX
Aplocheilus (Pseudepiplatys) annulatus

SYNONYMS: *Epiplatys annulatus, Pseudepiplatys annulatus*
FAMILY: Aplocheilidae (*sensu* Parenti and Nelson)
SUBFAMILY: Aplocheilinae (*sensu* Nelson)

TRADITIONALLY, THE CLOWN KILLIFISH AND ITS closest relatives have been classified as *Epiplatys*. In 1990, following an earlier paper on the subject, Scheel (*see* Bibliography)

CLOWN KILLIFISH
(APLOCHEILUS (PSEUDEPIPLATYS) ANNULATUS)

placed *Epiplatys* within *Aplocheilus*. Owing to distinct body patterning and unique caudal fin color distribution, along with some skeletal and behavioral differences, Scheel also regarded *A. annulatus* to be in a sufficiently "isolated position in *Aplocheilus*" to warrant its own subgenus, *Pseudepiplatys* (considered as a valid genus by some earlier authors). Scheel's classification is being followed for all *Epiplatys* species in this book, with the alternative names acknowledged.

DISTRIBUTION: *West Africa, including Guinea, Liberia and Sierra Leone*

SIZE: *Up to 1⅛in (4cm), but often smaller*

BEHAVIOR: *Peaceful surface swimmer; must not be housed with larger, boisterous tankmates*

DIET: *Livefoods preferred, but other formulations may be accepted*

AQUARIUM: *Well-planted, with some floating plants, peat substratum and subdued lighting. Softish, slightly acid water preferred. Temperature range: 73–79°F (23–26°C)*

BREEDING: *Eggs are laid among fine-leaved vegetation and are ignored by the spawners (a spawning mop—see Aphyosemion australe, p.262—will also be acceptable). Hatching takes about eight to ten days*

CHAPER'S PANCHAX

Aplocheilus chaperi

SYNONYM: *Epiplatys chaperi*
FAMILY: Aplocheilidae (*sensu* Parenti and Nelson)
SUBFAMILY: Aplocheilinae (*sensu* Nelson)

TWO SUBSPECIES OF *A. CHAPERI* ARE KNOWN: Chaper's Panchax (*A. c. chaperi*) and Schreiber's Panchax (*A. c. schreiberi*). Both have varying numbers of backward-slanting, narrow, oblique dark bands that are more pronounced in females than in males. The body is somewhat sturdier than in *A. annulatus*, and the caudal fin lacks the central fin-ray extensions.

DISTRIBUTION: *Western Africa: Ghana and Ivory Coast*

SIZE: *Up to 2¾in (7cm)*

BEHAVIOR: *Peaceful, though not quite as retiring as A. annulatus*

DIET: As for *A. annulatus*

AQUARIUM: As for *A. annulatus. Temperature range: 72–82°F (22–28°C)*

BREEDING: As for *A. annulatus*

BLUE PANCHAX

Aplocheilus panchax

FAMILY: Aplocheilidae (*sensu* Parenti and Nelson)
SUBFAMILY: Aplocheilinae (*sensu* Nelson)

THE BLUE PANCHAX IS ONE OF THE EARLIEST SPECIES imported into Europe (1899). Despite this, it has never become as widespread within the hobby as its undoubted beauty deserves.

DISTRIBUTION: *Southeast Asia*

SIZE: *Up to 3in (8cm)*

BEHAVIOR: *Relatively peaceful surface swimmer, although very small fry may be regarded as food; males somewhat aggressive toward each other*

DIET: *Livefoods preferred, but other diets also accepted*

AQUARIUM: *Well-covered, spacious, with some floating plants, dense plant shelter around edges and back, and some open swimming spaces along the front. Subdued lighting also advisable, as are bogwood and other types of shelter. Water chemistry not critical, but quality must be good. Temperature range: 68–77°F (20–25°C)*

BREEDING: *Eggs are laid among fine-leaved vegetation or spawning mops (see Aphyosemion australe, p.262) over a period of days. Hatching takes up to two weeks*

PLAYFAIR'S PANCHAX

Aplocheilus (Pachypanchax) playfairi

SYNONYM: *Pachypanchax playfairii*
FAMILY: Aplocheilidae (*sensu* Parenti and Nelson)
SUBFAMILY: Aplocheilinae (*sensu* Nelson)

PLAYFAIR'S PANCHAX WAS SUBSUMED WITHIN THE genus *Aplocheilus* by Scheel (*see* Bibliography) who nevertheless regarded it as sufficiently different to retain subgeneric, i.e. (*Pachypanchax*) status.

DISTRIBUTION: *Madagascar, Seychelles and Zanzibar*

SIZE: *Males around 4in (10cm); females smaller*

BEHAVIOR: *Aggressive and territorial toward conspecifics; preys on small fish, but may be kept with similar-sized tankmates*

DIET: *Livefoods preferred, but other diets also accepted*

AQUARIUM: *As for A. panchax, but water slightly acid to neutral and soft to medium-hard. Temperature range: 72–77°F (22–25°C)*

BREEDING: As for *A. panchax*

▲ CHAPER'S PANCHAX (APLOCHEILUS CHAPERI)

▼ BLUE PANCHAX (APLOCHEILUS PANCHAX)

SIX-BARRED PANCHAX (APLOCHEILUS SEXFASCIATUS)

SIX-BARRED PANCHAX
SIX-BARRED EPIPLATYS
Aplocheilus sexfasciatus

SYNONYM: *Epiplatys sexfasciatus*
FAMILY: Aplocheilidae (*sensu* Parenti and Nelson)
SUBFAMILY: Aplocheilinae (*sensu* Nelson)

THIS SPECIES HAS SIMILAR OBLIQUE BODY BANDS TO *A. chaperi*. It is also extremely variable, both in color and body patterning, with five sub-species, each exhibiting variability depending on location.

DISTRIBUTION: *Western Africa, including Togo, Gabon, Cameroon and (at least) Taylor Creek in Nigeria*

SIZE: *Around 3in (8cm), but up to 4¼in (11cm) reported*

BEHAVIOR: *A surface-living species that may prey on very small fish*

DIET: As for A. annulatus

AQUARIUM: As for A. annulatus. *Temperature range: 72–82°F (22–28°C)*

BREEDING: As for A. annulatus

GÜNTHER'S NOTHOBRANCH
Nothobranchius guentheri

FAMILY: Aplocheilidae (*sensu* Parenti and Nelson)
SUBFAMILY: Aplocheilinae (*sensu* Nelson)

THIS COLORFUL ANNUAL SPECIES, IN THE HOBBY since the mid-1910s, is one of the best-known representatives of its genus. *Notho-branchius* are highly variable, thus often causing confusion with regard to precise identification. Some aquarium strains are also known. Like many other killifishes, it is only occasionally available in general aquatic outlets.

DISTRIBUTION: *Island of Zanzibar, but also reported from the Tanzanian mainland*

SIZE: *Around 2in (5cm), but larger sizes sometimes quoted*

BEHAVIOR: *Males aggressive toward each other*

DIET: *Livefoods preferred, but other diets may be accepted*

AQUARIUM: *This species is best kept in a tank set aside specifically for it and in groups of one male and several females. To keep several males, the aquarium must be large enough to accommodate non-overlapping territories. Provide several shelters and some open swimming spaces surrounded by vegetation and a dark, soft*

OTHER *APLOCHEILUS* SPECIES

Aplocheilus (*sensu* Scheel, and thus including the species traditionally listed as *Epiplatys*, *Pseudepiplatys* and *Pachypanchax*) contains over 40 species, many of which are only infrequently seen outside specialist shops and killifish societies. As with *Aphyosemion*, aquarists wishing to keep these species should consult specialist literature (*see* Bibliography) and consider joining a specialist killifish society. Generally speaking, species listed elsewhere as *Epiplatys* or *Pseudepiplatys* have similar overall requirements and characteristics to those indicated in the accompanying entries for *Aplocheilus* (*Pseudepiplatys*) *annulatus*. For species listed elsewhere as *Pachypanchax*, the guidelines given here for *Aplocheilus* (*Pachypanchax*) *playfairi* generally apply.

substratum (peat is ideal). Soft, slightly acid water preferred. Temperature range: 72–79°F (22–26°C)

BREEDING: *Eggs are buried in the substratum. Treat these as for A. filamentosum for three to four months before resoaking. Adults die at the end of breeding season*

KORTHAUS' NOTHOBRANCH
MAFIA NOTHOBRANCH
Nothobranchius korthausae

FAMILY: Aplocheilidae (*sensu* Parenti and Nelson)
SUBFAMILY: Aplocheilinae (*sensu* Nelson)

SEVERAL COLOR FORMS OF THIS SPECIES ARE known, including one with a deep-red fin. There is a second red morph, in which the body is blue, plus two brown morphs that differ from each other in the intensity and distribution of the brown coloration, as well as in the yellow and black patterning (particularly) on the caudal fin.

DISTRIBUTION: *Mafia Island in Tanzania*

SIZE: *Around 1¾in (4.5cm), but up to 2½in (6cm) reported*

BEHAVIOR: As for N. guentheri

DIET: As for N. guentheri

AQUARIUM: As for N. guentheri. *Temperature range: 73–79°F (23–26°C)*

BREEDING: As for N. guentheri

KORTHAUS' NOTHOBRANCH
(NOTHOBRANCHIUS KORTHAUSAE)

PALMQVIST'S NOTHOBRANCH (NOTHOBRANCHIUS PALMQVISTI)

PALMQVIST'S NOTHOBRANCH

Nothobranchius palmqvisti

FAMILY: Aplocheilidae (*sensu* Parenti and Nelson)
SUBFAMILY: Aplocheilinae (*sensu* Nelson)

THIS IS ONE OF SEVERAL SPECIES IN WHICH THE caudal fin is blood-red throughout. As in so many other *Nothobranchius* species, the body coloration shows variation, depending on locality of origin.

DISTRIBUTION: *Coastal regions of southern Kenya and Tanzania*

SIZE: *Up to 2in (5cm)*

BEHAVIOR: *Males are particularly aggressive toward each other*

DIET: *Sometimes very reluctant to accept non-livefoods*

AQUARIUM: *As for* N. guentheri

BREEDING: *As for* N. guentheri

OTHER *NOTHOBRANCHIUS* SPECIES

Some 50 species and subspecies, plus a few hybrids, of *Nothobranchius* are known. The males of all the various types are beautifully colored. When kept in appropriate conditions (as described for *N. guentheri*), they hold their fins erect for much of the time, which makes for a dazzling display despite their relatively small size. One of the main reasons that *Nothobranchius* killifishes are not more widely available is that they are annual and therefore die at the end of the breeding season. It often takes eight to twelve weeks for males to develop their full coloration (females are generally drab-colored), which means that by the time such fish can be sold most are already about one quarter through their average lifespan. Owing to their long diapause and tough, resistant outer layers, *Nothobranchius* eggs are often exchanged between killie enthusiasts at club meetings or even by post. These hobbyists are among the best sources of supply, particularly of the less-frequently encountered species. Aquarists contemplating keeping *Nothobranchius* killifish would therefore be well-advised to seek membership of a killifish society.

RACHOW'S NOTHOBRANCH

Nothobranchius rachovii

FAMILY: Aplocheilidae (*sensu* Parenti and Nelson)
SUBFAMILY: Aplocheilinae (*sensu* Nelson)

SEVERAL COLOR FORMS ARE KNOWN TO EXIST IN the wild, along with a few aquarium-bred forms. Scheel (*see* Bibliography) states that the chromosomes of this species are the most specialized in the genus and that males from the northern parts of the range are the most colorful.

DISTRIBUTION: *From Quelimane (southern Mozambique) southward to northern parts of Krüger National Park (Republic of South Africa)*

SIZE: *Around 2in (5cm)*

BEHAVIOR: *Generally less aggressive than some other* Nothobranchius

DIET: *As for* N. guentheri

AQUARIUM: *As for* N. guentheri

BREEDING: *As for* N. guentheri

ARGENTINE PEARL

Cynolebias bellotti (but see box, opposite)

FAMILY: Aplocheilidae (*sensu* Nelson); Rivulidae (*sensu* Parenti)
SUBFAMILY: Rivulinae (*sensu* Nelson)

MIRRORING THE LIFESTYLE OF ITS OLD WORLD relatives belonging to the genus *Nothobranchius*, the Argentine Pearl and other *Cynolebias* species are annual fishes. Their reproductive behavior is virtually identical.

ARGENTINE PEARL (CYNOLEBIAS BELLOTTI)

BLACK-FINNED ARGENTINE PEARL (CYNOLEBIAS NIGRIPINNIS)

WHITE'S PEARL (CYNOLEBIAS WHITEI)

The Argentine Pearl was among the first New World killifish to be introduced into the hobby almost 100 years ago.

DISTRIBUTION: *Rio de la Plata basin (Argentina)*

SIZE: *Males up to 2¾in (7cm); females smaller*

BEHAVIOR: *Males, in particular, are active and sometimes aggressive*

DIET: *Livefoods preferred, but other diets also accepted*

AQUARIUM: *Single-species aquarium, with peat substratum and some clumps of vegetation as cover for females. Soft, slightly acid, good-quality water important. Temperature range: 59–72°F (15–22°C); extremely low temperatures, e.g. 39°F (4°C), and high temperatures, e.g. 86°F (30°C), will be temporarily tolerated*

BREEDING: *Use one male to two or three females. Eggs are buried in the peat, which should then be squeezed gently to remove excess water and stored in a small polythene bag or tub (in the dark) for three to four months, ensuring that the peat remains moist. When the eggs are then resoaked in aquarium water they will begin hatching, sometimes within hours. Females must be removed immediately after spawning, since they will be harassed by the male, which is able to spawn again straightaway*

BLACK-FINNED ARGENTINE PEARL
DWARF ARGENTINE PEARL

Cynolebias nigripinnis

FAMILY: Aplocheilidae (*sensu* Nelson); Rivulidae (*sensu* Parenti)
SUBFAMILY: Rivulinae (*sensu* Nelson)

MANY AUTHORS RECOGNIZE TWO SUBSPECIES OF *C. nigripinnis*: *C. n. nigripinnis* (Black-finned, or Dwarf, Argentine Pearl) and *C. n. alexandri* (Entre Rio Argentine Pearl). Others (perhaps a majority) consider each a valid species in its own right. While being overall similar to each other, *C. n. alexandri* males have brownish, almost vertical bands on the body; *C. n. nigripinnis* lacks these bands but has the characteristic black fins indicated in both the scientific and common names.

DISTRIBUTION: *Argentina. C. n. alexandri: Entre Rio Province (near Gualeguaychu); C. n. nigripinnis: Paraná (near Rosario de Santa Fe)*

SIZE: *Males up to 2in (5cm); females smaller*

BEHAVIOR: *Similar to C. bellotti*

DIET: *As for C. bellotti*

AQUARIUM: *As for C. bellotti. Temperature range: 64–77°F (18–25°C) recommended, but slightly higher and lower temperatures tolerated. C. n. alexandri prefers the higher end of the temperature scale*

BREEDING: *As for C. bellotti*

WHITE'S PEARL

Cynolebias whitei

FAMILY: Aplocheilidae (*sensu* Nelson); Rivulidae (*sensu* Parenti)
SUBFAMILY: Rivulinae (*sensu* Nelson)

AS IN THE OTHER SPECIES FEATURED, THE BODY IN male *C. whitei* is spangled with numerous white/cream/bluish "pearls." Males also exhibit a brownish base body color and elongated dorsal and anal fins. An aquarium-bred albino form is occasionally available.

DISTRIBUTION: *Near Rio de Janeiro (Brazil)*

SIZE: *Males up to 3in (8cm); females smaller*

BEHAVIOR: *As for C. bellotti*

OTHER *CYNOLEBIAS* SPECIES

The genus *Cynolebias* contains around 35 species. In addition to the ones featured here, only a few others are seen with any regularity. While availability will vary according to season and from country to country, the most frequently encountered of these other species are probably: *C. adloffi* (Banded Pearl), *C. boitonei* (Brazilian Pearl/Lyretail), *C. constanciae* (Featherfin Pearl), *C. dolichopterus* (Sicklefin Pearl), and *C. melanotaenia* (Fighting Gaucho). Some of the best sources of these and other *Cynolebias* species are members of killifish societies, although some of the more specialized retail outlets will also stock *Cynolebias*. The eggs of *C. melanotaenia* and *C. brucei* (Turner's Gaucho) are fertilized internally and then released. All *Cynolebias* species have similar aquarium requirements, with temperatures around 72–75°F (22–24°C) being generally acceptable. However, seek specialist advice for individual species. *Cynolebias* can be classified as *Austrolebias*, *Nematolebias* or *Simpsonichthys* by some authors

FIGHTING GAUCHO (CYNOLEBIAS MELANOTAENIA)

DIET: *Livefoods preferred; dried food accepted only reluctantly*

AQUARIUM: *As for* C. bellotti. *Temperature range: 68–73°F (20–23°C)*

Breeding: *As for* C. bellotti

LACE-FINNED KILLIFISH

Pterolebias zonatus

FAMILY: Aplocheilidae (*sensu* Nelson); Rivulidae (*sensu* Parenti)
SUBFAMILY: Rivulinae (*sensu* Nelson)

THIS IS A TRULY MAGNIFICENT SPECIES, WITH brownish speckling.and body bands on a light metallic blue base color. Fully mature males have an almost sail-like anal fin and substantial caudal fin. Of the other four species in the genus, *P. longipinnis* (Long-finned Killifish) is the most frequently encountered; it has similar requirements to Lace-finned Killifish.

DISTRIBUTION: *Venezuela*

SIZE: *Up to 6in (15cm) reported, but usually much smaller*

BEHAVIOR: *Males are aggressive toward each other; less so as they age*

DIET: *Predominantly livefoods; other diets usually accepted only with reluctance*

AQUARIUM: *As for* C. bellotti. *Temperature range: 64–73°F (18–23°C)*

BREEDING: *As for* C. bellotti

MAGDALENA SPOT-FINNED KILLIE

Rachovia brevis

FAMILY: Aplocheilidae (*sensu* Nelson): Rivulidae (*sensu* Parenti)
SUBFAMILY: Rivulinae (*sensu* Nelson)

OF THE SIX SPECIES IN THE GENUS (ALL ANNUALS), *R. brevis* is generally most available. Both males and females of this sturdy-looking species are attractively, though not spectacularly, colored.

DISTRIBUTION: *Colombia (largely, on coastal plains)*

SIZE: *Males around 3in (7.5cm); females slightly smaller*

BEHAVIOR: *Generally peaceful toward other fish, but males somewhat aggressive toward each other*

DIET: *Livefoods preferred, but other formulations—primarily deep-frozen and fresh—accepted*

AQUARIUM: *As for* C. bellotti. *Temperature range: around 77–81°F (25–27°C)*

BREEDING: *As for* C. bellotti. *Store eggs for about six weeks*

GREEN RIVULUS

BROWN, or CUBAN, RIVULUS

Rivulus cylindraceus

FAMILY: Aplocheilidae (*sensu* Nelson): Rivulidae (*sensu* Parenti)
SUBFAMILY: Rivulinae (*sensu* Nelson)

UNLIKE SOME OF THE OTHER MEMBERS OF THE family, *Rivulus* species do not bury their eggs. If pools dry out in the wild, the eggs of some species may withstand desiccation for a while—but do not go into the extended diapause exhibited by annual species. *Rivulus* species tend to live for 18 months or more, with Green Rivulus having a lifespan of up to four years.

DISTRIBUTION: *Cuba (in mountain streams)*

SIZE: *Around 2¼in (5.5cm)*

BEHAVIOR: *Generally peaceful, though active; exhibits good jumping ability*

DIET: *Predominantly livefoods, but other diets also accepted*

AQUARIUM: *Well-covered, with dark substratum, some clumps of fine-leaved vegetation, and subdued lighting. Water chemistry not critical, but neutral, medium-hard water preferred. Temperature range: 22–24°C (72–77°F) with some deviation either side*

BREEDING: *Use a trio of one male and two females. Eggs are laid, mainly, on fine-leaved vegetation or spawning mop (see Aphyosemion australe, p.262); spawning may occur on top of the mop, and the exposed eggs may survive exposure for a week or more. Hatching of submerged eggs takes 12–14 days*

▲ LACE-FINNED KILLIFISH (PTEROLEBIAS ZONATUS)　　▼ GREEN RIVULUS (RIVULUS CYLINDRACEUS)

BAR-TAILED RIVULUS

Rivulus magdalenae

FAMILY: Aplocheilidae (*sensu* Nelson): Rivulidae (*sensu* Parenti)

SUBFAMILY: Rivulinae (*sensu* Nelson)

BAR-TAILED RIVULUS IS ONE OF THE FIVE LARGEST species in the genus (the largest, *R. igneus*—Firebelly Rivulus—can attain 6in/15cm). While coloration will vary, depending on location, the body is always covered in numerous small reddish-brown spots and there is a distinct light-colored posterior edge to the caudal fin. The lifespan of this species is around two-and-a-half years.

DISTRIBUTION: *Colombia: Magdalena river basin, Caqueta tributaries, and (possibly) Cauca river basin*

SIZE: *Males up to 3½in (9cm); females smaller*

BEHAVIOR: *As for R. cylindraceus*

DIET: *As for R. cylindraceus*

AQUARIUM: *As for R. cylindraceus*

BREEDING: *Basically, as for R. cylindraceus. Hatching may take up to 35 days*

BLUE-STRIPED RIVULUS

BAND-TAILED RIVULUS

Rivulus xiphidius

FAMILY: Aplocheilidae (*sensu* Nelson): Rivulidae (*sensu* Parenti)

SUBFAMILY: Rivulinae (*sensu* Nelson)

THIS IS PROBABLY THE MOST SPECTACULARLY colored of all the *Rivulus* species. It is also one of the smallest and more challenging members of the genus—not a fish for beginners. It has a lifespan of about two-and-a-half years.

DISTRIBUTION: *French Guyana (forest springs); Amazon region (Brazil); also (possibly) Suriname, although the species found here may be R. frenatus*

SIZE: *Up to 1¾in (4.5cm), but often smaller*

BEHAVIOR: *Retiring, placid, with good jumping ability*

DIET: *Almost exclusively livefoods*

AQUARIUM: *Well covered, with subdued lighting and some plant thickets. Soft, slightly acid water important. Temperature range: 72–79°F (22–25°C)*

BREEDING: *Challenging in aquaria, but, basically, as for R. cylindraceus. Hatching takes around 14 days*

GOLDEN TOP MINNOW

GOLDEN-EARED KILLIFISH

Fundulus chrysotus

FAMILY: Fundulidae (*sensu* Nelson and Parenti)

THIS SPECIES HAS A CHARACTERISTIC GOLDEN patch on the gill cover, directly behind the

OTHER *RIVULUS* SPECIES

There are about 110 species in the genus *Rivulus* (defined in its broadest sense, i.e. including Parenti's "Rivulus"—*see* Bibliography). Few, however, are kept regularly in aquaria, more through lack of availability than difficulty of upkeep. A few species, e.g., *R. stellifer* (Stellate Rivulus) and *R. compactus* may be annual species that bury their eggs, as in *Nothobranchius* and *Cynolebias*; all others are longer-lived (average lifespan around three years). *R. urophthalmus* (The Golden Rivulus) may live for more than five years. Another long-lived species, *R. ocellatus* (Ocellate Rivulus)—traditionally referred to as *R. marmoratus*—is famous for being a hermaphrodite. While most species of *Rivulus* may be kept and bred following the general guidelines outlined for *R. cylindraceus*, detailed information should be sought from specialist literature (*see* Bibliography) and/or via membership of a killifish society.

BLUE-STRIPED RIVULUS (RIVULUS XIPHIDIUS)

eyes, hence its common names. In males, the greenish body is liberally covered in small reddish-brown spots; females are drabber but have numerous glistening light-colored spots.

DISTRIBUTION: *Gulf Coast plain of North America, including South Carolina and Florida and westward to the Trinity River drainage in Texas*

SIZE: *Up to 3in (7.5cm)*

BEHAVIOR: *Reasonably tolerant; rivalry intensifies between males at breeding time*

DIET: *Livefoods preferred, but other formulations, particularly deep-frozen ones, accepted*

AQUARIUM: *Spacious, well-covered, with surface vegetation, plant thickets and pieces of bogwood. Water chemistry not critical; a small amount of salt (about 1 teaspoonful per 1 Imp. gal/4.5–5 liters) may be added for stocks that originate from brackish-water regions. Temperature range: 64–72°F (18–22°C), with some deviation at either end*

BREEDING: *Use one male and two or more females. Eggs—which are laid, over a period of about a week, among fine-leaved vegetation—are ignored by the spawners. Hatching takes several days*

BLUEFIN KILLIFISH

Lucania goodei

FAMILY: Fundulidae (*sensu* Nelson and Parenti)

OF THE TWO MEMBERS OF THE GENUS, BLUEFIN Killifish is occasionally encountered in the hobby. It is a beautiful fish possessing blue coloration in both the dorsal and anal fins. The dorsal fin may also exhibit a small orange-red patch at the back, with similar coloration on the caudal and pelvic fins.

DISTRIBUTION: *Widespread in Florida*

SIZE: *Up to 2½in (6cm)*

BEHAVIOR: *An active shoaling species*

DIET: *Livefoods preferred, but some commercial diets—particularly deep-frozen ones—accepted*

AQUARIUM: *Well-covered, with some open space. Softish, slightly acid to neutral water preferred; partial water changes required about once a week/two weeks. Temperature range: 64–72°F (18–22°C), with some deviation at either end*

BREEDING: *Similar to B. chrysotus*

POECILIIDS AND CLOSE RELATIVES

Traditionally, poeciliid fishes have been considered synonymous with livebearers (as opposed to egglayers) such as platies, swordtails, mollies and guppies. However, following publication of the Parenti (1981) review of the cyprinodontiforms and subsequent work by Parenti and Rauchenberger (1989)—*see* Bibliography— the poeciliid concept was expanded. As a result, the former poeciliids (family Poeciliidae) were relegated to subfamily status, the Poeciliinae. Another former family—but not a livebearing one—was also relegated to subfamilial level and brought into the family Poeciliidae: the Aplocheilichthyidae (Lampeyes) which now became the Aplocheilichthyinae. The subfamily Fluviphylacinae—consisting of a single species, *Fluviphylax pygmaeus*—was, similarly, subsumed within Poeciliidae.

The four-eyed fishes (*Anableps*) and one-sided livebearers (*Jenynsia*) became amalgamated into a single subfamily, the Anablepinae, and with a new subfamily, the Oxyzygonectinae, formed the family Anablepidae.

Overall, these revisions resulted in just two families of poecilioid fishes: the Poeciliidae and the Anablepidae, whose similarities were deemed significant enough for them to be grouped into a single superfamily, the Poecilioidea.

This classification is becoming progressively more widely accepted within the scientific community. Nelson (1994)—whose classification is being followed in this book (*see* Bibliography)—is among those ichthyologists that have adopted it, although there remains much aquarium literature that has not.

In the pages that follow, the Parenti/Rauchenberger/Nelson interpretation of poecilioid fishes is adopted, with representatives of both families and three subfamilies being featured:

Family: Anablepidae
  Subfamily: Anablepinae
Family: Poeciliidae
  Subfamilies: Poeciliinae and Aplocheilichthyinae

FOUR-EYED FISH
STRIPED FOUR-EYED FISH, FOUR EYES

Anableps anableps

FAMILY: Anablepidae
SUBFAMILY: Anablepinae

THIS SPECIES' COMMON NAME IS DERIVED FROM the two pigmented horizontal flaps of tissue that extend across the eye to meet, but not fuse, in the center of the pupil, effectively dividing the eye into an upper and a lower portion. Modifications to the eye lens allow *Anableps* to see above and below the water simultaneously. This ability is further enhanced by a split retina: one part receives the incoming light rays from above the water, while the other receives those that originate underwater. The Four-eyed Fish is an interesting, but large and somewhat challenging species. Two other species with similar characteristics, size and requirements are also occasionally available: *A. dowei* (Pacific Four-eyed Fish), from Mexico to Nicaragua; and *A. microlepis* (Fine-scaled Four-eyed Fish), from the Orinoco delta to the Amazon delta.

DISTRIBUTION: *Southern Mexico to northern South America (in both freshwater and brackish water)*

SIZE: *Males approximately 6in (15cm); females up to 10½in (27cm)*

BEHAVIOR: *Surface-swimming shoaler*

DIET: *Livefoods preferred, but deep-frozen, freeze-dried and some other commercial diets accepted*

AQUARIUM: *Long, covered, and only half to three-quarters full so that the above/below-water eye orientation can be observed. Alkaline, moderately hard water; add 1 teaspoonful of salt per 1 Imp. gal (4.5–5 liters). Temperature range: 72–86°F (22–30°C), with some deviation at either end tolerated*

BREEDING: *The anal fin of males is modified into a tube-like mating organ (gonopodium) via which*

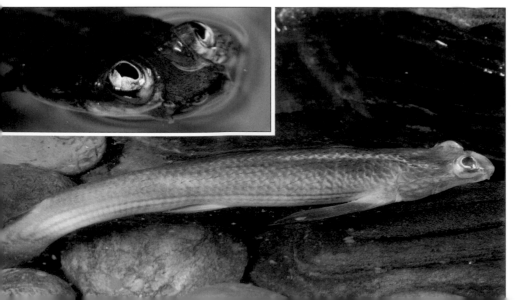

FOUR-EYED FISH (ANABLEPS ANABLEPS)

sperm are transferred into the vent of the female.
Eggs are fertilized internally and retained by
female, which gives birth to small broods (as few
as six offspring) of large fry (1¼–1½in/3–4cm)
about twice a year

ONE-SIDED LIVEBEARER
FALSE-STRIPED JENYNSIA
Jenynsia multidentata

SYNONYM: *Jenynsia lineata*
FAMILY: Anablepidae
SUBFAMILY: Anablepinae

TRADITIONALLY REGARDED AS CONSISTING OF JUST
one species (*J. lineata*), the genus *Jenynsia*
is now widely accepted as containing no
fewer than nine. Further, the species that
has always been referred to as *J. lineata* is,
in fact, *J. multidentata* (*see* Bibliography,
Ghedotti and Weitzman). These ichthyologists also claim that the one-sided mating
behavior responsible for the common
name of the species does not occur.

DISTRIBUTION: *South of the Amazon from
southern Brazil to Rio de la Plata (Argentina). Exact
distribution not clear, owing to the establishment
of similar-looking, but distinct, species (see above)*

SIZE: *Males around 1⅛in (4cm), females around
4¾in (12cm)*

BEHAVIOR: *May be timid in the presence of
boisterous tankmates; keep as a shoal*

DIET: *Wide range of diets accepted; regular
vegetable component recommended*

AQUARIUM: *Heavily planted, with some open
swimming space. Alkaline, moderately hard water
preferred; 1 teaspoonful of salt per 1 Imp. gal
(4.5–5 liters) may be added, but is not essential.
Temperature range 64–77°F (18–25°C), but
lower and higher temperatures also tolerated*

BREEDING: *Internal fertilization is followed by
nourishment of the 20 or so embryos for five to*

LAMPEYE PANCHAX (APLOCHEILICHTHYS LUXOPHTHALMUS)

seven weeks; consequently, the fry are quite
large at birth

LAMPEYE PANCHAX
BIG-EYE, OR IRIDESCENT, LAMPEYE
Aplocheilichthys luxophthalmus

SYNONYM: *Aplocheilichthys macrophthalmus*
FAMILY: Poeciliidae
SUBFAMILY: Aplocheilichthyinae

TWO SUBSPECIES OF THIS DELIGHTFUL LAMPEYE
are recognized: *A. l. luxophthalmus* (Lampeye Panchax itself), and *A. l. harnerzi* (Han-
nerz's Lampeye), from the lower Cross River
drainage in Nigeria. To see either fish at its
best, close attention must be paid to aquarium conditions.

DISTRIBUTION: *Western Africa, including
Cameroon, Nigeria (Niger Delta) and Togo*

SIZE: *Up to 1½in (4cm)*

BEHAVIOR: *Active, peaceful shoaler*

DIET: *Livefoods preferred, but other diets also
accepted*

AQUARIUM: *Heavily planted, with open swimming
spaces, surface vegetation, dark substratum and
subdued lighting. Neutral or slightly alkaline,
medium-hard water preferred. Temperature
range: 72–79°F (22–26°C)*

BREEDING: *Eggs are scattered among fine-leaved
vegetation or the finely divided roots of floating
plants. Lowering the water level is recommended.
Hatching takes 10–14 days*

TANGANYIKA
LAMPEYE
Aplocheilichthys pumilus

FAMILY: Poeciliidae
SUBFAMILY: Aplocheilichthyinae

IN REFLECTED LIGHT, THE SIDES OF THE BODY—
particularly in males in peak condition—
are silvery blue divided longitudinally by a
dark stripe. The caudal fin is thinly edged
in gold, while the other fins are orangey-
brown with some blue speckling. These
colors are only really apparent under ideal
aquarium conditions.

DISTRIBUTION: *East African crater lakes, including
Lake Tanganyika and Lake Victoria*

SIZE: *Around 2¼in (5.5cm)*

BEHAVIOR: *Timid, peaceful shoaler*

DIET: *As for* A. luxophthalmus

AQUARIUM: *As for* A. luxophthalmus; *aerate water
thoroughly. Temperature range: 75–79°F
(24–26°C)*

BREEDING: *As for* A. luxophthalmus, *but use soft,
slightly acid water*

TANGANYIKA LAMPEYE (APLOCHEILICHTHYS PUMILUS)

OTHER *APLOCHEILICHTHYS* SPECIES

Of the 40* or so *Aplocheilichthys* species, subspecies and undescribed types (sometimes offered for sale with a "code" added—as in *A. sp. aff. maculatus* "K86/1"), relatively few are encountered regularly in aquatic retail outlets. Of these, the following are among those most frequently seen. Their aquarium requirements are, basically, those described for *A. luxophthalmus*. Sizes given are approximate.

SCIENTIFIC NAME	COMMON NAME(S)	SIZE
A. johnstoni	Johnston's Lampeye	3⅛in (8.5cm)
A. katangae	Blackstripe, or Katanga, Lampeye	1¾in (4.5cm)
A. (Congopanchax) myersi	Myer's, or Hummingbird, Lampeye	1in (2.5cm)
A. normani	Norman's Lampeye/Blueye	1½in (4.0cm)
A. rancureli	Rancurel's, or Filamentosus, Lampeye	1⅝in (4.0cm)
A. scheeli	Scheel's Lampeye	1⅜in (3.5cm)

NOTE:

*This figure includes the species referred to as "*Aplocheilichthys*" by Parenti (1981)—*see* Bibliography.

NORMAN'S LAMPEYE (APLOCHEILICHTHYS NORMANI)

BANDED LAMPEYE
Aplocheilichthys spilauchen

FAMILY: Poeciliidae
SUBFAMILY: Poeciliinae

AT FIRST SIGHT, THIS LAMPEYE DOES NOT APPEAR to belong within the genus *Aplocheilichthys*: it looks a little more like some *Aplocheilus* species than either of the two previous *Aplocheilichthys* featured. Skeletal and other characteristics, however, prove otherwise. The vertical bands on the body and caudal fin help make the Banded Lampeye a very visually pleasing and desirable fish.

DISTRIBUTION: *Western Africa: from Senegal to lower Congo (Zaire), taking in Liberia, Gambia and northern Angola*

SIZE: *Up to 2¾in (7cm)*

BEHAVIOR: *Active shoaler*

DIET: *Livefoods preferred, but other diets accepted*

AQUARIUM: *As for A. luxophthalmus. Add 1 teaspoonful of salt per 1 Imp. gal (4.5–5 liters) of water. Temperature range: 75–90°F (24–32°C)*

BREEDING: *Similar to A. luxophthalmus, but add salt as above*

TANGANYIKA PEARL KILLIFISH
Lamprichthys tanganicus

FAMILY: Poeciliidae
SUBFAMILY: Aplocheilichthyinae

THIS EXCEPTIONALLY BEAUTIFUL SPECIES IS THE sole representative of its genus and the largest of the Aplocheilichthyinae. It is a streamlined fish with a series of lines of small, metallic-blue scales that are particularly resplendent in reflected light. It can prove challenging to keep in peak condition.

DISTRIBUTION: *Lake Tanganyika (Africa)*

SIZE: *Up to 5in (13cm)*

BEHAVIOR: *Active shoaler*

DIET: *Livefoods preferred, but other formulations also accepted*

AQUARIUM: *Spacious, covered, with some plant thickets and ample swimming space, and at least one group of rocks or blocks of bogwood, placed closely together to provide crevices. Top-quality alkaline medium-hard to hard water important. Temperature range: 72–77°F (22–25°C)*

BREEDING: *Eggs are generally deposited in cracks or crevices in rocks or bogwood and are best left to develop in the dark for over a week*

TANGANYIKA PEARL KILLIFISH
(LAMPRICHTHYS TANGANICUS)

GREEN LAMPEYE
BLUE-GREEN LAMPEYE

Procatopus aberrans

FAMILY: Poeciliidae
SUBFAMILY: Aplocheilichthyinae

OF THE THREE SPECIES IN THE GENUS, GREEN Lampeye is probably the one that is most often seen. Mature males in peak condition are particularly impressive, with their characteristic blue-green body coloration and red fin edges. The Large-finned Lampeye (*P. nototaenia*) and the Variable Lampeye (*P. similis*)—both from different locations within Cameroon—are also very attractive and worth searching for. None, however, is recommended for beginners.

DISTRIBUTION: *Western and southwestern Cameroon*

SIZE: *Around 2½in (6cm)*

BEHAVIOR: *Active, peaceful shoaler*

DIET: *As for* Lamprichthys tanganicus

AQUARIUM: *As for* Lamprichthys tanganicus

BREEDING: *As for* Lamprichthys tanganicus

KNIFE LIVEBEARER

Alfaro cultratus

FAMILY: Poeciliidae
SUBFAMILY: Poeciliinae

WHILE NOT THE MOST COLORFUL OF THE poeciliines, Knife Livebearer makes a dazzling display when kept in a shoal (but *see* below). The "knife" consists of a series of scales on the lower edge of the body between the vent and the beginning of the caudal fin. *A. huberi* (Orange Rocket), from Guatemala, Honduras and Nicaragua, has a central body spot, is smaller (around 2¾in/7cm), and is less frequently available.

DISTRIBUTION: *Costa Rica, Nicaragua and Panama*

SIZE: *Males reported up to 3½in (9cm); females slightly larger*

BEHAVIOR: *Can be shy and easily frightened in sparsely decorated aquaria. Males can sometimes be aggressive toward each other, but not excessively so when kept in a shoal that includes several other males; aggression is highest when only two males are present*

DIET: *Livefoods preferred, but other diets also accepted*

AQUARIUM: *Spacious, well-planted, and covered, with some open swimming spaces and shelters. Neutral or slightly alkaline medium-hard, well-filtered water with some movement (as produced by a powerhead outlet) recommended. Temperature range: 75–82°F (24–28°C)*

BREEDING: *Fertilization is internal. Females give birth to as many as 100 fry every four to five weeks (although broods are generally much smaller than this)*

PIKE TOP LIVEBEARER
PIKE TOP MINNOW/KILLIFISH

Belonesox belizanus

FAMILY: Poeciliidae
SUBFAMILY: Poeciliinae

THIS STREAMLINED, BEAK-MOUTHED, SABRE-toothed species has been in the hobby for nearly 100 years. One of the livebearers "with character," it is undoubtedly for the specialist who likes something a little different. Two subspecies are sometimes recognized: *B. b. belizanus* and *B. b. maxillosus* (Yellow Pike Top Livebearer) from the Yucatán in Mexico. Some authorities doubt the validity of the second subspecies.

DISTRIBUTION: B. b. belizanus: *from Veracruz (Mexico), southward to Guatemala, Honduras and Nicaragua;* B. b. maxillosus: *Yucatán Peninsula (Mexico)*

SIZE: *Males up to 4¾in (12cm); females 8in (20cm)*

BEHAVIOR: *Predatory; must be housed only with similar-sized tankmates; large females may even prey on small males of their own species*

DIET: *Livefoods, deep-frozen and freeze-dried diets*

AQUARIUM: *Spacious, covered, well-planted, with some shelters and well-filtered water. Neutral to alkaline hard water with 1 teaspoonful of salt per 2 Imp. gal (9–10 liters) preferred. Temperature range: 79–86°F (26–30°C) or slightly higher*

BREEDING: *Up to 100 large fry (up to 1in/2.5cm) produced every 4½–7 weeks, following internal fertilization*

THE BISHOP

Brachyraphis episcopi

FAMILY: Poeciliidae
SUBFAMILY: Poeciliinae

THE BISHOP IS PERHAPS THE BEST KNOWN OF THE nine or so *Brachyraphis* species (the total number is uncertain because some are awaiting scientific description). This is a distinctive fish, with netlike scale patterning, a red line and dark spots running down the body, red-edged dorsal fin, and the characteristic "Brachy" black spot around the vent and extending into the

KNIFE LIVEBEARER (*ALFARO CULTRATUS*)

anal fin. It is challenging to maintain in peak condition.

DISTRIBUTION: *Both oceanic slopes of Panama*

SIZE: *Males up to 1½in (3.5cm); females 2in (5cm)*

BEHAVIOR: *Relatively aggressive toward smaller and even some similar-sized tankmates; exhibits fin-nipping tendencies, but may be kept as a shoal*

DIET: *Predominantly livefoods, but other diets accepted (flakes often rejected)*

AQUARIUM: *Well-planted and well-filtered. Neutral to alkaline medium-hard water preferred. Temperature range: 75–79°F (24–26°C)*

BREEDING: *Small broods of around 20 fry produced every four weeks or so*

BANDED WIDOW
STUART'S LIVEBEARER

Carlhubbsia stuarti

FAMILY: Poeciliidae
SUBFAMILY: Poeciliinae

THIS LARGE-EYED SPECIES HAS ATTRACTIVE, THIN, black vertical stripes along the body—more pronounced in males than females; males have a black gonopodium with a white tip. A second species, *C. kidderi* (Kidder's Livebearer)—from Mexico and Guatemala—is similar but lacks the very well-marked stripes of Banded Widow. These stripes also distinguish Banded Widow from *Phallichthys amates* (see p.278).

DISTRIBUTION: *Rio Polochic system, Dulce and Sebol rivers, and Laguna Izabal (Guatemala)*

SIZE: *Males up to 2in (5cm); females up to 2½in (6cm), but usually smaller*

BEHAVIOR: *Can be a little timid, particularly in sparsely planted aquaria; should be kept as a shoal*

DIET: *Livefoods preferred, but some other diets also accepted*

AQUARIUM: *Well-planted, covered, with subdued lighting. Slightly alkaline hardish water preferred, but softer, more acid conditions also tolerated. Temperature range: 75–82°F (24–28°C)*

BREEDING: *Broods of between 10 and 50 fry are produced every five to seven weeks. Males of this genus have dextrally (right-handedly) or sinistrally (left-handedly) asymmetrical gonopodia*

TEN-SPOT LIVEBEARER

Cnesterodon decemmaculatus

FAMILY: Poeciliidae
SUBFAMILY: Poeciliinae

DEPENDING ON LOCALITY OR MOOD, THIS SPECIES can exhibit the ten spots (which are more like very short vertical bands than spherical marks) either brilliantly or not at all. The number of spots may also vary, from 7 to 11. Of the three species in the genus,

OTHER *BRACHYRAPHIS* SPECIES

Once the undescribed species (sometimes referred to in aquarium literature by a code, e.g. *Brachyraphis* sp. "FU35") have been named and the nature of others, e.g. *Brachyraphis cf. roseni* has been determined, this genus could end up with over 15 species. Currently, though, the following are fully recognized (in addition to *B. episcopi*) and are available with varying degrees of regularity from specialist aquatic outlets or from members of livebearer societies. All have the same basic characteristics and requirements as *B. episcopi*, but specialist literature should be consulted (see Bibliography). Sizes given are approximate, with that of males listed first.

SCIENTIFIC NAME	COMMON NAME(S)	SIZE
B. cascajalensis	Cascajal Brachy/Bishop	2⅜in (6cm); 3in (7.5cm)
B. hartwegi	Hartweg's Brachy/Bishop	1½in (3.5cm); 2in (5cm)
B. holdridgei	Holdridge's Brachy/Bishop	1½in (4cm); 2in (5cm)
B. parisima	Parisima Brachy/Bishop	1¾in (4.5cm); 2in (5cm)
B. punctifer	Spotted Brachy/Bishop	1¼in (3cm); 2in (5cm)
B. rhabdophora	Lace Brachy, Regan's Bishop	1½in (4cm); 2¾in (7cm)
B. roseni	The Cardinal, Cardinal Brachy	2in (5cm); 2½in (6.5cm)
B. terrabensis	Sailfin Brachy, Terraba Bishop	2in (5cm); 2½in (6.5cm)

only *C. carnegiei* (Carnegie's Livebearer) from southeastern Brazil and Uruguay is likely to be encountered in the hobby.

DISTRIBUTION: *Argentina, Bolivia, Brazil, Paraguay and Uruguay*

SIZE: *Males around 1in (2.5cm); females around 1¾in (4.5cm)*

BEHAVIOR: *Should be kept as a shoal in a species tank or only with other small nonaggressive species*

DIET: *Small livefoods preferred, but other diets may be accepted*

AQUARIUM: *Well-planted, covered, with well-oxygenated water; carry out regular partial water changes. Neutral, moderately soft water preferred, but a little deviation on either side is tolerated. Temperature range: 64–77°F (18–25°C)*

BREEDING: *Broods of around 20 fry are produced every four to six weeks*

BLACKLINE MOSQUITOFISH

Flexipenis vittata

SYNONYMS: *Flexipenis vittatus, Gambusia vittata*
FAMILY: Poeciliidae
SUBFAMILY: Poeciliinae

THERE IS CONSIDERABLE DEBATE REGARDING THE true identity of this beautiful fish. Some authorities believe it to be the single representative of the genus *Flexipenis*, while others (probably a majority) believe it to be a *Gambusia*.

DISTRIBUTION: *Atlantic side of Mexico*

SIZE: *Males around 1¾in (4.5cm); females around 2½in (6cm)*

BEHAVIOR: *Surprisingly unaggressive for a "Gambusia-type" species; may be kept in a shoal*

DIET: *Wide range of foods accepted*

AQUARIUM: *Well-planted, well-lit, covered. Neutral, softish water, with some deviation on either side, accepted. Temperature range: 72–77°F (22–25°C)*

BREEDING: *Broods of around 20 fry produced every four to six weeks*

WESTERN MOSQUITOFISH

Gambusia affinis

SYNONYM: *Gambusia affinis affinis*
FAMILY: Poeciliidae
SUBFAMILY: Poeciliinae

TOGETHER WITH ITS CLOSEST RELATIVE, *G. holbrooki* (Eastern Mosquitofish), this is undoubtedly the most widely distributed of all the livebearers, having been introduced into numerous tropical and sub-tropical regions as a biological means of malaria control. While effective in this role—by eating large quantities of malaria mosquito larvae—both these species have proved very invasive and have often displaced native species. Melanic (black or black-mottled) morphs of *G. holbrooki* are commonly found in the wild.

DISTRIBUTION: *G. affinis: From northern Veracruz (Mexico) northward to southern Indiana and eastward to Alabama; G. holbrooki: From central Alabama eastward to Florida and northward up to New Jersey. Both species also exist as exotic populations in numerous other locations*

SIZE: *Males up to 1½in (4cm); females up to 2¾in (7cm)*

BEHAVIOR: *Distinct fin-nipping tendencies; voracious appetite toward anything of a swallowable size. Both these species should be kept as a shoal*

DIET: *Livefoods preferred, but wide range of other diets also accepted*

AQUARIUM: *Well-planted, covered, and with surface vegetation with feathery roots (to offer protection for fry). Water chemistry not critical, but quality must be good. Temperature range: from below 50°F (10°C) to above 86°F (30°C)*

BREEDING: *Broods can vary from 10–80 fry and are produced every five to eight weeks during the warmer months. Parents are highly cannibalistic toward their offspring*

GOLDEN GAMBUSIA
GOLDEN MOSQUITOFISH
Gambusia aurata

FAMILY: Poeciliidae
SUBFAMILY: Poeciliinae

THIS VERY ATTRACTIVE SPECIES, WITH GOLDEN body color and rows of fine black body spots, is one of the stockier-looking representatives of the genus.

DISTRIBUTION: *State of Tamaulipas (Mexico)*

SIZE: *Males around 1in (2 5cm); females around 1½in (4cm)*

BEHAVIOR: *As for G. affinis*

DIET: *As for G. affinis*

AQUARIUM: *As for G. affinis, but temperatures should not go below 15°C (59°F) for extended periods*

BREEDING: *Broods of 10–20 fry produced every 4 6 weeks*

OTHER *GAMBUSIA* SPECIES

There are around 35 species of *Gambusia* so far described, with the possibility that this figure may rise slightly as some outstanding taxonomical queries are resolved. Most are hardy and relatively easy to keep and breed following the guidelines given for *G. affinis*, though not all exhibit the keen cannibalistic and fin-nipping characteristics of this species. Although most are comfortable at temperatures in the 72–77°F (22–25°C) range, quite a number can tolerate considerably lower temperatures, while a few, e.g. *G. luma* (Clawed Gambusia or Mosquitofish) from Guatemala and *G. nicaraguensis* (Nicaragua Gambusia or Mosquitofish) require warmer water in the 75–84°F (24–29°C) range. Before obtaining any *Gambusia* species, expert advice should be sought, both from specialist literature (*see* Bibliography) and specialist livebearer aquarists and societies.

MARSH'S GAMBUSIA
MARSH'S MOSQUITOFISH
Gambusia marshi

FAMILY: Poeciliidae
SUBFAMILY: Poeciliinae

THE YELLOWISH-BROWN BASE BODY COLOR, AND the distinct dark band that runs from the head to the caudal peduncle, make this species easily recognizable.

DISTRIBUTION: *Cuatro Ciénegas basin in Coahuila (Mexico)*

SIZE: *Males around 1⅜in (3.5cm); females up to 2½in (6cm)*

BEHAVIOR: *One of the more peaceful of the genus; should be kept in a shoal*

DIET: *Wide range of foods accepted*

AQUARIUM: *As for G. affinis. Temperature range: 72–77°F (22–25°C)*

BREEDING: *As for G. aurata*

GIRARDINUS TOPMINNOW
METALLIC, or BLACK-BELLIED METALLIC, TOPMINNOW
Girardinus metallicus

FAMILY: Poeciliidae
SUBFAMILY: Poeciliinae

THIS IS THE MOST FREQUENTLY SEEN OF THE EIGHT species making up this genus. In some males, the gonopodium has black coloration that extends forward into the chest area (hence the "black-bellied" part of one of the common names). Both males and females have a metallic sheen and vertical black body bands.

DISTRIBUTION: *Most of Cuba*

SIZE: *Males up to 2in (5cm); females up to 3½in (9cm)*

BEHAVIOR: *Lively shoaler*

GIRARDINUS TOPMINNOW (GIRARDINUS METALLICUS)

OTHER *GIRARDINUS* SPECIES

In addition to *G. metallicus*, seven other species are cited in current aquatic literature. All exhibit similar characteristics and have similar requirements to those outlined for *G. metallicus*, but specialist literature should be consulted (*see* Bibliography) or advice sought from experts. Sizes given below are approximate, that of males being listed first.

SCIENTIFIC NAME	COMMON NAME(S)	SIZE
G. creolus *	Creole Topminnow	1½in (4cm); 2¾in (7.5cm)
G. cubensis **	Cuban Topminnow	1¼in (3cm); 1¾in (4.5cm)
G. denticulatus	Toothy Topminnow	1½in (4cm); 2½in (6cm)
G. falcatus *	Goldbelly Topminnow	1½in (4cm); 2¾in (7cm)
G. microdactylus	Smallfinger Topminnow	1½in (3.5cm); 2½in (6cm)
G. serripensis	Taco Taco, or Serrated, Topminnow	1½in (4cm); 2½in (6.5cm)
G. uninotatus	Singlespot Topminnow	2in (5cm); 3in (8cm)

NOTE

* These two species are generally seen more frequently than the others listed

**There is some doubt regarding the validity of this species

DIET: *Wide range of foods accepted*

AQUARIUM: *Planted, covered, well-filtered, with some gentle water movement. Slightly alkaline, medium-hard water preferred. Temperature range: 72–84°F (22–29°C)*

BREEDING: *At the higher temperatures, broods of up to 100 fry (but usually fewer) are produced every five weeks or so*

MOSQUITO FISH

DWARF LIVEBEARER, DWARF TOPMINNOW, LEAST KILLIFISH

Heterandria formosa

FAMILY: Poeciliidae
SUBFAMILY: Poeciliinae

OF THE COMMON NAMES CITED, THE LAST SHOULD cease to be used because this delightful, minute species is not a killifish at all. It ranks among the smallest vertebrates known to science. A fish for the specialist, it should be regarded as a "must" by any aquarist who develops the appropriate level of husbandry skills.

DISTRIBUTION: *From southeastern North Carolina southward, including eastern and southern Georgia, Florida, the Gulf Coast (as far as New Orleans) and Louisiana*

SIZE: *Males up to ¾in (2cm); females up to 1¼in (3cm)*

BEHAVIOR: *Peaceful shoaler, best kept in a tank set up exclusively for it*

DIET: *Small livefoods preferred, but other diets also accepted; a regular vegetable supplement recommended*

AQUARIUM: *Thickly planted, covered. Alkaline hardish water preferred, but other conditions*

also accepted. Temperature range: from 61°F (16°C) to around 84°F (29°C)

BREEDING: *Small numbers of relatively large fry are released on an almost daily basis over a period of 10–14 days (this is known as superfetation)*

MILLER'S FLYER

Heterophallus milleri

SYNONYM: *Gambusia milleri*
FAMILY: Poeciliidae
SUBFAMILY: Poeciliinae

AS THE TWO SCIENTIFIC NAMES INDICATE, THERE is some debate regarding the true identity of this attractively finned species. In addition to the glistening coloration of some of the fins, the caudal—at least, in some specimens—has three rounded tips: one at the top, one in the middle and one on the bottom, the latter being slightly extended in some mature males. Two other species also occasionally available are: *H. echeagarayi* (Palenque Flyer) and *H. rachovii* (Rachow's Flyer)—both also from Mexico.

DISTRIBUTION: *Mainly Teapa river in Tabasco (Mexico)*

SIZE: *Males around 1in (2.5cm); females up to 1½in (4cm)*

BEHAVIOR: *Active shoaler*

DIET: *Livefoods preferred, but other diets may also be accepted*

AQUARIUM: *Thickly planted, with some water movement. Carry out regular partial water changes. Neutral, softish water seems to be preferred but*

MOSQUITO FISH (*HETERANDRIA FORMOSA*)

▲ DOMINICAN LIMIA (LIMIA DOMINICENSIS); SEE BOX P.278   ▼ HUMPBACKED LIMIA (LIMIA NIGROFASCIATA)

HUMPBACKED LIMIA
BLACK-BARRED LIMIA
Limia nigrofasciata

SYNONYM: *Poecilia nigrofasciata*
FAMILY: Poeciliidae
SUBFAMILY: Poeciliinae

THE HUMPED BACK OF ONE OF THE COMMON names is particularly evident in fully mature males, a group of which create an impressive sight in any aquarium. Hybridization with closely related species is not uncommon. Two very similar species: *L. grossidens* (Largetooth Limia) and *L. miragoanensis* (Miragoane Limia)—both also from Lake Miragoane—are thought by some authors to be synonymous with Humpbacked Limia.

DISTRIBUTION: *Lake Miragoane in Haiti*

SIZE: *Males around 2¼in (5.5cm); females up to 2½in (6cm)*

BEHAVIOR: *A peaceful shoaler*

DIET: *As for* L. melanogaster

AQUARIUM: *As for* L. melanogaster, *but water need not be as hard and alkaline. Temperature range: 75–82°F (24–28°C)*

BREEDING: *Temperature appears to affect the sex ratio of fry, with the higher end of the scale reportedly resulting in more females. Broods of around 60 fry are produced every four to ten weeks*

CUBAN LIMIA
Limia vittata

SYNONYM: *Poecilia vittata*
FAMILY: Poeciliidae
SUBFAMILY: Poeciliinae

THIS IS ANOTHER EXTREMELY ATTRACTIVE *LIMIA* species that hybridizes easily with its closest relatives. It is also highly variable, with some specimens having very little spotting, while others—particularly some of the aquarium-bred strains—being richly spotted in yellow and black.

DISTRIBUTION: *Cuba; some populations occur in brackish waters*

SIZE: *Males up to 2½in (6.5cm); females up to 4¾in (12cm), but usually smaller*

BEHAVIOR: *As for* L. melanogaster

DIET: *As for* L. melanogaster

AQUARIUM: *As for* L. melanogaster. *A little salt— about 1 teaspoonful per 1 Imp. gal (4.5–5 liters) may be added to the aquarium water, but this is not essential. Temperature range: 75–82°F (24–28°C)*

BREEDING: *Large broods of up to 100 fry are produced every four to six weeks*

some deviation acceptable. Temperature range: 64–84°F (18–29°C)

BREEDING: *Small broods (usually fewer than 20 fry) produced every four to six weeks*

BLACK-BELLIED LIMIA
Limia melanogaster

SYNONYM: *Poecilia melanogaster*
FAMILY: Poeciliidae
SUBFAMILY: Poeciliinae

IN PEAK CONDITION, THIS A SUPERB LITTLE FISH for a community aquarium. Males have a bluish sheen and yellow coloration in the caudal and dorsal fins, and females have a large black belly patch. Males, in particular, are always on the move, displaying to each other and attempting to mate, both with females of their own species and with those of closely related ones (when fertile hybrids may be produced).

DISTRIBUTION: *Jamaica*

SIZE: *Males up to 1¾in (4.5cm); females up to 2½in (6cm)*

BEHAVIOR: *Active shoaler*

DIET: *Wide range of foods accepted; regular vegetable component important*

AQUARIUM: *Well-planted, covered, with open swimming area, and good illumination to encourage growth of green encrusting algae (a natural source of vegetable food) on the aquarium panes (leave the sides and back unscraped during aquarium maintenance). Alkaline, hardish, good-quality water preferred. Temperature range: 72–82°F (22–28°C)*

BREEDING: *Broods of about 20 fry are produced every five to eight weeks. Considerable variation, however, exists, both in the size and frequency of these broods*

CUBAN LIMIA (LIMIA VITTATA)

OTHER *LIMIA* SPECIES

In addition to the featured species (plus the two mentioned in the *L. nigrofasciata* entry), there are 15 other limias currently recognized. Characteristics and requirements are generally similar, with all species preferring water conditions on the alkaline and harder end of the pH and hardness spectra and temperatures in the 75–82°F (24–28°C) region. The following are the most likely species to be encountered. Sizes given are approximate, that of males being listed first.

SCIENTIFIC NAME	COMMON NAME(S)	SIZE
L. dominicensis	Dominican, Haiti, or Tiburón Peninsula, Limia	1¼in (3cm); 2in (5cm)
L. ornata	Ornate Limia	2in (5cm); 2½in (6cm)
L. perugiae	Perugia's Limia	2¾in (7cm); 3⅓in (8.5cm)
L. sulphurophila	Sulphur Limia	1⅓in (3.5cm); 1⅓in (3.5cm)
L. tridens	Tiburón Limia	1¼in (3cm); 1¾in (4.5cm)
L. zonata	Striped, or Zoned, Limia	1⅓in (3cm); 2½in (6cm)

NOTE:

Some *Limia* species interbreed easily, in some cases producing fertile hybrids, so to maintain genetic "purity," it is important not to keep species together in the same aquarium.

PICTA

Micropoecilia picta

SYNONYM: *Poecilia picta*
FAMILY: Poeciliidae
SUBFAMILY: Poeciliinae

THIS TINY FISH IS SUPERFICIALLY SIMILAR TO (*Poecilia reticulata*—*see* p.279). Males are brilliantly colored and highly variable, as are those of the other species in the genus. Of these, the most frequently encountered is *M. branneri* (Branner's Livebearer) from Brazil. Neither species is suitable for beginners.

DISTRIBUTION: *Guyana and Trinidad*

SIZE: *Males up to 1¼in (3cm); females up to 2in (5cm)*

BEHAVIOR: *Active shoaler; should not be kept with large boisterous tankmates*

DIET: *Range of small foods accepted; vegetable component required*

AQUARIUM: *Thickly planted, covered. Add 1 teaspoonful salt per 1 Imp. gal (4.5–5 liters) of water for longterm health. Temperature range: 75–82°F (24–28°C)*

BREEDING: *Challenging; fewer than 20 fry may be produced every four to five weeks*

MERRY WIDOW

Phallichthys amates

SYNONYM: *Phallichthys amates amates*
FAMILY: Poeciliidae
SUBFAMILY: Poeciliinae

SUPERFICIALLY, MALES OF THIS SPECIES RESEMBLE those of *Carlhubbsia stuarti* (Banded Widow—*see* p.274), but lack the bold vertical body bands of the latter. Two other species are also occasionally available: *P. fairweatheri* (Elegant Widow) from Guatemala and *P. pittieri* (Orange-dorsal Widow) from Costa Rica, western Panama and Nicaragua.

DISTRIBUTION: *Atlantic slope of southern Guatemala and northern Honduras*

SIZE: *Males up to 1½in (4cm); females up to 2¾in (7cm)*

BEHAVIOR: *Quiet shoaler; must not be kept with active tankmates*

DIET: *Range of foods accepted; vegetable component necessary*

AQUARIUM: *Thickly planted, with little or no water movement and subdued lighting. Water chemistry not critical, but extremes must be avoided. Temperature range: 72–82°F (22–28°C)*

BREEDING: *Up to 150 fry may be produced by large females every four to six weeks*

MERRY WIDOW (PHALLICHTHYS AMATES)

ONE-SPOT LIVEBEARER

GOLDEN ONE-SPOT, SPOTTED, or GOLDEN SPOTTED, LIVEBEARER, THE CAUDO

Phalloceros caudimaculatus

SYNONYMS: *Phalloceros caudimaculatus auratus* and *P. c. a. reticulatus*
FAMILY: Poeciliidae
SUBFAMILY: Poeciliinae

OWING TO ITS GREAT VARIABILITY, WITH SOME specimens bearing one body spot, others none at all and yet others being golden and/or mottled (reticulated), this species has a wide range of both common and scientific names. Modern-day thinking is that all are representatives of a highly variable single species, *P. caudimaculatus*.

DISTRIBUTION: *Southern Brazil, Paraguay and Uruguay; introduced into some locations outside its range, e.g. Malawi and western Australia*

SIZE: *Males around 1¼in (3cm); females up to 2in (5cm)*

BEHAVIOR: *A peaceful shoaler*

DIET: *Range of foods accepted; vegetable component required*

AQUARIUM: *Well-planted, well-illuminated. Water chemistry not critical, but alkaline, medium-hard conditions preferred. Temperature range: 64–82°F (18–28°C)*

BREEDING: *Up to 80 fry may be produced every five to six weeks*

SAILFIN MOLLY

Poecilia latipinna

FAMILY: Poeciliidae
SUBFAMILY: Poeciliinae

DESPITE ITS COMMON NAME, NOT ALL WILD MALES of this species develop the full sail-like dorsal fin. The pure wild form of the species is hardly ever seen within the hobby. Instead, either cultivated color varieties or, more frequently, fertile hybrids between sailfins and two of their closest relatives, *P. sphenops* and *P. velifera*—*see* separate entries—are encountered.

DISTRIBUTION: *The Carolinas, Florida, Texas, Virginia and Atlantic coast of Mexico*

SIZE: *Males around 4in (10cm); females around 4¾in (12cm)*

BEHAVIOR: *Peaceful shoaler; males constantly display toward each other*

DIET: *Range of foods accepted; vegetable component essential*

AQUARIUM: *Spacious, planted, with some open swimming space. Alkaline, medium-hard water with 1 teaspoonful salt per 1 Imp. gal (4.5–5*

liters) important for longterm health. Temperature range: 77–82°F (25–28°C)

BREEDING: *Broods of well over 100 fry are common every eight to ten weeks*

GUPPY

MILLIONS FISH

Poecilia reticulata

FAMILY: Poeciliidae
SUBFAMILY: Poeciliinae

IN THE HOBBY SINCE THE EARLY 1900S, THE Guppy is one of the best known and popular aquarium fishes of all time. It is an adaptable, hardy fish whose inherent genetic variability has been exploited over the years to produce a bewildering array of fin and color permutations. As a result, the original short-finned wild type of the species is hardly ever seen, except in the aquaria of specialist livebearer enthusiasts. Endler's Livebearer is a particularly beautiful wild form.

DISTRIBUTION: *Widely distributed north of the Amazon and extensively introduced into tropical and subtropical regions outside of the range*

SIZE: *Wild males up to 1¼in (3cm); wild females around 2in (5cm); cultivated varieties generally larger*

BEHAVIOR: *Peaceful shoaler; should not be kept with boisterous or fin-nipping tankmates, e.g. Barbus tetrazona (Tiger Barb)*

DIET: *Wide range of foods accepted; vegetable component recommended*

GUPPY (POECILIA RETICULATA): RED VEILTAIL ▲
"ORIGINAL" WILD FORM (P. RETICULATA) ▶
BLUE-VARIEGATED DELTA GUPPY (P. RETICULATA VAR.) ▼

Aquarium: *Well-planted, well-illuminated, with some open swimming space. Water chemistry not critical, but alkaline, medium-hard conditions preferred. Temperature range: 64–82°F (18–28°C)*

Breeding: *Large females can produce over 150 fry every four to six weeks*

SPHENOPS MOLLY

Poecilia sphenops

GREEN, BLACK, LIBERTY, MEXICAN, or POINTED-MOUTH, MOLLY

Family: Poeciliidae
Subfamily: Poeciliinae

This highly variable, widely distributed species has given rise to a vast array of cultivated varieties (many through hybridization), the best known of which is the Black Molly. According to some authorities, it is the closely related—and very similar—*P. mexicana* (Atlantic Molly) that is the true ancestor of the aquarium strains. The confusion seems to have arisen from both species' being regarded as one and the same. The Liberty Molly, a form of Sphenops Molly, possesses a short, but very attractively colored and patterned dorsal fin. Both *P. mexicana* and Sphenops Molly hybridize with *P. latipinna* and *P. velifera* (*see* p.279 and below).

Distribution: *From Texas southward along both Mexican coasts, as far as Colombia; also introduced elsewhere*

Size: *Males around 2½in (6cm); females around 3¼in (8cm)*

Behavior: *Peaceful shoaler*

Diet: *Wide range of foods accepted; vegetable component essential*

Aquarium: *As for* P. latipinna

Breeding: *Broods of around 80 fry produced every five to seven weeks*

YUCATÁN MOLLY

SAILFIN MOLLY

Poecilia velifera

Family: Poeciliidae
Subfamily: Poeciliinae

Wild specimens of this species look similar to those of *P. latipinna* (*see* p.279). However, Yucatán Molly is larger, and has a fuller sail-like dorsal fin, with a higher number of fin rays (18 or 19, as opposed to 14). Ease of hybridization between this species, *P. latipinna* and/or *P. sphenops* has resulted in a spectacular range of aquarium varieties.

Black Molly (*Poecilia velifera var.*)

Distribution: *Yucatán Peninsula (Mexico)*

Size: *Males up to 6in (15cm); females up to 7in (18cm)*

Behavior: *As for* P. latipinna

Diet: *As for* P. latipinna

Aquarium: *As for* P. latipinna

Breeding: *Broods numbering 100 fry—and produced every six to eight weeks—are not uncommon*

OTHER *POECILIA* SPECIES

There are about 35 species in the genus *Poecilia*, most of which are only rarely available. However, stocks of most species are maintained by members of livebearer associations throughout the world. For a full listing of all the known species, as well as for specific guidance on aquarium care, consult specialist literature (*see* Bibliography). The following are the species most likely to be encountered. Sizes given are approximate, with that of males listed first.

SCIENTIFIC NAME	COMMON NAME(S)	SIZE
P. butleri	Pacific Molly	2¾in (7cm); 3in (8cm)
P. caucana	South American Molly	1¼in (3cm); 1½in (4cm)
P. chica	Dwarf Molly	1¼in (3cm); 1½in (3.5cm)
P. dominicensis	Santo Domingo Molly	1½in (3.5cm); 2½in (6cm)
P. "formosa" *	Amazon Molly	—*; 2½in (6cm)
P. gillii	Gill's Molly	1½in (4cm); 2in (5cm)
P. latipunctata	Tamesí Molly	2in (5cm); 2½in (6cm)
P. maylandi	Mayland's Molly	4in (10cm); 4¾in (12cm)
P. petenensis	Petén Molly	4in (10cm); 3in (8cm)
P. salvatoris	Salvator Molly	3in (8cm); 4in (10cm)
P. vivipara	One-spot Molly	2in (5cm); 2½in (6cm)

NOTE

* This is not a true species, but a hybrid in which eggs appear to develop after they are "penetrated" by sperm, but without fertilization actually taking place (gynogenesis). The species involved are generally thought to be *P. latipinna* and *P. mexicana*, but males of a number of species are known to produce the same effect. All *P. "formosa"* are females; males reported from time to time have not been unequivocally confirmed

▲▲▲ South American Molly (*Poecilia caucana*)
▲▲ Dwarf Molly (*Poecilia chica*) ▲ Gill's Molly (*Poecilia gillii*)

Orange and Black Sailfin Molly (Poecilia velifera var.)

PORTHOLE LIVEBEARER

Poeciliopsis gracilis

FAMILY: Poeciliidae
SUBFAMILY: Poeciliinae

THIS SILVERY-SIDED SPECIES HAS A NUMBER OF black spots along the body, which can vary in number (from 4 to 11) and in intensity.

DISTRIBUTION: *Southern Mexico to Honduras, along both the Atlantic and Pacific coasts*

SIZE: *Males up to 1½in (4cm); females reported up to 2¾in (7cm)*

BEHAVIOR: *Active shoaler*

DIET: *Livefoods preferred, but other diets accepted; vegetable component recommended*

AQUARIUM: *Well-planted, covered, with some open swimming space. Neutral to slightly alkaline, well-oxygenated, medium-hard water preferred. Temperature range: 72–82°F (22–28°C)*

BREEDING: *A few fry are produced every day over a period of some ten days (superfetation); up to 60 fry may be produced over this period*

MAYAN BLUE-EYE

SLAB-SIDED BLUE-EYE

Priapella compressa

FAMILY: Poeciliidae
SUBFAMILY: Poeciliinae

LIKE THE TWO OTHER MEMBERS OF ITS GENUS, *P. compressa* has beautiful blue eyes. It also has a compressed, beige-orange body,

and a "keel" running from the vent to the base of the caudal fin. *P. intermedia* (Oaxacan Blue-eye), from Oaxaca (Mexico) and *P. olmecae* (Olmecan Blue-eye), from around Veracruz (Mexico) are also occasionally available; the latter has very attractive fins with a good deal of orange coloration.

DISTRIBUTION: *Chiapas (Mexico)*

SIZE: *Males up to 1¾in (4.5cm); females 2¾in (7cm)*

BEHAVIOR: *Active shoalers with excellent jumping ability. (They are known to catch flying insects in the wild)*

DIET: *Strong preference for livefoods, but other formulations accepted*

AQUARIUM: *Spacious, planted and covered, with open swimming areas and water movement (as produced via the outlet of a powerhead or power filter). Clean, well-oxygenated water essential. Extremes of pH and hardness must be avoided. Temperature range: 72–82°F (22–28°C)*

BREEDING: *Up to 30 fry may be produced every four to eight weeks*

TWO-SPOT LIVEBEARER

COMMON TWIN-SPOT LIVEBEARER, SPOT-TAILED MOSQUITOFISH, PSEUDO HELLERI

Pseudoxiphophorus bimaculatus

SYNONYM: *Heterandria bimaculata*
FAMILY: Poeciliidae
SUBFAMILY: Poeciliinae

WITH THE POSSIBLE EXCEPTION OF *POECILIA velifera* (see p.280), this is the largest of the poeciliid livebearers. In peak condition, it is a truly impressive species. *P. joinesii* (Northern Twin-spot Livebearer)—also from Mexico, and the only other species seen with any frequency in the hobby does not possess the same intensity of coloration, but it is about half the size of *P. bimaculata* and therefore a little easier to maintain.

DISTRIBUTION: *From southern Veracruz and Oaxaca (Mexico), to Belize, Guatemala and Honduras*

SIZE: *Males around 2¾in (7cm); females 6in (15cm)*

BEHAVIOR: *Highly aggressive and predatory, but can be kept as a shoal of similar-sized individuals, as well as with similar-sized tankmates of other species*

DIET: *Livefoods strongly preferred, but some other formulations may be accepted*

AQUARIUM: *Spacious, well-planted, covered, with some open swimming areas and water current (as produced via a powerhead or power filter outlet). Clean, well-oxygenated water important, and extremes of pH and hardness should be avoided. Temperature range: 72–79°F (22–26°C)*

BREEDING: *Broods of over 100 fry are produced every four to eight weeks*

OTHER *POECILIOPSIS* SPECIES

There are just over 20 species in this genus, but only *P. gracilis* is seen on a regular basis. Several of these are spotted and can be easily confused with *P. gracilis*. Advice should therefore be sought, both from specialist literature and hobbyists (also the best source of supply). The following are probably the most frequently available of these. Sizes are approximate, with that of males listed first.

SCIENTIFIC NAME	COMMON NAME(S)	SIZE
P. baenschi *	Baensch's Topminnow	1¼in (3cm); 1¼in (3cm)
P. hnilickai *	Comitan Topminnow	1⅜in (3.5cm); 2in (5cm)
P. infans	Black Topminnow, or Rio Lerma, Mosquitofish	1⅜in (3.5cm); 2in (5cm)
P. latidens*	Broad-toothed Topminnow	1¼in (3cm); 2in (5cm)
P. prolifica	Prolific Topminnow	¾in (2cm); 1⅜in (3.5cm)
P. turrubarensis *	Pacific, or Costa Rican, Topminnow	1⅜in (4cm); 3in (8cm)
P. viriosa	Robust Topminnow	1⅜in (3.5cm); 2½in (6cm)

NOTE:

* These are some of the spotted species referred to in the opening paragraph.

BLACK-BARRED LIVEBEARER

BARRED TOPMINNOW

Quintana atrizona

FAMILY: Poeciliidae
SUBFAMILY: Poeciliinae

IN PEAK CONDITION, THIS IS A DELIGHTFUL SPECIES with black body bars, black patches in the dorsal fin, light blue in the pelvic and anal fins, and silvery chest and belly.

DISTRIBUTION: *Western Cuba*

SIZE: *Males up to 1in (2.5cm); females up to 1½in (4cm)*

BEHAVIOR: *Retiring shoaler; must not be kept with boisterous tankmates*

DIET: *Livefoods preferred, but other diets accepted; vegetable component recommended*

AQUARIUM: *Densely planted, with surface vegetation and little water movement. Clean, slightly alkaline, medium-hard water preferred. Temperature range: 75–82°F (24–28°C)*

BREEDING: *Broods numbering, on average, around 25–30 fry are produced every five to eight weeks*

SHEEPHEAD SWORDTAIL

Xiphophorus birchmanni

FAMILY: Poeciliidae
SUBFAMILY: Poeciliinae

THIS IS ONE OF THE "NEWER" SPECIES OF Swordtail and Platy described since the mid-1980s. It is a stocky fish in which males have a magnificent rounded dorsal fin and very short sword. Mature males also have a characteristic thickened (hump) area on the head, hence the common name.

DISTRIBUTION: *Southern part of the Pánuco river basin, San Pedro river system, Montezuma and Tuxpan rivers—all in Mexico*

SIZE: *Males around 2½–3in (6–8cm); females around 2¾in (7cm)*

BEHAVIOR: *Somewhat timid shoaler; either one male, or a group, should be maintained (if only two males are kept, one is likely to suffer)*

DIET: *Livefoods preferred, but other diets also accepted; vegetable component important*

AQUARIUM: *Heavily planted, covered, with some open space. Alkaline medium-hard water preferred. Temperature range: 70–77°F (21–25°C)*

BREEDING: *About 30 fry produced every four to five weeks*

PUEBLO PLATY

Xiphophorus evelynae

FAMILY: Poeciliidae
SUBFAMILY: Poeciliinae

THE "PEPPER-DUST" SPOTTING EXHIBITED BY THIS fish makes it very attractive. It is not dissimilar in overall body shape to the *X. variatus*—*see* p.283.

DISTRIBUTION: *Nexaca, and Tecolutla river system (Mexico)*

SIZE: *Males up to 1¾in (4.5cm); females around 2in (5cm)*

BEHAVIOR: *Peaceful shoaler (keep as outlined for X. birchmanni)*

DIET: *As for X. birchmanni*

AQUARIUM: *As for X. birchmanni*

BREEDING: *Around 50 fry are produced every four to five weeks*

SWORDTAIL

Xiphophorus helleri

FAMILY: Poeciliidae
SUBFAMILY: Poeciliinae

TRUE WILD-TYPE SWORDTAILS ARE HARDLY EVER seen within the general hobby today. Considerable numbers of this highly variable species are, however, kept by livebearer enthusiasts who represent the best source of such specimens. Elsewhere, the vast majority of swordtails are available in a wide range of color and fin varieties developed over many decades. Many of these cultivated fish are the result of crosses between Swordtail and one or other of two of its close relatives, *X. maculatus* and *X. variatus*—*see* separate entries.

DISTRIBUTION: *Atlantic drainages in central America from Mexico to northwestern Honduras; also introduced into numerous locations outside its range, including Sri Lanka and South Africa*

SIZE: *Males around 4in (10cm), excluding the sword; females around 4in (10cm); larger sizes also reported but generally not attained*

BEHAVIOR: *Active shoaler; males can be scrappy among themselves; keep as outlined for X. birchmanni*

DIET: *As for X. birchmanni*

AQUARIUM: *As for X. birchmanni*

BREEDING: *Up to 200 fry are produced every four to six weeks*

MARBLED RED SWORDTAIL (XIPHOPHORUS HELLERI *VAR.*)
(Inset) BLACK SWORDTAIL (XIPHOPHORUS HELLERI *VAR.*)

SOUTHERN PLATY

MOONFISH

Xiphophorus maculatus

FAMILY: Poeciliidae
SUBFAMILY: Poeciliinae

JUST LIKE ITS FAMOUS RELATIVE, *X. HELLERI*, THIS species is inherently highly variable and has been developed into numerous color varieties. It has also been hybridized with both *X. helleri* and *X. variatus*. The best source of true wild-type specimens is specialist livebearer societies (*see* photo p.3).

DISTRIBUTION: *From Veracruz in Mexico, to Belize and Guatemala*

SIZE: *Males to 1½in (4cm); females up to 2½in (6cm); cultivated varieties and hybrids may be larger*

BEHAVIOR: *Placid shoaler*

DIET: *As for* X. birchmanni

AQUARIUM: *As for* X. birchmanni. *Temperature range: 64–77°F (18–25°C)*

BREEDING: *Around 50 fry are produced every four to six weeks*

OTHER *XIPHOPHORUS* SPECIES

There are around 30 species in the genus *Xiphophorus*, relatively few of which are available in aquatic outlets with any regularity. Some species are under threat in the wild, but most (including the threatened ones) are kept and bred by members of livebearer societies in various countries. These societies are the best sources of supply for such species, as well as of maintenance and breeding information. Within the genus, some species are referred to as platies and some as swordtails, but the distinction between the two is not clear-cut. Numerous reports of sex reversal in swordtails may be found in aquarium literature, but these need to be regarded with great caution, since—in all cases that have been studied—the "females" that have apparently changed into males have all been late-developing males. The following are among the best known species. Sizes given are approximate, with that of males listed first. (In the case of swordtails, the length quoted excludes the sword).

SCIENTIFIC NAME	COMMON NAME(S)	SIZE
X. alvarezi	Upland Swordtail	2½in (6cm); 3in (7.5cm)
X. andersi	Ander's Platy	1¾in (4.5cm); 2¼in (5.5cm)
X. clemenciae	Yellow Swordtail	1½in (4cm); 2¼in (5.5cm)
X. cortezi *	Cortés Swordtail	1¾in (4.5cm); 2½in (6cm)
X. couchianus	Monterrey Platy	2in (5cm); 2½in (6cm)
X. gordoni	Cuatro Ciénegas Platy	1½in (3.5cm); 1½in (4cm)
X. malinche	Highland Swordtail	2in (5cm); 2in (5cm)
X. milleri	Catemaco Swordtail	1in (2.5cm); 1¾in (4.5cm)
X. multilineatus	High-backed Pygmy Swordtail	2in (5cm); 2in (5cm)
X. nezahualcoyotl	Northern Mountain Swordtail	2in (5cm); 2¼in (5.5cm)
X. nigrensis	El Abra Pygmy Swordtail	2¼in (5.5cm); 2¼in (5.5cm)
X. pygmaeus **	Slender Pygmy Swordtail	1½in (3.5cm); 1½in (4cm)
X. signum	Comma Swordtail	3in (8cm); 4in (10cm)
X. xiphidium ***	Spiketail Platy	1¼in (3cm); 1½in (4cm)

NOTES:

* *X. cortezi* has traditionally been known as the Montezuma Swordtail, but this common name should be reserved for *X. montezumae*

** Two naturally occurring color forms of *X. pygmaeus* are officially recognized: "Yellow" and "Blue"

*** *X. xiphidium* hybridizes easily with some other *Xiphophorus* species, such as *X. maculatus*, *X. alvarezi* and *X. nigrensis*. A naturally occurring hybrid with *X. variatus* is generally known as *X. "kosszanderi"*

MONTERREY PLATY (*XIPHOPHORUS COUCHIANUS*)

MONTEZUMA SWORDTAIL

Xiphophorus montezumae

FAMILY: Poeciliidae
SUBFAMILY: Poeciliinae

MALES OF THIS SLENDER-BODIED SPECIES PRODUCE an exceptionally long sword, making a shoal of such fish an unforgettable sight. A number of zigzag body stripes, plus speckling (not seen in all populations or specimens) add to the attraction of this species, particularly among livebearer enthusiasts.

DISTRIBUTION: *Mainly Tamesi river basin (Tamaulipas) and Panuco river basin (San Luis de Potosi) in Mexico*

SIZE: *Males up to 2½in (6cm)—excluding the sword; females up to 7.5 cm (3in); larger sizes also reported*

BEHAVIOR: *Active shoaler; keep as outlined for* X. birchmanni

DIET: *As for* X. birchmanni

AQUARIUM: *As for* X. birchmanni

BREEDING: *Up to 50 fry (but usually fewer) are produced every four to eight (usually four to five) weeks*

SUNSET PLATY

VARIATUS PLATY

Xiphophorus variatus

FAMILY: Poeciliidae
SUBFAMILY: Poeciliinae

THIS FISH IS MORE SLENDER THAN *X. MACULATUS* (*see* above) and carries a number of bars on its body (lacking in *X. maculatus*). Many aquarium Variatus specimens are hybrids between these two platy species or between *X. variatus* and *X. helleri*. At least one such variety even exhibits a pronounced sword, which is a characteristic of *X. helleri*, but not of either platy species.

DISTRIBUTION: *Atlantic slope of Mexico*

SIZE: *Males up to 2¼in (5.5cm); females approximately 2¾in (7cm); cultivated varieties may be larger*

BEHAVIOR: *A peaceful shoaler*

DIET: *As for* X. birchmanni

AQUARIUM: *As for* X. birchmanni. *Temperature range: 61–81°F (16–27°C)*

BREEDING: *Around 50 fry (but up to 100) produced every four to six weeks*

GOODEIDS AND THEIR RELATIVES

Goodeids—also frequently, but confusingly, referred to as Mexican livebearers or Highland carp—received a great deal of attention following the introduction of *Ameca splendens* (*see* below) in the early 1970s. The reason for this interest was the species' unusual reproductive strategy. Goodeids appeared to be related to poeciliids, but they also possessed some unique characteristics. Males do not have the characteristic poeciliid gonopodium (*see* Glossary); instead they have a distinct notch (spermatopodium). Fertilization of eggs is internal—as in poeciliid livebearers—but females cannot store sperm. Consequently, each brood requires a separate insemination. After an egg has been fertilized within its egg sac, the female ejects it into the ovarian cavity or lumen, where all subsequent development occurs. Bathed in nutrient-rich ovarian fluid, embryos develop whitish, strand-like structures (trophotaeniae) from their vent. These act as a means of nourishment absorption and waste product elimination, and result in enormous weight increases during gestation. As a consequence, the young are huge (relatively speaking) at birth when compared with poeciliid fry; weighing many thousand times more than the eggs from which they developed. The trophotaeniae are still present at birth, but are lost soon afterward.

At one time, these characteristics were deemed sufficiently significant to warrant the assignment of goodeids to their own family, the Goodeidae. Today, they are afforded subfamilial status, i.e. Goodeinae. A further subfamily, the Empetrichthyinae—which contains two egglaying genera that lack pelvic fins—now joins the goodeines within the family Goodeidae (*see* Parenti, 1981, and Parenti and Rauchenberger, 1989, in Bibliography).

Together with the family Cyprinodontidae, the goodeids are now regarded members of the superfamily Cyprinodontoidea. This is a similar arrangement as that described earlier for the poeciliids and anablepids (superfamily Poecilioidea).

In the pages that follow, representatives of the two families and of three subfamilies will be featured:

Family: Goodeidae
Subfamily: Goodeinae

Family: Cyprinodontidae
Subfamilies: Cubanichthyinae and Cyprinodontinae

GOLDEN BUMBLEBEE GOODEID

Allotoca dugesi

FAMILY: Goodeidae
SUBFAMILY: Goodeinae

MOST MALES EXHIBIT A BEAUTIFUL GOLDEN-yellow sheen in the lower half of the body (below a dark horizontal body stripe). Females are often mottled and exhibit some blue in the lower half of the body. This is the most commonly seen species in the genus, although *A. maculata* (Opal Allotoca), from Jalisco, *A. catarinae* (Green Allotoca), from Michoacán and *A. goslinei* (Banded Allotoca), from Jalisco, are also occasionally seen.

DISTRIBUTION: *Lerma river basin in Jalisco; several localities in Michoacán and Guanajuato (all Mexico)*

SIZE: *Males up to 2¼in (6cm), usually smaller; females slightly larger*

BEHAVIOR: *Can become aggressive; best kept as a pair or as trio of one male and two females*

DIET: *Live and dry foods accepted; vegetable component important*

AQUARIUM: *Well-planted, with some surface vegetation, subdued lighting and some rock shelter. Alkaline, medium-hard water is preferred. Temperature range: 64–75°F (18–24°C)*

BREEDING: *Up to 76 fry reported, but broods generally smaller and produced at around eight-week intervals during breeding season (spring/summer)*

AMECA
BUTTERFLY GOODEID

Ameca splendens

FAMILY: Goodeidae
SUBFAMILY: Goodeinae

THIS IS THE BEST-KNOWN OF ALL THE GOODEIDS. It caused a stir when it was first introduced into the hobby in the early 1970s owing, largely, to the unusual goodeid reproductive strategy (*see* introduction to this section above). Although *Ameca* is under threat in the wild, the species itself is relatively safe in that all specimens currently in the hobby are captive-bred. A dark aquarium strain of the species has been developed and is occasionally available.

DISTRIBUTION: *Ameca river basin in Jalisco (Mexico)*

SIZE: *Males up to 3in (8cm); females up to 4¾in (12cm)*

BEHAVIOR: *Active, generally tolerant species; older specimens may develop into fin-nippers*

DIET: *All foods accepted; vegetable component important*

AQUARIUM: *Spacious, well-planted, with some floating vegetation and some open swimming spaces. Alkaline, medium-hard water preferred. Temperature range: 64–84°F (18–29°C) tolerated, but 72–77°F (22–25°C) advisable longterm*

BREEDING: *Up to 40 large fry can be produced during the warmer months of the year at around eight-week intervals*

AMECA (AMECA SPLENDENS)

SPOTTED GOODEID

BARRED GOODEID

Chapalichthys encaustus

FAMILY: Goodeidae
SUBFAMILY: Goodeinae

OVERALL, THIS SPECIES IS SIMILAR TO AMECA *splendens* in body shape. The body patterning, however, consists of a number (around eight) of shortish black vertical bars stretching from just behind the gill cover to the caudal peduncle. *C. pardalis* (Polkadot Goodeid) and the rarely seen *C. peraticus*, both from Michoacán, are also similar in shape and requirements.

DISTRIBUTION: *Laguna de Chapala and Rio Grande de Santiago in Jalisco; Lago Cuitzeo and Tanhuato river in Michoacán (Mexico)*

SIZE: *Males around 2¼in (6cm); females around 3in (8cm)*

BEHAVIOR: *As for A. splendens*

DIET: *As for A. splendens*

AQUARIUM: *As for A. splendens*

BREEDING: *As for A. splendens. Temperature range: 64–82°F (18–28°C), but the higher temperatures should be avoided longterm*

RAINBOW GOODEID

Characodon lateralis

FAMILY: Goodeidae
SUBFAMILY: Goodeinae

THIS IS ONE OF THE MOST COLORFUL SPECIES IN THE family. It is also quite variable, although most males in peak condition exhibit a great deal of red coloration, bluish-green reflective scales and yellow-golden undersides. *C.*

audax (Black Prince or Bold Goodeid)—also from Durango, Mexico—lacks the red coloration, but has impressive black finnage.

DISTRIBUTION: *Durango, Mexico (mainly Los Beros and Upper Mezquital river)*

SIZE: *Males up to 2¼in (6cm), but usually smaller; females reported up to 3in (7.5cm), but usually smaller*

BEHAVIOR: *Generally retiring; best kept as a trio of one male and two females, or a mixed shoal in a species tank set up specifically for it*

DIET: *As for Ameca splendens*

AQUARIUM: *As for Ameca splendens. Temperature range: 64–75°F (18–24°C)*

BREEDING: *Generally fewer than 20 fry produced at eight-week intervals*

AMARILLO GOODEID

BLACK SAILFIN GOODEID

Girardinichthys viviparus

FAMILY: Goodeidae
SUBFAMILY: Goodeinae

MALES OF THIS SPECIES DEVELOP BLACK COLoration on most fins, with the large dorsal fin being particularly impressive. Females develop deep-black coloration along their bellies. *G. multiradiatus* (Golden Sailfin Goodeid) from Lago de Lerma and other localities within Mexico State, i.e. around Mexico City, has equally impressive yellow finnage.

DISTRIBUTION: *Several water bodies within Mexico City*

SIZE: *Males up to 2in (5cm), but usually smaller; females up to 2¾in (7cm)*

BEHAVIOR: *Generally retiring; may be kept as a shoal*

DIET: *As for Ameca splendens. Vegetable component essential.*

AQUARIUM: *As for Ameca splendens. Temperature range: 64–77°F (18–25°C)*

BREEDING: *Around 20 fry produced every seven to eight weeks*

BLACK-FINNED GOODEID

Goodea atripinnis

FAMILY: Goodeidae
SUBFAMILY: Goodeinae

AT LEAST FOUR SUBSPECIES OF THIS SUBSTANTIAL species are known: *G. a. atripinnis*, *G. a. martini* (Martin's Black-finned Goodeid), from Rio de Morelia and Lago de Cuitzeo (Michoacán), *G. a. luitpoldi* (Luitpold's Goodeid), from Lago de Patzcuaro (Michoacán), and *G. a. xaliscone*, from Laguna Chapala (Jalisco). They differ slightly in coloration and small details but have similar characteristics and requirements.

DISTRIBUTION: *Durango and Jalisco in Mexico*

SIZE: *Males up to 4¾in (12cm); females up to 8in (20cm)*

BEHAVIOR: *Occasional fin-nipper, best kept as a shoal in a species tank set up specifically for this species*

DIET: *As for Ameca splendens. Vegetable component essential.*

AQUARIUM: *As for Ameca splendens. Temperature range: 64–75°F (18–24°C)*

BREEDING: *Around 50 fry produced every six to eight weeks*

BLUE-TAILED GOODEID

Goodea toweri

SYNONYM: *Ataeniobius toweri*
FAMILY: Goodeidae
SUBFAMILY: Goodeinae

CONSIDERABLE DEBATE STILL SURROUNDS THE name of this species, with some authors still referring to it by its earlier name of *Ataeniobius*. This name refers to the absence of trophotaeniae (*see* introduction to this section, p.284, for explanation). In fact, this is not quite accurate: developing embryos do possess trophotaeniae, but they are tiny and virtually disappear before birth.

DISTRIBUTION: *San Luis de Potosí (Mexico)*

SIZE: *Males reported up to 3in (8cm); females up to 4in (10cm)*

BEHAVIOR: *Shoaler*

DIET: *As for Ameca splendens*

AQUARIUM: *As for Ameca splendens; subdued lighting recommended; vegetable component essential. Temperature range: 72–77°F (22–25°C)*

BREEDING: *Around 30 fry produced every seven to eight weeks during warmer months of the year*

GOLD-BREASTED ILYODON

Ilyodon furcidens

SYNONYMS: *See* below
FAMILY: Goodeidae
SUBFAMILY: Goodeinae

THERE IS CONSIDERABLE DIFFERENCE OF OPINION regarding the identity of the four *Ilyodon* "species." Some authors believe them to be valid species in their own right, others that they are all subspecies of *I. furcidens*. Generally speaking, though, *I. furcidens* and *I. xantusi* (Xantus' Ilyodon) are believed to be very similar to each other—possibly variants of the single species, *I. furcidens*. Similarly, *I. lennoni* (Lennon's Ilyodon) and *I. whitei* could be variants of *I. whitei* (White's Ilyodon). All have similar behavior characteristics and aquarium requirements.

DISTRIBUTION: *Mesa Central in Mexico*

SIZE: *Males around 3½in (9cm); females around 4in (10cm)*

BEHAVIOR: *Active, generally peaceful shoalers*

DIET: *As for Ameca splendens*

AQUARIUM: *As for Ameca splendens. Vegetable component important. Temperature range: 64–77°F (18–25°C)*

BREEDING: *Around 35 fry produced every seven to eight weeks during the warmer months*

SPECKLED SAWFIN GOODEID

Skiffia multipunctata

SYNONYMS: *Skiffia multipunctatus*
FAMILY: Goodeidae
SUBFAMILY: Goodeinae

THE "SAWFIN" IN THE COMMON NAME IS DERIVED from the deep notch that it bears (along with the other members of the genus) on the dorsal fin. Hybrids between this species and the *S. francesae* (Golden Sawfin Goodeid)—which is believed to be extinct in the wild—have been produced in aquaria. In this fertile hybrid—known as the Black Beauty—most of the body of the male is jet black. Other species in the genus (all having similar requirements) are *S. bilineata* (Two-lined or Elfin Goodeid) from Guanajuato, Jalisco and Michoacán, and *S. lermae* (Hooded Sawfin Goodeid), also from Michoacán.

DISTRIBUTION: *Jalisco and Michoacán in Mexico*

SIZE: *Males up to 2½in (6cm); females slightly larger*

BEHAVIOR: *Generally peaceful shoaler*

DIET: *As for Ameca splendens*

AQUARIUM: *As for Ameca splendens. Temperature range: 64–75°F (18–24°C)*

BREEDING: *Around 30 fry produced every seven to eight weeks*

GREEN GOODEID
CAPTIVUS

Xenoophorus captivus

FAMILY: Goodeidae
SUBFAMILY: Goodeinae

THIS ROBUST SPECIES IS SOMEWHAT SIMILAR IN overall appearance to *Ameca splendens*. Males in peak condition are richly adorned with greenish-blue reflective scales on a dark background.

DISTRIBUTION: *San Luis de Potosi (Mexico)*

SIZE: *Males up to 2½in (6cm); females slightly larger*

BEHAVIOR: *As for Ameca splendens*

DIET: *As for Ameca splendens*

AQUARIUM: *As for Ameca splendens. Temperature range: 68–77°F (20–25°C)*

BREEDING: *As for Ameca splendens*

ORANGE-TAILED GOODEID
RED-TAILED GOODEID

Xenotoca eiseni

FAMILY: Goodeidae
SUBFAMILY: Goodeinae

MATURE MALES POSSESS AN IMPRESSIVE HUMP behind the head and a very deep body. The two dominant colors in such males are blue, particularly on the posterior half of the body, and an orange or reddish caudal peduncular area. Several forms of the species are known: one with a great deal of blue in the body (Nayarit), a blotched one (San Marco) and one with some body spots (Spotted). Of these, the San Marco type is the only one found in the wild—around San Marco, in Jalisco, Mexico.

DISTRIBUTION: *Nayarit and Jalisco (Mexico)*

SIZE: *Males around 2½in (6cm); females around 2¾in (7cm)*

BEHAVIOR: *Shoaling; fin-nipping tendencies*

DIET: *As for Ameca splendens*

AQUARIUM: *As for Ameca splendens*

BREEDING: *Around 30 fry are produced every seven to eight weeks*

CUBAN KILLIFISH
CUBAN MINNOW

Cubanichthys cubensis

FAMILY: Cyprinodontidae
SUBFAMILY: Cubanichthyinae

THERE ARE ONLY TWO SPECIES IN THIS SUBFAMILY, *C. cubensis*, and *C. pengelleyi* (Jamaican Killifish). The Cuban Killie has a number of spotted bands consisting of sparkling bluish-green scales running along the body, from behind the head to the caudal peduncle. Males also have colorful dorsal, anal and caudal fins.

DISTRIBUTION: *Cuba*

SIZE: *Up to 1¾in (4.5cm)*

BEHAVIOR: *Peaceful; should be kept in a shoal*

DIET: *Livefoods preferred, but other diets accepted*

ORANGE-TAILED GOODEID (XENOTOCA EISENI)

OTHER *GOODEID* SPECIES

In addition to the featured species, other members of the subfamily Goodeinae become available from time to time, particularly via specialist aquatic societies. All require alkaline, medium-hard conditions, most prefer cool water (between 64–77°F/18–25°C), and all will accept a varied diet, which should include a vegetable component. However, behavioral characteristics differ. Specialist literature (or specialist aquarists) should be consulted prior to attempting to keep these species. Sizes given below are approximate, with that for males listed first.

SCIENTIFIC NAME	COMMON NAME(S)	SIZE	BEHAVIOR
Allodontichthys spp.	Darter Goodeids (several species)	Up to 2¾in (7cm); 2¾in (7cm)	Somewhat aggressive; best kept as pair or trio of one male and two females
Aloophorus robustus	Bulldog Goodeid (only one species)	Up to 6in (15cm); 6¼in (16cm)*	Aggressive and predatory; keep as a pair or a trio
Hubbsina turneri	Turner's Sailfin Goodeid (only one species)	2½in (6cm); 3in (7.5cm)	A peaceful shoaler
Xenotaenia resolanae	Leopard Goodeid (only one species)	Up to 2½in (6cm); 2½in (6cm)	Exhibits fin-nipping tendencies, but may be kept in a shoal
Xenotoca variata	Jewel Goodeid	Up to 3in (8cm); up to 3½in (9cm)	Shoaling; fin-nipping tendencies
Zoogoneticus quitzeoensis	Picoted Goodeid, Crescent Goodeid or Crescent Zoe (probably only one sp.)	Up to 2½in (6.5cm); up to 2¾in (7cm)	Shy shoaler

NOTE:

*Up to the late 1990s, this species was believed to attain a maximum size of around 4in (10cm) for males and 4¾in (12cm) for females.

ARABIAN KILLIFISH (APHANIUS DISPAR)

AQUARIUM: *Well-planted, well-filtered, with subdued lighting. Neutral to alkaline, medium-hard water recommended. Temperature range: 72–82°F (22–28°C)*

BREEDING: *Adhesive eggs are scattered among vegetation. Hatching takes about ten days*

ARABIAN KILLIFISH

MOTHER OF PEARL KILLIFISH

Aphanius dispar

FAMILY: Cyprinodontidae
SUBFAMILY: Cyprinodontinae

OF THE 30 OR SO SPECIES IN THIS GENUS, TWO ARE much more frequently encountered than any others: Arabian Killifish and *A. mento* (Black Persian Minnow/Killifish), mainly from Israel and Turkey. Two subspecies of Arabian Killifish are generally recognized: *A. d. dispar* and *A. d. richardsoni* from Jordan. Both have similar aquarium requirements. *A. mento*, on the other hand, has lower temperature requirements (50–77°F/10–25°C) and wider pH and hardness tolerance ranges (from slightly acid and soft, to alkaline and hard).

DISTRIBUTION: *Middle East, including Dubai, Jordan, Iran and north Somalia*

SIZE: *Around 2¾in (7cm)*

BEHAVIOR: *Adult males become scrappy*

DIET: *Wide range of foods accepted; vegetable component important*

AQUARIUM: *Well-planted (with salt-tolerant species), and suitable retreats. Well-filtered, hard, alkaline water important, with 1 teaspoonful salt per 1 Imp. gal (4.5–5 liters). Temperature range: 61–84°F (16–29°C)*

BREEDING: *Eggs are laid among fine-leaved vegetation or spawning mop (see* Aphyosemion australe, *p.262). Hatching takes about seven days*

FLORIDA FLAGFISH

AMERICAN FLAGFISH

Jordanella floridae

FAMILY: Cyprinodontidae
SUBFAMILY: Cyprinodontinae

THIS OLD FAVORITE (*SEE* PHOTO P.1) CONTINUES to hold its own against some of the more colorful killifishes of both the New and Old Worlds. It is a tough, easy-to-breed species in which mature males in peak condition constantly display toward each other, as well as toward prospective mates.

DISTRIBUTION: *From Florida southward to the Yucatán peninsula in Mexico*

SIZE: *Males up to 2½in (6.5cm); females slightly smaller*

BEHAVIOR: *Males territorial and often aggressive toward rivals, but more tolerant of other species*

DIET: *All types of food accepted; vegetable component important*

AQUARIUM: *Thickly planted, with some open swimming areas and fine-grained substratum. Water chemistry not critical, but quality must be good. Temperature range: 66–77°F (19–25°C)*

BREEDING: *Eggs are either scattered among fine-leaved vegetation or laid in a depression prepared by the male; male also guards eggs. Hatching takes six to nine days*

MISCELLANEOUS SPECIES

In addition to the families featured in the foregoing sections, there are many others represented in the aquarium hobby. Some have just a single representative, or only a few, but like *Oryzias latipes* (Medaka) they are well-known. In other instances, while the total number of species that can be obtained may be more numerous, many of these are little-known. The pages that follow contain a selection of both types. It does not claim to be exhaustive (indeed, it cannot be) and interested aquarists are advised to seek specialist advice for individual genera and species not covered here.

WRESTLING HALFBEAK (DERMOGENYS PUSILLUS)

WRESTLING HALFBEAK

MALAYAN HALFBEAK

Dermogenys pusillus

SYNONYM: *Dermogenys pusilla*
FAMILY: Hemirhamphidae
SUBFAMILY: Hemirhamphinae

OF THE 15 OR SO SPECIES IN THIS GENUS, *D. pusillus* is the only one encountered with any regularity. Two subspecies are generally recognized: *D. p. borealis* with bright-yellow and/or red coloration on the dorsal, caudal and anal fin, and *D. p. pusillus*, whose coloration is mainly restricted to the dorsal fin. A golden variant of *D. p. borealis* is occasionally available.

DISTRIBUTION: *Malaysia and surrounding regions*

SIZE: *Males reported up to 6cm (2¼in), but usually smaller; females up to 3in (8cm), but usually smaller*

BEHAVIOR: *Surface-swimming; often quarrelsome, sometimes nervous*

DIET: *Livefoods; floating freeze-dried, deep-frozen and other diets*

AQUARIUM: *Well-covered, with plenty of open surface space (i.e. free of vegetation), subdued lighting, and submerged vegetation planted in clumps along sides and back of aquarium. Neutral to alkaline medium-hard water with one teaspoonful of salt per 1 Imp. gal (4.5–5 liters) recommended. Temperature range: 64–86°F (18–30°C)*

BREEDING: *Up to 40 (but usually fewer) very large fry are produced every four to eight weeks*

CELEBES HALFBEAK

Nomorhamphus liemi

FAMILY: Hemirhamphidae
SUBFAMILY: Hemirhamphinae

OF THE EIGHT OR SO SPECIES IN THIS GENUS, THE Celebes Halfbeak (*see* photo p.6) is the one most frequently available. Its common name, appropriate in that the species is found in Sulawesi (Celebes), would seem better suited to *N. celebensis*—also from Sulawesi—which is normally referred to as Northern Harlequin Halfbeak. Two subspecies of *N. liemi* are recognized: *N. l. liemi* (known as both Celebes Halfbeak and Southern Harlequin Halfbeak), and *N. l. snijdersi* (Snijder's Halfbeak).

DISTRIBUTION: *Areas around Maros in southern Sulawesi*

SIZE: *Males around 6cm (2¼in); females reported up to 4in (10cm)*

BEHAVIOR: *Surface-swimming; considerably more peaceful than Dermogenys pusillus*

DIET: *As for Dermogenys pusillus*

AQUARIUM: *As for Dermogenys pusillus. No salt required. Temperature range: 72–79°F (22–26°C)*

Breeding: *As for Dermogenys pusillus. Produces 10–15 fry per brood*

OTHER HALFBEAK SPECIES

In addition to *Dermogenys* and *Nomorhamphus* halfbeaks, representatives of at least three other genera are occasionally available.

SCIENTIFIC NAME	COMMON NAME(S)	SIZE	NOTES
Hemirhamphodon spp.	Several species are encountered, the most frequent of these being the Thread Jaw, Long-nosed, or Longsnouted, Halfbeak (*H. pogonognathus*)	Up to 3½in (9cm)	No salt required
Tondanichthys kottelati	Kottelat's Halfbeak	Around 2½in (6.5cm)	Little aquarium data available; no salt required
Zenarchopterus spp.	Several species occasionally imported—most frequently Beaufort's Halfbeak (*Z. beauforti*) and *Z. dispar* (no common name)	Around 6in (15cm)	Predominantly marine, but enters freshwater: add salt (1 teaspoon per 1 Imp. gal (4.5–5 liters) to the aquarium water

JAPANESE MEDAKA

GOLDEN MEDAKA, JAPANESE RICE-FISH, GEISHA GIRL

Oryzias latipes

FAMILY: Oryziidae (referred to as Oryziatidae by some authors)

VIRTUALLY ALL THE MEDAKAS CURRENTLY IN THE hobby are golden—this being considerably more colorful than the wild type. Japanese Medaka is popular not just because of its color but because of its breeding behavior. Of the other ten or so species in the genus, the following are the most frequently seen: *O. celebensis* (Celebes Medaka), from Sulawesi, *O. javanicus* (Javanese Medaka), from Java, and *O. melastigma* (Spotted Medaka), from the area around Calcutta (India). *O. nigrimas* (Black Medaka) from Lake Poso in Sulawesi—in which some males are jet black—is rarely seen. All have similar requirements.

DISTRIBUTION: *China, Japan and South Korea; reported from Java and Malaysia*

SIZE: *Around 1¼in (4cm)*

BEHAVIOR: *Active shoaler*

DIET: *Wide range of foods accepted*

AQUARIUM: *Well-illuminated, well-planted, with open swimming areas, some clear surface area (i.e. free of floating vegetation), and water movement. Water chemistry not critical, but slightly alkaline, medium-hard water preferred. Temperature range: below 15℃ (59℉) to above 28℃ (82℉); these extremes should, however, be avoided longterm*

BREEDING: *Eggs may be fertilized internally or externally; either way, the female carries them attached to the vent for a time before depositing them among fine-leaved vegetation. Hatching takes seven to ten days*

INDIAN GLASSFISH

Parambassis ranga

SYNONYM: *Chanda ranga*
FAMILY: Chandidae (referred to as Ambassidae by some authors)

THIS IS THE MOST NATURALLY COLORFUL OF the three species generally available (*see* photo p.1). *Parambassis (Chanda) commersonii* (Commerson's Glassfish) and *P. (C). wolffii* (Wolff's Glassfish) are larger: in the wild—not in aquaria—the former attains around 4in (10cm) and the latter 20cm (7¾in). During the 1990s, "painted" glassfish—artificially colored (injected) fish—became widely available from Far East sources. Demand for these has declined dramatically, both from consumers and dealers, with the natural types regaining some of their former popularity. Injected specimens lose most of their color after several months and also appear to be prone to Lymphocystis (Cauliflower Disease)—a non-lethal virus infection.

DISTRIBUTION: *India, Myanmar and Thailand*

SIZE: *Up to 3in (8cm) reported, but usually smaller*

BEHAVIOR: *Somewhat territorial, but generally peaceful shoaler; sometimes timid, particularly in sparsely planted aquaria*

DIET: *Livefoods preferred, but deep-frozen and freeze-dried diets also readily accepted; dry foods only reluctantly taken*

AQUARIUM: *Heavily planted (with salt-tolerant or artificial plants), dark substratum, shelters, and subdued lighting. Mature, hard, alkaline water, with some salt (1 to 3 teaspoonfuls per 1 Imp. gal/4.5–5 liters) important for longterm health. Temperature range: 64–86℉ (18–30℃)*

BREEDING: *Challenging in aquaria. Eggs are scattered among fine-leaved vegetation—often following exposure of the aquarium to morning sun. Hatching takes one day. Fry are difficult to raise owing to their very small size*

ARCHER FISH

Toxotes jaculatrix

SYNONYM: *Toxotes jaculator*
FAMILY: Toxotidae

THIS IS THE MOST WIDELY AVAILABLE MEMBER OF its genus and family (*see* photo on p.1), although the *T. chatareus* (Seven-spotted Archer Fish) is also seen with increasing regularity. Two other species are also seen, but only rarely: *T. lorentzi* (Primitive Archer Fish) and *T. oligolepis* (Few-scaled Archer Fish). All possess the remarkable ability to eject powerful jets of water to shoot down prey, usually insects, from branches located as much as 5ft (1.5m) above the water.

DISTRIBUTION: *Widely distributed from Gulf of Aden, to Australia, including India and southeast Asia*

SIZE: *Up to 10in (25cm) reported, but usually much smaller*

BEHAVIOR: *Generally tolerant of tankmates, including conspecifics; may be kept in a shoal if accommodation sufficiently spacious*

DIET: *Almost exclusively livefoods, although floating freeze-dried and deep-frozen formulations may be accepted. If flying insects can be provided, these will be shot down over a period of time*

AQUARIUM: *Tightly covered. Deep-sided, but only partially filled to create an above-water space for twigs and/or branches that can act as perches for insects, e.g. crickets. Plants used for underwater decoration must be salt-tolerant or artificial. Neutral to alkaline, medium-hard water with one teaspoonful of salt per 1 Imp. gal (4.5 liters) important. Temperature range: 77–86℉ (25–30℃)*

BREEDING: *No documented accounts of aquarium breeding available*

SCAT

ARGUS FISH

Scatophagus argus

FAMILY: Scatophagidae

JUVENILE SCATS ARE VERY ATTRACTIVELY MARKED, although some of the intensity of coloration is lost as they grow. A reddish "species" or "subspecies" is also available

SCAT (SCATOPHAGUS ARGUS)

▲ MONO (MONODACTYLUS ARGENTEUS)　　　▼ SPOTTED PUFFER (TETRAODON SCHOUTEDENI). SEE BOX

and is referred to as *S. "rubrifrons"* or *S. argus atromaculatus*. However, it is generally accepted that it is just a naturally occurring color variety of *S. agrus*. *S. tetracanthus* (African Scat) is only rarely seen in the hobby. *Selenotoca multifasciata* (Silver Scat) from Australia—also known as Striped Butterfish or Striped Scat—is occasionally available and has similar characteristics and requirements. In the wild, adult Scats are generally estuarine or saltwater fish. Juveniles enter freshwater, and it is these that are usually available in shops.

DISTRIBUTION: *Widely distributed in brackish and marine waters in the Indian and Pacific oceans*

SIZE: *Up to 12in (30cm)*

BEHAVIOR: *Lively, peaceful shoaler*

DIET: *All foods accepted; vegetable component essential*

AQUARIUM: *Large, deep, with clumps of salt-tolerant (or artificial) plants*, and substantial open swimming areas. Well-filtered, alkaline, hard water important. Add 1 teaspoonful of salt per 1 Imp. gal (4.5–5 liters) to aquaria housing juveniles, gradually doubling this concentration as they grow. Eventually, nearly (or fully) saline conditions*

should be provided for adults. Temperature range: 68–82°F (20–28°C)*

BREEDING: *No documented accounts available*

*NOTE: It has been reported that the Java Fern (Microsorum pteropus) is toxic to Scats

MONO
MOON, or FINGER, FISH, SILVER BATFISH, BUTTER BREAM
Monodactylus argenteus
FAMILY: Monodactylidae

USUALLY SOLD AS JUVENILES, MONOS WILL—given appropriate conditions—eventually grow into large fish. Juveniles often occur in freshwater, but adults require brackish conditions. As juveniles grow, they lose their pelvic fins either partially or entirely. In *Psettus (Monodactylus) sebae* (Seba Mono), the body is deeper than long, particularly in young specimens. It is also a little less tolerant of freshwater conditions than the Mono.

DISTRIBUTION: *Widely distributed in brackish-water tropical regions from Africa to Asia and Australia*

SIZE: *Up to 10in (25cm), but usually smaller*

BEHAVIOR: *Peaceful shoaler, but larger specimens may prey on small fish*

DIET: *As for Scatophagus argus*

AQUARIUM: *As for Scatophagus argus*

BREEDING: *As for Scatophagus argus*

GREEN PUFFER
Tetraodon fluviatilis
FAMILY: Tetraodontidae

THIS IS PROBABLY THE SPECIES OF PUFFER MOST frequently seen in shops. As its species name indicates, this species can be found in at least some freshwater habitats in the wild. However, for peak longterm health, brackish conditions are recommended.

DISTRIBUTION: *Freshwater and brackish regions in southeast Asia*

SIZE: *Up to 6¾in (17cm)*

BEHAVIOR: *Increasingly intolerant and aggressive with age, particularly toward conspecifics; exhibits fin-nipping tendencies*

DIET: *Wide range of foods accepted, including aquatic snails and succulent plants*

AQUARIUM: *Spacious, with several shelters, fine-grained substratum, and tough and/or unpalatable plants (see Aquarium Plants)—or their artificial equivalents—arranged in clumps along sides and back, leaving open swimming area along front. Neutral to alkaline hard water with about 1 teaspoonful of salt per 1 Imp. gal (4.5–5 liters) recommended. Temperature range: 75–82°F (24–28°C)*

BREEDING: *Challenging in aquaria; brackish conditions important. Eggs are laid on stone and are guarded by male. Hatching takes around six to seven days*

SIAMESE TIGER
Datnioides microlepis
FAMILY: Lobotidae

THIS BEAUTIFULLY MARKED BRACKISH-WATER species grows to a large size and is therefore unsuitable for many aquaria. A second Siamese Tiger (*D. quadrifasciatus*), which is smaller (12in/30cm) and not as boldly marked, is also occasionally available.

DISTRIBUTION: *Borneo, Cambodia, Sumatra and Thailand*

SIZE: *Up to 16in (40cm), but usually much smaller*

BEHAVIOR: *Stalking predator; but can be kept with similar-sized tankmates*

DIET: *Predominantly large livefoods, including fish (a factor that requires consideration prior to purchase); it may be weaned off such foods and onto chunky deep-frozen, meaty and freeze-dried formulations*

OTHER PUFFER SPECIES

Several other species of puffer fish are available with varying degrees of regularity. They vary in size, requirements and behavior, so the main features of some of these species are listed below. Sizes given are approximate. Tank layouts should be as for *T. fluviatilis*.

SCIENTIFIC NAME	COMMON NAME(S)	SIZE	TEMPERATURE RANGE	NOTES
Carinotetraodon (Tetraodon) lorteti	Red-bellied Puffer	Up to 2¾in (7cm)	75–82°F (24–28°C)	Aggression increases with age; slightly acid, medium-hard water; no salt
Monotretus travanconicus	Red-green Dwarf Puffer	Around ¾in (2cm)	72–79°F (22–26°C)	A tiny shoaling species; slightly acid to slightly alkaline, softish water; no salt
Tetraodon biocellatus	Figure-of-eight Puffer	Up to 7in (18cm)	72–81°F (22–27°C)	Aggression increases with age; water as for *T. fluviatilis*
T. cutcutia	Mosaic Puffer	6in (15cm)	72–77°F (22–25°C)	Characteristics and water as for *T. fluviatilis*
T. mbu	Giant Puffer	Up to 12in (30cm)	75–82°F (24–28°C)	Keep alone; water conditions as for *T. fluviatilis*; no salt
T. schoutedeni	Spotted Congo Puffer	4in (10cm)	72–79°F (22–26°C)	One of the most peaceful species; tank as for *T. fluviatilis*; no salt
T. steindachneri	Steindachner's Puffer	2½in (6cm)	72–79°F (22–26°C)	Aggressive and intolerant; avid planteater; tank as for *T. fluviatilis*; no salt

ELEPHANTNOSE (GNATHONEMUS PETERSII)

AQUARIUM: *As for Tetraodon fluviatilis.*
Temperature range: 72–79°F (22–26°C)

BREEDING: *No documented accounts of aquarium breeding available*

BUTTERFLYFISH

Pantodon buchholzi

FAMILY: Pantodontidae

THIS CHALLENGING FISH, KNOWN IN THE HOBBY since the early 1900s, has never been available in large numbers. Contrary to reports, this species does not fly, i.e. it does not flap its wing-like pectoral fins. It is, however, able to glide for short distances.

DISTRIBUTION: *West Africa: Cameroon, Zaire and Nigeria*

SIZE: *Up to 10cm (4in)*

BEHAVIOR: *Surface predator; can be aggressive toward other surface swimmers but tolerant toward tankmates that occupy the lower levels of the aquarium*

DIET: *Predominantly livefoods, but will take deep-frozen and freeze-dried diets, and may accept some floating dry formulations,*

AQUARIUM: *Spacious, well-covered, with large open surface areas—but also incorporating some floating vegetation. Soft, slightly acid water, preferably tannin-stained (see Aquarium Setup), preferred, but some deviation tolerated. Temperature range: 73–86°F (23–30°C)*

BREEDING: *Challenging in aquaria; floating eggs are produced over several days. Hatching takes one-and-a-half to two days*

ELEPHANTNOSE

PETER'S ELEPHANTNOSE

Gnathonemus petersii

FAMILY: Mormyridae

ELEPHANTNOSES USE WEAK ELECTRICAL PULSES TO communicate with each other and to find their way around in the often-murky waters of their natural habitat. All species are challenging to keep, although modern-day foods and a deeper understanding of these somewhat unusual fish make their upkeep much easier than it used to be.

DISTRIBUTION: *Central and West Africa*

SIZE: *Up to 9in (23cm) reported, but usually smaller*

BEHAVIOR: *Predominantly bottom dwelling; crepuscular and nocturnal; territorial toward conspecifics; burrows in substratum in search of food*

DIET: *Distinct preference for livefoods, but will also accept other formulations, particularly deep-frozen and freeze-dried diets*

AQUARIUM: *Spacious, well-filtered, with clumps of vegetation, open spaces and fine-grained substratum (very important!). A "moonlight" fluorescent tube to facilitate nighttime viewing* recommended. Softish, slightly acid to neutral water preferred, but some deviation tolerated. Temperature range: 72–82°F (22–28°C)

BREEDING: *No documented accounts are available*

WHALE
WHALE-FACED MARCUSENIUS

Marcusenius brachyistius

SYNONYM: *Brienomyrus brachyistius*
FAMILY: Mormyridae

THIS IS ONE OF SEVERAL ELEPHANTNOSES THAT lack a "nose" and are referred to as "whales." Unlike *Gnathonemus petersii*, which has attractive body markings, the Whale is generally a uniform brownish coloration.

DISTRIBUTION: *West Africa*

SIZE: *Up to 7in (18cm) reported, but usually smaller*

BEHAVIOR: *Generally peaceful; crepuscular/nocturnal*

DIET: *As for* Gnathonemus petersii

AQUARIUM: *As for* Gnathonemus petersii

BREEDING: *As for* Gnathonemus petersii

CLOWN KNIFEFISH

Notopterus chitala

FAMILY: Notopteridae

THE CLOWN KNIFEFISH IS GENERALLY AVAILABLE as small, very attractively marked juveniles. Adults are very large (a factor that should be borne in mind at the time of purchase). If their needs can be catered to, they make very interesting fish for aquaria, but they are not suitable for new aquar-

OTHER ELEPHANTNOSES AND WHALES

Several members of the family Mormyridae are now regularly available, though not always in large numbers. All are, basically, similar in characteristics and aquarium requirements. The following are among the most frequently seen species. Sizes quoted are approximate.

SCIENTIFIC NAME	COMMON NAME(S)	SIZE
Campylomormyrus cassaicus	Angolan Elephantnose	10in (25cm)
Gnathonemus elephas	Blunt-nosed Elephantnose	8in (20cm)
G. tamandua	None	16in (40cm)
Marcusenius angolensis	Spotted Elephantnose or Whale	5½in (14cm)
M. longianalis	Slender Elephantnose or Whale	6in (15cm)
M. macrolepidotus	Large-scaled Elephantnose or Whale	10in (25cm)
Mormyrus longirostris	Short-faced Elephantnose	12in (30cm)
Petrocephalus catostoma	Big-nosed Whale	2½in (6cm)
Pollimyrus nigripinnis	Dusky Whale	4¼in (11cm)

ists. Two other species, *Papyrocranus (Notopterus) afer* (African Featherfin or Knifefish) and *N. notopterus* (Asian Knifefish) are also available. They have similar requirements to Clown Knifefish.

DISTRIBUTION: *Widely distributed in Southeast Asia*

SIZE: *Up to c.39in (1m) reported, but usually smaller*

BEHAVIOR: *Adults are solitary predators, active mainly at dusk and during the night; juveniles may be kept together, at least for a time*

DIET: *Large livefoods, including live fish, preferred—a factor that needs due consideration prior to purchase; chunky, meat-based or fish-based formulations also accepted*

AQUARIUM: *Large, well-covered, well-filtered, well-planted, with subdued lighting and large shelters, e.g. substantial pieces of bogwood. A "moonlight" fluorescent tube will facilitate nighttime viewing.*

Water chemistry not critical, but softish, slightly acid water preferred; quality must be good. Temperature range: 75–86°F (24–30°C)

BREEDING: *No documented accounts of aquarium breeding currently available*

AFRICAN KNIFEFISH

Xenomystus nigri

FAMILY: Notopteridae

WHILE LOOKING SUPERFICIALLY SIMILAR TO *Notopterus notopterus* (Asian Knifefish), and sharing a common name with *Papyrocranus (Notopterus) afer*—see under *N. chitala*—it can be easily distinguished by its total lack of a dorsal fin. This species is also considerably smaller than *Notopterus chitala* and can therefore be accommodated more easily.

DISTRIBUTION: *River Nile, Gabon, Liberia, Niger and Zaire*

SIZE: *Around 12in (30cm)*

BEHAVIOR: *As for* Notopterus chitala

DIET: *As for* Notopterus chitala

AQUARIUM: *As for* Notopterus chitala

BREEDING: *As for* Notopterus chitala

BLACK GHOST KNIFEFISH

Apteronotus albifrons

FAMILY: Apteronotidae

THIS IS A MOST ATTRACTIVELY MARKED SPECIES whose jet-black body contrasts sharply with a white streak, which runs from the snout to the top of the head, and two white patches in the caudal peduncular area. The somewhat less strikingly marked

AFRICAN KNIFEFISH (XENOMYSTUS NIGRI)

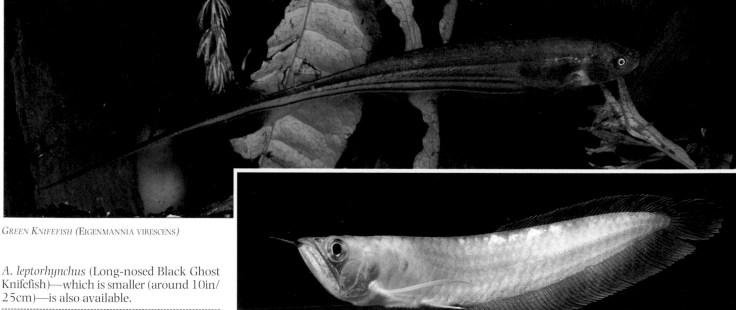

Green Knifefish (Eigenmannia virescens)

A. leptorhynchus (Long-nosed Black Ghost Knifefish)—which is smaller (around 10in/25cm)—is also available.

DISTRIBUTION: *Widely distributed in northern South America*

SIZE: *Up to 20in (50cm)*

BEHAVIOR: *Often timid, but can become aggressive, particularly toward conspecifics*

DIET: *Chunky livefoods and deep-frozen or freeze-dried formulations preferred*

AQUARIUM: *As for* Notopterus chitala. *Temperature range: 73–82°F (23–28°C)*

BREEDING: *As for* Notopterus chitala

GREEN KNIFEFISH

Eigenmannia virescens

FAMILY: Sternopygidae

THIS IS ONE OF THE SO-CALLED GLASS KNIFEFISHES grouped by some authors, along with other related species, within the family Rhamphichthyidae. However, according to the classification followed here (as in Nelson 1994—*see* Bibliography), the Rhamphichthyidae are known as the sand knifefishes and contain only two genera (not featured in this book). Green Knifefish look particularly impressive in a shoal, where the establishment of a strict pecking order prevents fighting and, thus, injuries. *Steatogenys duidae (elegans)* (Barred Knifefish), *Sternopygus macrurus* (Variable Ghost Knifefish), and various species of *Gymnotus*, especially *G. carapo* (Banded Knifefish), all of which have similar requirements, are occasionally available.

DISTRIBUTION: *Widely distributed in tropical regions of South America*

SIZE: *Males reported up to 18in (45cm), but usually smaller; females considerably smaller*

BEHAVIOR: *Shoaler with crepuscular and nocturnal habits*

DIET: *As for* Notopterus chitala

AQUARIUM: *As for* Notopterus chitala

Silver Arowana (Osteoglossum bicirrhosum)

BREEDING: *Adhesive eggs are laid among floating plants*

SILVER AROWANA

Osteoglossum bicirrhosum

FAMILY: Osteoglossidae

TWO SPECIES OF AMAZONIAN AROWANA ARE available, the Silver Arowana and *O. ferreirai* (Black Arowana) from the Rio Negro. The adults are very similar, although Silver Arowana is somewhat sturdier looking, with fewer lateral line scales, dorsal and anal fin rays and vertebrae. Juvenile *O. ferreirai* exhibit the characteristic black coloration responsible for the common name of the species. Both these arowanas are excellent jumpers that can pluck prey from branches above the water surface. This ability has earned them the local name of "macaco d'agua" (water monkey).

DISTRIBUTION: *Amazon drainage, western Orinoco and Guyana*

SIZE: *Up to c.39in (1m) reported, but often smaller*

BEHAVIOR: *Juveniles become progressively intolerant with age, but may be kept with similar-sized tankmates; exceptional jumping ability*

DIET: *Large livefoods, including fish, preferred, but a wide range of meat-based or fish-based formulations will also be accepted*

AQUARIUM: *Large, well-covered, well-filtered, with plenty of open swimming spaces near surface. Soft, slightly to moderately acid water recommended. Temperature range: 75–86°F (24–30°C)*

BREEDING: *Only occasionally achieved in aquaria. Eggs and (later) the young are carried orally by male for up to 60 days*

DRAGON FISH
ASIAN BONYTONGUE/AROWANA

Scleropages formosus

FAMILY: Osteoglossidae

THIS LEGENDARY FISH OF THE FAR EAST IS STEEPED in history and mystery and is one of the "greats" of the aquarium. In their native lands, Dragon Fish are said to bring health, wealth and luck to their owners; they are, consequently, much sought after. The only specimens that can be legally traded are those bred in captivity and approved by the Convention in International Trade in

Dragon Fish (Scleropages formosus)

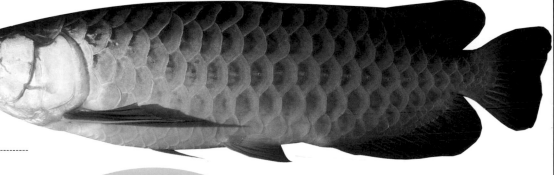

Endangered Species (CITES). However, this species is now bred in such large numbers in captivity that current demand can be satisfactorily met. There are three main color varieties: silver/green, gold and—the most highly sought and expensive—red. Several other varieties have now been added and more are likely to follow. An Australian species, *S. jardinii* (Gulf Saratoga) is also now being bred in captivity, while another Australian species, *S. leichardti* (Spotted Saratoga), is only rarely seen.

DISTRIBUTION: *Widely distributed in Southeast Asia*

Size: Up to 35in (90cm)

BEHAVIOR: *As for* Osteoglossum bicirrhosum

DIET: *As for* Osteoglossum bicirrhosum

AQUARIUM: *As for* Osteoglossum bicirrhosum

BREEDING: *As for* Osteoglossum bicirrhosum

SPECIAL NOTE

Arapaima gigas (Arapaima or Pirarucu) is another member of the Osteoglossidae that may, occasionally, be encountered. However, although it has similar requirements to both *Osteoglossum bicirrhosum* and *Scleropages formosus*, it can attain a length of up to 14.8ft (4.5m) and therefore cannot be regarded as an aquarium fish.

LESSER SPINY EEL
Macrognathus aculeatus

FAMILY: Mastacembelidae

THIS SPECIES IS CHARACTERIZED BY A NUMBER OF prominent eyespots along the base of the dorsal fin and a series of darker and lighter bands running from snout to caudal peduncle. As in all spiny eels, the dorsal fin is preceded by numerous isolated small spines that can be raised, hence the common name for these interesting fish.

DISTRIBUTION: *Southeast Asia*

SIZE: *Up to 14in (35cm) reported, but usually smaller*

BEHAVIOR: *Aggressive toward conspecifics when kept as pairs or trios; aggression subsides when kept in large groups of around ten specimens; a burrower that is most active at dusk and during the night; may prey on small fish*

DIET: *Bottom-dwelling livefoods preferred, but some commercial sinking formulations, e.g. deep-frozen, freeze-dried also accepted; may reluctantly accept pellet/tablet diets*

AQUARIUM: *Spacious, well-covered (spiny eels are expert escape artists), with fine-grained substratum, numerous hiding places, and clumps of plants protected from burrowing activities (see Aquarium Plants). A "moonlight" fluorescent tube will facilitate nighttime viewing. Neutral or slightly alkaline, soft to medium-hard water recommended. A small amount of salt, i.e. 1 teaspoonful per 2 Imp. gal (9–10 liters) may be added but is not essential. Temperature range: 73–82°F (23–28°C)*

BREEDING: *Rare in aquaria. Eggs are scattered and hatch in about three days*

FIRE EEL
SPOTTED FIRE, or ASIAN FIRE, EEL
Mastacembelus erythrotaenia

FAMILY: Mastacembelidae

THIS IS THE BEST KNOWN AND MOST COLORFUL OF all the spiny eels. It is also among the largest and perhaps the most sensitive to poor water conditions and parasitic infections and injuries. Special care must hence

FIRE EEL *(*MASTACEMBELUS ERYTHROTAENIA*)*

OTHER SPINY EELS

Spiny eel classification is still, after many years of study, in a slightly confused state, with *Macrognathus* and *Mastacembelus*, and *Afromastacembelus* and *Caecomastacembelus*, often being used interchangeably. Doubts also exist about the identification and validity of some species. The following are among the most frequently encountered spiny eels (but the number is increasing). All have the same basic characteristics and aquarium requirements described for *Macrognathus aculeatus*. Sizes quoted are approximate.

SCIENTIFIC NAME	COMMON NAME(S)	SIZE
Caecomastacembelus (Afromastacembelus) ellipsifer	Big-spot Spiny Eel	6in (15cm)
C. (A.) frenatus	Ladderback Spiny Eel	6in (15cm)
C. (A.) moorii	Mottled Spiny Eel	6¼in (16cm)
C. (A.) ophidium	Snaky Spiny Eel	4in (10cm)
C. (A.) tanganikae	Tanganyikan Spiny Eel	6in (15cm)
Macrognathus aral	Lesser Spiny Eel	12in (30cm)
M. circumcinctus	Banded, or Half-banded, Spiny Eel	10in (25cm)
M. maculatus	Spotted, or Black-spotted, Spiny Eel	18in (45cm)
M. pancalus	Common, Deep-bodied, or Spotted, Spiny Eel	8in (20cm)
M. siamensis	Clown, Spot-finned, or Siamese, Spiny Eel	14in (35cm)
M. zebrinus	Zebra Spiny Eel	18in (45cm)
Mastacembelus armatus	Giant, White-spotted Car-track, or Tire-track, Spiny Eel	30in (75cm)

be taken to ensure that its aquarium requirements are scrupulously met.

DISTRIBUTION: *Southeast Asia*

SIZE: *Up to c.39in (1m) reported, but usually smaller*

BEHAVIOR: *As for* Macrognathus aculeatus

DIET: *As for* Macrognathus aculeatus

AQUARIUM: *As for* Macrognathus aculeatus

BREEDING: *No documented accounts currently available*

AFRICAN LUNGFISH

Protopterus annectens

FAMILY: Protopteridae

THIS TOUGH, LARGE FISH IS, LIKE ALL OTHER lungfishes, able to tolerate a wide range of conditions. As their native pools dry up in the wild, all the African species bury into the substratum and secrete a mucus cocoon within which they aestivate (i.e. undergo a period of summer dormancy) until the rains return. The pectoral and pelvic fins of African Lungfish are long and whip-like rather than fin-like.

DISTRIBUTION: *Widespread in Africa*

SIZE: *Up to 28in (70cm) reported*

BEHAVIOR: *Intolerant and predatory*

DIET: *Large livefoods, including fish; chunky meat-based or fish-based formulations also accepted*

AQUARIUM: *Large, well-covered, well-filtered, with fine-grained substratum and large shelters and pieces of bogwood. Water chemistry not critical. Temperature range: 77–88°F (25–30°C)*

BREEDING: *No documented reports of aquarium breeding currently available*

BOWFIN

Amia calva

FAMILY: Amiidae

FOSSILS OF MEMBERS OF THIS FAMILY OCCUR IN rocks that are up to 180 million years old.

OTHER LUNGFISH SPECIES

There are only five other lungfish species living today, although these primitive fish (some authorities question whether they are fish at all) have a long fossil history going back perhaps 270–350 million years. All are rarely seen, other than in public aquaria, and all except *Neoceratodus forsteri* (*see* Notes below) have the same basic requirements and habits.

FAMILY	SPECIES	SIZE
Ceratodontidae*—one species	*Neoceratodus forsteri*** (Australian Lungfish)	Up to c.60in (150cm)
Lepidosirenidae—one species	*Lepidosiren paradoxa* (South American Lungfish)	Up to c.50in (125cm)
Protopteridae—three species (in addition to *Protopterus annectens*, see main entry)	*P. aethiopicus* (Ethiopian Lungfish) *P. amphibius* (no common name) *P. dolloi* (Spotted Lungfish)	Up to c.80in (200cm) Over 40in (100cm) 33in (85cm)

NOTES:

*Referred to as Neoceratodontidae by some authors

** *Neoceratodus forsteri* possesses only one lung, while the others possess two; its pectoral and pelvic fins are fin-like, rather than fleshy filaments; its newly hatched larvae lack the external gills possessed by the larvae of the other species; it does not build a cocoon and cannot therefore survive the summer by going into aestivation (dormancy); it has occasionally been bred in public aquaria.

Today, though, the family has just this one representative, which still retains some primitive features. Among these is a lung-like swimbladder, a heterocercal caudal fin, i.e. one that (at least, internally) has a longer upper lobe, and the remains of a spiral valve (a spiral infolding of the wall of the intestine—as found in true sharks). The dorsal fin is also interesting in that it extends more than half the length of the back.

DISTRIBUTION: *Widely distributed in eastern half of North America, extending as far north as the Great Lakes and a little beyond*

SIZE: *Males reported up to 20in (50cm), females larger*

BEHAVIOR: *Solitary predator; can only be kept with tankmates that are too large to swallow*

DIET: *Large livefoods, including fish; some chunky meat-based of fish-based formulations may be accepted*

AQUARIUM: *Large, with numerous shelters, clumps of stout vegetation, and subdued lighting. Water chemistry not critical, but avoid extremes of pH and hardness. Temperature range: from below 54°F (12°C) to around 68°F (20°C)*

BREEDING: *No documented accounts of aquarium breeding available*

REEDFISH

ROPE, or SNAKE, FISH

Erpetoichthys calabaricus

SYNONYM: *Calamoichthys calabaricus*
FAMILY: Polypteridae

CLOSELY RELATED TO THE BIRCHIRS (*POLYPTERUS* —*see* next entry), with which it shares several characteristics, such as the possession of a number of dorsal finlets (7–13)

REEDFISH (ERPETOICHTHYS CALABARICUS)

ORNATE BIRCHIR (POLYPTERUS ORNATIPINNIS)

rather than a single fin, and the ability to use its swimbladder as an auxiliary respiratory organ. It is distinguished from its relatives by its extremely elongated snake-like body and the lack of pelvic fins. Reed-fish can survive out of water for several hours, as long as the air is humid.

DISTRIBUTION: *Cameroon and Nigeria*

SIZE: *Up to 16in (40cm) reported, but usually smaller*

BEHAVIOR: *Peaceful toward tankmates that are too large to swallow; likes to burrow; active mainly at dusk and during the night*

DIET: *Livefoods and chunky or meaty formulations*

AQUARIUM: *Large, well-covered, with several shelters/hiding places and fine-grained substratum. Protect plants against burrowing (see Aquarium Plants). A "moonlight" fluorescent tube to facilitate nighttime viewing recommended. Slightly acid, medium-hard water preferred. Temperature range: 72–82°F (22–28°C)*

BREEDING: *No documented accounts available*

ORNATE BIRCHIR

Polypterus ornatipinnis

FAMILY: Polypteridae

THIS IS THE MOST WIDELY AVAILABLE MEMBER OF ITS genus. While having several characteristics in common with *Erpetoichthys calabaricus* (*see* previous entry), birchirs do not possess a snake-like body and do not lack a pelvic fin. Several other species are occasionally available: *P. congicus* (Congo Birchir), mainly from Zaire, *P. delhezi* (Armored Birchir), also from Zaire, *P. palmas* (Marbled Birchir), from Guinea, Liberia, Sierra Leone and Zaire, and *P. senegalus* (Cuvier's or Senegal Birchir), from Senegal, Gambia, the Niger, White Nile and several major lakes, such as

Lakes Albert, Chad and Rudolf. All have similar requirements.

DISTRIBUTION: *Widely distributed in central Africa*

SIZE: *Up to 18in (46cm) reported*

BEHAVIOR: *Generally tolerant of large tankmates, but less so of conspecifics; will prey on small fishes*

DIET: *Large livefoods, including live fish; chunky, meaty formulations also accepted*

AQUARIUM: *As for* Erpetoichthys calabaricus. *Temperature range: 79–82°F (26–28°C)*

BREEDING: *Tight spawning embraces—usually among vegetation—are accompanied by egg release and fertilization. Eggs are abandoned, and they hatch in four days*

LONGNOSED GAR

Lepisosteus osteus

FAMILY: Lepisosteidae

THIS IS A SLIM-BODIED SPECIES WITH A LONG, pointed mouth. Along with several other gar species, it is strictly a fish for specialists who can provide sufficiently large aquaria and an appropriate diet. Among the other gars occasionally on offer are the following: *L. oculatus* (Spotted Gar)—47in (120cm); *L. platostomus* (Shortnosed Gar)—24in (60cm); *Atractosteus (L.) spatula* (Alligator Gar)—118in (300cm); *Atractosteus (L.) tristoechus* (Cuban Gar)—reported up to 118in (300cm); and *L. platyrhincus* (Florida Gar)—52in (132cm), of which a golden variety is sometimes available.

DISTRIBUTION: *Atlantic slope of U.S.A. down to Florida; Great Lakes (except Lake Superior), Gulf Coast from Florida to Rio Grande; Texas and Mexico*

SIZE: *Up to 72in (183cm) reported*

BEHAVIOR: *Stalking predator; can only be kept with other large tankmates*

DIET: *As for* Datnioides microlepis

AQUARIUM: *Very large, covered, well-planted aquarium essential. Large decor, shelters and robust plants recommended. Temperature range: 54–64°F (12–18°C)*

BREEDING: *Very challenging in aquaria. Eggs are scattered among vegetation*

SHOVELNOSED STURGEON

Scaphirhynchus platorynchus

FAMILY: Acipenseridae

MOST STURGEONS CAN GROW TO VERY LARGE sizes—e.g. *Huso huso* (Beluga) can reach around 26ft (8m)—and are therefore totally unsuitable for aquaria. However, the Shovelnosed Sturgeon, along with *Acipenser ruthenus* (Sterlet) and *A. stellatus* (Stellate Sturgeon), are smaller, and can be housed in aquaria as long as these are spacious enough. One of the reasons for their growth in popularity in certain countries—beginning in the late 1980s/early 1990s—has been the expansion of the pondkeeping/watergardening hobby, in general, and that of Koi keeping in particular: Shovelnoses, Sterlets and Stellate Sturgeons are transferred to outside ponds once they outgrow their aquaria.

DISTRIBUTION: *Mississippi river basin, Mobile Bay drainage and upper Rio Grande, U.S.A.*

SIZE: *Around 39in (1m), but often smaller*

BEHAVIOR: *Peaceful; burrows in the substratum in search of food, and may prey on small fish*

DIET: *Chunky livefoods, deep-frozen and freeze-dried preparations, as well as sinking pellets and tablets*

AQUARIUM: *Very large, well-filtered, with open swimming areas and fine-grained substratum. Neutral, medium-hard water preferred, but some*

SHOVELNOSED STURGEON
(SCAPHIRHYNCHUS PLATORYNCHUS)

deviation accepted. Temperature range: 50–68°F (10–20°C)

BREEDING: *No documented accounts of aquarium breeding available*

OCELLATED STINGRAY
PEACOCK-EYE, or MOTORO, STINGRAY

Potamotrygon motoro

SYNONYM: *Potamotrygon laticeps*
FAMILY: Potamotrygonidae

THIS IS AN EXTREMELY VARIABLE SPECIES, WHICH, along with other members of the family, is becoming increasingly popular. Stingrays are most definitely not suitable for new aquarists and should in any case be treated with caution owing to the dangers posed by the sting. Seek specialist advice and consult specialist literature (*see* Bibliography) before purchase.

DISTRIBUTION: *Widespread in tropical South America*

SIZE: *Up to 20in (50cm)*

BEHAVIOR: *Tolerant; may be kept in a group; spends much time buried in the substratum with only the eyes showing*

DIET: *Bottom-dwelling livefoods, chunky meat-based or fish-based formulations, and sinking deep-frozen diets*

AQUARIUM: *Large, well-filtered, with some floating vegetation, well-bedded rocks or bogwood pieces, and deep fine-grained substratum. Slightly acid to neutral, soft to medium-hard water accepted. Temperature range: 75–79°F (24–26°C)*

BREEDING: *No documented accounts of aquarium breeding currently available*

OCELLATED STINGRAY (POTAMOTRYGON MOTORO)

GLOSSARY

adipose fin Second dorsal fin.

adsorption The "adhesion" of molecules to a porous surface; no chemical transformation of these molecules occurs.

aerobic Chemical and biological processes (or reactions) that require oxygen.

aestivation Period of summer dormancy exhibited by some species, e.g., African and South American lungfish.

anadromous Fish species that spend most of their life at sea but migrate into freshwater for breeding, e.g., salmon.

anaerobic Chemical and biological processes that can occur in the absence of oxygen.

anal fin Belly fin.

andropodium Term often used for the "gonopodium" of halfbeaks (Hemirhamphidae). *See* gonopodium and spermatopodium.

annual Of fish species that live for only one season.

barbels Fleshy filaments growing around the mouth of a fish.

benthic Bottom-dwelling.

branchiocranium The skeleton of the lower half of the skull, including the jawbones and gill covers.

branchiostegal ray Slender bony rod found on some of the bones that support the operculum (gill cover).

cable tidy Box that allows a number of pieces of electrical equipment to be connected to a central block with a single lead to the mains supply.

catadromous Fish species that spend most of their life in freshwater but migrate to the sea for spawning, e.g., eels.

caudal fin Tail fin.

caudal peduncle Base of the caudal fin.

chlorophyll Green pigment (found within chloroplasts) that traps light and is therefore essential for photosynthesis.

chloroplasts Tiny granular structures within the green tissues of plants (mainly the leaves) containing the green pigment chlorophyll.

chromosome Gene-carrying structure found in the nucleus of a living cell.

condensation tray Perspex or (less frequently) glass sheet installed between the aquarium and the hood to minimize evaporation and prevent electrical connections from becoming wet.

conspecific Of the same species.

dechloraminator Chloramine-removing agent.

dechlorinator Chlorine-removing agent.

denitrification The conversion of nitrate to nitrite and, thence, to nitrogen. In aquaria, this function is performed by anaerobic micro-organisms.

diapause A period of dormancy, e.g., in the eggs of some killifishes.

dorsal fin Back fin.

ectotherm An organism whose body/blood temperature matches that of the surrounding environment. Ectothermic organisms derive their heat from their environment, i.e., from an external source. (*Compare* endotherm and poikilotherm.)

endotherm A "warm-blooded" animal, i.e., one that is capable of generating its own body heat and thus able to maintain a more or less constant internal temperature, irrespective of ambient conditions. (*Compare* ectotherm and poikilotherm.)

facultative viviparity Scientific term for species formerly regarded as ovi-ovoviviparous (*see* ovi-ovoviviparity).

flocculation Clumping of small particles into larger agglomerations.

gamete Reproductive cell, i.e., egg or sperm.

GH General or Permanent Hardness of a water sample, determined primarily by the chlorides, nitrates and sulphates of calcium and magnesium.

gonopodium Copulatory organ possessed by males of livebearing families such as Anablepidae (e.g., Four-eyed Fish) and Poeciliidae (e.g., Guppy). It consists of highly modified rays of the anal fin and is used as a means of introducing sperm into the vent of the female during mating. (*See also* andropodium and spermatopodium.)

gravel tidy Mesh sheeting that can be laid on top of undergravel filter plates to prevent grains of substrate blocking the plate slits or pores.

gynogenesis Development of eggs after sperm penetration, but without actual fertilization taking place (as in *Poecilia* "formosa," see Other *Poecilia* species table, p.280).

hermaphrodite Animal possessing both male and female sex organs.

KH Temporary, Bicarbonate or Carbonate Hardness of a water sample, caused by the bicarbonates of calcium and magnesium. Temporary Hardness (unlike GH) can be reduced or eliminated by boiling.

labyrinth Specialized auxiliary breathing organ found in fish such as gouramis.

lamella Thin, plate-like structure as found in, e.g., the gills of mushrooms or fish gills, when it is often referred to as a gill filament. (Plural: lamellae.)

lateral line system A system of pores that run, to a greater or lesser extent, along a fish's body. These pores lead to nerve endings that allow a fish to sense vibrations in the water and help it locate prey, detect predators, avoid obstacles, and so on.

laterite Iron- and aluminum-oxide containing red soils common in tropical regions.

lignin Hard "woody" material found in the walls of plant cells; some species of fish—notably Whiptail Cats (family Loricariidae) consume lignin as part of their natural diet.

metabolism The collective term for the biochemical reactions that occur in living organisms.

moonlight fluorescent lamp A fluorescent tube that emits a weak bluish light that simulates moonlight. It is particularly recommended for aquaria housing fish that are active mainly at night.

neoteny The retention of larval characteristics in sexually mature adults, e.g., external gills in Axolotls.

neurocranium The top half of a fish skull, including the braincase.

neuromast A "pore" of the lateral line system.

nitrification The conversion of ammonia to nitrite and then to nitrate. In aquaria, this function is carried out by aerobic micro-organisms.

operculum Cover, consisting of bony plates, which encloses the gills.

ovarian follicle Egg sac.

ovi-ovoviviparity Term (no longer widely used) to describe reproductive strategies that consist of internal fertilization with subsequent release of the fertilized eggs.

oviparity Egglaying.

ovoviparity Livebearing reproductive strategies that consist of internal fertilization with most of the embryo nourishment originating from egg yolk.

oxidation Addition of oxygen, loss of hydrogen or loss of electrons, as a result of a chemical reaction.

pathogen Disease-causing agent.

peat sandwich A layer of (aquarium) peat sandwiched between two layers of a different medium, e.g., gravel, or wrapped in, e.g., muslin. This can be laid as the substratum of the aquarium or within a filter (for peat filtration).

pectoral fin Chest fin.

pelvic fin Hip fin.

pH A value indicating levels of acidity/alkalinity. The scale is logarithmic, i.e., each "unit" represents a tenfold increase/decrease. A value of pH 7 represents neutral conditions; lower values indicate increasing levels of acidity, while higher ones indicate increasing levels of alkalinity.

photosynthesis The process by which green plants (and photosynthetic bacteria) combine carbon dioxide and water in the presence of light and chlorophyll (green pigment) to form carbohydrate. Oxygen is a by-product of the process.

poikilotherm Cold-blooded organisms whose body temperature varies with that of their environment (*see* ectotherm and endotherm).

reduction Removal of oxygen, addition of hydrogen or addition of electrons, as a result of a chemical reaction.

rhizome A modified swollen plant stem that grows horizontally on or below the substratum and that acts as a food reserve from one season to the next. Rhizomes last for several years. (*See also* tuber.)

runner Creeping stem with embryonic plant at its tip; this young plant eventually roots, becomes detached from the mother plant and develops into a separate individual. Runners are produced by many aquarium plants, e.g., *Vallisneria* species.

spawning mop Strands of non-toxic material (e.g., wool) attached to a floater (e.g., a piece of cork). Mops are frequently used in killifish breeding aquaria to provide a spawning medium for species that—in the wild—deposit their eggs among vegetation (rather than in the substratum).

specific gravity The mass ("weight") of a volume of liquid, as compared to an equivalent one of pure water. Pure water has an SG of 1.000, while seawater has an SG of around 1.020, which varies according to the concentration of salts it contains.

spermatopodium The notched anal fin in males of livebearing species of the family Goodeidae. It is used to effect internal fertilization of eggs during mating. (*See also* andropodium and gonopodium.)

stratification Layering effect. In water, this consists of warm layers lying above colder ones.

substrate 1. A substance on which an enzyme acts, e.g., carbohydrates are acted upon by enzymes during respiration and are therefore substrates. 2. A medium to which: (a) fixed animals are attached, e.g., rocks onto which barnacles and mussels are attached; (b) plants are anchored or attached, e.g., a piece of bogwood on which an aquatic fern grows, or gravel/mud/s and/silt in which aquatic plants have their roots embedded. Used in the latter sense, substrate is interchangeable with substratum.

substratum See substrate.

superfetation Strategy exhibited by some livebearers in which a female can simultaneously carry several small broods of embryos at different stages of development.

surfactant Proteins, fats and other compounds that are attracted to, or trapped by, the interface between water and gas (see p.47).

T.D.S. Total Dissolved Solids (or Salts) in a water sample. It is the equivalent of Total Hardness.

Total Hardness The sum of all the dissolved salts in a water sample, i.e., Temporary/Bicarbonate/Carbonate Hardness, plus Permanent/General Hardness.

trophonemata Outgrowths of ovarian tissues found in a few species (e.g., Jenynsia) through which mothers nourish their developing embryos.

trophotaeniae Outgrowths from the vent area of goodeid embryos (family Goodeidae), through which they obtain nourishment during early their development.

tuber Similar in structure and function to a rhizome but usually smaller and lasting for only one growth season. (See also rhizome.)

venturi An aeration device incorporated within powerheads or power filters. It drags air from the atmosphere, via a tube, into the water, and dispels it in a stream of bubbles.

viviparity Livebearing, i.e., giving birth to live young.

zeolite Clay-based compounds that adsorb certain dissolved chemicals such as ammonia.

zoonosis Disease that can be transmitted from animals to humans. (Plural: zoonoses.)

BIBLIOGRAPHY

Allgayer, R. and Teton, J., The Complete Book of Aquarium Plants (Ward Lock Ltd., 1987).

Andrews, C., Exell, A. and Carrington, N., The Manual of Fish Health (Salamander Books Ltd., 1988).

Banister, K. and Campbell, A. (Eds), The Encyclopaedia of Underwater Life (George Allen & Unwin, 1985)

Bassleer, G., Colorguide of Tropical Fish Disease [on Freshwater Fish] (Bassleer Biofish, 1997).

Burgess, W. E., An Atlas of Freshwater and Marine Catfishes: A Preliminary Survey of the Siluriformes (T.F.H. Publications, Inc., 1989).

Burgess, W. E., Colored Atlas of Miniature Catfish: Every Species of Corydoras, Brochis & Aspidoras (T.F.H. Publications, Inc., 1992).

Dakin, N., The Questions & Answers Manual of The Marine Aquarium (Andromeda Oxford Ltd., 1996).

Dawes, J., Livebearing Fishes: A Guide to their Aquarium Care, Biology and Classification (Blandford, 1991).

Dawes, J., Lim, L. L. and Cheong, L. (Eds), The Dragon Fish (Kingdom Books, 1999).

Ghedotti, M. J. and Weitzman, S. H., A New Species of Jenynsia (Cyprinodontiformes: Anablepidae) from Brazil with Comments on the Composition and Taxonomy of the Genus, Occas. Pap. Mus. Nat. Hist. Univ. Kans., **179** (1996); 1.25.

Glaser, U. and Glaser, W., Loricariidae: All L-Numbers and all LDA-Numbers (Verlag A.C.S. GmbH, 1995).

Glaser, U. and Glaser, W., South American Cichlids: I, II and III (Verlag A.C.S. GmbH, 1996).

Glaser, U., Schäfer F. and Glaser, W., All Corydoras (Verlag A.C.S. GmbH, 1996).

Göbel, M. and Mayland, H. J., South American Cichlids: IV—Discus, Scalare (Verlag A.C.S. GmbH, 1998).

Helfman, G. S., Collette, B. B. and Facey, D. E., The Diversity of Fishes (Blackwell Science, 1997).

Hieronimus, H., Breathtaking Rainbows (Verlag A.C.S. GmbH, 1999).

Hoese, D. F. and Gill, A.C., Phylogenetic relationships of eleotrid fishes (Perciformes: Gobioidei), Bull. Mar. Sci. 52 (1) (1993); 415–440.

Horst, K. and Kipper, H. E., The Optimum Aquarium (AD Aquadocumenta Verlag, 1986).

Huber, J. H., Review of Rivulus: Ecobiogeography: Relationships (Musée National d'Histoire Naturelle, Paris, 1992).

James, B., A Fishkeeper's Guide to Aquarium Plants (Salamander Books Ltd., 1986).

Jinkings, K., Bristlenoses: Catfish with Character (Kingdom Books, 2000).

Kempes, M. and Schäfer, F., All Livebearers and Halfbeaks (Verlag A.C.S. GmbH, 1998).

Konings, A., Back to Nature Guide to Malawi Cichlids (Föhrman Aquaristik AB, 1997).

Konings, A., Back to Nature Guide to Tanganyika Cichlids (Föhrman Aquaristik AB, 1997).

Lambert, D. and Lambert, P., Platies and Swordtails: An Aquarist's Handbook (Blandford, 1995).

Linke, H., Labyrinth Fish: The Bubble-Nestbuilders (Tetra-Press, 1991).

Masters, Charles O., Encyclopedia of Live Foods (T.F.H. Publications, Inc., 1975).

Mayland, H. J. and Bork, D., South American Dwarf Cichlids: Apistogramma, Crenicara, Microgeophagus (Verlag A.C.S. GmbH, 1997).

Mühlberg, H., The Complete Guide to Water Plants (E. P. Publishing Ltd., 1982).

Nelson, J. S., Fishes of the World (3rd Edition) (John Wiley & Sons, Inc., 1994).

Parenti, L. R., A Phylogenetic and Biogeographic Analysis of Cyprinodontiform Fishes (Telcostei, Atherinomorpha), Bull. Am. Mus. Nat. Hist., **168 (4)** (1981); 335–557.

Parenti, L. R., and Rauchenberger, M., Systematic Overview of the Poeciliines, in Meffe, G. K. and Snelson Jr., F. F. (Eds): Ecology and Evolution of Livebearing Fishes (Poeciliidae) (Prentice-Hall, 1989).

Pethiyagoda, R., Freshwater Fishes of Sri Lanka (Wildlife Heritage Trust of Sri Lanka, 1991).

Pinter, H., Labyrinth Fish (Barrons Educational Series, Inc., 1986).

Post, G., Textbook of Fish Health (T.F.H. Publications, Inc., 1987).

Ross, R. A., Freshwater Stingrays of South America (Verlag A.C.S. GmbH, 1999).

Ross, R. A. and Schäfer, F., Freshwater Rays (Verlag A.C.S. GmbH, 2000).

Sandford, G., The Questions & Answers Manual of The Tropical Freshwater Aquarium (Andromeda Oxford Ltd., 1998).

Schäfer, F., All Labyrinths: Bettas, Gouramis, Snakeheads, Nandids (Verlag A.C.S. GmbH, 1997).

Scheel, J. J., Atlas of Killifishes of the Old World (T.F.H. Publications, Inc., 1990).

Schraml, E., African Cichlids: I—Malawi Mbuna (Verlag A.C.S. GmbH, 1998).

Seegers, L., Killifishes of the World: Old World Killies I—Aphyosemion, Lampeyes, Ricefishes (Verlag A.C.S. GmbH, 1997).

Seegers, L., Killifishes of the World: Old World Killies II—Aplocheilus, Epiplatys, Nothobranchius (Verlag A.C.S. GmbH, 1997).

Seegers, L., Killifishes of the World—New World Killies (Verlag A.C.S. GmbH, 2000).

Smartt, J. and Blundell, J. H., Goldfish Breeding and Genetics (T.F.H. Publications, Inc., 1996).

Tekriwal, K. L. and Rao, A. A., Ornamental Aquarium Fish of India (Kingdom Books, 1999).

Tepoot, P., Aquarium Plants: The Practical Guide (New Life Publications, 1998).

Wishnath, L., Atlas of Livebearers of the World (T.F.H. Publications, Inc., 1993).

INDEX

300

301

304